AF520473

Digital Library
&
Computer Science

About the Book

The value of a library is the reuse of the behavior. When a program invokes a library, it gains the behavior implemented inside that library without having to implement that behavior itself. Libraries encourage the sharing of code in a modular fashion, and ease the distribution of the code. The behavior implemented by a library can be connected to the invoking program at different program lifecycle phases. If the code of the library is accessed during the build of the invoking program, then the library is called a static library. An alternative is to build the executable of the invoking program and distribute that, independently from the library implementation.

About the Author

Pooja Singh, is an experienced java consultant currently residing in Belgium, and working for one of the leading financial companies in Belgium. She received her double Masters Degree in Computer and Communication Networks and Information Technology from Telecom Belgium and University of Belgium in 2014. She is a recipient of the prestigious Telecom Scholarship for Excellence provided by Foundation Telecom, Belgium. She received the Bachelor of Engineering degree in Computer Engineering from the University of Chhattisgarh, India in 2009. From 2010 to 2013, she was employed as a Software Engineer with Geometric Ltd, Maharashtra, India. Her major interests include Advanced Java Frameworks, Logging Frameworks, Network Security and Data Mining. She published many research papers National and Internationally.

Digital Library & Computer Science

Pooja Singh

AMIGA PRESS INC.

(DELHI (INDIA

AMIGA PRESS INC.
H.O.: 28-A, Indra Park,
Chander Nagar, Delhi-110051 (India)
Tel.: 011-22504028, +91-98736-57000
E-mail: amigapress@gmail.com
amigaeditorial@gmail.com
amigapub@gmail.com
info@amigapress.co.in
Website : www.amigapress.co.in

This edition is published by Amiga Press Inc.

ISBN: 978-93-87295-50-6

Copyright© Reserved

First Published 2020

All rights reserved, no part of this publication may be reproduced, stored in a retrieval system or transmitted in any form or by any means, electronic, mechanical, photocopying, recording or otherwise without the prior written permission of the publisher or the copyright holder.

This book contains information obtained from authentic and highly regarded sources. Reasonable efforts have been made to publish reliable data and information, but the author's, editor/s and publisher cannot assume responsibility for the validity of all materials or the consequences of their use. The author/s, editor/s and publishers have attempted to trace and acknowledge the copyright holders of all materials reproduced in this publication and apologize to copyright holders, if permission and acknowledgements to publish in the form have not been taken. If any copyright material has not been acknowledge please write and let us know so we may rectify it, in subsequent reprints.

***Publisher Notice:* -** Presentations, Logos (the way they are written/ Presented), in this book are under the copyright of the publisher and hence, if copied/resembled the copier will be prosecuted under the law.

Printed and bound in India by Replika Press Pvt. Ltd.

Preface

A library is a collection of implementations of behavior, written in terms of a language that has a well-defined interface by which the behavior is invoked. This means that as long as a higher level program uses a library to make system calls, it does not need to be re-written to implement those system calls over and over again. In addition, the behavior is provided for reuse by multiple independent programs. A program invokes the library-provided behavior via a mechanism of the language. For example, in a simple imperative language such as C, the behavior in a library is invoked by using C's normal function-call. What distinguishes the call as being to a library, versus being to another function in the same program, is the way that the code is organized in the system. Library code is organized in such a way that it can be used by multiple programs that have no connection to each other, while code that is part of a program is organized to only be used within that one program. This distinction can gain a hierarchical notion when a program grows large, such as a multi-million-line program. In that case, there may be internal libraries that are reused by independent sub-portions of the large program. The distinguishing feature is that a library is organized for the purposes of being reused by independent programs or sub-programs, and the user only needs to know the interface, and not the internal details of the library.

The value of a library is the reuse of the behavior. When a program invokes a library, it gains the behavior implemented inside that library without having to implement that behavior itself. Libraries encourage the sharing of code in a modular fashion, and ease the distribution of the code. The behavior implemented by a library can be connected to the invoking program at different program lifecycle phases. If the code of the library is accessed during the build of the invoking program, then the library is called a static library. An alternative is to build the executable of the invoking program and distribute that, independently from the library implementation. The library behavior is connected after the executable has been invoked to be executed, either as part of the process of starting the execution, or in the middle of execution. In this case the library is called a dynamic library. A dynamic library can be loaded and linked as part of preparing a program for execution, by the linker.

Alternatively, in the middle of execution, an application may explicitly request that a module be loaded. Most compiled languages have a standard library although programmers can also create their own custom libraries. Most modern software systems provide libraries that implement the majority of system services. Such libraries have commoditized the services which a modern application requires. As such, most code used by modern applications is provided in these system libraries.

–Author

Contents

❐

1

Barcode Technology

INTRODUCTION

The circulation work in an automated library involves keying in a large amount of data. Sometimes, the library staff at the counter has to retype the same information due to error in data entry. All this results in long queues at the circulation desk in our libraries. This voluminous work can be handled in a smooth manner in a much less time by the application of barcoding, one of the simplest coding technologies available in the market. The speed of data capture is three times faster than the speed at which a skilled data entry operator can input data' and also the error rate is negligibly small2. The barcode technology originated out of the need of retail stores and big industries to track down their inventory errors in a faster way. Due to the cheap human labour available in our country, the estimated barcoding market was a mere 12 crores in 1995-96', out of which libraries and miscellaneous services accounted for only 1 crore. Libraries need to adopt this technology as it helps retrieve and collect data quickly and efficiently.

BARCODE DATA TRANSFER

The information that can be encoded on the barcodes is rather limited and hence, it is up to the individual libraries to decide what information they need to barcode for efficient handling of collection and for better operation of services. Libraries can use accession numbers of books, the unique information that distinguish their collection, as the vital information entity to barcode their collection. Similarly, the identification number of a user stands distinct for each member, which can be used to barcode the user's cards. Accession number/borrower number exported from the library database/borrower database is converted to a series of black and white lines by the barcode software.

This can be printed by a dot-matrix/laser printer and pasted on all books and borrower cards. The light beam flashed from the barcode scanner on the barcode label undergoes reflection at the white lines and absorption on the dark bands.

This reflected light is collected back and is converted into electric pulses by the photoelectric circuitry of the scanner. Further, these pulses are converted into binary information by the interface circuitry of the scanner before they are fed to the computer, for further processing. So, the information read from barcode acts as a substitute for the same information entered through keyboard, to handle circulation/other routines of the library database.

The barcode technology is essentially a data transfer device and hence, it works in perfect harmony with any of the computerised database systems.

Any customisation needed at the user end can be done either by the in-house system personnel or by local solution providers.

The barcoding setup includes the barcode scanner to read the barcode dinformation, its interfacing with the library computer, the software to convert the requisite information to barcodes, and the printer.

The barcode scanners may be classified into different groups like:

- As per design (handheld and fixed-mount).
- As per light source (infrared or visible).

Hand-held scanners contain no moving parts. They are compact, light and cheaper as compared to fixed-mount models. Hence, they are of interest to libraries desiring to optimise their budgetary resources. Infrared scanners can read mutilated labels; however, they need special printers. But recent times saw the dominant categorisation, as per technology, into CCD and laser scanners.

In CCD scanners, light from the LEDs is used to read the barcode information, whereas laser light is used in the latter. Accordingly, laser scanners have increased scan width and range (distance from which the labels are scanned), but they are comparatively expensive. The vendors used to offer requisite software to generate barcodes from suggested fields of library database. Since, materials and readers are added only in prescribed number in a library, it will be better to avoid commercial printing of barcode labels.

All required lables can be printed either on normal paper or on purchased blank labels on a dot-matrixllaser printer, as per their availability in the library. While generating lables, provision may also be made to print some other fields like author/title/user riame in normal text to identify the labels easily, as one is more comfortable with text than numbers like accession/identification number. The user cards are normally laminated and to ensure long life of the labels on books (defective labels always lead to wrong/no reading of data), transparent cellotape can be pasted over these.

CODING FORMATS/ SYMBOLOGIES

The different code formats and how the information is encoded in bars is available in the litreature4. The same information can be encoded by different schemes; however, at the user and application level, it doesn't make much distinction and the user may use any of the schemes. The same information can be encoded to and satisfactorily decoded from more than one scheme without hampering efficiency or time. Limitations are imposed by the barcoding software one uses, and it is better to consult the individual operational manual for such information.

Some of the common formats are:

- Universal Product Code (UPC): US standard to encode only digits, UPC-A to encode 12 digits or UPC-E to encode 6 digits.
- European Article Number (EAN): European code to encode digits, available in two variations:. EAN-8 to encode 8 digits and EAN-13 to encode 13 digits.
- Interleaved 2 of 5. (ITF): Supports only numeric characters but can be used for variable length.
- Code-39: Encodes capital alphabets, numerical and few special characters like $, +, per cent. Asterisk (*) must be used as the start and stop character. Lowercase alphabets cannot be encoded.
- Code-1 28: Encodes both the lower and the upper case letters, numeric and special characters found on the keyboard.
- Codabar: Encodes only numeric and few special characters and is the most widely used coding format. Generally, libraries use this symbology to encode books and borrower cards.

BARCODING AT THE IIT KHARAGPUR CENTRAL LIBRARY

The Central Library of the Indian Institute of Technology, Kharagpur, is one of the few libraries in the country to have a huge database of their entire collections. Initially, the computerised issue return of books6 was done by keying in the accession number of books and identification number of borrower, but this mechanism was prone to errors and. also resulted in long queues at the circulation grant desk. Out of the project of ` 10 lakh received from AICTE in 1994 for the conversion of the conventional central library into the electronic library, the Library procured 5 CCD barcode scanners and one HP-5Si Mx Laser Printer. It was decided to barcode books and hence, the details of books brought for issue/ return were exported from the library database for generating barcode labels with accession number as the key field and the labels were printed on the laser printer using 'Softbar vl' software supplied by the vendor.

The Library also received a consignment of 'Nashua Laser Labels' in 30 labels per page format as gift from one of its alumni settled in US. The system generates three labels for each book to be pasted on the back of title page, secret page and last page. To fasten the process, personnel were given honorarium and encouraged to work overtime/on holidays to barcode the entire book collection. Side by side, new books processed by the technical processing section were also barcoded before release. Out of a special operating fund of ₹ 1 lakh received from the Institute in 1998, all the pending old books were also barcoded.

Now, the entire collection of over 2 lakh books is barcoded. From the academic year 1998-99, all B.Tech and M.Tech students were given a laminated barcoded library identity card and the practice of issuing separate borrower cards as per the entitlement was discontinued.

This facility will be further extended to faculty, researchers, and other staff in near future. This practice not only resulted in saving a large amount of stationery for printing numerous borrower cards but also a total saving of staff time which would have otherwise been spent for filing those cards. The user can have a book in one third of the pre-barcode issue time. The faculty, students and the personnel manning the circulation desk find the barcode technology user-friendly, efficient and fast.

ADOPTION IN OTHER LIBRARIES IN INDIA

Few of the computerised libraries in the country like American Centre, British Council, other ITs, some R&D libraries have already started barcoded circulation. With an investment of less than a lakh, the computerised libraries can procure barcode related hardware and software. A CCD scanner can be purchased for ₹ 15,000 and a laser scanner for ₹ 25,000 with comparable costs for relevant software. It is always better to have a feedback from the nearby libraries who use this technology before procuring one. Also, the potential vendors may be called to give a demonstration of this technology.

The procurement may be carried out in one go or in stages, so that those required for barcoding active collection may be purchased first and on completion of that work, more scanners may be bought. The accrued savings for the first few years will be more than what has been invested. Further, it will also improve the status of the library which will move one step closer to realise the fourth law of library science.

APPLICATIONS OF BARCODING

Barcoding offers a lot of comfort and ease to handle bulk routine tasks efficiently. The application of this technology for issue/return of books is widely identified and practiced in the developed countries of thc world. A few of the computerised libraries in our country have also started experiencing the fruits of this technology. It is important to emphasise that this technology is not limited to circulation work. Newnham describes the barcoding of DNA samples in Britain. It is not out of place to ponder over future barcoding applications in a library. With the help of a data gathering device, the barcodes can be used to verify stock, as libraries have to resort to stock verification, at intervals.

If the provision for multiple barcodes or multidimensional barcoding is incorporated to handle call number information also, wrong shelving of books can be autodetected which would help the staff to rectify the same. The individual journal volumes are handled in a library with lots of intricacies. Many a time these issues have to be taken out of the display area for Xerox work. There are also chances of their shelving in wrong cabinets.

These problems are tackled by using a control number for the current journal issues and barcoding them accordingly. A database of journal issues can thus be generated so that their management through cards can be avoided. If the parent institution also has a computerised accounting system, all the bills can be routed after barcoding so that their follow up and processing are done efficiently. Barcoding has come a long way and it is here to stay for faster and efficient library work.

AUTOMATED LIBRARY STOCK VERIFICATION WITH BARCODE AND LIBSYS

The modern technology has enabled automation and integration of the various processes of libraries and information centres to reduce or avoid human intervention and to increase the efficiency and speed. As the libraries provide open access service to make the holdings available to the users, the loss, damage, and misplacement of books are inevitable. To know and replace the lost books, and to maintain balance between various subjects, and to take adequate precautionary measures, it is necessary to do periodical inventory and accounting of the library collection of the library.

The term stock verification thus came into existance with regard to libraries. It is also referred as stock taking, physical verification or checking, stock inspection, and inventory, taking meaning physical checkup of any article on record.

Libraries of Govt. of India and its other organisations has to do a mandatory physical verification of all their holdings as per the following guidelines:

- Complete annual physical verification of books should be done every year in the case of libraries having not more than 20,000 holdings and not fewer than one qualified library staff. In case there is only one qualified staff, the verification may be done as per sub-para.
- Complete physical verification at intervals of not more than three years should be done in the case of libraries having more than 20,000 but not more than 50,000 volumes.
- Sample physical verification at intervals of not more than five years may be done in the case of libraries having more than 50,000 volumes. If such sample verification reveals unusual or unreasonable shortage, complete verification shall be done.

Libraries traditionally perform the periodic stock verification by adopting any one of the following methods: Verification by accession register; using a separate register with accession numbers; slips containing accession numbers; numerical counting; and shelf register cards or shelf list cards. The methods are cumbersome, time-consuming, and error prone as these are done manually.

The automated stock verification procedure adopted at Raja Ramanna Centre for Advanced Technology (RRCAT) library by employing barcode and LibSys facilities library stock verification could be performed easily with less manpower; one person scanned the barcode label (accession number) of documents and other person marked the documents by putting month and year stamp at the inside back cover to ensure that the document was physically verified. Besides, identification of damaged and worn out documents for repair, binding of obsolete volumes, and rearrangement and cleaning can also be done simultaneously. During the stock verification period, the returned (check-in) documents were also verified before shelving. Once the data capturing was over, the verification and generation of report with LibSys could also be done in a short period of time.

IMPLEMENTATION OF BARCODE TECHNOLOGY AND LIBSYS AT RRCAT LIBRARY

To improve the library service and to have an efficient control over the entire operation, the LibSys, which is a commercially available integrated multi-user library automation package, was implemented at RRCAT in 1995. To improve the services further, the barcode technology (print-related automatic identification technology) was implemented in 2000. The hardware installed to implement these technologies at RRCAT are: Laser barcode scanner for reading labels (at circulation counter); portable data capturing terminal with build-in laser scanner for inventory (stock verification); and accessories such as cradle, cable, battery and other items. The softwares for interfacing the data capturing terminal with computer are: PowerGen, SysTools and Label Works for Windows for label designing.

BARCODE AND BARCODE SCANNER

The barcodes are being used effectively to speed up, avoid human error, and automate the processes in industry for production planning control, materials management, purchase/ sale, and inventory control. In libraries, barcode is being used to automate the data-capturing process, for stock verification, and in the circulation counter for issue/return of documents.

A barcode is a sequence of dark bars on a light background or the equivalent of this with respect to the light-reflecting properties of the surface. The coding comprises in the relative widths or spacing of the dark bars and light spaces. A barcode scanner is an optical device that reads the code by scanning a focussed beam of light, generally a laser beam, across the barcode and detecting the variations in reflected light. The scanner converts these light variations into electrical variations, which are subsequently digitised and fed into the decoding unit programmed to convert the relative widths of the digitised dark/light spacings into numbers and/or letters.

BARCODE LABELLING

Each document in a library should be uniquely identified for barcode labelling purpose. Most of the libraries in India use accession number for this purpose. RRCAT has also used the same for printing barcode labels. The labels designed using Label Works for Windows, which supports major barcode symbologies.

Code 128, a high density linear symbology that can encode text, numbers, several functions and the entire 128 ASCII character set was selected for designing the labels. Figure shows the barcode label design specifications.

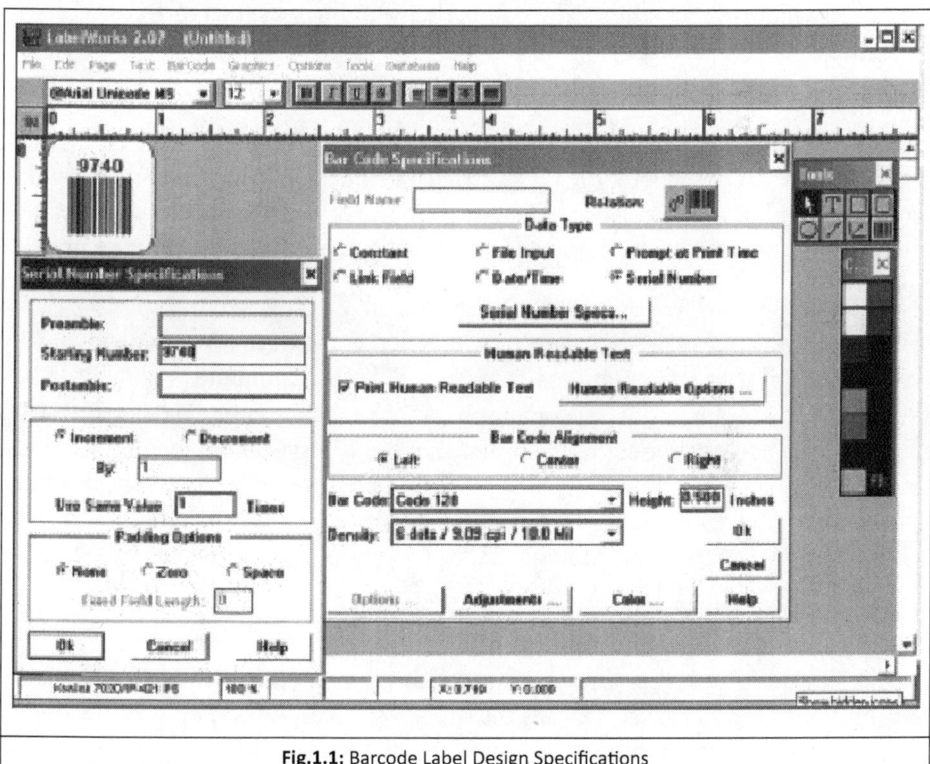

Fig.1.1: Barcode Label Design Specifications

DATA CAPTURING, MODIFICATION AND UPLOADING

The datalogic formula 732 wizard terminal was used to capture the data. The portable data collection laser scanner terminal scans the encoded data and automatically decodes and stores up to 128 KB of data in the memory. As the accession number differs from one to other, the terminal stores approx. 2500 accession numbers.

The data was downloaded into the PC using Systool's (software utility for data exchange) and was saved in a data file (*.dat). Later downloads were also appended to the same file. The PowerGen was the other software utility used to build personalised settings as per the requirements.

Each document was scanned and stamped (month and year) manually at the inside back cover to avoid duplication. During scanning, the terminal stores the accession number of each document and automatically displays the document number for a moment. If a data scanned is wrong, it can be manually updated or rescanned, and if a document has been inadvertantly scanned multiple times, the terminal simply stores the documents with duplicate accession numbers.

The downloaded data in the PC shows a vertical bar '|' (pipe) character after each accession number. The '|' characters were manually removed from the file using the windows text editor. The comprehensive file was then moved to LibSys work file ('wfilexx' directory).

DATA PROCESSING

As the entire collection of RRCAT was catalogued in the LibSys, the data analyses and report generation was carried out through the LibSys cataloguing stock verification module. The initiation of stock verification function is executed at once. This operation sets the system for the big exercise on inventory entails.

Data Analysis

The LibSys provides data verification in two ways; accession numbers one by one, and list of accession numbers in a file. All accession numbers are stored in a file. The system registers accession numbers for verification in the database. After matching the accession number from the file, the LibSys automatically generates an exception case file with extension '*. exp' and saves it in the work file path, i.e., in the wfilexx directory. This file enlists the list of mis-matching accession numbers and wrongly scanned numbers.

CONCLUSION

Barcode technology is reliable and easy to use. It improves accuracy and accelerates the processing time, eliminates the typing errors, decreases the costs and improves the services. During the stock verification period, routine library activities can be carried out without any disturbance. Data-capturing terminal is handy and portable, and there is no problem of scanning the data multiple times. The only disadvantage being like libraries assign simple accession numbers 1 to n for books, R1 to Rn for reports, and S1 to Sn for standards (R and S are the accession series of specific publication type). If libraries carry out stock verification for books alone LibSys has no option to carry out stock verification by an accession series wise. It process as the data and generates a report for all records available in the cataloguing module. Overall, the technology is beneficial for carrying out stock verifications in libraries. Since, there is no human intervention, the verification report generated by the system is perfect and accurate.

❐

2

Computer Service Perspectives for the Digital Library

A digital library is a library in which collections are stored in digital formats (as opposed to print, microform, or other media) and accessible by computers. The digital content may be stored locally, or accessed remotely via computer networks. A digital library is a type of information retrieval system.

The DELOS Digital Library Reference Model defines a digital library as: An organization, which might be virtual, that comprehensively collects, manages and preserves for the long term rich digital content, and offers to its user communities specialized functionality on that content, of measurable quality and according to codified policies.

The first use of the term digital library in print may have been in a 1988 report to the Corporation for National Research Initiatives The term digital libraries was first popularized by the NSF/DARPA/NASA Digital Libraries Initiative in 1994.

These draw heavily on As We May Think by Vannevar Bush in 1945, which set out a vision not in terms of technology, but user experience. The term virtual library was initially used interchangeably with digital library, but is now primarily used for libraries that are virtual in other senses (such as libraries which aggregate distributed content).

TYPES OF DIGITAL LIBRARIES

The term digital library is diffuse enough to be applied to a wide range of collections and organizations, but, to be considered a digital library, an online collection of information must be managed by and made accessible to a community of users. Thus, some web sites can be considered digital libraries, but far from all. Many of the best known digital libraries are older than the web including Project Perseus, Project Gutenberg, and ibiblio. Nevertheless, as a result of the development of the internet and its search potential, digital libraries such as the European Library and the Library of Congress are now developing in a Web-based environment. Public, school and college libraries are also able to develop digital download websites, featuring eBooks, audiobooks, music and video.

A distinction is often made between content that was created in a digital format, known as born-digital, and information that has been converted from a physical medium, e.g., paper, by digitizing. The term hybrid library is sometimes used for libraries that have both physical collections and digital collections. For example, American Memory is a digital library within the Library of Congress. Some important digital libraries also serve as long term archives, for example, the ePrint arXiv, and the Internet Archive.

Academic Repositories

Many academic libraries are actively involved in building institutional repositories of the institution's books, papers, theses, and other works which can be digitized or were 'born digital'. Many of these repositories are made available to the general public with few restrictions, in accordance with the goals of open access, in contrast to the publication of research in commercial journals, where the publishers often limit access rights. Institutional, truly free, and corporate repositories are sometimes referred to as digital libraries.

Digital Archives

Physical archives differ from physical libraries in several ways.
Traditionally, archives were defined as:

- Containing primary sources of information (typically letters and papers directly produced by an individual or organization) rather han the secondary sources found in a library (books, periodicals, etc);
- Having their contents organized in groups rather than individual items;
- Having unique contents.

The technology used to create digital libraries has been even more revolutionary for archives since it breaks down the second and third of these general rules. In other words, "digital archives" or "online archives" will still generally contain primary sources, but they are likely to be described individually rather than (or in addition to) in groups or collections, and because they are digital their contents are easily reproducible and may indeed have been reproduced from elsewhere. The Oxford Text Archive is generally considered to be the oldest digital archive of academic physical primary source materials.

Leaders in the Field

Project Gutenberg, Google Book Search, Windows Live Search Books (shutdown), Internet Archive, Cornell University, The Library of Congress World Digital Library, The Digital Library at the University of Michigan, and Carnegie Mellon University's Million Book Project are considered leaders in the field of digital library creation and management.

The Future

Large scale digitization projects are underway at Google, the Million Book Project, and Internet Archive. With continued improvements in book handling and presentation technologies such as optical character recognition and ebooks, and development of alternative depositories and business models, digital libraries are rapidly growing in popularity as demonstrated by Google, Yahoo!, and MSN's efforts. Just as libraries have ventured into audio and video collections, so have digital libraries such as the Internet Archive.

Searching

Most digital libraries provide a search interface which allows resources to be found. These resources are typically deep web (or invisible web) resources since they frequently cannot be located by search engine crawlers. Some digital libraries create special pages or sitemaps to allow search engines to find all their resources.

Digital libraries frequently use the Open Archives Initiative Protocol for Metadata Harvesting (OAI-PMH) to expose their metadata to other digital libraries, and search engines like Google Scholar, Yahoo! and Scirus can also use OAI-PMH to find these deep web resources.

There are two general strategies for searching a federation of digital libraries:

- Distributed searching, and
- Searching previously harvested metadata.

Distributed searching typically involves a client sending multiple search requests in parallel to a number of servers in the federation. The results are gathered, duplicates are eliminated or clustered, and the remaining items are sorted and presented back to the client. Protocols like Z39.50 are frequently used in distributed searching.

A benefit to this approach is that the resource-intensive tasks of indexing and storage are left to the respective servers in the federation. A drawback to this approach is that the search mechanism is limited by the different indexing and ranking capabilities of each database, making it difficult to assemble a combined result consisting of the most relevant found items. Searching over previously harvested metadata involves searching a locally stored index of information that has previously been collected from the libraries in the federation. When a search is performed, the search mechanism does not need to make connections with the digital libraries it is searching - it already has a local representation of the information.

This approach requires the creation of an indexing and harvesting mechanism which operates regularly, connecting to all the digital libraries and querying the whole collection in order to discover new and updated resources. OAI-PMH is frequently used by digital libraries for allowing metadata to be harvested. A benefit to this approach is that the search mechanism has full control over indexing and ranking algorithms, possibly allowing more consistent results. A drawback is that harvesting and indexing systems are more resource-intensive and therefore expensive.

CONSTRUCTION AND ORGANIZATION

Frameworks

A digital library can be built around specific repository software. The best known examples of this are DSpace, Eprints, Fedora, dLibra(Poland), and Greenstone Digital Library Software. In 2009, Fedora Commons and the DSpace Foundation merged to create a new organization, DuraSpace

The Reference Model for an Open Archival Information System (OAIS) provides a framework to address digital preservation.

Other formal frameworks include the DELOS Reference Model(Agosti, et al., 2006) and the Streams, Structures, Spaces, Scenarios, Societies (5S) formal framework.

Digitization

In the past few years, procedures for digitizing books at high speed and comparatively low cost have improved considerably with the result that it is now possible to plan the digitization of millions of books per year for creating digital libraries.

ADVANTAGES

The advantages of digital libraries as a means of easily and rapidly accessing books, archives and images of various types are now widely recognized by commercial interests and public bodies alike.

Traditional libraries are limited by storage space; digital libraries have the potential to store much more information, simply because digital information requires very little physical space to contain it. As such, the cost of maintaining a digital library is much lower than that of a traditional library. A traditional library must spend large sums of money paying for staff, book maintenance, rent, and additional books. Digital libraries do away with these fees. Both types of library require cataloguing input to allow users to locate and retrieve material.

Digital libraries may be more willing to adopt innovations in technology providing users with improvements in electronic and audio book technology as well as presenting new forms of communication such as wikis and blogs; conventional libraries may consider that providing online access to their OPAC catalogue is sufficient.

An important advantage to digital conversion is increased accessibility to users. There in also availability to individuals who may not be traditional patrons of a library, due to geographic location or organizational affiliation.

- **No Physical Boundary:** The user of a digital library need not to go to the library physically; people from all over the world can gain access to the same information, as long as an Internet connection is available.
- **Round the Clock Availability:** A major advantage of digital libraries is that people can gain access to the information at any time, night or day.
- **Multiple Access:** The same resources can be used simultaneously by a number of institutions and patrons. This may not be the case for copyrighted material: a library may have a license for "lending out" only one copy at a time; this is achieved with a system of digital rights management where a resource can become inaccessible after expiration of the lending period or after the lender chooses to make it inaccessible (equivalent to returning the resource).
- **Information Retrieval:** The user is able to use any search term (word, phrase, title, name, subject) to search the entire collection. Digital libraries can provide very user-friendly interfaces, giving clickable access to its resources.
- **Preservation and Conservation:** Digitization is not a long-term preservation solution for physical collections, but does succeed in providing access copies for materials that would otherwise fall to degradation from repeated use. Digitized collections and born-digital objects pose many preservation and conservation concerns that analog materials do not.
- **Space:** Whereas traditional libraries are limited by storage space, digital libraries have the potential to store much more information, simply because digital information requires very little physical space to contain them and media storage technologies are more affordable than ever before.
- **Added Value:** Certain characteristics of objects, primarily the quality of images, may be improved. Digitization can enhance legibility and remove visible flaws such as stains and discoloration.

PROBLEMS

Digital Preservation

The work needed to ensure that digital content is maintained and accessible into the future is beginning to be addressed.

Technological standards change over time and forward migration must be a constant consideration of every library. Migration is a means of transferring an unstable digital object to another more stable format, operating system, or programming language. Migration allows the ability to retrieve and display digital objects that are in danger of becoming extinct.

This is a rather successful short-term solution for the problem of aging and obsolete digital formats, but with the ever-changing nature of computer technologies, migration becomes this never-ending race to transfer digital objects to new and more stable formats. Migration is also flawed in the sense that when the digital files are being transferred, the new platform may not be able to capture the full integrity of the original object.

There are countless artifacts sitting in libraries all over the world that are essentially useless because the technology required to access the source is obsolete. In addition to obsolescence, there are rising costs that result from continually replacing the older technologies. This issue can dominate preservation policy and may put more focus on instant user access in place of physical preservation.

Copyright and Licensing

Some people have criticized that digital libraries are hampered by copyright law, because works cannot be shared over different periods of time in the manner of a traditional library. The republication of material on the Web by libraries may require permission from rights holders, and there is a conflict of interest between them and publishers who may wish to create Web versions of their content for commercial purposes. There is a dilution of responsibility that occurs as a result of the spread-out nature of digital resources. Complex intellectual property matters may become involved since digital material isn't always owned by a library.

The content is, in many cases, public domain or self-generated content only. Some digital libraries, such as Project Gutenberg, work to digitize out-of-copyright works and make them freely available to the public. An estimate of the number of distinct books still existent in library catalogues from 2000BC to 1960, has been made. The Fair Use Provisions (17 USC § 107) under copyright law provide specific guidelines under which circumstances libraries are allowed to copy digital resources. Four factors that constitute fair use are purpose of use, nature of the work, market impact, and amount or substantiality used. Some digital libraries acquire a license to "lend out" its resources. This may involve the restriction of lending out only one copy at a time for each license, and applying a system of digital rights management for this purpose.

Metadata Creation

The ability to find works of interest in large libraries is directly related to how well they are catalogued. While cataloguing electronic works digitised from a libraries' existing holding may be as simple as copying moving a record for the print to the electronic item, with complex and born-digital works require substantially more effort. While full text search can be used for some searches, there are many common catalog searches which can't be performed using full text, including:

- Finding texts which are the translation of other texts
- Linking texts published under pseudonyms to the real author (Samuel Clemens and Mark Twain, for example)

- Differentiating non-fiction from parody (The Onion from The New York Times, for example)

FRAMEWORK FOR BUILDING DIGITAL LIBRARY

The Greenstone digital library software provides a wide range of tools for building digital library collections. Based on our own extensive and varied experience, and that of others, we have designed a new framework for building digital library collections. We call it “Greenstone 3” to distinguish it from the earlier system, “Greenstone 2”. The new framework is supported by a fresh implementation that is completely independent of the existing one.

It capitalizes on the best ideas from the existing system, which we have urther refined and developed to open new avenues through which users can tailor their digital library collections.

Several pertinent new open standards have emerged since the original design many years ago, and a key objective is to incorporate them into the new design. The trend towards increasingly open, flexible architectures can be traced in the development of digital library protocols.

The Open Archives Protocol for Metadata Harvesting has provided a simple base-line for metadata access, and subsequent work strives to base component-based, modular protocols upon it. The METS document framework provides an open, extensible system for representing documents in digital repositories. Greenstone 3 adopts the same approach for a range of digital library functions, as this chapter demonstrates.

Set against the move towards standard protocols, today’s digital library systems must confront an increasing range of document formats and media, architectural designs for browsing and classification, indexing requirements, and user interface techniques. This drives the demand for open architectures, but makes it hard to provide well-formed and supportive infrastructures that maximise reuse of individual components and the reliability of the system as a whole. This chapter proceeds as follows.

First we introduce and describe the configuration structure and document representation used through our new building architecture. The second section describes the building process itself.

This is followed by the model that we have adopted to ensure that the new architecture is extensible. Fourth, we compare this with the previous Greenstone 2 design and present an example use-case scenario, identifying the key advantages of the new open collection-building architecture. We conclude by relating the new architecture to existing collection-building systems.

COLLECTION CONFIGURATION AND DOCUMENT REPRESENTATION

Before describing the process by which collections are built, we will show how the collection-building process is configured, and how documents are represented internally within the system. In we described our “plugin” mechanism and showed how it provides great flexibility for such varied tasks as ingesting both document files and metadata files, extracting text and metadata from different file formats, and expanding compressed files.

It has proved so successful that we have adopted it in the new framework. However, we depart radically from our earlier system by using the METS framework (which postdates that system) throughout for internal document representation.

Configuration

Collections are designed individually, and the structure of a collection is encapsulated in an XML file called the "collection configuration file." Its contents include build-time configuration options such as:

- The document types that the collection should recognise
- The metadata access structures or "classifiers" that are to be provided for users to browse the collection, such as by Titles A–Z
- The full-text indexes to build for searching the collection. The configuration file also contains run-time information about the collections, for example display options.

The bulk of an example configuration file can be seen in Figure—all that is omitted is the part concerning the purely runtime configuration. It defines a simple collection of HTML pages and plain text files, along with XML files that define metadata that is to be associated with these documents.

A document may consist of several separate files—for example, in this collection any images associated with the HTML pages will be contained within the HTML document rather than being identified as documents in their own right. Or a document may comprise complementary pairs of files—like a Word file and matching PDF version.

A collection configuration file

```
<documenttypes>
<document type="HTML">
<document type="Text">
<document type="MetadataXML">
</doctypes>
<search type="mg">
<index name="dtx" level="document" field="text">
<displayItem name="name" lang="en">entire documents</displayItem>
<displayItem name="name" lang="fr">documents entiers</displayItem>
<displayItem name="name" lang="es">documentos enteros</displayItem>
</index>
<index name="stx" level="section" field="text">
<displayItem name="name" lang="en">chapters</displayItem>
<displayItem name="name" lang="fr">chapitres</displayItem>
<displayItem name="name" lang="es">cap?tulos</displayItem>
```

```
</index>
<index name="stt" level="section" field="title">
<displayItem name="name" lang="en">section titles</displayItem>
<displayItem name="name" lang="fr">titres des sections</displayItem>
<displayItem name="name" lang="es">t?tulos de las secciones</displayItem>
</index>
<format>
<gsf:templatematch="documentNode">
<tdvalign="top"><gsf:link><gsf:icon/></gsf:link>
</td><td><gsf:metadata name="Title"/></td></gsf:template>
</format>
</search>
<browse>
<classifiername="CLSubject"type="Hierarchy"file="subject.xml"
field="Subject"/>
<classifier name="CLTitle" type="AZList" />
<classifiername="CLOrganization" file="organization.xml"
field="Organization"/>
<classifier name="CLKeyword" type="List" file="howto.xml"
field="HowTo">
<displayItem name="name" lang="en">HowTo</displayItem>
</classifier>
</browse>
```

The search block in Figure defines the full-text-searchable indexes that will be built. In this case the MG indexer will be used to build document-level and section-level indexes of the main text, and a section-level index of Title metadata. The browse block defines the metadata-based browsing mechanisms through which users can access the collection.

This configuration file specifies a hierarchical subject browser by defining a Hierarchy-type classifier of each document's Subject metadata, and the file that defines that hierarchy is named.

Other browsing classifiers are also defined. Run-time configuration items can be seen in both the classification and indexation parts of the file. For example. the "displayItem" nodes give names for the indexes (in English, French and Spanish) and for one of the browsers.

The Greenstone 3 building programme reads this file and configures the components to be used by the collection-building process. Many default options are implied. For instance, this collection would automatically expand Zip files—because the Zip expansion plugin is enabled by default. The process followed during building will be described later. type="Hierarchy"

METS and Document Representation

We were eager to adopt an open, standard form for modelling the content and metadata of a document. The METS framework supports a free selection of metadata formats and avoids duplicating data that is already stored in constituent files. Using this standard, open framework should facilitate interoperation with other digital library systems. These are the METS Header, Administrative Metadata, Descriptive Metadata, File lists and Structural lists.

The structural content is the only required section, and the content of the remaining sections is mapped onto the encoded structure. For the sake of clarity, this example shows only the connections between sections and the descriptive metadata and files.

A document is encoded into METS form by a plugin that corresponds to the type of the document. Each such plugin extracts any appropriate metadata from the document files (e.g. title), catalogues the files that comprise the document, and extracts the document text in subsequent phases.

In other words, it encapsulates the document content and acts as a standard gateway to its METS representation. This means that other phases of the building process are able to access data without having to understand the particulars of each file format—even if the data is stored as a binary object.

Document text can be provided in one of three ways, as the processing component requires. Plain Unicode is a simple baseline recognized throughout the system. At a higher level of sophistication, an XML representation is supported.

Finally, indexers can use the underlying binary files if they so desire. A complete document plugin provides all these formats, though the XML representation is optional. In any case, a document may have no textual content whatsoever (in which case all forms are empty).

For example, a PostScript file can be translated into an XML format. The PostScript plugin allows a plain-text reduction of this, but if an indexer wishes to treat PostScript files in a special way, it can access the original files directly. METS documents are partitioned into several components, the most common elements being structure, files, administrative metadata and descriptive metadata.

A given document may form part of a single file, or be an agglomeration of individual files and parts of files. Metadata can be associated with a document as a whole or with any part of its structure. A document may also have more than one structural form.

For instance, it may have both a page based structure and a logical chapter-and-section based structure. Metadata may be provided in several different formats and standards, and this allows for the native coding of metadata on the document in different formats—for instance RFC1807 and Dublin Core.

When a document first enters the library, it is given a unique identifier. That identifier will remain with the document throughout any subsequent revisions, and is recorded within the METS framework. Having described the configuration controls and document representation that underpin the new collection-building architecture, we now describe the building process itself.

Building Digital Library Collections

In our new architecture, collections are built in several distinct phases, which occur in sequence.

- **Expansion:** Compressed files such as Zip archives are expanded, and links to web sites are expanded into lists of constituent web pages.
- **Recognition:** All files are sent to the Recognition Manager, which identifies groups of files as documents.
- **Encoding:** All the recognised documents are catalogued for the subsequent phases of building.
- **Extraction:** Every document is passed through extractors, which use special processing algorithms to extract information from the document (e.g. title, keyphrases) or add metadata stored in special files.
- **Classification:** Documents are assigned to classifiers (e.g. topical classifiers, ordered list classifiers) depending on their inherent and extracted metadata.
- **Indexation:** Documents are sent to indexers to build indexes that support later searching.
- **Validation:** Post-building checks are carried out on the collection as a whole, and on its constituent documents.

Expansion

Before any individual documents are identified, any files that are compressed, or refer to external sources, are expanded. The case of a Zip archive has already been mentioned; other cases include OAI repositories, and links to web sites via a file of URLs.

The purpose of this phase is to create a complete list of all files that are available for building the collection. These raw files are then passed to the next phase for grouping into documents.

Recognition

The relationship between files and documents is complex. A file of emails may be seen as one file that contains many documents. Conversely, a JPEG image and a plain text file that describes it may constitute a two-file document. Our architecture uses special "recogniser" plugins to address the problem of distinguishing documents from files.

When the building process is initialised, all plugins listed in the collection configuration file are registered by a "Recogniser Manager." When the Expansion phase terminates, this Manager is handed each file in the collection in turn. It sends these files to each plugin.

For some simple cases—like a plain text document comprising a single file—the plugins are trivial. However, in other circumstances conflicts can emerge, and the Recogniser Manager includes a scheme for resolving these. For example, suppose a collection includes both web pages and digital photographs. A single JPEG file may be a document in its own right, or form part of a web page. By default, JPEG files that are referred to by web pages, being constituent parts of a larger whole, are not treated as documents in their own right, while JPEGs that do not appear in the web pages are identified as separate, discrete documents. This default behaviour can be adjusted, if desired, to allow all JPEG files to be treated as documents, even ones that also appear in a web document.

The same issue arises with any image file on a web page. Furthermore, such a file (for instance a logo) could well be part of more than one document. In this case it is treated as a subcomponent of all the documents in which it appears. A web page and associated files cannot form a strict subset of another web page, because the.html files must necessarily differ. The same strategy is used in other cases.

Once the Recogniser Manager has taken a pass through the entire inventory of files and identified the documents, it resolves any conflicts that occur and hands the output on to the Encoding phase.

At this stage all that is known of a document is the list of files that constitute its content. No metadata has yet been assigned—even that found within the document itself. The content and representation of any metadata internal to the document is identified in the next phase.

Encoding

Documents appear in a wide variety of forms, textual encodings and file formats. The Encoding phase creates the document framework that is used throughout the remainder of the building process.

This framework supports the retrieval of the full text of the document. It contains metadata defined within the document, and will also contain any metadata added to it. Finally, it binds the document, with its representation, into the classification and indexation structures. The METS document framework is used to encapsulate the files, metadata and structure of each document. At the end of the Encoding phase, documents are ready to be processed by extracting further metadata, indexation and storage.

Extraction

The Extraction phase is controlled by the Extraction Manager, which filters the documents through a series of extraction plugins. These can have one of two origins:

- Metadata-only files identified in the recognition phase above
- Explicit mention in the collection configuration file

The former method is typically used for files of descriptive metadata that are provided with the documents. The latter is used to invoke automatic extraction tools such as the KEA Keyphrase Extractor.

At the conclusion of the Extraction phase, all metadata has been collected and stored in the METS document representation. The next two phases place the documents into the context of the collection as a whole.

Classification

The Classification phase uses each document's metadata to site it within the browsing structures, or "classifiers," that are supplied by the collection to access the documents it contains. Each classification is represented by a plugin specified in the collection configuration file.

There may be more than one instance of any given classification type, achieved by initiating a separate copy of the plugin for each classification. Classifications are stored in a database, and when a document is matched to a node in a classification, this fact is recorded in both the document and the classification node.

Indexation

Indexing follows classification. To support the widest range of indexing systems, indexers are also treated as plugins. Again, the indexer—or indexers—used when building a collection are determined by the collection configuration file. For each indexer, parameters can be supplied that control its behaviour.

Indexers can build several different indexes, each with its own parameters. In the case of MG, for example, the structure level (e.g. document, section) and field (full text, title, etc.) can be controlled.

Validation

Validation plugins are used to control the quality of the collection by checking the final form of each document, and the collection as a whole. For example, a collection may insist on a complete metadata set—that is, all compulsory fields must be present.

Or the databases may be checked for empty classification nodes, which may be suppressed. Validation could be done in earlier phases, but we separate it into a final phase for architectural clarity.

Summary

Greenstone 3 uses a seven-phase build architecture. The first three phases identify and store each document. The next three phases enrich and index those documents. The final phase provides for quality control. The phases support different behaviours and activities that are required by different types of software, and a set of distinct functions that should assist programmers in extending any given implementation of the architecture.

Individual documents are recorded in the METS framework, which provides a standard form that gives access to different metadata formats, file formats and document structures. The document plugins give the indexation and classification components access to content without having to decode or transcribe documents.

EXTENDIBILITY: MANAGERS AND PLUGINS

The central role of plugins in each phase should now be apparent. However, we have made little mention of the structure of plugins themselves, or how they connect to the core system. The architecture achieves extensibility through Plugins and Managers. Each phase of the building process is controlled by a Manager—e.g. the Recogniser Manager, the Indexer Manager.

Managers are configured through the collection configuration file when the building process starts; and in some cases further configuration occurs when special files—like metadata-only files—are found when building.

Each manager coordinates the plugins for its phase of the build cycle.Each manager works in the same way. It initialises and configures its plugins. Then, when its phase runs, it takes each plugin in turn and tells it to do any necessary preparatory work. Next it passes each document or file in turn to that plugin. Finally it sends the plugin a termination message. Document plugins are unique in that they apply to several different phases of the building operation, whereas other plugins appear only within one phase. Managers accept a list of plugins from the configuration file.

New plugins are readily installed into the system by placing them into the plugin directory corresponding to their type, and adding them to the configuration file of one or more collections.

There is a standardised interface for all extraction, indexation and classification plugins.

This includes:

- Get Number Of Passes Return the number of passes required by the plugin
- Start Pass(int) Begin a pass for this plugin
- Process Documen t(Document) Process the given document
- End Pass(int) Terminate a given pass
- Tidyup Close the plugin
- Configure (Node)

Pass configuration information to the plugin. The configuration information mentioned in the last method is taken from the collection configuration file, where it is specified as an XML node. It is particular to each plugin. The get Number Of Passes method allows plugins to request multiple passes over the documents.

The MG indexation plugin, for example, requires a minimum of two passes plus a further two passes for each index it builds. Running each plugin separately and serially keeps memory overheads down.

ADVANCE OVER EARLIER WORK

The architecture that we have described capitalizes on lessons learned from the existing Greenstone digital library system, and incorporates some very significant improvements. At the time the earlier system was designed several important open standards did not exist, or were available only in draft form.

For example, the METS Document Framework, a key component of the new architecture, was unborn. The original Greenstone design adopted ad hoc file formats that became inconsistent with emerging norms.

Collection configuration was viewed as a compilation process directed by a configuration file whose format was similar to the Makefile format rather than by directives couched in a structured markup language. It used an HTML-like structure, the Greenstone Archive format, to store documents and metadata, which is less structured than modern XML.

The internal formats were also inconsistent with each other—configuration files being flat files whereas document files were derived from HTML. These simple and apparently cosmetic differences magnified into large-scale divergence.

Architecture

In Greenstone 2, collections are constructed in two phases: importing and building. The first parallels the Expansion, Recognition and Encoding phases of Greenstone 3, while the second mirrors the Extraction, Classification and Indexation phases. Both phases use the same set of plugins, which are listed in the collection's configuration file and loaded separately in each phase—despite the fact that some plugins only pertain to one phase.

Document plugins, like HTMLPlug, played a rather different role from that described above. Documents were identified by a single key file—e.g. an HTML file—and complex document structures were poorly supported.

A special generic plugin was later developed that recognized multi-component documents such as a Word file and its corresponding PDF version. However, the plugins had to be carefully ordered in the configuration file to recognize this compound document.

Once a file was captured by a plugin, subsequent plugins could not see it. The Recognition phase described above facilitates complex document forms and arbitrates competing claims for a file by different document types.

Plugin Details

Document plugins handle Encoding very differently in the new design. Originally, all documents were encoded into the standard Greenstone Archive Format as soon as they were encountered. This duplicated content, and could lose, or render inaccessible, some information in the original file.

The benefit was that all documents were presented to subsequent phases in a standardised format. In the new architecture, plugins convert document content to either plain text or well-formed XML, which allows formats such as TEI to be retained verbatim.

The METS Framework provides a standard container for metadata and structural information. This open public standard retains the benefits of the original Greenstone Archive Format, and goes further by allowing multiple structures within the same document. Plugins in Greenstone 2 could be of three types—Expansion (then called "structural"), Document, and Extraction (called "metadata").

All were placed in the same pipeline. The new architecture makes a clearer distinction between phases and allows a richer variety of documents. For most tasks, it supports clearer, more compact, interfaces. In addition, monolithic parts of the old design, such as indexation, are now readily adjusted and extended in the flexible manner exhibited by other phases (such as Expansion).

Example: The Kids Digital Library

We briefly present an actual digital libraries that was difficult to accommodate within the earlier design, and show how it benefits from the new architecture. In the Kids Digital Library each document can belong to several collections. Some collections are private (e.g. a child's own documents), others public. Some documents are unchanging (accepted final essays); others are under continually revision by a restricted group of users.

Students can annotate the work of others, and teachers provide feedback too. All collections support full-text searching and metadata-based browsing; some have additional browsing facilities. Collections sometimes change rapidly over a short period—e.g. during a scheduled class. Using the new architecture, many of these requirements can be delivered far more easily.

Consistent document identifiers and explicit change history allows revisions of a document, and comments made between changes, to be tracked. Incremental indexing is supported by recording accession and revision data as METS administrative metadata. The METS framework allows files to be duplicated between collections yet reside in only one location.

The Kids Digital Library featured some unusual browsing classifiers such as the "Top ten" and "Latest ten" stories. These require simple support for feature extraction. In the earlier design, this could only be done by altering the building scripts—which caused portability problems, and made it difficult to install new versions of the software. The new architecture circumvents the problem by modularizing feature extraction.

Comparison with other Digital Library Systems

Cheshire II emphasises the construction of digital libraries from original scanned documents. The process described for collection building reveals a system of fixed metadata fields and a strict control of the format in which documents are presented to the system.

Nowhere is support for feature extraction, expansion of compressed files, or novel indexes described. The CORR 2 is built on the NCSTRL software. The CORR documentation reports that the system requires documents to be submitted in a standard source format. No documentation on CORR or NCSTRL describes the parameters for collection configuration.

Conclusion

In the new collection building architecture we have described, the building process is segmented into a number of distinct phases. Once documents are identified, they are encoded into a flexible, open framework (METS) and are passed in that form to the succeeding phases of the build process. Within each phase, the elements are componentised to support greater portability and simpler development.

The build process is configured through a simple XML format file which is readily extensible for future components. We have implemented this architecture in a practical digital library system.

The use of a document framework rather than standardised document encoding has not created any obstacle to providing existing features. Rather, it supports our move to more complex document file structures and permits any processing of the document (e.g. by an indexer) to either refer to the original binary or to extracted content as it chooses.

We believe that the challenge of providing effective, portable solutions to building digital library collections is an important one. As file formats diversify, the issue of digital preservation grows. Similarly, if extraction and indexation technologies are not made more portable their adoption will slow. Our new architecture provides a step forward in meeting these challenges.

CONSTRUCTION OF DYNAMIC DIGITAL LIBRARY

This chapter describes a digital library architecture and implementation that is configurable, extensible and dynamic in the way it presents content and in the services it provides. The design manifests itself as a network of modules that communicate in terms of XML messages. All modules characterize the functionality they implement in response to a "describe yourself" message, and can transform messages using XSLT to support different levels of configurability.

Traditional library values such as backwards compatibility and multiplatform operation are combined with the ability to add new collections and services adaptively. The paper describes the new design and shows how it can be used to build four different digital library systems.

We conclude by showing how the design fits existing interoperability frameworks. This chapter describes a digital library design that improves upon the Greenstone toolkit. First, it provides more flexible ways of dynamically configuring the run-time system and adding new services to it.

Second, it lowers the overhead incurred by collection developers when accessing this flexibility to organize and present their content. Third, it modularizes the internal structure and simplifies the addition of new modules.

The design is based on widely-accepted standards such as XML, current software practices such as simple protocols (like SOAP), cross-platform development strategies (Java), and contemporary schemes for software modularization and dynamic updates.

Most important of all, it is informed by our experience with the current Greenstone system and the problems and challenges faced by real users, international collection developers, and practicing librarians.

The structure of the paper is as follows. First we give some background out of which the requirements for the digital library software arose. Next we describe the new design, called Greenstone, and discuss how it meets the identified needs. Fundamental to the approach is the use of XML throughout for data representation, combined with XSL Transforms to provide a flexible mechanism for adjusting the functionality of the runtime system without having to modify and recompile the source code.

To promote cross-platform independence (which has consumed inordinate human resources in the present Greenstone system) and facilitate the dynamic loading of services and other modules, the implementation uses Java.

Following this we describe four very different examples built using the new design. The first demonstrates backwards compatibility, and, in addition, operates within a distributed environment. The second augments text at display time, using an established software tool for text mining developed elsewhere, to show how functionality can be enriched through the introduction of a new service. The third is a map-based digital library that introduces two new services to support geographic functionality and, while still accessed through a web-based interface, is highly tailored to the specific domain of its source documents. The fourth is a radically different interface for the interactive viewing of search results as a hierarchically organized cluster of documents, and illustrates the versatility of the design in coping with fine-grained interaction. We conclude with a commentary on how the design fits existing interoperability frameworks, from which many valuable lessons have been learned.

Background

Over the years the Greenstone digital library software has been employed by many users internationally to develop a wide variety of digital libraries. In addition to operation over the Web, an early application, and still a major one, is collections of humanitarian information in the form of CD-ROMs that run on any Windows computer (including Windows 3.1).

There are now over two dozen of these collections, and they have been distributed widely by the United Nations and other non government agencies.

Many other styles of collection have been developed under Greenstone. They range from numerous personal collections based around common document formats such as E-mail, photographs, Word, and PDF documents through to largescale bibliographic catalogs such as the BBC radio and TV archives.

There are mixed media collections involving text, images and audio drawn from data such as historic newspapers and oral history. Several demonstration music collections support direct content-based retrieval through "query by humming." Many customized and branded user interfaces exist, such as the New York Botanical Gardens, and many international collections in local languages created by institutions in China, India, Croatia, Russia and Israel.

The software is distributed in source form, and for convenience binaries are available for Windows, Linux and MacOS X. The user interface is available in 30 languages. A recent addition is a graphical interface for collection design and construction which is also multilingual.

A portfolio of demonstration collections is available at www.nzdl.org, and selected example collections built internationally can be found at www.greenstone.org.

Weaknesses

Many experimental interfaces have been built for Greenstone, some of which make use of a CORBA-based protocol to support distributed client-server interaction. These include a Venn diagram tool for formulating Boolean queries graphically, and a bibliographic visualization tool that plots matching citations on an x-y grid based on publication year and ranked relevance score to the query terms. However, while perfectly functional, some of these variants are implemented inelegantly, exposing limitations caused by certain aspects of the design. For instance, the immutable nature of the index files generated during the building process makes incremental adjustments to a collection expensive. Another hindrance is the low level of functional customization supported by the runtime system.

Although minor presentation tweaks are easy, more extensive changes involve modifying and recompiling the source code. The strongly typed nature of the CORBA protocol was also found to be overly restrictive in many practical situations.

Requirements

From these and other considerations arose the following requirements for an improved design.

- **Backwards Compatibility:** Naturally we wish to retain the existing system's strengths. This is accomplished by ensuring that the new design is backward compatible, which has the added benefit of providing existing developers and users with an easy migration path.

- **Levels of Customization:** To match the different categories of people involved in constructing digital libraries, different levels of customization are required. For instance, a content developer may wish to include source documents in a new format; a collection editor may seek influence over diverse issues of presentation.
- **Software Modularity:** To facilitate development and long-term management of the software, code modularization—a mantra of any software engineering approach—is essential. This is promoted by adopting off-the-shelf technology such as a database system, indexing tools, and page rendering software; and by the use of standards.
- **Service Based:** Basing a digital library around a set of services is another way to accomplish modularity—in this case, modularity of function.
- **Distributed Architecture:** A rich digital library infrastructure can only be supported by a distributed architecture, and the addition of an open protocol helps to foster interoperability.
- **Future Compatibility:** Libraries are long-term institutions with a mandate for preservation, and it is essential that old collections can be presented by future versions of the system. This is a more ambitious requirement than mere extensibility which, although an admirable quality in any design, does not necessarily ensure that future versions can safely interact with current ones.
- **Dynamic**: Many aspects of the library should be dynamic, for example content, whereby documents and metadata can be added, revised and removed while a repository remains on-line, and configuration, where presentational issues can be adjusted and services added at runtime.
- **Integrated Documentation:** Large-scale software systems such as digital libraries benefit immensely from the use of an integrated documentation system.
- **Self-Describing Modules:** This goes a stage further than the previous item: modules describe themselves in a machine-readable format so that other modules can interact with them without the need for explicit control. Computer environment integration. A digital library should mesh well into a user's existing computer environment. Full integration makes a digital library become a seamless component of each user's work environment.

SOFTWARE DESIGN

The new software design has evolved from the requirements articulated above, our own experience of developing digital library systems, and studies of other open source software and research projects.

This section provides an overview of modularity and inter-module communication, and then works through a simple, stand-alone example. The next section describes four very different examples built using the new design, to illustrate the general applicability of the approach.

Modularity

We decided that the best way to meet the challenges posed by the list of requirements was to reimplement Greenstone using a modular topology. In the design, a digital library manifests itself as a network of modules, and communication between them is expressed through an instantiation of XML.

A mandatory requirement for a module—enforced through its base class definition—is that it handles “describe yourself” messages. What kinds of messages follow typically depend on the outcome of an initial “describe yourself”.

Modules have the ability to transform messages by applying an XSL Transform. This is a particularly useful mechanism for dynamically controlling levels of configurability—one of our requirements. Within the network of modules comprising a digital library, a set of services are defined that prescribe the functionality supported by that particular digital library configuration.

Communication

Modules communicate using synchronous request-response pairs. Figure shows an example XML exchange, where the Text Query module in a collection called “demo” is asked to describe itself. It does this, providing information about the structure of the service as well as fragments of text to be used for display. These are returned in the language specified in the request. While the language used is structured and typed, it has been crafted in such a way that the information it contains can be open-ended.

For example the paramList structure allows other items to be included, such as whether stemming is on or off. In addition to supporting optional parameters, extensions can be introduced without having to update the protocol’s API, thereby avoiding the need to propagate code changes to the entire distributed network (which may require taking it off-line while the changes are made).

Programming for a sample XML exchange as a request/response pair.

```
<request to=’demo/TextQuery’ lang=’en’ type=’describe’ uid=’21’/>
<response from=’demo/TextQuery’ lang=’en’ type=’describe’>
<service name=’TextQuery’ type=’query’>
<displayItem name=’name’>Search</displayItem>
<displayItem name=’description’>Full text search</displayItem>
<displayItem name=’submit’>Search</displayItem>
<paramList>
<param name=’index’ type=’enum_single’ default=’stx’>
<displayItem name=”name”>Index to search in</displayItem>
<option name=”dtx”>
<displayItem name=”name”>entire documents</displayItem>
</option>
<option name=”stx”>
<displayItem name=”name”>chapters</displayItem>
```

```
</option>
</param>
<param name='maxDocs' type='integer' default='10'>
<displayItem name="name">Maximum hits to return</displayItem>
</param>
<param name="query" type="string">
<displayItem name="name">Query string</displayItem>
</param>
</paramList>
</service>
</response>
```

A Simple Stand-alone Example

The simple stand-alone example shown in Figure encapsulates many of the design's key features. It comprises a "back end" server, termed a digital library site in our design, coupled to a "front end" that provides the user interface.

The modules' names were chosen to emphasize the roles they play. The Receptionist's point of contact with the server is the Message Router (MR) module—all communication with the site occurs through this module.

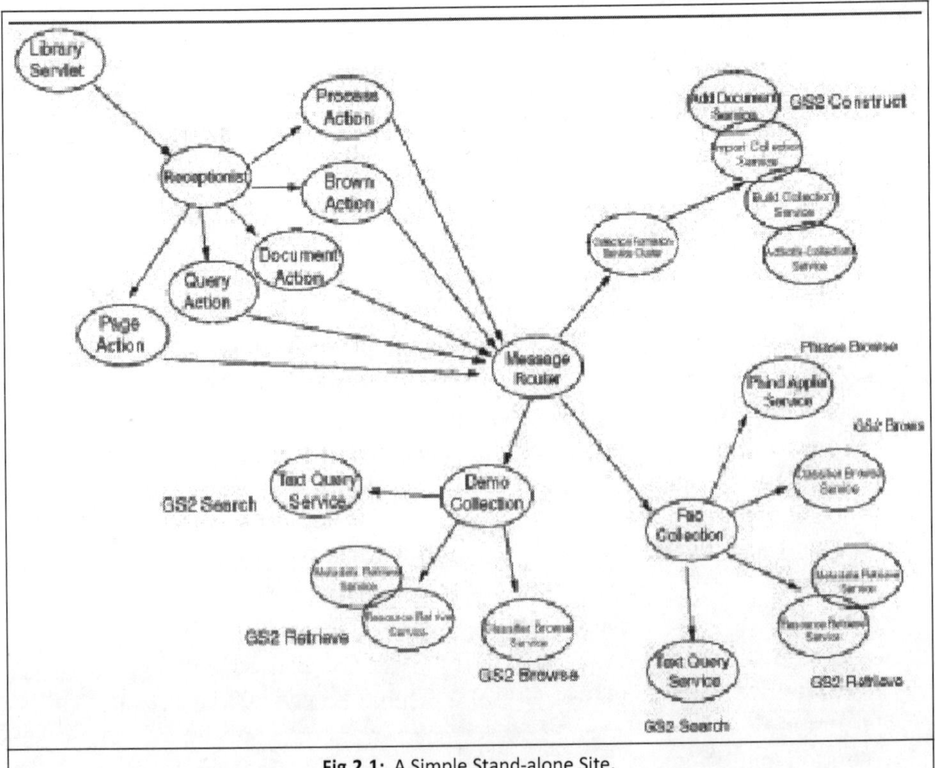

Fig.2.1: A Simple Stand-alone Site.

The configuration is designed to generalize to a distributed environment. The digital library back end in Figure contains two collections, demo and fao, and a cluster of collection-formation services. Add Document is a service that adds a document to a collection. Import Collection imports into the system all documents associated with a collection, converting them where necessary from their original form. Build Collection builds all indexes and browsing structures that are associated with a collection. Activate Collection makes a newly-built collection active, so that it can be seen by digital library users.

These services are all concerned with creating a digital library collection. Being related, they are grouped together into a “service cluster.” In Figure the services just listed are accessed through the Collection Formation service cluster module. As far as the digital library user is concerned, a “collection” is a focused group of documents with a uniform means of access. For the system, it is a service cluster that groups a set of services that are related by the data they work on.

For example, the demo collection towards the lower left of Figure contains three modules providing four services to the user. The modules are called “Search,” which provides a Text Query service, “Retrieve,” which provides a document retrieval service Resource Retrieve and a metadata retrieval service Metadata Retrieve, and “Browse,” which provides a metadata browsing service Classifier Browse.

The Web-based front end at the upper left of Figure centers around the Receptionist, which is the point of contact for the interface generator. A servlet (labeled “Library Servlet”) takes HTTP commands in the form of URLs and arguments and translates them into XML for the Receptionist.

The Receptionist is capable of executing various different actions, each of which involves (usually) many calls to the digital library’s Message Router. The builtin ability for Receptionist modules to transform XML messages using XSLT is used—in conjunction with a style sheet—to generate the HTML that is finally presented to the user.

Examples

For pedagogical purposes, the example configuration in Figure is rudimentary. The front and back ends (receptionist and site server) are compiled together into a single executable process with a single Message Router handling all communication between them.

However, the design supports a far richer infrastructure than this. Message Routers have the capability to communicate across a distributed network with other Message Routers and with Receptionists.

Different implementations of the same service can be switched in and out to give a digital library site different algorithmic behaviour (such as incremental building); and new services can be introduced and brought on-line, dynamically if necessary. The library can also have many different user interfaces.

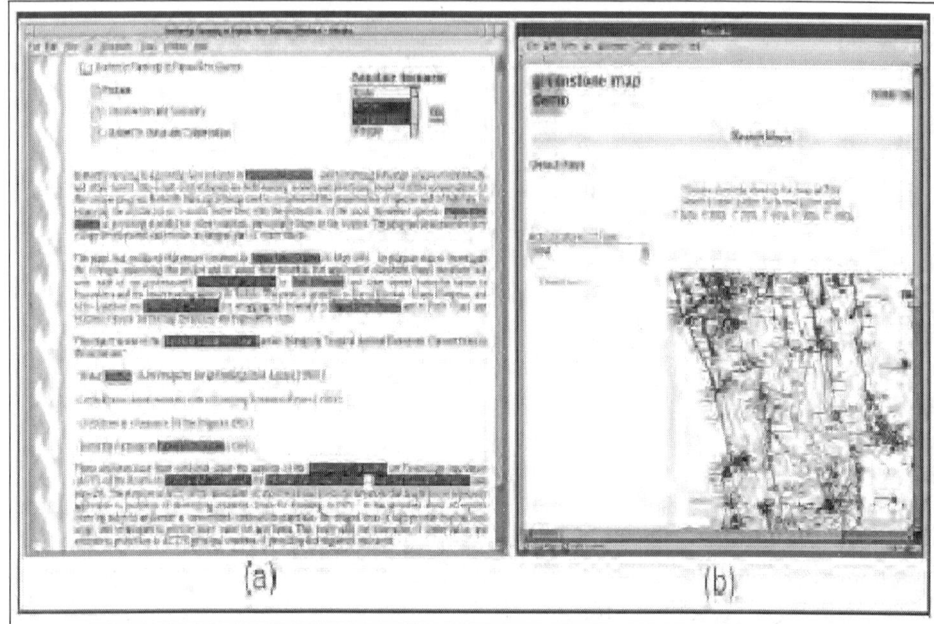

Fig. 2.2: Additional Services to Augment run-time Functionally (a) text Augmentation of place names; (b) a novel map-based Interface.

We now describe four more interesting scenarios. The first emulates "classic" Greenstone to demonstrate backwards compatibility, with a distributed configuration a straightforward addition. The second augments text at display time, to show how functionality can be enriched through the introduction of a new service.

The third and fourth utilize novel interfaces to enrich the interaction: the former is specialized for geographic maps, and the latter for text based collections.

Classic Greenstone, with collections on remote sites

To provide backwards compatibility, a set of Greenstone services have been implemented that access index and database files generated by a Greenstone system. Indeed we have already seen these in Figure.

Moreover, using Cascading Style Sheets (CSS), the look and feel of the traditional interface has been matched one-for-one, so that the user's experience of the digital library remains the same. Of course with the more versatile design, more sophisticated internal structures can be built within the digital libary.

For instance, because of the design decision that all communication be XML based, it is straightforward to arrange for the XML messages sent between modules to be seamlessly streamed across remote machines.

For this we employ the Simple Object Access Protocol (SOAP), but any protocol that can process text can be used. To the user there is no disernable difference accessing collections this way. Backwards compatability is not the sole aim, however, and the structure allows increasingly interesting digital library designs—ones that do provide a distinctly different expierence for the user. We discuss three such examples next.

Dynamic Text Mining

The next example shows how a new Greenstone service can be provided that enhances documents for the reader, based upon the open source GATE system for text mining. The motivation is that highlighting selected items in documents can make it easier for users to scan them for particular pieces of information.

In this implementation, digital library documents, once located, are mined on the fly marking up entities such as keywords and place names before presenting them to the user. Figure shows a section of a book on Butterfly Farming in Papua New Guinea (from the Humanity Development Library at www.nzdl.org) that the user is reading.

The Annotate document menu at the top right calls the display time text mining feature. When items on this menu are selected, text of the selected type is highlighted in the document displayed. In this case the user has selected Places and Organizations, and these are highlighted wherever they occur, in different colors (simulated by white-on-grey and black-on grey in the illustration).

The selectable items in Figure were identified and extracted by ANNIE, GATE's information extraction system. Whenever an annotation type is selected from the menu, Greenstone calls the information extraction module dynamically to identify items of that type.

This incurs a delay that depends on the document's size but is usually short: the system processes text at the average rate of 15 Kb/sec on a typical workstation. In order to achieve this the software is loaded when the Greenstone server is executed and remains resident in memory thereafter, to avoid a start-up delay (of about 10 seconds) in which all the text processors are initialized and prepared for use.

In Greenstone3, GATE is encapsulated in a module as just another service. It takes messages with two parameters, the type of annotation and a document, and returns the document with relevant items marked up with XML tags.

A style sheet in the server module chooses the colors in which the items are displayed. In order to generate the menu in the figure, a "describe yourself" message is sent to the GATE module, which returns a list of the annotations that are available. Apart from this one module, the rest of the digital library system knows nothing of GATE.

However, it does know about a general class of services, Enrich, that take a document and return the same document with some elements marked up. To add this text-mining ability to an existing Greenstone site dynamically the Java class files for the new service need to added to the correct folder on the DL site's file system, the site's configuration file updated to name the new service, and a "reconfigure" signal sent (which can be initiated through a web browser) to the DL site server.

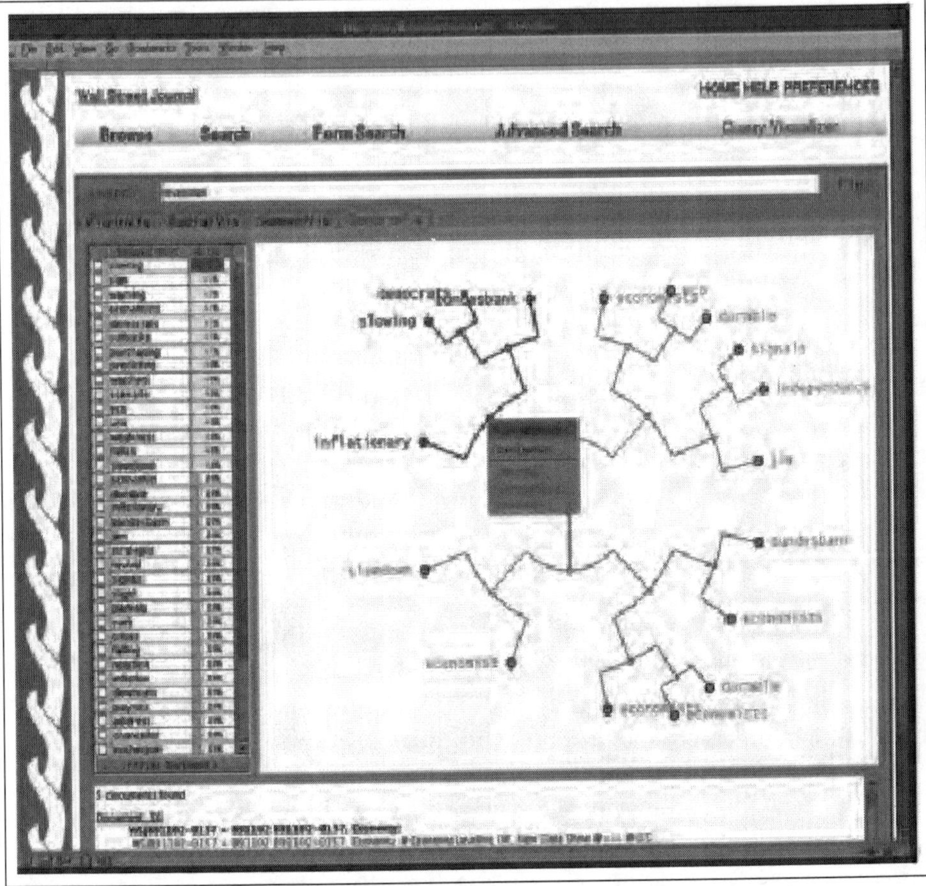

Fig. 2.3: Applet based Dendro Visualization of Clustered Documents Matching query.

Geographical map based interface Figure is taken from a site configured to support map searching based on a small collection of New Zealand maps drawn between 1770 and 1953, part of our university library's special collections.

It shows the result of searching for "Rangiriri"—a township in the North Island of New Zealand and, on a hill nearby of the same name, the scene of a battle in 1863 between Maori and British soldiers. Two crosses (colored red when viewed online) have been overlaid on the map showing the position of the township and hill, and can be seen slightly above the centre of the map.

The query interface and presentation of the results is similar to the traditional interface, except that against each matching item a thumbnail of the map containing the place name is given.

Figure is the result of honing in on one such map appearing in the result set. Through the interface the user can change the level of magnification of the map and request that additional features such as cemeteries, bridges, and estuaries be marked.

This new functionality is provided by adding two new services, including geographic metadata with the collection's source documents (the maps), and a gazetteer of over 40,000 entries from Land Information New Zealand (LINZ).

Searching is handled by the Map Query service. For each place name query term that is located in the gazetteer, its longitude and latitude are checked against each map to see if it falls within its boundaries.

Once all cross-referencing is complete, the list of maps with matching entries is sorted by the number of query terms on each map. Image manipulation and the results display are handled by the Map Retrieve service, which makes use of the open source Image Magick toolkit for copying, annotating (such as placing a cross at an x, y location) and resizing images.

Cluster Visualizations

Figure shows a web-based interface, but there may be other forms, ranging from standalone applications and applets that display documents in different ways to alert services that recognize when new information becomes available in one of the collections and formulate appropriate E-mail to users. Figure is one such instance: a Java applet that supports browsing result sets as document clusters through a multi-viewed, interactive interface. To function it needs the addition of a new build-time service, Vis Construct, which is responsible for computing additional statistics about the collection necessary to perform subsequent document clustering operations, and a sub-classing of the Applet service, tailored for the HTML necessary to embed the visualization applet within a web page.

Besides this, the visualization can interact with any text-based Greenstone collection that defines keyword metadata. The distinctly different interface behaviour is achieved through fine-grained interaction with the existing Text Query and Metadata Retrieve services using SOAP. Derived from the query term entered, there are four views in the visualization.

The first is the standard result list format; the other three are based around a shared model of hierarchically clustered documents.

In Figure the user has entered the query term "recession" to a collection based on the Wall Street Journal and is viewing the result as a Dendro map—the circular arranged tree displayed in the main panel—which contains words like slowing, slowdown and inflationary around the circumference. The size of nodes in the tree represents the number of documents clustered at that point in the hierarchy, and for reasons of space only 5 levels of the tree are shown at a time. Clicking on a node shows a popup menu with the precise number of documents in the cluster and the option of "drilling down" as shown in the figure.

The consequence of choosing this option is for the tree to be redrawn with the selected node at the centre of the map, thereby exposing more of the detail in that part of the hierarchy. While all this is going on, the left-panel displays the keywords relevant to the selected cluster, and the bottom panel lists the documents involved. Within the left panel, keywords can be activated or deactivated and the bottom panel dynamically filtered to reflect the changes.

INTEROPERABILITY FRAMEWORKS

This modular, service-based and dynamically configurable approach to digital library architecture can be found in other designs and systems. Two key examples are the Extended Open Archives Initiative protocol (XOAI) proposed by Suleman and Fox and the Open DLib system of Castelli and Pagano.

The XOAI protocol, based upon XML and related technologies, builds upon the basic OAI Protocol for Metadata Harvesting. It is a modular protocol which represents each service as a different type of OAI request. This service-based approach is readily seen in Greenstone's protocol, where each service has its own request and response format.

Like OAI and XOAI, Greenstone uses XML for representing requests and responses; providing a gateway between Greenstone and XOAI servers and clients should be readily achievable. The Open DLib system also takes a modular approach to service communication and library construction.

Many of its features are similar to those of XOAI and Greenstone, and the handling of requests to the library map as readily as for XOAI. However, Open DLib is centered upon a "manager" service that coordinates services, responding to the introduction of new services and alterations to existing ones.

Coordination is achieved through a communication protocol between the manager and each service. Individual services, including each library in a federation, acquire data from the manager.

The manager does not itself control or direct requests for searches, documents, and so on but instead coordinates between services to ensure consistency. Greenstone provides many of these features—for instance, service description requests—without requiring a centralized manager.

The similarity of protocols between Greenstone, XOAI and OpenDLib echoes experience with the previous generation of DL protocols and augers well for interoperability. Greenstone's widespread adoption and free availability allows others to adopt it as a platform for experimenting with the service-centered design approach.

It facilitates the addition of new digital library features which would have been hampered by the less open structures of Greenstone and its contemporaries. Greenstone retains and extends the lightweight configurability of its predecessor without requiring centralized management processes.

This chapter has presented a new digital library design which is significantly different from the present Greenstone, but strongly rooted in past success. To meet a broad range of requirements a modular based topology is utilized to provide a flexible infrastructure.

Written in Java to promote portability, dynamic loading of objects and internationalization, modules communicate by streaming XML messages between each other. Using SOAP this communication can be distributed across a network. All modules have the ability to describe themselves in a machine readable form, and to apply an XSLT to transform messages.

The latter is instrumental in providing different levels of configurability, an important ability given the different types of people involved in the life-cycle of a digital library. Several working examples have been given to convey the general applicability of the design.

The first example demonstrated backwards compatibility to collections built with Greenstone, and satisfies another of the identified requirements: to help minimize the migration path of existing developers and users. It also demonstrated the design functioning in a distributed environment.

The second example augmented an existing DL site with text mining capabilities with the introduction of a new service. The third and fourth examples illustrated substantially different user interfaces: one specialized for maps that required two extra services to provide the necessary geographical functionality; the other provided an interactive visualization to search results through a Java applet that was applicable to a wider realm of text-based collections.

Numerous aspects of the design contribute to its dynamic configurability. The "describe yourself" feature allows receptionists to adapt to the facilities that a server presents. Through XSLT a corpus editor can exert significant control over the function and appearance of a digital library such as modifying the structure of a generated page, for example adding a transform that sorts the query results alphabetically by title rather than ranked score. Alternatively they may reformat the results according to OAI syntax in preparation for exporting.

Previously such changes required editing the source code and restarting the digital library software after recompilation. Implementing the design in Java has promoted dynamic attributes in the system, particularly through the ease in which modules can be loaded at runtime.

The re-reading of configuration files is also straightforward to arrange and adds dynamic abilities that a digital library administrator can take advantage of. In addition to integrating the documentation with the software using JavaDoc and other techniques, usability of the software also benefits from the development of self-documenting collections that both demonstrate and describe particular aspects of design.

The list of requirements is ambitious, however, and not all of them have been proven yet. For example, while none of the sample implementations demonstrate computer environment integration, the design is capable of supporting the idea through specialized receptionists. For future compatibility, more time is needed to establish if the design successfully meets such a criteria.

DIGITAL LIBRARY EVALUATION

When an animal bred in captivity runs, flaps or slithers into the wilderness for the first time, scientists do not simply wave goodbye, wish it well and move on to the next project. Usually the animal is tracked and observed for a long time thereafter—the point of release is where the research really begins.

However, this has been less true for grant-funded digital library projects. Administrative and institutional barriers tend to confine evaluation to the funding period when the system is being designed, and when its uses and effects can only be guessed at. In this short paper I will discuss a digital library project in environmental science where some of these evaluation issues arose, the value of eliciting narrative data from users, and some ways to take better advantage of existing but underused mechanisms for long-term evaluation of digital libraries.

Viewing information technologies and society as inextricably co-determined makes it necessary to gather data both on the design process and on how the finished systems are used by people—often in quite unexpected ways.

Iterative design and formative evaluation are ways to introduce user feedback into ongoing design, but while these strategies can serve as an effective translation layer between users, designers and builders, the focus is on how an evolving system might be used.

How it is actually used can be more accurately determined when the system is in the wild, when the designers and their formal evaluation instruments have gone away. Digital libraries are social entities. They tell stories about a culture, a science, a place or a time, through the items represented and organized in the collection, and in use, they help generate new stories as well.

Manovich has advanced the idea of database and narrative as two ends of same continuum; both structure information, but where a database aims for access, a narrative aims for psychological immersion in the story. From an institutional standpoint, digital libraries are rarely ends in themselves.

The social missions of the funding organizations—the stories they wish to tell— often drive the creation of digital libraries, but how well a finished system supports the mission can't be fully evaluated until the digital library has had some time to develop a user base. This line of research began with a participant observation of the design of a digital library of environmental science collections. Funded by an Library Services and Technology Act (LSTA) grant, the project involved diverse designers, content, metadata and institutional participants.

As one of the participants in the environmental science digital library noted, "Part of the art of grant writing is interpreting vague language in a way that lets you do what you want to do," or in other words, making project proposals and achievements dovetail with the mission and goals of the funding agency. These goals included outreach and evaluation, so a usability component was included in the grant proposal. My initial role in the project was to develop the instruments and conduct the evaluation.

Understandably, digital library designers tend to create evaluation instruments that demonstrate in a measurable way the work they've done, a tacit statement of the value produced for the grant funds received. For example, the design of the interface, the appropriateness of descriptive metadata, and user success at canned search tasks are classic evaluative measures.

However, in an analysis of the Perseus Digital Library (PDL), Marchionini writes: "Operational data are powerful components in a chain of inferences that address impact but the PDL evaluation illustrates the value of anecdotes and "stories" that illustrate new effects, i.e., how DLs augment existing capabilities with new ones. These augmentations garner public support for a DL and should not be underestimated in assessing impact.

Integrating multiple views is more naturally done with narratives than summary statistics and integrating these forms of evidence can aid in assessing complex change." In the evaluation, statistical and demographic data were not hard to come by.

Observation, interviews, document analysis, narrative analysis and social network analysis were effective ways to construct as complete a picture as possible about the interactions of the designers. But the usability component needed to be completed at the same time as the digital library, in time for the results to be included in the final LSTA grant report (though the exact LSTA grant regulations vary by state, most LSTA grantees must submit a final grant report within 15-30 days of project completion).

Participants in the usability study were evaluating a still evolving system, and had to project potential uses into their responses to open-ended interview questions. By the time they might integrate the collections into their professional lives, and perhaps surprise themselves with unexpected dimensions of usefulness, the evaluation would be long over. This is certainly not to say that there is no such thing as continuing evaluation of grant-funded digital libraries.

But the mechanisms for long-term evaluation are usually little more than Web forms or e-mail links, not organic components of the digital library. In practice, designers are more concerned with present and future digital library projects than with continuing evaluation of those of the past.

Digital library researchers have an opportunity to conduct this longer-term research, to question and reveal the impacts of digital libraries as social entities, and to apply the resulting knowledge to future projects.

The good news is that in some situations, a mechanism for longer term evaluation already exists. For example, the State Library of Ohio's LSTA grant process makes use of a "year-after" evaluation form (http://winslo.state.oh.us/publib/lstayraft.html), which includes questions such as "Did the project produce any unexpected results?" and encourages narrative ("Please provide a success story of how your project has impacted someone's life or had a positive impact on the community.").

This is precisely the sort of openended data collection instrument that can reveal how a digital library is actually being used—but even this document is only the length of a one-page questionnaire. Subsequent research will attempt to evaluate the usefulness of this and other longer-term evaluation instruments, and how they might be expanded. While longer-term evaluation should include quantitative data such as transaction logs and perhaps a list of external sites that link to collection content, evaluation instruments should also be open-ended, designed to encourage narrative expressions of unexpected use, the kind of data that reveal to funding agencies the real impact of their grants. Iterative digital library design philosophies have always had at their core the sense that user input should feed back into ongoing system design. I propose here simply a wider iterative design circle, one that allows for more naturalistic data about longer-term use to be fed back into future systems.

In sum, lessons learned that will be explored in future research include an increased emphasis on:

- Long-term evaluation of digital libraries
- Narrative data; allowing users to tell stories
- Unexpected uses
- Evaluating social outcomes, not just the design process or product
- Linking findings more directly to the higherlevel goals of funding agencies

DIGITAL LIBRARY INFORMATION APPLIANCES

Although digital libraries are intended to support education and knowledge work, current digital library interfaces are narrowly focused on retrieval.

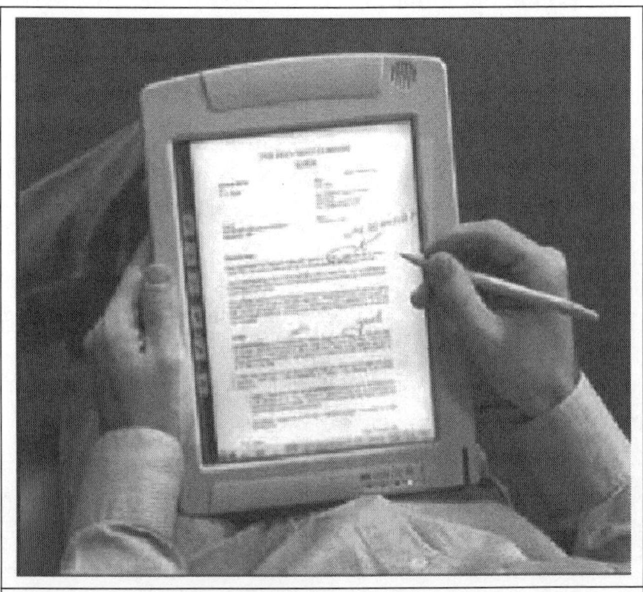

Fig. 2.4: XLibris Prototype in a Reader's lap.

Furthermore, they are designed for desktop computers with keyboards, mice, and high-speed network connections. Desktop computers fail to support many key aspects of knowledge work, including active reading, free form ink annotation, fluid movement among document activities, and physical mobility.

This chapter proposes portable computers specialized for knowledge work, or digital library information appliances, as a new platform for accessing digital libraries. We present a number of ways that knowledge work can be augmented and transformed by the use of such appliances. These insights are based on our implementation of two research prototype systems: XLibris, an "active reading machine," and Tele- Web, a mobile World Wide Web browser.

The standard platform for accessing today's digital libraries is a desktop computer with a keyboard, a mouse, information retrieval software, and a network connection. Unfortunately, desktop computers are not suitable for many types of knowledge work.

Studies of people using electronic and paper documents show that desktop systems fail to support four important activities:

- Active reading
- Free form ink annotation
- Fluid movement among document activities
- Physical mobility

As a result of focusing on the desktop, today's interfaces for accessing digital libraries support retrieval in isolation, without addressing these broader work practices. We propose a new platform for accessing digital libraries: specialized portable computers designed for knowledge work, or digital library information appliances.

In this chapter, we draw on our experience designing and building two research prototype information appliances— the XLibris "active reading machine" and the TeleWeb mobile Web browser— to show how these devices can support a broad range of activities in the digital library.

READING AND DIGITAL LIBRARIES

The first and most fundamental document activity is reading. "Reading" encompasses a broad range of complex and poorly understood practices involving documents, including skimming, searching, browsing, speed-reading, surfing, reviewing, and rereading. Although we often take it for granted, reading can be hard work. We use the term active reading to distinguish this rich collection of activities from simply looking at words on a page.

Desktop computers do not support active reading. Once expected to create a paperless office, computers have instead produced ever-increasing quantities of paper documents. Dataquest predicts printers and copiers will generate over 1012 pages in the U.S. in 1997.

This statistic suggests that people do not use computers to read. The reason for this is obvious: paper supports extended, focused, deep reading practices better.

Current research on digital libraries does not address a broad range of reading activities. Instead, as David Levy points out, digital libraries support shallower, more fragmented, and less concentrated reading.

The research focus in this field is on tools for search, selection, and distillation, tools that promote identification and extraction of information fragments. Because digital library interfaces do not support active reading, people search online and then print documents to read them. This "search and print" reality contrasts with the "search and read" ideal held by researchers.

Although a dual online/paper system is not a priori undesirable, we will show the many advantages of an online system that enables a variety of reading practices. The XLibris active reading machine supports a broad class of reading activities by employing a "paper document metaphor" (as opposed to the desktop metaphor) that imitates the physical experience of reading and marking on paper.

The paper document metaphor follows lessons learned from a number of studies comparing reading online to reading on paper, summarized below.

TANGIBILITY

Readers often move paper documents to avoid glare, to speed up handwriting, or to adjust their perspective of a text. In contrast, most computer displays are stationary while in use, so that readers must move themselves—their heads, their bodies, and their arms— rather than their display. XLibris supports paper document-like tangibility by running on tablet displays.

Although XLibris has not been deployed for real use, people say that holding a page-sized display in their lap and being able to easily reposition it changes their online reading experience.

The tangibility of paper documents also supports navigation. Turning paper pages seems easy and natural, and the weight and thickness of a paper document convey length and location.

In XLibris, pressure strips on the case of the device provide a tangible interface for page turning: pressing on one side of a sensor moves to the next or previous page, and holding down initiates riffling through pages. The harder you press, the faster you move. A quick animated transition indicates the direction of turning.

Finally, "location guides" of varying thickness drawn in the top cor- ners of each page provide feedback about the length of the document and the reader's current location.

Page Orientation & Fixed Layout

Paper documents are laid out on fixed-size pages. The page layout often communicates the type of the document (e.g., business letter versus technical article) and where to find important information (e.g., a return address). The fixed layout also supports spatial memory and helps readers find old information.

In these and other ways, paper pages give readers an excellent "sense of the document." This sense of the document is often lost online.

Most CRT monitors cannot display a full page of text legibly, leading to awkward scrolling and zooming. Word processors and Web browsers commonly re-flow the text on a "page." And hypertext versions of paper documents can lead to disorientation and a sense of being lost. XLibris respects pages by displaying the image of a single page at a time.

Because the LCD panels we use are designed for landscape viewing, XLibris rotates the image 90° to approximate the portrait orientation of a typicalprinted page. XLibris stores the image of each page and the underlying text; this "image + text" file format is compatible with printed and with scanned documents.

Multiple Displays

People often work with multiple pieces of paper simultaneously, either with several pages from one document or with several documents. Most of today's computers provide multiple virtual displays through use of a windowing system. Unfortunately, the effort of managing window layout and switching among windows can interfere with reading.

Therefore XLibris displays a single page image and does not support windows. Since limiting the digital library information appliance to a single page image is problematic, we have considered a number of ways to address the need for collateral displays.

Presenting two full-page images side by side, as in Book Emulator, makes text unreadable on current tablet displays, but may be feasible as LCD technology evolves. A form factor with multiple physical displays is another approach. (Bush's vision of a Memex desk included multiple displays). In our case, to maintain mobility, a book (instead of a tablet or desk) with two opposable LCD panels may be appropriate. Weiser presents an enticing vision of ubiquitous computing with devices so cheap they can be scattered and used as paper.

In the near term, however, a small number of pen computers in conjunction with nearby desktop displays or even paper may provide the most practical solution to the problem of collateral document work. In summary, XLibris employs tangibility, page orientation, and fixed layout to provide an online reading experience comparable, in many ways, to reading from paper.

FREE FORM INK ANNOTATION

"Until we provide support for smooth integration of annotation with reading, it is likely that people will continue to annotate paper materials, even as they read materials in a digital library." – Cathy Marshall The second key document activity is annotation.

Knowledge work involves reading combined with categorizing, speculating, remembering, judging, or, more broadly, critical thinking. This active reading process is facilitated by underlining, highlighting and making notes on the text or in a separate notebook. Marking on paper helps readers "make the text their own" and is a common practice associated with deep understanding of written information. In a nutshell, readers write.

Unfortunately, annotation online is quite different from its paper-based cousin. Interfaces for annotating often involve selecting a command, pointing with a mouse, and typing on a keyboard. They generally require much more effort than scribbling with a pen.

Text annotations are not as visually distinct as ink marks, and online annotations often cause changes in the layout of the document. We believe that the ability to make unstructured, free-form, idiosyncratic ink marks is a crucial feature of any interface to digital libraries. Although such marks may not have explicit meaning to the computer, they have rich semantic meaning, supporting visual and episodic memory. An essential aspect of ink on paper is its lack of modality: users can write anything they want, anywhere on the page.

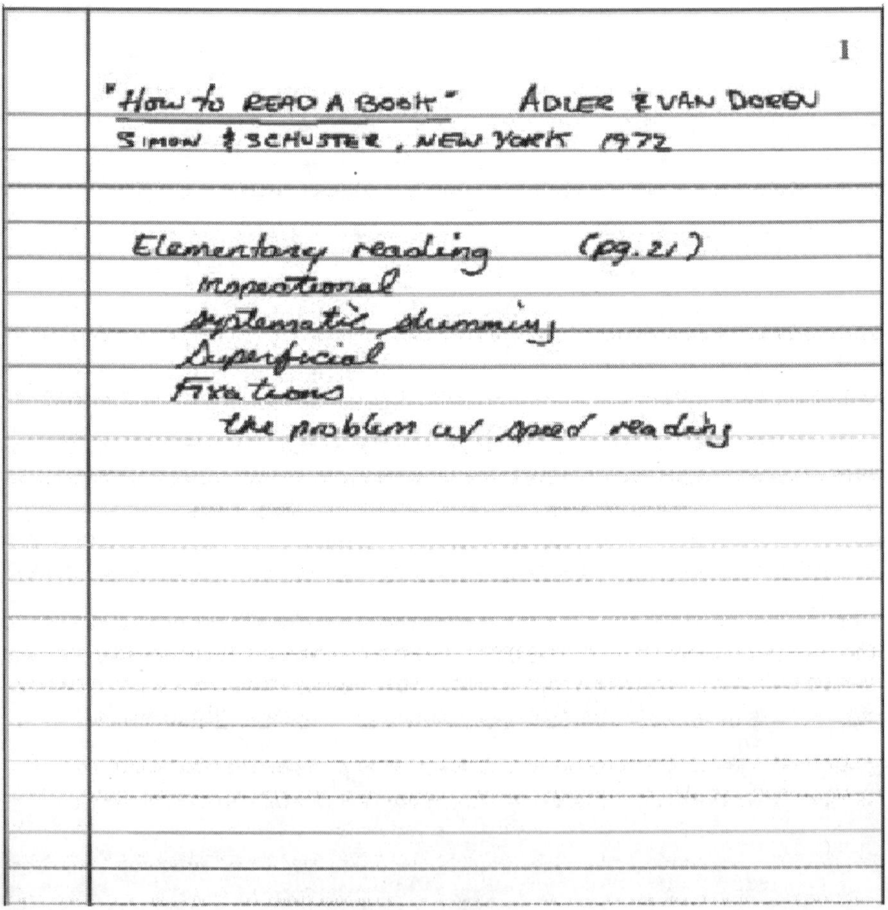

Fig. 2.5: A Notebook page from XLibris.

In XLibris, we followed this principle by letting users scribble notes, draw figures, highlight, or annotate text, all without switching modes or applications. Readers highlight and mark-up document page images as they read or flip to a blank page in a lined notebook for more space. XLibris provides several colors of ink, several highlighter pens, and a stroke-based eraser.

FLUID MOVEMENT AMONG DOCUMENT ACTIVITIES

The third key aspect of knowledge work is fluid movement among different styles of reading and different document activities. As an example, consider the process of "information triage" where an analyst skims through a pile of search results and reduces them to a manageable set.

The current practice is to fire off a query to a search engine, retrieve the 100 top-ranked documents, print them out, mark them up with highlighters, and put them into piles. Analysts then read the most relevant passages to answer the original question. Consider an alternative scenario where the analyst owns a digital library information appliance.

After conducting a search, the analyst skims the documents online. The appliance enhances skimming by emphasizing important material. As on paper, the analyst marks up important information as it is found. Instead of reviewing the collected information by thumbing through piles of paper, the analyst views a concise collection of his or her text annotations.

If any of the annotated material is worth reading in greater depth, the analyst can do so comfortably online. If the analyst needs more information, the text that has already been highlighted can be used to generate the next query. At a high level, this scenario demonstrates fluid movement among document activities. The analyst quickly moves among searching, skimming, annotating, reviewing, and deep reading.

There is no waiting for a printer. Because skimming and deep reading are tightly integrated with retrieval, analysts can determine if the information they are collecting is useful before they invest much effort. This scenario also demonstrates how computation can enhance skimming, reviewing, and searching.

Because the interface is based on a paper document metaphor, the reading and annotation activities remain much the same as on paper. In our design, the "computer" remains in the background and, when requested, rises to the surface to assist the reader with the tasks of skimming, reviewing, and searching. Below we describe how XLibris supports and augments these three activities.

Skimming Mode

Skimming is one way readers gain a quick impression of a text. When skimming, the reader's eyes typically search for and alight on key words or sentences and take in short passages before moving on. Sometimes the reader becomes engaged and shifts into deep reading, or is distracted and moves into quicker skimming or into riffling.

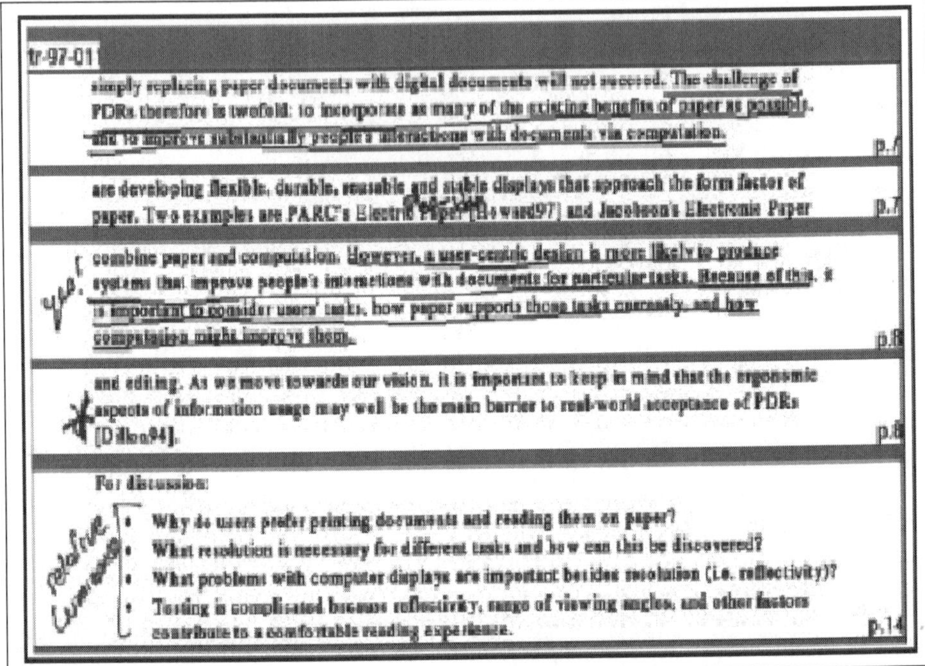

Fig. 2.6: The Reader's Notebook shows annotated clippings of documents laid end-to-end. Clippings are labeled with document title and page number and are linked to the corresponding pages.

XLibris' "skimming mode" highlights phrases and sentences that are characteristic of the document being skimmed. We call out key phrases because they can be read at a glance and tend to reflect the topic of the nearby text.

This assists with the activity of scanning the text for relevant portions to read. The Wall Street Journal and People Magazine use a similar technique of boldfacing company names and Hollywood celebrities' name to help readers find information. We also highlight summary sentences to support a speedreading– like activity. Skimming mode uses a commercial text summarizer to identify summary sentences that are emphasized. Skimming through a document of highlighted summary sentences provides a narrative overview that is not available by just reading key phrases.

Both of these highlighting techniques permit a smooth transition from skimming to deep reading: key terms and sentences can help readers decide whether a passage is worth reading and are likely to be appropriate places to transition to deep reading. Skimming mode uses shades from gray to black to indicate term importance. Meaningful terms are identified by heuristics that select noun phrases.

The shade for each term is then based on a statistical information retrieval measure: terms that occur frequently in the document but occur rarely in other documents are colored black, while terms common to many documents are colored light gray. For example, the term "digital library information appliance" would be colored black when it appears in this document.

Skimming is a common practice: a study of college students' reading habits reported that skimming occupied 32% of their reading time, and that "86% of the descriptions of skimming strategies mentioned a selection process based on key words and/or particular sentences and paragraphs in certain text locations".

Although our design requires empirical evaluation to confirm its utility, from our experiences thus far, we are optimistic that computers can improve the skimming activity and that augmented skimming is a useful function for a digital library information appliance.

Reviewing the Reader's Notebook

Reviewing paper documents is facilitated by the marks made during reading: marks not only record information but are also used to organize it for later review. There are three common venues for marking: annotating on the page, taking notes in a notebook, and writing on loose-leaf paper.

Annotations on the page highlight key information but tend to be lost in piles of paper. Notebooks are compact and can be reviewed quickly, but taking notes can be tedious and error-prone.

Unbound notes can be reorganized flexibly, but require even more effort by the note taker. XLibris' Reader's Notebook combines the best features of annotating directly on the page, of taking notes in a separate notebook, and of organizing index cards. As with paper documents, readers mark on the page in the context of the document, yet without the laborious and imprecise step of copying.

As with a bound notebook, readers can review concise annotations by time. Finally, as with note cards, flexible filtering and sorting of the view allow readers to reorganize their information as needs change. The Reader's Notebook extracts "clippings" of annotated text and lays them end to end in a separate, multipage view.

Each clipping is linked to the corresponding annotated page, so readers can move fluidly between notes and documents. Each clipping includes some surrounding text, and is labeled with document title and page number to help readers understand the meaning of the marks. In designing clippings, we had to decide how much of the document should be shown for each annotation.

Starting with the bounding rectangle of each ink stroke, we expand it horizontally to the width of the page and vertically to include complete words.

Snippets that overlap are merged together resulting in reasonably sized clippings of annotated text.

The Reader's Notebook can display, sort, and filter clippings from one document or from all documents. By default, clippings are sorted by document page number, which is analogous to rummaging through a pile of paper, but should be faster because readers do not see the less important (i.e., un-annotated) information. Clippings can also be sorted by time so that new information appears at the end, as in a paper notebook.

Finally, readers can filter the clippings by ink colour to search for different kinds of marks or to group related items together. Many readers already use different pens to mark different types of information. For example, some lawyers highlight "pro" information in green and "con" information in red.

Finding Information Related to Readers' Annotations

Readers often search for related material and move from one text to another. For example, an ecology student studying the effects of acid rain in the Appalachian Mountains decides to search the Internet for information on the economy of West Virginia. A doctor reading up on a drug she has never prescribed decides to follow a reference to a study of its side effects.

Unfortunately, in both online and offline situations, finding related materials and reading are not well integrated. Typical information retrieval interfaces force users to stop reading, to identify related documents, and then to print them.

References found in paper documents are even more timeconsuming to track down. Although hypertext was designed to address some of these problems, authors cannot anticipate the information needs of all readers. Ironically, despite the fact that readers' interests may change rapidly, interfaces for moving from reading to finding and back to reading again are time consuming and disruptive.

Clearly this is another example where fluid movement across document activities is desirable. XLibris facilitates fluid transitions among reading, searching and browsing by creating a dynamic hypertext from readers' marks.

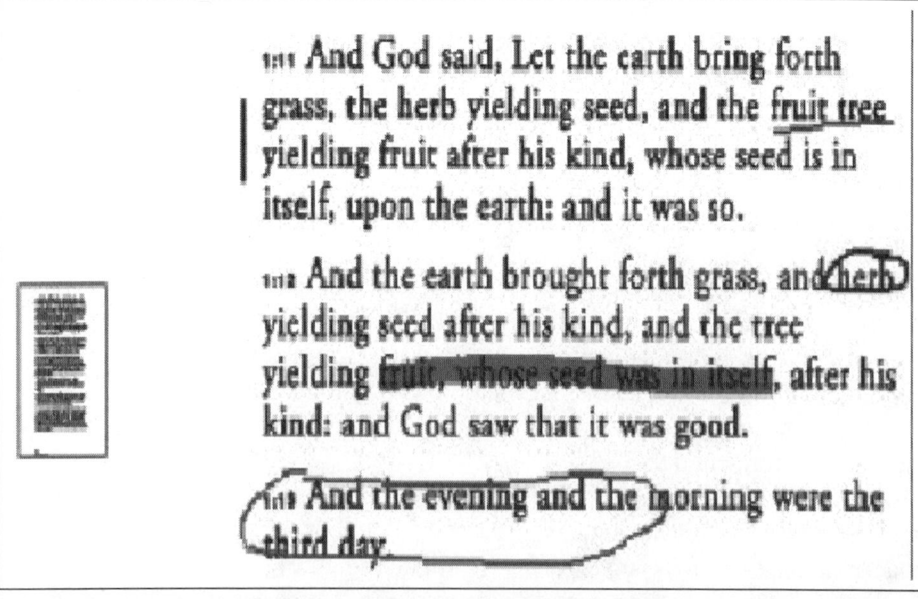

Fig. 2.7: Examples of Highlighting, Underlining, Circling, and margin Annotations. Each Annotation Generates a Query. If a good match is found, XLibris adds a margin link (Rectangle on the left) that shows the thumbnail of the Destination page.

The system observes readers' annotations and the text of the underlying document and generates hypertext links (margin links) to related documents: no additional effort from readers or authors is required. Because XLibris suggests links of interest to particular readers at particular times— based on the passages they are marking— people can discover useful information serendipitously. This type of serendipitous retrieval is a benefit of paper libraries: as people walk to the shelf for a particular book, walls of related books surround them, making it possible to find interesting material accidentally.

Although serendipity in the library is often a rewarding experience, it is generally lacking in online systems. XLibris provides two user interfaces that integrate reading, searching, browsing, and serendipity. These are described below.

MARGIN LINKS

Margin links provide serendipitous access to related documents during the active reading process. As readers mark up passages, the system finds related documents and presents links unobtrusively in the margin; our intent is to provide a modeless link suggestion mechanism. Because margin links persist, readers can follow links at their leisure.

We use thumbnail images of the target page as anchors. The reader taps on an anchor to move to that page. For the most part, link creation does not disrupt the reading process since the reader is free to disregard the suggestion and to continue reading. In the current design, however, margin links intrude on the reading process more than we would like.

One problem is that XLibris computes a separate query for each stroke (although strokes often do not result in margin links because of a similarity threshold).

We have begun to address this by adding a button to turn links off and by designing ways to manage the frequency with which margin links appear.

FURTHER READING LISTS

When readers reach the end of a document, they often want to know more. The document may not emphasize the topic they are most interested in, or it may spark an interest in a new topic without providing enough depth or detail. Sometimes this need is addressed.

For example, articles in Scientific American typically describe an area of research at a high level, without providing much technical detail. To help readers go into more depth, the editors create a further reading list at the end of each article.

The Scientific American example illustrates the limitations of authored reading lists. The article describes a technological vision for protecting digital copyrights. Consider a reader with a narrower interest, such as "how digital copyright affects librarians."

Further Reading

LEGALLY SPEAKING: REGULATION OF TECHNOLOGIES TO PROTECT COPYRIGHTED WORKS. Pamela Samuelson in *Communications of the ACM*, Vol. 39, No. 7, pages 17–22; July 1996.

FORUM ON TECHNOLOGY-BASED INTELLECTUAL PROPERTY MANAGEMENT: ELECTRONIC COMMERCE FOR CONTENT. Edited by Brian Kahin and Kate Arms. Special issue of the *Interactive Multimedia News*, Vol. 2; August 1996.

LETTING LOOSE THE LIGHT: IGNITING COMMERCE IN ELECTRONIC PUBLICATION. Mark Stefik in *Internet Dreams: Archetypes, Myths, and Metaphors*. Edited by Mark Stefik. MIT Press, 1996.

SCIENTIFIC AMERICAN March 1997 81

Fig.2.8: A Further Reading list from Scientific American

The reference to a six-page article on digital copyright law may help track down this information, but the reference is unlikely to answer the question directly. Furthermore, by the time the reader scans the further reading list, more appropriate articles may have been written. XLibris augments this traditional editorial practice by automatically generating further reading lists for each document. Unlike static references, these lists reflect the interests of a specific reader at a specific point in time. As with margin links, the reader's interests are inferred from annotations, and no additional intervention from the reader is required.

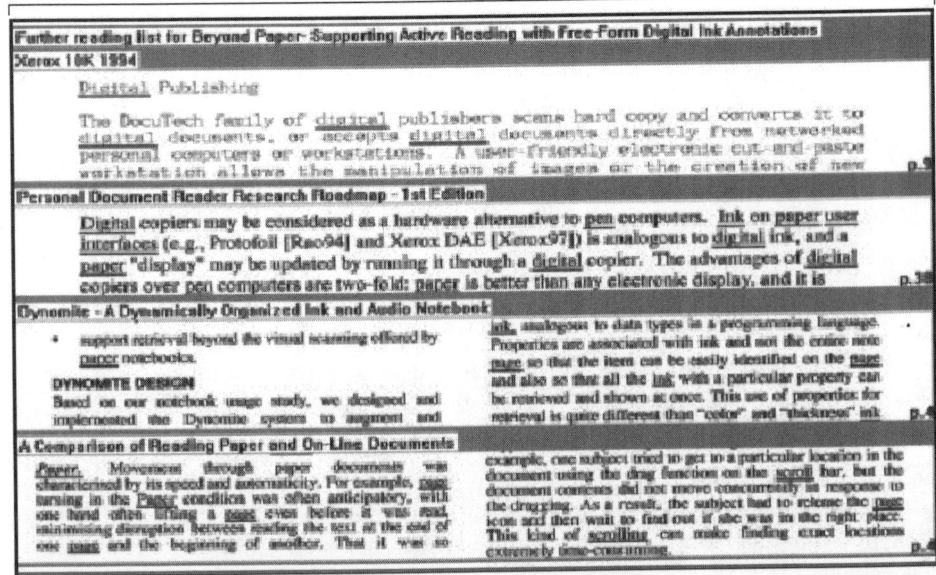

Further reading list for Beyond Paper: Supporting Active Reading with Free-Form Digital Ink Annotations

Xerox 10K 1994

Digital Publishing

The DocuTech family of digital publishers scans hard copy and converts it to digital documents, or accepts digital documents directly from networked personal computers or workstations. A user-friendly electronic cut-and-paste workstation allows the manipulation of images or the creation of new

Personal Document Reader Research Roadmap - 1st Edition

Digital copiers may be considered as a hardware alternative to pen computers. Ink on paper user interfaces (e.g., Protofoil [Rao94] and Xerox DAE [Xerox97]) is analogous to digital ink, and a paper "display" may be updated by running it through a digital copier. The advantages of digital copiers over pen computers are two-fold: paper is better than any electronic display, and it is

Dynomite - A Dynamically Organized Ink and Audio Notebook

- support retrieval beyond the visual scanning offered by paper notebooks.

DYNOMITE DESIGN

Based on our notebook usage study, we designed and implemented the Dynomite system to augment and

ink, analogous to data types in a programming language. Properties are associated with ink and not the entire note page so that the item can be easily identified on the page and also so that all the ink with a particular property can be retrieved and shown at once. This use of properties for retrieval is quite different than "color" and "thickness" ink

A Comparison of Reading Paper and On-Line Documents

Paper. Movement through paper documents was characterized by its speed and automaticity. For example, page turning in the Paper condition was often anticipatory, with one hand often lifting a page even before it was read, minimizing disruption between reading the text at the end of one page and the beginning of another. That it was so

example, one subject tried to get to a particular location in the document using the drag function on the scroll bar, but the document contents did not move concurrently in response to the dragging. As a result, the subject had to release the page icon and then wait to find out if she was in the right place. This kind of scrolling can make finding exact locations extremely time-consuming.

Fig. 2.9: A Further Reading list in XLibris. Each related Document is Presented as a Clipping of the most Relevant Sentence with key Phrases Underlined.

Further reading lists are presented as a separate set of pages, or view, associated with each document. Readers can access this view at any time, whether or not they have annotated the current document.

Of course, the more annotations the user has made, the more focused the resulting list is on the reader's interest as opposed to the document as a whole. Visually, the further reading list looks like a Reader's Notebook of annotations except that each clipping is a segment of a related document obtained from a search engine.

These clippings, with matching terms underlined, help readers understand the destination of the link and also make the target passage more recognizable if they choose to follow the link.

Query-mediated Links

Both margin links and further reading lists use a technique called query-mediated links. Query-mediated links derive a query from a user's interaction with a document and use that query to identify related documents.

Golovchinsky has shown that query-mediated links based on explicitly selected words and passages are effective in supporting information exploration tasks. XLibris computes margin links from the words, phrases and passages that are implicitly selected by the reader's marks. (We do not expect readers to make marks for querying explicitly, but rather as part of their existing annotation practice.)

Marks are converted into text selections, which are then expressed as full-text queries that yield a best-matching passage. The system adds a margin link to the best match if its similarity value (or belief score) is above a threshold.

For further reading lists, each annotation is interpreted as a text selection and is transformed into a list of word scores.

The scores for each word are then summed across all annotations. If several annotations select the same instance of a word, then the maximum score for that instance is used.

The words along with their scores are used to generate a query. If not many words have been included, then terms that are most characteristic of the document can be added.

This padding reduces the chance that a query based on a small number of annotations will return documents that are entirely unrelated.

Ink Annotations as Queries

XLibris recognizes several distinct ink patterns from which queries are computed. These include underlined words, highlighted words, circled words, circled passages, and margin annotations. We emphasize that there is no "vocabulary of marks" that readers must learn; rather, our heuristics are based on general annotation practices. Each type of annotation results in a slightly different query for the search engine. Marks that select specific words translate into queries that retrieve other instances of the same term. Marks that select longer passages generate queries that search for similar passages.

PHYSICAL MOBILITY

The fourth and final document activity supported by digital library information appliances is mobility. Until now we have discussed reading in XLibris; in this section we describe mobile information access in TeleWeb. Desktop access to digital libraries is not adequate for mobile workers.

A doctor making hospital rounds has no desktop with her to access a digital library. This could have grim repercussions: a recent study concluded that patients for whom prompt MEDLINE searches were conducted have significantly lower costs and shorter hospital stays. Mobile work is not limited to physicians and traveling salespeople; even office workers often work with documents away from their desks.

For these people, portable information appliances can provide access to digital libraries anywhere, anytime. Unfortunately, it is not possible to give mobile people the same network access that they would have in their office. Compared to wired desktop networks, wireless networks are slow, expensive (with different billing schemes), and only intermittently available. As workers move from place to place, they are likely to experience three levels of connectivity: high quality connectivity from an office network, lower quality connectivity from a wireless network, and no connectivity at all when disconnected.

How can people use digital library appliances to access distributed information sources across this range of operating conditions? Aside from the variable networking conditions, there are two other issues that affect mobile access to digital libraries. First, downloading a document over a wireless network can be very expensive, and current interfaces for search engines and Web browsers do not help people manage these costs.

Second, user interaction is punctuated by surprises: an information request may return right away (when data is locally stored), take a while (when data is remote), or take forever (when the network is down). The TeleWeb mobile Web browser was designed and built to explore these three issues.

TeleWeb runs on a laptop computer with multiple communication channels: it may be docked to an office Ethernet, used from home over a telephone line, used while traveling over a wireless network such as a cell phone, or operated while not connected to a network. The lessons learned from TeleWeb apply not only to the Web but also to digital libraries.

In the design of TeleWeb, we assumed that at least some of the time users would be disconnected but would still want to browse the Web. Some mobile networks are so limited in bandwidth compared to office networks that users may feel like they are disconnected.

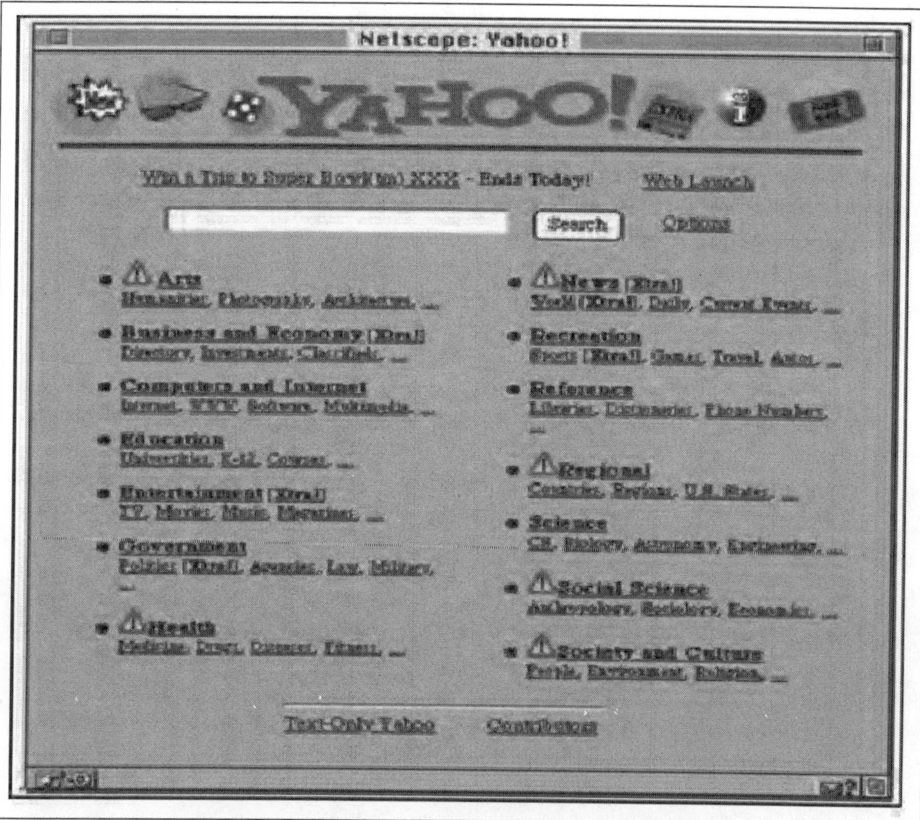

Fig. 2.10: A Document Annotated with road sign icons to show Hypertext anchors Absent from the cache. Networking not ubiquitous

How can people browse the Web when disconnected? TeleWeb uses “caching for availability,” the standard solution for this problem. This means that the system loads documents into a local cache when fully connected.

Later, if the user needs the document while the network is not available, the locally cached copy is returned. Caching for availability only works if the system knows the user’s information needs ahead of time. The system can use past history to predict future needs. In addition, the user can tell the system what documents belong in the cache; unfortunately, in practice people find it difficult to articulate which documents they need.

Furthermore, both techniques share the drawback that information needs often change in unpredictable ways. Overall, caching for availability often works, but is frustrating when it does not.

An alternative solution is to replace synchronous interaction (a user request followed immediately by a response from the network) with asynchronous interaction. For example, when the user requests a document not in the cache, TeleWeb asks the user if the system should download it later.

If so, Tele- Web downloads the information the next time the user connects and adds the document to a "to read" list that the user can browse. This interaction style is analogous to sending a request for a book from an out of state library, and eventually receiving it in the mail.

There are other reasons to postpone downloading a document. For example, if a user is connected over a cellular telephone, downloading a large document is going to be expensive, and can tie up the network connection for hours.

Given the choice, the user might be happy to download this document overnight or upon returning to the office. There is a tradeoff here between how urgently people need information and how much they are willing to pay for it in time and money.

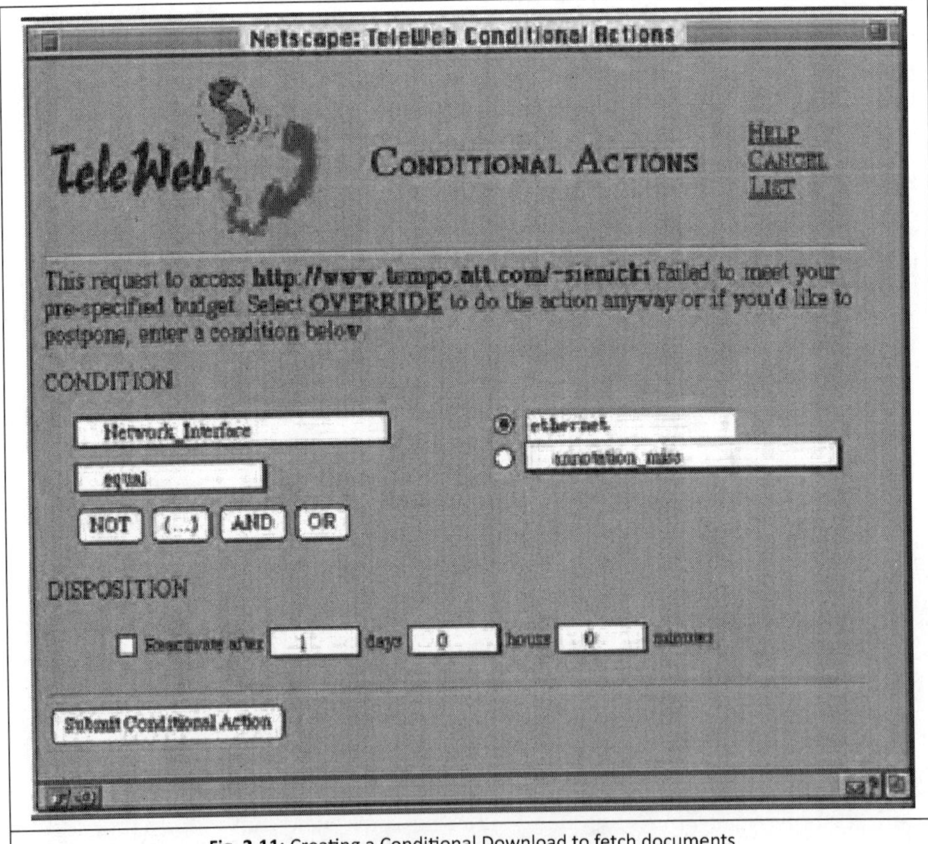

Fig. 2.11: Creating a Conditional Download to fetch documents when Reconnected. No feedback on cost

With a mobile information appliance, users should be able to decide how much they are willing to pay for each document and how quickly they need that document. With this principle in mind, TeleWeb includes a budget monitor that sits between the user and the network. If a request is made for a document that is not in the cache and downloading the document will break the user's budget, then

TeleWeb presents a "conditional download" form instead of the document. Users can override their budget to fetch the document immediately, or they can request that the document be fetched at a later time.

Unpredictable Systems are Frustrating

The third problem of mobile appliances is unpredictable behaviour. Those using computer networks already know this problem: sometimes they hit a key and nothing happens. In wireless computing, this experience is magnified many-fold.

TeleWeb's solution is to show the user what is going on inside the cache and network manager. Specifically, Tele- Web labels links that will be slow to download with a "road work" icon.

If there is no road sign, then either the link destination is cached, or a high-speed connection to the information superhighway is available. This simple change— essentially exposing the state of the system— makes mobile Web browsing much more predictable. This contrasts with the traditional approach of trying to simplify the user's view of the system by concealing the state of the network.

THE FUTURE

The development of tomorrow's digital library information appliances is an iterative process. Our current cycle, however, is not complete until we evaluate the ideas presented in this chapter.

Towards this end, we have begun a series of laboratory user interface experiments and are in the planning stage for a real-world deployment. One experiment suggests that free-form ink marks made while reading are better for query formulation than traditional relevance feedback.

People who have tried XLibris agree that our approach of taking a work practice and augmenting it— rather than redefining it— makes the system immediately accessible. Information appliances must be accessible. The digital library community must decide whether digital libraries should, as we propose, support users throughout the process of turning information into knowledge. If so, there are many issues that must be addressed.

One reviewer of this chapter asked: "Where is the digital library?" We purposely avoided describing protocols, services, and architectures because we believe infrastructure should support the vision of working with a digital library information appliance, not define it.

The next step is to understand how users of digital library information appliances should interact with external repositories. For example, should users pay authors to cache documents on their devices, even when they do not read them? How should users search repositories that are not always accessible?

How should searches be distributed between local and remote databases?

These and other issues require further investigation. We have shown how information appliances based on the paper document metaphor can support active reading. Because these systems allow people to work on digital documents much as they would on paper, this provides an alternative to the standard "search and print" model of digital libraries.

Furthermore, by integrating a wide variety of document activities, and by allowing fluid movement among them, disruptive transitions between paper and digital media can be eliminated.

The combination of the paper-like and the digital allows us to augment these activities without redefining them. Finally, the mobility of a digital library information appliance supports work away from the desk.

With all these benefits, digital library information appliances can create a rich, universally accessible, digital library experience that improves the way we work. Clearly there is an exciting future for digital library information appliances in the digital library.

ELECTRONIC RESERVE AND ON-DEMAND PUBLISHING

The term 'electronic reserve collection' may be a misnomer as it implies rationed access whereas 'the digital environment removes the need for this form of rationing as a single digitisation can simultaneously be accessed by any number of readers'.

Nevertheless, the term is used to describe collections of resources, including journal papers and extracts from texts and newspapers, that have been digitised and mounted on campus networks to be accessed by students.

The rationale for this is that hard copy can be accessed by only one person at a time but access to digital copy is limited only by the infrastructure required to use it. Electronic reserve collections (ERCs) have been developed with a view to meeting more effectively the needs of large undergraduate classes which rely increasingly on the library for core reading materials. Development of ERCs is more widespread in the US than it is in the UK.

In the early 1990s, many of those developing ERCs in the US considered it 'fair use' to digitize copyright resources and make them available electronically.

The Conference on Fair Use (CONFU) guidelines were intended to formalise this reading of the law but publishers and librarians were unable to agree on guidelines for electronic reserve use of copyright materials (http://www.utsystem.edu/ogc/intellectualproperty/confu.htm). Nevertheless, many libraries continue to interpret the law in this way (follow links from the following URL for examples http://www.cc.columbia.edu/~rosedale/#Sites).

Use of copyright resources in ERCs in the US must now be licensed just as it is in the UK. In the UK, HE ERC developers have assumed that ER use of copyright materials is not 'fair dealing' and guidelines published recently by the Publishers' Association and the JISC confirm that this is so (http://www.ukoln.ac.uk/services/elib/papers/pa/licence/fairnote.html).

Clearly, the cost of obtaining permissions is important to the economic viability of the whole exercise. This cost includes not only the price for using copyright material but also time spent identifying right sholders, seeking permission to use their copyright material and, often, chasing that request.

The total figure can be as high as ten times the actual copyright fee. The cost to rightsholders of administering permissions requests is also significant. At present the Association for Computing Machinery (ACM) grants blanket permission to copy its copyright materials for educational use because the cost of administering applications exceeds the revenue generated. This suggests that if licensing digital use of copyright materials is to become a viable revenue stream for publishers, copyright fees must be relatively high.

Although publishers have been willing to grant permissions free of charge to limited life ER projects, i.e. during development, they charge fees to use their material in ongoing ER services.

This may not be a viable revenue stream but many publishers consider ER use of their material to be a threat to their core business. Charging deters widespread adoption of ER as an alternative to text provision or recommendation. On the other hand, as long as ER systems do not cannibalise publishers' primary income, a streamlined process may actually generate incremental revenue for them.

Another significant cost associated with ERCs is the cost of digitising text. Odlyzko cites an example of a company that will digitise text for $0.60 per page but recent eLib supporting study established £2.50 as a reasonable estimate. Obviously, cost varies with a number of factors such as the cost of identifying and obtaining the original, the condition of the original, the presence or otherwise of special characters, i.e. the degree of manual intervention required to produce a useful file.

If publishers begin to supply their texts in electronic form and offer the facility to buy subsections of texts, then the need for HEIs to digitise a significant amount of text will vanish. However, unless publishers digitise all back runs of journals and text back lists, there will be a need to digitise older material.

At present, developments in delivering texts in electronic form are embryonic, so material selected for reserve collections from texts must almost always be digitised if it is to be delivered in electronic form. However, duplication of effort may be avoided if institutions collaborate. Very little has been published on the economics of running an ERC. The ACORN Project at Loughborough University compared the costs of traditional and electronic reserve collections of journal papers.

A more comprehensive study of the costs and benefits of ERCs was published as an eLib supporting study in 1998. This study was informed by all eLib studies in the electronic reserves (ER) and ondemand publishing (ODP) programme areas, including ACORN. Another relevant study comparing charging mechanisms was conducted on behalf of a JISC/PA working party following a seminar on pricing in July of that year.

This study arose from debate among and between librarians and publishers regarding appropriate pricing mechanisms that would not cannibalise publishers' primary income stream. It considered only licensing of digitised copy from printed books and journals; not licensing of electronic products.

The report from the study called for a pricing mechanism that is 'simple and therefore inexpensive to administer … susceptible to centralised administration [and produces] predictable costs for users and revenues for rights holders'.

Furthermore, the report recommended that two models be adopted to reflect different types of use of digitised material; a 'textbook substitution' model and a 'library substitution' model. The former would be applied to materials that, in print, publishers would expect students to buy.

The pricing mechanism would be based on student numbers and a licence would be granted for a fixed period; probably an academic year. The latter model would be applied to material that, in print, publishers would have expected libraries to buy. In this case, a licence would be granted in perpetuity.

The report referred also to the high cost of digitisation and commended the idea of a central repository of digitised text which would avoid duplication of effort among HEIs and would make it easy for HEIs to identify material for which permission is likely to be granted, as it had been in the past. The report from this study is particularly useful because it resulted from an ongoing collaborative attempt by publishers and HE representative to resolve many issues that hindered progress with ERC developments.

Many of the recommendations in the report appear to have informed the Copyright Licensing Agency (CLA) Higher Education Digitisation White Paper which details the terms on which copyright materials are now licensed by the CLA for digitisation and distribution.

The CLA will continue to require institutions to request rights on a transactional basis and prices will be set individually by publishers. Publishers will differentiate between material that is likely to substitute for sales of texts to libraries and material that is likely to substitute for sales of texts to students.

The latter will be more expensive to compensate for many more 'lost sales'. This differentiation will refer to specific titles; it will not vary between institutions depending on their patterns of use of that title. Thus, although institution A may refer students to title X for further reading while at institution B it is required reading for all students in a class, both institutions A and B will be required to pay at the prescribed rate, be it 'text substitution' or 'library substitution'. This system is not ideal but the alternative, i.e. setting prices with reference to both the title and the institution requesting permission to digitise it would be extremely complex and thus expensive.

The CLA White Paper also specifies the format of digitised text; it should be an 'exact page representation' of the print original. As pages designed to be printed tend not to be suitable for on-screen reading students can be expected to print.

At present, students tend to photocopy materials borrowed from a reserve collection so the library could recover print costs from students without increasing student expenditure. However, support for networked printing is likely to be a significant cost associated with the introduction of an ER system.

The CLA does not expect institutions to comply with the 'exact page representation' criterion by creating and delivering bitmapped images from printed originals. The White Paper acknowledges that bitmapped images are large files and thus are bandwidth hungry.

However, licences may specify the degree of qualitative and quantitative accuracy in digitised text. It may be possible to comply with terms by using suitable software and including disclaimers regarding accuracy (and the CLA anticipates that this will be the case) but there is no guarantee that this will be the case. As OCR programs tend to generate errors, it may be necessary to proof-read digitised text.

This adds considerably to the digitisation cost. It is not immediately apparent that the eCLA (the name of the new CLA service) will be more efficient than the often criticised CLARCS system for clearing rights in materials to be used in course packs (containing photocopies).

A transactional payment mechanism is expensive. The Copyright Clearance Centre in the US has operated a transactional system for electronic reserve materials since 1997.

In addition to any permission fee it charges $5 per request regardless of whether or not permission is obtained and claims that this charge is required to cover costs. The CLA requires from each publisher a mandate to license that publisher's material for use in electronic form in HEIs. The Publishers Licensing Society (PLS) has published a template which publishers can use to mandate the CLA Some of the terminology in this template differs from that used by the CLA, i.e. the PLS refers to a 'Bookshop Materials' model and a 'Library Materials' model instead of, respectively, a 'text substitution' and a 'library substitution' model. One more substantial difference between the CLA White Paper and the PLS mandate is that the latter restricts a licence for 'library materials' to 5 years rather than granting it in perpetuity.

The PLS mandate also sets the 'Bookshop Materials' model as default and recommends a default price of 5 pence per page. Thus, libraries will be expected to pay for copyright at a rate of 5 pence per page per student in a class. A single 20-page extract for a class of 200 students would cost £200 (£235 inc. VAT) in copyright fees alone. If widely adopted, the terms of this mandate will probably render ER prohibitively expensive.

HERON

HERON is an eLib-funded project developing a national database and resource bank of electronic texts to be selected and accessed by HEIs throughout the UK. HEIs will supply details of materials that they require in digital form.

HERON will obtain permission for their use and will digitise these materials. HERON is collaborating with rights holders and representative bodies to determine appropriate fee levels and conditions of digitised text and to streamline copyright clearance procedures.

The Project will normally clear rights through the CLA and when an institution requires permission to use material that is owned by a publisher or other person who has not mandated the CLA, HERON will seek to secure an agreement directly with the rightsholder.

Thus, when HERON has agreed terms with a publisher and an institution seeks to use material owned by that publisher, HERON can approach the company with confidence not only that permission will be granted but that the terms agreed previously will suffice and no lengthy negotiation will be required. Gradually, HERON will accumulate a collection of such agreements making it more efficient for HERON than for any individual institution to seek to clear rights in material to be included in an ER system. Furthermore, HERON aims to become a repository for digital copy.

HEIs seeking permission to digitise material from the CLA, either through HERON or directly, will be asked by the CLA to place a digital copy in a repository such as HERON so that it may be accessed by other users thereafter, thus avoiding duplication of effort.

Clearly, any future use of the digital copy would also have to be licensed. The model described later in this report is informed by the eLib supporting study of ODP/ER services, by cost and charge developments such as those published by the CLA and the PLS, and by HERON. The economic impact of rationalisation of licence negotiation and of digitisation will be explored using the model as will the ramifications for libraries of the CLA White Paper and the PLS mandate.

For example, the textbook substitution model (referred to by the PLS as the Bookshop Materials model) reflects the fact that libraries increasingly provide access to core reading materials that, previously, students would have bought from booksellers. Libraries cannot afford to pay to provide all students with core texts and further reading.

The crisis that libraries now face has been precipitated to some degree by student demands that they do so. However, librarians are uncomfortable with the prospect of charging for student reading materials. To do so would be to qualitatively change the role of academic libraries which would then be open to competition from other organisations which charge to supply information. Booksellers also would be affected by a move to supply core texts directly through the library.

INFORMATION GATEWAYS

Very little work has been done on the economics of information (or subject) gateways, also known as portals and hubs. Cataloguing the Internet is an activity undertaken by various types of organisation to attract users to their sites with a view to promoting their primary products/services or enhancing their reputations. Examples of this type of activity include:

- BioMedNet which, offering pointers to useful sites among manyother discipline-based services, is effectively a discipline-based Internet community owned by Elsevier Science and funded, in part, by advertising (http://www.biomednet.com/gateways/bac);
- The Wiley student resource centre which includes subject-specific sub-sites each of which revolves around specific high-volume Wiley texts (http://www.wiley.co.uk/products/worldwide/canada/src/ index.htm#links);
- Oppedahl & Larson LLP Patent Law Web Server, a site created and maintained by a professional law firm, which includes links to sources about all aspects of intellectual property (http://www.patents.com/index.sht);
- Various HE sites which having created pointers for their own users make them universally available (http://www.stir.ac.uk/infoserv/).

The perceived quality of these types of pointers is related to the site on which they are located. For example, links from an HEI may be considered more credible or impartial than those from a commercial organisation. Information gateways whose primary purpose is to provide pointers to other networked resources without promoting a different primary product would appear to be unique to the UK.

The eLib subject-based gateways (SBGs) have co-ordinated identification and evaluation of Internet resources and provide links to Internet resources within specific subject areas. Every resource which is linked from an SBG has been assessed by an expert in the relevant subject area and deemed to be of high-quality.

None of the SBG projects developed an economic model for maintenance and development of a service beyond the grant-funded period. However, an eLib supporting study conducted by Haynes et al. evaluated three different models for the transition of the SBGs from project to service status.

These models varied depending on the proposed funding sources. The first was a JISC-funded service, i.e. one which would continue to rely on 100% grant funding. The structure of SBG organisation would remain unchanged.

The second model would increase JISC funding in the first two years with a view to migrating to a service funded 50:50 between JISC and other sponsors. This model includes a considerable degree of rationalisation in the organisation of SBG activities. The third model would end JISC funding and require services to find alternative sources to fund their activities.

The Haynes report recommended that the JISC pursue the second of these models. This required additional JISC funding for two years to employ a managing director who would seek complementary funding for an ongoing service.

Many of the functions undertaken individually by eLib SBG projects would be rationalised and centralised to reduce duplication of effort and to allow for greater.

PRESERVATION AND ARCHIVING

Acceptable archiving and preservation strategies are essential preconditions to the widespread acceptance of electronic journals by authors and librarians. Many questions relating to archiving and preservation require answers before economic factors can be explored. For example, there is the question of who should archive. Publishers are reluctant to accept what, traditionally, has been a library responsibility.

They are waiting to find out what the role of national libraries will be in a digital environment before they commit themselves in this regard.

Furthermore, the long-term commitment of publishers and other stakeholder groups is questionable. It has been suggested that the only way to ensure 'systematic archiving of electronic publishing would be to assign that role to national institutions funded to do so and backed up by legislation'.

The UK research community generally agrees that preservation should be the responsibility of a publicly funded national agency. Preservation issues are of great concern to the UK HE community.

They have been the subject of several eLib supporting studies, of a British Library Research Study and issues continue to be explored by the CEDARS project. Economic modelling however, has not yet been undertaken.

JSTOR

Successful attempt to develop a model for archiving and preservation in electronic form of scholarly journals is JSTOR. One of the aims of JSTOR is to help libraries with space problems. JSTOR is also designed to be a trusted archive. Development of the archive has depended on the cooperation of publishers holding copyright in the journals included therein. It is important to those publishers that JSTOR should not cannibalise subscription income.

Thus, current issues of journals are not included in the JSTOR archive. JSTOR operates a 'moving wall' whereby entire backruns of journal issues are included in the archive except those published during the previous X years. Every year the contents from X-1 years ago are added to the archive.

The duration of X varies from publisher to publisher but generally is between 3 and 5 years. The JSTOR archive is funded by fees from institutions accessing the contents. The JSTOR team has calculated and compared the costs associated with:

- A centrally managed electronic text archive (including the cost of migrating content to keep pace with technological development);
- Storage, processing, reshelving and maintenance of a hard-copy collection.

A key factor in making JSTOR financially viable is that it is available widely and thus, costs are spread across a large number of institutions both in the US, and now also in the UK. JSTOR aims to be as equitable as possible in pricing access to the archive. Price discrimination is applied with a view to setting prices according to the value derived by each institution. Thus, institutions are banded according to size and annual access fees are varied on that basis. Pay-per-use was dismissed as a possible pricing mechanism because it ‘usually yields prices higher than the marginal cost of providing the product’ and JSTOR ‘did not want to force students and scholars to have to decide whether it would really be ‘worth it’ to download and print an article’.

This contrasts with the view that it is prudent to charge a print fee as this discourages indiscriminate use of printing resources, i.e. a fee would encourage users to filter information before rather than after they have printed. JSTOR received start-up funding from the Andrew Mellon Foundation but is expected to be self-sustaining over the longer term. STOR appears to be a pragmatic and useful model for archiving andproviding electronic access to backruns of journals. The capacity of JSTOR, however, is limited; currently the project aims to include backruns of a minimum of 100 journals before the year 2000.

To preserve in electronic form and make available worldwide all developments in scholarly communication is a monumental task requiring co-operation on an international scale.

It is notoriously difficult to secure international agreement for any type of activity and it is beyond the scope of this project to explore the ramifications of such an initiative.

PRE-PRINT ARCHIVES

The most famous example of an electronic pre-print archive is the Physics archive developed by Paul Ginsparg at the Los Alamos National Laboratory (LANL) (http://xxx.lanl.gov). The archive is very successful and is used by authors and readers throughout the world.

Development of the archive was funded by a grant from the US National Science Foundation. The full cost of developing and running the archive is not clear. Odlyzko estimated the cost per paper at $5. Then, to pre-empt disagreement on this figure he recalculated using wildly extravagant estimates of the costs of personnel and storage space.

He estimated that the upper limit would be $75, i.e. that it could not possibly cost more than $75 per paper to run such an archive. In the absence of grant funding, a cost-recovery model would be required.

Given Odlyzko’s figures, if the international physics community were to subscribe to this service either on an individual or institutional basis, the subscription charge would be small. Nevertheless, the administration of subscriptions would increase the total cost. An alternative model might charge authors to place pre-prints in the archive.

This would be unlikely to succeed however as authors are reluctant to pay page charges even to submit papers tojournals where the benefits of publication are clear. Harnad is trying to establish a similar pre-print archive in the cognitive sciences. This project (CogPrints) is funded by eLib. Other than grant funding, no economic model for a pre-print archive has been published and so no model will be explored here.

It should be noted however, that increasing use of preprints effectively transfers the information filtering function either to libraries or to end users.

Publication in a specific journal confers on a paper a mark of quality that is recognised by the readers. When all papers are freely available and unrefereed, the user must seek to identify high quality papers for herself. The time taken to do so is a cost; thus, in economic terms, preprints are not free. Physicists reading material from the Ginsparg archive tend to read only articles written by colleagues with whose work they are familiar This suggests that they are unwilling to filter the material for themselves. It also makes it difficult for newcomers to establish themselves in the field. Issues Related to Digital Library Service and Resource delivery.

Licensing

The application of national copyright law to the electronic environment is not straightforward; legislation tends to predate the digital era. Furthermore, the business of providing access to copyright materials in electronic form tends to be international.

Combined with the Internet 'gift culture' whereby users expect electronic content to be available free of charge, copyright on its own is inadequate for regulating use of copyright materials. Rather than relying on copyright law, content suppliers tend to use licences to detail precisely the terms on which their copyright material is made available to end users.

In the words of Karen Hunter of Elsevier Science, 'publishers view licences 48 and contracts as a more robust, clearer method of resolving what might otherwise be ambiguities as to permitted use and limitations'. Licence terms have important implications for libraries.

As the availability of an increasing proportion of library material depends on relationships beyond the organisational boundary, library managers must consider the impact that this has, among other things, on their ability to control budgets and guarantee access beyond the current licence term.

Clearly, the pricing model detailed in a licence and the level of prices are important in determining the costs and benefits to licensor and licensee. At present, prices tend to be very high for a variety of reasons including:

- That publishers often tie the price of electronic copy to the print price and offer both formats as a bundle;
- That by becoming the source site, the publisher takes on some of the library roles and costs.

Although pricing is an important element of a licence agreement it is only one of many issues that determine the costs and benefits conferred on the licensor and licensee. At present, pricing models offered by individual publishers vary considerably and are complex. Negotiation on a licence terms requires expertise, and takes a great deal of time. As licensing becomes increasingly important and common so do legal advice and staff with the knowledge and experience required to negotiate favourable and consistent licence terms.

Guidelines published by the US Association of Research Libraries (ARL) in 1997 recommend that institutions 'create a contract team' consisting of 'appropriate staff from the library, legal office, purchasing department and information technology division to provide information and develop contract expertise'. This type of recommendation suggests that licensing electronic resources is very much more expensive in terms of personnel than acquisition of print resources by library staff.

Furthermore, it illustrates the importance to all stakeholders that licences be kept simple and terms be standardised wherever possible. This is the rationale behind CHEST and behind initiatives like the UK National Electronic Site Licence Initiative (NESLI).

NESLI has based its model licence on one developed by a collaborative working party of representatives from the JISC and from the Publishers Association (PA) (http://www.nesli.ac.uk/nesli-licence.html). This model has been revised by NESLI in an iterative process involving all stakeholder groups.

When electronic resources were first offered to libraries by publishers, licences tended to be extremely restrictive with regard, for example, to use and users. This can be understood with reference to the size and importance of the market to academic publishers and the apparent naivety about copyright among users accustomed to the internet 'gift culture'. A great deal of progress has been made towards increased trust, goodwill and understanding between different stakeholder groups.

Librarians have identified licensing issues of importance to them and initiated dialogue with publishers. In the US an informal organisation calling itself the International Coalition of Library Consortia (ICOLC) and representing initially US library consortia, but later also consortia from Australia, the UK and the Netherlands, published a Statement on Current Perspectives and Preferred Practices for the Selection and Purchase of Electronic Infrastructure (http://www.library.yale.edu/consortia/statement.html).

This is essentially a wish list which elicited responses from several publishers thus initiating dialogue which continues at annual meetings of the ICOLC. The most recent (7th) draft of the NESLI model contract, published in September 1998 (http://www.nelsi.ac.uk/nesli7.html) addresses many of the issues raised by the ICOLC 50 and by writers on licensing such as Okerson.

For example, terms dictate that access to licensed material will not be withdrawn when subscriptions are cancelled and that licensees will be given the opportunity to subscribe to electronic copy only. NESLI is also considering the type of usage data that it can feasibly provide and is working towards seamless access from OPAC entry to abstracts, Tables of Contents, and full text.

By offering standardised terms, NESLI aims to minimise negotiation costs for both parties but acknowledges that the terms in this contract will not be acceptable to all publishers. There are often stark differences between the commercial interests of publishers and the library mission and negotiation is not often straightforward. The US experience to date is that negotiation of terms of use of electronic journals is often adversarial and protracted, and the resulting licences are lengthy and complex but clearly there is a willingness to simplify the licensing process and thus reduce costs for all parties.

User Behaviour in the Online Environment

User acceptance is key to the success of digital library resources and services. A resource can be technically impressive but unless it is acceptable to the target audience it will not be used. Research on user needs should be practical rather than hypothetical as potential users' reported needs differ from those of experienced users.

Thus, studies which provide access over a sufficient period to allow users to learn and repeatedly use a system are likely to be most useful. Research on user behaviour tends to focus on electronic journals but user needs and behaviour with reference to electronic texts and monographs have also been explored.

There is a remarkable degree of consensus among researchers of user behaviour in the online 51 environment. It would appear that researchers consistently identify the same essential pre-requisites for a successful online resource and the same deterrents to use.

Core Functionality

Identification of core functionality is important as journal readers use only those functions that meet their needs. As additional functionality increases production costs and may impact on price, superfluous functions should be avoided.

Users consider the core functions to be the facility to browse, search and print from an electronic journals service. Research repeatedly emphasises the fact that users do not read on screen but prefer to use print copy.

There are various reasons for this, including portability, the facility to annotate and guaranteed future access. Some users claim that a virtual filebox may reduce the need to print.

This would reduce anxiety about accessing materials in the future but does nothing to address the requirement for annotation and portability. Although Butterworth reports that scientists' interest in electronic journals relates primarily to improved functionality and lists linking to references as one of the required functions, the SuperJournal project found that users consider linking to be 'nice to have' rather than essential.

Creating links to references can be expensive especially for journals that are published in PDF format so it is essential that the importance of this feature to users be established.

Critical Mass and Currency

Users consider it essential that any service should offer a critical mass of resources both in terms of breadth and depth. Access to a limited selection of journal titles, whether they be published by a single publisher or by a range of publishers, is not considered sufficient incentive to learn to use a new system. Users also expect an electronic journal service to offer a backfile of a minimum duration.

The SuperJournal Project found that users consider the minimum requirement for a journal service to be a backfile of 5–10 years. Others consider the minimum useful backfile to be 25 years.

Furthermore, many users expect an electronic journals service to offer a wider range of titles than is currently available in print from the library.

System Performance

System performance is a necessary prerequisite if users are expected to use digital resources and services. Both academics and students are subject to time constraints and users are reluctant to learn to use new systems unless there are clear benefits.

Lowlevel problems demoralise users and it is difficult to entice them back if they have been disappointed. Time taken to download and print materials from a system is also important.

At present many users consider the delay to be excessive and consequently, would not print. Staff from the library at the University of Columbia have found that the online books system is used as a sophisticated catalogue. Users search for items of interest in the digital environment but when they have identified an item and wish to read more than a few lines, they seek a print copy from the library shelf.

This finding echoes that, noted earlier, of the ELINOR project at De Montfort University. It is no surprise that users consider the online books system to be an adjunct rather than a replacement for print.

Convenient, Fast Desktop Access to a one-stop Shop

Desktop access is considered to be important as is speed and ease of use. Users prefer not to have to login at all and complicated login procedures invariably deter use. The SuperJournal project found that when users experienced difficulty with the login procedures they did not attempt to use the system again. Furthermore, 90% of requests for user support from the SuperJournal helpdesk were from users who had forgotten their personal ID for logging in. Having accessed the system, the time taken to identify and retrieve material is important; users are not prepared to follow long chains of links to access relevant content. A single common interface is also an important feature and the interface should be familiar so frequent upgrading and redesign is unacceptable. Furthermore, users expect an electronic journals service to offer seamless discovery and access. The user should have the facility first to identify material that she wishes to read by searching or browsing tables of contents, second to link to the abstract of any items that interests her, and third to link to the full-text of any article that she wishes to read in full.

Format

A significant proportion of electronic journals are delivered as portable document format (PDF) documents especially when the electronic format is produced as a parallel of the print format. It is claimed that PDF is cheap to produce in these circumstances but is inappropriate for electronic delivery especially when pages have two or more columns.

Nevertheless, PDF currently has advantages over HTML. Users of Super Journal service claimed to prefer reading HTML on screen but when offered a document in either HTML or PDF format, the majority selected the latter.

This may be related to the fact that users prefer not to read on screen and print material if they intend to read more than a few lines. Super Journal users claim to prefer prints from PDF because they look like printed journal pages and, unlike HTML documents, they have page numbers. Benefits of an Electronic Service

Access to digital library resources tends not to be restricted to library opening hours and generally, two or more users may access an item simultaneously. Improved access is considered to be a benefit of digital library services. However, although Super Journal users claimed that access outside library opening hours is important, most use occurred during office hours.

Users also believe that the digital medium should facilitate faster publication; where items are published in both print and digital formats, users expect the latter to be published before or at the same time as the former. Benefits of Print and Photocopies

Generally, studies of user needs and behaviour in the digital library have revealed a range of different functions associated with print and photocopies that users consider to be 55 important. Until equivalent or improved features are available in an electronic environment many users will remain attached to print. These features include ease of browsing and reading; most current users have been familiar with print since childhood and are skilled in its use. A ubiquitous equivalent level of familiarity and skill is likely to be available to future users who are currently in the primary education system. Studies also report an emotional attachment to print.

Whether or not this attachment will remain among future lifelong users of electronic media remains to be seen. Another feature of print that currently give it an edge is its portability. Users tend not to read at their computers and often read journal papers at home or when travelling. The facility to annotate a print copy is also important as is the fact that they can legally cache materials for future use. Finally, some users consider presentation in print resources to be superior to that in digital resources. For example, high-quality graphics cannot be satisfactorily reproduced on prints from electronic resources. This is particularly important with regard to colour images.

Disciplines

Although many research findings apply to all users, differences between disciplines should be recognised. The Los-Alamos pre-print archive is commonly cited as an example of discipline-specific behaviour which has contributed to the success of a digital library resource.

There has long been a culture among physicists of distributing preprints. Physicists differ from other sciences in this respect and it is argued that the success of the Los Alamos archive derives in part from 56 this culture.

It is reported also that electronic journals are embraced more readily by those in disciplines that have not been adequately catered for in a print environment, for example musicology and other disciples to which non-printable elements are important.

Future research on user behaviour in the online environment should differentiate between users from different disciplines. Unfortunately, initiatives such as ATHENS which are designed to streamline delivery of digital resources can subvert attempts to gather data on different types of user.

MEASUREMENT OF USE AND PERFORMANCE INDICATORS IN THE DIGITAL LIBRARY

International Standards for Performance Measurement

The ability to monitor use and interpret the results is essential if any information resource or service is to be deemed a success or otherwise. Internationally standardised performance indicators have been developed for traditional library services.

However, recent studies of usage measurement and performance indicators for digital libraries have found no evidence of standardisation and continue to recommend that international standards be developed and applied. An initiative in this direction has been taken by the ICOLC who have published guidelines for statistical measures of usage of electronic resources. An eLib supporting study published in 1997 investigated Management Information Systems and Performance Measurement for the Electronic Library. The authors described a three-fold approach to library management with regard to performance measurement:

- The day-to-day needs of library managers;
- The need for information that can be used by planners for forecasting;

The need for indicators of value for strategic review. Although they found that some indicators used in traditional libraries can be adapted, it was necessary to devise other 57 new indicators. For example, the number of documents accessed was considered not to be important in an electronic environment; the range and depth of resources available was deemed far more important.

Furthermore, Brophy and Wynne identified a number of issues which must be addressed if progress is to be made in this area. While acknowledging the significant contribution of the eLib programme in this regard, they called for a clearer definition and understanding of what is meant by the term 'electronic library'.

A requirement for international standards is clear but development of such standards is a lengthy process. While this process is ongoing, each individual digital library initiative requires feedback to inform development and, thus, must unilaterally adopt an approach to performance measurement.

Electronic library projects in the UK, Europe and the USA have used a variety of different definitions and methods of usage measurement and analysis. Thus, neither analyses nor data from different projects can be compared.

Most Internet usage analysis tools are applicable to digital library activities and WWW server log file analysis programs still predominate. In 1997 the eLib supporting study referred to above found that most work in the electronic library field relied on transaction logging for management information.

If users are authenticated (i.e. have usernames and passwords), it is possible using these tools, to monitor individual use by logging the username alongside the URL. Hits can also be time stamped. In this way, an individual's progress can be tracked from page to page. It is possible also, using cookies, for a service supplier to track an individual's movements on the Internet beyond that supplier's site. However, this is likely to be considered a breach of privacy and librarians 58 make it an issue in negotiation with content suppliers.

To comply with the library ethos, performance indicators should not rely on information about individuals' reading habits. Many academic subscription services authenticate whole sites by registering and restricting access a list of IP addresses.

Not only does this overcome privacy issues related to individual users as names and time stamps cannot be recorded on accesses, but it also removes the need for costly password management. An alternative means of reducing the cost of authentication in the UK is use of the ATHENS service which provides an individual with a username and password which may be used to access a variety of services.

Unfortunately, use of ATHENS greatly reduces the management information that can be gathered by individual service suppliers. This is deliberate to protect the privacy of individual users. For example, it is not possible for a supplier to monitor use of her service within a specific discipline if neither individuals nor even whole classes are identifiable by user ID.

Limitations of Current usage Measurement Tools

It is important when designing performance measurement activities that they be justified in terms of the benefits derived. Because it is automatic, transaction logging is a cheap way of gathering data in an electronic environment.

Unfortunately, the type of data that can be collected is often restricted by the delivery format. In 1996, when Michigan University intended to test economic models during the TULIP Project, it was unable to do so because 'the Web does not support the kind of data collection required to test economic models'.

Project MUSE is still unable to distinguish between downloading/printing and browsing as the Web is a stateless environment. SuperJournal know that although users claim to prefer HTML documents for onscreen viewing, given a choice of formats, a large majority 59 chooses PDF over HTML. As most users print documents if they intend to read more than a few lines, it can be assumed that they select PDF as a superior format for printing.

Unfortunately, SuperJournal cannot verify this assumption by monitoring use as it is not possible to differentiate downloading from printing. Thus, although data gathering is cheap, as yet, it is also limited. Furthermore, analysis of such data tends to be time consuming and thus expensive and interpretation is not always straightforward.

For example, it may be assumed that more hits indicate a better service, as a high number suggests that users return and that they recommend a site to others but, of course, this may not always be the case. A subject-based gateway which generates search results that closely match a users needs will cord very few hits before that user leaves the site satisfied with the result. If the search results supplied are poor and include a number of extraneous links or if the user is required to conduct several searches before she retrieves useful links, the gateway will record many more hits before the user leaves.

However, if a subject-based gateway offers not only access to a database of catalogue records but also holds a local archive, it should record a larger number of hits as users are likely both to search the database and to retrieve local resources. Furthermore, attempts to make more efficient use of internet bandwidth by caching and mirroring can subvert attempts to monitor use.

Access to resources from site A from a cache or mirror held at site B will not be included in usage measurement unless site B informs site A about the cache and agrees to supply site A with use data. This type of shortfall makes WWW statistics unreliable or, worse, misleading.

Inferring user Behaviour from Transaction Logs

Use of transaction logs for performance measurement requires digital library practitioners to infer meaning from specific types of user act in a digital environment. For example, A. Dawson of the BUBL service (http://www.bubl.ac.uk) suggests that to view a list of journal issues with dates and contents is the equivalent of browsing a library shelf. He also asserts that searching is a deliberate activity which is not easily mistaken and that to access full-text is a likely indication that the user is reading the article.

The latter assertion is qualified by the acknowledgement that the reader may access text to scan for relevance rather than, necessarily, to read the article. However, Dawson argues that this ambiguity need not influence the accuracy of any performance measure as it applies to all journals. This type of inference helps digital library practitioners to make sense of quantitative data. However, knowledge of user behaviour in the digital environment is limited and it can be dangerous to base inference entirely on assumptions and prior experience.

For example, Dawson's assumption that the frequency with which a reader accessing full text is in fact scanning for relevance will apply equally to all journals is contradicted by the findings of the SuperJournal project.

SuperJournal found evidence that the way in which scientists and social scientists use journal elements differs. For example, scientists are more likely than social scientists to identify a relevant article from its title and to print it on that basis. Social scientists more often read the abstract to establish relevance because article titles in the social sciences can be more ambiguous. There may be similar differences in the way that scientists and social scientists approach full text. It is clearly difficult to derive qualitative research findings from quantitative information. Qualitative methods such as interviews and 61 observation should be used to inform assumptions about the meaning of quantitative information and for triangulation.

Training and Awareness

Some of the eLib projects in the Training and Awareness programme area have now migrated to a service model and offer training courses in the use of new technologies for teaching and learning. HEIs are likely to continue to pay for this type of training from staff development budgets.

Training of users in the use of IT is unlikely to fall within the remit of libraries although libraries will probably continue to offer training in information skills and the use of specific resources.

It is beyond the scope of this project to explore the economics of this activity and compare the costs and benefits of training academics and students in the use of electronic and print resources. Clearly, the transition from a traditional to a digital or hybrid library involves dramatic changes in the infrastructure that supports the production and use of information resources. At present people prefer not to read on screen so they print articles from electronic journals.

As resources for teaching, learning and research are increasingly delivered in electronic form there is likely to be a mass shift from photocopying to printing; the latter is more expensive than the former but the total opportunity cost of an individual operating a photocopier is not incurred so costs are probably very similar.

As people become more familiar with technology, users may no longer need print copies.

This could lead to a net reduction in the cost of using information. The report of a recent study on the impact of electronic journals on networked printing suggested that one of the reasons for printing material from the Internet is to ensure future access; networked access is not always reliable.

In effect users create a personal print cache of networked resources. The report predicted that improved access to networked resources would 62 reduce the need to print but suggested that it may also increase use of the network, which in turn would increase the print load. The net effect of a combination of such changes is virtually impossible to predict.

Another factor impacting on the economics of digital information is the pace of technological change; new technologies become obsolete at an alarming rate, making it expensive for organisations to meet the changing needs of users. However, technological advances are reducing some costs, for example the cost of storing digital resources.

It is not possible within the scope of this project to estimate the infrastructure costs associated with delivering electronic resources in such an unstable and unpredictable climate. Investment in infrastructure that effectively enables all stakeholders to conduct much of their business electronically will be required. The models described here will be based on the assumption that the HE sector will invest in sufficient infrastructure to support digital/hybrid library activities.

At present there is no coherent model of the digital library, nor is there yet any developed model of the hybrid library. Furthermore, economic issues tend to be tested after solutions have been found to the more pressing technical, cultural and legal issues. Many specific digital library activities are insufficiently mature to have generated economic models. Where a model exists it has been evaluated and where alternatives exist these have been compared.

It is clear that a great deal of progress has been made over the last decade towards a greater understanding of how digital library activities may be integrated in HE. Nevertheless, a considerable amount of work remains, specifically in the areas of preservation and archiving and in standardisation of usage measurement and performance indicators. Conclusions regarding specific issues relating to digital library activities are outlined in the remainder of this report.

THE HYBRID DIGITAL LIBRARY

I shall propose some reflections upon the open access topic which is at the heart of our meeting, focussing upon its implications in the domain of cultural heritage. I will insist espeçially on the transition of museums in the web. When compared to the scientific production published in books and journals, the transition of museums into the cyberspace poses different challenges both in the production and organization of digital information and in the modalities of granting it access.

I shall first focus upon the way in which the virtual museums should be conceived in the web. In the second part of my presentation I shall then introduce my view of the compromise we will have to accept when dealing with museums in the perspective of an open access policy to cultural heritage.

I am obviously aware that it is extremely daring to formulate a long-term vision of the transition of cultural heritage in the web, and that I risk being engaged in an exercise of purely wishful thinking.

Visibility on the web is today one of the major concerns for museums the world over. Many efforts are devoted to web presentations of Museums and their collections and of cultural heritage at large. The transition of museums in the cyberspace is still largely conceived as a linear development of traditional procedures. This means that the style and traditional conception of documentation and information tends to exhibit a strong inertia in the new medium.

As a consequence of this inertia, the museum world seems still to be a long way from having fully exploited the potential of the web revolution. In this new dimension it becomes ever more difficult to accept the constraints which characterize the traditional activity of documentation and information. Let me schematically remind you of two of the basic constraints which are at work in the documentation strategies of the museums of the real world:

- Catalogues are conceived as rigorously confined to the objects preserved by individual museums.
- Objects are treated as isolated items; only limited attention is devoted to the cultural and social context to which they pertain, and to enhance their conceptual genesis and meanings.

It may be worth recalling that Museums, libraries and archives of the real world are the result of a process which began many centuries ago. Museums started out in 16th century Europe as promiscuous bodies where art objects, instruments, artifacts of various nature, natural items, books and documents were intrinsically integrated and displayed alongside one another.

The conceptual glue of what we would today rate as a promiscuous ensemble was the exceptional character and the uniqueness of all the collected entities and the curiosity that they aroused in the visitor. Later evolution of museums might be portrayed as a story of ever stronger specialization. First, the separation of art collections from scientific collections (during the Enlightenment).

Then art collections underwent a further process of specialization with the separation of paintings (this marks the origins of the Pinacotheca) from sculpture (sculpture galleries), from drawings (print and drawing rooms) and from minor arts (decorative arts departments). The same process took place with regard to scientific collections.

After their separation from art collections, specialization progressed through the division of mathematical and physical objects from natural history items;

moreover, in the mid- 19th century, technological and industrial collections gave rise, under the impulse of the Universal Exhibitions, to new independent museums. Later on, new institutions devoted to the preservation and presentation of bio-medical and ethnoanthropological collections were founded.

This evolution has produced a fragmentation of cultural documentation and cultural heritage according not only to disciplines, but also to the various categories of objects (books, documents, drawings, paintings etc.) and to their different material supports (canvas, marble or stone, paper, fabrics, timber, metal etc.). This specialization and fragmentation process has placed all museums in a difficult position, when it comes to making explicit to visitors the value of the collection they preserve. The same holds true for libraries and archives. These limitations derive from the fact that objects are presented in museums atomized and de-contextualized. This makes it almost impossible for visitors to grasp their real meaning and to perceive their importance. When dedicating our energies to the digital conversion of cultural heritage, we have first of all to avoid the mistake of reproducing the fragmentation of objects and records in the different containers of all real world, and their isolation in specialized and totally unrelated structures (as museums, archives and libraries are today).

The new format of the humanities in the digital Age will have then to coincide with the re-composition of what the material history of cultural patrimony has fragmented. Once the information has been processed and transformed into a digital entity, it has no more to follow the fate of its physical support. There is thus no reason to store it according to the same systems used to preserve the object it emulates. The logical consequence of what I have been saying is that we can finally re-arrange the records which digitally mirror the real objects in a totally new orderly architecture. We will thus build new hybrid repositories.

Hybrid not in the sense that this adjective has in the librarian jargon (where hybrid library means a combination of digital and analogical contents), but hybrid because the web repository is heterogeneously populated by a variety of different digital objects, which represent material objects, preserved in different containers. In recent years, growing use has been made of information technology especially through the development of so-called virtual museums model. The idea of the virtual museum which seems to be asserting itself, is, in fact, the idea of the digital clone of the real museum, accepting all of its structural features. To have meaning and utility, the "virtual" museum of the web should rather be constructed with a radically different configuration from the 'real' museum.

In cyberspace the real museum should constitute only the point of departure and return of journeys that are confined neither to the internal perimeter of the museum, nor to the same typology of items or the same discipline or genre to which it relates. The visitor should be permitted explorations not only of objects, but also of ideas and persons, of places and events, of books and documents, whenever this information is preserved.

The transition of cultural heritage in the cyberspace has thus to be conceived as the creation of a totally new architecture of knowledge: a meta-museum/library/ archive, with no walls nor physical separations.

A totally different construct from the way in which cultural heritage is arranged in the real world. In order to make this vision of the future of virtual museum to come true, the keywords and guidelines to keep in mind will thus be hybridisation, re-composition, and systematic enhancement of the network of meaningful connections among the items of the cultural heritage.

On the sociological ground, one of the corollaries of this new vision of the future web of cultural heritage is that the traditional division of labour will have to be rebalanced. There is no question that in the cultural institutions of he real world (in museums, above all) curatorial concerns have played a crucial role in shaping the physical organization of the heritage.

The understandable priority of the curatorial vision has also deeply affected the development of traditional documentation and communication strategies, with their strong selective emphasis upon the patrimony preserved in individual institutions. In the cyberspace the documentation and communication strategies can be finally conceived independently of the curatorial priorities and vision. The autonomy of documentation activity from curatorial concerns will permit to stress the connections and conceptual relations among items of cultural heritage which in the real world are preserved in different places and containers.

In the long run, this new perspective will produce an unheard of integration of knowledge, thanks to the enhancement of the enormous multiplicity of threads which connect the various digital items stored in the immense repository of the web. All this obviously implies the establishment of new forms of programmatic cooperation among content providers. It will obviously be necessary to offer the possibility of vertical exploration of collections preserved in individual institutions.

But the crucial step is represented by the possibility of an effective horizontal navigation in the endless virtual shelves of the web repository. We have vertical exploration often at hand in the actual web. Much more challenging appears the solution of the problem of an effective horizontal navigation among the digital surrogates of cultural heritage items in the web space. In order to achieve this goal, a strong change of paradigm in the standard procedures of web content production has to be put into practice.

Only the adoption of common standards of classifications on the part of content providers – which is still a rare phenomenon – will permit the user to navigate among data stored in different archives. Today interoperability among different digital archives is guaranteed on a large scale only by search engines; that is by a third party (the other two being content-providers and users), which has no role in the content production. Search engines work from the outside, ignoring the conceptual structure of data that they filter.

As everybody well knows, search engines use above all statistic methods and string search. Because of their extrinsic filtering procedures, search engines cannot guarantee content-driven search. I fully agree with Jürgen Renn presentation in our conference and with the ECHO Network Agorà vision that the schizophrenia between content and link providers is one of the major limits of the actual web. It represents a serious obstacle to the exploitation of the web as a universal and hybrid repository of cultural heritage.

We need then first of all to integrate and tune these two crucial functions. Moreover, in order to be really satisfactory, especially in the cultural heritage, links among the documents which are disseminated in the web should adhere to the representation of knowledge embedded in them. Search engines filter the web using words and strings, that is textual elements.

But textual search is very inadequate in order to filter conceptually coherent content in a federal digital repository, like the web. First of all, it is ambiguous, suffering the misleading effects of word polisemia (both in queries and in answers); moreover, it is almost impossible to effectively manage the multi-linguistical character of the web; finally, it is not appropriate to represent and filter extra-textual documentation (sounds, images, audiovisual materials etc.), which constitute an ever growing dimension in the web.

Even if some of these limits can be overcome by the adoption of community multilingual controlled dictionaries, textual classification and search in the web repository remains inadequate if we look for content-sensitive linking. In fact content-sensitive linking constitutes a fundamental challenge for the development of a web of cultural heritage intended as a universal and hybrid repository. In order to achieve this goal we will have to shift emphasis in document description and hyper-linking from words and textual elements to meanings.

It is at this very point that the semantic web comes appropriately into play. In the scenario which I have sketched of the future web as a universal hybrid metarepository of cultural heritage, the shift from textual elements to associations based upon meanings has to be considered as a crucial step.

The re-composition and recontextualization of the fragmented items of cultural heritage in the cyberspace implies in fact the systematic production of content-sensitive hyperlinks. The latter will be fully effective only if they are based upon semantic relationships.

Ontological system of classifications, shared by the specific web community involved in cultural heritage exploitation - a community formed by subjects who are, at the same time, users and providers, clients and servers - will guarantee both the rational construction of a universal hybrid repository and the possibility of effective navigation in it.

Ontologies will serve both as content-sensitive search engines and as effective representations of the structures of knowledge embedded in the web repositories, thus paving the way for their use as tools for e-learning activity and giving the users the possibility of designing personal itineraries. Users will also have the chance of improving the efficacy of ontologies, by producing standardized descriptive metadata which will become shared knowledge for the community. They will not simply access data provided by others, but will be able to create added value to be exploited by the community. Content-sensitive hyper-linking is a need strongly felt by members of the international community who work in the humanities and in cultural heritage.

This crucial need inspires the vision of the ECHO Network project, with its strong emphasis upon a shared service infrastructure to help intelligent and interoperable implementation of the web of Cultural Heritage. I come now to my second point. Once we have been able to effectively promote in the web the heritage preserved in the museums, will it be possible to grant open access to it? It is obvious that the vision of the web of the virtual museums which I have schematically outlined presupposes a largely open access to the web of cultural heritage.

The fantastic cumulation of knowledge in the shared environment of the web produced by different actors would be much less productive and profitable within the framework of commercial copyright or in the so-called "deep web" model. This is certainly true, but we cannot utopically remove the economical dimension of the complex process with which we are dealing.

We are in a phase in which everywhere – and very strongly also in Europe – national policies (and also European Union policy) are insisting upon the need to reduce public investments in the preservation and promotion of cultural heritage and upon the necessity of involving private entrepreneurs in the management of museums in order to obtain the best commercial exploitation of cultural patrimony.

In this conjuncture a radical emphasis upon open access policy might turn out lacking a firm grounding and appear without concrete prospects. We cannot simply ignore these political trends and the reason and expectations behind them. So, in my view, we have to work in order to find a way of integrating our open access vision with a strategy of cultural, educational and touristic services provided on payment by museums through the web.

One of the possible strategic directions might thus be that of granting free per view access to the information published by museums in the web, providing payment services for advanced interaction with the published content (like unloading images, publishing unloaded material for commercial purpose, e-learning activity and so on).

I have no detailed proposal to advance here, but I want to stress once more that the view of a fully open access policy to cultural heritage in the web will have very little chance of imposing itself, unless we find a balanced solution between the moral duty of granting universal access to cultural heritage and the need of at least partially recovering the costs of producing, maintaining, updating and integrating the digital representation of cultural heritage in the web. This is, to my mind, a crucial point. I fear that we will not cover any distance by simply contrasting the present commercially driven national and communitarian policies for the promotion of digital cultural heritage through information technology with our noble vision of open access. We have to operate in order to find an acceptable compromise and a sustainable economic model between these diverging opposite conceptions.

Otherwise, we might well obtain good results in our battle for open access to research papers and journals in the web, but we will receive little satisfaction in the crucial area of museums - especially of the great art museums – where commercial interests, due to the enormously superior number of potential customers, are much stronger. In this area we will have to guarantee the user new services, opportunities and creative access strategies without a commercial approach, even if this will involve some fair form of payment.

I would like to go back, in my concluding remarks, to the vision of the virtual museum of the future which I have sketched in the first part of my presentation. The real world museums, archives and libraries tell us incomplete, fragmented and often incomprehensible stories. The items that they preserve are organized according to extrinsic criteria (format, physical supports, typological categories, state of preservation, and so on) which do not help to catch their conceptual value and relationships.

In the future web of cultural heritage museums will have to be, at the same time, individual entities (that is faithful representations of the real museums) and global and hybrid repositories.

Global, in the sense that the items they preserve will be linked to all conceptually connected items. Hybrid, because those connections will not be limited to items of the same typology but will include all kinds of documentation.

If the cultural heritage in the web does not look something like this, let us say, ten years from now, and if we will not have been able to guarantee a fair level of open access to this shared repository, we will have to candidly acknowledge that the revolutionary potential of the transition of cultural heritage in the cyberspace has not been fully exploited.

I am personally convinced that the vision of the future of museums in the web which I have proposed will prove to be more than wishful thinking. This vision will represent a real cultural revolution, on condition that we are able to avoid the risk both of ignoring the concrete economical constraints and of passively accepting the transferral of the pay per view model to the web of cultural heritage and research.

CO-USAGE OF DOCUMENTS IN A LARGE DIGITAL LIBRARY

Creating relationships between similar documents is an activity that has a long distinguished history in Information Retrieval. In his textbook on the subject Korfhage (1997) writes "Probably the single key concept behind information storage and retrieval is document similarity". A practical motivation for the search for similarity is to improve information retrieval. When users have found one document they can be directed to similar documents that may be worth their attention.

A more theoretical motivation is the discovery of patterns of thought within a body of knowledge that is dispersed across a collection of documents. There are, of course, many ways in which similarity between documents can be assessed. One way is to use the judgment of an expert.

This is typically done by classifying documents according to a subject classification. This is a tried and trusted method. However, it requires human expertise and labour. These do not come cheap these days.

Therefore many collections have no classification data. Within the collection of documents that we study in this chapter, three in four documents do not have a subject classification. Other classic measures of relationship between academic papers are the strengths of co-citation and bibliographic coupling. Such an analysis presumes that a citation index for the papers is available. Producing one manually is even more expensive than subject classification.

It is possible to use recently available software for autonomous citation indexing. Barrueco Cruz and Krichel report on on recent effort s using the same digital library that we study here. In this chapter, we introduce a completely new concept of similarity that is user-centered.

We start with the idea that two documents are similar if they respond to the same information need. Thus roughly speaking we can think of two document as similar, if many users will withdraw the papers together while they are working on the system. Provided that we have a digital library with a long log of usage, we can find which papers have frequently been used together. This is what we will refer to as "co-usage" in the following. We are not aware of a study that has developed and tested this concept within a digital library context. We are, of course, aware that commercial systems use a related concept. Amazon.com, for example, suggests to a customer who is considering to purchase an item x that other people who bought x also bought item y. But since users are anonymous in our digital library, within the scope of our collection, the evidence on common usage is more difficult to gather.

MEASURING CO-USAGE

Our dataset comes from logs of the usage of the RePEc digital library. We have built this library over many years. RePEc is the largest free distributed academic digital library in the world. It is a pioneering effort in three respects.

First, RePEc pioneered the business model of the Open Archives Initiative distinction between data providers and service providers. RePEc has grown over 200 archives that are used in 10 different user services.

Second, RePEc is more than a collection of data about documents. RePEc offers a comprehensive picture of academic output by describing collection of documents, persons that are involved as authors of documents or editors of collections, and the institutions to which they belong in a relational database scheme. Third, RePEc is essentially volunteer driven and has no owner. It is a public good much like the Internet. The data that we examine comes from the WoPEc user service. This service, founded in 1993 is available on the web at three locations since 1994.

These are Hitotsubashi University in Tokyo, Japan, Manchester Computing in the UK, and Washington University in St. Louis in the USA. The web site has static pages for each paper. In addition, there are a number of pages that link different papers together.

There are pages that list papers that have been issued within same series, and there are pages that group papers with the same subject classification. The log data also contains indication about what searches users have been making. However, as far as we are concerned, only the access to the description of the individual papers is relevant.

To begin with, recall that WoPEc is a non-commercial service. WoPEc does not enter into a contractual arrangement with a customer, with or without an exchange of money. Contractual arrangements with customers are expensive to arrange because they involve complicated negotiations, privacy issues etc. On the other hand contractual arrangement—even without exchange of money—generate customer data. The customer data itself has considerable value.

In the period that we examine, cookies have not been used. Therefore we need to wade through the log to find traces of usage by the same persons. All that the log offers is a trace to the Internet address (i.e. IP number) of the client machine, a file or action performed, and a time when this happened. Over recent years, the Internet is more and more accessed through personal computers rather than through multi-user systems.

However, we can not be completely sure that an IP number corresponds to the machine of an individual user, because there are caching sites. Therefore we must be watchful of IP addresses that appear particularly frequently. Let us for the moment make the assumption that the usage data from one single machine comes from one single user. We are then in the happy situation that we have identified the user.

However, to be able to claim that papers that are appearing together are joined together because they correspond to the same user need, we still have to assume that the information need of the user remains the same throughout the period of observation. This is problematic. Typically users will regard WoPEc as a reference source, and therefore naturally turn to it with different information needs. Therefore it is likely that the log contains material that corresponds to different information needs, even if they are expressed by the same user.

Therefore, we have chosen to think of users using the system within sessions. We typically think of a session as an academic, using a web browser on a desktop machine, going to the WoPEc site, make a few searches and look at a few results. Or we can think of it as a student, walking into a computer lab, uses a search engine, finds a page on the WoPEc service and navigates it for further data.

Technically, we define a session as a subset of the total log that comes from the same IP address within a certain time frame. In fact we assume that there must not be more than one hour between two consecutive log entries for them to qualify to be within the same session. In addition, we do not consider repeat access to the same paper as two different accesses to that paper. Such access is likely to occur mainly for technical reasons, such as that the user did not have time to read the article at the first discovery.

Under these restrictions it appears to be convenient to model sessions as sets of papers. We can now proceed to a formal definition of co-usage. Let D be the set documents in the library and S be the set of sessions. Each session s contains a subset of the set of documents, i.e. s Ì D. Introduce | • | as as notation for the number of elements in a set. Let there be two documents di and dj. Let u(di, dj) be the set of all sessions that contain both di and dj. For convenience of notation, write u(di) = u(di, di). Then we propose to call the co-usage coefficient c(di, dj) as follows:

$$c\left(d_1, d_j\right) = \frac{\left|u\left(d_i, d_j\right)\right|}{\left|u\,(di)\right|\left|u\left(d_j\right)\right|}$$

The motivation for introducing the product in the denominator is to ensure that we do not have situations where one paper appears frequently with another by the sheer size of its own usage. It also leads c(di, dj) to gain the attractive properties that 0 <= c(di, dj) <= 1 and that c(di, di) = 1. It is clear that the measure that we propose here is an intuitive one. It is not a scientifically developed metric of the likelihood that, whatever size the session is, we will see the two papers appearing together in the session.

It is possible to evaluate that probability. However that calculation is not attempted here. It is left for future work. Even if we can theoretically ascertain how to calculate the probability, we can not in practice calculate it for all possible document couples, because of the amount of calculations that would have to be made within a large digital library as ours.

Results

We ran a programme to search for co-usage on a log for three years 1999–2001. There are 102551867 lines in the log. We discarded 24836221 requests for images, 401614 requests for CSS files, and 9315 contained another error. 3164598 requests contained a 404 error and were omitted. Most of them went to robots.txt. 3966837 distinct hosts accessed the system.

We exclude all accesses from hosts that accessed robots.txt. In addition, there are cache and proxy sites that we would like to remove as well. This is a more difficult terrain. The rule that we chose was to look at each day's log, and detect all hosts that issued more than 100 requests. In total, we detected 23068 such hosts, and discarded 17484961 lines because they were made by these hosts.

This left us with 23413849 to analyzed. We detected 5251337 sessions. We limited ourselves to sessions that had more than 3 accesses and less than 100, and that included at least one search. There were 69179 sessions that remained for analysis. We can not make the results available here, for obvious reasons of space. Therefore we have placed them at http://openlib.org/home/krichel/kumegawa/report.htm. We print the top couples that have the highest co-usage, up to a rounded coefficient of 50%. The following results appear when we look through the data.

First, papers in the same series seem to be much more prone to co-usage than papers from different series. It is often papers by the same authors, over different periods of time, available in the same working paper series or journal that appeared to be co-used a lot.

This observation suggests that the original split of the data in different series does not only provide an organizational layer to the data, but also a semantic one.

Second, from reading through the related couples, it appears that a key concept that appears in the title immediately explains the co-usage. Thus, it should be possible to gain insights into key concepts that are of user interest by looking at the title data of papers that are co-used, and find the common words. This would be an interesting subject for further research.

This chapter has introduced co-usage as a means to make document to document relationships. The concept of co-usage has been found to lead to excellent empirical results. Our results suggests that the concept of co-usage is a valid and interesting one.

Any remaining problems that we are experiencing to make it work in practice are consequences of poor measurement of usage, rather than flaws in the underlying theoretical reasoning. Just in the case of co-citation and bibliographic coupling, there will be a debate on how useful co-usage analysis really is. We have opened that debate with this chapter.

There are two further consequences from this chapter. In the short run, we intend to incorporate co-usage similarity into future developments of WoPEc, to build links from the description of one paper to the description of another as suggested by co-usage analysis. In the longer run, we believe that our work can be seen as simple, but pioneering step towards information retrieval systems that are learning. Instead of having a system that has a fixed procedure that is applicable whatever the query an the collection, we can imagine that future information systems will learn from past user behaviour to better serve the present user. Co-usage appears as a key concept to move things forward in that direction.

❐

3

Expansion of Web-based Library Services

INTRODUCTION

The Due to the tremendous growth and continuous development of technology, the role of library becomes more responsive in making the users techno-savvy. Technological developments have affected not only the formats and sources of the information, but also how and where to provide library services. Libraries and their resources have partially moved to the virtual world of the Internet.

As a result, library users can access the resources from outside the physical library. In an effort to reach users accessing the library via their computers, many libraries and library consortia are extending their services to include virtual reference.

Technology now allows users to submit their queries to the library at any time from any place in the world. Web Based Services, Digital Library Services, Internet Library Services and Electronic Library Services are terms with similar meanings. As more libraries move towards providing services in a digital environment, the improved access to remote library collections is making the use of electronic information resources more realistic and more attractive.

Traditional online services had transformed themselves into internet-based online services using web-based technologies. From traditional online services to today, four generations of information retrieval tools have passed that assist users in searching the World Wide Web.

The first generation of information retrieval tools was designed for use with bibliographic databases. The first generation provided access to references to the end documents rather than to the documents themselves, and indexing and searching were thus applied to document surrogates, such as titles or abstracts. These tools require considerable human efforts to collect, arrange, code, and annotate the various resources.

A primary benefit of the first generation of tools is providing users with easy browsing capabilities. The second generation of tools attempts to collect and index resources as an automated function. Automatic collection and indexing reduces the amount of human effort. The ability to search through massive amounts of information and locate the desired information for the user is the primary benefit of the second generation of tools. The third generation deals with World Wide Web Meta search engines, such as Harvester and Meta crawler.

The fourth generation involves new ideas such as search agent technology currently being developed to search for information on the web. Web-based search engines are as a means of finding relevant pages on the Internet. Different search engines, directory, meta-search engines, gateways, subject portals, electronic journals and on line databases each type could be used in a different way, from simple keyword searching up to peer reviewed web sites.

WHAT IS WEB BASED LIBRARY SERVICE

A digital Library service manages and develops electronic services, the library web sites and library staff. It can be defined broadly as ‘an information access service in which users ask questions via electronic means, e.g., e-mail or web forms’.

WHY WEB BASED LIBRARY SERVICE

Library service on the internet requires many of the same qualities as traditional references: accuracy, promptness, courtesy, an understanding of the information need. It provides users with the convenience of accessing information in their own time, saving them traveling cost and time and new options for answering reference questions. The provision of these services is not constrained by the traditional opening hours but can be offered on a 24-hour, seven-days-a-week basis known as 24/7. And while there may be a disadvantage in not having a face-to face encounter, there are many advantages to this new medium and the greatest advantage is that many more users can be helped by using electronic library services. Advantages and disadvantages of electronic access over printed form access are showed in table.

Web based services are established due to the following reasons.

- Ensuring the needs of users and the accessible information sources are suitable matched at all times.
- Delivering those information sources to the user in a timely and appropriate fashion.

- Ensuring the information provided is high quality, accurate and appropriate.
- Assisting the user in interpreting the materials, if necessary.
- Promoting user awareness of new services and information sources as they develop.
- Providing users with individualised guidance and support as they build their information search and application skills.

TABLE: Advantages and Disavantages of Printed from over Electronic Access.

S.No.	Advantages of Print Form	Electronic Form
1.	Format is tested and standardised	Format is in the early stages of dvelopment
2.	Easy for users to use	Requires some training for users to use
3.	No special equipment needed sofware, printers, etc.)	Special equipment required (hardware, softwar, printers, etc.)
4.	Easy to locate (if shelved properly) problems, internet connection	Access is currently unreliable (URL problems, etc.)
5.	Use in limited only to copyright laws licensing	Use is limited by copyright laws and agreements.
6.	Archiving is effective and permanent	Archiving is "up in the air".

TABLE: Advantages and Disadvantages of Printed Form over Electronic Access.

S.No.	Disadvantages of Print Form	Electronic Form
1.	Operating costs are considerable (ordering, cataloging, claiming, and binding)	Operating costs are iminimal (no cataloging, binding, or claiming)
2.	Requires shelving	No shelving required
3.	Often mutialted, stolen, or misshelved	Cannot be mutilated, stolen, or misshelved
4.	Requires extensive storage space	Saves considerable storage space
5.	Allows only one user at a time	Allows for multiple users with simultaneous access
6.	Slow delivery via "snail mail"	No more missing issues
7.	Issues are easily lost in the mail or missing	Fast publication
8.	Slow publication	

DIFFERENT RESOURCES FOR WEB BASED LIBRARY SERVICES

Today, users may have access a variety of textual information resources. There are different kinds of webbased reference resources and services for accessing information from libraries such as OPAC, Gateways, Portals, Subject Portals, Electronic Journals, Online Databases, Subject Directories and Search Engines. These resources overlap considerably in the type of information they cover, and sometimes it is difficult to distinguish between some of them.

A library should have a good collection of these resources like selected Web links, subscription resources, and library materials in well-organised pages for serving better services to their users. Many libraries and organisations are providing digital reference service through collaborative services. Existing library consortia are adding digital reference to current shared services, and networks of libraries. Some regional library consortia are offering member libraries the opportunity to share reference questions with each other using the Internet and other technologies.

OPAC

OPAS's - On Line Public Access Catalogues, form an important part of many digital library's collections. It allows users to search for the bibliographic records contained within a library's collections. Now days, some OPAC also provide access to electronic resources and databases, in addition to the traditional bibliographic records.

GATEWAYS

A gateway is defined as a facility that allows easier access to network based resources in a given subject area. Gateways provide a simple search facility and a much-enhanced service through a resource database and indexes, which can be searched through a web based interface. Information provided by gateways is catalogued by hand. Gateways cover a wide range of subjects, through some areas, such as music and religious studies, currently lack subject gateways.
Some well-known gateways are as follows:

- Internet Public Library (IPL),
- Bulletin Board for Libraries (BUBL),
- National Information Services and Systems (NISS),

PORTALS

In the library community, portals may be defined as an amalgamation of services to the users where the amalgamation is achieved through seamless integration of existing services by using binding agents such as customisation and authentication services, search protocols such as Z39.50, loan protocols such as ISO10161, and e-commerce. The result is a personalised service which allows the individual to access the rich content of both print-based and electronic systems.

Portals are either commercial or free web facilities that offer information services to a specific audience. The facilities include web search to communication to e-mail to news, etc.

There are three kinds of portals; Consumer (or horizontal), Vertical and Enterprise.

1. Consumer portals are aimed at consumer audiences and offer free e-mail, games, chat, etc. Examples are Yahoo!, MSN and AOL.
2. Vertical portals, target a specified audience, such as a particular industry, and offer many of the consumer portal features. Example includes VerticalNet.
3. Enterprise portals on the other hand are similar to consumer portals, but they are offered only to corporations or similar organisations.
4. Examples include Epicentric and Corporate Yahoo! These portals can be best understood as electronic pathfinders for users, pulling together in one place in a web site selected links to subjects or interest-oriented resources located on the WWW.

SUBJECT PORTALS

Web Search Engines had been developed initially by computer scientists, by borrowing techniques from information retrieval search such as best match searching and relevance ranking. Information professional are increasing bringing their skills to help organise the growing wealth of Internet resources.

A good example of their influence is the development of subject-specific web search engines known as subject portals, where evaluation of material covered is a major concern. Two prime UK subject portals are SOSIG Social Science Information Gateway, covering social science resources and OMNI Organising medical networked information covering medical resources. Subject portal sites can be very helpful, but they should be used with care.

Users should bear the following points in their mind:

- The aim of the subject portal is to list and review the most important sites on the web relevant to that subject. The sites are usually constantly peer-reviewed to ensure that the site is relevant and up to date.
- New sites are appearing all the time. Relying on a subject portal site to find everything users require may mean that they miss an important site that has recently appeared and has not yet been reviewed by the producers of the particular subject portal.
- A subject portal is a one stop shop for information on the topic it covers. Users don't have to carry out extensive Internet searches in order to find the information require. They can simply go to the required subject portal site.

- Subject portals save users having to have long lists of bookmarks (saved addresses of web pages), which are often, cumbersome and time consuming to arrange and keep up to date. However, if users do prefer to use bookmarks they can arrange them in an order to suit the way they work and not have an order forced on them by the subject portal.
- A subject portal site is only as good as the reviewers who peer-review the site listed. The reviewers need to have a policy of keeping the portal sites up to date and of constantly reviewing the sites they list, to make sure that they are still relevant and still contain good, timely information.
- A subject portal may be available to everyone who needs to use it to only certain groups of users. A good portal should be publicly available to anyone who needs it.

ELECTRONIC JOURNALS

Electronic journals form a large part of the collection of a library for providing web based services. Today many journals are available electronically - some are full text and some contain only bibliographic information with abstract. Major advantage of electronic journals is that they are constantly updated and easy to access but disadvantage is that breaching of copyright law is very easy. They are available as bitmaps, PostScript, PDF, ASCII, SGML and HTML. Library services may be delivering to users on CDRom, through e-mail or through web. Some international societies and associations have developed their own digital libraries through which users can get access to all their publications. Services are available to the members of society or associations through subscription.

ONLINE DATABASES

These are large collections of machine-readable data that are maintained by commercial agencies and are accessed through communication lines. Many libraries subscribe to them for easy access and use of current information. The disadvantage is that only bibliographic data is presented and not full text. The information cannot be accessed when the system is down for any reason. Examples Ei Compendex, SciFinder Scholar, Web of Science, Current Contents, etc.

SEARCH ENGINES

Search Engines are huge databases of web page files that have been assembled automatically by machines where as the subject directories are human-compiled and maintained. Search engine indexes every page of a web site and subject directories linked only homepages. Search Engine is the popular term for an information retrieval (IR) system. A search engine is computer software that searches a collection of electronic materials to retrieve citations, documents, or information that matches or answers a user's query. The retrieved materials may be text documents, facts that have been extracted from text, images, or sounds.

A query is a question phrased so that it can be interpreted properly by search engine. Depending on the type of software, it may be a collection of commands, a statement in either full or partial sentences, one or more keywords, or in the case of non-text searching, an image or sequence of sounds to be matched.

SUBJECT DIRECTORIES

Subject directories differ from search engines in that search engines are populated by robots that finds and index sites whereas humans making editorial decisions that populate subject directories. Subject directories are basically index home pages of sites and can be classified as general, academic, commercial or portal. Among the well known subject directories are the Argus Clearinghouse and Yahoo. Strengths include relevance, effectiveness and relative high quality of content. Weaknesses are that they lack depth in their coverage of the subjects.

NEW WEB BASED LIBRARY SERVICES

VIRTUAL LIBRARY TOURS

Web sites of libraries provides virtual library guide to the physical facilities including collections, services and infrastructure available in the library. The combination of library maps and floor plans, library departments and photographic views are used for the tour. Virtual library tours are also using new technologies such as QuickTime movies etc and are beginning to replace image maps on main campus Web sites.

ASK-A-LIBRARIAN

Ask-A-Librarian services are Internet-based question and answer service that connects users with individuals who possess specialised subject knowledge and skill in conducting precision searches. Most "Ask-a-Librarians" services have a web-based question submission form or an e-mail address or both. Users are invited to submit their queries by using web forms or through e-mail. Once a query is read by a service, it is assigned to an individual expert for answering. An expert responds to the query with factual information and or a list of information resources.

The response is either sent to the user's e-mail account or is posted on the web so that the user can access it after a certain period of time. Many services have informative web sites that include archives of questions and answers and a set of FAQs. Users are usually encouraged to browse archives and FAQs before submitting a question in case sufficient information already exists.

REAL TIME SERVICES

A new and exciting method of digital reference service that libraries are attempting to provide more and more now is live reference. These are real- time, interactive reference services in which the users can talk to a real, live reference librarian at any time, from anywhere in the world. User and librarian can interact using chat technologies, and unlike with e-mail reference the librarian can perform a reference interview of sorts by asking the users to elaborate or clarify if needed before proceeding to answer the question. The librarian can perform Internet searches and push web sites onto the user's browser, and can receive immediate feedback from the users as to whether their question have been answered to satisfaction.

BULLETIN BOARDS

A bulletin board is an electronic communications forum that hosts posted messages and articles connected to a common subject or theme or interest. It allows users to call in and either leaves or retrieves messages. The messages may be directed to all users of the bulletin board or only to particular users. But all messages can be read by all users. Several libraries are using bulletin boards for their web-based library services. The bulletin board system is also used as an interactive interface to invite suggestions on activities and services of a library. It can also be used as an interface to distribute library services.

WEB-BASED USER EDUCATION

Web guides and teaching tools are found everywhere on the Web because they are easily updated, accessed, and printed on demand. The web-based user education provides a high degree of interactivity and flexibility to the users. The library web sites can use web-based user education for imparting training to users in teaching the basic library skills along with glossary of library terms, using Library OPAC, locating books, magazines, biographical data and other library materials, understanding how to navigate the libraries web site and how to select the most relevant database, instructions for searching CD ROM and guidance in locating web-based databases and other electronic resources and instructions on subject searching training, using Boolean operators and searching internet resources through search engines.

WEB FORMS

Library web sites have some web forms for suggestions and comments on the Library Services. Different types of Web Forms are available on web that may be an Indent form for acquiring some publications, interlibrary loan request form for document delivery, Ask-a-Librarian forms, on line reservation form or user survey form, etc.

INDIAN SCENARIO

The Indian libraries also have realised to give web based services to users and they have recognised that working together can accomplish for more than they can do individually.

Many Indian libraries in India are not geared up for accessing e-journals due to various reasons including user ignorance, infrastructure and initial funds.

The library and information networks in India were initiated in early eighties. The growth during this period can be linked to some of the policies that Government of India pursued. Some institutions like CSIR, ISRO, DRDO, DAE, ICAR, SIRNET, NICNET, NISSAT, INFLIBNET, MHRD and IIM libraries are actively working continuously to improve the present situation.

They spend annually a huge amount of money towards library acquisition, especially towards journals, e-journals and e-databases. Some initiative include, Indian Institute of Management for accessing bibliographic databases, CSIR laboratories for Science Direct, FORSA for accessing Astronomy and Astrophysics journals, Hyderabad Knowledge park members of J-gate, INFLIBNET (UGC–INFONET) initiative for full text and databases like BIOSIS and CAS and INDEST for a host of full text sources and few bibliographic databases for the benefit of IITs, IISc, NITs and Engineering colleges. In India, library consortia are emerging as one of the important service to users. The Indian consortiums will help the library to provide better services to the users by investing meagre amount. To expand the access for more number of e-journals, e-books and other resources, we have to develop the digital library infrastructure as a platform for e-learning.

THE FUTURE OF WEB BASED SERVICES

Library Web services will continue to spread out, offering more full-text electronic journals and indexes that do not now include full text will begin to do so, or link to external resources.

Bibliographic access to full-text periodicals either through cataloging, databases, or vendors will be in improved form. There will be more Web forms for user feedback, and perhaps a virtual librarian who interacts in real time chat or video conferencing. More Document delivery services to distance education or users and Savings on Interlibrary Loan and user convenience are incentives.

Information resources through creative consortia purchasing will be popular. A well-developed user education modules or tutorials, especially to support independent exploration of library and Web resources. Somebody will have to figure out how to keep Word users from saving print documents as XML, without thinking in terms of Web, not print, space. XML will be embraced as a way to control page appearance and behaviour, but it will take a while for people to figure out how to use it well and there will be trends we haven't thought of yet...

WEB PUBLISHING: GETTING STARTED

WEB PUBLISHING

The Oracle's Hyperion® Data Relationship Management Web Publishing module provides an auxiliary means of accessing Data Relationship Management system functionality.

This application provides the following capabilities through a Web browser interface:

- Viewing hierarchies and node properties.
- Running exports.
- Printing hierarchy trees.
- Searching for nodes in a given hierarchy.

Data Relationship Management Web Publishing connects to the Data Relationship Management application server, but operates in a read-only mode. Various requests can be made using HTTP to either retrieve information or execute a command such as running exports or reloading from the database.

Figure provides a top-level view of Data Relationship Management Web Publishing in relation to the Data Relationship Management architecture. Web Publishing can be run on its own server or hosted on the Data Relationship Management multi-tier Web Server or the primary application server.

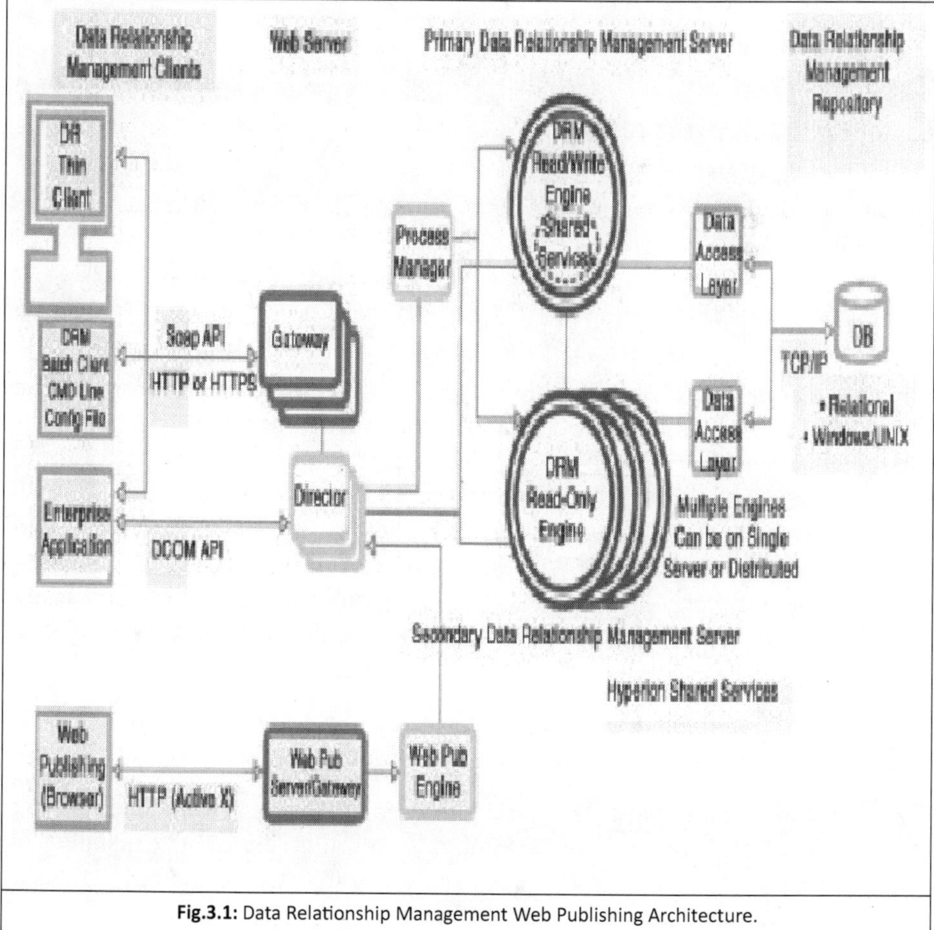

Fig.3.1: Data Relationship Management Web Publishing Architecture.

SYSTEM REQUIREMENTS

The following topics describe the Data Relationship Management Web Publishing system requirements for the Web server and the client computers.

Web Server Requirements:

- Windows 2000 Server or Windows Server 2003.
- Internet Information Services (IIS) version 5 or later.
- Microsoft Data Access Components (MDAC) 2.7 or later (required only for MS SQL.)

Windows 2000 or later (ME, 2000, XP, Server 2003)

- Internet Explorer version 5 or later.
- Client Computer Requirements:

INSTALLING, CONFIGURING, AND UNINSTALLING

PRE-INSTALLATION TASKS

The following topics describe tasks that must be performed before you can install and use Data Relationship Management Web Publishing.

System Administrator Tasks

Your Data Relationship Management system administrator must complete the following tasks before you can install and use Data Relationship Management Web Publishing:

- Ensure that the Data Relationship Management system Release 9.3 is currently installed and operational.
- Create a new Data Relationship Management user name specifically for accessing Data Relationship Management Web Publishing (for example: mdm_Web). Assign the desired access rights to the user.
- Since the engine needs access to all paths that might be used for exports, provide a list of these paths to the network administrator.
- The system preference WebExDir controls the directory root for file storage location on the Web Publishing server.
- Configure the appropriate Data Relationship Management system preferences related to Data Relationship Management Web Publishing.

Network Administrator Tasks

Your network administrator must complete the following tasks before you can install and use Data Relationship Management Web Publishing:

- Create a new network user/application id that the Engine can use to login to the system. This id should have full access rights (including file creation) to any network shares that are designated for Data Relationship Management exports.

- Verify that IE browser policies allow for the use of digitally-signed ActiveX controls. While most Data Relationship Management Web Publishing implementations provide for browser access, some may be used strictly for automating exports. Configuring the browser can be skipped if interactive access is not desired.

General Tasks

In addition to system administrator and network administrator tasks described in the preceding topics, the following tasks must be performed before you can install and use Data Relationship Management Web Publishing:

- You must manually uninstall prior versions of Data Relationship Management Web Publishing before installing Data Relationship Management Web Publishing Release 9.3.
- Ensure that the intended host machine(s) meet or exceed the minimum system requirements defined in this document.
- Ensure that the user performing the installation has administrative rights to the Web server machine.
- Ensure that the Data Relationship Management Web Publishing release package is available.

INSTALLING DATA RELATIONSHIP MANAGEMENT WEB PUBLISHING

To install Data Relationship Management Web Publishing:

- Do one of these tasks:
  - f you have a Data Relationship Management Web Publishing CD or DVD, insert the CD or DVD into your CD or DVD drive.
  - If you downloaded the Data Relationship Management Web Publishing software from the Download Center
    a. Navigate to the directory where you downloaded the installation programme.
    b. Select File > Run or Start > Run and enter Drive:\Folder\mdm_web_pub_server_setup.exe, where Drive and Folder are the installation programme location.
- Review the Welcome box and click Next.
- Read the license agreement, select I AGREE and click Next.
  From Web Publishing Installation Options, do one of the following:
  - Click Next if the computer where you are installing Data Relationship Management Web Publishing is also a Data Relationship Management Web server.
  - Select Ntier Director if Data Relationship Management Web Publishing is being added to a computer that is not a Data Relationship Management Web server or if it is a standalone server, and click Next.

- Click Next to accept the default installation directory, or click Change to select another directory, and click Next.
- Do one of the following:
  - If you are installing Ntier Director, continue with the next step.
  - If you are not installing Ntier Director, continue with step 8.
- Enter the machine name or IP address of the Data Relationship Management primary application server and click Next.
- From Windows COM+ Logon, enter a user name and password for a user who has rights to perform the following actions and click Next:
  - Edit registry settings
  - Read and write to the local file system
  - Launch processes
  - Run as a service
- Click Install.
- Optional: After installation completes, you can select Launch Data Relationship Management Web Publishing Console.
- Click Finish.

MANUALLY CONFIGURING DATA RELATIONSHIP MANAGEMENT WEB PUBLISHING

Configuration must be completed for the following:

- Data Relationship Management Web Publishing Service
- IIS Virtual Directory/Pool Configuration
- Data Relationship Management Web Publishing Engine
- When installing on a stand-alone server: COM+ Director and Process Manager Proxy Components

Configuring Data Relationship Management Web Publishing Service To configure the service:

- Select Start > Programmes > Administrative Tools > Services.
- Select the Hyperion Data Relationship Management Web Publishing
- service.
- Right-click the service and select Properties.
- On the General tab, ensure that Startup Type is set to Automatic.
- On the Log On tab, select This Account.
- Enter a username and password for a Windows administrative user.
- Click OK.
- Close the Services dialog box.

Configuring Internet Information Services

For IIS 5.0:

- Select Start > Programmes > Administrative Tools > Internet
- Services Manager (or Internet Information Services (IIS) Manager).

- Expand to the default Web site.
- Select the mdm_web virtual directory.
- Right-click and select Properties.
  On the Virtual Directory tab, verify the following:
  - The Local Path is pointing to the Data Relationship Management Web directory.
  - The Read option is selected.
  - Execute Permissions is set to Scripts and Executables.
  - The Application Protection is set to High (Isolated). Selecting this option enables you to unload the mdm_web application without restarting IIS.
- On the Directory Security tab, enable and configure anonymous access.
- Click OK.
- Click OK.
- Close the IIS Manager.

For IIS 6.0 or later:

- Select Start > Programmes > Administrative Tools > Internet
- Services Manager (or Internet Information Services (IIS) Manager).
- Expand to the default Web site.
- Select the mdm_web virtual directory.
- Right-click and select Properties.

On the Virtual Directory tab, verify the following:

  - The Local Path is pointing to the Data Relationship Management Web directory.
  - The Read option is selected.
  - Execute Permissions is set to Scripts and Executables.
  - Application Pool is WebPool. This setting enables you to unload the mdm_web application without restarting IIS.
- Click OK.
- Select the Web Service Extensions node and select Active Server Pages from the list of Web Service Extensions on the right.
- Verify that the Status column displays the status Allowed.
- Create a new Web service extension namedmdm_web_pub_gateway that points to mdm_web_pub_gateway.dll and is set to Allowed.
- Close the IIS Manager.

Verifying System Access

To verify system access: At the prompt, select to install the mdm_web_client ActiveX control:

- This digitally signed control is safe to install. If you are not rompted to install the component, then it may be necessary to adjust the current browser settings to allow download and installation of ActiveX controls.

- Click OK: The Data Relationship Management Web Client page is displayed. No data (versions or hierarchies) is displayed until the service is started at the end of the installation/configuration/ startup process.

Configuring Data Relationship Management Web Publishing Engine

To configure the Web Publishing Engine:

- Select Start > Administrative Tools > Component Services.
- Expand the Component Services node to the DCOM Config folder.
- In the DCOM Config folder, select the mdm_Web_Pub_Engine object, right-click and select Properties.

For Windows 2000 only: From a command line prompt, type: dcomcnfg.

  - In the list of applications, select the mdm_Web_Pub_Engine object and click Properties.
  - On the General tab, set Authentication Level to None.
- On the Identity tab, select This User and enter the same user and password that were configured for the Data Relationship Management Web Publishing Service.
- On the Security tab, under Launch and Activation Permissions, select Customise and click Edit.
- Add the user that is configured for IIS anonymous access to the mdm_web virtual directory.
- Allow Local Activation for this user.
- Repeat this process for the Access Permissions section, by selecting
- Customise > Edit, and adding the same user and enabling the Local Access permission.
- Click OK to close the Properties dialog box.

Configuring Director

If you install on a stand-alone server where Director does not already exist, you must configure the COM+ Director component.

To configure the COM+ Director component:

- Select Start > Programmes > Administrative Tools > Component Services.
- Drill down and select the Director component.
- Right-click and select Properties.
- On the Security tab, verify that Enforce Access Checks for this Application is not selected.
- On the Identity tab, verify that the appropriate user is setup and then close the Properties dialog box.
- Drill down to the Components folder of Director.
- Select all components by pressing CTRL-A, then right-click and select Properties.

- Verify that Enable Object Pooling is selected on the Activation tab and then close the Properties dialog box.
- Close the Component Services window.

Configuring Process Manager

If you install on a stand-alone server where Process Manager does not already exist, you must configure the COM+ Process Manager Proxy component.

To configure the COM+ Process Manager Proxy component:

- Select Start > Programmes > Administrative Tools > Component Services.
- Drill down and select the Process Manager component.
- Right-click the component and select Properties.
- On the Activation tab, verify that the remote server is correct.
- Close the Component Services window.

USING THE DATA RELATIONSHIP MANAGEMENT WEB PUBLISHING ONSOLE

The Data Relationship Management Web Publishing Console is designed to allow configuration, control and monitoring of the Web Publishing system. The Server Monitor Page allows the Web Publishing Service to be controlled (Start, Stop, Restart, Force Shutdown) and displays the current status of the service.

In addition there are three tabs for further information:

- System Status.
- Event Log.
- Web Server.

The System Status tab shows some basic operating system information as well as information on COM+ and DCOM (Out of Process) applications. Currently Web Publishing does not use any COM+ so this section is blank.

The Event Log tab filters the application event log to show events for the Web Publishing module. Clicking on an event in the top panel shows the detail for the event in the lower panel. Events shown are filtered to include only events after the console was started. To see historical events you can check the Show History and click Refresh. Clear resets the filter time to the current date and time.

The Web Server tab provides two browser views to validate access to the Web Server system. The first panel displays the test HTML in the mdm_web virtual directory and validates access to the virtual directory for Web Publishing. The second view tests the Web Publishing Gateway to perform the List Versions command. If the system is up and running, the list of versions available for Web Publishing is displayed. When stopping and starting services such as IIS, you may need to refresh these views. To refresh, right-click on the view and select Refresh.

You can set the Data Relationship Management username and password for the Web Publishing module on the Configuration page. This user is the Data Relationship Management user that the Web Publishing engine uses to retrieve the data for display on the Web client. Limiting access to this user allows the Web Publishing to be restricted. It is important that the user specified for Web Publishing be exempt from session timeout. Thus, the system preference IdleTimeExcludeUsers should be set to include the name of the user for Web Publishing. If this user is not excluded from session timeout, then the Web Publishing service needs to be restarted each time the user session expires.

CONFIGURING DATA RELATIONSHIP MANAGEMENT WEB CLIENT

Data Relationship Management Web provides a specific set of frequently-used Data Relationship Management functionality in a Web browser. This document assumes that the user is already familiar with the overall Data Relationship Management system, including its terminology and feature set. The appearance and behaviour of Data Relationship Management Web Publishing can be configured using both System Preferences and embedded parameters.

LECTRONIC THESES AND DISSERTATIONS FOR INDIAN UNIVERSITIES: A FRAMEWORK

Even though the electronic publishing and writing offer demanding environment in academic scholarship, the theses and dissertations are still written and published in print and archived in shelves in university libraries where the vast majority gather dust, read by perhaps one or two interested researchers who access them in print with lot of difficulty, often for a fee and most are never consulted at all. Digital libraries of electronic theses and dissertations (ETDs) offer an alternative to this waste of valuable academic scholarship and offer researchers and University Libraries in India opportunities to explore the possibilities electronic publishing trend in academic sector. The emergence of UGC Infonet, the aspiring and dream project of University Grants Commission, which also aims at Content Creation by Indian Academic Sector, will definitely boost this idea.

UGC-INFONET

As technology is becoming a driving force in the contemporary education systems, University Grant Commission has launched an ambitious programme to bring about a qualitative change in the academic infrastructure, especially for higher education. Under this initiative UGC is modernising the University Campuses with State-of-the-art campus wide networks and setting up its own nationwide communication network named UGC-Infonet. UGC-Infonet will be a boon to the higher education systems in several ways to facilitate spread of quality education all over the country. This will function as a tool to distribute education material and journals to the remotest of areas and a resource centre for researchers and scholars for tapping the most up-to-date information. As a main feature of UGC Infonet, a data center with large server capacity is being set up, where content of common interest can be maintained. Each University will have the option of hosting their web site, digital content like ETDs and the E-journals subscribed through INFLIBNET Consortia.

THESES AND DISSERTATIONS IN INDIA

Indian universities play a major role in generation and dissemination of knowledge by conducting research works and producing Ph D theses as a unique genre of information sources. Every year, nearly 8000- 10000 Ph Ds are awarding in India. The purpose of the thesis is to provide an experience in scholarship, which will be of enduring value to the student in understanding how new knowledge is acquired and communicated within the chosen field. These works contain valuable content, including focused literature reviews and details on research, which are not generally made available elsewhere.

At present there are some lacunas in publication, control and access theses information in India, and some attempts have been made to address them. At the moment, most unpublished theses are hard to get hold of, as they are filed only in the university library where the student has worked. The Indian thesis literature is beset with many problems like Lack of Systematic acquisition, Lack of Access, Uncertain publication practice, Enormous Growth in the number of theses, etc. In western countries, these problems were addressed already and serious attempts have been made to solve them. In North America, less than 5 per cent of all accepted dissertations and masters' theses are initially conceived of and executed as electronic documents.

BENEFITS OF ETD

- Broader exposure of university research through greater accessibility;
- Opportunities to use new forms of creative scholarship through use of interactive elements, multimedia, hyperlinks, etc.;
- Ability to have a hyperlink to the thesis/dissertation on homepages and electronic CVs;
- Professional development experience for research students as they learn the basic skills of scholarly publishing in an electronic format;
- Conservation of paper, library storage space and of library staff time;
- Theses and dissertations more immediately accessible: publication occurs near point of submission rather than three to four months later; and
- The option to have theses or dissertations accessible to any potential reader every day at any time.

ELECTRONIC THESES AND DISSERTATIONS FOR YOUR UNIVERSITY

Format to Create ETD

PDF stands for Portable Document Format: Adobe Systems developed the PDF standard and provides the premiere package for creating and manipulating PDF files, Adobe Acrobat. The process of converting to PDF takes instructions that would ordinarily be sent to a specific printer and prepares them to be viewed or printed on any computer with the free Acrobat Reader installed. Postscript is a standard language developed by Adobe Systems, which is used to send instructions to postscript compatible printers. These instructions describe the contents of all text and graphics to be printed, and where on the page each piece of content is to be printed. Ordinarily, these instructions are transferred to a Postscript printer, which interprets them, creates a printed copy based on the instructions, and then discards the instructions.Other file types for image files can be.gif.jpeg, or.tif; for video files.mov.mpg, or.avi; and for audio files.aif.midi.snd.wav, or as CD-DA, CD-ROM/XA, or MPEG-2.

Facilities Required

Researchers need to create their original thesis using a word processor, such as Microsoft Word or WordPerfect and once it is done, then it can be converted to a PDF file, which will retain the original document format (for the purpose of future editing). Conversion into a PDF file is a straightforward process. Libraries and Campus labs have to be equipped with Windows based computers set up to convert theses and dissertations written in Microsoft Word to Adobe Acrobat format. This application will allow us to convert the word processing document to PDF format as well as create bookmarks. Researchers must submit the document on disk, CD, or Zip drive; the conversion machines are not attached to the network. Library staff can provide assistance with using the software to convert files, but cannot assist with document preparation.

SOFTWARE TO MANAGE ETDS

D-Space is a groundbreaking digital library system that captures, stores, indexes, preserves and redistributes the intellectual output of a university's research faculty in digital formats. The future of Etheses and of archiving and searching in general depends on institutions being able to deliver top quality services, with a high degree of interoperability. This means, among other things, that systems must continue to be developed and they must be able to handle many different types of digital object. It is believed that DSpace will fulfill these requirements to a higher degree and will continue to improve in this way in the future.

As an open source system, DSpace is now freely available to other institutions to run as-is, or to modify and extend as they require to meet local needs. From the outset, HP and MIT designed the system to be run by institutions other than MIT, and to support federation among its adopters, in both the technical and the social sense. INFLIBNET believes that it is our responsibility to lead the charge for a realistic assessment of how we can head off an otherwise inevitable loss of academic resources. Awareness building in Open Archives and Institutional Repositories in Indian academic Institutions will be the main focus of INFLIBNET in coming future. For long-term preservation of our knowledge base and cultures, we have to find out an economical way to save digital content for future generations.

Institutions in India started using variety of open source archiving solutions like Green Stone, E-Print, DSpace etc since 2000. After experimenting all popular solutions, INFLIBNET decided to opt DSpace for its Institutional Repository and archive its publications, conference proceedings, lecture notes, etc. The capability of Dspace to handle multilingual content, even at Metadata level using globally accepted UNICODE standard was the important issue for selecting this solution, especially a country like India with its mullti-lingual dilemma in digital content creation and storage.

It has been installed in test-bed and experimented its capabilities and performance. After all sorts of testing required, Dspace was customised according to our requirements and it was installed on one of the WWW Server on Linux platform. Then we have requested Corporation for National Research Initiatives (CNRI) site for providing Persistent Identifiers (CNRI Handles) which promotes interoperability among open archives through Open Archives Initiative Protocol for Metadata Harvesting (OAI-PMH). The Handle System® covers assignment, management, and resolution of these persistent identifiers and are compliant with the IETF's Uniform Resource Name (URN) specification.

ROLE OF THE FACULTY AND REVIEW PROCESS

Faculty will continue to be responsible for upholding the quality of the thesis or dissertation, whether that thesis or dissertation is submitted using electronic formats or through paper. The electronic format can facilitate communication among members of the dissertation committee and the student. Electronic distribution of drafts allows multiple readers to markup and comment within one copy of the work simultaneously, regardless of the readers' physical location, and to see others' comments. It also allows the student to collate the comments of all readers within one document.

For defence, some committees may require that students provide all members of the committee with a paper copy of the ETD before the defence; others may elect to read on-screen or to have committee members take individual responsibility for working from screen or paper they print out themselves. Printed versions of the textual components of an ETD can always be made available to committee members at their request. If non-text elements of the ETD are part of the defence, the committee can consider the most effective way to ensure that all members of the committee have access to non-text elements during the defence. After the committee approves thesis or dissertation, it can be sent to a particular contact person in the library for processing, who will be responsible for processing ETDs by making sure that the file's formatting is correct, the links work, etc. Metadata of ETD can be created and made available for searching and accessing.

ISSUE OF COPYRIGHT

The copyright issue involves two components: Protecting the information/work produced as part of the research programme; and Granting license to University or to any ETD Programme to make the work available for use. This also includes obtaining permission to use parts of the work that have already been published in other sources. If the material we are quoting or reproducing does not fall under the general guidelines of "fair use" then as suggested, need to get written permission from the copyright owner. Since a dissertation or thesis is published for non-profit educational purposes, the author is permitted limited use of copyrighted material under the guidelines of "fair use." The purpose, amount, nature and effect of the work reproduced determine whether or not one must seek permission from the copyright owner.

INDIAN INITIATIVES

As a bibliographical tool to know about theses of awarded Ph Ds, Association of Indian Universities started publishing of Doctoral Bibliographies in all subjects and Theses of the Month column through its weekly publication University News. In 1994, INFLIBNET hosted a regularly updated free online union database of Ph D theses submitted to Indian universities. At present it is freely available for searching at INFLIBNET web site and contains around 1,40,000 of unique bibliographical records covering all subjects and all universities. Being the data supplied by the Universities themselves, it is considered as the only authoritative online-tool available to find-out the research out put of Indian Universities.

Recently University of Mysore, in collaboration with NISSAT and Ford Foundation initiated a project called Vidyanithi to host individual full-text thesis from various universities who are willing to become a member of this project. Even though, this project tries to evolve as a national depository for Indian theses, but it is not compulsory for Universities to become a part of this project. All these efforts are, off course, helpful for researchers in locating theses, but in the case of access, still we need remedies.

IN THE END WE CAN SAY

Popularisation of ETDs and its full advantages for faculty, students, and researchers are the foremost attempt to be start of. Brochures, communications, web sites etc conveying this information need to be written, designed, published and disseminated to all affected by this far-reaching change. Workshops and training programmes for both students and faculty need to be developed that cover issues of copyright and choice of access, and that encourage research scholars to carefully consider the ethics of restricting their research from access by the national and international scholarly community. Well-equipped computer labs must be put in place to provide workstations, software, and technical support staff for students writing ETDs. And standards need to be developed for the presentation of dissertation research—standards which facilitate the development of a useful and easily navigable digital collection of works, but which do not unnecessarily constrain the use of software and design considerations graduate students deem essential to their research. Careful consideration of these requirements and their full support will contribute substantially to making this transition smoothly. The potential ETDs have to transform graduate education in ways that benefit both students and the scholarly community depends upon it.

SEARCH TECHNIQUES FOR ACCESSING CD-ROM DATABASES

Due to the development of information technology, information is increasingly recorded in digital format and electronic databases which are continually becoming more complex, information storage and retrieval As the technology obsolete very fast, CD-ROM is also facing problems due to emergence of the DVD. In today's business, education, and government environments the amount of information, data and software being archived and distributed on CD-ROM and DVD-ROM media is overwhelming. For years the medium of choice for storing, archiving and distributing digital content has been the CD-ROM.

As capacity requirements of data intensive applications and databases grow, DVD-ROM, with a capacity potential over 13 times that of CD-ROM, is fast becoming the most popular medium. (CD-ROM media can store up to 700 MB of data). Single-sided, single layer DVD-ROM media can store up to 4.7 GB of data. Doublesided, single layer DVD-ROM media store up to 9.4 GB of data). DVD which is used primarily with movie/ video features will not affect the CD-ROM, but DVD-ROMs will be, which can carry information on both sides of the disc. DVD-ROM will replace the CD-ROM, but that it will take a few years.

As information is increasingly recorded in digital format and electronic databases are continually becoming more complex, information storage and retrieval processes have profoundly changed. Over the past decades three major migrations have occurred in library academic services: from printed resources to online electronic databases; from online databases to bibliographic and full-text CD-ROM databases; and from CD-ROM databases to online Internet access to bibliographic and full-text/full-image databases.

CD-ROM DATABASES

CD-ROM is abbreviation for 'Compact Disc-Read-Only Memory' a type of optical disk capable of storing large amounts of data up to 1GB, although the most common size is 650 MB (megabytes). The term 'database' has been used in the literature in two different connotations. In Computer Science this is referred to as a database management system. In this sense a database has a logically consistent structure in which records are actually linked. In library and Information science, these are referred to as bibliographic or inventory in nature and comprise a collection of related logical records here a database is defined as an organised and generally unlinked set of machine, or it can be said, these databases are the electronic version of published literature traditionally appearing in printed form in various field.

Databases are produced by different agencies in a computer readable form, the contents of which are accessible in various ways according to requirements with the help of suitable software. Various agencies (governmental and non-governmental) are involved in developing databases by collecting information from varieties of sources and packaging the information in the form of databases. Databases can be stored on CD-ROM, on the Internet, or on commercial sites that are accessible only if user's library has a subscription.

CD-Rom in the library contains periodical indexes, abstracts, statistics, directories, and other complete texts. Some databases provide information that is primarily numeric, such as data from a recent government census and some contain information that is primarily textual. Database some time also called data bank.

USE CD-ROM DATABASES IN LIBRARIES

Access to Cd-Rom databases is fast, accurate and thorough. A clever search by a users may get them in seconds most of the information they need. In contrast, traditional print services may take months for same task, with still great deal of information left out. As a matter of fact, libraries can not possibly continue with the sluggish manual information service methods and hope to remain in business tomorrow.

Libraries can have economic access to information, space saving and users friendly Libraries and information centers used these databases in providing various library services as mentioned below:

- Literature search services, current and retrospective literature
- searches
- Current awareness services in various forms including SDI
- Full text databases may be utilised for search services
- Document delivery services
- For producing digest trend reports, etc.
- Compilations of bibliographies
- Abstracting and Indexing Services

WHY WE DON'T WANT TO USE CD-ROM DATABASES

It is always beneficial to know about the pros and cons of any information so that one can proceed systematically.

- CD-ROM databases are not updated in time, some web journals or indexing services are available online even before their print editions roll out of the press. For example, Engineering Index on disc is updated quarterly, and Dissertation Abstracts on disc only once in a year.
- Retrieval from CD-ROM databases take seconds, as against online databases, which take only milliseconds, however complex the command

search statement may be (of courses with higher bandwidth telecom pipes provided) If not acquired from a single producer, CD/DVD Rom databases require skills in using different search engines. Making menu-driven index searching or single keyword searching at command prompt may be easy to use in each system. But, users must make command, or Boolean searches, to get at exacter or less abstract hits. Sometimes users have been found key boarding DIALOG syntax instead of SPIRS one to search into MathSci Disc or PsycLIT from SilverPlatter, and vice versa. Both the search engines are so dissimilar in construct.

- Again, generally, users keyboard a collection of key words at the command prompt. They are flummoxed to discover that one access engine parses the search statement with "or" operator between words, and the other with 'and' operator. The former results come in too many hits and the latter in too few. Therefore, all new uses require basic education in the techniques of bibliographic database searching.
- If adequate jukeboxes are not provided for permanent mounting of optical databases, it is a great hassle for users to switch from one disc to another for either a different file or part of the same file. By comparison, on online services, like DIALOG's the process is just a click away.

Yet another disadvantage of CD-ROM, they are vulnerable to damage by dust, fingerprints and scratches, etc. Therefore they need very careful handing. Libraries will have to make backup copy of each CDS disc to be kept in safe custody, so fresh copies can be made.

SEARCHING CD-ROM DATABASE

Conducting effective searches requires knowledge of a number of techniques. Users should not only have been an understanding of the nature, content and structure of the database, but also be familiar with the various option available in the search screen, the tools and techniques for searching, and the techniques and formats for display of the search output. The search features commonly available are Keyword Search, Phrase Search, Boolean Search, Truncation, Index and/or Thesaurus Support, Proximity Search, Field-Specific Searches, Free-Text Search, Combing Search Sets and Search Refinement, Limiting or Range Search, Searching through the Retrieved Records and they may vary from one CD-ROM to another.

SELECTION OF DATABASES FOR COMPARISON

Four CD-ROM Databases have been selected for a discussion on the various search and retrieval features available, 'Ulrich's on disc', 'Books in Print' from the category of general or ready reference sources, 'Ei Compendex', 'LISA plus' are Bibliographic databases containing details of documents including abstracts and Emerald full-text database of journal articles.

Ulrich's on Disc

Ulrich's on Disc from R. R. Bowker provides the ability to search and browse the entire Ulrich's family of databases. They included nearly 250,000 titles from over 200 countries, Information on about 11,000 new titles per year, annotations for almost 90,000 titles, full text reviews from Magazines for Libraries and Library Journal for over 8,700 publications, indicators for over 21,000 refereed publications and complete names and addresses for 80,000 serials publishers and distributors. The main screen of Ulrich's is shown in figure.

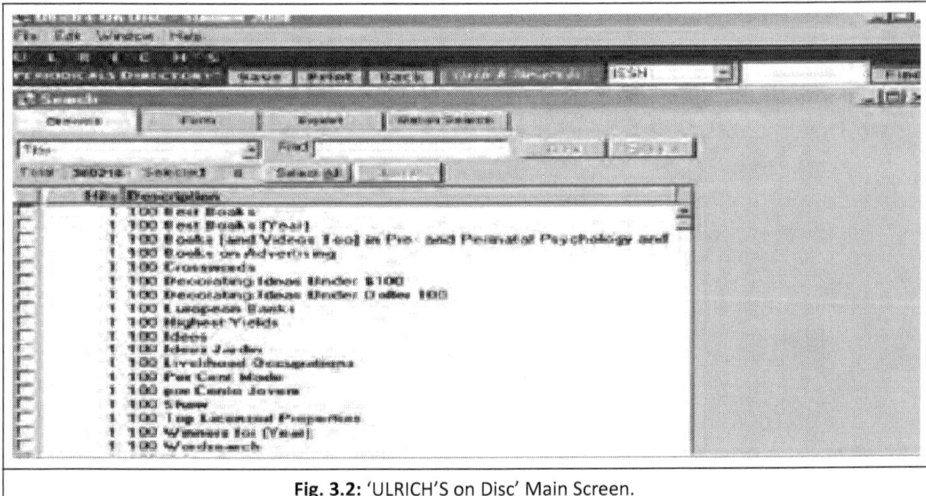

Fig. 3.2: 'ULRICH'S on Disc' Main Screen.

EI COMPENDEX BIBLOGRAPHIC DATABASE

DIALOG OnDisc® Compendex, produced by (Ei) Engineering Information Inc., provides coverage of the world's significant engineering and technical literature.

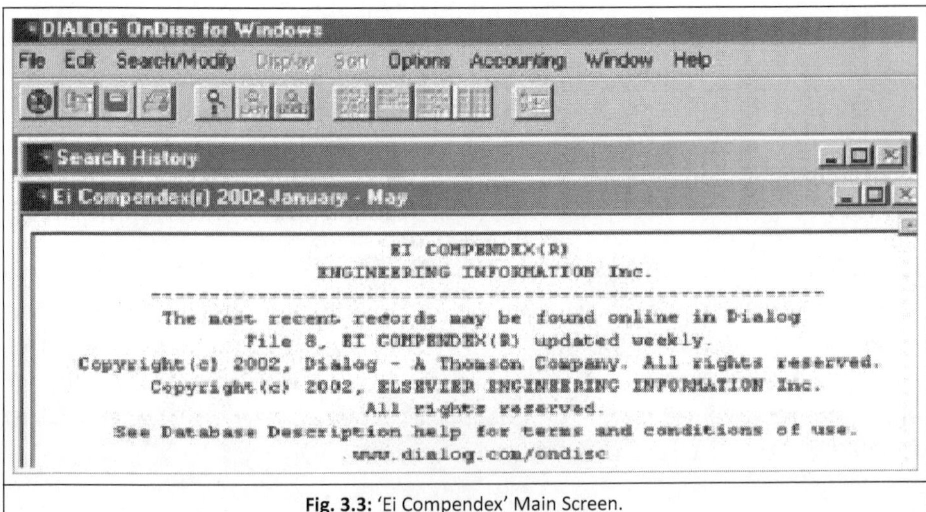

Fig. 3.3: 'Ei Compendex' Main Screen.

Subject coverage includes but is not limited to the various disciplines of engineering, applied physics, electronics and instrumentation, light and optical technologies, and other areas of significant technology. Compendex contains references to and abstracts from journals, technical reports, books, proceedings and conference papers, and more. Author-prepared abstracts are used when available. Publications from around the world are indexed, including approximately 4,500 journals and 2,000 conference proceedings per year.

Approximately 10 percent of the documents indexed are in a language other than English.

LIBRARY AND INFORMATION SCIENCE ABSTRACTS (LISA PLUS)

LISA plus is the world's best known resource for the coverage of ongoing research in all aspects of library and information studies. Over 245,000 abstracts keep user well informed about such topics as artificial intelligence, information and knowledge management, publishing and copyright, World Wide Web resources and much more since 1969. Lisa plus main screen is as figure.

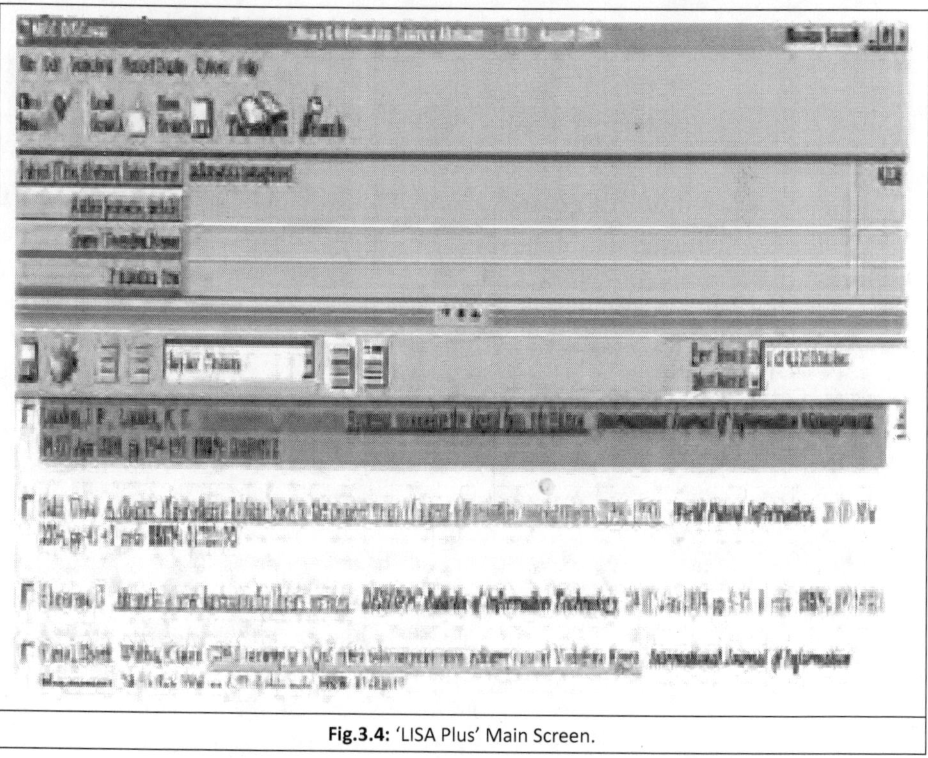

Fig.3.4: 'LISA Plus' Main Screen.

EMERALD FULL-TEXT DATABASE OF JOURNAL ARTICLES

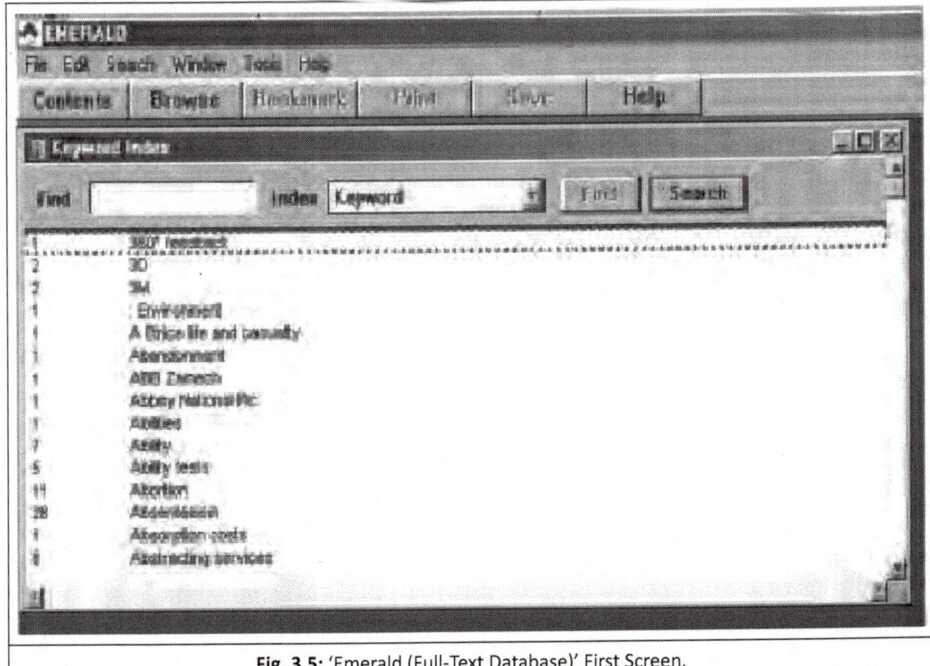

Fig. 3.5: 'Emerald (Full-Text Database)' First Screen.

Emerald is a full text database from MCB, covers more than 82 top journal across ten broad subject areas. It provides access to the full text of articles in PDF and HTML format published from 1994 to date. The subjects covered include Marketing, Human Resources, Quality Management, Information Management, Library and Information Services, Training and Education, General Management Property, Operations and Production Management, etc. Users can choose any subject and get a list of all the journals covered in that subject. First screen of Emerald is as figure

ACCESSING DIFFERENT DATABASES

Searching in Specific Field of Selected CD-ROM Databases

There are two forms of searching for information in CD-ROM databases – field-specific and free-text search. A user may know which field to search, or might like to restrict a given search to one or more fields. This is a field specific search. If the user are not sure of the field to be searched, they can conduct a free-text search, which means that the search is not restricted to any particular field. While the free-text search is not universally available, field specific search is the simplest form of search, and CD-ROM databases offer various options to conduct searches on one or more specific fields. The simplest option is the form search, where the user can select a specific box for a particular field and can key in the search term/phrase. Which search field can be searched in a database depends on the content and structure of the database concerned, and there fore they differ from one database to another.

Ulrich's on Disc

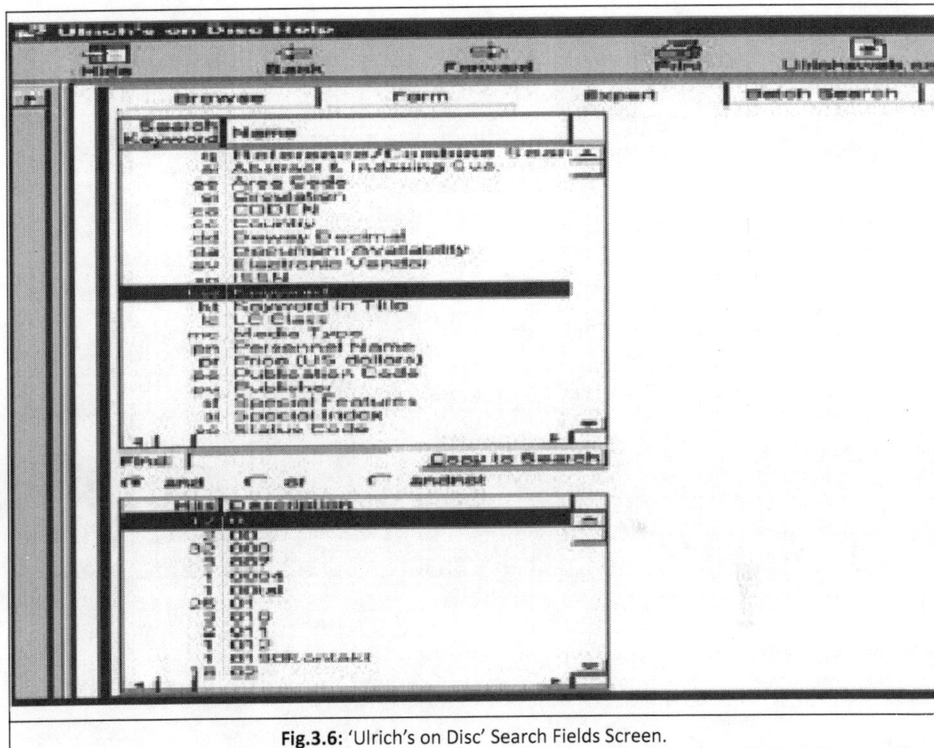

Fig.3.6: 'Ulrich's on Disc' Search Fields Screen.

Search fields are Abstracting and Indexing Service, Area Code, Circulation, CODEN Number, Country, Dewey Number, Document Availability, Electronic Vendor, ISSN, Keyword, Keyword In Title, LC Class, Media Type, Personnel Name, Price (US Dollar), Publication Code, Publisher, Special Features, Special Index, Status Code, Subjects, Title, US State/Zip, Year First Published. Search screen is shown by figure.

Ei Compendex

Under option 'Search/Modify' search fields are Word/Phrase Index, EI Subject Headings, Author Name, Author Affiliation, Title Words, Journal Name, Conference Search Options (Conference Title, Conference Location, Conference Sponsor, Conference Year), Limit Options 'English…', Additional Search Options (Words/Phrases, EI Classification Codes, Major Subject Headings, Treatment Codes, Year of Publications, Language) different fields and Search results screen shown in figure.

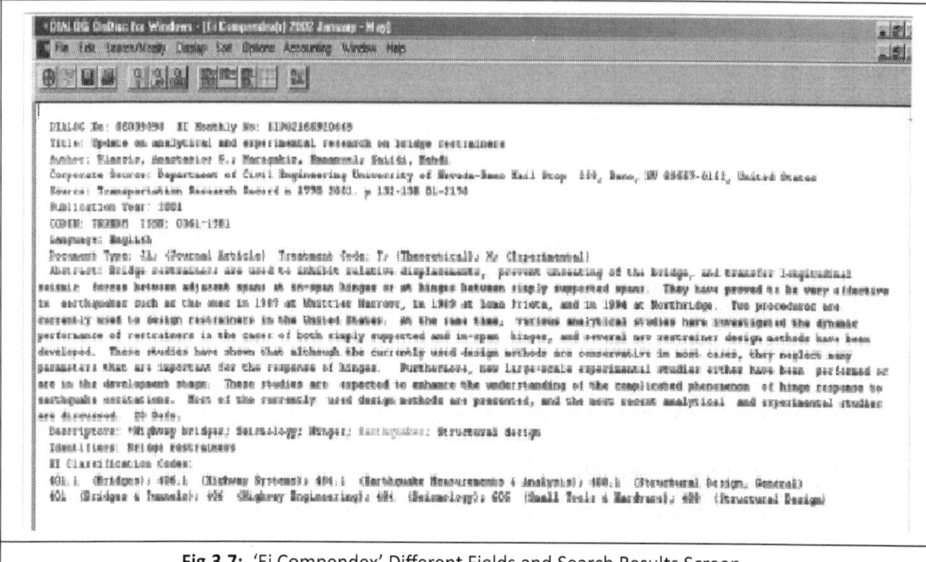

Fig.3.7: 'Ei Compendex' Different Fields and Search Results Screen.

LISA Plus

Subject, Title, Abstract, Index Term Or Keyword, Author, Source, Title Database Name,, Keyword, Language, Publication Date, Author Affiliation, Country Of Research, Record Number, CODEN, CATNI name, ISSN, Thesaurus term

Boolen Search

Combine terms to make the search broader or narrower. How broad or narrow the search is depends on the search logic used to combine search terms. Three logical connectors, or Boolean operators, are used to define the relationship between search terms: "and", "or ", and "not". The Boolean operators may be used to join search terms within search fields in all search modes and to join search criteria between search fields in the Advanced and Expert search modes only. (Novice mode always uses a Boolean AND between search fields). Boolean searches can not be conducted in the 'browse index' mode of CD-ROM.-

Ulrich's on Disc

Operators are AND, OR, NOT/AND NOT and Options are, In the Form Search mode user can combine terms/phrases with Boolean operators in achosen field box, or can type one term/phrase in each box and click on a Boolean operator in the box next to the box next to the term on the right. In the search mode user have to type the Boolean operator to combine terms/phares from the same or different fields. Ei Compendex: Operators are AND, OR, NOT and Options are: use these operators to combine search terms in the 'Modify Search Option'

LISA Plus

Operators are AND, OR, ANDNOT (not can also be used in free-text search mode) Options: In the Easy Search mode, user can combine terms/phrases with Boolean operators in a chosen field box, or can type one term/phrase in each box and click on a Boolean operators in the box next to the term on the right. In the Expert Search Mode, user has to type the Boolean operator to combine terms/ phases from the same or different fields. No nesting is possible. Emerald: Operators are And or, not and Options enter theses operators in the search in the search as well as Advanced Search Mode

Truncation Search

Truncation of the three kinds of truncation (left, right and middle truncation), left truncation is not commonly available in CD-ROM databases. The symbols for truncation and their syntax and effect vary, and the user has to learn these to conduct an effective search.

Ulrich's on disc

Ulrich's on disc: * or $ substitute for any number of characters and can be used for right truncation only. '?' Substitutes for one character, can be used anywhere in a word, or user can use multiple '?'Symbols. LISA: Truncation is the substitution of a wildcard symbol for any portion of a word to retrieve a group of words. Most often, truncation is used to abbreviate a word — to trim a term back to its stem, or root word.

Truncating lets user search for word variants thereby broadening the search. The asterisk * is a multicharacter wildcard and the question mark ? is a single character wildcard. Wildcards are typically used at the end of a word but may be embedded within a word as well. Right and middle or internal truncation is allowed. Both the symbols can be used for right as well as middle truncation. User can enter the symbol as appropriate in the Easy Search as well as the Expert Search mode. Multiple ? can be used. Wildcards are typically used at the end of a word but may be embedded within a word as well. Avoid truncating words to less than five characters or user may retrieve unwanted results.

Index Search and Thesaurus Search

The indexes allow users to select the search terms/phrases from the term index, and a thesaurus allows users to consult a map of available terms to widen or narrow down a given search, as required. CD-ROM retrieval software provides index search facilities, ie users can select an index to browse and select from the index for searching. There may be an index file or a separate index for each searchable field so that the user can choose a field and then browse the corresponding index file. Index search facilities are more commonly available than thesaurus facilities. Thesauri are hierarchically structured. This means that they go from broad terms to narrower, more specific, terms.

Ulrich's on disc

User can choose a field from either the search or the From Search mode. In each case user can display and browse the corresponding index and select a term/ phrase from the index.

Ei Compendex

In order to conduct a search, user need to choose an index: author, subject heading, keywords, etc, and then the corresponding index will be open for user to browse and to select the search term

LISA plus

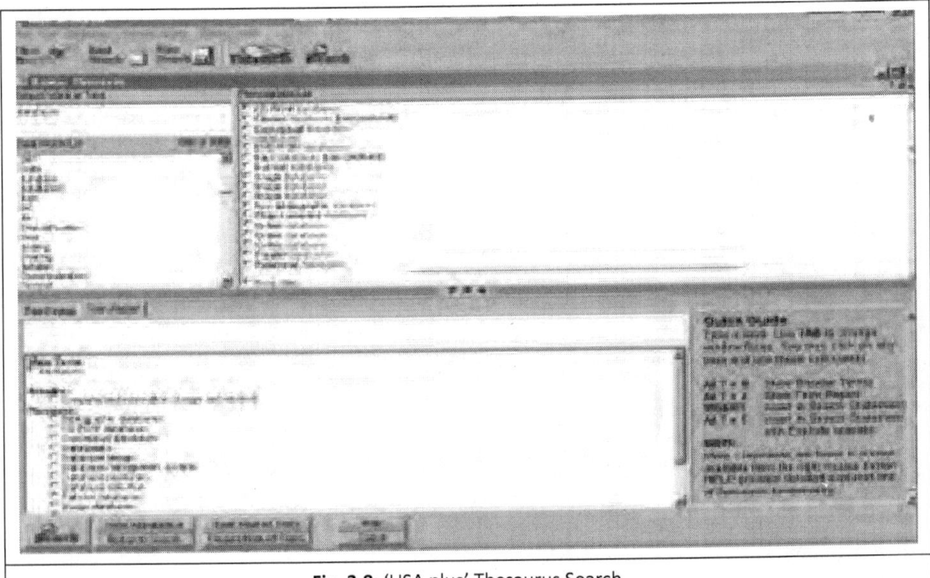

Fig. 3.8: 'LISA plus' Thesaurus Search

The thesaurus may be accessed via the Browse window by clicking on the Index drop-down list and selecting Thesaurus Term; highlight the required term and click View Titles. In the Expert Search mode enter the thesaurus term in the Search Query Box, click on ok or press Enter. Press the 'View Brief' button to display the results of the search ie the thesaurus block. A thesaurus term can be selected to conduct a search in the database as shown in figure.

Emerald

In the Advanced Search mode, user can choose one or more fields to search, and once users have entered a search term correspond to a field, they can click on the 'Thesaurus' button to get other words correspond to the search term.

Proximity Search

With a proximity search, user can specify the number of words allowed between the search terms. In a general sense, there is a correlation between the number of intervening words (the words creating the "distance" between search terms) and the topical relevance of users search results.

The closer the distance between users search words, e.g., 5 words, the more relevant but fewer the results may be. Likewise, the wider the distance between the search words, e.g., 20 words, the less relevant but larger the CD-ROM results may be. The type of proximity search operator to use depends upon whether user need search terms to be found in the same order as listed in the search statement (adjX) or found in the same or reverse order of what user originally specified (nearX).

RESULTS

After the comparison we come to know that all databases have almost same basic accessing techniques as keyword search, Phrase Search, Boolean Search, Truncation, Index and/or Thesaurus Support, Proximity Search, Field-Specific Searches, Free-Text Search, Combing Search Sets and Search Refinement, Limiting or Range Search, Searching through the Retrieved Records and they may vary from one CD-ROM to another with a slight variation as given below

- Boolean searching is possible in all the CD-ROM database, through how it is carried out varies. Boolean searches cannot be conducted in the 'browse index' mode of a CD-ROM database for the obvious reason that only one term/phrase can be keyed in to display the corresponding portion of the index. None of the sample databases provides left-truncations facilities.
- The symbols for truncation vary from one database to another. Search refinement of a given search can be refined by adding or dropping one or more search terms or criteria, such as limiting the output to a given language, year of publication, price range, and so on.
- Some CD-ROM products have more than one search interface, for example, Ulrich's on disc, while others have on search interface giving options for both - simple, novice and other advanced/ expert search.
- Some retrieval system such as EI Compendex show the result instantly, while in others the user has to chose the view/display option, as in LISA plus Proximity search in CD-ROM databases allows users to conduct proximity searches in order to specify how closely the terms prescribed in a search expression.
- Two types of indexing practice are followed word index and phrase index. in the word index, each individual word in a field is indexed, while in the phrase index, a given phrase that may comprise several keyboard, is indexed. The user may need to check whether a field is a word- or phrase-indexed, by browsing through the index for the particular field, before entering a search term/phrase.

- CD-Rome databases do not usually provide facilities for ranking the search results according to relevance.

CONCLUSION

The standards for organising web-based resources are still in the early stages of development, and librarians are forced to utilise standards for print resources that were not designed for electronic resources. Additionally web-based information resources are volatile in the sense that may be moved from one site to another or may be removed altogether from web. Web-based library services will become more widespread and sophisticated as the web becomes common place throughout the world, and to be successful players in the E-world.

Libraries must continue to address the web design and implementation issues. As we actively transfer library services, our central purpose remain the same, to serve and teach users to find, evaluate, and use information effectively. The librarians should be expert to hold the hands of the users who are moving towards new communication paradigm a shift from face to face human contact to human machine interaction, from paper to electronic delivery, from text centered mode to multimedia and from physical presence to virtual presence. Despite these changes in communication technology, the reference interview will remain at the heart of the reference transaction. To meet these challenges the librarians may play a leadership role in providing better Web Based library Services facilities to their current techno savvy users.

❐

4

Internet

Internet is the network of networks, i.e., a global network which make WWW.

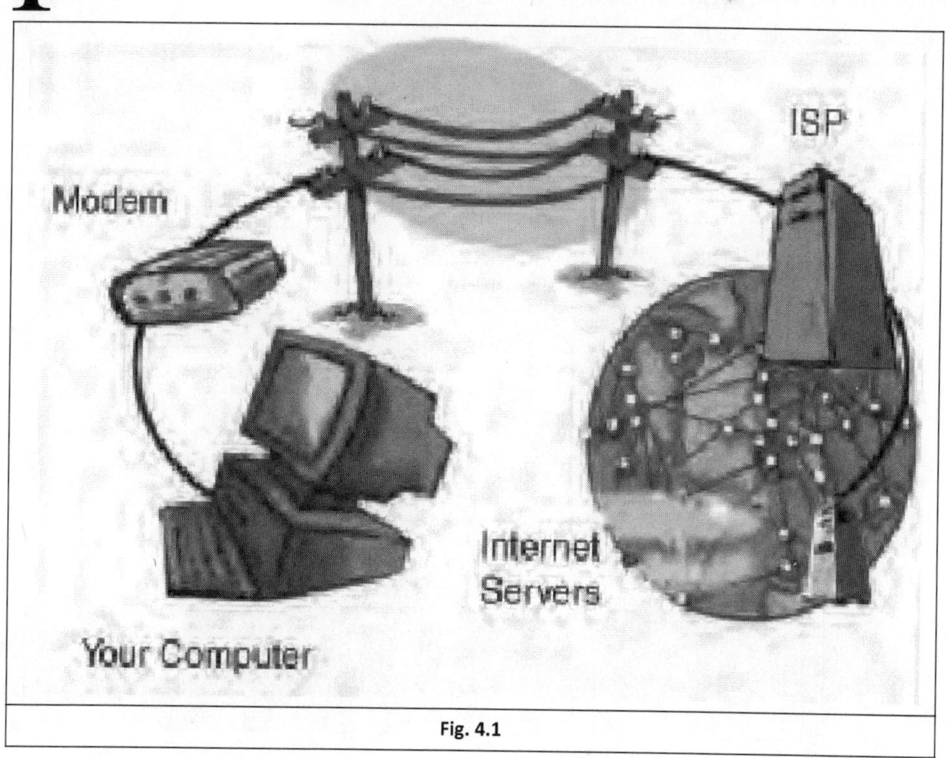

Fig. 4.1

BIRTH OF THE NET

The Internet grew out of an experiment in the 1960s by the U.S. Department of Defence. The DoD wanted to create a computer network that would continue to function in the event of a disaster, such as a nuclear war. If part of the network was damaged or destroyed, the rest of the system still had to work. That network was ARPANET, which linked U.S., scientific and academic researchers.

It was the forerunner of today's Internet. In 1985, the National Science Foundation (NSF), an American research organisation, created NSFNET, a series of networks for research and education communication. Based on ARPANET protocols, the NSFNET created a national backbone service, provided free to any American research and educational institution. At the same time, regional networks were created to link individual institutions with the national backbone service. NSFNET grew rapidly as people discovered its potential and as new software applications were created to make access easier. Corporations such as Sprint and MCI began to build their own networks that they then linked to NSFNET.

When commercial firms and other regional network providers took over the operation of the major Internet arteries, NSF withdrew from the backbone business. NSF also coordinated a service called InterNIC that registered all addresses on the Internet so that data could be routed to the right system. This service has now been taken over by Network Solutions, Inc. and other Internet registration services in cooperation with NSF

NET ANATOMY

The Web physically consists of your personal computer, web browser software, a connection to an Internet service provider, computers called servers that host digital data, and routers and switches to direct the flow of information.

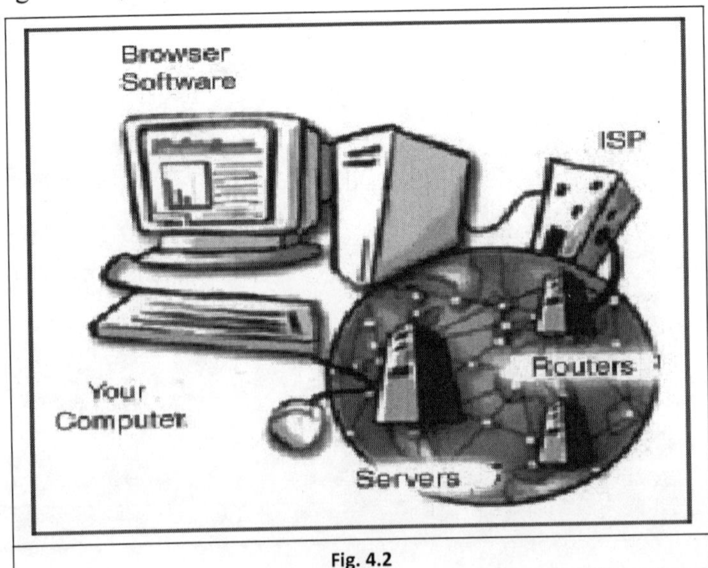

Fig. 4.2

WEB BROWSERS

A web browser is the software programme you use to access the World Wide Web, the graphical portion of the Internet. The first browser, called NCSA Mosaic, was developed at the National Centre for Supercomputing Applications in the early 1990s. The easy-to-use point-and-click interface helped popularise the Web. Microsoft Internet Explorer and Netscape Navigator are the two most popular ones.

NAVIGATING THE WEB

The Web is known as a client-server system. Your computer is the client; the remote computers that store electronic files are the servers. To visit the web site, enter the address or URL of the web site in your web browser. Browser requests the web page from the web server that hosts the requested site. The server sends the data over the Internet to your computer. Your web browser interprets the data, displaying it on your computer screen.

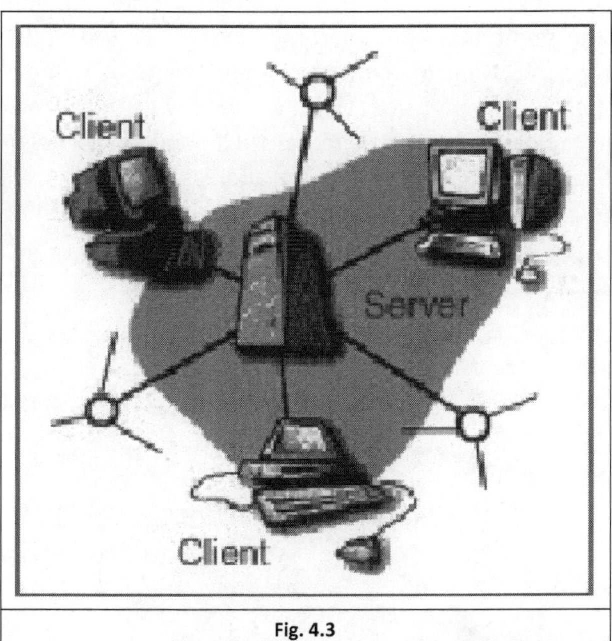

Fig. 4.3

The 'glue' that holds the Web together is called hypertext and hyperlinks. This feature allows electronic files on the Web to be linked so you can jump easily between them. On the Web, you navigate through pages of information--commonly known as browsing or surfing-based on what interests you at that particular moment. Web pages are written in a computer language called Hypertext Markup Language or HTML

W3C

The World Wide Web was originally developed in 1990 at CERN, the European Laboratory for Particle Physics. The original idea came from a youngcomputer scientist, Tim Berners-Lee. It is now managed by The World Wide Web Consortium. The WWW Consortium is funded by a large number of corporate members, including AT&T, Adobe Systems, Inc., Microsoft Corporation and Sun Microsystems, Inc. Its purpose is to promote the growth of the Web by developing technical specifications and reference software that will be freely available to everyone.

WEB ADDRESSES

World Wide Web is a network of electronic files stored on millions of computers all around the world. Hypertext links these resources together. Uniform Resource Locators or URLs are the addresses used to locate the files. Every URL is unique and identifies one specific file.

DOMAIN NAMES

Every computer that hosts data on the Internet has a unique numerical address. For example, the numerical address for the White House is 198.137.240.100. But since, few people want to remember long strings of numbers, the Domain Name System (DNS) was invented. DNS, a critical part of the Internet's technical infrastructure, correlates a numerical address to a word. To access the White House web site, you could type its number into the address box of your web browser. But most people prefer to use 'www.whitehouse.gov.' In this case, the domain name is whitehouse.gov.

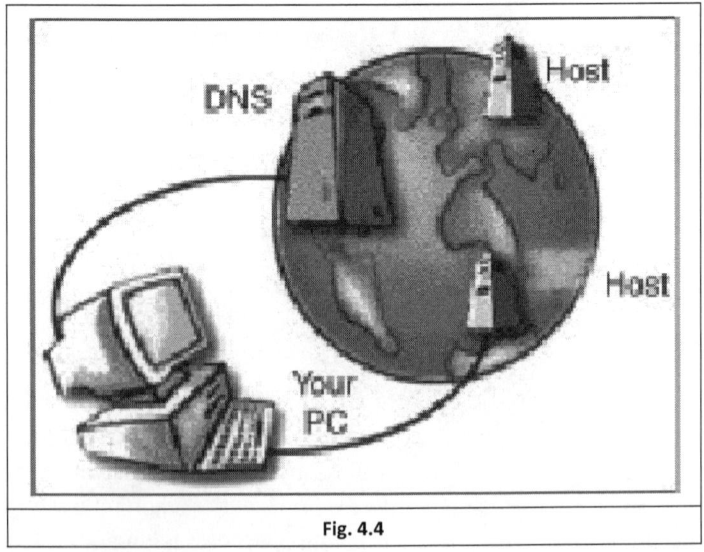

Fig. 4.4

THE STRUCTURE OF A DOMAIN NAME

A domain name has two or more parts separated by dots and consists of some form of an organisation's name and a three letter or more suffix. For example, the domain name for IBM is 'ibm.com'; the United Nations is 'un.org.'

The domain name suffix is known as a generic top-level domain (gTLD). It describes the type of organisation. Currently in use gTLDs:

- aero--For the air-transport industry
- biz--Reserved for businesses
- com--For businesses, commercial enterprises
- edu--For educational institutions and universities
- gov--Reserved for United States government agencies
- info--For all uses
- mil--For the United States military
- net--For networks; usually reserved for organisations such as Internet service providers
- org--For non-commercial organisations

BOOKMARKS AND FAVOURITES

Bookmarks and Favourites save Web addresses so you can return to them quickly. To save a web page, go to the Bookmarks or Favourites menu or click on its icon and select Add. When you click on the icon again, the title of the page you recorded will appear at the bottom of the list. To access the page, just double-click on the title.

To organise your Favourites, Click on the Favourites button on the toolbar to open the Favourites window.

Now select Organise Favourites. Click on the folder icon to create a new folder, then name it.

Now click on each Favourite once, hold down your left mouse button and drag the Favourite into the appropriate subject folder.

Fig. 4.5

ABUSING INSECURE FEATURES OF INTERNET EXPLORER

INTERNET EXPLORER SECURITY MODEL

First, let us start with a description of the security framework used by Internet Explorer to classify resources and to enforce security policies when they are:

Restricted Sites Zone: Used for Web sites that contain content that can cause processed. Internet Explorer 4 introduced the concept of URL Security Zones as a means to classify web content according to its trustworthiness. Using this, framework security policies are configured for each of five pre-established Security Zones, then while it is running Internet Explorer dynamically assigns content received from the Web to a corresponding Security Zone based on the content's origin and the settings configured for that Security Zone are then used to enforce the security controls associated to its trust level. Thus, a web application executed by Internet Explorer will be granted authorisation to perform actions depending on the privileges set for the Security Zone to which it was assigned by Internet Explorer.

These are the five Security Zones of Internet Explorer listed by increasing level of trust:

- Restricted Sites Zone: Used for Web sites that contain content that can cause problems when downloaded. Use this zone to cause Internet Explorer to alert that potentially-unsafe content is about to download, or to prevent that content from downloading. The user explicitly adds the URLs of untrusted Web sites to this zone, Internet Zone: For Web sites on the Internet that do not belong to another zone. This default setting causes Internet Explorer to prompt the user whenever potentially unsafe content is about to download.
- Web sites that are not mapped into other zones automatically fall into this zone, Local Intranet Zone: For content located on an organisation's intranet.
- Because the servers and information are within an organisation's firewall, it is reasonable to assign a higher trust level to content on the intranet,
- Trusted Sites Zone: For content located on Web sites that are considered more reputable or trustworthy than other sites on the Internet. Assigning a higher trust level to these sites minimizes the number of authentication requests. The user explicitly adds the URLs of these trusted Web sites to this zone.
- Local Machine Zone: The Local Machine zone is an implicit zone for content that exists on the local computer. The content found on the user's computer is treated with a high level of trust.
- Although the default settings for each Security Zone have varied over time since, their introduction in Internet Explorer 4, the number of Security Zones and their implied level of trust have not changed.

For the purpose of this chapter there are two generic types of attacks to the Security Zone framework that are relevant:

- Security Zone elevation attacks, in which web content that should normally be assigned to a Security Zone with trust level X ends up assigned to a Security Zone with trust level Y where Y > X; and
- Security Zone restrictions bypass attacks, in which web content that ended up correctly assigned to a Security Zone successfully performs actions that require privileg es not granted to that Security Zone.

WHEN A DOOR CLOSES, A WINDOW IS OPENED

Bad design decisions or flawed design sometimes result in features that leave an open door for different kinds of attacks and under the eternal alibi of backward compatibility, it often seems that they will never be closed.

In this section, as suggested, describe some of these weak Internet Explorer features. Keep in mind that, as minimal as the security implications of these features may seem at a first glance, they have proved to be key components o the exploitation scenarios exposed herein, where the attacker can compromise a user desktop system by abusing nothing but these features.

Hiding the Key Under the Doormat

HTTP cookies and web navigation history are stored by Internet Explorer in several files and folders in the local file system. Apparently as a security measure random names are used for both files and folders. However, since, they need to be accessed by Internet Explorer in an efficient manner the names and location of the randomly named files are kept inside different mapping files named index.dat. Here are some examples:

- %USERPROFILE%\Localsettings\History\History.IE5\index.dat
- %USERPROFILE%\Localsettings\IECompatCache\index.dat
- %USERPROFILE%\Cookies\index.dat

Although the format of these index files is not entirely plain text, the security sensitive content is being stored in plain text. Since, these index files are used to reference content stored in randomly named files, obtaining them would result in obtaining the actual locations of the aforementioned files and folders. Hence, the increase in security gained by storing potentially sensitive information in file system objects with randomly select names is dependent on the ability to prevent read access of index files from an attacker. If an attacker is able to inspect the contents of these indexing files, she can easily determine the exact location of the sensitive content that was protected by storing it in hidden files.

A Chip off the Old Block

Internet Explorer and Windows Explorer use common underlying components and resemble each other in many aspects. They both support access to file systems object on SMB shares and use of UNC (Universal Naming

Convention) paths to reference them. The use of common components and the idiosyncrasies of both programmes allow a user to do some tricks with Internet Explorer when accessing special files and folders that yield similar results when done using Windows Explorer. For example, when directly accessing the History folder with Windows Explorer, the actual files stored in there are not shown.

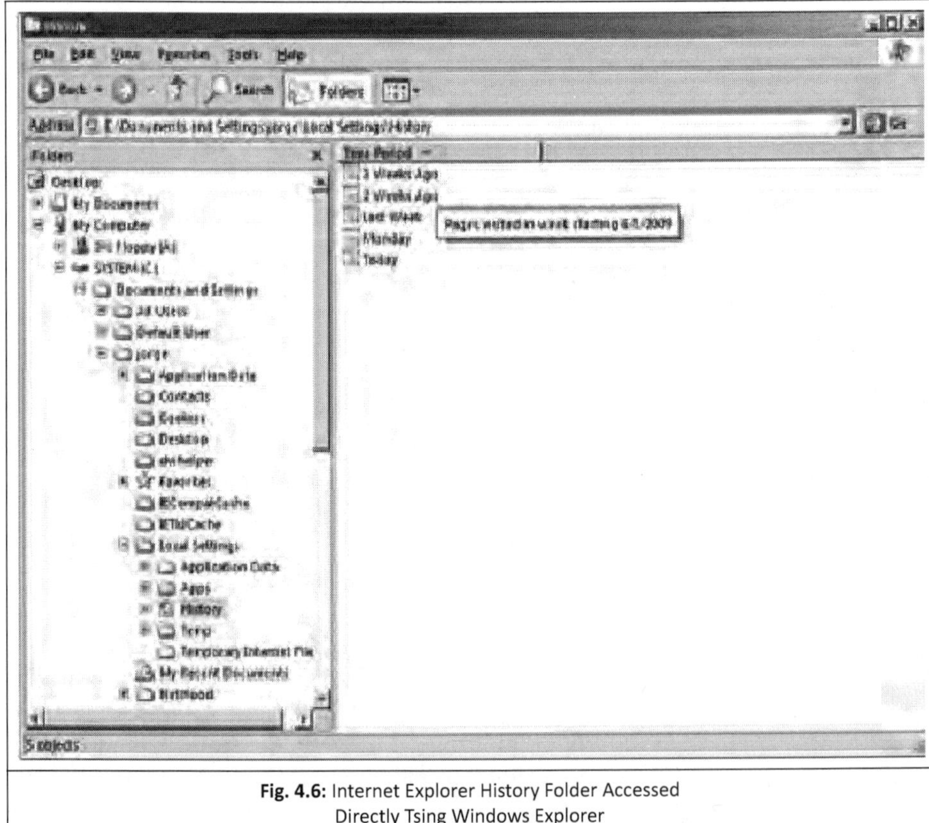

Fig. 4.6: Internet Explorer History Folder Accessed Directly Tsing Windows Explorer

However, accessing the same folder as a network resource requested using an UNC path will show the actual contents of this folder.

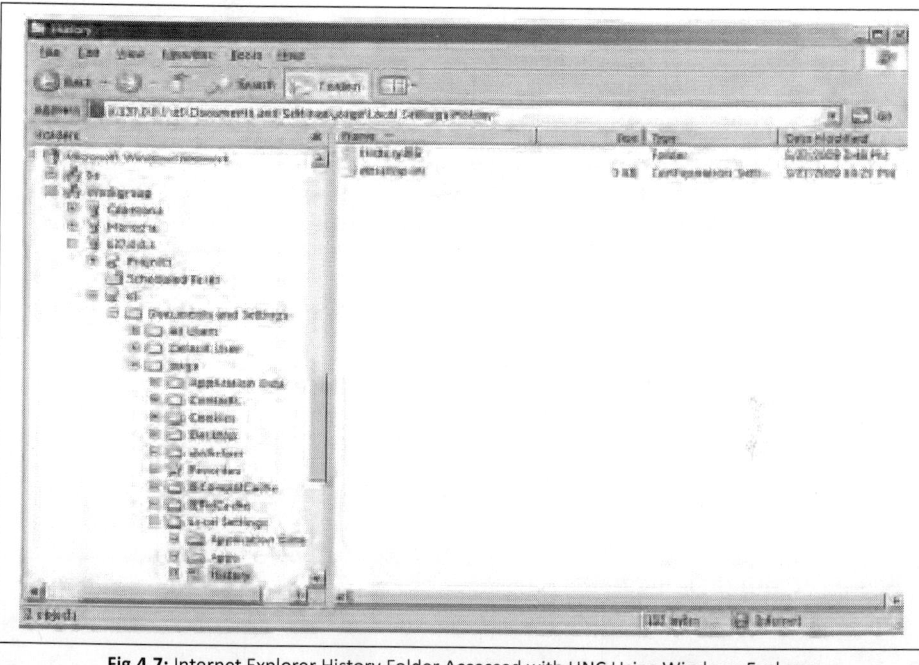

Fig.4.7: Internet Explorer History Folder Accessed with UNC Using Windows Explorer

As it was stated, Internet Explorer behaves alike when accessing these files and folders:

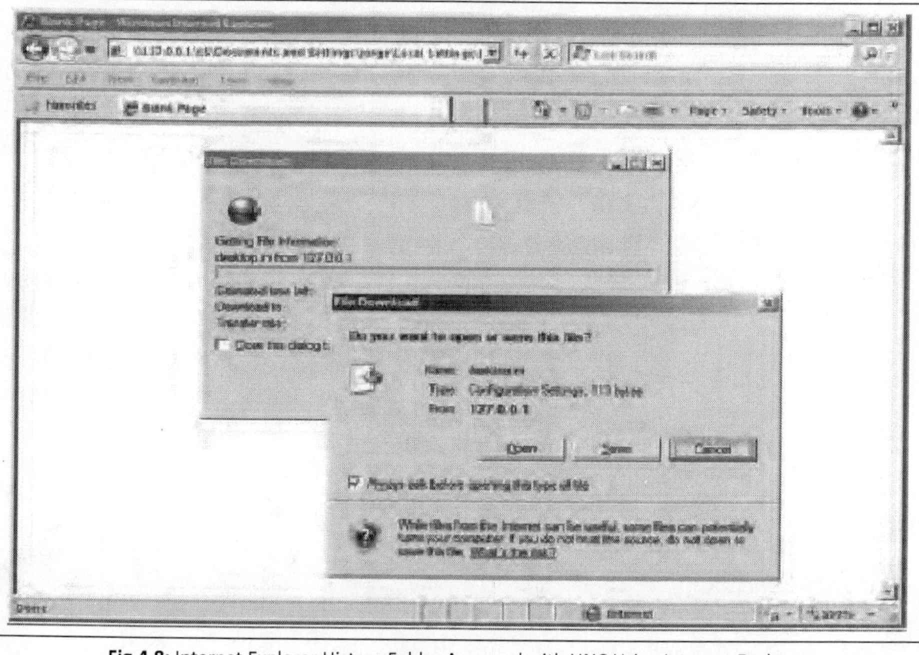

Fig.4.8: Internet Explorer History Folder Accessed with UNC Using Internet Explorer

Furthermore, the fact that Internet Explorer supports UNC and SMB has an important security implication. As this naming conventions and protocols can be used without restrictions inside web pages in the Internet zone or above, a web page in those zones can include an HTML tag such as the following:

<img src='\\[WEB SERVER IP ADDRESS]\image.jpg'>

When Internet Explorer renders this tag, it triggers an SMB request to a server at the IP address specified in the <img> tag. The NTLM authentication negotiation proceeds as follows: anonymous access is first tried and, if failed, the client starts the challenge-response negotiation. The server sends the client a challenge value and the client automatically responds back with the ciphered challenge.

Thus, as part of the challenge-response negotiation, the client sends to the server the following information about itself:

- Windows user name.
- Windows domain name.
- Windows computer name.

A challenge value chosen by the web server ciphered with the LM/NTLM hash of this user's password.

This ciphered challenge could then be brute-forced to obtain the plaintext password for the currently logged user.

This achievement opens a variety of security implications:

- If the victim's computer is directly connected to the Internet, it could be compromised as easy as accessing it trough SMB.
- If the attacker knows something more about the victim, she could try this password for accessing other systems.

Even if the attacker is not able to obtain the plaintext password from that the SMB request, the rest of the information obtained can still be useful for other attack vectors as will be shown later on.

Two Zones, the Same Place

The Security Zones model mentioned at the beginning of this article requires Internet Explorer to determine to which zone it will assign a web resource based on its origin. is: The Security Zone assigned to a given object referenced using the UNC convention.

- The Internet Security Zone if the UNC path contains the IP address to specify the target machine.
- The Local Intranet Security Zone if the UNC path contains a NetBIOS name to specify the target machine.

So far this does not sound bad. It makes sense as NetBIOS names can only be resolved within the scope of the local network segment if not mapped explicitly in the lmhosts file. But what happens with IP address 127.0.0.1? As trivial as it may sound, it is not.

In fact, this is one of the root causes of the problems that Microsoft staff has mentioned for closing the attack scenarios described afterwards in this document. After several discussions with MSRC team members, they agreed that the issue is a kind of dead end, given that due to expected functionality and design decisions forcing this address to belong to one zone or another cannot be done without high impact on either security or backward compatibility with existing applications. Since, Internet Explorer makes extensive use of cached files enforcing access control to them is not a minor issue. The assumptions and constrains of the Security Zones model make things ecome more complicated. Consider, for example, an Internet web site redirecting the navigation flow towards the following URL:

\\127.0.0.1\PATH_TO_RESOURCE

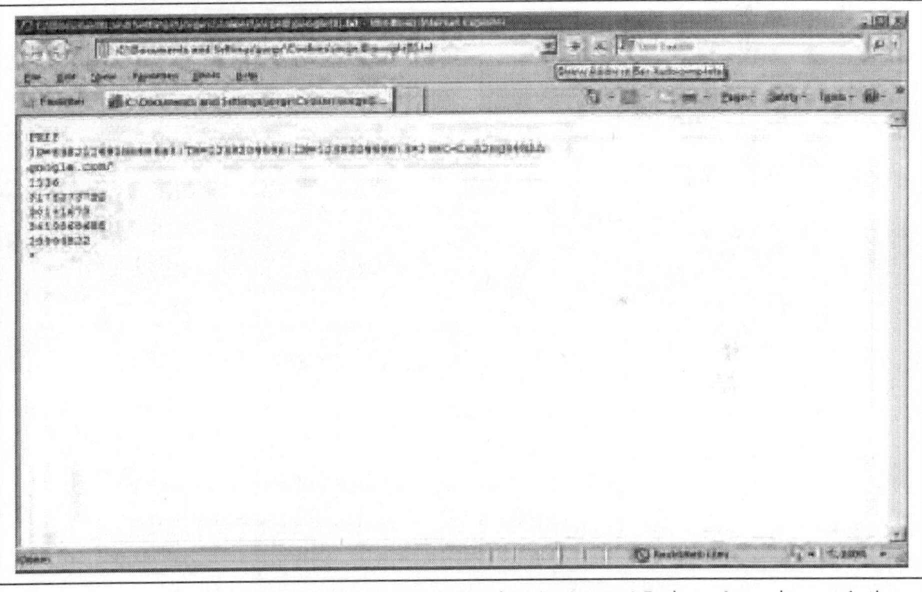

Fig. 4.9: Internet Explorer Cookie Folder Accessed Directly Using Internet Explorer. As can be seen in the Status Bar, the Folder is Treated as a Restricted Site

The Security Zones scheme, a web site located in a less trusted zone could never provide content for and redirect its navigation flow towards a web site in a more trusted zone. This behaviour is known as Zone Elevation. However, in the case above Internet Explorer will erroneously apply Zone Elevation restrictions and the redirection will effectively occur. Content will be treated as belonging to the Internet zone, in spite of being stored in the local machine. Let us consider a different way to bypass Security Zones restrictions: suppose that example.com was explicitly added to the Restricted Sites Security Zone. Then the following URI will be treated with the privileges of that zone:

http://example.com/index.html

However, if the same resource is requested using the UNC notation:

\\10.1.1.1\index.html

It will be treated as belonging to the Internet Security Zone. As can be seen Internet Explorer fails to apply zone restrictions to a given resource if it is accessed using a different protocol.

Fig. 4.10: Internet Explorer Cookie Folder Accessed with UNC Using Internet Explorer. As can be seen in the Status Bar, this Time the Folder is Treated as if it Belongs to the Internet Zone

Ways to Put Arbitrary HTML/Script Code in the Victim's Computer

While not straightforward there are at least three different ways for remote servers to write arbitrary HTML/script code in the local file system of clients running Internet Explorer:

- Navigation history files;
- Cookies; and
- History tracking files.

Even though these features are common to every modern web browser, the problem is not in the features themselves but in the way they are implemented:

- The content that a remote server sends to the client is written to various files on the local file system as they are received with little or no transformations/overhead;
- Internet Explorer allows rendering of HTML content read from local files that are not pure HTML. The non-HTML portions that cannot be rendered are simply ignored.

Due to this a remote server that managed to write arbitrary but partially controlled HTML/script code inside these files could eventually force Internet

Everything That Glitters is Not Gold

The way Internet Explorer determines how to process the contents of a given file is based on what is known as MIME type detection. This is basically a best-effort heuristic used to determine the content type of a given resource and then launch the corresponding object server/application to process it. Security problems may arise if type detection fails. In some cases, unknown content type is defaulted to be treated as HTML which could, obviously, include scripting code also. Besides, this mechanism has been proved not to be consistent when accessing the same resource through different methods. For example, the proof of concept code for the vulnerability reported in the CORE-2008-0826 Security Advisory took advantage from the fact that Internet Explorer was reacting different when an unknown MIME format resource was directly accessed from an <object> tag than when it was invoked from a script.

OVERALL IMPACT

As can be seen from what has been discussed so far, by chaining the exploitation of a series of weak features an attacker is able to store HTML and scripting code in the victim's computer and then force the victim's browser to load and render it. Even though 127.0.0.1 is in the Internet Zone an attacker can still do some other interesting things: as code is actually stored in the victim's computer, it has enough privileges to access other files in the same origin allowing blind but full access to every file in the victim's local file systems. Thus, interesting files such as the SAM backup file, all of the user's HTTP cookies and history files or any other file on the local system may become available to the attacker.

For example: if the computer compromised has IIS running, an attacker could get the source code of files stored in the Inetpub\wwwroot folder. Even more, as many applications store sensitive information inside configuration files, an attacker could gain complete access to these files if they exist. These attack scenarios have been proven to work in the past in at least three different cases. In each of those cases the same generic approach was applied with the only variations in the way to use Internet Explorer to render internal tracking files as HTML.

For each new attack scenario Microsoft addressed the specific way in which Internet Explorer internal files can be used to deliver malicious HTML/script content but it is very likely that as long as all the other components of the attack scenario could be chained together using the other individual weaknesses of Internet Explorer, an attacker will be just a single step away from successfully compromising the victim's system.

CORRIGENDA

Contrary to what has been stated in the Common Vulnerabilities and Exposures database for the CVE-2009-1140, it is not just a cross-domain information disclosure vulnerability. That is just a subset of the information you could get. In fact, CVE-2008-1448 description says something more precise: allows remote attackers to bypass intended access restrictions and read arbitrary files. And both of them are the same set of features abused by different means.

SOLUTIONS AND WORKAROUNDS

By the moment of the publication of this document official hot fixes will not be available for the latest variant of the attack exposed herein. Then, users could apply the following workarounds so to protect them from exploitation of these vulnerabilities in the wild.

Internet Explorer Network Protocol Lockdown

Internet Explorer can be configured to lock down HTML content from particular network protocols in additional zones besides the Local Machine zone. This feature allows an administrator to extend the same restrictions of the Local Machine Zone Lockdown to be applied to any content on any arbitrary protocol in any security zone.

In this case, in order to prevent this attack from occur, an administrator can configure Internet Explorer to lock down HTML content hosted on the file: protocol if it is in the Internet zone.

Since, the file: protocol's most common use is for either Local Machine or Local Intranet content and not Internet content, this mitigation should not imply huge compatibility issues.

Set the Security Level setting for the Internet and Intranet Zones to High

This setting will prevent Internet Explorer from running scripts or ActiveX controls in both Security Zones. Nonetheless, the impact on existing applications could render them unusable.

Disable Active Scripting for the Internet and Intranet Zone with a custom setting

This means to manually adjust the security level for that particular item instead of switching to an entirely different preset as in the previous workaround. Anyway, this could also have a considerable impact in multiple applications.

Only Run Internet Explorer in Protected Mode

If it is available on the operating system you should enable Protected Mode to mitigate this vector. However, as some applications stopped working properly when this working mode was introduced, many users have opted for disabling it.

Use a Different Web Browser to Navigate Untrusted Web Sites

As will be explained next, other browsers different than Internet Explorer can not be exploited the same way. Even so, using other browsers implies that users will be exposed to other risks those browsers are vulnerable to. It is up to the users to evaluate which is the best option.

SEARCH ENGINES

A web search engine is designed to search for information on the World Wide Web. The search results are generally presented in a list of results often referred to as search engine results pages (SERPs). The information may consist of web pages, images, information and other types of files. Some search engines also mine data available in databases or open directories. Unlike web directories, which are maintained only by human editors, search engines also maintain real-time information by running an algorithm on a web crawler.

During the early development of the web, there was a list of webservers edited by Tim Berners-Lee and hosted on the CERN webserver.

One historical snapshot from 1992 remains. As more webservers went online the central list could not keep up. On the NCSA site new servers were announced under the title 'What's New!' The very first tool used for searching on the Internet was Archie. The name stands for 'archive' without the 'v'. It was created in 1990 by Alan Emtage, Bill Heelan and J. Peter Deutsch, computer science students at McGill University in Montreal.

The programme downloaded the directory listings of all the files located on public anonymous FTP sites, creating a searchable database of file names; however, Archie did not index the contents of these sites since, the amount of data was so limited it could be readily searched manually. The rise of Gopher led to two new search programmes, Veronica and Jughead. Like Archie, they searched the file names and titles stored in Gopher index systems. Veronica provided a keyword search of most Gopher menu titles in the entire Gopher listings. Jughead was a tool for obtaining menu information from specific Gopher servers.

While the name of the search engine 'Archie' was not a reference to the Archie comic book series, 'Veronica' and 'Jughead' are characters in the series, thus referencing their predecessor. In the summer of 1993, no search engine existed yet for the web, though numerous specialised catalogues were maintained by hand. Oscar Nierstrasz at the University of Geneva wrote a series of Perl scripts that would periodically mirror these pages and rewrite them into a standard format which formed the basis for W3Catalog, the web's first primitive search engine, released on September 2, 1993. In June 1993, Matthew Gray, then at MIT, produced what was probably the first web robot, the Perl-based World Wide Web Wanderer, and used it to generate an index called 'Wandex'.

The purpose of the Wanderer was to measure the size of the World Wide Web, which it did until late 1995. The web's second search engine Aliweb appeared in November 1993. Aliweb did not use a web robot, but instead depended on being notified by web site administrators of the existence at each site of an index file in a particular format. JumpStation used a web robot to find web pages and to build its index, and used a web form as the interface to its query programme.

It was thus the first WWW resource-discovery tool to combine the three essential features of a web search engine. Because of the limited resources available on the platform on which it ran, its indexing and hence, searching were limited to the titles and headings found in the web pages the crawler encountered. One of the first 'full text' crawler-based search engines was WebCrawler, which came out in 1994.

Unlike its predecessors, it let users search for any word in any webpage, which has become the standard for all major search engines since. It was also the first one to be widely known by the public. Also in 1994, Lycos was launched and became a major commercial endeavour. Soon after, many search engines appeared and vied for popularity. These included Magellan, Excite, Infoseek, Inktomi, Northern Light, and AltaVista. Yahoo! was among the most popular ways for people to find web pages of interest, but its search function operated on its web directory, rather than full-text copies of web pages.

Information seekers could also browse the directory instead of doing a keyword-based search. In 1996, Netscape was looking to give a single search engine an exclusive deal to be the featured search engine on Netscape's web browser. There was so much interest that instead a deal was struck with Netscape by five of the major search engines, where for $5 million per year each search engine would be in rotation on the Netscape search engine page. The five engines were Yahoo!, Magellan, Lycos, Infoseek, and Excite. Search engines were also known as some of the brightest stars in the Internet investing frenzy that occurred in the late 1990s. Several companies entered the market spectacularly, receiving record gains during their initial public offerings.

Some have taken down their public search engine, and are marketing enterprise-only editions, such as Northern Light. Many search engine companies were caught up in the dot-com bubble, a speculation-driven market boom that peaked in 1999 and ended in 2001. Around 2000, Google's search engine rose to prominence. The company achieved better results for many searches with an innovation called PageRank. This iterative algorithm ranks web pages based on the number and PageRank of other web sites and pages that link there, on the premise that good or desirable pages are linked to more than others. Google also maintained a minimalist interface to its search engine.

In contrast, many of its competitors embedded a search engine in a web portal. By 2000, Yahoo! was providing search services based on Inktomi's search engine. Yahoo! acquired Inktomi in 2002, and Overture in 2003. Yahoo! switched to Google's search engine until 2004, when it launched its own search engine based on the combined technologies of its acquisitions. Microsoft first launched MSN Search in the fall of 1998 using search results from Inktomi. In early 1999 the site began to display listings from Looksmart blended with results from Inktomi except for a short time in 1999 when results from AltaVista were used instead.

In 2004, Microsoft began a transition to its own search technology, powered by its own web crawler. Microsoft's rebranded search engine, Bing, was launched on June 1, 2009. On July 29, 2009, Yahoo! and Microsoft finalised a deal in which Yahoo! Search would be powered by Microsoft Bing technology.

HOW WEB SEARCH ENGINES WORK

A search engine operates in the following order:

- Web crawling
- Indexing
- Searching

Web search engines work by storing information about many web pages, which they retrieve from the HTML itself. These pages are retrieved by a Web crawler—an automated Web browser which follows every link on the site. Exclusions can be made by the use of robots.txt. The contents of each page are then analysed to determine how it should be indexed. Data about web pages are stored in an index database for use in later queries. A query can be a single word.

The purpose of an index is to allow information to be found as quickly as possible. Some search engines, such as Google, store all or part of the source page as well as information about the web pages, whereas others, such as AltaVista, store every word of every page they find. This cached page always holds the actual search text since, it is the one that was actually indexed, so it can be very useful when the content of the current page has been updated and the search terms are no longer in it.

This problem might be considered to be a mild form of linkrot, and Google's handling of it increases usability by satisfying user expectations that the search terms will be on the returned webpage. This satisfies the principle of least astonishment since, the user normally expects the search terms to be on the returned pages. Increased search relevance makes these cached pages very useful, even beyond the fact that they may contain data that may no longer be available elsewhere. When a user enters a query into a search engine, the engine examines its index and provides a listing of best-matching web pages according to its criteria, usually with a short summary containing the document's title and sometimes parts of the text. The index is built from the information stored with the data and the method by which the information is indexed. As early as 2007 the Google.com search engine has allowed one to search by date by clicking 'Show search tools' in the leftmost column of the initial search results page, and then selecting the desired date range. Most search engines support the use of the boolean operators AND, OR and NOT to further specify the search query. Boolean operators are for litreal searches that allow the user to refine and extend the terms of the search. The engine looks for the words or phrases exactly as entered. Some search engines provide an advanced feature called proximity search which allows users to define the distance between keywords.

There is also concept-based searching where the research involves using statistical analysis on pages containing the words or phrases you search for.

As well, natural language queries allow the user to type a question in the same form one would ask it to a human. A site like this would be ask.com. The usefulness of a search engine depends on the relevance of the result set it gives back. While there may be millions of web pages that include a particular word or phrase, some pages may be more relevant, popular, or authoritative than others. Most search engines employ methods to rank the results to provide the 'best' results first.

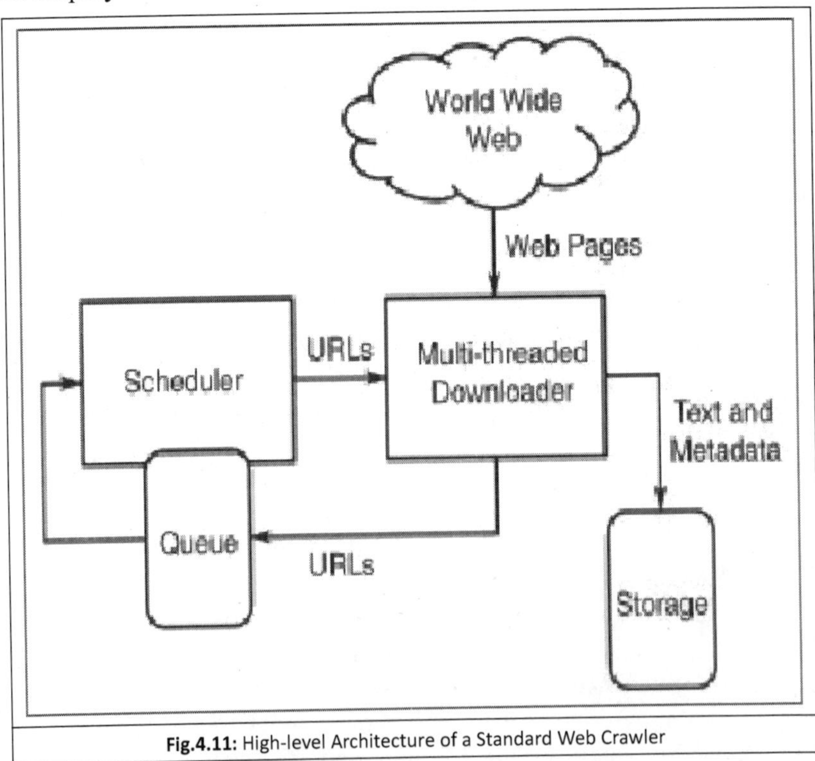

Fig.4.11: High-level Architecture of a Standard Web Crawler

How a search engine decides which pages are the best matches, and what order the results should be shown in, varies widely from one engine to another. The methods also change over time as Internet usage changes and new techniques evolve. There are two main types of search engine that have evolved: one is a system of predefined and hierarchically ordered keywords that humans have programmed extensively. The other is a system that generates an 'inverted index' by analysing texts it locates. This second form relies much more heavily on the computer itself to do the bulk of the work. Most Web search engines are commercial ventures supported by advertising revenue and, as a result, some employ the practice of allowing advertisers to pay money to have their listings ranked higher in search results.

Those search engines which do not accept money for their search engine results make money by running search related ads alongside the regular search engine results. The search engines make money every time someone clicks on one of these ads.

SEARCH ENGINE BIAS

Although search engines are programmed to rank web sites based on their popularity and relevancy, empirical studies indicate various political, economic, and social biases in the information they provide. These biases could be a direct result of economic and commercial processes, and political processes.Google Bombing is one example of an attempt to manipulate search results for political, social or commercial reasons.

CUSTOMISED RESULTS AND FILTER BUBBLES

Many search engines such as Google and Bing provide customised results based on the user's activity history. This leads to an effect that has been called a filter bubble. The term describes a phenomenon in which web sites use algorithms to selectively guess what information a user would like to see, based on information about the user. As a result, web sites tend to show only information which agrees with the user's past viewpoint, effectively isolating the user in a bubble that tends to exclude contrary information. Prime examples are Google's personalised search results and Facebook's personalised news stream. Eli Pariser, who coined the term, users get less exposure to conflicting viewpoints and are isolated intellectually in their own informational bubble. Pariser related an example in which one user searched Google for 'BP' and got investment news about British Petroleum while another searcher got information about the Deepwater Horizon oil spill and that the two search results pages were 'strikingly different.'

The bubble effect may have negative implications for civic discourse, Pariser, but there are contrasting views suggesting the effect is minimal and addressable. Since, this problem has been identified, competing search engines have emerged that seek to avoid this problem by not tracking or 'bubbling' users. One example is DuckDuckGo.

INTERNET SEARCHING

In 300 B.C., the Library of Alexandria held some half million scrolls and served as a cultural centre for the world, uniting the thoughts of Greek, Egyptian, Macedonian and Babylonian culture. The Letter of Aristeas, the library had "a large budget in order to collect, if possible, all the books in the world." Whole fields of study such as geometry and grammar grew from the scholars who had the fortune to travel to and study at Alexandria. In 2003 A.D., the Internet forms a distributed library of billions of pages, one that is accessible to anyone, anywhere in the world, at the click of a mouse. Every day hundreds of millions of 'trips' to the library start with a query to an Internet search engine. If I want to research a topic such as 'Library of Alexandria,' I can type those words to a search engine and in less than a second have access to a list of 14,000 pages, sorted by their usefulness to the query. This unprecedented ease of access to information has revolutionised the way research is done by students, scientists, journalists, shoppers, and others. It opens up an online marketplace of products, services, and ideas that benefits both information providers and seekers; sellers and buyers; consumers and advertisers.

How is it that an Internet Search engine can find the answers to a query so quickly? It is a four-step process:

- Crawling the Web, following links to find pages;
- Indexing the pages to create an index from every word to every place it occurs;
- Ranking the pages so the best ones show up first; and
- Displaying the results in a way that is easy for the user tounderstand.

Crawling is conceptually quite simple: starting at some well-known sites on the web, recursively follow every hypertext link, recording the pages encountered along the way. In computer science this is called the transitive closure of the link relation. However, the conceptual simplicity hides a large number of practical complications: sites may be busy or down at one point, and come back to life later; pages may be duplicated at multiple sites and must be dealt with accordingly; many pages have text that does not conform to the standards for HTML, HTTP redirection, robot exclusion, or other protocols; some information is hard to access because it is hidden behind a form, Flash animation or Javascript programme.

Finally, the necessity of crawling 100 million pages a day means that building a crawler is an exercise in distributed computing, requiring many computers that must work together and schedule their actions so as to get to all the pages without overwhelming any one site with too many requests at once. A search engine's index is similar to the index in the back of a book: it is used to find the pages on which a word occurs. There are two main differences: the search engine's index lists every occurrence of every word, not just the important concepts, and the number of pages is in the billions, not hundreds. Various techniques of compression and clever representation are used to keep the index 'small,' but it is still measured in terabytes, which again means that distributed computing is required. Most modern search engines index link data as well as word data. It is useful to know how many pages link to a given page, and what are the quality of those pages. This kind of analysis is similar to citation analysis in bibliographic work, and helps establish which pages are authoritative. Algorithms such as PageRank and HITS are used to assign a numeric measure of authority to each page. For example, the PageRank algorithm says that the rank of a page is a function of the sum of the ranks of the pages that link to the page. If we let PR(p) be the PageRank of page p, Out(p) be the number of outgoing links from page p, Links(p) be the set of pages that link to page p and N be the total number of pages in the index, then we can define PageRank by

$$PR \to p \to r / N \to | \, | \, 1 \to r \, | \, | \, i \to \text{Links}$$

$$PR \to i \to / \text{ Out } i$$

where r is a parameter that indicates the probability that a user will choose not to follow a link, but will instead restart at some other page. The r/N term means that each of the N pages is equally likely to be the restart point, although it is also possible to use a smaller subset of well-known pages as the restart candidates. Note that the formula for PageRank is recursive— PR appears on both the right- and left-hand sides of the equation.

The equation can be solved by iterating several times, or by standard linear algebra techniques for computing the Eigen values of a matrix. The two steps are query independent—they do not depend on the user's query, and thus can be done before a query is issued with the cost shared among all users. This is why a search takes a second or less, rather than the days it would take if a search engine had to crawl the web anew for each query. We now consider what happens when a user types a query. Consider the query, where the square brackets denote the beginning and end of the query, and the quotation marks indicate that the enclosed words must be found as an exact phrase match.

The first step in responding to this query is to look in the index for the hit lists corresponding to each of the four words 'National,' 'Academies,' 'computer' and 'science.' These four lists are then intersected to yield the set of pages that mention all four words. Because 'National Academies' was entered as a phrase, only hits where these two words appear adjacent and in that order are counted. The result is a list of 19,000 or so pages. The next step is ranking these 19,000 pages to decide which ones are most relevant. In traditional information retrieval this is done by counting the number of occurrences of each word, weighing rare words more heavily than frequent words, and normalising for the length of the page.

A number of refinements on this scheme have been developed, so it is common to give more credit for pages where the words occur near each other, where the words are in bold or large font, or in a title, or where the words occur in the anchor text of a link that points to the page. In addition the query-independent authority of each page is factored in. The result is a numeric score for each page that can be used to sort them best-first. Traditionally this is done by listing a short description of each result in rank-sorted order. The description will include the title of the page and may include additional information such as a short abstract or excerpt from the page.

Some search engines generate query-independent abstracts while others customise each excerpt to show at least some of the words from the query. Displaying this kind of query-dependent excerpt means that the search engine must keep a copy of the full text of the pages at a cost of several more terabytes. Some search engines attempt to cluster the result pages into coherent categories or folders, although this technology is not yet mature. Studies have shown that the most popular uses of computers are e-mail, word processing and Internet searching. Of the three, Internet searching is by far the most sophisticated example of computer science technology. Building a high-quality search engine requires extensive knowledge and experience in information retrieval, data structure design, user interfaces, and distributed systems implementation.

Future advances in searching will increasingly depend on statistical natural language processing and machine learning techniques. With so much data—billions of pages, tens of billions of links, and hundreds of millions of queries per day—it makes sense to use data mining approaches to automatically improve the system. For example, several search engines now do spelling correction of user queries.

It turns out that the vast amount of correctly and incorrectly spelled text available to a search engine makes it easier to create a good spelling corrector than traditional techniques based on dictionaries. It is likely that there will be other examples of text understanding that can be done better with a data-oriented approach; this is an area that search engines are just beginning to explore.

❒

5

Retrieval System in Libraries and information Search

INTRODUCTION

The explosion of literature in the form of micro documents on the one hand and the growing number of users demanding more specialised literature/ information on the other hand have led to information scientists to develop an efficient information retrieval systems for the realisation of retrieval suspend on advances in technology and its associated techniques. Database creation of the library resources and the sophistication in indexing techniques has eased the problems of storing and handling of large volumes of data. At the best, it enhanced the retrieval of the items.

Therefore, the focus of the information scientist for the recent past few decades is on the design and development of more powerful information search and retrieval systems.

INFORMATION SYSTEMS

Computer based information system is categorised into:

- Information Storage and Retrieval systems.
- Database Management systems.
- Management Information Systems.
- Decision support systems.

All these systems exhibit similarities to some extent in the area of information processing but differ in their functionalities.

OBJECTIVES OF THE INFORMATION RETRIEVAL SYSTEM

M.L. Pao, "user's input is an important consideration to be incorporated in setting the overall objective of the system for service point of view", as follows:

- Information content of information resources collected.
- Utility of information resources.
- Users.
- Documentary resources.
- Performance resources.
- Economics.

Information retrieval (IR) is the main purpose of any library. The librarian is a nodal point in the IR process and in the traditional library.

INFORMATION SEARCH AND RETRIEVAL IN DIGITAL LIBRARIES

Information search and retrieval of an object from digital library software is a vital feature of the system. The search enables quick retrieval of information. Search services help users to select relevant information from digital library. Digital library's service provides fast access to exact information which is looking for. The success of a search service in digital library relies on the implementation of a powerful retrieval engine and a flexible user interface for metadata support. The Search interface allows users to do "across database" searching without having to modify a query. Search service also covers searching beyond text to multiple media formats, including images, sound and video.

The retrieval formats should be flexible and should provide users to manipulate the search process and results by retrieving search history, adjusting search strategies, editing and sorting search results and choosing preferable delivery formats.

Users should also be able to get statistical analysis of the searches they have carried out. Many digital libraries provide different search options to users based on the metadata fields along with the facilities for federated search across a number of digital libraries.

TABLE: Data Retrieval vs. Information Retrieval.

	Data Retrieval (DR)	Information Retrieval (IR)
Matching	Exact match	Partial match, best match
Inference	Deduction	Induction
Model	Deterministic	Probabilistic
Classification	Monothetic	Polythetic
Query language	Artificial	Natural

Query specification	Complete	Incomplete
Items wanted	Matching	Relevant
Error response	Sensitive	Insensitive

Most digital libraries offer search by Boolean operator, keyword, and phrase and field searches. In the case of information retrieval, evaluation is often focused on the effectiveness of a result set in a specific search. Browsing and searching are two major paradigms for exploring digital libraries. Boolean, proximity and truncation searching are commonly used in digital libraries.

They are often provided as separate services. Searching is popular because it is useful when appropriate search keyword are unavailable to users. Table presents the difference between data retrieval and information retrieval.

The use of Information Retrieval is motivated by an information need.

This information need can be explicitly or implicitly verbalised. In a 'real world' setting the person seeking information (i.e., the user) formulates such a question and poses it to an expert.

The expert calls upon his internal representation of the knowledge space and external documents and formulates answers. From the answers received the user extracts relevant points and gives feedback to the expert. This "conversational loop" can also be found in the use of an Information Retrieval System (IRS).

As the IRS is not capable to understand the information need, thus, an abstraction matching in the IRS is needed. This abstraction is called query.

Analogously to the expert, the IRS formulates an answer based upon the internal representation of the knowledge space and external documents.

The answer is composed of documents perceived relevant or links to such documents. The user extracts those documents that are indeed relevant.

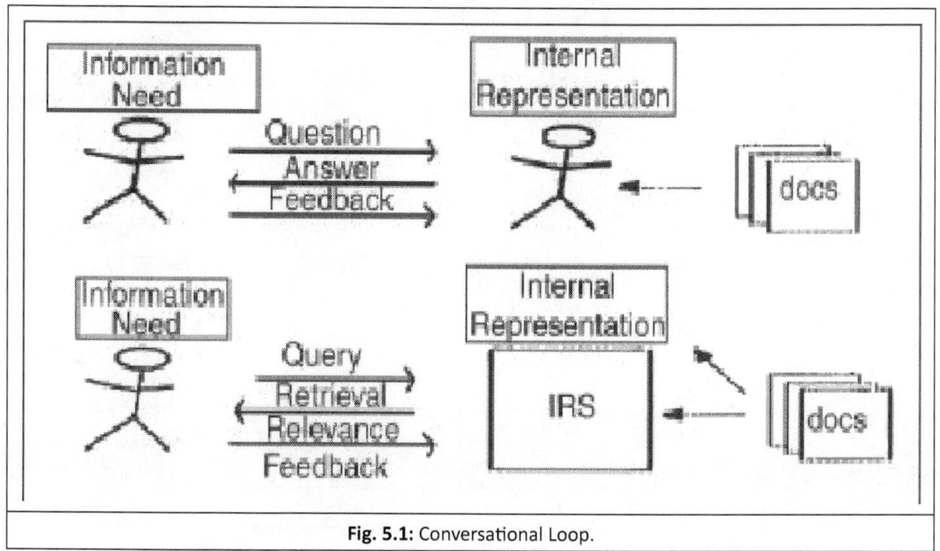

Fig. 5.1: Conversational Loop.

In some systems relevance feedback can be given. These two forms of the conversational loop are detailed in figure.

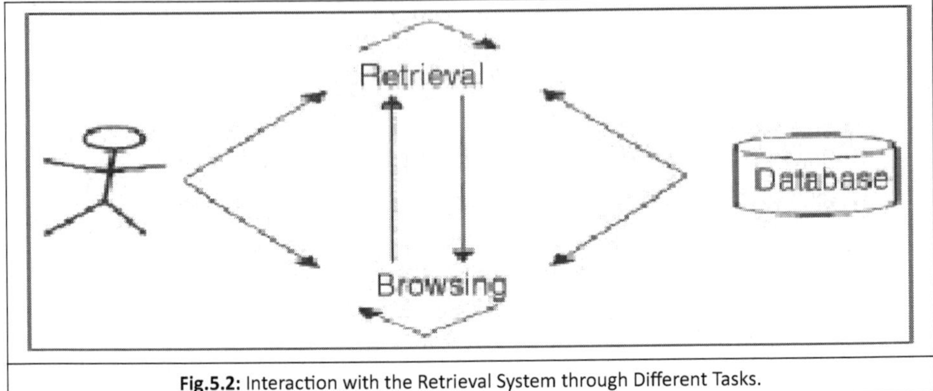

Fig.5.2: Interaction with the Retrieval System through Different Tasks.

RETRIEVAL VS. BROWSING

The sequence of action taken to satisfy the information need is called retrieval or searching. Retrieval is used in the case of an explicit information need. The explicit need can be formulated into a query. Searching usually results in lists of results. Sometimes the information need is non-explicit and no query can be formulated. In this case the information need can be satisfied by browsing through the documents of a collection. Browsing is also necessary to find relevant documents from the results of a retrieval process.

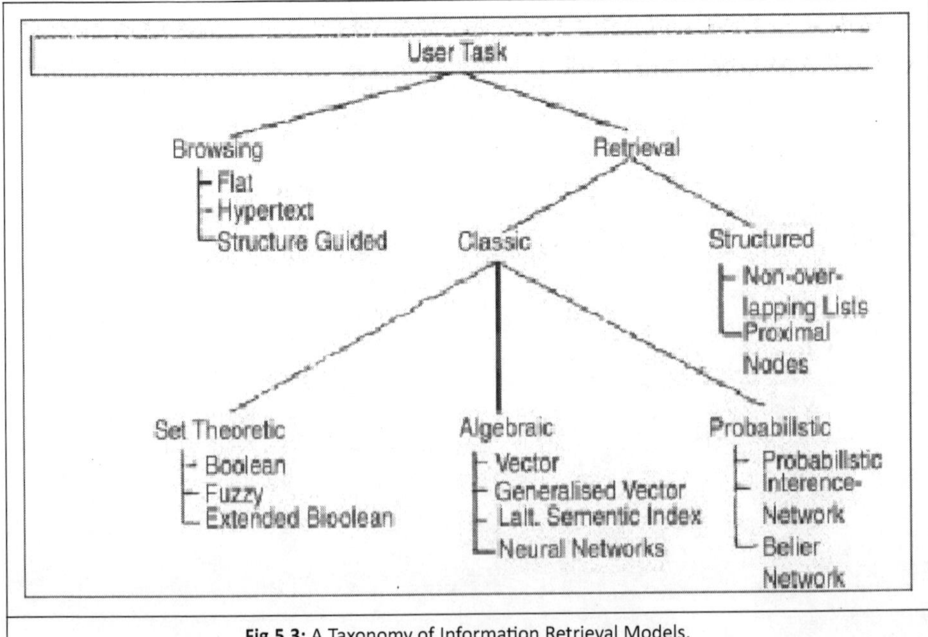

Fig.5.3: A Taxonomy of Information Retrieval Models.

Figure illustrates the relation of these two concepts. Both actions are pulling actions interpreting to the user makes request of information interactively. Searching for information in such a manner is called ad hoc searching. Alternatively the information may be provided in an automatic and permanent fashion for information by the user. This is called information push and is used in the case of a varying document collection and an unchanging information need.

In the same context as information push, filtering can be applied. Again the document collection is varying while the information need stays the same, but in contrast information push is an active task of the user, while in the case of filtering the information is passively provided by software agents or the like.

Browsing can be discerned into flat browsing, structure guided browsing and hypertext browsing. In the case of "flat browsing" the document collection is organised in a flat structure, like a list of search results. The term "structure guided" browsing describes the browsing of collections in structured and hierarchical manner.

The "king" of browsing allowing the highest flexibility is "hypertext browsing". In this case, documents are multiplied connected by hyperlinks. The Information Retrieval Model (IRM) needs introduction to the digital library for describing relevancy in the search results. Such a model describes the fundamental premises forming the basis for a ranking. Over the years, different IRM have been proposed.

The following parts will give an overview of those models which are relevant in the later part of this chapter. In order to build a model, a representation for the documents and its need for the users have to be found. These representations lead to the framework in which they can be modeled. For example, in the vector space model, the framework is composed of a t-dimensional vector space and standard linear algebra operations on vectors. In text based IR the information need and the documents are represented with words. In case of the documents these are called index terms. An index term is a word whose semantics matches the document's main themes. These index terms vary in relevance, as the more frequent words in the document collection are less relevant for the retrieval process.

Boolean Model

This simple retrieval model, which was adopted by many early commercial bibliographic systems, is based on set theory and Boolean algebra. The advantages are the intuitiveness of the concept of a set and the precise semantics of Boolean expressions, which form the queries. The major drawback of the model is that the retrieval is based on a binary decision leaving relevancy of the search result.

Moreover it is often not simple to translate an information need into a Boolean expression. In this model, index terms are either considered present or absent in a document, resulting in binary weights. Due to this binary value for relevancy, no partial match to the query is defined. So, if a document includes only one index term it is considered not relevant. As a result, the Boolean model often retrieves very less or too many documents.

Vector Model

The vector model heeds the fact that the use of binary weights is limiting and proposes a framework that allows a partial match. Non- binary term weights are used to compute a degree of similarity. The resulting set of documents retrieved is returned in decreasing order of this degree of similarity.

Though various term weighting techniques exist, only the main idea of the most effective techniques shall be discussed. The basic idea is to separate a document collection into two parts to satisfy the information need. One of the parts is composed of the objects related to the information need while the other is not. To accomplish this separation clustering techniques are utilised. Two sets of features are used to discern sets of related elements from those that are not.

The first set of features describes the intra-cluster similarity while the second describes inter-cluster dissimilarity. The improved retrieval performance resulting from the term-weighting scheme is one of the main advantages of the vector model. The second main advantage is the partial matching strategy and the fact that the cosine ranking function sorts the documents according to the degree of similarity to the query. Efficient implementations for the vector model are possible.

Finally, the vector model allows easy relevance feedback. Disadvantages of the vector model include the fact that the term "independency" is not fully given. In fact, real term independency might hurt the retrieval process. Moreover, syntactic information remains unconsidered.

Generalised Vector Space Model

The term "independence" in the classic vector space model is addressed by the generalised vector space model. The independence is interpreted as pair-wise orthogonality among the index term vectors that forms the vector space. Wong et al., proposed an alternate view which leads to the generalised vector space model. In this model, the index term vectors are assumed linearly independent but are not pair wise orthogonal. As such, they are not as like in the classic vector space model where the vectors compose the basis of the space.

They are composed of smaller components derived from the collection. These pair wise orthogonal so called min-term vectors compose the bases of the space. The main advantage of the generalised vector space model is the dependence of the index term. However, this dependence is still a controversial issue. Thus, the advantage of the generalised vector space model in practical situations is not yet proved. The main drawback is the high cost of computation due to the fact that the number of min-terms might be proportional to the number of documents in the collection.

Probabilistic Model

The third of the classic IR models, the probabilistic model, attempts to capture the IR problem within a probabilistic framework. To that end, a set of documents is defined for each user query, which contains only the relevant documents. This set is referred to as the ideal answer set. If the properties of this ideal answer would be known, the documents could be retrieved. The querying process can be described as the process of specifying these initially unknown properties.

The main advantage of the probabilistic model is the ranking by the probability to be relevant. The main disadvantages include the need to guess the initial separation into relevant and non-relevant documents. Moreover, the weights for the index terms are binary. Finally, as in the classic vector space model, the index terms are assumed to be independent. Although experiment exist which show better performance of the probabilistic model when compared to the vector space model, it can be expected that it is outperformed by the latter with general collections.

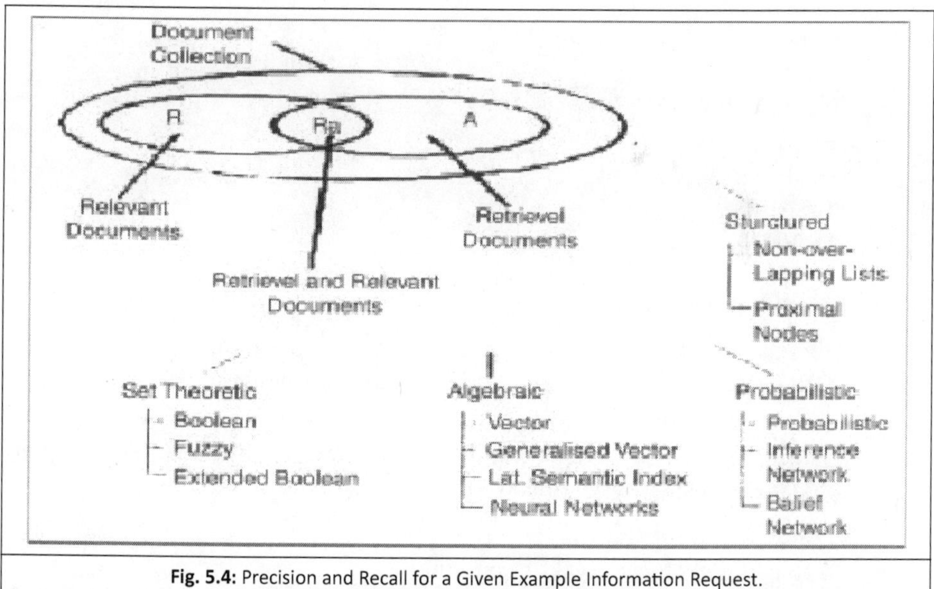

Fig. 5.4: Precision and Recall for a Given Example Information Request.

INFORMATION RETRIEVAL CONCEPTS IN DIGITAL LIBRARIES

Digital libraries rely on effective retrieval methods with easy access to the information. Thus, the success of digital libraries is depends on the quality of retrieval. Research in the IR has traditionally been important in the research pertaining to the digital libraries. One important topic in this context is the search in distributed collections.

As the document collection is managed by different organisational units or even the document collections of different digital libraries are used, the interfaces and functionality of these systems are supposedly inhomogeneous. Gutl part of the difficulties in this context are the variable IR methods and interfaces, like representation and relevance ranking, as well as the scope of the search results.

Another difficulty is the merging of the individual results and the inter-system ranking. The second important topic in this context is the multimedia content in document collection. Baeza-Yates et al., states the need for suiting query languages for different media, like a visual query for image search. In a multimedia environment, the task is even more complex, as the combined search in different media, as Gutl points out.

BROWSING FEATURES

The browsing feature is important for retrieval of neither information that is nor already known in part. Browsing enables people to look through a digital library and discover things that they had no previous knowledge of.
Users should be able to browse digital objects by:

- Author/ Creator/ Contributor.
- Title of the document/ article/ book.
- Issue Date/ Date of Publication.
- Collection.
- Communities.
- Subject browsing.
- Publisher wise browsing.
- Table of contents browsing.
- Multi-dimensional browsing.

SEARCHING FEATURES

Searching in any digital library is one of the important aspects. Hence, it is necessary to know what type of search features are supported by the software.

While, evaluating the software it is necessary to do functional testing of the software, i.e., determining the extent to which a digital library, in whole or in part, is able to perform desired operations.

- Full text searching.
- Boolean (AND, OR, NOT) searching.
- Basic Search.
- Advanced search.
- Truncation/Wild card searching.
- Exact words/phrases searching.
- Proximity searching.
- Stemming search.
- Fuzzy search.
- Phonetic search.
- Case sensitive.
- Case insensitive.

- Boosting the term.
- Range searching.
- Expand search.
- Lateral search.
- Multilingual search.
- Refine search.

QUALITY OF SEARCH RESULTS

Generally IR systems have to cope with a vaguely described information need of the user; the results of an IR process are not exactly matches to this information needs, but are ranked by relevance. The evaluation of the precision of this answer is called information retrieval evaluation. Besides, the performance measures generally important for a software system, like response time, space, and the like, this retrieval performance is the key to an IR system.

Information retrieval evaluation is performed by querying a standardised reference collection. These reference collections consist of a set of documents, a set of example information needs, and corresponding sets of relevant documents.

The relevant documents for example information requests are determined by experts. For a given retrieval strategy, the documents retrieved are compared to the set of relevant documents determined by experts. The similarity between these two sets is quantified by the test collection's evaluation measure and leads to the goodness of the tested retrieval strategy.

RECALL AND PRECISION

Recall and precision are basic evaluation parameters. The drawback of recall and precision is the fact that the examination of all documents of the answer set is assumed. This, however, is contrary to the usual fact that the user is presented only a part of the retrieved documents, ranked by the degree of relevance. Thus, the recall and precision values vary as the user proceeds through his examination of the retrieved documents.

In order to record this development, a precision versus recall curve is plotted. Usually recall and precision values resulting from averaging various queries are used to compare the performance of IR systems. Such average recall versus precision plots trade the advantage of a better overview on the overall retrieval performance for that fact that single mavericks remain undetected. In various situations, such as, to discover the superiority between the single value summary of the recall and precision plots. One possibility is to calculate the Average Precision at Seen Relevant Documents. To that end the precision figures obtained are averaged after each new relevant document which is observed.

CONCLUSION

Digital libraries present still another new environment for information retrieval, presenting new and different challenges and an expanded research agenda. Some of these challenges arise from the nature of the content in digital libraries, others from the nature of the tasks performed and the characteristics of the users of digital libraries. Like the Web, digital libraries incorporate mixed data types. The data may be structured, semi structured, or unstructured; and incorporate text, images, video, and audio information. Information retrieval from this mix of structure and formats is relatively unstudied, since research has usually been based on an assumption of a homogenous collection, and metadata, where available, has been treated as unstructured text.

How do we incorporate evidence from these multiple sources to create an ordered list? Since digital libraries are by definition often distributed or federated systems, another level of complexity is added by the need to make retrieval from multiple sites and multiple collections transparent to the user. Given multiple sites, we need to give priority for search to sites with the highest probability of success.

Searching on multiple sites leads to a data fusion problem as the system must integrate and rank information from different datasets, with different data and metadata. Furthermore the importance and challenges of distributed document collections have been analysed. Though the Web may appear as a distributed digital library at the first glance, there are numerous differences. Information Retrieval system which presents the basic layer applied in conceptualisation processes and discussed the models of the IR system.

❐

6

Library Automation and Networking

AN INTRODUCTION

Since, the 1960s, libraries have used technology in general, and computers in particular, to automate a wide range of administrative, public, and technical services tasks. Designed as an overview of major facets of automation activity, this chapter surveys the current state of computer applications in six areas of library work: circulation control, descriptive cataloguing, catalogue maintenance and production, reference service, acquisitions, and serials control. For each area, the discussion briefly indicates the motives for automation and describes current dominant approaches, citing examples of representative products and services.

CIRCULATION CONTROL

Library interest in automated circulation control is, in large part, based on a long-standing awareness of the problems inherent in manual circulation systems. These problems include labour-intensive and time-consuming record keeping work routines, inaccuracy, high personnel turnover, an inability to generate statistics about circulation activity, and the lack of an interface between circulation files and other library files which contain much the same bibliographic data. Circulation control is one of the most widely automated library operations, and it is often the first and simplest activity to be automated in a given library, possibly because circulation control systems bear an obvious resemblance to inventory management, retail charge card operations, and other transaction processing activities which have been successfully automated in general business applications.

While specific circulation policies and procedures may be subject to considerable local variation, the major component of circulation control-the check-out/check-in procedure—is typically performed in a straight forward manner that is easily understood by computer application developers and systems analysts lacking formal library training. As library users, many data processing professionals have experienced the circulation activity firsthand and are at least broadly familiar with its purpose and nature. Because the bibliographic data required for automated circulation control are often less extensive and complex than those required to computerise such activities as cataloguing and acquisitions, data conversion costs, software development time, and storage requirements may be substantially reduced. Perhaps more than any other library activity, the historical development of automated circulation control has reflected changes in state- of-the-art data processing technology.

Through the mid-1970s, most automated circulation control systems were custom-developed for a single library or library system. As early as the 1930s and extending into the 1960s, a number of libraries used keypunched cards in combination with sorters, collators, and other unit record equipment as an alternative to manual record keeping. Tabulating keypunched cards with information about books, borrowers, and due dates could be sorted to select overdue items or to identify all books on loan to a given person. Such 'precomputer' data processing systems, several of which were developed for academic libraries by methods and procedures analysts and operations research specialists, were typically based on inventory control models used in business.

With the introduction of computers for business applications in the mid-1960s, a number of libraries developed computerised circulation control systems based on batch processing techniques. Such systems were usually mplemented on a computer located in a data processing centre operated by a university, municipality, corporation, or government agency with which the library was affiliated. In the typical installation, keypunch or key-to-tape devices were used to convert information about individual circulation transactions to computer-processible form.

The resulting data were then hatched for processing at predetermined intervals, a computer writing individual borrower numbers into item records contained in a master circulation file maintained on magnetic tape and printing a list of all items in circulation for library reference. While some of these batch-processing circulation control systems remain in use, they are now mainly of interest for their limitations and impact on the design of subsequent systems.

As a particular disadvantage, the printed lists produced by batch-processing systems necessarily reflect the status of a library's circulating collection at the time when the last batch of transaction records was processed. Part of the information contained in such lists is necessarily invalidated by circulation transactions occurring after that time. By the mid-l970s, library automation specialists had begun to concentrate on the development of online, real-time circulation control systems which process circulation transactions as they occur.

Because pertinent data files are updated immediately, such real-time systems accurately reflect the status of a library's circulating collection. Printed lists are replaced by online terminal enquiries to determine the circulation status of specific items.

While real-time circulation control systems have been custom-developed for individual libraries, a number of vendors offer generalised, preformulated approaches to the computerisation of circulation control that eliminate the need for customised system development and speed the implementation process.

Such preformulated approaches, currently the dominant method of automating circulation control, can be divided into two related groups:

- Prewritten circulation control software intended for execution on a computer system operated by or for a given library; and
- Turnkey systems, consisting of preconfigured combinations of hardware and software marketed as self-contained products.

Introduced in the early 1970s, the earliest prewritten circulation control software packages and turnkey circulation systems were single-purpose products designed specifically and exclusively for library circulation activities.

While such single-purpose systems remain available, library administrators, systems analysts, automation planners, and pro- duct developers are increasingly emphasising integrated, multifunctional turnkey systems and software packages which combine circulation control with other capabilities.

In addition to circulation control, the most complete integrated system implementations include interrelated application modules for cataloguing, online catalogue access by library users and/or staff, acquisitions, and serials control, a community bulletin board system, and electronic message transmission. In some cases, circulation is a standard integrated system component which may be implemented alone or in conjunction with other functions; in others, circulation control is an optional application module which must be purchased separately. Whether designed as single-purpose products or as integrated system components, prewritten circulation software packages and turnkey systems can be implemented far more quickly than customised circulation control systems which may require months or perhaps years to develop. Speed of implementation is an especially important consideration in applications where automation of the circulation activity will result in a cost reduction.

Similarly, prewritten software packages and turnkey systems minimize or eliminate requirements for local software expertise. Libraries acquiring such products usually do not need to hire programmers. In fact, customer programming is specifically prohibited by most vendors. Because the system design is predetermined, user training is limited to operational considerations.

As a distinctive advantage of turnkey implementations, procurement-related tasks are greatly simplified by the availability of a preconfigured combination of hardware and software components that are specifically designed to work together. With a single source for central processing equipment and peripheral devices, the necessity of dealing with multiple hardware vendors is eliminated, as are potential problems of equipment compatibility.

While prewritten circulation control software packages are available for computers of all types and sizes, medium-sized and larger public and academic libraries have typically relied on mainframe—and minicomputer-based products. Examples for IBM mainframes include the NOTIS software package, originally developed by Northwestern University for its own use; IBM's own DOBIULIBIS programme; and the TECHLIB/STATS implementation of the BASIS software package which is marketed by the Information Dimensions subsidiary of Battelle.

Originally developed by libraries in the Minnesota State University system, the PALS software package is marketed by Unisys for use with its own mainframe computers, while the LIAS system, developed by Pennsylvania State University, operates on Honeywell computers. Examples of circulation software packages for popular minicomputer systems include Comstow's Bibliotech system for Digital Equipment's VAX product line; the Georgetown Library Information System (LIS) for Digital's PDP-11 Series models; the Washington University BACS system for Data General and other minicomputers which run under the MIIS operating environment; and the VTLS and Index systems for the Hewlett-Packard HP-3000 product line.

Minicomputer- based turnkey circulation control systems are available from CLSI, Geac, Data Research Associates (DRA), Dynix, OCLC, Universal Library Systems, and other vendors.

Reasonably priced and designed for readily available hardware configurations, microcomputer-based circulation control programmes have proven particularly popular with small public, school, and special libraries. Vendors include Follett, Gaylord, Easy Data, Data Trek, Aball Software, Nichols Advanced Technologies, Scribe Software, Winnebago Software, and Richmond Software. While the earliest circulation control programmes and turnkey systems forced libraries to accept predetermined loan periods, borrower categories, and other operating parameters, most newer products flexibly support a varied range of library requirements.

Unlike earlier systems which contained rigidly coded procedures to control charging, discharging, and related activities, all newer products are parameterised, i.e., they allow libraries to specify the conditions under which items will be circulated, file enquiries made, and printed output produced. Rather than being written into programmes, particular operating parameters are selected by libraries from a range of possibilities. The resulting flexibility broadens the range of applications which a given system can address and is particularly important in installations where a single prewritten software package or turnkey system will be shared by many libraries.

AUTOMATED CATALOGUING

Descriptive cataloguing is an intellectual activity requiring considerable decision-making and one that is time-consuming. As a result, many libraries experience cataloguing backlogs which impede the flow of materials into circulating and reference collections thereby preventing library catalogues from representing those collections fully and accurately. Recognising that the cost of descriptive cataloguing can approach or even exceed the value of certain materials, many libraries do not catalogue paperbound books, low-cost government publications, or other relatively inexpensive items.

In some research libraries, materials of presumably limited interest may be placed in off-site storage facilities with only an abbreviated catalogue record created. In most libraries, conventional descriptive cataloguing is not even considered for individual titles in large microform sets, even though such materials may significantly augment a library's resources in particular subject areas, and the failure to catalogue them impairs their utility. To simplify decision-making, to save time, and to reduce costs associated with descriptive cataloguing, libraries have historically relied on cataloguing copy, i.e., descriptive cataloguing information prepared by other libraries, especially the Library of Congress.

The automation of descriptive cataloguing depends on the availability of such cataloguing copy in computer-processible form. In the late 1960s, the Library of Congress developed the MARC format for the communication of bibliographic data on magnetic tape and began distributing machine- readable cataloguing copy through its MARC Distribution Service. Since, the late 1960s, MARC formats have been developed for various types of library materials, and the scope of the MARC programme-once limited to English-language monographs—has broadened steadily and significantly. The LC MARC database-the accumulation of Library of Congress cataloguing data in machine-readable form-now contains more than 2.5 million records, most of them catalogued since, the inception of the MARC programme.

Although MARC tapes can be purchased from the Library of Congress for input to local computer systems, most libraries obtain access to MARC data through products and services developed by publishers, computer system developers, time-sharing services, and other intermediaries. Among the earliest of these MARC-derivative products were computer-generated micropublications such as MARCFICHE, produced by MARC Applied Research, and Books in English produced by the British Library. Created by Computer-output Microfilm (COM) technology, both products provided more timely and varied access to LC cataloguing data than could be obtained through the conventionally printed National Union Catalogue, which was itself discontinued in favour of a COM implementation in the early 1980s.As an equally timely and flexible alternative, several search services, including DIALOG and WILSONLINE, offer online access to the LCMARC database.

A growing number of vendors supply the MARC database on CD-ROM disks or digital optical videodiscs accompanied by software which supports the retrieval of specific cataloguing records and the printing of card sets. Examples include the BIBLIOFILE system from the Library Corporation in Washington, D.C., the LASERSEARCH system from General Pesearch Corporation, and the MINI MARC II system from Library Systems and Services Incorporated. Although these products and services are important, most libraries obtain access to machine-readable cataloguing records through one of the bibliographic utilities-organisations which maintain large databases of cataloguing records and offer online access and other services to subscribing libraries.

Examples include the Online Union Catalogue implemented by the Online Computer Library Centre (OCLC), the Research Libraries Information Network (RLIN) operated by the Research Libraries Group, the cataloguing support service operated by the Western Library Network (WLN), the Cataloguing Support System (CATSS) offered by Utlas International, the LIONS system operated by the New York Public Library, the AGILE II service offered by Auto- Graphics Incorporated, and Brodart's Interactive Access System (IAS).

While they differ in database size and composition, the number and nature of their subscribers, and the specific capabilities they support, these bibliographic utilities each maintain a database of MARC records obtained from the Library of Congress and other sources, supplemented by original MARC-format cataloguing contributed by subscribing libraries. Working at local terminals, participating libraries can retrieve cataloguing copy, modify it to meet local requirements, and order printed card sets, machine-readable cataloguing records on magnetic tape, and other bibliographic products.

Local workstations are also used to input original cataloguing records for use by other subscribers. Supporting thousands of online terminals accessing millions of machine-readable records, the bibliographic utilities are among the world's largest and most intensively utilised computer-based information services.

COMPUTER-PRODUCED CATALOGUES

The automation of descriptive cataloguing addresses only one part of the cataloguing activity. In addition to using computers to facilitate access to cataloguing copy, libraries are interested in computer-based solutions to the much discussed problems of card catalogues. The most frequently cited of such problems include substantial space consumption; the purchase of expensive cabinets and supporting furniture; labour-intensive and time-consuming catalogue maintenance routines which are intensified by changes in cataloguing rules affecting the choice and form of entries; and limited convenience and retrieval capabilities.

These problems can be minimized or eliminated by the replacement of card catalogues with computer-based book-form or online catalogues. Broadly defined, a book-form catalogue contains successive bibliographic records listed in a page format on paper or microforms. Among the earliest applications of library automation, computer preparation of book-form catalogues can lower production time and costs while eliminating the labour-intensive file maintenance routines associated with card catalogues.

As an alternative to computer printed or typeset catalogues, computer- output microfilm catalogues have been widely implemented by libraries and library systems since, the early 1970s. A number of service bureaus, book jobbers, bibliographic utilities, and other vendors have developed software to produce COM catalogues from library-supplied data, thereby eliminating the need for in-house COM recorders and customised programming catalogues. Broadly defined, an online catalogue is an organised, machine- readable accumulation of bibliographic records which are maintained on disks or other direct-access computer storage media for retrieval by library users and staff members working at inter- active terminals or appropriately configured microcomputer workstations. In addition to saving space and automating file maintenance, online catalogues permit remote access by authorised persons equipped with compatible terminals, and they can support information retrieval operations—such as keyword searching of titles and series names—which are not conveniently possible with card or book-form catalogues.

Online catalogues may be custom-developed for specific library installations or purchased as prewritten software packages or turnkey systems. Examples of custom-developed online catalogues include the Library of Congress Computerised Catalogue, the MELVYL system at the University of California, the LIAS system at Pennsylvania State University, the Library Computer System (LCS) at Ohio State University, and the Dartmouth College Online Catalogue.

Prewritten software packages suitable for online catalogue implementations include BRS/SEARCH from BRS Information Technologies, a powerful information retrieval programme that is available in mainframe, minicomputer, and microcomputer versions; INMAGIC, a versatile data management programme for dominated by integrated library systems which combine database management and catalogue access capabilities with circulation control, acquisitions, serials control, and other operations.

Such systems may be implemented as complete turnkey configurations of hardware and software or as prewritten software packages designed to operate on a library owned mainframe, minicomputer, or microcomputer. Vendors include CLSI, Geac, Notis, Dynix, OCLC, Virginia Tech, Data Research Associates, Carlyle, Comstow Information Systems, Universal Library Systems, Sobeco, Sigma Data/Centel, George- town Medical Library, Washington University, IBM, Inlex, Sirsi, Utlas, Innovative Interfaces, Eyring Research Institute, Easy Data, Data Trek, and Unisys. Among the newest and most widely publicised approaches to online catalogue implementation, a growing number of vendors offer public access catalogue systems which employ CD-ROM storage technology. Examples include the IMPACT system from Auto-Graphics, LASERGUIDE from General Research, THE INTELLIGENT CATALOGUE from the Library Corporation, and the LEPAC system from Brodart.

In such implementations, the library provides a machine- readable version of its catalogue, typically consisting of MARC format records on magnetic tapes obtained from bibliographic utilities or other sources, to a CD-ROM system vendor who indexes and otherwise prepares it for conversion to one or more CD-ROM disks. The disks themselves are created by a mastering process in special manufacturing facilities, and the library receives a specified number of disk copies plus menu-driven software designed for public catalogue access at microcomputer-based workstations. Updated by periodic replacement in the manner of book-form catalogues, such CD-ROM catalogues are increasingly mentioned as an alternative to computer output microfilm for union catalogues and similar implementations.

AUTOMATED REFERENCE SERVICE

Since, the late 1960s, many publishers of printed bibliographies, indexing and abstracting journals, and other reference works have offered machine-readable versions of their products for use in computer assisted reference applications. Initially intended for government, corporate, and academic libraries supporting research in scientific and technical disciplines, such machine-readable reference sources have become widely available in business, the social sciences, and the humanities. In addition to databases which correspond to printed publications, a growing number of reference sources have been developed specifically for use in computer-based systems and have no printed counterparts.

While the earliest machine-readable databases were bibliographic in character, non-bibliographic numeric and directory-type databases are increasingly commonplace. During the late 1960s and early 1970s, a number of libraries purchased machine-readable bibliographic and non-bibliographic data- bases for processing on in-house computers using custom-developed information retrieval software. Most libraries, however, lacked access to the hardware and software resources required to implement such systems. Through the early 1970s,the needs of such libraries were addressed by fee- based search services operated by the producers of machine-readable databases or other organisations such as large research libraries. Such services, which operated in the offline, batch processing mode, were replaced in the mid-1970sby services offering online database searching on a time sharing basis to libraries equipped with conventional terminals.

Now widely utilised by libraries of all types and sizes, online search services can be divided into two broad groups:

- Multidisciplinary services—including DIALOG, BRS, ORBIT, WILSONLINE, DATA-STAR, and ESA-IRS-that provide database coverage of a varied range of subjects for a broad clientele; and

- Specialised services-such as the NLM SEARCH SERVICE, STN INTERNATIONAL, LEXIS, and WESTLAW-that provide online access to one or more databases relevant to a single subject discipline, profession, or activity, such as medicine, law, orngineering.

Various types of specialised search services provide online access to databases containing a specific type of information such as news. Examples include the NEXIS, VUITEXT, DATA TIMES, and NEWSNET search services. While they differ in the number and type of databases offered and in the specific retrieval capabilities supported, multidisciplinary and specialised search services share a common operating methodology: they purchase or otherwise obtain bibliographic and non-bibliographic data-bases in machine-readable form from their producers, convert the dataases to a form required for storage on their computers, and allow libraries or other subscribers to perform various retrieval operations on such data using prewritten data-base management software. The software features a non-procedural query language which permits a user at an online terminal to initiate litreature searches or other information retrieval operations by entering specified commands.

While their query languages are relatively easy to learn, online search services are more often providing menu-driven interfaces for novice users. Some services also offer private file capabilities which allow libraries to establish their own databases.

As a recently implemented supplement or alternative to online search services, an increasing number of bibliographic and non-bibliographic databases are available on CD-ROM disks. Accompanied by information retrieval software, such CD-ROM reference products permit database searching at local microcomputer workstations (over 100 titles were available at the time of this writing). Offered on a subscription basis, they can prove less expensive than online searching for databases that are accessed frequently, although infrequent updating, slow response time for complex searches, and other performance limitations may make them unsuitable for some applications.

As a hybrid implementation with potentially attractive cost/performance characteristics, several vendors combine CD-ROM searching of back file data with online access to the most current information.

ACQUISITIONS

More informed decision-making through improved statistical analysis and reporting of procurement activity is the most frequently cited motive for automating acquisitions operations. Since, the 1960s, automated acquisitions systems have been implemented in at least four different ways: as a custom-developed programme designed to operate on a computer owned by a library or its parent organisation; as an acquisitions-specific prewritten software package or turnkey system; as an application module supported by a multifunctional integrated library system;

or as a time-sharing service offered by a bibliographic utility or a book jobber. Each method has advantages and limitations. Customised acquisitions systems, an implementation option in any automated application, can be developed to a particular library's specifications but are expensive and time-consuming to create. Prewritten acquisitions-specific software, and the acquisitions application modules supported by integrated library systems, can minimize the worst implementation problems associated with customised software development, but a library must have access to required hardware and system software components. Turnkey systems, consisting of preconfigured combinations of hardware and software, are available as both acquisitions—specific products and as integrated systems.

In the latter group, the integration of acquisitions with cataloguing and circulation in a single system offers several advantages, including the ability to establish a preliminary bibliographic record at the time an item is ordered. All of the foregoing approaches require a substantial capital investment which can be minimized if automated acquisitions capabilities are obtained on a time-sharing basis through a bibliographic utility or bookseller. Because chargesare incurred as the acquisitions facility is used, this approach is especially attractive to libraries with modest annual volumes of acquisitions activity.

Use of a bibliographic utility for acquisitions offers other advantages as well. Its database can be used for bibliographic verification, and data can be transferred from cataloguing records to facilitate order preparation. In addition, the use of a single system for acquisitions and cataloguing simplifies staff training requirements, while the immediate online availability of information about the holdings of other libraries supports cooperative collection development. Acquisitions systems offered by booksellers typically feature online access to inventory data with electronic ordering capabilities.

SERIALSCONTROL

Current serials automation activities are directed towards two types of tasks-the bibliographic control of serial publications and the management of serials collections in individual libraries. The task of bibliographic control is the establishment of definitive bibliographic information about serial publications. Among automated approaches to this task, R.R. Bowker offers machine-readable versions of its various printed guides to serial publications including Ulrich's International Periodicals Directory.

The International Serials Data System (ISDS) and the International Centre for the Registration of Serials are charged with responsibility for the establishment and maintenance of a comprehensive machine-readable registry of bibliographic information about serials published through out the world. In the United States, the Library of Congress has developed a MARC format for serial publications and participates in the CONSER programme which creates and maintains a high-quality machine-readable database of cataloguing records. The CONSER database is maintained by OCLC, and CONSER records are disseminated through the MARC distribution service.

To manage local collections, a number of libraries and several vendors have developed systems which automate one or more aspects of serials processing, including union list production, ordering, check-in, claiming, and the routing of received issues to designated persons. Computer-based production of union lists of serials is routinely sup- ported by data management software or word processing systems. Such lists may be printed on paper or microfiche. The last option is especially useful for very long lists that will be mailed or otherwise distributed to multiple locations. As an example, microfiche is the output medium for the California Union List of Periodicals (CULP) which contains information for over 63,000 periodicals held by 700 California libraries.

The CULP database is also accessible online through BRS. As with conventional book acquisitions, computers can be used to minimize the labour-intensive sorting, filing, and other paper-handling work routines associated with manual serials processing. A number of libraries developed customised serials control systems during the 1960s and 1970s. The PHILSOM system, developed by the Washington University School of Medicine Library, is perhaps the most famous example. As an alternative to the time and expense associated with customised system development, libraries can obtain access to serials control capabilities on a time-sharing basis through subscription ser-vice companies. Examples of such time-shared serials control services include F.W. Faxon's LYNX system and the EBSCONET system offered by EBSCO Subscription Services.

Several companies and other organisations have developed pre- written software and turnkey systems designed specifically for serials control. The INNOVACQ Acquisitions and Serials Control System, for example, offers a comprehensive range of serials ordering, check-in, and claiming capabilities.

It can download records from bibliographic utilities and transfer serials records to a local circulation control or public access catalogue system. Among microcomputer-based products, OCLC's SC350 Serials Control System can retrieve bibliographic information, local data, and publishers' addresses from the OCLC online union catalogue.

It facilitates the check-in of received issues, produces claims and claim cancellations, maintains binding instructions, and prints bindery slips. It can also transmit serials records to OCLC's union list component. As an alternative to single-purpose implementations, several integrated library systems support serials control modules, and others have announced such capabilities for future implementation.

PLANNING FOR LIBRARY AUTOMATION ACADEMIC LIBRARIES

Library Automation refers to the use of computers to serve the needs of library users. The operations of a library get a quantum jump with the introductions of computers. The computers help to provide fast and reliable access to the resources available in the library as well as elsewhere. The application of computers in the library operations avoids repetitive jobs and saves lot of labour, time, speeds up operations, increases use of library resources. Computers are not only used as a tool for processing the data, but also for data storage and accessing. Planning for an automated system, no matter how big or small, should be part of an overall long-range plan for the library. Automation should always be used as a means to achieve overall better patron service. Careful planning for technology will assure that your automation project is 'sustainable', i.e., enhances the organisation's ability to meet its service mission without disrupting the organisational stability of the institution.

- Vastly expanded storage of indexes, statistical data bases, and document databases within the library.
- Full-text storage of documents, complete with full-text keyword searching and on-demand printing.
- Access by users to library databases from home or office, with direct downloading of information and text on demand.
- The ability to access remote databases across the country and the world, and to download information and text on demand.
- Storage of pictorial and graphic material.
- Availability of 'intelligent systems' providing transparent, one-step searching and access to various library in-house and remote databases.

These capabilities and far more have become reality. Accordingly, today's integrated system must not only provide access to the traditional cataloguing, circulation, public catalogue (OPAC) and acquisitions modules, but must be capable of connecting through the local system into the systems of other vendors, remote bibliographic databases, CD-ROM drives on a local area network (LAN), and the Internet.

Users are expecting that their library systems be capable of, among other things:

- Providing seamless integration between system gateway and OPAC modules.
- Providing access for external users on the Internet to the library's OPAC.
- Monitoring the usage of remote databases that have been accessed through the gateway.
- Accessing the Internet using a variety of graphical interfaces.

Essentially, what this means is that libraries must plan to use a local library system as a vehicle for achieving access to resources outside that system.

Stimulated by the Internet, which has created universal connectivity to information resources heretofore unknown and/or inaccessible, and by Z39.50 interoperability standards and 'gateways,' users of individual local systems are expecting to access the resources of other systems—anywhere and anytime. Moreover, the traditional definition of 'publishing' has been stretched by the creation and instant availability of informational home pages and Web sites worldwide.

Given such increased complexities and heightened levels of expectation, libraries must learn all the more how to plan for the introduction of automation in an organised and systematic fashion. There is little mystery involved here: It is entirely a matter of building upon what you already know about your library, using tools that are readily at hand and, most importantly of all, involving the people—staff and users—who must live with the consequences of any automation decisions.

WHAT IS LIBRARY AUTOMATION

Traditional library work consisting of acquisitions, technical processing, serials control, circulation and reference services all entail time consuming manual work. Though these activities are essential to proper functioning of a library, they consume professional staff time that might otherwise go towards user services and library development. Library computerisation is now gaining importance necessitating the establishment of profession-wide standards. Comprehensive studies of library computer systems world over include discussions of machine-managed acquisitions, cataloguing, serials control, circulation and bibliographic service modules. The litreature in this area highlights major aspects of computer's role in the library environment. Similar to several aspects of library management, the demand for more and faster information services and the decline in library resources are compelling librarians to appreciate the role of computers within their operations.

In general, librarians are looking to maximize the benefits of automation by spreading computer use to as many aspects of library activities as possible by taking advantage of developments in computer hardware and software and telecommunications.

NEED FOR LIBRARY AUTOMATION

Even though this question seems to be very fundamental it is essential to emphasise this aspect, as the library automation is yet to take off in majority of the Indian libraries. Secondly, while justifying need for library automation more than cost-effectiveness the benefits derived by the library users become the major consideration. To appreciate the advantages it becomes necessary to highlight the different levels of library automation. Following are considered as important factors for Library Automation:

- Information explosion.
- Increase in the collection of libraries.
- Inability of users to explore the unlimited litreature and information of their interest.
- Advances in the computer and communication technology. astage of user/ staff time in locating the information.
- Provide wide access to resources within the libraries and elsewhere.
- Better access.
- Quality in service.
- Cooperative efforts (Resource Sharing).

Out of all libraries an academic library has a difficult task of defining its mission and operating objectives. The automation programme will have to mange a wide range of litreature associated with numerous departments and educational programmes of the academic institution. Furthermore, in an academic library the collections will be diverse unlike a special research library where the collection is relatively homogeneous.

The user group will also range widely, including faculty, staff, students, scholars, administrators and the general public. The position of an academic library funded largely by the government further complicates the process of identifying and prioritising objectives.

As difficult as the task might at first appear, it is nevertheless essential to the process of establishing automated systems of any type. In addition the overall health of ones library operation will benefit from a modicum of intellectual rigour in this area.

AREAS OF LIBRARY AUTOMATION

As a first step in a planning process, it is desirable to formulate a model for computerisation listing all itemised and prioritised information systems being maintained on a manual basis by the library. For this exercise it is necessary to break down these procedures into their constituent parts. When further subdividing these activities, each item is to be considered of its functional elements. The systems and subsystems listed below are only indicative and may vary with differing library system environments.

These are:

- Acquisitions:
  - — Selection
  - — Ordering
  - — Claiming/cancellation
  - — Receiving/invoice processing
  - — Extended procurements
  - — Gift tracking
  - — Fund Control

- Maintains information about all library related funds
- Ability to group funds (nesting)
- Track fund allocations and adjustments
- Fund encumbrance
- Fund expenditure
- Cash Balance
- Free Balance
- Automatic updating of fiscal information through recording of specific transactions
- Track year-to-date expenditures
- Create Purchase Orders

• Technical Services:
- Books
- Serials
- Special Collections

• Cataloguing:
- Books
- Serials
- Special Collections

• Circulation:
- Charge/Renewal
- Discharge
- Loan Periods
- Processing schedules
- Holds
- Messages
- Blocks
- Notices
- Transaction Recording Devices for off-line processing
- Member control
- Inventory control

• Serials Control:
- Receipt (check-in)
- Claiming
- Bindery control
- Replacements
- Monographic serials
- Invoice processing

• Reference Services:
- Desk services

• User tools

• Bibliographic utilisation

- Reprography
- Inter-library communications
- General Administration
- Grants Administratiuon
- Library Publications
- Bindery
- Periodical Citation Searching
- OPAC
- Bibliographic Database

PLANNING OF LIBRARY AUTOMATION

Planning for library automation has been defined as planning for 'integrated systems' that computerise an array of traditional library functions using a common database. While this is still generally true, rapid technological change is forcing a re-examination of what it means to 'automate the library.' As physical, spatial and temporal barriers to acquiring information are crumbling, libraries must plan for a broader and more comprehensive approach to providing automated services.

DEVELOPING A LIBRARY 'PROFILE'

One of the most important planning tools involves collecting basic statistical information on the library and its operations.

You will find that the same basic data will be needed again and again—whether for vendors from whom you are requesting cost estimates, or for other libraries with whom you may be seeking to cooperate in implementing automation. The following are examples of commonly needed data:

- Number of titles and volumes in the collection, current and projected.
- Number of borrowers, current and projected.
- Number of materials circulated, current and projected.
- Number of new materials acquired, current and projected.
- Interlibrary loans, lent to and borrowed from other libraries.
- Description of any cooperative arrangements involving the library.
- Library address and hours of operation.

In addition, it is important to take stock of any existing automation in the library by compiling the following data:

- Percentage of collection that has catalogue records in machine- readable form.
- Description of collection without machine-readable records, by category, (monographs, audiovisuals).
- Description of currently-automated library functions (if any).
- Estimates of the location and number of workstations (to show where you intend to have equipment in any future system).

- Specifications for any existing equipment to be re-used with any future system (if any).

At the same time that this data is being assembled, it is important to assess user needs and set service priorities. This can be accomplished by undertaking a focused, strategic planning process designed to involve the library's 'stakeholders.'

DEVELOPING A STRATEGIC PLAN

A library planning to automate should undertake a process by which representative staff and users can identify service needs and objectives. The purpose of such an effort is to allow participants to articulate their interests and concerns, share perspectives and learn about possibilities in a collaborative setting. Group interaction is an important contributing factor in the success of the goal, which is to develop and sustain library automation in the years ahead.

Here are the basic steps involved in this process:

- Plan on a two-day, intensive planning effort.
- Ask participants to identify strengths, weaknesses, opportunities and threats in the library's environment (known as 'SWOT' factors in strategic planning) that are characteristic of or that confront the library.
- Group these factors into critical issue areas that are likely to have an impact on the libraries' future in developing and sustaining automation.
- Ask participants to identify ideas and perceptions in relation to the question: "How do you see the library providing user-friendly, cost-effective automated services in five years?
- Through a method of your own devising, ask participants to prioritise all of the ideas that come out of the above two 'brainstorming' exercises.
- Ask participants to shape these priorities into the draft of a strategic 'vision' for automation development consisting of a statement ofpurpose, goals and objectives for the library.

SETTING SERVICE PRIORITIES

Your strategic vision must now provide the framework or context for the next step in the automation process, which is to determine which library functions should be automated and in what order of priority. For example, processes that are repetitive, occupy large amounts of staff time, require retrieving information from large, unwieldy files, or are high-profile functions of the library (such as the public catalogue) are prime candidates for automation. Determining the functions that you wish to automate and their priorities relative to each other is important for all sorts of reasons.

If needs and priorities are clear, functions can be automated in phases, allowing for more effective use of frequently scarce funding. Moreover, it is a way to develop credibility with funding agencies and be able to take advantage of 'sudden' funding opportunities. Finally, evaluations of systems and options will be easier and more productive if you are able to match your highest functional priorities against the corresponding modules available in the marketplace.

A WORD ABOUT COSTS

Speaking of funding, planners need to be aware that there are certain cost elements involved in the installation and operation of any automated system. These may be summarised as follows:

- Planning and consulting costs include direct, out-of-pocket costs, (e.g., hiring a consultant) and indirect costs, (e.g., training staff) associated with getting started.
- Purchase of the system includes the cost of acquiring the initial system hardware and software, as well as the cost of preparing a site for the computer system.
- Telecommunication costs are those fees paid to telephone companies for connecting remote terminals or workstations to a central computer system.
- Conversion costs are those associated with the creation of machine-readable bibliographic and, for circulation systems, patron, records.

On-Going Operating costs include:

— Maintenance fees

— Utility costs

— Bar code labels

— Miscellaneous supply costs

— Telecommunications costs

— Salaries and benefits (if extra staff are hired).

Additions to the existing system may be required to maintain performance specifications, to accommodate new users, or to allow for additional automated functions.

SYSTEM SPECIFICATIONS

At some point, you will need to re-formulate your functional priorities into 'functional specifications,' which may be defined as what you want an automated system to do for you, including things that your current manual system cannot do. 'Technical specifications' must also be established. These include standards that must be adhered to, system performance, operation, and maintenance, as well as infrastructure requirements, such as stable sources of electricity and telecommunications, and sufficient bandwidth. Developing clear and accurate functional and technical specifications that are specific to your library is one of the most important, if not THE most important, activity that you will engage in as you plan for your automated system.

These specifications will carry you through the entire procurement process, and will ensure that the system which most closely matches them will be the most useful and the most responsive to your needs.

DEVELOPING A FORMAL SPECIFICATIONS DOCUMENT

It is very difficult to compare systems sensibly and pragmatically solely by randomly looking at systems, talking to sales representatives, reading litreature or comparing broad cost quotations. For this reason, libraries use a formal document—often known as a 'Request for Proposal,' or RFP—that organises and standardises the information provided to and requested from the various system vendors. Utilising an RFP to solicit written responses from vendors makes it possible for you to systematically compare functionality, cost, maintenance, support, and all the other issues that are involved in system procurements. The process can save you money and will result in a wiser decision.

- An RFP document should include these essential elements, among others: Background information on the library.
- A description of how the proposals should be arranged and submitted.
- Instructions on receiving vendor business and financial information.
- Criteria the library will use to evaluate vendor proposals.
- Questions regarding vendor training and documentation.
- Your functional and technical specifications.

Also, vendors should be asked to describe:

- How they will create bibliographic, item and borrower databases.
- Their system maintenance programmes and services.
- Their site preparation requirements.
- Their delivery and installation methodologies.
- Their system performance guarantees.
- Their pricing and cost strategies, in detail.

EVALUATING VENDOR PROPOSALS

Upon the receipt of vendor proposals, it will be time to begin the process of system evaluation and selection.

This process involves a number of key steps:

- If possible, form a project team of persons to assist with the evaluations and the selection who have some knowledge of automation or who work in the area(s) being automated. People involved in the strategic planning process would be a good choice.
- Try to weed out proposals that are 'fatally flawed,' e.g., where the vendor fails to reply to any of the functional specifications or the system is missing a module for a high-priority function.
- Begin in-depth reading of the 'surviving' proposals, carefully noting both deviations from the requirements as defined by the RFP and any aspect that is handled unusually well. Make a list of any parts of the response that are not clear and require further clarification.

- Schedule system demonstrations. They are an important component of the evaluation process. Allow the vendors to show off the vendor's system in the most attractive light; however, be prepared with a list of what you want to see along with questions you would like answered. Use the same list with each vendor. This permits more effective cross-comparisons.
- Consider using computerised spreadsheet software in order to compare and evaluate vendor cost proposals. Costs may not be what they seem at first glance.
- Contact some of each vendor's current clients—sites of the same library type, and of similar size, where the hardware and software modules that have been proposed to you are currently in use.
- Assign point values to the criteria listed in the RFP and assign scores to the different proposals. The system with the highest score becomes the number one finalist, the system with the second highest score number two and so on. To maintain a negotiating edge, it is better to cut to two vendors rather than one. If that is impossible, maintain the illusion anyway. Remember: The selection process is not over until the contract is signed. Until that point, never let any vendors know that they have been eliminated, including those with fatal flaws.

PUTTING SYSTEMS INTO PLACE

After the system selection process is complete, there are several important steps which must occur. You and your vendor will have to negotiate and sign a contract. You will want to test the system and make sure it suits your needs. You will want to make provisions for system maintenance. Finally, you will want to train both your staff and your users as much as possible to prepare them for when the system is up and running.

With regard to training, the following must be considered: In thinking of automation planning, there is often a tendency to focus on the hardware and software aspects of planning, and to ignore the human aspects of automation—training and public relations. Without these, however, even the most carefully designed system may not be accepted by library staff or library users. To assure the success of your hard planning work, a training and public relations plan should be part of any automation project.

Fortunately, training can begin long before the system is installed. By involving staff at all levels in the analysis of operations, the identification of needs, the setting of priorities, the development of specifications, and the evaluation of systems, staff will gain much of the knowledge they need as the planning progresses. User acceptance and enthusiasm for your new automated system is certainly an important ingredient in a successful planning effort. If you are implementing a public access catalogue, it is probably the most important measure of success.

Public relations can allow you to accomplish three things:

- Make users aware of your new system and services;
- Motivate them to use the system; and
- Train them in using the new system and services effectively.

RETROSPECTIVE CONVERSION

In the rush to acquire hardware and software, librarians often forget that their most valuable product is the library's database. The creation of a high-quality machine-readable database provides the cornerstone upon which all present and future automation efforts rest. Vendors will come and go, hardware will become obsolete, software will be replaced, but a well-constructed, well-maintained database, with its accompanying local holdings, will be the library's transportable and viable link from system to system. Moreover, as library users begin to access not only their local system but systems in other libraries as well, the quality of respective databases will influence both the outcome of search strategies and the availability of materials.

Database readiness has several important facets:

- Catalogue records must be carefully converted from manual to machine-readable formats.
- Collections must be prepared for conversion through effective and ongoing weeding and inventory programmes.
- Once converted, collections must be properly maintained as titles are added, withdrawn, transferred and recataloged.
- Standards—for bibliographic, item and patron records as well—must be adhered to. In particular, adherence to well-established and accepted standards of description for bibliographic information in a machine-readable database is critical because: without standards, files cannot easily be transferred from one automated system to another.
- It is essential for libraries wishing to participate in resource sharing arrangements with other libraries, who will require such adherence as a condition of participation.

LIBRARY AUTOMATION IN DEVELOPING COUNTRIES THE LAST 25 YEARS

When Information Development was launched in 1984, library automation was, looked at from today's perspective, very much in its infancy. The largest libraries in the world such as the Library of Congress and the British Library had sizeable databases of catalogue records.

University library catalogues were available on-line within their institutional four walls and library circulation was also automated, but data was generally confined to the institution that held it since, there was no network resembling the internet. In 1983 the JANET network had begun to connect the universities in the United Kingdom, and some catalogues were beginning to be available online from other institutions.

The most common way of accessing remote data if there was a possibility at all was by dial-up modem using ordinary phone lines and a modem or an acoustic coupler in which the phone handset was pushed into a rubber holder to ensure no extraneous noise seeped into the phone line when it was transferring electronic signals between computers. Businesses including libraries were also connected by dedicated phone lines to locations where their computers were located when they were remote. But most automation was firmly confined to the institution where it was based. Twenty five years ago was also the beginning of the period when computers were being introduced as desk top computers, with IBM PCs and subsequently IBM PC lookalikes. Personal computers were about to make a huge impact on automation in libraries as no longer was it necessary to have a dedicated air-conditioned room to house computers.

In the early days cataloguers had to have terminals on their desks to enable access to the catalogue but eventually all staff had PCs for general administration so no longer was it was the responsibility of the library budget to purchase desk-top computers. Modems were in fact used to access remotely catalogues for bibliographical purposes, to search databases like Medline. It was already possible to dial up databases such as the British Library's BLAISE database or the US National Library of Medicine's Medline. But these facilities required good phone lines and were not available outside Western Europe and the United States.

There was no such thing as 'full text' then. Computers did not have the capacity to store so much data and data stored was often coded to ensure that it did not take up more space than was necessary. 25 years ago, while most libraries in industrialised countries had not only computerised their catalogues but also computerised their circulation, in developing countries there was very little library automation outside that organised by the United Nations agencies such as FAO's AGRIS and IAEA's INIS and these were very much in their infancy or in their planning stages.

To return to the situation in industrialised countries. In the early 1990's catalogues began to be accessible on the internet but were not web-based and required the catalogue software to be run interactively across the Internet using various different protocols. By the end of the decade, true web-based catalogues using the power of hypertext were available. Libraries began to include in their catalogues digital resources internally held and externally held (predominantly external). MARC formats thenceforward incorporated a field 856 used to link to an external resource by means of a URL (the internet address).

Users of the catalogue could click on a link and go straight to a digital resource that could be anywhere in the world. Subscriptions were possible to electronic journals but they were often not available in developing countries or if they were available the bandwidth of tehinternet in those countries was not enough to enable the materials to be read. Digital library software became available and UNESCO encouraged its implementation in developing countries by making Greenstone available free-of-charge, a digital library software package developed at Waikatu in New Zealand. Links could be made from a library catalogue to material in such a digital library. Material available on the internet which might not be easily accessible in institutions in developing countries with low bandwidth could be downloaded or sent on CD-ROM to the digital libraries and hosted locally.

The Soros Foundation set up eIFL (Electronic Information for Libraries) with the aim of creating national purchasing consortia. They have since, become involved in supporting other activities such as promoting library automation systems, mindful of the fact that without a catalogue of print and digital materials the library user cannot easily find out what is accessible. eIFL supported the European Union funded project to implement NewGenLib, a system under development in India, in Aleppo and Al Baath university libraries in Syria alongside providing them with licences at a reasonable price to access electronic resources.

INASP, the International Network for the Availability of Scientific Publications, was set up by the International Council of Scientific Unions (ICSU) in 1992. Aware of the need to establish good catalogues in order to access scientific litreature, they have also participated in some library automation projects. The Andrew W. Mellon Foundation, well known for philanthropic projects in developing countries, is also supporting the development of a new library automation system at Duke University, the Open Library Environment (OLE). Although there is no participation from developing countries at this stage it is likely that any open source package developed would be supported with necessary tailoring in line with the needs of developing countries wherever they might be different.

The main feature in the last 25 years then has been in the expansion ofcomputers into every aspect of libraries. Possibly the biggest change has been the development of digital libraries, acquiring, transforming or accessing data in digital format. In developing countries this methods of digitisation has taken place to a certain extent.

TRENDS IN THE INDUSTRIALISED WORLD

Library systems in developing countries have obviously developed alongside systems in the industrialised world. First we should look at systems for large institutions. The majority of library systems have been developed in the United States. Many commercially available integrated library systems were developed by universities for their own use and later made available to a wider audience. Dynix was one such, developed for a university library and later sold around the world to universities, public libraries and special libraries. Other systems were based from the outset on cooperatives, such as TALIS which originated as BLS, the system of BLCMP (Birmingham Libraries Cooperative Management Project) which was a cooperative set up with government funding in the 1960s.

This project was one of two established from the beginning by OSTI, the UK Office of Scientific and Technological Information, to support cooperative cataloguing. They had less incentive to expand outside their country of origin as it was their aim to serve a cooperative all of whose members were equal. In 1967, the Ohio Colleges Library Centre was established to bring library automation to Ohio academic institutions by sharing costs. OCLC as it is now has developed from being a cooperative between libraries in Ohio to being an international cooperative, and at one time promoted a library management system. Then they ceased to support it returning eventually to the market by acquiring OLIB, an Oracle based library system. Its vision is to connect libraries of the world. Originally, as with BLCMP, it was a shared cataloguing system receiving records from participating libraries and adding them to a database which in turn could be used by member libraries to populate their own catalogues. Records were transferred between computers initially by sending large magnetic tapes, a thing of the past, from the Centre to the remote libraries. Later they were transferred by telephone lines and subsequently the transfer was done by a client computer, a PC in a remote institution, accessing the Centre's servers by the Internet. Jumping to the present, OCLC have established

Worldcat which could act as a large union catalogue for the world if every library in the world added its holdings. This concept is called Cloud Computing, on the basis that the computer is somewhere remote and no one knows or cares where exactly it is! To return to library systems established in individual institutions, VTLS (Virginia Tech Library System), another large library automation system, always had an interest in working with developing countries and have a large number of installations in the Third World after having expanded into Eastern Europe as well. Another popular system, Aleph, is based in Jerusalem surrounded by a number of developing countries some of which have considered installation though by far the largest share of the market is in Europe.

As for cooperatives like OCLC, there has existed for many years in former Yugoslavia a miniature version of OCLC, COBISS (Co-operative Online Bibliographic System and Service), which since, the break-up of Yugoslavia has expanded to include Albania and Bulgaria on the same basis as other ex-Yugoslav states. They act as a cooperative cataloguing agency but they also keep data on research projects. This institution would be a good model for other regions to adopt. Now and again a commercial library system has been licenced to a developing country institution which has subsequently found it difficult to pay the maintenance fees. Maintenance in any case is often more expensive in a developing country because of economies of scale and distance from the supplier. Additionally there may be problems caused by shortages of foreign exchange.

Now the internet reaches much of the world, distance is not so important. But there have been many instances of institutions retaining a package but not paying maintenance fees and therefore not updating it. Marshall Breeding keeps records of as many library automation packages and the sites where they are used as he can find the information. He publishes the results each year in Library Journal. The latest was published on the web in January 2009.

He reviews the market as well as providing statistics about library automation suppliers. This is a useful guide to make comparisons with developing countries. Unfortunately in his tables he makes only the distinction between the US and the rest of the world. However he also includes a general review and this year he reported that the use of Open Source packages is increasing mainly bring provided by third parties. For example, a company called Equinox provides support for the Open Source package Evergreen.

PACKAGES WHICH HAVE HAD AN IMPACT IN DEVELOPING COUNTRIES

Large libraries in developing countries had always had a certain amount of access to library automation systems. For example, the National Library of Venezuela had a system found in many US academic libraries called NOTIS.

However this library's catalogue is still not available on the web. A number of countries in the former Soviet Union use IRBIS, the CDS/ISIS clone developed by the Russian National Library for Science and Technology. But ordinary libraries, public and academic, in developing countries have always lacked a wealth of possibilities for library automation. Hardware used to be expensive, and relatively speaking is still expensive for developing countries. Other problems raised by writers on the subject range from the power supply to the problems of training staff. Another issue not often raised is the need for collaboration both within and between institutions to get library automation project off the ground and then maintain it.

This is a much more complex activity than a pre-automation situation where there is a library card catalogue maintained by cataloguers and used manually by staff and library patrons. Smaller systems than the ones developed for universities or networks have been developed which could be regarded as being similar sized to CDS/ISIS, for instance Inmagic and Tinlib. Some of these were not very easy to use and were not well maintained. Others were adopted by consortia or organisations in the industrialised world with branches in developing countries such as the British Council.

The main problem in developing countries has been support because of their remoteness and so those packages offering less support would be more attractive as they would be less expensive overall. This may well change in the future with the increase in the power of the internet and the next 25 years will surely see a difference in the availability of and the charges for support.

CDS/ISIS

CDS/ISIS has undoubtedly had a huge influence on library automation in developing countries. This author reviewed the package onits twentieth anniversary. Time and again, libraries have begun automation. There is even a reference to a library which began with Tinlib and has migrated to CDS/ ISIS. Since, CDS/ISIS is well mentioned in the litreature, concerning library automation in developing countries, it will not be covered here. However the most interesting feature which has become available over the last five years in CDS/ISIS is a Z39.50 import facility which is available as part of IsisMARC, and which enables MARC records from external sources to be downloaded into a CDS/ISIS database compatible with the version of MARC of the records.

CDS/ISIS is not essentially a library management system, rather a database management system aimed at bibliographic records which by their very nature are variable length (with for example book titles being of indeterminate length) rather than fixed length which is the case for most data processing systems. Because it is attractive to small institutions with little funding and because of its parentage (UNESCO), it has attracted a certain kind of institution, for example those in the development community. UNESCO developed a DOS version in 1985 and a Windows version which was available for many years as a beta test version but was eventually released around 1998.

However libraries were already requiring to place their catalogues on the web and a number of organisations began to develop compatible web-based systems which could be used by institutions which were developing databases for in-house use on Windows or DOS versions of CDS/ISIS. The main developer of the official version was BIREME with WWWISIS but already others were available such as Webisis. CDS/ISIS is no longer being developed by UNESCO but BIREME in cooperation with UNESCO is leading the development of ABCD on an Open Source basis.

Tinlib

Tinlib was a package which was used extensively in British Council libraries. In Ilorin Nigeria it was used from 1996 as reported by Adewoye. The library had by 2001 almost replaced its card catalogue by the OPAC. The chapter was optimistic about the future and reporting on the use of other electronic resources. However e-mail and the internet were not then available. However, TINLIB had its problems. It was not an easy system to use and contracts for it dwindled outside developing countries and it ceased to be supported. Adeyoyin describes in 2004 how the Development Policy Centre Library in Ibadan migrated their catalogue from Tinlib to CDS/ISIS.

DEVELOPING COUNTRY SCENARIOS

It is of course a fallacy to make assumptions that all developing countries will have approached and will approach library automation in the same way. The wealth of the country the distribution of that wealth and the culture of the residents will make a difference.

Nigeria and other African Countries

Nigeria has oil money and had automation early, being one of the first users of CDS/ISIS for mainframe computers. Already in1989 Eyitayo could write a paper on the attitude of automated library system vendors to investing in Nigeria. Many respondents hoped to open an office and increase their marketing. Enakrire describes a few instances in Africa where automation has been implemented, indicating that, except for branches of international organisations, it depends on the generosity of donors. In Makerere University in Uganda, the library has benefited from donor funding through the African Virtual University Library Initiative of the World Bank to equip the library with computers and installed Internet connectivity. Other university libraries are developing their information service as they are also benefiting from the Programme for thc Enhancement of Research of (PERI) under the sponsorship of the International Network for the Availability of Scientific Publications (INASP).

Through PERI, donors have paid subscriptions on behalf of libraries in Africa to access web-based journals. The University of Ibadan had a long history of automation, having begun in 1979. Georgina D. Ekpenyong wrote in 1997 about the history so far. The University of Ibadan Library was already seen as a leader in Nigeria. At that time they used CD-Rom extensively to provide bibliographic data. They took training seriously but did not yet have an OPAC. In 2008, the John D. and Catherine T. MacArthur Foundation in Chicago awarded grants totalling US $7.1 million to expand academic and research programme and strengthen staff development at two Nigerian universities as part of the Foundation's efforts to improve higher education in Africa. The result is that they signed up to VTLS, Virginia Tech Library System a commercially availabl package developed originally as Virginia Tech's own system.

Thailand

In Thailand there were efforts in the 1990s to computerise the libraries with foreign-based systems being purchased. Thammasat University library had Dynix, supported from Ameritech's Australia office, and planned to move to Ameritech's new system Horizon. In 1997 the university library sent three cataloguers to Middlesex University to learn to use Horizon. Since, then they have implemented Horizon and exchange of experience took place between Middlesex University and Thammasat University until the Systems librarian at Thammasat moved to a different post around 2006. Many universities in Thailand are able to purchase these systems often through local distributors of international or American packages. Early on though, CDS/ISIS was used and at Thammasat University they used it for databases of journal articles.

OPTIONS FOR DEVELOPING COUNTRIES

Developing countries depend on developments in the industrialised world but they do not necessarily benefit from the same options as the industrialised world can use. Moreover, some of the options may be much more attractive in developing countries or at least may seem to be so.

Developing a Library System

One solution for organisations in developing countries which might have problems with paying organisations in foreign currency but which have good local technical staff is to develop their own software system. One interesting example of this is the University of Colombo in Sri Lanka. They had begun to automate in 1991 by using CDS/ISIS and then later adopted CDS/ISIS for Windows when it became available. In 2002, Seneviratne and Amaraweera reported in Information Development that in Sri Lanka there was discussion on developing a library automation system to bridge the gap between CDS/ ISIS and what commercial software was able to provide, such as Alice for Windows (UK commercial) and LibSys (Indian).

In 1997 the National Agency for Research Energy, Science and Agriculture (NARESA) now the National Science Foundation, used the CDS/ISIS DOS version to handler acquisitions, cataloguing, serials management, Current Awareness Services as well as cataloguing and indexing; this package called PURNA was then used in 34 special and academic libraries. AGRIS using CDS/ISIS was widely influencing libraries in the agricultural sector and the Windows version was then used in the National Library of Sri Lanka for its union catalogue.

Now they are using Genisis, a package to make it easy to implement BIREME's WWWISIS on the web, development of which was undertaken in France by Pierre Chabet but for which a manual was written in Sri Lanka (partially a translation from the documentation in French) by Ms. Deepali Talagala Director/Information of the Sri Lanka Scientific and Technical Information Centre based at the National Science Foundation in Colombo Seneviratne and Amaraweera discussed in their paper the features a system would need and the platforms, hardware and operating system, most used and as a result decided to make a prototype using MS Access on Windows.

Development took two Phases.

Firstly a web-based interface to physically dispersed databases with a user-friendly front-end reported by Kumara et al in 1998, and a library automation system described in a BSc dissertation by DMS Dilrukshi, 1999 NetLib—a library management system through the Internet. In 2002 a prototype had been developed and the system was due to be maintained by the Computing Service Centre of the University of Colombo. Unfortunately there is a high overhead in developing and maintaining systems especially for a small client base.

In the UK all university libraries have commercial systems. Newcastle, used to have their own system in the 1980s but only Lancaster remained, eventually contracting with Ex Libris to take Aleph in 2001. By 2008 both the University of Colombo and the National Library of Sri Lanka had signed up to Softlink Europe's Alice system, a system used by the British Council worldwide (for example in Oman, Jordan and Sudan: the catalogue of the British Council in Sudan is available on the internet) and so has proven maintenance in developing countries. So developing one's own system is not to be recommended: Eyitayo noted that despite the availability of numerous off-the-shelf systems, most libraries in Nigeria that have attempted automation have chosen to commission expensive and time-consuming in-house projects, most of which have suffered severe set-backs and in most cases are not adequate for library work and often lack the capability for sharing information and interconnection with other systems.

Open Source

In the context of moving towards commercially supported systems, it is interesting to see that CDS/ISIS was attractive to libraries in developing countries. It was available without charge and so there was no danger of not being able to pay for it.

Of course it was supported by an organisation with as much prestige though not so much turnover as many industrial companies. It also operated on a legal footing. Institutions had to sign a licence agreement to use the software. No doubt many institutions obtained the software illegally but the software was protected in law by the licence agreement. UNESCO were more concerned with illegal copies being made and sold for illegal profit than with institutions using the software without being officially licenced since, the spirit of the software following the ethos of the developer Giampaolo Delbigio was that it should enable institutions to participate in worldwide record sharing at many different levels.

Nevertheless there was established a network of distributors which is still in place. Some acted merely as local distributors sending out the software on diskettes by post and thereby easing the burden of the hard-pressed office in UNESCO dealing with this. Other distributors were able to provide support usually of a limited nature though sometimes of a more extensive nature akin to the commercial support that is found in the large-scale library automation systems. The shareware movement was in place when CDS/ISIS was released in 1985.

In 1984, Andrew Fluegleman programmed a communications software package, PC-Talk and Jim Knopf a file management application called PC-File a year before the IBM PC was released and called it Freeware. The developers wanted to avoid commercial distribution networks and distribute the software over the now seemingly primitive and slow dial up systems whereby PC users could transfer programmes by dialling up a central computer using a modem and phone lines. The idea was that users would download the software, test it and if they liked it make a small contribution to the developer to support further development. Knopf established the term freeware as his own and no one else could use it.

There were other microcomputers around at the time, most notably the Apple Macintosh and others which are only part of history such as the BBC Microcomputer, though none ever reached the level of popularity that the IBM PC with the Microsoft Windows operating system has now reached.

Incidentally Fluegleman distributed his software with the source code which led to many other developers producing their own versions and PC-Talk was improved and sold on by other developers such that Fluegleman lost control of it. Knopf however established a multi-million dollar company on the basis of PC-File.

In 1983 Bob Wallace created PC-Write which became a well used word processor and was used extensively in developing countries. Because the word freeware was reserved he called it shareware. The concept was pretty much the same. Over the years, freeware and shareware became less used as concepts probably because the most used programmes for business purposes were monopolised by Microsoft with the operating system and Microsoft Office applications. Shareware was in a sense reborn with the open source movement. It is difficult to see any difference between Open Source and shareware but the Open Source Movement has been supported from the outset by large foundations such as the Soros Foundation which founded the Open Society Initiative.

In English 'Open Source' means freely available source software which developers can use to advance the software in question. In all these cases, software developed is free though usually developers ask for a voluntary contribution. They cannot be sold on. Open Source does not necessarily mean free-of-charge but there is an implication that the availability of the source code will enable organisations to acquire and develop it for free. CDS/ISIS was no shareware or open source but many of the features of open source and shareware were responsible for the popularity of CDS/ISIS.

For example, Open Source has the possibility for users with access to programming skills to make their own developments. CDS/ISIS has a feature of being able to write programme exits which enable further development. Unlike open source the source code was not made widely available but UNESCO did make it available to BIREME in Brazil where further developments have taken place. Moreover, in the Soviet Union the Russian National Library for Science and Technology developed with permission from UNESCO IRBIS, a functionally equivalent package copied from the DOS version of ISIS.

The Open Source movement gained much greater political credibility than the earlier movements did and UNESCO came under pressure to support the movement. They now have on their web site a Free and Open Source software portal. Because of UNESCO's lead in this concept, CDS/ISIS came under pressure to be declared open source in the early 2000s. But the source code is 100 Encyclopaedia of still not available. This author believes it would lead to many different versions of the software that could generate records in databases that were no longer compatible with each other. Moreover, Open Source is seen by some as the solution to some of the problems facing the library software industry. Is Open Source all it promises to be? Over the last few years there has been a spate of mergers in the library systems industry led by the equity market resulting in a trend to discontinue the development if not the support of library systems when a company has acquired more than one such package. This severely inconveniences the using institutions which have to migrate from one system to another. Would open source be a protection against this? Open Source has become so much a fashionable option for library software that the International Federation of Library Associations and Institutions held a meeting in Senegal prior to the annual conference's meeting in Durban South Africa.

The proceedings are illustrative of the views on Open Source. The argument in Savard's introduction goes that Open Source may help to smooth out the inequalities between industrialised and developing countries. The connection with commerce is weaker than with commercial software but it is not non-existent. In industrialised countries libraries often use third-party services to support Open

Source. This means the connection with the commercial world strengthens. There is no way put from paying for support. The question is who pays and there is not much difference between paying a developer or a third party.

In the conclusion of these proceedings, Diop feels there are clearly economic advantages to adopting an open source software solution but agrees that mastering open source software can take a lot of time and effort because library and information professionals are often isolated. User communities need to be built up to provide mutual help. However it remains to be seen what will be the impact of open source on library automation, particularly integrated library systems in the industrialised world. A pessimistic outcome might be that the institutions using such software feel no differently being supported by the commercial open source support companies than by the current range of commercial companies who promote systems they themselves own.

THE CURRENT SITUATION AND FUTURE PROSPECTS

Making predictions is a very hazardous occupation in anything to do with computers since, the future only tends to bring surprises. Developments in many developing countries are not as advanced as might be expected and in some places there is still a problem with electric supply: Adebibo reporting on usage of catalogues by students at the University of Ilorin in Nigeria stated: "Most respondents claimed to know how to use the card catalogues and OPAC but only a few use them. The possible reason for this low level use of the OPAC is power outages, which have become the rule in Nigeria rather than an exception. Overall, as the power of the internet increases, particularly its bandwidth and its reliability, library automation in developing countries will have the same capabilities as the industrialised world, but not the finance to support it.

In developed countries it is felt by some that the future of library automation lies in open source (outside the control of commercial suppliers) or 'Cloud Computing' (very much controlled by commercial suppliers who provide software on their own hardware and the clients access the data via the Internet). However if solutions to library automation are hosted services in the industrialised world, the suppliers of the service would be able to charge developing countries as little as they wish on the basis that every amount, however little, is profit. This has happened with hosted electronic journals where deals have been made by publishers to cover entire countries which are less than the licence fee required for a university in the west. As suggested, see if this happens. As with e-journals, it needs a champion like eIFL to promote to the suppliers the benefits of their working with developing institutions in what may be perceived as an altruistic way.

LIBRARY AUTOMATION IN ACADEMIC LIBRARIES IN INDIA PROBLEMS AND PROSPECTS

The history of library automation is sufficiently old now. It started in early fifties in the Untied States of America. The landmark was the initiation of MARC project by the Library of Congress. During 1960s some experiments were carried out in India in this field but very sparingly. During late seventies there were some achievements like production of National Union Catalogue of Scientific Serials by INSDOC, production of Union Catalogue of DRDO libraries of Western Region by the Institute of Armament Technology at Pune. Then came eighties and the whole focus of the librarians shifted towards library automation.

A number of seminars were organised on the library automation and still being done so. We graduated from simple library operations to specialised functions including networking. Now we talk about digital libraries and e-journals.

We have come a long way. But we are a country where bullock cart and cars are seen on the same road so blocking the fast moving traffic and those bullock carts restrict the speed of the cars to its own speed. To overcome this problem there are only two ways. First, replace the bullock cart with a car, and second, bypass the bullock cart and leave it behind. The state of library automation in our university libraries is more or less the same. We have the libraries like IIT libraries which are highly automated and also totally manual libraries which are really restricting the speed of academic and research in the country.

FACTORS RESPONSIBLE FOR AUTOMATION IN ACADEMIC LIBRARIES

There are several reasons which can be cited for this difference.
Some of them are:

- Attitude and awareness of the management
- Attitude and awareness of the Users specially faculty

- Resources available
- Non-availability of suitable software
- Level and skill of staff
- Geographical locations.

Attitude and Initiative of the Management

Attitude and initiative on the part of the management has played major role in library automation in Indian University Libraries. The management here includes both the university management and the librarian as a secretary of the management whose task is to carry out the decisions taken by the executive bodies of the university, such as Syndicate, Executive Council, etc. If the Librarian had the initiative then he was able to convince the authorities about this emergent need. In some of the cases, the initiative also came from top and the Librarian was forced (or bypassed) to do it. But the best blend was when the initiative of both the Librarian and University Authorities was synergised. If there was no initiative on both the ends than there was no progress.

Attitude and Initiative of the Uses

A library may be as smart as its readers. If the readers are smart and well aware they may force the authorities to work towards library automation. If the readers are knowledgeable about the development being taking place in the information technology, they have influenced the use of computers in library to a great extent. This is more true about faculty as they are the people who participate in decision making process. The good examples are the libraries of IITs and other higher engineering educational institutions.

Resources Available

The third important factor is the resources available with the university libraries. The resources include both financial as well as human resources. In most of the universities, the librarians are given funds only for books and journals. Some libraries do not want to or are not allowed the funds received for books and journals to be used for any other purpose, even though the University Grants Commission (UGC) guidelines permit the use of a certain percentage towards such activities (In VIII Plan it was 15 per cent and in IX plan 10 per cent).

Most of the libraries depend on the funds provided by the UGC under Inflibnet project. The distribution of the money under this project was not done logically. Big and small libraries were equated at par and as a result while some libraries remained fund starved some were not able to use the funds. Before distributing funds to libraries there should have been a survey of the requirement and certain guidelines laid down. Besides this there are no other financial resources available with the university libraries.

In order to save the university libraries from going further down UGC must do something in this direction. Another very serious problem, may be more serious than the financial one, is the lack of trained manpower.

Many of our library science schools have not based their curricula on the automation requirement of the university libraries. Some of them are even teaching today what was designed thirty or forty years back although that has become totally outdated. Not many library schools produce a candidate who can straight away go the Automation Department of a University Library and can independently work without any further training. The bifurcation of the library science schools from libraries are perhaps the one of the main important reasons for that.

As a result our profession became the only profession where practice went far ahead of the teaching. In the country people are talking about digital libraries and web-OPACs and we are teaching fundamental of computers in our library schools. This is the only profession where getting a professional degree does not require any professional training. Can you imagine a doctor without hospital training or an engineer without a training in Industry.

Non-availability of Suitable Software

Non-availability of suitable software has also played an important role. Though there are a number of software available for library management but most of them are non- standard. The main reason behind is that most of the software have been developed without the help of a qualified librarian. As a result there were a stream of non-standard software. Some of these softwares have been developed by big corporations like CMC but have not been proved very successful. The software developed by institutions (for example DESIDOC, INSDOC, etc.,) could not be successful as they were lacking in marketing and after sales service. The librarian is confused as he is not in a position to decide what to select.

Level of Skill of Library Staff

The level of skill of library staff also played a very important role. In our country there are no standard for level of subordinate staff to be recruited in academic libraries. There educational and professional qualification vary from state to state. In some of the cases the library assistants are recruited with 12th pass and a six months certificate in library science while in Central institutions like IITs and Central Universities it is minimum graduation and degree in library science. The institutions having better stuff went far ahead (though there are exceptions to that). The better qualified staff was better oriented towards progressive thinking which could move the things fast. This point emphasises the requirement of a uniform qualification policy for the recruitment of staff in academic institutions.

Geographical Location

Geographical location of an institution also played a very important role. The institutions near to a metro city were benefited by the availability of the resources. They were having better approach to hardware and software market and also the manpower for data entry. They were having approach to better training facilities. Hyderabad is a good example which can be cited.

PRESENT STATUS OF LIBRARY AUTOMATION IN UNIVERSITY LIBRARIES

The real boost in library automation came from the establishment of the INFLIBNET Centre. Before Inflibnet scattered efforts were being made in academic libraries specially in the institutions of special characters like IITs, IIMs, etc. INFLIBNET proved a real catalyst. Inflibnet started with scratch. At that time there were no financial assistance available to the University Libraries for automation. For the first time it was established that automation was the need of hour. The finances were allocated for the first time. The standards were established about the data capturing. The format was finalised and the Karvan started. As one estimate at present about 120 university libraries have been using computers in their activities. Some of the University libraries are even establishing digital libraries not only of already available digital resources but are digitising their own litreature. About 50 university libraries have their web pages.

AREAS WHERE COMPUTERS ARE BEING USED

The following are the areas where computer are being used at present:

- Online public access catalogue
- Circulation
- Acquisition
- Serial control
- Intranet
- Internet
- CD-ROM services

Online Public Access Catalogue (OPACs)

The problem being faced by the users in locating the document was the first to be targeted in the library automation. As a result the work first started in this direction. There was one more reason for this and that was the availability of CDS/ ISIS software which had the facility of catalogue only. It was in contrast of the special libraries where the work first started on providing information services like CD-ROM search. Even today this area of automation has more activity than any other area. It has now graduated to Web-OPAC (web based online public access catalogues) where university libraries have made their databases available on their web sites. This has eliminated the need of installation of search software on the user's terminal. One potential which remains unutilised is the use of search data for research purpose as the search history can provide very useful tools for the librarians to formulate their collection development plans.

Circulation

Circulation is one of the main activities of a university library or any library per say. In university libraries, however, the number of books issued and retuned are more than in special libraries. Therefore, the next area which was taken up was the circulation. In some of the libraries the number of books issued/returned may be more than one thousand per day. We at IIT Roorkee (formerly University of Roorkee) has experience of issuing 1500 books in six working hours. Sometimes there used to be a queue of more than 100 students, since, the free hours for all students used to be the same, before automated circulation started.

Use of barcodes had made the life very simple due to added accuracy and speed. Besides speeding up the issue/return, printing reports, sending reminders also become very easy. Circulation data also provides a very important insight into the book use pattern. Librarians should try to use this data for research and development purpose.

Acquisition

Use of computers in acquisition remains a low priority area. Not many libraries are using computers in acquisition. On reason may be the continuously reducing budget for purchase of books. But this area needs to be strengthened.

Computerisation at the stage can help not only in order processing but also can be a very effective tool in budget control. You can allocate funds to different departments based on a set formula, can send department heads about non-availability of funds, can control over ordering and also utilise the data entered at this stage for technical processing and OPAC.

Serial Control

Idiosyncracies involved in serial control affects the use of computers in serial control and hence, the area is not very well represented at automation scenario. One more reason is the unsuitability of serial control modules available in most of the library Management Softwares. The procedures developed by these softwares are so cumbersome that sometimes it looks easier to use normal method rather than automation. However, this area provides very good stage for use of computers as it can help tracking the missing issues very efficiently and provide the current awareness services and even the SDI services besides budget control.

Intranet

Making the information available on intranet is also growing popularity as it eliminates the need of installing the software on the users' terminals. Users can access the catalogue through intranet or they can find the status of the books issued to them through web access. CD-ROM resources and other digital resources can be accessed on intranet. The beauty is that one need not be conversant with the software as the web links are available through the web page. Growing installation of campus wide networks is also playing a positive role in this direction.

Internet

Use of Internet for academic purposes is also increasing day by day. More and more libraries are putting their resources on Internet. Internet is the medium both to access and disseminate information. Internet has emerged as a very big virtual library which has information on practically every subject and in every media may it be text, audio or video. Libraries should use this facility to the best of their capability. They should provide links to similar type of libraries through web pages. One very good use can be designing of e-gates where user can have access to the electronic resources through a common user interface.

Digital Libraries

Digital library has recently become the buzzword for librarians. In the last year most of the seminars and the conferences had 'digital libraries' as their theme. Digital libraries can be of two types, i.e., digital libraries of the digital text available in the market such as e-journals, CD-ROM databases, e-books, software, etc., or it can be developed from the printed text available in the library. If a library takes a decision to develop a digital library of its collection specially theses, dissertations and old journals, it can solve the problem of space and preservation both. But the decision about creating such decision is taken to be very carefully as it will prove a very costly venture both in terms of money and manpower.

PROSPECTS

Having talked about the problems and areas of applications let us talk about future prospects. I can definitely say that the things are changing for the good. Now University authorities are realising that there is no way to escape library automation. They are finding various ways to finance their library automation projects. Librarians are also realising that they can not remain indifferent to the change, otherwise they will be labelled outdated. One area of concern is the library science graduates being produced by our library schools It is surprising that UGC is giving responsibility of refresher courses of library science to the library science school and not to the libraries who are established themselves as advanced libraries and uses the technology far ahead than the library science schools. Existing staff is getting rid of the fear of computerisation. They are coming forward to learn and make themselves suitable to face the challenges of the new millennium. Standardisation is increasing and the better softwares are available.

LIBRARY AUTOMATION AND ORGANISATIONAL CHANGE IDENTIFICATION OF THE ISSUE

The example is only one instance of the large-scale changes that affect people's work lives. These types of changes raise many important issues for managers, from the level of director to unit supervisor. Some issues are primarily technological. What equipment will be needed? Is the technological infrastructure in place? Will the system crash when the date changes to January 1, 2000? Other issues are more social. How will the employees react? Will they accept the change or resist it? Can the change process be made easier?

Unfortunately, this second group of issues can be easily overlooked. Managers often do not address human issues adequately, even though they are aware of them, and even though they consider their employees, clients, and other people to be important.

CHANGE ISSUES IN THE PUBLIC AND PRIVATE SECTORS

While the specific issue of library automation is located principally in the public sector, the processes and challenges of change are common to both areas.

HUMAN FACTORS IN LIBRARY AUTOMATION

Librarians, staff and patrons must make a number of adjustments as a result of any library automation project, whether it is an original implementation or a migration. One key area is the relationship between people and technology. People have to change the way they behave and think to work effectively in an automated environment. They skim through cards to find a catalogue record in a manual system. To find a catalogue record in an automated system they use computer commands. In a migration scenario, this might be a change from typing keyboard commands to choosing buttons or menu items on a graphical interface. For long-term employees, this requires yet a third 'mental map.' These demands for change easily lead to stress reactions of fear or anger, especially when they are large-scale or frequent. Smith mentions several sources for these emotions, such as loss of control, worries about identity and security in the workplace, and breakdowns in interpersonal relationships. It is no wonder that people often resist change.

However, Smith cautions against regarding human responses solely as a barrier to change. For leaders who pay attention to social issues, these responses provide valuable feedback and help to implement a more successful system.

HISTORICAL PERSPECTIVE

The early history of library automation can be divided into three phases, the Developmental Phase, the Operational Phase, and the Integrative Phase. The development phasse was the period of early experimentation up to the early seventies. During this period a small number of institutions engaged in automation projects. While management hoped that systems could be transferred from one institution to another, this was not the case with these early efforts. Libraries did not have similar computer operating systems, they did not have standardised procedures, and they could not agree on outputs.

However, the development of the MARC record was a significant development that allowed libraries to communicate bibliographic records in a standard format. The operational phase, in the mid-to-late seventies, saw the expansion of automation in a wider variety of libraries. Vendor-supplied systems, shared computer resources, and networking made this possible. Since, libraries were no longer forced to develop their own systems from scratch, it was an easier and less expensive task. During this phase most library automation projects still focussed on discrete tasks, such as check-in or circulation. Operational areas were not integrated, and the overall workflow stayed basically the same, "it has been utterly possible to use the automated system as inefficiently and ineffectively and with as little knowledge of what is going on as with the manual system". Montague proposed that the next phase would be an integrative phase, in which the automation systems would cut across operational lines, actually change the way libraries do business, and improve service.

There were a number of obstacles during these stages of library automation:

- Lack of direction and oversight from library managers to systems staff;
- Lack of technical training for library managers;
- Failure to develop long-range plans;
- Lack of up and down communication between managers and staff;
- Lack of staff input;
- Lack of staff training;
- Lack of feedback mechanisms.

Overall, it appears that the several problems, training, oversight, input, feedback, all involved a general lack of communication.

MIGRATION—SECOND GENERATION SYSTEMS

Since, many libraries, including Notre Dame, have or plan to migrate to second generation library systems, it is important to consider whether the obstacles are the same. One view is that they are not the same. Migrations are said to be easier than initial implementations. Although there may be some staff apprehensions, staff morale is reported to improve. A significant advantage is that second-time buyers have a better understanding of what they want in a system, and focus more on quality and customer support, instead of low bids. There is one potential source of resistance, which is never present in an initial automation project, that is a hostile 'soon-to-be former vendor.' Another important distinction is whether the library is migrating after successful implementation of a system which simply no longer meets their needs, or whether the library is desperately seeking a new system after a failed effort.

The reaction of librarians to this viewpoint is to be mixed. Some libraries have reported a very similar degree of 'techno stress' during migration projects, with similar emotional responses. Staff are required to change procedures, and in many cases the new procedures are not clear-cut—of course, the procedures in the 'old' system were not clear-cut in the beginning either. On the other hand, the majority of directors in a survey of 33 libraries that had undergone system migrations felt that 'promoting' the system change to the staff was unnecessary. This seems to be primarily due to staff frustration with the old systems, providing a clear motivation for change.

The worse the original system, the less staff resistance there was to migration. However, there were still some symptoms of technostress. Many found the vendors training programmes to be inadequate, consisting of 'canned' presentations were did not apply to local needs. Due to 'rush jobs,' the staff at many libraries did not have adequate time to become familiar with the new system before it was made available to the public. In one particularly egregious case, the staff and patrons were given access to the system at the same time. The staff 'hated this.' A two-month lead-time between staff and public access gave optimum results.

PRIVATE SECTOR EXPERIENCES

While library automation, per se, is not a major issue in the for-profit world, automation in general definitely is. As such, experiences in the private sector provide helpful comparisons. One very familiar theme from corporate settings in the need to consult with users prior to any sort of migration or automation project. This is true even with systems that are not central to the users' jobs. Gaudin relates several stories of companies that tried to implement new systems without consulting users. One case involved replacing a mainframe e-mail system with a desktop system. After the company spent $3 million, the employees rejected it because it was not fast or stable enough.

In another case, FedEx introduced a scheduling system without consulting their own employees. This became one of the issues in a potential strike against the company. One manager pointed out the importance of remembering that 'users might like their old systems'. This is an important lesson for library managers to remember in a migration, especially when the original system was basically successful. Even a failed system may have features the employees liked. Another illustration is provided by Norman's study of a failed automation effort. An attempt to introduce the CASE system in a management information firm provides valuable lessons for both sectors.

The goal of the CASE project was to establish a 2-1 ratio of CASE workstation usage among the MIS staff and achieve a 10 to 15 per cent increase in productivity. The project is considered to be a failure, because people are not using it. The company has lost business to competitors who do use the system. Norman identifies a number of factors in the CASE implementation, which contributed to its failure.

From the beginning, the decision to implement CASE was made by a small high-level committee, without involving staff.

There was a successful pilot project, following which the company attempted to expand the system.

Their main methodology was a staff-training programme. Management assumed that if they provided training, the programmers would use the system.

While the training was described as 'adequate,' it was informational only, and there was no effort made to change attitudes. The most critical barrier identified in the study was the high learning curve for using CASE. Management did not make any effort to reduce this learning curve. Instead, each work group that attempted to use the system had to learn it on their own. There was no sharing of tricks or shortcuts, or any help given by those who had already started using the product to new users. Interdepartmental friction and a rigid chain-of-command that stifled communication between units prevented this type of cooperation.

A related factor was the lack of any visible benefits or rewards for using CASE. Instead rewards were based on completing projects under-time and under-budget. Since, CASE is intended to increase productivity, it might seem that this would reward its use. But "this means that the rewards are indirect and totally dependent upon the successful use of the tool". In conjunction with the high learning curve, this becomes a negative incentive – the system is likely to slow production in the short-term, until the learning curve is past. If the programmer fails to learn it quickly, rewards are lost rather than gained.

THEORIES AND STRATEGIES FOR CHANGE

In discussing theories of organisational change, many theorists divide changes into different types. Before delving too deeply into specific strategies for change, I would like to examine the relationship between library automation projects and descriptive theories.

CONTINUITY

In the Age of Unreason, Handy tells us that "Change is not what it used to be". He distinguishes continuous and discontinuous change. Continuous change is gradual and predictable, with one situation leading into the next. This is relatively comfortable for most people. But he asserts that the changes in the workplace now are discontinuous. That is, changes are abrupt and unpredictable, and hence, far less comfortable. Handy frequently links discontinuous change to technology. As such, it is easy to reach the conclusion that a library automation project is a discontinuous change.

People who worked with paper switch to online systems, and their jobs are altered or even eliminated. But we should not be too quick to classify it this way. Particularly in the early automation projects, automated tasks were substituted for manual tasks on a one-to-one basis. Because of this, there was no drastic change in the overall workflow; even when specific tasks were drastically altered. It could be argued that automation has had a more significant impact since, that time, as library systems have become integrated.

CALM AND TURBULENT WATERS

Robbins focuses on the frequency of change. He uses two metaphors, 'calm waters' and 'whitewater rapids.' In the calm-waters scenario, change is the exception. Most of the time is spent in a state of equilibrium, until some crisis forces a change. After the change is past, the organisation regains a new state of equilibrium. In the white-water scenario, change is continuous, though in a different sense than Handy uses the word.

There is no state of equilibrium; instead one period of change is followed directly by another. It is very tempting to identify library automation projects with the 'calm water' metaphor. In fact, Saunders uses a very similar model in her article on library system migration. First various forces bring about a need for change, which requires unfreesing process. This is followed by a period of instability. When this is over, the library establishes a new state of equilibrium, as new patterns and procedures are frozen into place. Because automation efforts are not made frequently, this model appears to be a good match.

In an original automation project, the library has been using a manual system as long as it has been in existence. Once the project has been completed, the library will continue to use the new system indefinitely. Even in a migration project, the library may have been using its old system for many years, and certainly would hope the new system would be long-lived. One potential problem with this model is that it ignores the wider picture of overall changes. At the same time as a library is contemplating an integrated library system, the staff may be dealing with new online indexes, electronic journals, e-mail systems, computer operating systems, and even a building renovation.

Taken in this larger context, the white water metaphor seems more appropriate to the library environment. It is often not just the project at hand that causes problems for staff and users, but the 'unrelenting demand' of changes in many areas. Another issue is the continuing change following the implementation of an automated system due to new releases and upgrades to the system.

Even after a new system is fully implemented, it may not be as 'calm' as the old manual system. One significant problem with the white-water model as a model for change is that it suggests a reactive style of management with unplanned changes. But most library automation and migration projects are planned, as are many of the other changes affecting the library staff. This model seems most apt for dealing with the external changes impacting an organisation.

THE FOUR MOTORS OF CHANGE

Van de Ven and Poole give a more fully fleshed taxonomy of change. They identify two crosscutting distinctions, the level and the mode of change. The level of change is whether the change involves single or multiple entities.

The mode of change is either prescribed or emergent. A priori changes are planned, predictable or follow set rules or patterns. Emergent change is discontinuous and unpredictable.

This combination yields four 'motors of change:'

- Life-cycle (single entity, prescribed);
- eleological (single entity, emergent);
- Dialectical (multiple entities, emergent); and
- Evolutionary (multiple entities, prescribed).

While these motors can be separated in theory, most real-life changes involve interaction between them. The four motors model provides a more complete description of organisational change, and avoids over simplification problems. If we examine library automation projects in this e-context of the four motors of change that Van de Ven describes, as suggested, find rather complex interactions. The teleological theory, which is characterised by planning and goal setting, provides the closest description of the first stage in an automation project. Libraries may have a variety of motivations for undertaking an automation or migration project.

In the case of migration, this might include negative factors, like dissatisfaction with the current vendor, as well as positive ones, like a desire to expand capabilities. These motivations provide the Aristotelian final cause for the project. Most libraries engage in goal setting activities, such as compiling lists of desired features. This stage may be described as teleological in Van de Ven's scheme because it primarily involves one entity and the process is emergent. At the beginning of this stage, it is not clear where it will finish. Although the process is planned the goals are identified during the process, and may provide a dramatic break with the existing manual or automated system.

The dialectical motor may be present to a lessor extant, as different stakeholders interact with each other, and occasionally present conflicting goals. This teleological description fits most, but not all migration projects. For 79 per cent of cases in a migration survey, the projects were planned. But in some cases, the libraries did not have time to develop plans due to legal or financial problems. In those cases, the teleological motor would only apply in a trivial sense, if at all.

Those cases are obviously not ideal scenarios. Towards the end of the selection process, the library must compare its goals and desires to the actual systems available. At this point, the process could be described as dialectical, involving the library and the vendors who would like to supply the system. Vendors and librarians both regard this process as different for migration projects compared to first-time automation efforts.

In a first-time automation, libraries tend to rely on numerical evaluation of vendors' proposals and claims. In migration projects, libraries find site visits to be the most effective way to evaluate quality and hands-on work issues. At some point either during the final selection process or shortly after a vendor is chosen, the process shifts to a life-cycle model. The life-cycle motor is also primarily concerned with the library as a single entity. At this point, the plan, which was developed in earlier stages, becomes the guide for the process.

The library engages is a series of steps that were laid out in the plan, possibly on a strict timeschedule. This includes all of the steps technically necessary to implement the system as well as steps to prepare the users. This process is imminent in, or prescribed by the plan, and is much more predictable than the earlier stages. The library may have even planned for contingencies. Once the actual conversion in done, and the new system is live, the process become somewhat less predictable. Procedures that worked on paper or in test may fail under the pressure of real-life use.

While none of the motors seem to be completely dominant at this point, the evolutionary theory is closest. Procedures that work 'survive' while others are discarded. The changes may still be described as imminent, however, because they are constrained by the system. The others motors continue to play some role, as plans are made and carried out, and different stakeholders disagree on various issues. The dialectical motor may become dominant from time-to-time as the vendor announces new releases, or the library recommends enhancements for the system. At these times the possibilities for change are less constrained, and the results become more emergent.

STRATEGIES

The authors who describe actual automation projects also list key lessons and make recommendations. There are a number of general, and some very specific, suggestions along with a couple of common threads. One of the common threads is communication. Whether it is between management and employees, between systems and users, or between the employees at large, it seems that more communication is always better. A related thread is the need to involve the users in the process as early as possible. Several of the authors suggested that users should be involved at the very beginning, during the selection process. Montage, Norman, Gaudin, Hallmark and Smith all cite lack of user involvement in the selection or planning stage as an obstacle to successful implementation. Since, these two threads stand out, we may conclude that if any overall strategy is too be effective, it must include a high level of communication and user participation.

STRATEGIES FROM THE CASE IMPLEMENTATION

Norman described three change strategies in his evaluation of the CASE implementation. These strategies could be used independently or in conjunction with each other.

Rational-empirical

This strategy focuses on training and information. It is presumed that teaching people to use the system and providing a rational explanation of why it is better will lead them to use it. This strategy could easily be applied to a library automation or migration project, as many of the authors indicated the importance of training programmes.

Normative-educational

This strategy focuses on group strategies for promoting acceptance of the new systems and providing motivation to use it. First, identify the attitudes that create resistance, and then develop programmes to change them. This is similar to developing training sessions in the rational-empirical strategy. The difference is that the sessions are intended to develop positive attitudes instead imparting information.

Power-Coercive

In this strategy individuals are induced to use the new system by the threat of loosing their job or other benefits. This can be a fairly direct approach to implement change, but it also runs a high risk creating bad feelings, job dissatisfaction, and tension between management and employees. Threats, whether explicit or implicit, will also add to the fear and anxiety already identified as an obstacle to change. A variation of this strategy can be applied in a positive way by offering employees incentives for change. While this is can be regarded as a power-exercise it is less confrontational. In the CASE implementation, the main strategy that was applied was the rational-empirical strategy.

The normative-educational strategy was largely ignored, and the power-coercive strategy was inconsistently applied. Management made statements that employees were required to use the system, but did not follow-up when it was not used. Management also did not provide any direct positive incentives. This strategy may also be applied to library systems in the sense that when the old system is shut-off, employees will not be able to perform their duties without using the new system.

PHASED IMPLEMENTATION

Saunders recommends a strategy of phased implementation. The idea of this strategy is to minimize the impact of the new system has on staff by introducing modules in a gradual fashion. For example, a library might implement cataloguing or acquisitions functions first, and circulation latter. This strategy has some advantages. Successful implementation of one module should increase staff willingness to use another. Also, management can deal with the staff in smaller groups, concentrating on the area currently being automated, instead of dealing with all areas at once. The chief drawback of this strategy is found when the current system is already well integrated.

In this case, phased implementation may mean that user's are initially presented with a system that has fewer features than their previous system. There may also be technical difficulties that preclude phased implementation, as the two systems are not likely to communicate with each other well, if at all. Where it is usable, this strategy should also be combined with other strategies. Saunders specifically emphasises the importance of training and communication issues.

PARTICIPANT-ORIENTED CHANGE

Zeffane advocates the strategy of participant-oriented change, which is based on the premise that change works best when comes from the bottom up rather than from the top down. One reason for this premise is that if the employees introduce change, then they will not have an authority figure to rebel against. It is also based on the idea that collegial affiliation is a positive motivation for change. That is, employees will be more motivated to help with a changes initiated by someone at, or close to, their level. To use participant oriented change, management needs to shift the responsibility for change awayfrom themselves and towards the employees.

This strategy goes beyond considering the users' needs, or soliciting input, to actually delegating authority to the participants. This strategy takes advantage of the fact that the employees who are closest to the hands-on work have the most detailed knowledge about it. This also frees the upper management from concentrating on this level of detail, and to concentrate on overall strategic planning. This strategy may not be effective in all types of organisations.

There are some essential elements for participative strategies to work. First, the employees given responsibilities for change must be well informed. Second, the employees must understand and agree with the mission of the organisation. Unless these requirements are met, management cannot expect that the decisions will be beneficial to the organisation. The third requirement is that this style of change must be supported by the organisation culture. The management must be comfortable with this type of delegation.

MANAGEMENT FUNCTIONS

The traditional roles of management are planning, organisation, coordination and control. These can be applied to these change strategies.

RATIONAL-EMPIRICAL

The rational-empirical strategy is primarily concerned with dispensing information, presuming that the plans for change have already been made. It involves the organising function of management, in the sense that the managers determine what information needs to be given to which employees in order to implement the changes. It also involves the control function, in that the management is seeking to influence behaviour through the information it dispenses.

NORMATIVE-EDUCATIONAL

The normative-education strategy is concerned with influencing attitudes and behaviour. As such, it involves the control function of management, but in an indirect manner. That is, rather than controlling behaviour directly, the management attempts to instill attitudes which are likely to result in the desired behaviour. Like the rational-empirical strategy, it also involves the coordinating function, as managers decide who should be involved in which programmes.

POWER-COERCIVE

The power-coercive strategy concerns the management role of control in a straight- forward fashion. It is mainly concerned with seeing to it that the schange decisions are carried out as directed. To ensure this, it dispenses rewards or penalties to individuals or groups depending or whether they have implemented the changes. In the extreme, employees who fail to change are fired.

PHASED IMPLEMENTATION

Phased implementation involves both the planning and coordinating functions to a large degree. Planning includes determining the order in which to implement the modules and setting timetables for each phase. Coordination includes meshing together the efforts of different groups associated with each phase, and ensuring that each module is integrated with the previous ones when it is brought into production. As more modules are brought into the 'live' mode, coordination becomes essential in order to see that the different areas function smoothly.

PARTICIPANT-ORIENTED CHANGE

Participant oriented change involves the coordinating function of management. Since, much of the planning and decision making is delegated downward to the staff, management must integrate these plans and decisions. This is particularly important when implementing an integrated library system, as the activities of staff in one area will have more impact on other areas than they are accustomed to. The actual delegation of these responsibilities to employees involves the organising function. Determining how and to whom these responsibilities are delegated is in important part of the change process.

This may involve organising employees into self-managed teams, work groups, or interdepartmental task forces. How these groups are organised, the amount of authority they have, and how they will interact with each other are crucial decisions.

The participant oriented change strategy provides the best overall approach to managing library automation and migration projects. Of the strategies which have been outlined, it offers the highest degree of employee communication and participation. These are the same areas that caused the most problems if they were inadequate. One of the chief advantages of this strategy is that it involves the users of the system at the earliest possible stage of the project. That is during the teleological process of identifying reasons for the project and setting goals or criteria for a new system. Involving the employees at this stage reduces the need for normative attitude-adjusting sessions latter in the process.

This is not to say that managers who adopt this strategy can just ignore employee attitudes later on. Change will still be stressful, and people may still resist it at various points. But, management will not have to invest as much effort in convincing staff that the new system is better if the staff were involved in selecting it. The rational-empirical strategies of employee training programmes will still have a role to play, as the process moves on. As was demonstrated in the failed attempt at implementing the CASE system, this strategy is not sufficient by itself. But users must learn how a new system works if they are to use it at all. Within the overall context of participant oriented strategy, other employees provide much of that training. With their hands-on experience, employee led training can be more effective than vendor supplied 'canned presentations'.

This also promotes an atmosphere in which employees will be comfortable sharing their learning experiences, tricks and shortcuts following implementation. The other two strategies, phased implementation and power-coercive can not be recommended across the board. The power-coercive strategy is divisive, and is likely make the change harder instead of easier. This strategy aggravates fears about job security, which is one of the sources of change anxiety. While a degree of control needs to be maintained, a threatening approach is not desirable as a general strategy.

The strategy of phased implementation will be helpful for some situations, but not for all. For libraries currently using manual systems or automated systems that are not integrated, this method may help to ease the transition. For libraries that already have a well-integrated system, it could create even more chaos. Within the context of participant-oriented change, the choice of whether to include it rests with the employees who actually work with the system.

PROBLEMS OF LIBRARY AUTOMATION

In old civilizations like India and other Asian countries, libraries have been in existence since, early times. Recent political and economic developments which have brought about various types of changes in these countries are also reflected in the evolution of information systems. India's educational system had a definite elitist slant in mediaeval times and the legacy of feudalism during the British period nurtured this trend. Libraries with very rich collections of manuscripts and other rare reading material were mainly the property of the elite. The infrastructure of the country was, moreover, not congenial for the kind of wide-ranged library system which one can envisage today. Library development has shown a marked change since, 1947. It is estimated that India now has approximately 90,000 libraries of different types. The Indian library system can be divided into four broad categories: public, academic, special and national libraries.

PUBLIC LIBRARIES

India is divided into states, union territories, districts, sub districts and villages. The state central libraries serve as public libraries. There are also district central libraries, but village libraries are few and far between. Libraries and library development are included in the broad category of education which, under India's constitution, is considered the responsibility of each state. Some states, namely Tamil Nadu, Karnataka, Andhra and Maharashtra, have very progressive library legislator! which provides the necessary framework and finances for developing good state public library systems. Despite this, only a very small percentage of the total population of India has access to public libraries.

ACADEMIC LIBRARIES

There has been some improvement in the standards and status of university and college libraries in recent years. At present there are more than 100 universities and 8000 colleges throughout the country. Most of these have library facilities which are in different stages of evolution. School libraries, however, have not been given sufficient attention. Primary and middle-level schools rarely have library facilities, and barely 20 per cent of the secondary schools have adequate library facilities.

SPECIAL LIBRARIES

These are mainly the boon of the post-independence period. Government departments, research institutions, business and industrial houses have established libraries for their own research and development programmes. Currently there are approximately 1500 of these special libraries in India; they are also at different stages of development.

NATIONAL LIBRARIES

Under the national library system, the National Library of India is situated in Calcutta. There are regional libraries of national stature at Bombay and Madras. Some libraries on special subjects are now being given the status of national libraries, e.g., the National Medical Library and the Indian Agricultural Research Institute Library. The major activites of the different categories of Indian libraries are mainly routine work, such as acquisition, circulation, smanagement, processing, reference and bibliographic service, periodical holdings, information retrieval, inventory, and so on.

The services and techniques utilised in the different libraries, however, tend to make these activities very cumbersome and slow. The acquisitions of most libraries are done independently, and involve unnecessary duplication of work and lengthy procedures.

Cataloguing and classification methods differ from one library to another and are generally time-consuming and labour-oriented. This is very confusing for the users as they must thus switch from one classification and cataloguing system to another when using more than one library.

There is also a lack of bibliographic control at the national level. The Indian National Bibliography suffers from a large time lag. Almost all library activities involve long hours of manual work, tending to make library service very unpopular. Therefore, users still cannot envisage a librarian as a giver of information but consider him or her a custodian of books. In order to improve the services of libraries, application of newer methods, such as information, computer and communication technologies, will be needed. I am only concerned here with computer applications in libraries and believe that for efficient functioning of our library systems, as suggested, need automated services at some point. But serious thought must first be given to which areas will be automated, while keeping in mind the national need.

NATIONAL SCENE ON LIBRARY AUTOMATION

Elaborate automated library systems are still far off in the context of any developing country. The priorities of each country may vary, but the emphasis is mainly on providing the basic necessities of life to its people. The use of computers started in India with the establishment of computer centres at the Indian Institute of Technology and the Tata Institute of Fundamental Research during 1963-64. At present, there are about 400 computers installed at different places. The size and variety range from a Honeywell 400 to the large IBM 370/155 and DEC-1077.

These computers are used mainly for scientific calculations, business applications and data processing for decision-making. Computerised library activities are found in very few organisations, and consist primarily of the use of spare capacity of available computer facilities suitable for off-line use.

Although the number of institutions which have computerised library applications is still very small, the awareness of quickly and easily available information is gradually increasing.

I conducted a short survey in this connection through a questionnaire and personal letters sent to different institutions and business houses outside Delhi which have automated library facilities. Like most questionnaire surveys, this one did not prove very successful, although the personal letters I received from some heads of institutions were encouraging. I then visited some of these major institutions in and around Delhi, and interviewed many of those who work with computerised systems or have plans to do so in the future. The institutions visited were: Indian National Scientific Documentation Centre (INSDOC) and National Informatics Centre, New Delhi; Bhabha Atomic Research Centre (BARC) and Tata Institute of Fundamental Research (TIFR), both in Bombay; Documentation Research Training Centre (DRTC), Hindustan Machine Tools, Ltd. (HMT) and Central Machine Tools of India (CMTI), all in Bangalore; and Small Industries Extension Training (SIET) Institute and the Administrative Staff College of India in Hyderabad. Altogether, twenty-five organisations were contacted. While this survey may not have been comprehensive in its coverage, the extensive discussions gave a good picture of the problems facing Indian organisations using library automation.

INSDOC, NEW DELHI

Automation is used for indexes, a union catalogue of serial publications, data processing of Indian periodicals on science and technology, directory compilation, and the centralised acquisition of periodicals for thirty laboratories. The IBM 360 model 44 and IBM 1620 are used on a rental basis.

TIFR, BOMBAY

Automated operations include recent additi ns list, cumulative classified catalogue of books, weekly list of preprints/reports of TIFR, catalogues of progress serials and periodical holdings, and evaluations of journals from the user's point of view. The CDC 3600/160-A and DEC- 1077 computers are available in-house.

NATIONAL INFORMATICS CENTRE, NEW DELHI

Bibliographic citations are available so far only for books in its library; periodical articles are to be added. The centre is a member of INSPEC tape service and a subscriber to a patent bibliographic information system since, 1978. The HP 2 I/MX is used.s

INDIAN INSTITUTE OF TECHNOLOGY (IIT), MADRAS

In collaboration with INSDOC, IIT handled the CHEM/SDI project, a computer-based SDI system using the IBM 370 model 155 system and the CA Condensates data base. The CHEM/SDI uses a subset of CAN/SDI software made available by CISTI through UNESCO for its regional pilot project. The project was also handled by NISSAT during 1976-77. The project has been upgraded into a national SDI service using CAC, INSPEC and Compendex data bases; there are more than 500 users.

DRTC, BANGALORE

This group provides education and training, and researches methods for designing and developing computer-based information systems and services. A set of fourteen programmes have been developed in COBOL for creation and updating of the data base, retrieval of bibliographical references in response to specific queries, provision of current awareness and SDI services, retrieval of factual data, provision of a referral service, the semi-automatic generation of a microthesaurus, indexing, and so on.

BARC, BOMBAY

The computer unit of the Library and Information Services of BARC uses the in-house computer Honeywell 400 and BESM 6 for information processing. Computerisation activities include: preparation of a monthly current awareness bulletin, Bibliography of Current Reports; an SDI service offered regularly to some seventy-five users since, May 1972; retrospective litreature searches based on stored data on request from BARC scientists; subject bibliographies; documentation lists; compilation of periodical holdings; loan and issue system of the library; and inventory. An SDI service using the DEC-1077 computer of the National Centre for Software Development and Computing Techniques and TIFR and the magnetic tape output of the International Nuclear Information System is being developed and will be in operation shortly.

SIET, HYDERABAD

This group has automated its Index to Product Profile, which is a list of literature available in the library to April 1976. A TDC 12 is used on a rental basis.

CMTI, BANGALORE

Here work is being done on automating an in-depth index of periodical articles to compile a data base. They have a PDF/ 11 in-house. Future plans include classifying the trade catalogue.

HMT, BANGALORE

Currently under consideration is computerisation of the comparative product profile and the issue system. The computer used is ICL 1903.

PHYSICAL RESEARCH LABORATORY, AHMEDABAD

This laboratory has a mechanised catalogue of its publications holdings and information retrieval facilities. They have discontinued CAS and plan to start SDL In use is the IBM 360 model.

OTHERS

Some industrial units, such as Asian Paints India, Ltd., Hindustan Zinc, Ltd., and Institute of Armament Technology have automated catalogues of holdings. Along with all these ventures in automated library services, a weeklong on-line demonstration of the ESRIN/RECON data base system used at Frascati, Italy was arranged at TIFR during September 1976, with the assistance of UNESCO and the European Space Agency. The Frascati centre had 10 data bases and provided access to about 7.5 million references at the time.

NISSSAT

Although these organisations and some other institutions have plans for future automation, the most important plan in India is the National Information System for Science and Technology (NISSAT). In 1971, for the first time, it was seriously felt that a strong national network of documentation and information services was necessary to meet the evergrowing need of scientists and research scholars. The Indian government created the high-powered National Committee on Science and Technology in October 1971. A report submitted by the committee in 1973 recommended the establishment of NISSAT under the Department of Science and Technology. The NISSAT network comprises a sectoral system, a regional system and other specialised services.

SECTORAL SYSTEM

All major areas of science and technology are classified into information sectors based on discipline, mission and product, e.g., leather technology, machine tools, drugs and Pharmaceuticals, etc., Organisations of national stature, such as INSDOC, Defence Scientific Documentation Centre, BARC and Small Enterprises Documentation Centre, will continue to provide services at the national level.

REGIONAL SYSTEM

Because of India's size, more than one sectoral centre for each discipline is necessary. Therefore, regional centres will act as NISSAT contact points. These will be located in major areas of research, development, educational and industrial activities, e.g., one centre is in Delhi and another in Bangalore. Similar centres will be started in Bombay, Calcutta, Madras and Kanpur.

OTHER SPECIALISED SERVICES

Efforts such as the experimental computer-based SDI services of IIT and the on-line demonstration of ESRIN/ RECON at TIFR fall into this category. The ESRIN/RECON demonstration was a success and attracted considerable interest, and there is now a proposal to provide permanent terminals at Bombay and Delhi. NISSAT also includes plans to create and maintain data bases on themes of national importance, and technical and statistical data banks on such topics as minerals, resources, etc. NISSAT is the most ambitious information network plan in India today. Although the social sciences have also been brought within its fold, its emphasis is mainly on science and technology.

Therefore, social scientists are of the opinion that a parallel system for the social sciences and humanities would make the circle effectively complete. India's library system, as described earlier, can make use of automation in different ways for more effective functioning. Thus far, the specialised libraries and documentation centres have laid emphasis primarily on information retrieval, which has been substantially developed in many areas. The major need for computerised bibliographical control has not yet been s.

TABLE: Possible Computerized Activities for Different Types of Libraries

	Types of Library			
	Activity	**Public**	**Academic**	**Specia National**
Acquisition and distribution	×	×	×	×
Management and administration	×			×
Cataloguing and bibliographies		×	×	×
Periodical holding information retrieval		×		×
Circulation	×	×		

*Special libraries include documentation centres

PROBLEMS OF LIBRARY AUTOMATION

Presently, the system of computerised library activities is growing, although it is still in its infancy compared with system in developed countries. While at the sophisticated research level there appears to be general acceptance that computerised library activities will lead to increased efficiency, the hindrances to such a goal are many and any efforts to achieve it are the exception rather than the rule. Computerised library service is likely to be beset with technological, economic and attitudinal problems peculiar to most developing countries.

TECHNOLOGICAL PROBLEMS

Technological problems include both the hardware, i.e., the computer as an instrument for information processing, and the software, i.e., the methodology which is applied. The major problems faced today in terms of the hardware are due to the variety of computers being used in different types of research and business institutions. The computers, manufactured by various firms are not compatible. Developing countries sometimes receive sophisticated technology like computers as gifts from more developed countries; these often become obsolete from the manufacturer's point of view.

Such machines are not only unsuitable for most complex work but any technical problems which come up cannot be repaired. Information retrieval work requires machines more sophisticated than those manufactured indigenously, and few imported machines are capable of handling information retrieval applications. The random access facility and disks large enough for storage of bibliographic information are not readily available. In most institutions, organisational goals receive priority over the library's requirements, meaning that the librarian must use the computer available rather than what is actually required according to specifications. Library activities in all institutions are done through sharing disk space as well as computer time. Therefore, when the storage capacity is not large enough to accommodate various types of data, bibliographic data are given the lowest priority. On-line facilities are rare in India. In fact, only TIFR's library has access to an on-line terminal for bibliographic data, the DEC-1077 computer of the National Centre for Software Development and Computing Techniques.

The communication infrastructure of India is still not suitable for extensive on-line information facilities; the telephone system is not reliable enough to support an effective network facility. Software problems arise because programmes must be developed in terms of the machine on which they are to operate. Therefore, the incompatibility of equipment tends to make the software incompatible as well, especially when programmes are written in machine or assembly language. While using languages which are not machine-bound, such as FORTRAN, COBOL, ALGOL, etc., may seem like a solution, in actual practice such languages cannot be interchanged without suitable modifications.

A software package developed for the IBM 360 model 30 would require many changes not only in the programme but also in the programming language if it were to run on any other computer. Development of a programme suitable for the available machine is therefore preferable to acceptance of a package programme. This makes the development and use of package programmes difficult and leads to a lack of standardisation in programming language as well as in output. Machine-readable data bases are byproducts of international information network systems and are available on magnetic tapes.

These are useful in building information resources and for retrospective search and current awareness services. Again, however, the tape service is expensive and suitably sophisticated computers are scarce. The data bases have a standard format which requires extensive changes to fit existing hardware and other system requirements. Also, relevant bibliographic information has to be selected from the data base and stored. Often this storage space is scarce and expensive.

ECONOMIC PROBLEMS

The major obstacle for any innovations in developing countries is the lack of resources. The initial cost of establishing a computer system is beyond the reach of most organisations and institutions. Library and information processing is done either with spare computer capacity made available by the institution itself, or with computer time hired from another institution. The cost of hiring computer time and storage space is very high and often cannot be justified at the management level by cost-benefit analysis. At IIT, for example, CPU time per hour costs ₹ 1000 for educational purposes and ₹.2000 for business and industrial use.

Moreover, the computer provides only paper printout, and the paper often costs more than the processing. Few developing countries can afford the smachinereadable data bases, either. The tapes are very expensive and because foreign exchange is involved in subscribing to them, it is even more difficult for most organisations in India and other developing countries to afford them. The annual subscription rate of one data base is now $8000. Library tasks often overlap and their peculiar nature seldom makes the advantages of computerisation seem very convincing in the light of cost-benefit analysis.

In India, libraries and information centres are attached to government organisations or research institutions, so library services cannot be calculated on a profit/loss basis. Long-term benefits have to be kept in mind while justifying such services. The libraries that have computerised some of their services or operations often have not taken such steps as a result of serious thought. Computerisation has a glamour of its own in the minds of many librarians. Overly enthusiastic librarians often run uneconomical programmes, producing lengthy listings, for instance, in the name of computerised service.

Often the manual method is used concurrently with the computerised system because of a lack of faith on the part of staff and users. The duplication of work and the cost involved in these cases is obviously unjustifiable; the librarian should know which aspects of service should be mechanised. An example of an economically viable computerised library activity is the centralised acquisition of periodicals in operation at INSDOC. This facility serves thirty laboratories, which not only frees the facilities from the tedious task of periodical acquisitions but also eliminates the cost of duplicate purchasing.

ATTITUDINAL PROBLEMS

Computers appear very awesome to developing countries. They are powerful machines which can perform many functions and therefore offer a solution to the many types of manual inefficiency which often plague the developing countries. Among librarians there are two different attitudes towards computerised facilities. One group is taken in by the glamour of modern technology and believes that computers can perform miracles. Members of this group often give insufficient thought to the real value of the computer to the organisation/institution and make uneconomical, haphazard use of the facility.

The other group, still the majority in developing countries, lacks knowledge of the potential and consequences of library automation. There is constant tension between this traditional librarian group and the 'new-wave' librarians. Professionals of the majority group do not realise that computers cannot replace human intelligence. Due to the accuracy essential for data input in library services, the librarian/information scientist is indispensable. The National Library of Calcutta conducted an experiment to computerise the Indian National Bibliography in 1968.

The scheme failed, however, because labour unions opposed it fearing retrenchment of library staff. Among developing countries, the attitudes of India's librarians are typical. They are not confident about automated services.

Library staffs should therefore be trained in programming and thus be made aware of the work involved in automation. They will then realise that utomation will not take away their jobs. They will also realise that computers are machines which have their limitations as well as their advantages. The communication gap between the librarian and the computer specialist is another major hindrance in establishing any effective automated system in a library.

There is often disagreement among the librarian, the programmer and the systems analyst. Librarians should be trained in computer programming and computer specialists should be versed in the special needs of library automation. Only then can a common language evolve among the three and a project be started. Administrative personnel assume a very important role in decisionmaking. Their enthusiasm, support and conviction can help realise any new plan, just as their apathy and lack of understanding of the need for accurate and speedy information can jeopardise any effort. Although many things have taken a favourable turn in India, the majority of those at the management level unfortunately are not conversant with the development of information science and are unaware of the important role of information in all areas of national development.

This very often results in insufficient planning, which in turn curbs the enthusiasm of imaginative information scientists and librarians. Due to this lack of appreciation, priorities are poorly ordered and funds are not well allocated. Administrators also have a tendency to underestimate or overestimate the capacity of automation. Any information system or service is planned for the best possible benefit to its users. Unless the users are mentally prepared to accept a new system, however, it cannot be effective. Indian users are still unfamiliar and overawed by computers, so computer awareness and interest has to be fostered to enable proper utilizaton of a system.

They should neither overestimate computer capabilities nor be afriad of interacting with the computer systems. Another obstacle is that, because batch processing systems are still in use in India, there are bulky printouts in monotonous type faces and formats which prove to be a headache not only for the librarian, but also for the user. There is no dearth of manpower in systems analysis and computer programming in India. We are already exporting software packages to countries that find them less expensive than developing their own.

Library automation is still neglected, however; it is an area which has not attracted young people with appropriate expertise. Training should be given to both the librarian and the computer specialist about each other's functions and possibilities. Both INSDOC and DRTC conduct courses on automated systems in libraries. Under the forthcoming NISSAT plan, steps are being taken to build the requisite technical manpower.s

Moreover, the Indian government's Department of Electronics is developing training programmes for the National Informatics Centre. There are two main objectives in training for library automation: to orient the programmers and system analysts to writing programmes suitable for automating library facilities, and to persuade librarians to accept the utility of automation and teach them to prepare accurate inputs to make the system sworthwhile.

RECOMMENDED IMPROVEMENTS

- The computers used in India should not vary so widely. Production of computers with special capacity for library automation should be taken into consideration.
- Government policy has taken a positive step in establishing large computer systems, with one sophisticated central computer capable of handling complex information to be connected to indigenous minicomputers. The National Informatics Centre project dealing with agricultural and other governmental data processing is designed along siilar lines. Such plans should be pursued.
- Indigenous, inexpensive library package programmes are very necessary. These should be usable on a large variety of machines and be capable of handling different activities in the library. The MARC format would be ideal if it could be adapted for the smaller indigenous computers. DRTC is currently involved in preparing software packages for information retrieval.
- The international data bases are being used by some organisations. However, these are expensive and often not applicable to Indian research needs. Indigenous data bases with our specific requirements should be prepared. Core periodicals in each subject relevant to India, and litreature from important Indian periodicals, should be used as input for such data bases.
- A national standard or common language for bibliographic information exchange is necessary. Efforts are being made to achieve a standard language compatible with any international standard.
- Training of personnel, i.e., proper communication among the librarian, computer programmer and systems analyst is very important. Courses offering training in library automation are being taught, but there is a general need for better understanding among these three architects of library automation.
- User awareness and orientation is very much needed. The users scomprise managerial policy-makers as well as the research scholars and regular clientele of a library. The need for, as well as the possibilities of, automated library facilities have to be highlighted by professionals and experts in this area. A few seminars and workshops have been conducted at New Delhi and Bangalore, namely the UNISIST workshop in August 1975 and the Indo-U.S., seminar in 1977; however, little else has been accomplished in this area.

Do we need library automation now? In developing countries the problems are many and though they are not insurmountable, they are certainly very difficult to face and live with. The most pertinent question for our profession in this regard, however, is whether we really need computerised library services on a large scale. A colleague from Bangladesh said: "The library and information sciences are a 'least-priority area' in this country. Only 20 percent of the people can write their names. There is an acute shortage of readers.... Most of the nation's resources are utilised for food, shelter, flood control and health problems."

Although the Indian situation differs from that of Bangladesh in many ways, the first priority of any developing country is to provide the basic necessities to its people. Litreacy and education are still at the primary level. Information of a very basic nature, such as the essentials for healthful living, must be presented in simple terms and communicated through media which will reach the people. Library activities of even the most primitive nature will not be within the intellectual grasp of most people unless the library is turned into a proper communication centre. We cannot take as our model the community information centre as developed in the West. The economic and social problems here are so acute and diverse that no one model for all parts of the country can be established.

As discussed earlier, library facilities may have to cater to a sophisticated and highly academic clientele in different organisations even though it is a minority. Libraries have had a long tradition here, but academia has yet to develop a tradition of data-oriented search for knowledge. The concept of libraries as storehouses of books remains very strong. Information is still sought in books rather than in microform. Because profundity in knowledge is the tradition of Eastern culture, the modern trend towards fast, accurate information is still not expected.

That is exactly what a computer is supposed to provide for a scholar. Information is often treated as a commodity in the West. In industrially developed countries it is believed that any information which is economically profitable should be considered worthwhile and made quickly available. Can the same be said of the Indian situation? In highly developed industries, such as Hindustan Machine Tools, Ltd., a survey of the information needs of engineers revealed that the time factor was not important. Even if the information were received a day or two after it had been requested it would still be accepted and used. The competition in the industrial field is not sufficiently keen to require immediate information. Industrial research is done in a relatively leisurely fashion in India.

At the documentation centre of SIET, the need for computerising library and information work has not been perceived. I quote: "As of today, there does not seem to be adequate justification for computerising library and information work here. Our intake is not that sizable, nor are the demands on us yet so enormous that we should think of using computers."

The genuine need of the country is to provide usable resources for spreading litreacy and to develop libraries at the school and college levels in order to give students the opportunity to acquire the taste for information. I do not intend to belittle the efforts to build a sophisticated information system such as NISSAT. India is a country in which the levels Proposals of development are varied in different areas. Its planners must therefore cater to the needs of each area in its own right. On the whole, however, our priorities still differ. Both librarians and clientele must be made information- conscious before anything as expensive, sophisticated and dumb as a computer can become a tool in their hands.

SUPPORTING MULTILINGUALITY IN LIBRARY AUTOMATION

Today's libraries have automated their everyday transactions such as acquisition, cataloguing, and circulation. An automated library appears to users as an online public access catalogue (OPAC) through which they can quickly search and obtain the desired information. Such systems support bibliographic search according to author name, title, publication year, etc., and provide free text and keyword facilities. Hence, computer systems have replaced the librarian's role as intermediary between user and library, and expert systems that simulate this role providing general information to the user have been developed.

Moreover, the application of AI to information retrieval has recently attracted the attention of information scientists. Advanced applications of natural language processing (NLP), such as machine translation, have already improved the capabilities of several systems in this area. Translation-based methods for translingual information retrieval require the query be translated into the target language. In this case, full-fledged machine translation is not applicable. Experience shows that of three well-known translation approaches, which is dictionary-based term translation (DICT), example-based term translation (EBT), and example- based term-to-sentence (EBS), DICT presents the best solution for queries consisting of isolated words, or at best, short phrases. Other approaches in information retrieval are concerned with systems with cross-language functionality. A few of them, especially in trade trans-actions and Web-based information services, make use of a controlled language in order to improve the recall and precision rates. The majority of these systems utilise free text retrieval.

The corpus-baseds approach, MIRTH, supports within- language retrieval in English and Chinese and in specific areas, such as computing, linguistics and litreature. The limitations of this system lie in the lack of a complete linguistic tool to guide translation, as well as in the absence of any maintenance system to deal with tasks such as add, insert, delete, update, replace, and sort links with their keywords. Knowledge- based information retrieval is used in Gilarranz where the features of the EuroWordNet multilingual lexical knowledge base are described.

However, although both approaches tackle the cross- language functionality of the retrieval, they do not consider as yet the localizability of their system by adopting, for instance, an internationalised methodology in their design. In addition, libraries have not paid special attention to multilingual features of OPACs, despite the fact that it is a serious problem.

The National Library of Canada was one of the first libraries to offer multilingual access to its users, in the form of controlled bilingual that is English and French, authority files. It is also worthwhile mentioning the ETHICS project that produced an OPAC with multilingual user interface and help screens and a subject index in three languages.

So far, multilinguality in OPACs has been dictated by the needs of a specific multilingual community and restricted to the provision of bilingual or multilingual lists of controlled terms such as controlled authority files, subject headings, and thesauri. Multilinguality as a potential problem for the common user of the library was only explicitly investigated in the NORDINFO survey. According to the results of this survey, multilingual access to online catalogues can improve remarkably the quality of the provided services. Similar user surveys were undertaken by the Central Library of the University of Patras, the Library of the Spanish Agency of International Co-operation, and the Municipal Library of Patras.

The main outcomes of the surveys have been as follows: in a conventional OPAC by using controlled:

- Searching or uncontrolled terms is time consuming, requiring repeated effort from the user who in a lot of cases remains unsatisfied.
- The libraries express their interest in a multilingual access tool, because they understand that multilinguality poses problems to their users as well as to the interconnection with libraries from other countries.
- The translation tool, if any, should be able to retrieve information from the title, subject, and author fields.
- An important indication is that the specific national conditions should be taken very seriously into account, especially with respect to dialects and unofficial languages. A very good example is the relatively high interest of the Spanish library in the Catalan language.

These surveys were aimed at an analysis of the attitude of the users towards the OPAC they used and investigation about their eventual need for a multilingual tool.

The results of these surveys are essentially independent of the sex, educational status, familiarity of computer use, and frequency of the use of the OPAC by sample users.

The analysis of the results was very illuminating:

- Approximatsely 75 per cent of the users were either moderately satisfied or dissatisfied with the results of their searches in the OPAC.
- Over 80 per cent of the dissatisfied users noted that the hits werenot in the user's native language or that the search was based only on a single language;

- Approximately 70 per cent of the users were interested in bibliographies written in foreign languages.
- 65 per cent of those who used books in only one language considered being able to search in multiple languages either useful or very useful.

In this chapter, we present Translib, a multilingual interface system to library automation systems. It takes full advantage of tools such as bilingual dictionaries, conversion tables, terminology lexica, intelligent thesauri, and simplified translation tools in order to support multilingual access to library catalogues.

This system stemmed from the integration of new and existing multilingual information tools and has been tested in existing medium-sized bibliographic databases in Greece and Spain. The tools are characterised by a high degree of modularity and user- friendliness that allow easy and low-cost maintenance. The following section contains an overview of the Translib system, describes briefly its architecture and gives its basic features.

OVERVIEW OF TRANSLIB

The global Translib perspective is shown in figure.

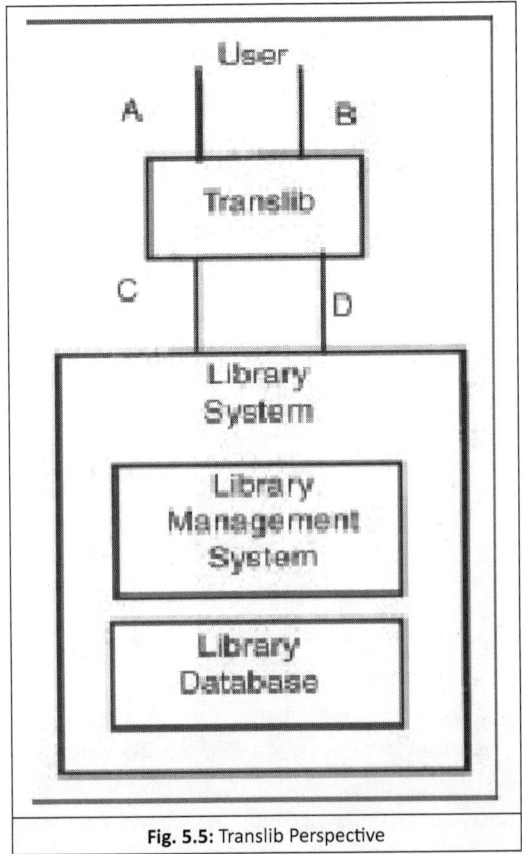

Fig. 5.5: Translib Perspective

Notes: A: Input, message, search, output language (S).
B: Presented query results, fields, labels, message.
C: Search topic query D: Received records.

The user interacts with the Translib module by choosing the languages to be used as well as the search fields, the search key topics, and the type of searching to be initiated. Translib combines all this information to support multilingual access to the library system, by sending it a query for each key topic and receiving from it the records that match the users' query. Finally, Translib presents the query results to the user in the preferred language as well as the predefined search field labels, information windows, and all messages. If the query results are empty, Translib allows the user to repeat the search using synonyms, super categories, or subcategories of the search keywords. Translib is an OPAC that provides the users with a capability for multilingual access to library catalogues.

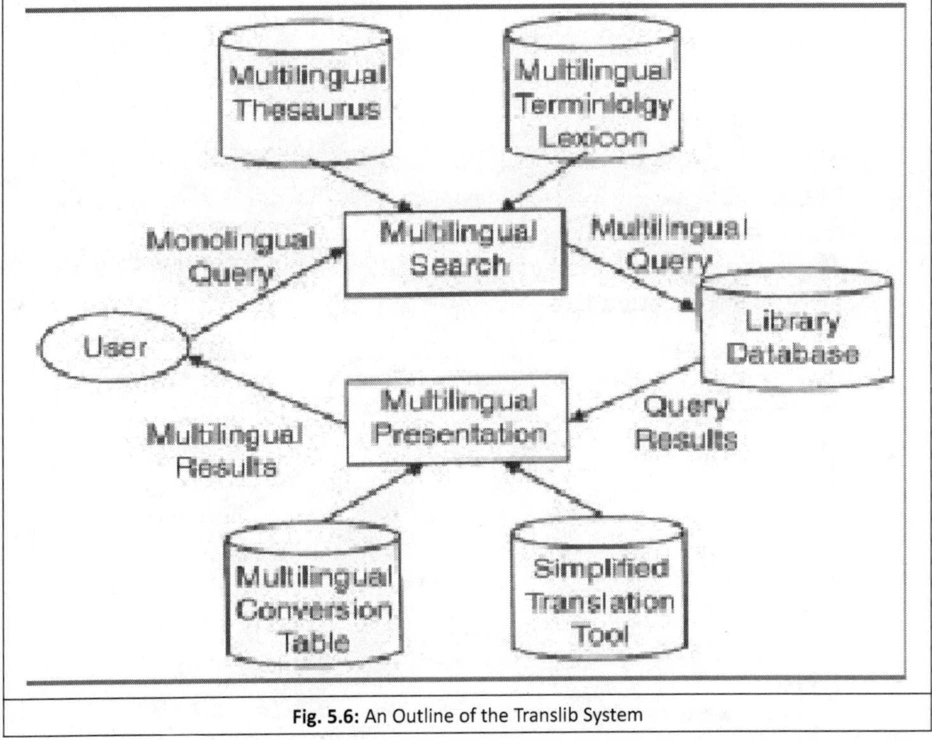

Fig. 5.6: An Outline of the Translib System

Translib is fully implemented, runs under Windows 95, and currently supports three languages, that is English, Greek, and Spanish. These three languages are considered to be sufficient to both demonstrate the feasibility of this type of multilingual access and to highlight potential problems in the future adoption of additional European or non-European languages. An outline of the system is given in figure.

Translib offers bibliographic information retrieval, whether from a local library database or from remote databases, through servers that support the Z39.50 standard, that is, a standard specifying a client/server- based protocol for information retrieval that was originally proposed for use with bibliographic information.

One of the main characteristics of Translib is its ability to be easily integrated into the majority of library automation tools.

In order to achieve this objective, we have had to consider seriously the following problems:

- All library automation systems do not use the same type of database;
- There will be libraries that will not give access to their databases to developers' groups so that they can be connected with the Translib system.

Our solution has been to integrate a Z39.50 client tool into Translib. Thus, the Translib interface can now connect with any library automation system that supports the Z39.50 protocol. All other processes, such as retrieving bibliographic information in any language and translating the titles and keywords into English are also supported by the new Translib with the Z39.50 client module.

Translib comprises two basic tools:

- The multilingual search tool that supports the retrieval of multilingual bibliographic information; and
- The multilingual presentation tool that allows multilingual presentation of the retrieved information.

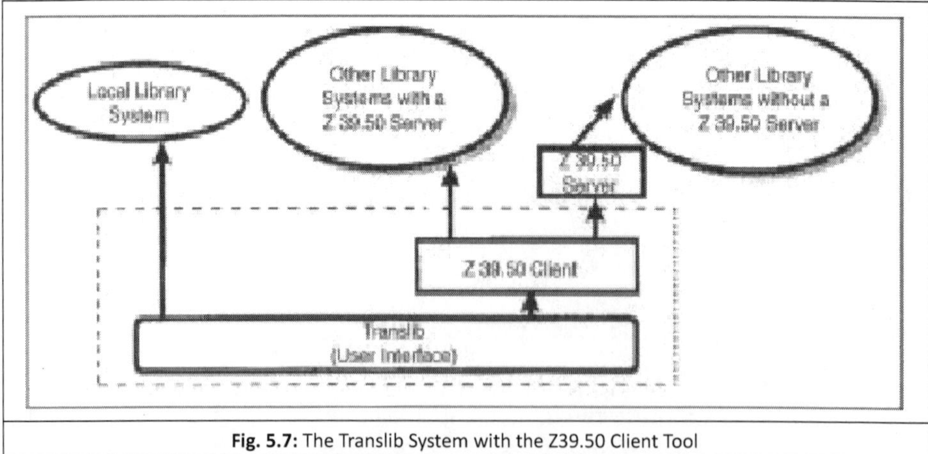

Fig. 5.7: The Translib System with the Z39.50 Client Tool

The following subsections illustrate the features of these tools.

By taking advantage of them, Translib offers the following facilities in contrast to up-to-date library systems:

- Localisation of user-interface is supported.
- The user is able to enter a query in his/her native language and search for

entries that match this query in all the possible languages for which there is at least one entry in the current database.

- The retrieval of all the entries for a given query as well as for its synonyms in any language is possible. Furthermore, the user is able to indicate the type of search, which can be based on narrower and/or broader terms of the query.
- Finally, translation of the retrieved books/journals titles and keywords in any language is provided in order to give the user an idea of the content of these books/journals.

MULTILINGUAL SEARCH TOOL

This tool enables the user to enter the query in the language (s)he prefers and select the languages in which the matching entries have to be found. Essentially, this tool performs a conversion from monolingual to multilingual queries.

The user can select the input language and the search languages (s)he prefers:

- **Input language:** The language used to introduce the search criteria, that is, the title, author, publication year, etc.
- **Search language(s):** One or more languages in which the user wishes to find some documents matching his queries.

Furthermore, the user is able to determine the search depth by selecting to search with synonyms, and/or narrower terms, and/or broader terms of the search criteria.

The multilingual search tool utilises:

- A multilingual terminology lexicon, allowing the search of keywords in several languages, and
- A multilingual thesaurus, enabling sophisticated bibliographic information retrieval by means of synonyms, narrower and broader terms.

An example of broader and narrower terms of some keywords is shown in table.

TABLE: Example for Broader/Narrower Terms

Keyword	Broader Terms	Narrower Terms
Academic	Journal	–
Book	Publication	Manual, Introduction
Brochure	Publication	–
Industrial	Journal	–
Journal	Publication	Academic, Industrial
`Manual	Book	Tutorial, Reference
Publication	–	Book, Brochure, Journal
Reference	Manual	–
Tutorial	Manual	–

The search criteria can be specified in a search screen. A search can be started for publications that match the search criteria. For instance, if the user types part of a keyword in the field Keyword and selects the button Keyword Search, the application searches the multilingual terminology lexicon for keywords to match.

Fig.5.8: Search Screen

The results can be shown in a drop down list. Then a keyword from this list can be selected.

The multilingual terminology lexicon contains a list of key topics in three languages, that is, Greek, English, and Spanish.

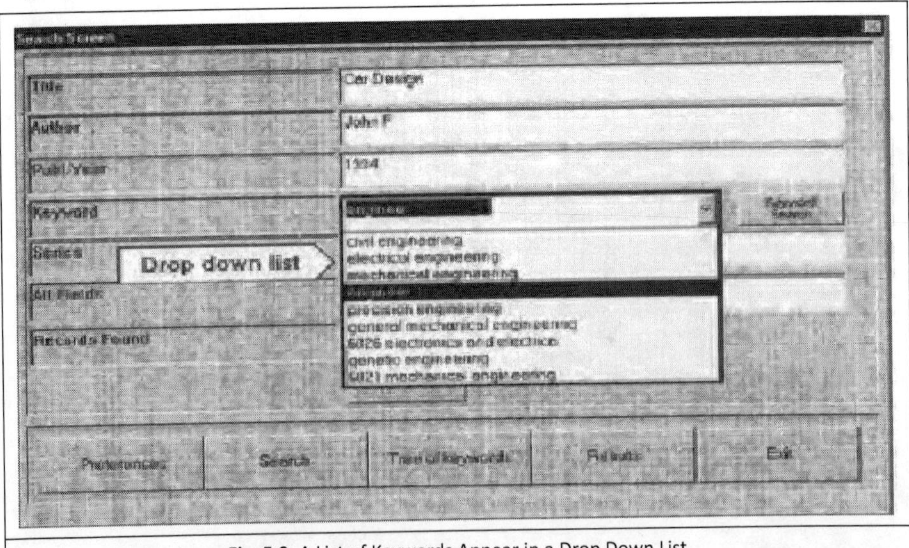

Fig. 5.9: A List of Keywords Appear in a Drop Down List

A search for publications that match the search criteria is executed when the button Search is selected from the Search Screen. The number of publications found appears in the field Records Found.

The search fields are as follows:

- **Title:** The title or part of the title of a publications.
- **Author:** The name or part of the name of an author.
- **Publishing year:** The issuing year of a publication.
- **Keyword:** A Keyword or part of a keyword.
- **Series:** The series or part of the series of a publication.
- **All fields:** All the fields associated with a publication.

When a search starts, all the fields associated with a publication are searched for a string that matches the string typed in this field. The application searches for matching publications by using the 'OR' operator between data entered in the search fields. For example, if the search criteria contain the title 'Democracy', the author 'Cat Stevens,' and the keyword 'Ancient Greece,' a search is performed for publications with the title 'Democracy' or publications written by "Cat Stevens" or publications that contain the keyword "Ancient Greece." Finally, fields that are left blank are not included in the search criteria. For example, if the user leaves the fields Publishing Year, Keyword, Series, and All Fields blank, the search criteria include only the fields Title and Author.

MULTILINGUAL PRESENTATION TOOL

This tool allows localisation of the user interface as well as presentation of the library database entries matching the user query in any of the sup- ported languages. This can be achieved by translating publication titles and keywords, if needed. Particularly, the user has the capability of selecting the Message Language and the Output Languages (s) he prefers.

More specifically, these languages stand for:

- Message language: The language used for presenting labels and messages to the user as well as help screens.
- Output language(s): One or more languages used for presenting the query results. The multilingual presentation tool utilises.
- A multilingual conversion table, converting labels and messages into the Message Language.
- A simplified translation tool, supporting the translation of book and journal titles and/or keywords into the specified Output Language(s).

A CLARIFYING EXAMPLE

The following clarifying example aims at further illustrating the definitions. Let us assume that the user selects English as the Input Language, English and Greek as the Search Language(s), English, Greek, and Spanish as the Output Language(s), and the search criteria contain the keyword democracy. The multilingual search tool searches the library data- base for entries containing the keywords democracy and the multilingual presentation tool lists the publications that match these keywords and translates their titles and keywords into Spanish as is shown in table.

TABLE: A Clarifying Example

Inpot Language	**Search Language (r)**	**Output Language (s)**	
English	English, Creek	English, Greek, Spanish	
Search Criterla (Leyword)	Search for	Results	
Search Crkerla (Leyword)	Search for	Remarks (Title)	(Keywords)
Democracy	Democrayc sympoxpaxia	Democracy in Ancient Greece (English translation)	Democracy, Ancient Greece
		La Democracia on Greecia Ancigwa (Spanish translation)	Democracia. Grecia Anagwa
		II sympoxpaxia own spzaia Ellsisa (conigmal language)	sympoxpaxia, spraia Ellssa

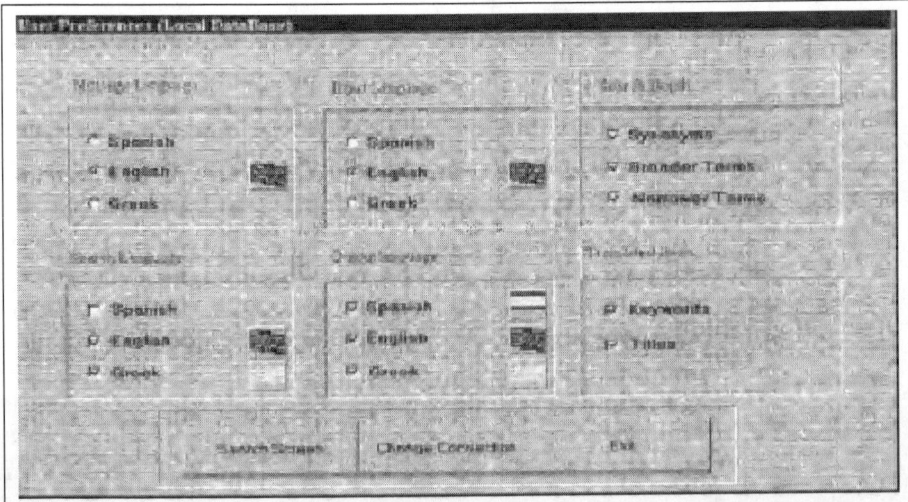

Fig. 5.10: The Screen Where the User Enters His/Her Choices for This Search

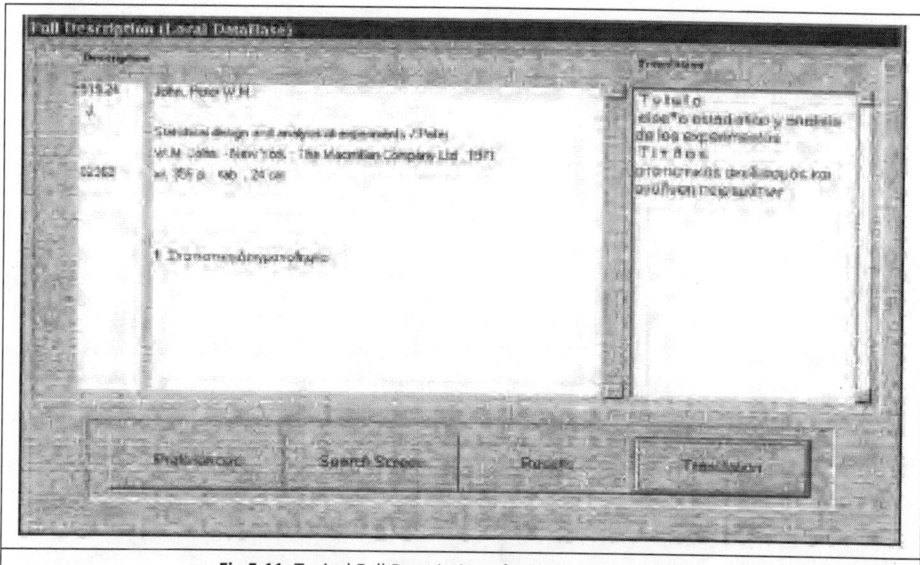

Fig.5.11: Typical Full Description of a Retrieved Book Entry

Figure shows a typical full description of another retrieved book entry that also contains its translation from English into Greek and Spanish.

The system can also present the query results by using a short description of the retrieved book entry. At times a query can retrieve multiple records. In this case, the records are presented to the user ranked in alphabetical order. The original language of these records is also clearly labelled.

MULTILINGUAL RESOURCES

Translib is a system built through the integration of both new and existing information tools. Since, the advantages of the use of reusable resources are well known, we tried to utilise general purpose and state-of-the-art resources where possible, in order to avoid the excessive cost of building a resource from scratch, as well as to ensure the quality and the adequacy of the resources.

MULTILINGUAL THESAURUS

After an extensive market survey and taking into account the advantages and disadvantages of using an existing multilingual thesaurus, we decided that EUROVOC suits the needs of the Translib system. EUROVOC is based on ISO-5964/85, which is an international standard for the development of multilingual thesauri. EUROVOC is a multilingual thesaurus, which was originally built specifically for processing documentation of the European commission. It is implemented in the official languages of the European community.

The edition we used was compiled in 1994 in nine languages:

- Danish
- Dutch

- English
- French
- German
- Greek
- Italian
- Portuguese
- Spanish

Our version of EUROVOC contains only the following languages, which cover the needs of the current Translib system: English, Greek, and Spanish. All these languages have equal status—each descriptor in one language necessarily matches a descriptor in each of the other languages.

At the specific level of descriptors and non-descriptors, the internal structure of EUROVOC depends on semantic relations:

- Scope note (SN)
- Microthesaurus relationship (MT)
- Equivalence relationship (UF, USE)
- Hierarchical relationship (BT, NT)
- Associative relationship (RT)

The EUROVOC thesaurus covers all the subjects that are of importance to the activities of the European community institutions:

- Politics, international relations, European communities, law, economics, trade;
- Finance, social questions, education and communications, science, environment;
- Business and competition, employment and working conditions, transport, energy;
- Agriculture, forestry and fisheries, agri-food stuffs, production;
- Technology and research, industry, geography, international organisations.

We mainly focused on the use of the following subjects: economics, trade, finance, education and communications, science, business and competition, production, technology and research, energy, industry, without excluding the others. Technically speaking, EUROVOC is a single file that contains a significant number of terms relevant to the subjects. EUROVOC's architecture consists of a number of micro- thesauri. Each one of them consists of a set of terms for a given topic.

Each record in a micro thesaurus has several fields indicating the relation between the records and the terms themselves in the nine languages of the European community. Each term is given in two forms for each language. Two terms can have a hierarchical relation, that is, one can be narrower or broader than the other. Each record in the EUROVOC file fits on a single line. The fields occupy fixed positions on the line and have concrete names. Our goal was to transfer the data from EUROVOC to a commercial database. A set of routines was thus developed for the compilation of the EUROVOC thesaurus into files with a special format that can be easily read by database procedures. Several files constitute the Translib multilingual thesaurus derived from EUROVOC. There are separate files for the terms of each language. The terms are stored in the same order in each of the three files, so that the files are matching. If a term has no equivalents in one or more languages, there is a blank line in the corresponding position. The line number of each term in the files is used as a unique code during the building of the tree, which is stored in another file and does not include the terms themselves.

Thus, the multilingual thesaurus of TRANSLIB has been designed as a simple ASCII table file which contains all the material that is included in the EUROVOC thesaurus. Software was written in order to be able to extract the terms and relevant terms from this huge data store quickly. B+ trees algorithms have been used to make the extraction process as quick as possible.

In conclusion, the multilingual thesaurus helps the user retrieve bibliography related to the relevant keywords (s) he has entered, as its sophisticated search mechanism automatically builds the tree structure of the keywords in all the preferred search languages and sends a complex query to the data-base. In the case where the user does not use the thesaurus, he may not retrieve all the available bibliographic records, since, the keyword he uses to describe his query may not be the same as that used by the librarian for the record classification.

Even when the user enters a query which has no keywords in the multilingual thesaurus, it is possible to update it by means of an editing tool that caters for a number of data entry fields, such as New Keyword, Related Keyword, Keyword Language, Kind of Relationship, etc.

MULTILINGUAL TERMINOLOGY LEXICON

The result of another extensive market survey encouraged us to adopt EURODICAUTOM as a terminology tool. However, after we had completed the decoding of EURODICAUTOM, a problem emerged. The terms of the multilingual thesaurus were entirely incompatible with those of the multilingual terminology lexicon. This meant that the library database could not be searched using keywords from the multilingual terminology lexicon, nor by using synonyms, broader or narrower terms of it. The solution decided on was to create a multilingual terminology lexicon from the terms of EUROVOC.
This was analysed into two sections:

- The informative part; and
- The data retrieval part.

The former mainly consists of a file containing all the terms that are used as keywords in all the Translib supported languages. This file is a three- column file, which contains the same term in each line for all the supported languages. The latter uses a binary search algorithm to achieve maximum efficiency. In this case, it was necessary to create a sequence of files, which contain an upper case description of terms and a numeric label used to locate the term and its description in all languages.

The multilingual terminology lexicon helps the user choose one term in the preferred Input Language, and search the database for this term as well as for all the equivalent terms in all the preferred Search Languages. Again the user can check the new keywords to be included in the multilingual terminology lexicon by means of an editing tool that caters for a number of data entry fields, such as New Keyword, English Keyword, Spanish Keyword, Greek Keyword, etc.

MULTILINGUAL CONVERSION TABLE

The multilingual conversion table is responsible for the interaction between the user and the system in the user's preferred language. It contains all the label fields, messages, and help screens of the user interface in all the supported languages and provides the user with the ability to both choose the language of the user interface and effectively change it at runtime according to his/her preferences. It is independent of any actual data store that is used as the base of the information storage. Finally, the information kept in the Multilingual Conversion Table is logically grouped into three files, one for each language.

A new file can be used for a new supported language, so that maximum source independence and management can be achieved. The Multilingual Conversion Table is stored at the client's site in relational database tables. One table in the database includes the label fields, messages and on- line help information in the three languages supported by the project. Its internal structure is compatible with a future addition of equivalent terms in other European languages.
The table has the following attributes:

- **Code:** A unique number that acts as the tuple's identifier.
- **Kind:** Reflects the type of the user interface item that is contained in the tuple.
- **EngContent:** Content in English.
- **SpaContent:** Content in Spanish.
- **GreContent:** Content in Greek.

When the user wants to customise any label fields, messages, or help screens, this can be accomplished through an editing tool that caters for a number of data entry fields, such as code label, Greek message, Spanish message, etc.

LIBRARY DATABASE

The Translib system follows the UNIMARC standard so as to be easily portable to all library automation systems following the same standard. Regarding the library database, two medium- sized bibliographic data- bases have been utilised. The Greek one possesses about 10,000 titles concerning mainly engineering and computer science sectors, while the Spanish one possesses about

20,000 titles regarding political and financial topics. More specifically, the Greek library database contains 5,500 Greek titles, 3,500 English titles, and 1,000 titles in other European languages. On the contrary, the Spanish library database contains 12,000 Spanish titles, 6,300 English titles, and 1,700 titles in other European languages. Both data- bases were considered appropriate and representative to test the performance of the TRANSLIB system.

SIMPLIFIED TRANSLATION TOOL

The translation of the titles carried out by this tool should give the user an idea of the content of a retrieved book/journal. Even when the translation is not completely correct, it should help the user understand the subject of the document.

Translating titles is, in general, easier than translating a whole sentence or even entire texts. The simplest title is a single noun while the most complex one may be a whole phrase. Few titles, however, are composed of a long phrase, i.e., the combination of both noun and prepositional phrases. Furthermore, a title is selected carefully by the author to represent the content of a book.

This fact means that a title must not be ambiguous in order to be comprehensible immediately by the reader. In most cases, syntactic or referential ambiguities can easily be solved. Additionally, titles are usually typed carefully by the editors of a book, so that no grammatical or syntactic errors occur. Needless to say, the titles of books and journals are totally different from those found in a newspaper. Looking at the translation of the titles from a computational point-of-view, the translation process can be facilitated further by making a set of assumptions.
These can be described as follows:

- Translation from one language into another is realised via English which is used as an interlingua.
- For each title only one translation is provided. In addition, a set of titles may have the same translation.
- Only the main title of a bibliographic entry is translated. Subtitles, version numbers, etc., are ignored.
- The titles are considered to be linguistically correct. Hence, syntactically incorrect interpretations are ignored.
- No semantic and/or pragmatic information is used. All the titles are referred to the scientific domain of engineering and computer science. Moreover, for every word in the dictionary there is only one translation.
- Finally, the input as well as the output files of the translators are ASCII files containing one title per line. If a title cannot be translated, the output file contains an empty line for it.

The selection of an interlingua was adopted to achieve system robustness and reduce the translation costs. Translation between a pair of languages implies translation to and from interlingua. Additionally, the upgrade of the system with a new supported language would only require the implementation of a ling ware for the new language, able to provide translation to and from interlingua. We selected English as the interlingua, since, it was found that it is the most widespread foreign language among the OPAC users. In fact, our interlingua is not plain English but an artificial language, that is, an abstract form that represents the structure of the title based on the English translations of its consisting words. Thus, the interlingua is composed of a list of structures that correspond to the words of the title. These structures have the following form in PROLOG language for a given word of the line: where English-Lemma is the English translation of the Greek or Spanish word of the title, and Part-of-Speech, Number, and Case are the corresponding morphological information of this word in the source language.

Taking all the points into account and in order to strengthen our claim that an AI-based translation tool is needed in the translation process, we tried two translation scenarios. We first implemented a simple word-by-word translation, in order to simplify the translation process and consequently minimize the computational cost.

The evaluation of this approach has shown that only a small percentage of the translated titles were comprehensible, particularly in translations from Greek to English, Spanish to English, and vice versa.

We decided, then, to implement a more sophisticated approach that would improve the quality of the translations by taking advantage of AI- based methods.

For instance, the following tools for the implementation of the Greek and English ling-ware were used:

- An existing two-level morphological analyser for morphological recognition and synthesis of Modern Greek words. This is a PC KIMMO-based analyser that was designed for general purpose morphological analysis of Modern Greek and uses a 30,000-word lexicon. According to the two-level morphological model, the surface form of a word is derived by applying a set of rules to the lexical form of that word and vice versa. The main advantage of such a model is that these rules are applied in parallel and in both directions, that is, surface to lexical form and lexical to surface form. In linguistic terms, the two- level rules are not processing rules, but more like the realisation rules of stratification linguistics.
- A public domain two-level morphological analyser for morphological recognition and synthesis of English words. This is a PC KIMMO-based analyser that was designed for general purpose morphological analysis of English and uses a 10,000-word lexicon.
- Two syntactic parsers built from scratch and able to recognise the basic phrase structures of the title. These parsers are based on a context-free grammar model consisting of 28 rewriting rules for each one of them. As an example, the four first rules of the modern Greek grammar are given below:

— Title Ü Phrase.
— Title Ü Phrase, Conjunction, Phrase.
— Phrase Ü NounPhrases, Prepositional Phrases.
— Phrase Ü Prepositional Phrases.

- Two medium-sized bilingual morphological dictionaries containing words from the scientific domains of engineering and computer science found in the Central Library of the University of Patras. In particular, these dictionaries stemmed from the PC KIMMO-based dictionaries and translation information as well as new words from the previous scientific domains were added.
- Similar tools for the implementation of the Spanish ling ware were utilised.
- Just to illustrate the translation process from a Greek title into a corresponding English one, we give below the sequence of transitions among the different tools:
- Greek Title→Greek Morphological Analyser→ Morphologically Analyser Greek Title
- Morphologically Analysed Greek Title→Greek Syntactic Parser→Abstract Syntactical Form→Abstract Syntactical Form→Greek-English Translator,
- Greek-English→Bilingual→Dictionary→Translated→Abstract→F ormTranslated→AbstractForm→EnglishMorphological→Analyser →Morphologically Correct English Title
- Morphologically Correct English Title→English Syntactic
- Parser→Well-Formed English Title

An outline of the simplified translation tool is shown in figure.

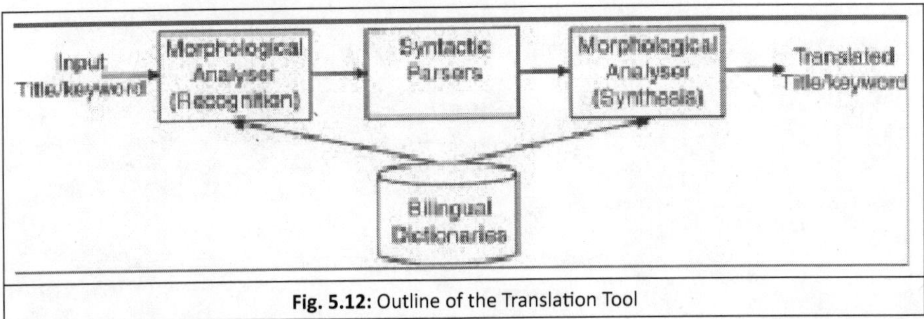

Fig. 5.12: Outline of the Translation Tool

In contrast to the word- by- word translation, approximately 86 per cent of the translated titles are comprehensible.* It has to be noted here that the quality and comprehension of the provided translations depend on the scientific domain of the library database.

For instance, the Greek word has two meanings:

- Series; and
- Line.

Hence, if the library database comprises books/journals concerning the scientific domain of mathematics, then the former translation should be included in the bilingual dictionaries. Finally, an editing tool is used for updating entries in the English-Greek and Greek-English dictionaries. The user is able to update the nouns and adjectives that are included in the selected bilingual dictionary.

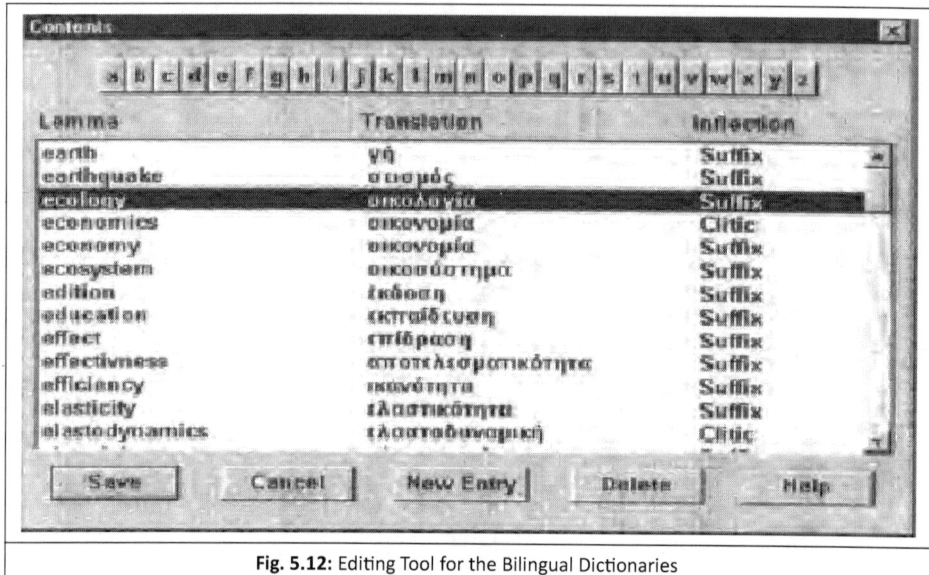

Fig. 5.12: Editing Tool for the Bilingual Dictionaries

A new entry may be inserted or an existing one may be changed or deleted. When inserting a new entry, the user must insert the new lemma as well as its translation. Additionally, (s)he should also select an inflectional category in order to determine the various word forms of the new entry.

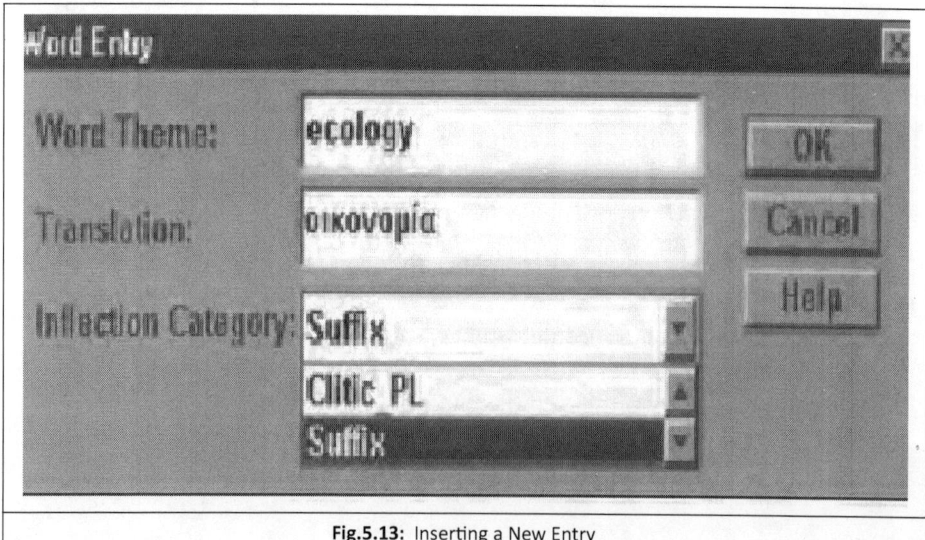

Fig.5.13: Inserting a New Entry

EVALUATION

The Translib system has been tested in the library databases in both Greece and Spain under real life conditions.
Two parameters were evaluated:

- The subject search, i.e., the proportion of citations found by the user referring to a given subject, and
- The user satisfaction, i.e., the impression of the user with respect to the quality of the service provided.

The first parameter was measured by means of the standard 11- point average precision for our DICT method. The 11- point average precision is a conventional performance measure for evaluation of text retrieval systems. Given a query, for recall thresholds of 0 per cent, 10 per cent, 20 per cent..., 100 per cent, the system assigns in decreasing score order as many titles as needed until a given recall level is achieved, and computes the precision value at that point. Then, the precision values of individual queries are averaged over all test queries.

TABLE: Recall- Precision Values for the DICT Approach

Monolingual Retrieval		Multilingual Retrieveal	
Recall	**Precision**	**Recall**	**Prcision**
0.0	0.90	0.0	0.63
0.1	0.86	0.1	0.50
0.2	0.93	0.2	0.45
0.3	0.80	0.3	0.39
0.4	0.77	0.4	0.34
0.5	0.72	0.5	0.30
0.6	0.68	0.6	0.23
0.7	0.86	0.7	0.21
0.8	0.52	0.8	0.18
0.9	0.50	0.9	0.12
1.0	0.35	1.0	0.10

Monolingual Retrieval

These averaged precision values can be further averaged over the recall thresholds, to obtain a single-numbered global measure. The resulting global average is referred to as the 11- point average precision. We carried out the measurement of the first parameter in the Greek library database, initially with the previous OPAC system and then with the Translib system. We used 1,000 test queries from the scientific domain of engineering and computer science. The input language for these queries was either Greek or English, and the search criteria comprised either a unique search field or a combination of two or more search fields.

The vast majority of these queries consisted of isolated words or short phrases. Only 15 per cent of the above queries formed long phrases. The recall-precision values for these two systems are shown in table.

The DICT approach proves efficient enough for queries consisting of isolated words or at best short phrases. The second parameter was evaluated by means of a short questionnaire which was used to gather the general impression on the system and its features.

This questionnaire comprised 27 questions, which were classified in four distinct parts:

- Personal information regarding the evaluator;
- Results on the use of Translib;
- Personal opinion of Translib.;
- Comments.

In some cases, the questionnaire reply boxes ranged from 1 to 5 by degree of satisfaction. Finally, a total of 42 library users filled the questionnaires.
They were selected on the basis of the following criteria:

- Encyclopaedia of Computers in Library Services
- To possess a good knowledge of English and/or Spanish;
- To have different sex and age;
- To be willing to participate in the evaluation process.

The results of the evaluation are encouraging and pinpoint the strength as well as the potential weaknesses of this system. Some of the most important results are listed below:
Multilingual Search:

- 95 per cent of the users performed multilingual searches in thelibrary database rather than monolingual ones.
- Approximately 45 per cent of the users felt rather satisfied or completely satisfied about the results of their search, while 9 per cent of them were dissatisfied.
- Less than 25 per cent of the dissatisfied users considered multilingual aspects not supported in Translib responsible for their dissatisfaction.
- Approximately 85 per cent of the users considered the search via the multilingual thesaurus more accurate and complete.

Translation of Titles:

- Approximately 80 per cent of the users considered the translationof titles rather useful or very useful.
- Over 55 per cent of the users considered the translations of titles comprehensible. Note that users with high familiarity with OPACs tended to be slightly more satisfied with the quality of the translation.
- Over 90 per cent of the users found the functionality of the translation component very easy.

Multilingual Presentation:

- Over 70 per cent of the users considered the system easy to use by anyone, not just experts.
- Over 60 per cent of the users considered Translib more friendly, useful, and easier to understand than other OPACs they had used in the past. It is noteworthy that users with a high familiarity in OPACs were considerably more satisfied.
- Finally, over 65 per cent of the users found the help and error messages of Translib clear, useful, and adequate.

As noted earlier, the selection of an interlingua affects the quality as well as the comprehension of the translation of titles. Hence, translations to and from English are more comprehensible than from Greek to Spanish and vice versa. Nevertheless, approximately 95 per cent of the performed translations are translations to and from English, since, the vast majority of the book/journal titles contained in a library consists of titles in the local language and English.

The satisfaction of the users with the multilingual thesaurus and the overall search results they obtained from the system in contrast to other OPACs was remarkable. The localisation of the user interface was one of the main reasons why the users favoured this system.

In conclusion, the reaction of the users to the Translib system appears to be closely dependent on their previous experience:

- Users find multilingual search very useful.
- Users with a higher familiarity with OPACs find Translib a simple, friendly, and easy to learn system. Users with a lower familiarity with OPACs find it more difficult to use Translib. This is a satisfactory conclusion, as Translib neither intends to replace OPAC nor makes its baseline operation simpler. It is simply intended to overcome the linguistic barriers posed by multilingual library holdings.
- Users appear to search for titles in languages in which they are familiar. For this reason they tend to show limited appreciation of the usefulness of the translation of titles, while they expect a better translation.
- Although the user reaction is positive, there appears to be room for improvement with respect to the terminology used, the help and error messages, and the way that the system keeps the user informed of what is being done at any time.
- The satisfaction of the users depends highly on both the Translib system as well as on the bibliographic database and the library holdings. As a result it is difficult to assess the impact of Translib on the quality of the search results. More extensive experiments would be needed for this purpose, preferably in a distributed, transnational bibliographic database.

CONCLUSION

As we described earlier, despite the fact that there are several OPACs supporting the automation of retrieving bibliographic information, only a few of them support some kind of bilingual or even multilingual access to libraries catalogues. In this chapter, we presented a system that aims at solving this problem. Translib allows multilingual search as well as multilingual presentation of the query results and consists of an integration of state-of-the-art existing information tools and tools built from scratch. The integration of these tools was a difficult task, since, the former were built for different purposes and, some of them, for different operating systems.

The multilingual functionalities of Translib help the user, to a high degree, improve significantly the results of a query and allow him/her to select the presentation of the results in the preferred language. For all these reasons, we feel that libraries, book trade enterprises, appropriate consultancy services and library schools can directly benefit from a system of this type. Translib should have a remarkable impact on the improvement of library services as well as on the easy access to the wealth of knowledge held in libraries. The results of its performance on the Greek library database and its pilot installation in the Central Library of University of Patras strongly encourage us to believe that it will have a successful commercial exploitation in the near future.

Our short-term goal is to endow Translib with the capability to support bibliographic information retrieval from remote databases through INTERNET servers. In addition, we plan to further improve the present system by adding new languages in the existing framework. Our long-term goal is to enrich it with new AI tools. In particular, we intend to provide the translation of entire abstracts rather than just the titles and improve the accuracy of the search results based on intelligent information extraction.

❐

7

Information Technology Impact and Library

INTRODUCTION

Information technology has transformed the whole world into a global village with a global economy, which is increasingly dependant on the creative management and distribution of information. Over the past decades the world has been experiencing significant changes in which the need to acquire, utilise and share knowledge has become increasingly essential. Now, in the 21st century, the age of knowledge and information is in its higher gear. This is an age when invisible knowledge and information take the role of prime movers leading all sector.

The World Bank has used metaphor "knowledge is development". Lack of knowledge is largely responsible for underdevelopment. In a knowledge and information-oriented society, creative brains become leaders of economy and knowledge workers are in great demand. If knowledge can be equated with development, then the wider the knowledge gap, the broader the development gap.

EMERGENCE OF INFORMATION AND KNOWLEDGE SOCIETIES

Some 10,000 year ago the early ancestor of mankind, subsisted by hunting and gathering, started to building agrarian societies. The old agrarian societies began their transitions to industrial societies in mid-18th centuries. Expansion of intellectual activities in industrial societies, such as industrial production, international trade and transactions, and technological advancement, stimulated mass distribution of education and creation of libraries. Industrial societies continued their enormous material development throughout the 20th scentury.

The information society has passed through four transformational stages of development, the most radical stage starting at the tail end of the 20th century. This stage has brought a never-ending revolution, particularly with the introduction of information and communication technologies. During this period, there have been unprecedented developments, profoundly affecting the social structure – the decline of manufacturing sector as compared to the prospering information-rich service sector is one example of such developments.

The concept of knowledge societies is often used to denote a development in or second generation of information society. Whereas the information society aims to make information available and provide the necessary technology, the knowledge society aims to generate knowledge, create culture of sharing and develop applications that operate mainly via the Internet.

The goal of knowledge society is to fill social needs, create wealth and enhance the quality of life in a sustainable manner. India is moving fast towards becoming an information society as the Government of India is paying due attention to the use of information technology (IT).

The Prime Minister of India constituted a National Task Force on IT and Software Development in May 1998 with the purpose of formulating a long- term National IT Policy to convert India into an IT software superpower. These steps are helping India to shift from an "economy of goods" to a "knowledge economy" or "knowledge driven economy".

The beginning of the knowledge society has been made through creation of parks and corridors, and the Prime Minister has given a mission of converting India into a "knowledge society" by the year 2008. Today, India is one of the largest exporters of knowledge workers.

ROLE OF LIBRARIES

In the modern knowledge society libraries have a new role and there are various types of library models. In the modern society, where the use of electronic services and Web-based information sources constantly increases, libraries are managed in a more democratic way, have more flexible communication system and work organisation, and their service development is based on the quality and user-orientation of services. In the modern knowledge society libraries have a new role and there are various types of library models.

These are as follows:

- Traditional library as a memory institution.
- Library as a learning and research centre.
- Library as a cultural and communication centre.
- Electronic library.
- Digital library.
- Virtual library as library without walls.

Libraries had been performed many important roles in the past agrarian and industrial societies. But those roles were limited in scope. In the 21st century, libraries have to perform pivotal roles in disseminating and sharing the culture of knowledge. In this age of knowledge libraries should be repositories of all of the knowledge and information accumulated by human kind.

They will have to store all kinds and forms of material and information and disseminate beyond the geographical boundaries. Today's advanced information technology is enabling libraries to accomplish this immense task. Exchange of knowledge has always been the most important objectives of libraries. Various systems have been developed to share and exchange the records of human knowledge.

Universal Bibliographic Control and Universal Availability of Publications are two major programmes of IFLA (International Federation of Library Associations and Institutions) to exchange knowledge world over. OCLC is the world leading library network in USA for sharing intellectual knowledge among academic community in all over the world. But libraries in the 21st century should fulfill more dynamic role. They should exchange knowledge and information with users inside and outside their country, thus going beyond their traditional reference and lending services. This would possible when libraries agreed to expand their roles beyond the geographical boundaries by using sate of art technologies.

The modern libraries certainly can not be passive repository for books and other printed materials. The opposite requirements of storing increasing collection in various forms and of maintaining easy access to most part of it can only be balanced by deploying information and communication technologies. Libraries should upgrade their services by digitising their resources for online use.

These services should be accessible to anyone, regardless of time or location, through digital communication devices. Libraries can play significant role in providing a good education and knowledge of high quality. Individuals around the world, no matter how poor they may be, can access whatever knowledge and information they need by visiting libraries via the internet, such as the library of congress.

PROBLEMS AND OPPORTUNITIES FACING LIBRARIES IN INDIA

Library and information services are fundamental to the goals of creating, disseminating, optimally utilising and preserving knowledge. They are instrumental in transforming an unequal society into an egalitarian, progressive knowledge-based society. It is well known that in India most of the libraries function in the government sector. These are in academic and research institutions and under the public library system, which is again under the state and central governments. At present, education being a state subject and coming under the purview of different apex agencies, there is no common direction or coordination among them.

It is imperative that all libraries (public, academic, research and special) change gear and develop at an accelerated pace. Developments in information communication technology (ICT) have enabled libraries to provide access to all, and also bridge the gap between the local, the national and the global. Yet the Library and Information Services (LIS) sector in India has not kept pace with the paradigmatic changes taking place in society. There are a few libraries which are using state of art technologies to disseminate knowledge to their respective user community. There is lack of cooperation among the libraries of different organisations and which cause the lack of union catalogues at national level.

The national library failed even to do this immense task. One of the major problems faced by LIS sector in India is lack of bibliographic control at national level which causes duplication in research. A considerable number of libraries had not been developed bibliographic databases of their documents for putting them on network.

To summarise, the major constraints faced by the libraries which militate against effective dissemination and use of information are:

- A considerable percentage of the population is illiterate or functionally literate making libraries of minimal use to them.
- Poor resource allocation for infrastructure improvement and collection development for public libraries.
- Lack of sufficient sanctioned posts, forcing most services to be operated by voluntary non-professional staff, which damages information organisation and services.
- Lack of national policies promoting ICT as a tool for development of library systems and services.
- Lack of adequate trained manpower in the use of IT.
- Lack of funds for acquiring necessary hardware and software facilities.
- Resistance on the part of library staff to change from their traditional practices to the use of IT.

Despite the problems, Library and Information Services (LIS) sector in India has got remarkable achievements. Efforts had been made to set up networks at local, regional and national level to deploy information and communication technologies and to build electronic information sources.

Besides INFLIBNET at the national level to support university and college libraries, a number of other national networks and various library networks have also been developed including:

- NICNET (National Informatics Centers Network),
- ERNET (Education and Research Network),
- CALIBNET (Calcutta Library Network),
- DELNET (Developing Library Network), etc.

A number of educational institutions are members of such networks. These networks, especially INFLIBNET and DELNET, are engaged in compiling union catalogs, creating various databases of experts, providing training to library staff, ILL, online facilities, reference service, assistance in retrospective conversion, etc. To overcome the problem of financial crunch and the rising costs of journals, librarians have formed consortia to subscribe all the required journals and databases.

Some special libraries and research organisations have established consortia known as FORSA (Forum for Resource Sharing in Astronomy) to share electronic access to journal literature. NISCAIR (National Institutes of Science Communication and Information Resources), one of CSIR labs, has formed a consortium for CSIR labs for accessing e-journals and databases.

In order to solve the problem of universities and college libraries, UGC launched a major initiative called UGC-INFONET that provides high speed Internet connections so as to have electronic access to professional literature including research journals, abstracts, review publications, and databases from all areas in science and technology, as well as in social sciences and humanities.

The Ministry of Human Resource Development (MHRD) has set up the "Indian National Digital Library in Science and Technology (INDEST) Consortium" for the subscription to electronic resources for 38 academic institutions, including the Indian Institute of Sciences, Indian Institute of Technology, Regional Engineering Colleges, Indian Institute of Managements, and about 60 centrally-funded/aided government institutions through the consortium.

For the improvement of quality of library and information services through the systematic acquisition, organisation and dissemination of knowledge, various library associations have been set up at national and state level. They annually organised conferences, seminars and training programmes to trained and update library professionals with latest development in LIS. Recently libraries and research organisations realise the importance of digital libraries and they started the work of digitisation of important documents.

NISCAIR and the Department of Indian Systems of Medicine and Homoeopathy (ISM&H) have entered into an agreement for establishing a Traditional Knowledge Digital Library (TKDL) on Ayurveda. TKDL will be available in English, German, French, Spanish and Japanese since these languages account for more than 98 per cent of the international patent applications. TKDL in the first phase targets Ayurveda. But as a whole it would encompass, in addition to Ayurveda, Siddha, Unani, Yoga, Naturopathy and Folklore medicine.

The Indian Institute of Science (IISc), Carnegie Mellon University (CMU), the International Institute of Information Technology, Hyderabad (IIITH) and many other academic, religious and government organisations, totaling about 21 "Content Creation Centers", have become partners in the Digital Library of India (DLI) initiative for the digitisation and preservation of Indian heritage present in the form of books, manuscripts, art and music. Each centre brings its own unique collection of literature into the digital library. DLI has a vision to build a universal digital library of world knowledge. One million books have already been available through this project.

India perhaps has one of the oldest and largest collections of Manuscripts in the world. These manuscripts are in different languages and scripts; written on different materials such as birch bark, palm leaf, cloth, paper, etc. They are in the custody of libraries, museums, monasteries, mutts and individuals. A significant proportion is not preserved scientifically. Experts estimate that almost all palm leaf manuscripts may perish due to wear and tear over next 50 to 100 years.

In this regard the National Mission for Manuscripts has taken a step to save the most valuable, intellectual property of our cultural inheritance. The missions has started a pilot project for digitising the manuscripts in five states across India covering five caches of manuscripts and for the same four digitising agencies have been selected. Importance of open access archives, institutional repositories and open access journals has been realised by the library and information professionals in India.

This movement has been accelerated by the availability of open source software namely DSpace, EPrints, Greenstone, etc. Indian Institute of Science, Bangalore, INFLIBNET Centre, Ahmedabad and Documentation Research and Training Centre (DRTC), Bangalore are the leading institutions who made this movement a great success.

Among the top 25 publishing countries, India ranks 12th for the overall number of journals, but drops to 18th for journals with online content. At present there are more than 150 open access journals in India. The open access journals in India are mainly initiated by six journal publishers, namely, Indian Academy of Sciences, Indian National Science Academy, Indian Medlars Centre of National Informatics Centre, Medknow Publications, and Kamla-Raj Enterprises. The Indian Institute of Science was the first in the country to set up and interoperable institutional archive. The archive now has more than 7000 records, with over 90 percent having full text. Presently there are 25 institutional archives in India which are registered in the Registry of Open Access Repositories (ROAR). An open access statement is likely to be ready by this year.

The CSIR also has a plan to setup a national digital repository of research literature. NISCAIR has already started to work on the project known as National Science Digital Library. National knowledge Commission is also formulating similar open access policies and guidelines for the higher education and R & D sectors to improve access to research literature and disseminate research literature to the global communities. The National Knowledge Commission has submitted its report to the government on how to redefine the information services sector. The report of Knowledge Commission on library sector suggests that "Every state should establish a registry and archives of knowledge based digital resources which should be made accessible to all".

CONCLUSION

The acquisition of knowledge has therefore been the thrust area throughout the world. The economy of present times depends no longer on visible resources and capital goods but on invisible knowledge and information. Therefore, poor nations as well as poor individuals can create wealth through active contacts and use of knowledge and information. Libraries of thse 21st century can help fight poverty and narrow the gap between rich and poor. For the first time in history poor are getting opportunity to enhance their wealth through the creation and use of knowledge. And libraries are taking a central role in this notable movement.

❐

8

Strategic Planning

A DEFINITION OF STRATEGIC PLANNING

Strategic planning is a tool for organising the present on the basis of the projections of the desired future. That is, a strategic plan is a road map to lead an organisation from where it is now to where it would like to be in five or ten years. It is necessary to have a strategic plan for your chapter or division. In order to develop a comprehensive plan for your chapter or division which would include both long- range and strategic elements, we suggest the methods and mechanisms outlined in this manual.

The plan must be:

- Simple
- Written
- Clear
- Based on the real current situation

Have enough time allowed to give it a time to settle. It should not be rushed. Rushing the plan will cause problems.

BENEFITS AND PITFALLS IN STRATEGIC PLANNING

Since, the beginning of Special Libraries Association in 1909, it has experienced phenomenal growth in membership and influence. In the past ten years, growth has been particularly significant. Changes in the fields of special librarianship and information science have been dramatic and fundamental to the very way of doing business. The advent of on line systems and the computer age rapidly changed the way librarians/information smanagers operate. The Association recognises that it can no longer merely react to issues as they emerge. If it is to continue as a leader in improving the profession, it must begin to anticipate future change rather than merely react to change. The Association as well as each chapter and division needs to consider this long-term future. Drawing on the resources it has, both human and financial, it needs to continue to grow. These resources are limited, and careful thought must be given to the allocation osf these resources.

To meet obligations to the profession, the public, and the membership, it is essential that the Association and its units use these resources in the most efficient manner by determining priority areas on which to concentrate. This means the identification of goals, pursuing those goals, and achieving them.

Strategic planning will help build continuity in the Association's programmes, particularly in the areas of continuing education and publications. The Association has the gift of a great deal of diversity among the membership. The Association draws its strength from this diversity but at the same time, that diversity lessens the Association's impact in key areas because of a lack of cohesive focus by the organisation.

Therefore, it is necessary for each chapter and division to have a plan that is compatible with the overall strategic plan of SLA thus concentrating its efforts and greatly increasing its impact. There are several pitfalls associated with strategic planning. First, the plan may not turn out as well as expected because of changes in the environment in which the plan is supposed to operate. Also, strategic planning is worthless in getting an organisation out of a major crisis.

sA crisis is a current problem not solved by a strategic plan. And, if the planning process itself is weak, the resulting plan may be weak and not satisfactory to the organisation. George Steiner in his Strategic Planning lists 50 major common pitfalls in starting, doing, and using strategic planning.

STRATEGIC PLANNING MODEL

In choosing the strategic planning model, two main things need to be considered. The first is whether you want the Association unit to plan as a not-for-profit, or as a profit organisation. Association planning is not the same as the planning for universities or businesses or government agencies.

Associations need to be consistently receptive to the needs of the membership-at-large. The main purpose is to serve the members more than to make a profit or to increase the size of the organisation. The strategic plan needs to include a Mission Statement, Objectives, Goals, and an Action (or Implementation) sPlan.

MISSION STATEMENT

This is the agreed-upon statement by the organisation and explains the reason for its existence. It is necessarily broad to encompass the diversity within the Association. The statement is not precise in its measurements nor does it need to be, but it does need to be periodically revisewed by the Association to see whether it still encompasses all of the relevant activities of the Association.

OBJECTIVES

The objectives are the areas of emphasis within the Association. Rather than specific statements with a specific goal, objectives state that the Association plans to continue to do quality work in the following areas. These objectives or areas of emphasis need to be attained by discussion and review of the organisation's current activities as well as activities in which it would like to participate.

GOALS

These need to bes both long-term and short-term goals; six months, one-year, threeyears, and ten-year goals need to be set so that the strategy for reaching these goals can be outlined in the plan. Most organisations recommend setting the long-term goals first and then setting short-term goals: those goals which can be reached as steps to attaining the long-term goal.

ACTION PLAN

The Action Plan should be designed after the main goals and objectives have been set in order to attain the mission in a straightforward and measurable way. With an Action Plan, the goals themselves can be obtained. Without the Action Plan, and the measures it entails, it would be impossible to implement the plan and measure its success. Being able to measure success would certainly be important both for maintaining our tax status as a not-for-profit organisation as well as to explain the use of it to the membership-at-large.

STRATEGIC PLANNING PROCESSES AND MECHANISMS

The publications 'A Guide to Nominal Group and Delphi Processes' by Andre L. Blebecq, et al, and "Guide for Leaders Using Nominal Group Technique" by James G. Cope and Carl Moore, describe the combination of nominal group and Delphi processes. Using these techniques, an organisation that is geographically separate can communicate and develop the working document in fairly rapid fashion.

GATHERING OF BACKGROUND INFORMATION

Background information is used by your Strategic Planning Committee for its review. By shifting through that information, the Committee would be able to develop a sound basis to continue their work. After existing information has been gathered, another information gathering activity should take place.

Develop a survey questionnaire to poll all members for their viewpoints on the directions your chapter or division should take. After the information has been synthesised from the questionnaires as well as from information already gathered, move to the second step.

A PLANNING WORKSHOP

The title of the article is 'Strategic Planning: Lead Your Association With a Plan for Tomorrow'.

Based on this article, your chapter or division needs to gather information on five basic questions:

- Where are we now? (The Situation);
- How did we get there? (Our Momentum);
- Where are we going? (The Direction);
- Where should we be going? (Desired Direction);
- How will we get there? (The Strategic Plan).

Bailey recommends that after gathering the background information, the planning workshop should take place. The first session would assess the current situation and how you arrived at that present situation. The second activity of this first workshop is to try to figure out where you are going and where you want to be. This is a very hard-hitting and difficult time for any association or business given the economic conditions and the change within sour profession itself.

DESIGNING A PLANNING WORKBOOK

The planning Workbook will bring together all of the information gathered during the Planning Workshop, sift through the ideas put forward, and organise them into a meaningful body for review by the Planning Workshop attendees and other interested parties in the organisation.

SECOND PLANNING WORKSHOP

After the Planning Workshop information has been gathered into a workbook, another workshop should be planned. At this workshop (which should not be held too long after the first one), several things need to be accomplished. In the first half-day a Mission Statement should be adopted for the Association. The Mission Statement will include what the Association intends to stand for; what it hopes to contribute to the world-at-large. It should set goals for the Association and then, having set the goals, fulfill the Mission Statement by translating each goal into a specific objective. This means that the Mission Statement will be carried forth into a strategic plan.

THE COMMITTEE STRUCTURE

The Strategic Planning Committee should be composed of people who understand the organisation of Special Libraries Association, but also who have a constant feel for the Association and your chapter and division in general, and where it is moving. The Strategic Planning Committee should be made a permanent standing committee within the chapters and divisions with a rotating membership. This will encourage constant review and updating by the membership.

THOUGHTS REGARDING SHORT AND LONG RANGE PLANNING

In order to achieve a sound basis for the development of programmes and activities, systematic planning efforts must be undertaken. The following is a stream of ideas about planning which have been able to find their way to paper. They are presented merely for a point of departure and not meant for any other purpose--a 'Plan for Planning' so to speak.

PLANNING

Planning includes the ability to identify opportunities, analyse problems, establish priorities and needs, and allocate available resources. This also includes the establishment of priorities and needs, and allocate available resources.

This also includes the establishment of policies and procedures, objectives and standards of performance, forecasts and budgets, programmes and schedules:

- Planning is necessary:
  - — Provides direction
  - — Gives perspective
- Planning facilitates:
  - — Involvement of concerned people and groups.
  - — Communication
  - — Coordination
- Steps in Planning:
  - — Organising
    - a. Establish a structure
    - b. Group involvement
  - — Setting objectives
    - a. Nature of objectives
    - b. Basis for objectives
  - — Establishing priorities—based on needs, opportunities, interrelationships between elements.
  - — Designing activities
  - — Dividing action into feasible steps
    - a. Short range
    - b. Long range
  - — Implementing action
  - — Disseminating information
  - — Evaluating—a continual process
  - — Revising—at least annually

PROGRAMME

Conceptual—why the programme should be undertaken:

- — Problem statement

- Objectives
- Hypothesis
- Review of existing information

- Methodological—what has to be done and how it will be done:
  - Design Programme
  - Sampling
  - Analysis
    a. Qsuantitativse
    b. Qualitative
  - Instrumentation selection or development.
- Statement of ssphilosophy:
  - General philosophy of the organisation
  - Philosophy of special libraries
- Needs assessment
- Goal of the Association
- Objectives of the Association
  - Something we want
  - Output—end product
  - Means—end product
- Establish programme alternatives
  - Fiscal—costs of conducting the programme:
    a. Time
    b. Resources
      i. Humans
      ii. Non-humansss
    c. Money
  - Programme—set of activities which are combined into some structure and are carried out to achieve some previously stated objective.
  - Limits and constraints:
    a. An analysis of what we have to work with and work against
    b. Specify time, money, programme requirements, people, and facilities within which the Association must operate

CONTENTS OF PLANNING DOCUMENT

The statement of ground rules under which the Association must operate Types of constraints:

a. Social
b. Technological
c. Administrative
d. Political

e. Legal
f. Economic

Forces affecting programme development:

a. Political
b. Outside interest groups
c. Administrative hierarchy
d. Users
e. Professional organisations
   - Establish programme priorities
   - Select best programme alternative
   - Action plan
   - Evaluation of programme

❐

9

Libraries: Resources and Services

For this chapter information was collected from library staff using a squestionnaire about the administration, organization, resources, services and facilities of libraries of colleges of education under study. An attempt was also made to ascertain the problems being faced by them in managing these sslibraries.

YEAR OF ESTABLISHMENT

Libraries constitute an integral part of colleges. These are supposed to be established simultaneously with their parent institutions. Realizing their crucial role in education, all the libraries have been established together with the inception of colleges. All libraries, except one had been existing for more than 30 years. Library of University College of Education (UCE) came into existence in 2001 along with the college.

LIBRARY STAFF

Library is the trinity of collection, staff and readers, where staff brings together other two elements. Qualified and adequate staff is pre-requisite for effective functioning of libraries.

Librarians

Libraries need the services of professionally qualified librarians for proper administration of the system. A library having good collection and adequate staff may not essentially provide effective library services, unless it is managed by a professionally qualified librarian having managerial capabilities. All the colleges, except UCE had sanctioned posts of librarians. The UCE library had a post of an assistant librarian as incharge, which was lying vacant since the establishment of college in 2001. It was being managed by a library assistant.

Two Government. Colleges of Education (GCE) had two posts of librarians seach. Out of these, in a college a post was vacant and one librarian was managing library. Table reveals the prevailing position of librarian's posts in colleges under study.

Andhra Pradesh

TABLE: Prevailing Position of Librarians Posts

S.No.	Particulars	No. of Libraries	Percentage
1.	Permanent Librarians	13	72.22
2.	Adhoc based librarians	01	05.56
3.	Post vacant	04	22.22
	Total	18	100.00

It is evident from Table above that out of the 18 libraries having sanctioned posts of librarians, 13 (72.22%) libraries had permanent librarians, whereas, a government aided college appointed a librarian on adhoc basis. In four (22.22%) colleges posts of librarians wesre lying vacant.

Out of these, a government. aided college appointed a professional and designated her as an assistant librarian, inspite of the fact that the college did not have any sanctioned post of an assistant librarian. The remaining three libraries were being run by restorers.

The National Council for Teacher Education (NCTE) required each college to have a full time librarian. Analysis of the responses revealed that libraries of six (31.58%) colleges consisting of four Government. Aided Colleges of Education (GACE), one government. college of education and UCE did not meet the NCTE norms about full time librarian.

Educational Qualification of Librarians

Educational qualifications of librarians influence the organizational health of libraries. Higher academic and professional qualification leads to better library management, ultimately better library services.

Table shows that out of 15 librarians serving 14 libraries, six (40.00%) possessed master's degree in arts/science and ssbachelors' degree in Library and Information Science (LIS), while four (26.66%) librarians had master's degrees in arts/ science in addition to masters' degree in LIS. Three librarians had bachelors' degree in arts/ science and master's degree in LIS.

A librarian possessed Ph.D. degree in the subject of History and bachelor's degree in LIS. Only one librarian had Ph.D. degree in LIS and master's degree in another discipline. Out of the seven librarians having master's degree in LIS, three had qualified National Eligibility Test (NET) for Lectureship, while a librarian qualified State Eligibility Test (SET) for Lectureship.

TABLE: Educational Qualification of Librarians.

S.No.	Qualification No. of		% age	
	Academic	Professional	Librarians	
1.	M.A./Sc./M/Ed./ Ph.D. M.Com	01	06.67	
2.	M. Phil/Ph. D.B. Lib & I.Sc.	01	06.67	
3.	M.A./M.Sc.	M.Lib & Sc.	04	26.66
4.	M.A./M.Sc.	B.Lib & Sc.	06	40.00
5.	B.A./B.Sc.	M.Lib & Sc.	03	20.00
	Total		**15**	**100.00**

It has been found that all three librarians serving GCE libraries had bachelor's degree in LIS, whereas all the librarians having master's degree in LIS were serving at GACE. The NCTE has revised its norms regarding qualification of librarians. These are now only bachelors degree in Library and Information Science whereas as per NCTE these were "As prescribed by State Government/UT Administration concerned." The qualifications laid by State Government were as per University Grant Commission. But the qualifications prescribed by NCTE are only B.Lib. & I.Sc. Therefore, this amounts to the degradation of librarians and eventually libraries.

Table depicts that out of 15 librarians, 09 (60.00%) had experience of more than 20 years. Out of these, 07 librarians possessed bachelor's degree and two had master's degree in LIS. Five (33.33%) librarians had experience of less than 10 years, while a remaining librarian's experience ranged between 16-20 years. All three librarians serving GCE had experience of more than 20 years each. Analysis of the responses tabulated in tables reveals that all the librarians having only bachelor's degree in LIS were appointed more than 20 years ago. On the other hand, all the librarians appointed thereafter had master's degree in LIS.

TABLE: Experience of Librarians.

S.No.	Experience in Years	No. of Librarians	Percentage
1.	Up to 5	02	13.33
2.	6-10	03	20.00
3.	11-15	–	–
4.	16-20	01	06.67
5.	21-25	03	20.00

6.	26-30	03	20.00
7.	More than	30.03	20.00
	Total	**15**	**100.00**

Refresher Courses sAttended

Librarians were asked if they had attended any refresher course, orientation programme, workshop, etc. Responses revealed that out of 15 librarians, 07 (46.67%) attended refresher courses, two (13.33%) had attended orientation programmes and a librarian also participated in a workshop. It has been found that about 50% librarians had not participated in refresher courses and workshops, which are imperative for updating professionals and essential for Continuous Professional Development.

Library Assistants

The UCE and a government aided college had a post of library assistant each. Out of the two library assistants serving respective libraries, one possessed bachelors' degree in LIS, while another was only matriculate not having any degree or diploma in LIS.

Library Restorers

Thirteen (68.42%) libraries had sanctioned posts of restorers, while remaining six (31.58%) did not. In 12 (92.30%) of 13 libraries, restorers were working against the sanctioned posts, while in a government college library post was vacant.

Two colleges out of the six not having sanctioned posts, appointed restorers on adhoc basis, while remaining four had not made such effort. All the GCE had sanctioned posts of restorers. About two-thirds of the library restorers serving libraries possessed either diploma or bachelor's degree in LIS, while remaining five did not.

Library Attendants

Eight (42.10%) libraries did not have sanctioned posts of library attendants. In two libraries, out of the 11 (57.90%) having sanctioned posts of attendants, posts were vacant.

All the GCE had sanctioned posts of library attendants. But it was shocking to find that in Desh Bhagat Pandit Chetan Dev Government College of Education, Faridkot the previous principal had assigned the job of a 'gardener' to a graduate library attendant and replaced him with an illiterate peon in the library to provide library services to the users.

This shows the ignorance and lack of importance of libraries on the part of authorities. Out of the nine attendants serving libraries, one third had either degree or diploma in LIS, whereas, the remaining two third did not.

LIBRARY COMMITTEE

Generally, library committee comprises of three types of authorities principal as the chairman of committee, librarian as secretary and teachers and students as members. Keeping in view its significance, librarians were asked about the existence, structure and functions of library committees.

Existence of Library Committees

Out of a total 19 libraries, 18 (94.73%) had library committees, whereas a government aided college did not. In a college it was named as 'Book Purchase Committee'.

Chairperson of Library Committee

Table below reveals that in 12 (66.67%) libraries out of the 18 having library committees, principals were serving as the chairpersons of the committees, whereas in two GACE libraries, librarians themselves led these. In two colleges, lecturers were the heads of committees. Out of these, a college did not have regular principal. In two colleges, library committees did not have any chairman. In one of these, college principal was the convener of committee and librarian and lecturers were members, while in a remaining library, committee comprised of members only.

TABLE: Chairperson of Library Committee.

S.No.	Chairperson of Committee	No. of Libraries	Percentage
1.	Principal	12	66.67
2.	Librarian	02	11.11
3.	Lecturer	02	11.11
4.	No Chairman	02	11.11
	Total	18	100.00

Secretary of Library Committee

It is worth mentioning here that in majority of the libraries i.e. eight (44.44%), librarians were serving as secretaries of the committees, while in six (33.33%) libraries lecturers did the job table. Four libraries did not have any secretary of the library committees.

In a library, it comprised of principal as convener and librarian and lecturers as members, while in two libraries these had only members including librarians. In a remaining library, where librarian was head of the committee, it consisted of lecturers as members. Survey revealed that only one library had students' representatives as members in the committee.

TABLE: Secretary of Library Committee.

S.No.	Secretary Committee	No. of Libraries	%age
1.	Librarian	08	44.44
2.	Lecturers	06	33.33
3.	No One	04	22.23
	Total	**18**	**100.00**

Nature of Work of Library Committee

In majority of the libraries forming 66.67%, library committees were advisory bodies. In remaining one third libraries these were executive in nature because of lack of full time librarians.

COLLECTION DEVELOPMENT

The Working Group on Libraries set up by National Knowledge Commission emphasized for collection building based on the information needs of users. In its recommendations the Group added: "To fulfil its role in the present and changing context, each library must have a well-rounded collection relevant to its user community". A balanced and need based collection, adequate to meet the present as well as future information needs of users depends upon a well prepared collection development policy. Library staff of ten colleges responded that they had prepared and were following collection development policy, while staff of remaining nine libraries responded otherwise. It was very disappointing to find that none of the libraries had any written guidelines for collection development.

Who Makes Selection of Subject Related Books

Subject books are meant to meet the curriculum based information needs of users and enable them to explore the concerned subjects in depth. Library staff was asked to give ranking in order of preference to the different authorities mentioned in Questionnaire I, according to their role in selection of subject books.

TABLE: Selection of Subject Related Books.

S.No.	Persons who Select Books	Scores	Ranking
1.	Teachers	66	01
2.	Principal	60	02
3.	Library Committee	43	03
4.	Librarian	39	04
5.	Others (Students and College management)	15	05

Sum total of the scores assigned to different options on the basis of ranking given by librarians reveals that teachers occupied the leading role in selection of subject books, followed by the principals and library committees respectively. Librarians attained the fourth position in order of ranking for subject related document selection, while others earned least scores.

GENERAL AND REFERENCE COLLECTION

As in case of subject books, scores have been assigned to the different authorities involved in selection of general and reference collection also, which are tabulated in table below:

TABLE: Selection of General and Refrence Books.

S.No.	Persons Who Who Books	Scores	Ranking
1.	Teachers	62	01
2.	Principal	60	02
3.	Librarian	45	03
4.	Library Committee	43	04
5.	Others (students and college management)	05	05s

Table shows that teachers have earned the highest scores in selection of general and reference collection too. Principals and librarians were given second and third preferences, while library committees and others attained fourth and fifth positions respectively. Analysis of the responses given in tables makes it clear that the teachers and principals played a leading role in selection of subject related as well as general and reference collection.

Document Selection Tools

Scores have been assigned to the various document selection tools on the basis of preference ranking given by librarians. Rank '1' was given the highest score '8' followed by others in descending order of 1 score at each stage.

Table depicts that teacher's suggestions have earned the highest scores as sources of document selection, while publisher's catalogues and student's suggestions earned the second and third position respectively. Book reviews and other bibliographical tools were given least ranking as document selection tools.

TABLE: Document Selection Tools.

S.No.	Sources of Book Selection	Scores	Ranking
1.	Teachers' Suggestions	132	01
2.	Publishers' Catalogue	101	02

3.	Students' Suggestions	71	03
4.	Books on Approval	54	04
5.	Book Sellers' List	42	05
6.	Book Exhibitions	40	06
7.	Book Reviews	16	07
8.	Other Bibliographical Tools	11	08

COLLECTION OF LIBRARIES

Among three components of libraries i. e. collection, staff and readers, collection occupies the key position. It is collection which determines the use of a library. Collection is a wider term covering books, periodicals, microforms, electronic form documents, etc. Information was gathered about the nature and size of collection of libraries under study.

Total Book Collection

Responses received about the total collection of libraries were arranged into different ranges of 5000 each. It is evident from table that majority of the libraries under study i.e. 10 (52.63%) possessed 15,000-25,000 volumes, while four (21.06%) libraries had 10,000-15,000 books. Only two GCE libraries crossed the figure of 30,000 volumes.

The UCE library had less than 5000 volumes due to its recent origin in 2001.

The GCE were found rich in collection size than GACE and UCE. Main factor affecting this was that GCE received recurring grants for reading material from both the University Grants Commission (UGC) and the State Government, while GACE got grants for library from UGC only.

TABLE: Book Collection of Libraries.

S.No.	Total Number of Books Possessed	No. of Libraries	%age
1.	0-5000	01	05.27
2.	5000-10000	02	10.53
3.	10000-15000	04	21.06
4.	15000-20000	05	26.31
5.	20000-25000	05	26.31
6.	25000-30000	–	–
7.	More than 30000	02	10.52
	Total	19	100.00

The NCTE require each college to have a minimum 1000 titles and 3000 books for B.Ed. Course and minimum 2000 titles for M.Ed course in libraries to get recognition. The UCE had less than 5000 volumes though it was offering both B.Ed. and M.Ed. courses. The NCTE further mentioned that a library should add 200 titles annually wherever B.Ed. course is being run. In addition it requires annual addition of '100 quality books' where M.Ed. course is also being run.

It has been found that libraries of only two GACE were fulfilling the NCTE norms for M.Ed. course. Whereas, for B.Ed. course libraries of total seven colleges were adding 200 volumes annually on an average including the two mentioned earlier.

Text Book Collection

Table shows the textbook collection of libraries of colleges of education in Punjab.

TABLE: Text Book Collection of Libraries.

S.No.	Number of Text Books Possessed	No. of Libraries	%age
1.	0-4000	06	31.58
2.	4000-8000	07	36.84
3.	8000-12000	03	15.79
4.	12000-16000	03	15.79
	Total	**19**	**100.00s**

Table above reveals that majority of the libraries had 4000-8000 textbooks. Six libraries had less than 4000 volumes and three possessed 8000-12000 textbooks. Three libraries had 12000-16000 volumes of textbooks. It is evident from the table that textbooks constitute a large part of the total collection of libraries.

Reference Collection

A good reference collection is the soul for sound reference service. It has been observed that all libraries maintained separate reference sections. Responses received about the strength of reference collection are shown in table below.

TABLE: Reference Collection of Libraries.

S.No.	Number of Reference Books Possessed	No. of Libraries	%age
1.	0-200	02	10.53
2.	200-500	05	26.31
3.	500-1000s	02	10.53
4.	1000-1500	03	15.79
5.	1500-2500	03	15.79
6.	More than 2500	04	21.05
	Toral	**19**	**100.00**

Table above depicts that five (26.31%) libraries possessed 200-500 reference volumes, while other five had 500-1500 books. About 21.05% libraries had more than 2500 volumes in reference sections. In majority of the libraries, the reference collection was found to be satisfactory in proportion to their total collection. It was noticed that though the libraries of two GCE were richest in their total collection, still libraries of four GACE had more volumes in reference sections.

Book Bank

Fifteen libraries (78.94%) had book banks to help poor and needy students, while remaining 04 did not. Out of the 15 libraries, 14 maintained separate book bank sections, while a librarian shared that they did not have any separate book bank section, but lend books to needy students for the full session from text books section. Table below furnishes the number of volumes in book banks of 14 libraries.

TABLE: Size of Book Bank Collection.

S.No.	Number of Books in Book Bank	No. of Libraries	%age
1.	0-500	04	28.58
2.	500-1000	04	28.58
3.	1000-2000	03	21.42
4.	2000-3000	01	07.14
5.	More than 3000	02	14.28
	Total	**14**	**100.00**

Table above discloses that out of 14 libraries having separate book bank sections, eight had less than 1000 volumes in their respective book banks. Four libraries had 1000-3000 books and two possessed more than 3000 volumes. It was learnt that majority of the libraries added only gifted books to book banks.

Non-Book Material

Non-book material constitutes an important source of information. The NCTE also requires libraries to have electronic publications (CD-ROMs) in collection. But, it has not gained the desired momentum in the libraries of colleges of education.

It was found that only nine libraries had non-book material in meager quantity. Out of these, seven libraries possessed a few CD's and one had cassettes that came free with books. Another library had approximately 400 maps.

Dissertations

Out of 15 colleges running M.Ed. course, libraries of 13 had dissertations. Eight libraries possessed less than 300 dissertations and three had 300-400 titles. Two libraries possessed more than 400 dissertations. Number of the dissertations possessed by libraries varied according to the year of starting M.Ed. course.

The University College of Education, Bathinda and SDS College of Education, Lopon started M.Ed. courses during the academic sessions 2006-07 and 2007-08 respectively. Libraries of both of these colleges did not have dissertations.

Periodical Literature

Periodical publications serve the purpose of both information and recreation. These include journals, magazines and all other publications, which are issued at regular intervals.

Journals

Journals are the subject specific periodicals, usually containing primary information. Table below represents data about the number of journals on subscription of libraries.

TABLE: Number of Journals on Subscription.

S. No.	Number of Journals	No. of Libraries	%age
1.	0-10	04	21.05
2.	11-20	10	52.63
3.	21-30	03	15.79
4.	More than	30.02	10.53
	Total	**19**	**100.00**

Table above reveals that majority of the libraries forming 52.63% were subscribing to 11-20 journals. Three libraries had 21-30 journals on subscription, while two libraries were subscribing to more than 30 journals. Only one library subscribed two international journals.

A government aided college library was subscribing to merely two journals. The NCTE has prescribed for B.Ed. and M.Ed. colleges to subscribe to a minimum of 10 and 15 journals respectively.

But libraries of two colleges offering B.Ed. course and three colleges offering M.Ed. course in addition to B.Ed. also did not meet these standards. The NCTE provided revised norms regarding journals for M.Ed. course. It requires each library to have subscription to at least one international publication.

Back Volumes of Journals

Back volumes of journals are the vital sources of information for furtherance of research. All the libraries except one had back volumes of journals.

Table below depicts that eight (44.44%) out of a total 18 libraries having back volumes of journals had less than 100 back volumes, while three (16.67%) had 100-200 volumes.

Three libraries possessed 200-400 volumes, whereas other three libraries were having more than 400 back volumes of journals.

One librarian had not specified the number of back volumes of journals available in library.

Survey brought to notice that back volumes of journals were not properly organized as six libraries had loose issues, while in three libraries these were partially bound.

TABLE: Back Volumes of Journals.

S. No.	Number of Volumes	No. of Libraries	%age
1.	0-100	08	44.44
2.	100-200	03	16.67
3.	200-400	03	16.67
4.	More than 400	03	16.67
5.	No Response	01	05.55
	Total	**18**	**100.00**

In addition to journals, libraries provide general magazines to users for reading. Majority of the of libraries i. e. 13 (68.42%) were subscribing to less than 20 magazines, while four had 21-30 magazine titles on subscription. Two libraries were making available more than 30 magazine titles for users.

Newspapers

Sometimes, newspapers contain information not available from other sources. Fifteen libraries were subscribing to 05-10 newspaper titles, whereas two had 05 or less newspapers on subscription. A library was subscribing to more than 10 newspapers daily in English, Punjabi and Hindi.

LIBRARY BUILDING

Libraries are dynamic institutions which continue to grow in terms of collection, staff and readers. In order to tackle the resultant growth it becomes necessary to house a library in an independent, functional and modular building. Keeping in view the significance of library building, query was made to ascertain whether libraries have their own independent buildings. Responses revealed that only one government aided college library had an independent building used exclusively for library purpose.

The remaining 18 libraries were housed in buildings forming part of college premises. During visit, it was observed that library of GHG Khalsa College of Education, Gurusar Sadhar was sharing building with canteen. Library was located on first floor while canteen was sited on ground floor, causing disturbance to library users.

Majority of the libraries i. e. seven (36.84%) were housed in single rooms, while six (31.58%) libraries had two rooms each. Three libraries consisted of four rooms and one had more than five rooms. It was astounding to find during visit to

Khalsa College of Education, Mukatsar that a teacher was taking class in library. When asked, assistant librarian shared that it was a usual practice.

Majority of the libraries were housed in one or two rooms, which can not be considered sufficient for effective functioning of libraries. The NCTE norm about library building need to be revised. These require each college to have "a library-cum-reading room."

Separate Reading Room

A separate reading room with sufficient seating capacity and free from disturbance is the essence of all types of libraries. Survey revealed that only five (26.31%) libraries had separate reading rooms for users, while in remaining libraries chairs were arranged within stack area. Similarly, five libraries had separate librarian's offices to perform the documentary work. In remaining libraries these were in the form of tables or cabins in corners of libraries.

USERS' VISIT TO LIBRARIES

Libraries exist to meet the information needs of users. The strength of users, their information needs and subjects of study, etc. greatly influence the resources and services of libraries. Table below reveals the average number of visitors to libraries.

TABLE: Average Number of Visitors to Libraries.

S.No.	Number of Visitors	No. of Libraries	%age
1.	0-40	03	15.79
2.	40-80	06	31.58
3.	80-120	06	31.58
4.	More than 120	04	21.05
	Total	**19**	**100.00**

It is evident from the table above that six (31.58%) libraries were being visited by 80-120 users and other six libraries were visited by 40-80 users everyday. Four libraries were visited by more than 120 users daily on an average. In three libraries less than 40 users were visiting a day. The number of daily visitors to libraries varied due to variation in the students' strength with colleges.

SEATING CAPACITY

A library is supposed to provide adequate seating arrangement to users for reading inside library premises. Following table reveals the seating capacity of libraries. Table shows that majority of the libraries had seating capacity for 26-50 users, while 04 libraries could accommodate 76- 100 users at a time. Three libraries had less than 25 seats each for users.

A library had seating arrangement for more than 100 users. Six libraries had separate seating arrangement for M.Ed. students, while libraries of remaining nine colleges offering M.Ed. course did not have such facility. Ten libraries had separate seating arrangement for teachers. The NCTE prescribed for each college to provide seating arrangement in libraries for at least 25% of their B.Ed. students and for 10 students of M.Ed. course, but 08 libraries did not meet this requirement.

TABLE: Seating Capacity for Users.

S.No.	Number of Visitors	No. of Libraries	%age
1.	0-25	03	15.79
2.	26-50	08	42.10
3.	51-75	03	15.79
4.	76-100	04	21.05
5.	More than 100	01	05.27
	Total	**19**	**100.00**

NCTE has revised norms regarding seating capacity of libraries for B.Ed course. It requires libraries to have seating arrangement for at least fifty per cent of B.Ed students. Only one library had drinking water facility for users. Similarly, Library of DAV College of Education, Abohar had toilet facility for faculty members. Students were not allowed to use that.

LIBRARY BUDGET AND SOURCES OF FINANCE

The impact of Information and Communication Technologies (ICTs) on libraries has brought structural changes to library practices. Effective library management and provision of services depends upon the availability of adequate funds.

It was disappointing to find that none of the libraries except one had provision for library budget. Only UCE, Bathinda had provision of ₹ 50,000 each year for reading material. But since its establishment in 2001 no increase has been made in this amount. Libraries of GCE and GACE mainly depended up on the UGC grants.

Moreover, NCTE is silent about the financial provision for libraries. In libraries of colleges of education under study, the sources of finance varied considerably. Major sources of finance for purchase of reading material are given below:

- University Grants Commission (UGC) Grants
- Library Fees
- Library Development Funds and
- Amalgamated Funds

UGC Grants

The UGC plays a significant role in funding libraries through out the country. An attempt was made to find whether libraries have received any grant from UGC during the period 2002-2007. Only 13 (68.42%) libraries responded.

Table shows that out of 13 libraries, 10 (76.92%) received recurring grants under tenth five year plan, while a library got nonrecurring grant from UGC during the period 2002-2007. Office superintendent of the government aided college shared that the college had received special grant for library meant for 'Backward District College'. Libraries of two colleges including UCE and a government aided college had not received any recurring or non-recurring grant from UGC. The government aided college had not demanded grants from UGC because of the conflict between members of college management committee.

TABLE: Type of Grants Received from UGC.

S.No.	Type of Grant Received	No. of Libraries	%age
1.	Recurring	10	76.92
2.	Non-Recurring	01	07.70
3.	No Grant	02	15.38
	Total	**13**	**100.00**

Amount of Grants Received by Libraries

Librarians were asked to mention the amount of grants received from UGC during the period 2002-2007. Responses received were arranged into different ranges of one lakh each.

Table below reveals a considerable variation in the amount of grants received by 11 libraries. Majority of the libraries received less than ₹ 01 lakh as UGC grant for purchase of reading material under tenth five year plan, while 36.36% received 1-2 lakhs. A library received grant of more than rupees three lakhs from UGC.

TABLE: Extent of Grants Recevid.

S.No.	Amount of Grants Received (Rs.)	No. of Libraries	%age
1.	Up to one Lakh	06	54.54
2.	1-2	04	36.36
3.	2-3	–	–
4.	3-4	01	09.10
	Total	**11**	**100.00**

Grants from State Government

None of the libraries under study received grants from the State Government during the period 2002-2007. The State Government had earlier given grants to libraries of GCE only, as reported by librarians.

Amalgamated Fund

Amalgamated fund is collected from students each year at the time of admission to colleges. This amount is to be used for various purposes i. e. cultural activities, games, library and for some other similar purposes. Allocation of amalgamated funds towards library depends upon the discretion of the principals of colleges.

Library Fee and Library Development Funds

As like amalgamated fund, Library Fee and Library Development Fund are also charged from students at the time of admission to colleges. Out of the 13 responding colleges, eight charged library fee at varying rates from Rs.200-400. In four colleges it was termed as 'Books and Journals Fee'. Similarly four colleges charged library development fund from students at different rates of 100-200. In a government aided college it was being charged under the head 'Books Replacement Fund'.

Overdue Fine

The negligible amount of overdue fine can not be considered as reliable and sufficient source of funds for libraries. In UCE, the amount of overdue fine goes to the University Account.

TECHNICAL PROCESSING

Technical processing of documents takes place after accessioning. It covers all the activities related with their classification, cataloguing and physical processing. Classification provides systematic order among documents and catalogue guide the users to retrieve needed documents easily from large collection, through various access points.

Classification

Collection has to be classified and the classification scheme has to be user friendly. Survey revealed that out of a total 19 libraries, 18 had classified their collection. On the other hand, in the library of Dev Samaj College of Education for Women, Ferozepur City that was established in 1942, collection was not classified at all. Almirah numbers were written on catalogue cards instead of call numbers. The following table furnishes data about the extent of classification of documents in libraries:

Table below reveals that in majority of the libraries i. e. 11 (57.90%) collection was fully classified, while in seven (36.84%) libraries it was classified partially. In a remaining library documents were not classified at all. It has been found that all libraries were using Dewey Decimal Classification (DDC) scheme ranging from 16th to 21st edition to classify collection. Earlier UCE library was using Colon Classification (CC), but later on it switched over to DDC.

Three librarians responded of facing problems in classifying collection. A librarian having 18th edition of DDC shared that the respective library had an old edition of DDC which did not contain detailed class numbers for the subject of Computer. Librarian of Government College of Education, Jalandhar said, "It becomes very difficult to decide the main class of a book in case of interdisciplinary subject books".

A librarian stated lack of professionally qualified staff as one of the obstacles in organizing collection.

TABLE: Status of Classification of Collection.

S.No.	Extent of Classification	No. of Colleges	%age
1.	Fully Classified	11	57.90
2.	Partially Classified	07	36.84
3.	Not At All Classified	01	05.26
	Total	**19**	**100.00**

Cataloguing

Survey revealed that 11 (57.90%) libraries had partially catalogued their collection, not providing access points for all documents in possession. On the other hand, eight libraries had fully catalogued their holdings.

Majority of the libraries i.e. 11 (57.90%) were following Anglo American Cataloguing Rules-II and remaining eight (42.10%) libraries were using Anglo-American Cataloguing Rules-I for cataloging. This reflects the popularity of dictionary catalogue over classified catalogue among college libraries.

Number of Entries Prepared for Each Document

Users may approach a document through different access points i.e. subject, author, title, etc. Table shows the number of entries prepared for each volume in libraries to provide access to their holdings.

Table below reveals that in nine (47.37%) libraries, only two entries, and in six libraries only one entry for each document was prepared. Three librarians responded that they prepared all possible entries for each book in possession. Librarians were further asked to state the time taken to process new arrivals.

Table above depicts that in eight libraries, it was taking 1-2 weeks to process new arrivals, whereas, in other eight libraries books were being processed with in a week.

Three librarians responded of taking more than two weeks to process documents, due to inadequate staff.

TABLE: Number of Entries Prepared for each Document.

S.No.	No. of Entries Pepared	No. of Libraries	%age
1.	One Entry	06	31.58
2.	Two Entries	09	47.37
3.	Three Entries	01	05.26
4.	All Possible Entries	03	15.79
	Total	**19**	**100.00**

All libraries maintained card catalogue. Eight libraries using computers also prepared computer-based databases of books. Five librarians mentioned the problems they faced in cataloguing, whereas, remaining majority responded otherwise.

TABLE: Time Taken to Process Books from Date of Acquisition.

S.No.	Average Time Taken	No. of Libraries	%age
1.	Less than a Week	08	42.11
2.	1-2 Weeks	08	42.11
3.	More than Two Weeks	03	15.78

Three librarians complained of lack of professional staff and one of them further added that his college principal did not sanction funds even to purchase catalogue cards and cabinet. A librarian responded that they did not have catalogue code to get clarity in case of any doubt about cataloguing rules, while another shared that their library did not have standard subject heading list and they faced problem in assigning subject headings.

STOCK VERIFICATION

Stock verification, also known as physical verification brings to light the number of volumes missing from a library. It also helps to rectify the misplaced documents, and enable to take out books for repairing and binding. It has been found that 18 libraries were undertaking stock verification regularly, whereas in the library of UCE it was done since its establishment in 2001.

Frequency of Stock Verification

Responses revealed that out of 18 libraries, 11 (61.11%) undertook stock verification once in two years, whereas in seven (38.89%) libraries it was undertaken every year. Majority of libraries i.e. 15 did stock verification during vacations and a library carried out it during the period of examination. A librarian responded that, "It depends upon the availability of time" and another preferred to perform this job before the commencement of the new academic session. There are various tools to undertake stock verification i.e. stock taking registers, accession register, separate sheets with accession numbers, computers etc.

Table below depicts that out of the 18 libraries, 88.88% were using stock verification register for this purpose. A library was using accession register for stock verification, while in a government aided college library computer was used for the purpose.

TABLE: Method used for Stock Varification.

S.No.	Method of Stock Verification	No. of Libraries	%age
1.	Stock Verification Register	16	88.88
2.	Computer	01	05.56
3.	Accession Register	01	05.56
	Total	**18**	**100.00**

Average Loss of Books

Librarians were asked to mention the quantum of loss of documents suffered annually on an average. Responses received are shown in table below:

TABLE: Quantum of Loss of Books.

S.No.	Average Loss of Books	No. of Libraries	%age
1.	0-20	05	27.77
2.	21-40	07	38.89
3.	41-80	07	38.89
4.	No Loss	01	05.58
5.	Loss Not Calculated	01	05.56
6.	Not Specified	03	16.66
	Total	**18**	**100.00**

It is obvious from Table above that out of 18 libraries, in 07 (38.89%) libraries average loss of collection per year ranged from 20 to 40 books, whereas in 05 libraries it was below 20 documents. In a library average loss of documents went beyond 40. Three librarians had not specified any number representing loss of book, but responded that it was very low. A librarian responded that they never found any book missing from library. Another shared that they did stock verification every year, but never calculated the loss of books because of shortage of time and adequate staff, which makes stock verification useless.

Responsibility for Loss of Books

Responses revealed that in 14 libraries out of the 18 undertaking stock verification, missing books were written off against loss of books, while staff of four libraries responded that they were held responsible for the loss. On asking about the policy for writing off books, staff of 16 libraries responded that maximum three books were being written off for every thousand books with the permission of library committee. Whereas two librarians responded, “there is no such policy, library committee takes the decision for writing off books”.

CIRCULATION SERVICE

Circulation is highly used service of a college library. Survey revealed that in two libraries ‘demand boxes’ were placed for B.Ed. students. The students were required to put slips in demand box giving details of needed books and their identification.

The demand boxes were being opened next day morning to take out the needed books from almirahs for lending to students. Similarly, a library adopted slip system for lending books to B.Ed. students. In these libraries the M.Ed. students were entitled to borrow books at any time. The remaining 16 libraries had practice of lending books on the spot when demanded. Number of Books Users were Entitled to Borrow

An attempt was made to find the maximum number of books that a user could borrow from library at a time. Responses received are organized according to category of users.

B.Ed. Students

No uniformity was found among libraries on the number of books that users were entitled to borrow at a time. Majority of the libraries i.e. 11 (57.90%) entitled users to borrow three or less books at a time, whereas remaining eight (42.10%) libraries had this limit between books.

M.Ed. Students

Total 5.24 colleges were offering M.Ed. course in addition to B.Ed. In libraries of 12 (80%) of these colleges, users were entitled to borrow 04-06 books, whereas in two libraries they were allowed to borrow up to three books only at a time. In a government aided college library M.Ed. students were entitled to borrow up to 10 books at a time.

TABLE: Number of Books Entitled to Borrow (M.ED. Sutdent).

S.No.	No. of Books Being Issued at a Time	No. of Libraries	%age
1.	1-3	02	13.33
2.	4-6	12	80.00
3.	7-10	01	06.67
	Total	15	100.00

Teachers

Table below reveals that eight libraries had no limit over the number of books a teacher could borrow at a time. Six libraries entitled teachers to borrow 06-10 books, while a library gave privilege to teachers to borrow up to 30 books at a time in case he or she was guiding M.Ed. students for dissertation.

TABLE: Number of Books Entitled to Borrow (Teachers).

S.No.	No. of Books Being Issued at a Time	No. of Libraries	%age
1.	1-5	–	–
2.	6-10	06	31.57
3.	11-15	03	15.79
4.	15-20	01	05.27
5.	20-30	01	05.27
6.	No Limit	08	42.10
	Total	**19**	**100.00**

Loan Period

Students

It has been found that majority of the libraries were lending books to B.Ed. and M.Ed. students for 14-15 days.

In a government aided college library users were entitled to keep books with them for seven days only. In case of M.Ed. students, a library had practice of lending books for a month.

Teachers

Ten (52.63%) libraries had not fixed any loan period for teachers. They were entitled to keep books with them as long as desired. Four libraries had practice of lending books for one month, while in three libraries teachers were privileged to retain books with them for the full session. A library had practice of lending books to teachers for the period of one year, while another fixed loan period as three months.

System of Circulation

TABLE: System of Circulation.

S.No.	System of Circulation	No. of Libraries	%age
1.	Ledger System	17	89.48
2.	Browne System	01	05.26
3.	Computer	01	05.26
	Total	**19**	**100.00**

It is evident from the Table above that 17 (89.48%) libraries were using ledger system for circulation of books, while one was using Browne system. In library of a government aided college computer was being used for circulation. In two libraries, B.Ed. students were allowed to borrow books during particular fixed time only. In a government aided college library books were issued to students during the period of tea break and lunch break only, while in another library circulation time was fixed as 11 a.m. to 3.30 p.m., though the library was kept open for 9 a.m. to 4 p.m. In remaining libraries there was no such restriction of time for lending books to students. A few libraries had fixed days for different sections of students for circulation.

AVERAGE NUMBER OF BOOKS ISSUED DAILY

B.Ed Students

Table shows that in five (26.32%) libraries up to 30 books were being issued daily. Four (21.05%) libraries were lending 31-60 books and other four were lending 61-90 books to B.Ed. students per day on an average.

In 04 (21.05%) libraries more than 120 books and in two libraries 91-120 books were being issued everyday. The variation in number of books being circulated by libraries was caused by variation in student's strength with colleges also.

TABLE: Number of Books Issued Daily.

S.No.	Average Number of Books Issued	No. of Libraries	%age
1.	0-30	05	26.32
2.	31-60	04	21.05
3.	61-90	04	21.05
4.	90-120	02	10.53
5.	More than 120	04	21.05
	Total	**19**	**100.00**

M.Ed. Students

In case of M.Ed. students, five libraries were lending 21-30 books and other five were lending 11-20 books daily. Responses revealed that two libraries were lending more than 30 books everyday.

In proportion to the strength of M.Ed. students considerable number of books were being circulated daily. In two libraries dissertations were also being issued to M.Ed students for two days only.

Teachers

In 11 libraries up to 10 books and in seven libraries 11-20 books were being issued to teachers daily. A library was lending more than 20 books to teachers on an average.

Return of Books

Responses revealed that in 17 libraries students return books in time with in the prescribed loan period, whereas two librarians responded otherwise. The majority of the libraries had not fixed any loan period for teachers, therefore no question of timely return of books by them arises. Responses revealed that out of remaining nine libraries having prescribed loan period, teachers of five colleges did not return books by the due date.

OVERDUE FINE

Sixteen (84.21%) libraries were charging overdue fine from users for return of books after due date, whereas remaining 03 libraries did not. Out of the 16 libraries charging overdue fine from students, 15 could not dare to charge it from teachers. Only UCE library was charging overdue fine from teachers for late return of books.

Rate of Charges

Majority of the libraries were charging overdue fine from users at a nominal rate of ₹ 1 or less per book per day. It is interesting to mention here that in a government college library overdue fine was being charged from students @ Rs.10 per book per day.

RESERVATION OF BOOKS

Librarians were asked whether they had provision for reservation service in case the needed books were already issued to other users. Response revealed that majority of the libraries comprising 17 (89.48%) were providing reservation service to users, while remaining two libraries did not.

MOST USED COLLECTION

Responses revealed that in 17 libraries textbooks were used by students and teachers more frequently than other documents. Of remaining two libraries, a librarian responded that books of all categories were used equally, while, another shared that text books and reference books were used more frequently.

EXPECTATION OF THE INTERNET CONNECTIVITY

Responses of the library staff revealed that the users of 12 libraries did not expect the Internet connectivity in libraries because of its availability in computer labs, whereas seven librarians responded that users do expect this service. Six libraries were already providing the Internet service to users.

Librarians responded that users expect the Internet in libraries for academic purpose i.e. to access research papers and objects in the subject of education.

SERVICES

Our education system is becoming more and more complex. The classroom instruction alone cannot be considered sufficient to attain educational objectives. College libraries exist to supplement their parent institutions in achieving educational goals. Therefore, these are expected to provide the necessary services and facilities to users. Services provided by libraries under study are discussed here.

Opening Hours of Libraries

Opening hours of libraries have direct bearing on the use of their resources and services. Survey brought to notice that 15 (78.94%) libraries were being kept open for 6-7 hours a day, while remaining 04 (21.06%) libraries were being opened for 7-8 hours daily. Working hours of majority of the libraries coincided with class hours. All libraries remained closed with colleges on Sunday and holidays, but were kept open during vacations.

It has been found that during vacations also majority of the libraries were kept open for 6-7 hours a day, while a library remained open for 4-5 hours only. Three librarians shared that there was no specific timing for opening libraries during vacations.

REFERENCE SERVICE

Responses revealed that all libraries were providing reference service. Librarians were further asked to indicate the type of reference service being rendered.

Table below makes it clear that 17 libraries were providing only short-range reference service while two librarians accepted of providing long-range reference service also in addition to short-range reference service.

TABLE: Provision of Reference Service.

S.No.	Type of Reference Service	No. of Libraries	%age
1.	Short Range	17	89.48
2.	Short Range and Long range	02	10.52
	Total	**19**	**100.00**

Current Awareness Service (CAS)/Selective Dissemination of Information (SDI)

Current Awareness Service is aimed at keeping users abreast with the latest developments in concerned field. As reported by librarians, 11 libraries were providing CAS, while remaining 08 did not. None of the libraries had provision for SDI service. Librarians were further asked about the methods of providing CAS.

The responses received for multi-choice options are given in Table:

TABLE: Method of Providing Current Awareness Service.

S.No.	Methods of CAS	No. of Libraries	%age
1.	Display of List of Recent Acquisitions	03	27.28
2.	Recent Acquisitions Display	06	54.54
3.	Routing of Periodicals	05	45.46
4.	Verbal Discussion with Users	01	09.10
	Total	**15**	**100.00**

Table above reveals that majority of the libraries were providing CAS through display of recent acquisitions and 03 were rendering it by display of recent acquisition lists. Five libraries were circulating periodicals among teacher. A librarian shared that he provided CAS through verbal discussion with the users. But on the other hand, only one student of a college was familiar about this service.

Book Exhibitions

Only four libraries were organizing book exhibitions. Two librarians responded of organizing these on the 'important occasions' i.e. Gandhi Jayanti, Maharishi Dayanand Anniversary etc. A library organized book exhibition on the occasion of annual convocation, while remaining one arranged that on the college functions.

A few librarians invited booksellers to organize book exhibitions in their libraries. Three librarians responded of providing bibliographical services, while remaining responded otherwise.

Photocopy Service

The NCTE provided in its norms and standards that a college library shall have photocopying facility. Only 08 (42.10%) libraries had provision of photocopy service, while remaining majority i.e. 11 (57.90%) did not. In majority of the libraries it was offered at a genuine rate of 50 paise to ₹1 per copy, whereas in a library photocopy charges were fixed @ ₹1.50 per copy for students and ₹ 1 for teachers.

All libraries except one had no limit over number of pages a user could get copied at a time. The remaining library had fixed this limit to a maximum of 20 flashes.

Resource Sharing

Resource sharing enables libraries to provide access to the users to the resources and services beyond their means and help to overcome the problem of paucity of funds. Only five libraries of GACE were participating in resource sharing programmes with other libraries. It has been found that resource haring was limited to books only. These libraries were co-operating with the libraries of other institutes run by the same management.

Referral Service and Newspaper Clipping

Referral service is very useful as no library can acquire all the available information. Survey revealed that 14 libraries were providing referral service, while library staff of remaining five libraries responded otherwise. Staff of all libraries except one library had maintained newspaper clipping files of important newspaper objects on education and of news related to NCTE and their colleges.

ORIENTATION

Responses revealed that library staff of all libraries, except one was giving orientation to users towards libraries. Library staff was asked about the method of providing orientation. Response received is tabulated below table:

TABLE.: Methods of Providing Orientation.

S.No.	Mathod Used	No. of Libraries	%age
1.	Lecture	10	55.56
2.	Visit Around Library	03	16.67
3.	Notice Board	01	05.55
4.	Lecture and Visit Around Library	03	16.67
5.	Other Method	01	05.55
	Total	**18**	**100.00**

It is evident from Table above that in 55.56% of the 18 libraries giving orientation to users, it was provided through lecture method, while in three (16.67%) libraries users were taken around libraries. In three libraries, a combination of the aforesaid methods was used to give orientation. In UCE library users were given orientation individually at the time of giving them membership.

Access

Open access is essential to facilitate maximum use of library collection. It gives users opportunities to browse documents on their own and enable them to find most relevant information. Survey brought to notice that only five libraries had open access system and eight libraries were providing partially open access. The remaining six libraries had close access to collection. Fear of theft and lack of adequate number of staff members were the main reasons for following close access. During visit to DAV College of Education, Abohar it was observed that books were kept in almirahs touching the ceiling of library, leaving no scope for browsing.

USE OF COMPUTERS

The ICTs has greatly enhanced the efficiency of library services. Computers are used to provide various library services and perform the routine, repetitive and clerical jobs. The functioning of all types of libraries is influenced by this vital machine. Libraries of college of education are also adapting to this need of the day. It was found that out of total 19 libraries, 10 libraries had computers, while remaining nine did not.

Eight libraries were using computers for automation, and one had two computers to provide the Internet service. In a library computer was kept side in a corner without any use as library did not have any library automation software and the Internet connectivity. Librarians were further asked to indicate the softwares being used for library automation. The responses received from library staff of eight libraries using computers for library automation are discussed here.

TABLE: Software Being used for Automation of Libraries.

S.No.	Name of the Software	No. of Libraries	%age
1.	SOUL	01	12.50
2.	CDS/ISIS	01	12.50
3.	WINSIS	01	12.50
4.	Alice for Windows	01	12.50
5.	Local	02	25.00
6.	Not Use Any Software	02	25.00
	Total	**08**	**100.00**

Table above shows that out of a total eight libraries using computers for automation, two libraries were using locally developed softwares, while another implemented SOUL for automation.

A library has implemented CDS/ ISIS and other two were using WINSIS and Alice for Windows respectively.

Two libraries had not used any library automation software but prepared databases of documents in 'Microsoft Word' and 'Microsoft Access' respectively.

It was observed that majority of the libraries were using computer to perform housekeeping operations. All libraries were using computers to create databases of books.

Five of these also created databases of journals, magazines and newspapers in addition to databases of books.

INTERNET

Majority of the libraries did not have the Internet connectivity, though the NCTE requires a library to have computer with the Internet facility for the use of faculty and student-teachers. Only six libraries were providing the Internet service to users.

ATTEMPTS TO PROMOTE USE OF LIBRARIES

Library staff of 17 libraries responded of making efforts to promote use of libraries, whereas in remaining two libraries no such attempts were being made.

Both of these libraries did not have librarians and these were being run by restorers. Library staff of 17 libraries responded of ascertaining information needs of users to improve the resources and services to promote use of libraries.

Responses revealed that in three libraries, the library staff displayed the lists of recent arrivals and in six libraries they displayed the recent acquisitions to promote use of libraries. Librarians were further asked to indicate the methods used to ascertain information needs of users.

TABLE: Methods Used to Ascertain Information Needs of Users

S.No.	Method to Ascertain Information Needs	No. of Libraries	%age
1.	Discussion with Users	17	100.00
2.	Maintain Suggestion	06	35.50
3.	Record Queries	03	17.64
4.	Conduct Survey	02	11.77
	Total	**28**	**100.00**

It is obvious from Table above that discussion with users was the most useful method to ascertain their information needs, as the staff of all 17 libraries ascertaining information needs of users was using this method. In addition, six libraries had maintained suggestion boxes.

Two librarians reported about conducting user surveys to ascertain the information needs of their users and take necessary action wherever applicable.

Three librarians responded of maintaining record of users' queries. Inadequate staff was the major problem faced by librarians in promoting use of libraries. Nine librarians expressed the need to appoint more staff to serve users effectively.

A librarian of a government aided college not having adequate supporting staff in library commented "I remain busy in locking and unlocking almirahs throughout the day and do not get time for this."

PROBLEMS FACED BY LIBRARIANS

Librarians were asked to express the problems being faced by them in managing libraries.

Inadequate Staff

Lack of adequate staff was the major obstacle in functioning of libraries, influencing their organization and administration. Nine librarians responded that they did not have adequate staff to serve the users. It has been found that three libraries were being run by restorers. Many GACE did not have the sanctioned posts of library restorers and library attendants. Librarians were overburdened with the non-professionals jobs due to lack of adequate staff.

Problem of Space

Some libraries including library of Government College of Education, Jalandhar were suffering from the problem of insufficient space. Only five libraries had separate reading room for users whereas, in remaining libraries chairs were arranged in stack area. A librarian complained of shortage of furniture.

Paucity of Funds

Funds are the nerve centre of an organization. Responses of the library staff of four colleges revealed that they were facing the problem of scarcity of funds for purchase of reading material. Purchase of documents largely depended upon the UGC grants. The administration of colleges contributed less towards libraries. A librarian shared that they did not have funds even to purchase catalogue cabinet and cards.

Status

Society has not recognized librarians equivalent to teachers. Three librarians complained that they were not given equal recognition with teaching staff. In spite of the higher academic and professional qualification they were thought as a part of clerical staff. One of the librarians went to the extent of saying that they were on a par with the teachers in terms of salary only but not in status.

SUGGESTIONS OF LIBRARY STAFF

Library staff was required to give suggestions to improve the services of libraries to make them more effective. Library staff of 10 libraries made suggestions for the provision of more staff in libraries to serve the users, as majority of the libraries did not have adequate staff. A restorer serving at a government aided college library, where post of librarian was vacant responded that college should appoint librarian to relieve her from the responsibility of managing library. Four librarians expressed the need for supporting staff to assist them in proper organization of libraries. Staff of five libraries suggested that libraries should be provided independent buildings to accommodate the growing collection and users.

A librarian demanded the provision of adequate furniture in library. Library staff of four colleges suggested for the provision of adequate funds for purchase of reading material, furniture and equipment to make library services more effective.

A librarian responded that he has computer in library, but it was not being used for any purpose as the authorities had not sanctioned the requisite funds to purchase library automation software. Three librarians suggested for computerization of library operations for effective functioning.

FUTURE PLANS

Librarians of only five colleges expressed their future plans regarding libraries, whereas library staff of majority of the colleges had not responded to questions. Librarians of DAV College of Education, Hoshiarpur and Dev Samaj College of

Education for Women, Ferozepur City had plans to develop local area network with in college campus.

They also planned to introduce the Internet service in respective libraries. A librarian responded that he want to develop library as per the requirements of National Assessment and Accreditation Council (NAAC). Library of Khalsa College of Education, Amritsar had two computers to provide the Internet service. Its librarian was planning for automation of library operations using standard software. Similarly, two more librarians had plans to implement computers in libraries. One of them was interested in using SOUL software for library automation.

CONCLUSION

To conclude, libraries did not have adequate staff leaving librarians overburdened with the semi-professional and nonprofessional jobs. Six libraries did not have regular librarians, having its influence on the organization and administration of libraries. Moreover, the NCTE has not provided any detailed norms regarding library staff.

It has been found that the functioning of library committees was restricted to acquisition and writing off missing books rather than the overall development of libraries. Student's involvement in committees was almost absent, as only one college library had students' representatives as members of library committee. By and large libraries did not have any collection development policy.

Analysis brought forward that teachers and principals were playing leading role in selection of documents, while librarians had little say in selection of subject related books. Availability of financial support influenced the collection size of libraries. Libraries of GCE had more volumes than libraries of GACE and UCE. Non-book material was almost absent in libraries. A few libraries had CD's that came free with books, though the NCTE prescribed for colleges to have 'electronic publications' in collection. Many libraries did not meet the NCTE norms regarding annual addition of books and minimum number of journals on subscription.

Only five libraries had separate reading rooms, while in remaining libraries chairs were arranged with in stack area. The NCTE norms about library buildings need to be revised, as it requires each college to have library-cum-reading room.

It was observed that in a government aided college library books were arranged on shelves touching the ceiling. When users need books they express heir demand to library staff and then library attendant take out books from shelves using ladder. Except UCE, none of the colleges had provision for library budget.

The UGC grants, library fee, library development fund and amalgamated fund constituted the regular source of finance. The NCTE remained silent about financial provision for libraries. Survey revealed the lack of standardization for technical processing of collection. In seven libraries, collection was partially classified, whereas in the library of a college established in 1942, collection has not yet been classified.

Eleven libraries had partially catalogued collection. Eight libraries gave the privilege to the teachers to borrow as many books as they wish, while 10 libraries allowed them to keep books with themselves for as long as desired. Shockingly, two libraries were using demand box system and another was using slip system for lending books to B.Ed. students. Majority of the libraries were being opened for 6-7 hours a day, leaving users with little time to use libraries.

In addition to circulation, reference service was the only service provided by all libraries. Eleven librarians admitted of providing Current Awareness Service (CAS), but on the other hand only one student and a few teachers were aware about this service.

Eight libraries were rendering photocopy service. Libraries did not provide any advance library services. Only eight libraries were using computer for automation of their operations. In addition, a library had two computers to provide the Internet service.

Only six libraries had the Internet connectivity, though the NCTE prescribed that college library should have computer with the Internet connectivity. Library staff of 17 libraries responded of ascertaining information needs of users to improve resources and services to promote use of libraries.

Discussion with users was the most useful method to ascertain information needs of users. In addition, two librarians reported about conducting user surveys to find information needs of users. Lack of staff and paucity of the funds were the major problems faced by librarians. Another major problem is related with the status of library staff vis-à-vis. teachers, they feel that that they are not on a par with the teaching staff and this leads to frustration and apathetic mind set of library staff. It is in the hands of the library staff also to change this attitude and make a place for themselves in the college. It was good to find that many librarians were planning to implement computers and provide the Internet services in libraries.

❐

10

Understanding the Participatory Networks

AN OVERVIEW

Knowledge is created through conversation. Conversations can take place between friends and colleagues in the 'here and now.' But, they can also take place over centuries, with the participants changing but the theme remaining the same, and the conversation being recorded in thousands of artifacts, like books, pictures, and digital files. In many conversations users need sophisticated processes to facilitate the conversation. Facilitation not only enriches conversations with diverse and deep information, it also serves as a memory keeper, documenting agreements and outcomes to facilitate future conversations.

The library serves this vital role for many communities. The implication of this rather abstract concept is that libraries are in the conversation business. This theoretical argument can be seen in traditional brick-and-mortar libraries as library speaker series, book groups, and even the collection development processes. Yet online, the library has fallen far short of this ideal of conversation facilitator. Key library systems, such as the catalogue for example, are at best one-way conversations.

Libraries have a great opportunity to provide invaluable conversational, participatory infrastructure to their communities online. By adopting concepts and technologies from Web 2.0 and tightly integrating them into their services, libraries can advance not just their communities but also their positions within them.

The opportunities inherent in participatory networks have not emerged because of current Internet developments such as Web 2.0, but, rather, these technologies make it easier to meet an identified and long-standing role of libraries. Wikis, blogs, and recommender systems replace dial-up bulletin boards and local databases as a means to empower our communities.

What's more, these technologies can bring the ideal of the participatory model to our most fundamental library systems. Libraries should adopt participatory network concepts and software not because they are new or sexy, but because they match our most fundamental mission: knowledge creation and dissemination. This document describes the participatory model of libraries and provides an overview of current Web 2.0 technologies and a brief discussion of how current Library 2.0 efforts point the way to an even greater change in library as a facilitator of conversations. Specific challenges and opportunities of participatory networking are reviewed. Finally, the authors recommend the creation of a shared participatory test bed for libraries.

This network would not only experiment with new collaborative Web technologies, but also work with library organisations and vendors to speed innovation in traditional library systems. Finally, the network test bed would create a shared infrastructure to provide participatory technologies – such as Wikis, blogs, and RSS feeds—to libraries for inclusion in their day-to-day services.

THE GOAL

Knowledge is created through conversation. Libraries are in the knowledge business. Therefore, libraries are in the conversation business. Some of those conversations span millennia, while others only span a few seconds. Some of these conversations happen in real time. In some conversations, there is a broadcast of ideas from one author to multiple audiences. Some conversations are sparked by a book or a video or a Web page. Some of these conversations are as trivial as directing someone to the bathroom. Other conversations centre on the foundations of ourselves and our humanity. It may be odd to start a technology brief with such seemingly abstract comments. Yet, without this firm, if theoretical, footing the advent of Web 2.0, social networking, Library 2.0, and participatory networks seems like a clutter of new terminology, tools, and acronyms.

In fact, as will be discussed, without this conceptual footing, many library functions can seem disconnected, and the field that serves lawyers, doctors, single mothers, and 8 year olds fragmented. The scale of this technology brief is limited; it is to present library decision makers with the opportunities and challenges of participatory networks. It is only a single piece of a much larger puzzle that seeks to present a cohesive framework for libraries. This framework will not only fit tools such as blogs and Wikis into their offerings, but also will show how a more participatory, conversational approach to libraries in general can help libraries better integrate current and future functions.

Think of this document as an overview or introduction to participatory librarianship. Readers will find plenty of examples and definitions of Web 2.0 and social networking later in this chapter. However, to jump right into the technology without a larger framework invites the rightful skepticism of a library organisation that feels constantly buffeted by new technological advances. In any environment with no larger conceptual founding to measure the importance of an advance in technology or practice selection of any one technology or practice is nearly arbitrary. Without a framework the field becomes open to the influence of personalities and trendy technology.

Therefore, it is vital to ground any technological, social, or policy conversation into a larger, rooted concept. As Susser said, "...to practice without theory is to sail an uncharted sea; theory without practice is not to set sail at all." For this chapter, the chart will be conversation theory.

The core of this brief is in four sections that follow:

- A conceptual framework for understanding and evaluating participatory networks;
- A discussion of key concepts and technologies in participator networks drawn primarily from Web 2.0 and Library 2.0;
- A merging of the conceptual framework with the technological discussion to present a sort of roadmap for library systems development; and
- A set of recommendations to foster greater discussion and action on the topic of participatory networks and, more broadly, participatory librarianship.

LIBRARY AS A FACILITATOR OF CONVERSATION

So let us return to the concept that knowledge is created through conversation. This notion stretches back to Socrates and the Socratic Method. However, the specific foundation for this statement comes from 'Conversation Theory,' a means of explaining cognition and how people learn. It is not the purpose of this chapter to provide a detailed description of Conversation Theory, a task already admirably accomplished by Pask. Rather, let us use the theory as a structure upon which to hang an exploration of participatory networking and, more broadly, participatory librarianship.

The core of conversation theory is simple: people learn through conversation. Different communities have different standards for conversations, from the scientific community's rigourous formalisms to the religious community's embedded meaning in scripture to the sometimes impenetrable dialect of teens. The point remains, however, that different actors establish meaning through determining common definitions and building upon shared concepts. The library has been a place where we facilitate conversations, though often implicitly. The concept of learning through conversations is evidenced in libraries in large initiatives like information litreacy and teaching critical thinking skills and in the smaller events of book groups, reference interviews, and speaker series. Library activities such as building collections of artifacts inform scholars' research through a formal conversation process where ideas are supported with evidence and methods.

Similarly, preservation efforts, perhaps of wax cylinders with spoken word content or of ancient maps that embody an ongoing dialogue about the shape and nature of the physical world, seek to save, or at least document, important conversations. Common use of the word 'conversation' is completely in accordance with the use of the term in Conversation Theory.

The term is, however, more specifically defined as an act of communication and agreement between a set of agents. So, a conversation can be between two people, two organisations, two countries, or even within an individual. How can a conversation take place within an individual? Educators and school librarians may be familiar with the term 'metacognition,' or the act of reflecting on one's learning. Yet, even the most casual reader will be familiar with the concept of debating oneself. The point is that a conversation is with at least two agents trying to come to an understanding. Also note that those two agents can change over time. So, while Socrates and Plato are dead the conversation they started about the nature of knowledge and the world is carried forward by new generations of thinkers...same conversation, different agents. People converse, organisations converse, states converse, societies converse.

The requirements, in the terms of Conversation Theory, are two cognitive systems seeking agreement. The results of these conversations, what Pask would call 'cognitive entanglements,' are books, videos, and artifacts that either document, expand, or result from conversations. So, while one cannot converse with a book that book certainly can be a starting point for many conversations within the reader and within a larger community.

If the theory is that conversation creates knowledge, the library community has added a corollary: the best knowledge comes from an 'optimal information environment,' one in which the most diverse and complete information is available to the conversant. Library ethics show an implicit understanding of this corollary in the advocacy of intellectual freedom and unfettered access. Libraries seek to create rich environments for knowledge and have taken the stance that they are not in the job of arbitrating the conversations that occur or the 'appropriateness' of the information used to inform those conversations. As will be discussed later, this belief in openness of conversations will have some far-reaching implications for the library collection and is an ideal that can never truly be met.

For now, the reader may take away that conversation theory is very much in line with current and past library practice, and it also shows a clear trajectory for the future. The value to this viewpoint is not just theoretical; it has real consequences and uses. For example, much of library evaluation has been based in numeric counts of tangible outputs: books circulated, collection size, reference transactions, and so on. Yet this quantitative approach has been frustrating to many who feel they are counting outcomes but not getting at true impact of library service. Librarians may ask themselves, "Which numbers are important...and why?" If libraries focused on conversations there might be some clarity and cohesion between statistics and other outcomes. Suddenly, the number of reference questions can be linked to items cataloged or to circulation numbers...they are all markers of the scope and scale of conversations within the library context.

This approach might enable the library community to better identify 'important' conversations and demonstrate direct contributions to these conversations across functions. For example, a school district identifies early litreacy as important. There is a discussion about public policy options, new programmes, and school goals to achieve greater litreacy in the K-5 grades.

The library should be able to track two streams in this conversation. The first is the one libraries are used to counting; that is, the library's contribution to K-5 litreacy. But the library can also document and demonstrate how it furthered the conversation about children's litreacy in general. It could show the resources provided to community officials. It could show the litreacy pathfinders that were created. The point of this example is that the library is both participant in the conversation and facilitator of conversation. The theoretical discussion leads us to a discussion about the second topic of this technology brief: pragmatic aspects of the knowledge as conversation approach, or a participatory approach as it will be called.

As new technologies are developed and deployed in the current environment of limited resources, there must be some means of evaluating their utility. The utility of a technology is appropriately measured against a given library's mission, which is in turn developed to respond to the needs of the community that library serves. First, however, let us identify some of the new technologies and describe them briefly.

PARTICIPATORY NETWORKING SOCIAL NETWORKS, AND WEB 2.0

Let us now move from the theoretical to the operational. The impetus behind this chapter is the relatively recent emergence of a new group of Internet services and capabilities. Suddenly, terms like Wiki, blog, mashup, Web 2.0, and biblioblogosphere have become commonplace. As with any new wave of technological creation, these terms can seem ambiguous and they also come wrapped in varying amounts of hype. They may all, however, be grouped under the phenomenon of participatory networking. While we now have a conceptual framework to evaluate these technologies that support participatory networking, we still need to know the basics of the terminology and technologies. This section outlines key concepts in the pragmatics of participatory networking. The section after this one will join the theoretical and operational to outline key challenges and opportunities for the library world. We begin with Web 2.0

WEB 2.0

Much of what we call participatory networking, at least the technological foundation of it, stems from developments in 'Web 2.0.' As with many buzzwords, the exact definition of Web 2.0 is not clear. It is more an aggregation of concepts that range from software development to abstractions. What pervades the Web 2.0 approach is the notion that Internet services are increasingly facilitators of conversations.

Web 2.0 Characteristic: Social Networks

A core concept of Web 2.0 is that people are the content of sites; that is, a site is not populated with information for users to consume. Instead, services are provided to individual users for them to build networks of friends and other groups. The content of a site, then, comprises user-provided information that attracts new members of an ever-expanding network.

Examples:

- **Flickr:** Flickr provides users with free Web space to upload images and create photo albums. Users can then share these photos with friends or with the public at large. Flickr facilitates the creation of shared photo galleries around themes and places.
- **The Cheshire Public Library:** The Teen Book Blog at the Cheshire Public Library offers book reviews created only by the students who use the library.
- **Memorial Hall Library:** The Memorial Hall Library in Andover.
- Massachusetts offers podcasts of poetry contests in which the content is created by students.
- **Libraries in My Space:** MySpace searches show that there are MySpace sites for hundreds of individual libraries and scores of library groups.
- **Alexandrian Public Library:** This practice is growing among public libraries and is an attempt to reach out to users in their preferred online environments. In this venue, the more friends a library My Space site has the more successful it may be considered. The Alexandrian Public Library has 75 friends and 15 comments. The Brooklyn College Library has 2195 friends and 270 comments.

Web 2.0 Characteristic: Wisdom of Crowds

There has been some research into the quality of mass decision-making. That research shows how remarkably accurate groups are in their judgements. Web 2.0 pools large groups of users to comment on decisions. This aggregation of input is facilitated by the ready availability of social networking sites. Certainly, this approach of community organisation and verification of knowledge also has its detractors. Many, for example, question the wisdom seen in some entries of

Wikipedia. Yet, recent articles have compared this mass editing process favourably to traditional sources of information such as the Encyclopaedia Britannica.

Examples

eBay

eBay has perhaps the most studied and copied community policing and reputation systems. All buyers and sellers can be rated. The aggregation of many users' experiences create a 'Feedback Score' that is equivalent to a group credibility rating. These kinds of group feedback systems can now be seen in most major Internet retailers.

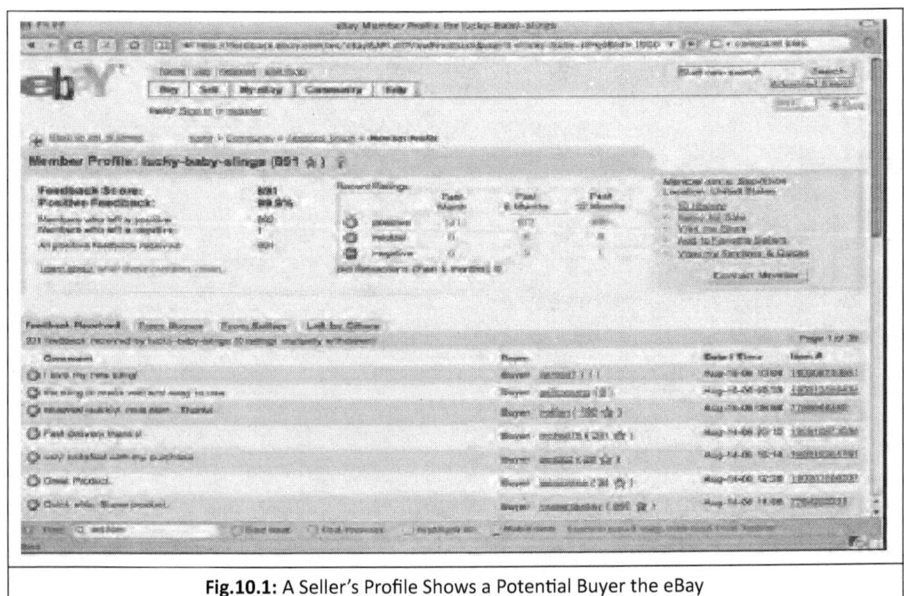

Fig.10.1: A Seller's Profile Shows a Potential Buyer the eBay Community's Current Estimation of a Seller's Credibility

LibraryThing

LibraryThing.com makes book recommendations based on the collective intelligence of all users of the site. The greater the pool of collective intelligence the more information is available to the user for decision-making.

The Diary Project

The Diary Project Library is a non-profit organisation that encourages teens to write about their day-to-day experiences growing up. The goal of this site is to encourage communication among teens of all cultures and backgrounds, provide peer-to-peer support, stimulate discussion, and generate feedback that can help ease some of the concerns encountered along the way and let them know that they are not alone. To that end, the site comprises thousands of entries in 24 categories. Because of the great number of entries, most youth can find helpful materials.

Web 2.0 Characteristic: Loosely Coupled APIs

API is short hand for 'Application Programming Interface.' It provides a set of instructions that a programmer can use to communicate between applications.

APIs allow programmers to incorporate one piece of software they may not be able to directly manipulate into another. For example, Google Maps has made a public API that allows Web page designers to include satellite images into their Web pages with little more than a latitude and longitude. APIs vary in their ease of integration. Loosely coupled APIs allow for very easy integration using high-level scripting languages.

Examples

Google Maps

Google Maps displays street or satellite map showing markers on specific locations provided by an external source with simple sets of longitudes and latitudes. So, it becomes extremely easy to create Geographic Information Systems with little knowledge of GIS principles.

Flickr

Flickr provides easy means to integrate these hosted images into other Web pages or applications.

YouTube

YouTube provides users with the capability to upload and comment upon video on the Internet. It also allows for easy integration of the videos into other Web pages and blogs. With a simple line of HTML code anyone can access streaming video for their content.

Web 2.0 Characteristic: Mashups

Mashups are combinations of APIs and data that result in new information resources and services. This ease of incorporation has led to an assumption of a 'right to remix.' In the world of open source software and the creative commons, the right to remix refers to a growing expectation among Internet users that they are not limited by the interfaces and uses presented to them by a single organisation.

Examples

ChicagoCrime.org

An often-cited example of a mashup is ChicagoCrime.org, which uses Google Maps to plot crime data for the city of Chicago. Users can now see exactly which street corner had the most murders.

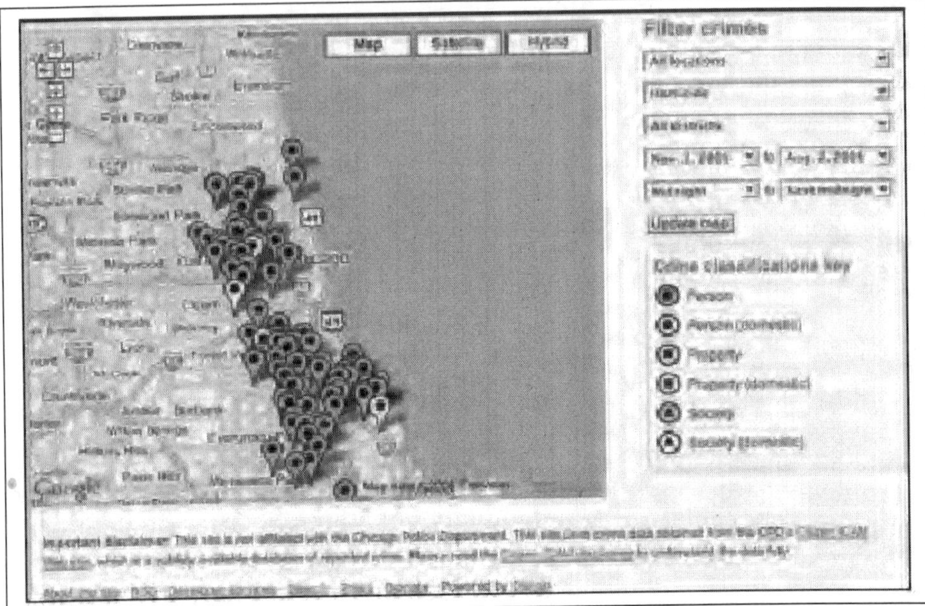

Fig. 10.2: Screen Shot of Chicagocrime.org. The Map, Generated by Google Maps, is showing a Marker at the Location of Every Homicide in Chicago from November 2, 2005 to August 2, 2006.

Book Burro

Book Burro "is a Web 2.0 extension for Firefox and Flock. When it senses you are looking at a page that contains a book, it will overlay a small panel which when opened lists prices at online bookstores such as Amazon, Buy, Half and whether the book is available at your library."

Web 2.0 Characteristic: Permanent Betas

The concept of a permanent beta is, in part, a realisation that no software is ever truly complete so long as the user community is still commenting upon it. For example, Google does not release services from beta until it has achieved a sufficient user base no matter how fixed the underlying source code is. Permanent beta is also a design strategy. Large applications are broken into smaller constituent parts that can be manipulated separately. This allows large applications to be continually developed by a more diverse and distributed community.

Examples

MIT Libraries

The MIT Libraries are experimenting with new technologies to help make access to information easier.

The tools are offered to the public with an appeal for feedback and additional tools, and the there is a permanent address designed just to collect feedback from the beta-phase tools, which include:

- The New Humanities Virtual Browsery, which highlights new books and incorporates an RSS feed, the ability to comment on books, links to book reviews, availability information, and links to other books by the same author.
- The LibXMIT Edition, which is a Firefox toolbar that allows users to search the Barton catalogue, Vera, Google Scholar, the SFX FullText Finder, and other search tools; it embeds links to MIT-only resources in Amazon, Barnes and Noble, Google Scholar, and NYT Book Reviews.
- The Dewey Research Advisor Business and Economics: Q&A, which provides starting points for specific research questions in the fields of business, management, and economics.

Google Labs

Google has a site named 'Google Labs' that puts out company-generated tools and services. In fact, part of a Google employee's work time is dedicated to creating the resources and tools through personal projects and exploration.

These tools and services remain a part of the 'Lab' until they are finished and have sufficient user bases. Projects range from the simple to the extensive.

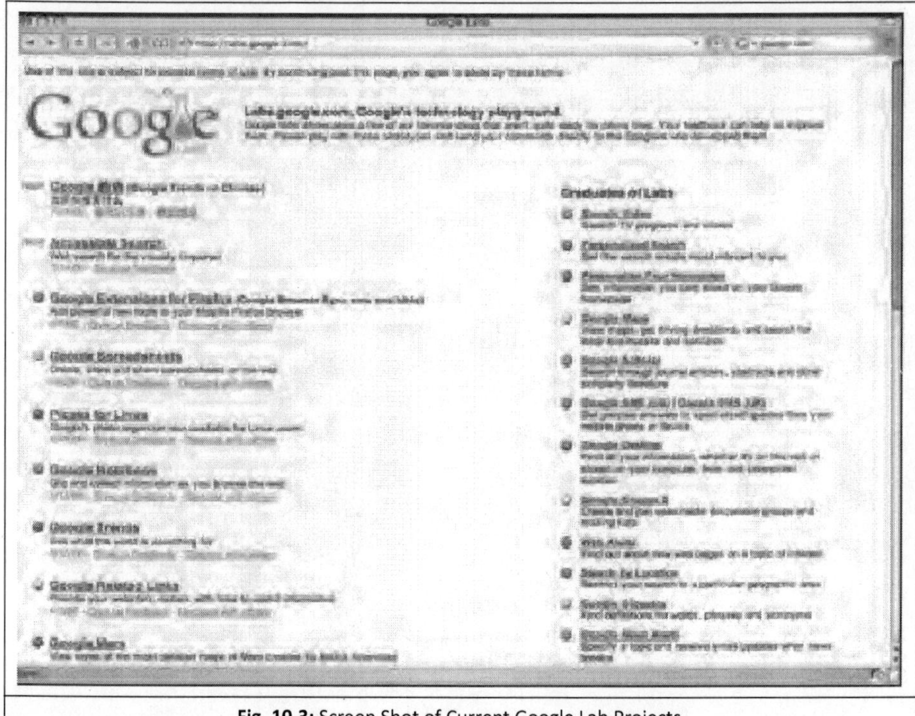

Fig. 10.3: Screen Shot of Current Google Lab Projects.

Web 2.0 Characteristic: Software Gets Better the More People Use It

An increasing number of Web 2.0 sites emphasise social networks, where these services gain value only as they gain users. Malcolm Gladwell recounts this principle and the work of Kevin Kelly with an earlier telecommunications network, the network of fax machines connected to the phone system: "The first fax machine ever made...cost about $2,000 at retail. But it was worth nothing because there was no other fax machine for it to communicate with.

The second fax machine made the first fax machine more valuable, and the third fax made the first two more valuable, and so on...When you buy a fax machine, then, what you are really buying is access to the entire fax network—which is infinitely more valuable than the machine itself." With social networking sites, and all sites that seek to capitalise on user input, the true value of each site is defined by the number of people it can bring together.

Examples

Amazon

A classic example of this characteristic is Amazon.com. Amazon sells books and other merchandise, but, in reality, Amazon is very much about the marketing of information. Amazon gains tremendous value by allowing its users to review and rate items. The more people use Amazon and the more they comment, the more visibility these active users gain and the more credibility markers they take on.

Web 2.0 Characteristic: Folksonomies

A folksonomy is a classification system created in a bottom-up fashion and with no central coordination. This differs from the deductive approach of classifications systems like the Dewey Decimal System, where the world of ideas is broken into ten nominal classes. It also differs from other means of developing classifications where some central authority determines if a term should be included. In a folksonomy, the members of a group simply attach terms to items and the aggregate of these terms is seen as the classification.What emerges is a classification scheme that prioritises common usage over semantic clarity.

Examples

PennTags

PennTags is a social bookmarking tool for locating, organising, and sharing one's favourite online resources. Members of the Penn Community can collect and maintain URLs, links to journal articles, and records in Franklin, the online catalogue, and VCat, the online video catalogue. Once resources are compiled, users can organise them by assigning tags and/or by grouping them into projects, according to specific preferences. PennTags can also be used collaboratively, because it acts as a repository of the varied interests and academic pursuits of the Penn community, and a user can find topics and other users related to his or her own favourite online resources.

Hillsdale Teen Library

The Hillsdale Teen Library uses Flickr to post pictures of events at the Hillsdale Teen Library, as in this figure.

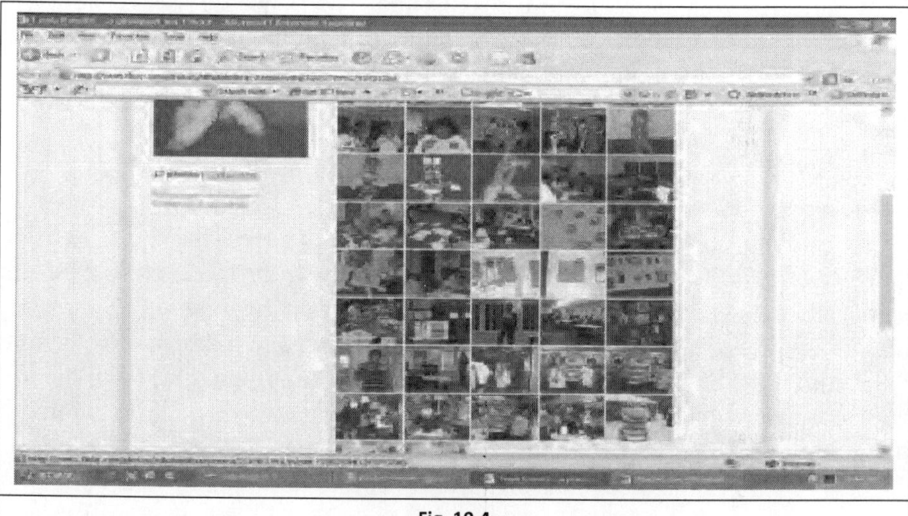

Fig. 10.4

The resulting tag view is represented in the next figure. These tags allow users to easily retrieve the images in which they are interested.

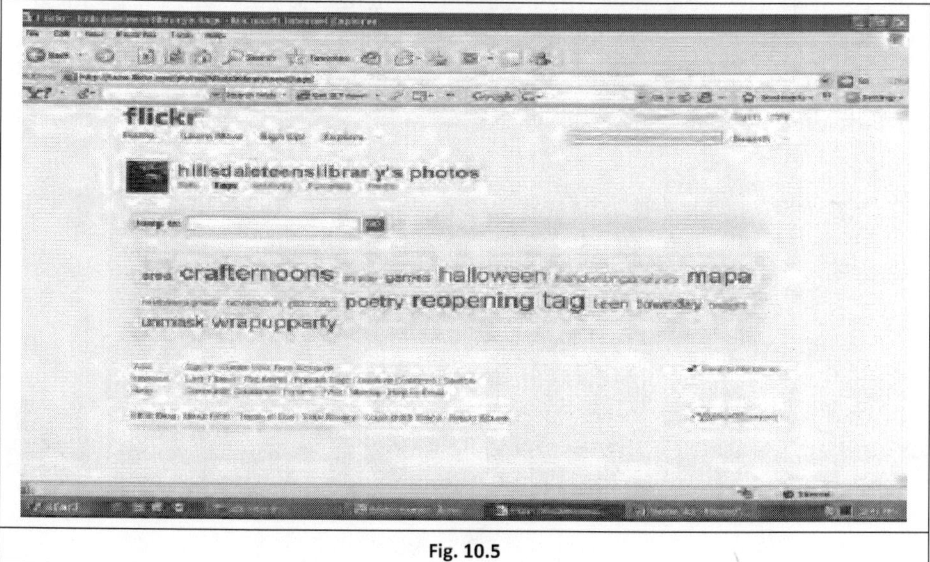

Fig. 10.5

There are more characteristics of Web 2.0, but these give some overall concepts.

CORE NEW TECHNOLOGIES: AJAX AND WEB SERVICES

As we have jut discussed, Web 2.0 is little more than set of related concepts, albeit with a lot of value being currently attached to these concepts. These concepts are supported by two underlying technologies that have facilitated Web 2.0 development and brought a substantially new user experience to the Web. The first is AJAX, which allows a more desktop-like experience for users. The second is the advent of Web services. These technologies are not necessary for Web 2.0 concepts, but they have made Web 2.0 sites much more compelling.

AJAX

AJAX stands for Asynchronous JavaScript and XML. It is a set of existing Web technologies brought together. At the most basic, AJAX allows a browser and a server to send data back and forth without needing to refresh the entire Web page being worked on. Think about the Web sites you work with. You click on a link, the browser freezes and waits for the data, then draws it on the screen. Early versions of sites like MapQuest would show a map. If you wanted to zoom into the map, you would press a zoom icon and wait while the new map, and the rest of the Web page was redrawn. Compare this to Google Maps, where you click in the middle of a map and drag left or right and the map moves dynamically.

This kind of interaction we are used to in desktop applications. Click and drag has become second nature on the desktop and AJAX is making it second nature on the Web, too. Another advantage of AJAX is that it is open and requires only light programming skills. Javascript on the client and almost any server side scripting language are easily accessible languages. This fact allows for both fast development and easier integration with existing systems. As an example, it should now be easier to bring more interactive Web interfaces to existing online catalogues.

Web Services

Web services allow for software-to-software interactions on the Web. Using Web protocols and XML, applications exchange queries and information in order to facilitate the larger functioning of a system. One example would be a system that uses an ISBN number to query multiple online catalogues and commercial vendors for availability of a book. This simple process might be part of a much larger library catalogue that shows users a book and its availability.

The point is that unlike federated search systems such as Z39.50, Web services are small. They also tend to be lightweight, and are aggregated for greater functionality.

LIBRARY 2.0

Library 2.0 is a somewhat diffuse concept. Walt Crawford, in his extended essay Library 2.0 and 'Library 2.0' found 62 different views and seven distinct definitions of Library 2.0. It is no wonder that people are confused. However, it is natural for emerging ideas and groups to function in an environment of high ambiguity. For use in this technology brief the authors see Library 2.0 as an attempt to apply Web 2.0 concepts to the purpose of the library. In the words of Ormsby, "The purpose of a library is not to … showcase new gadgetry …; rather, it is to make possible that instant of insight when all the facts come together in the shape of new knowledge."

How the applications are used will determine whether they support Ormsby's "instant of insight." Many libraries and librarians are already pursuing this goal. Some, for instance, are using blogs to reach other librarians, their own users, and potential users.

They are using Wikis to deliver reports, teach information litreacy, and serve as repositories. One has developed an API that allows WordPress posts to be directly integrated into a library catalogue. Clearly, the Internet and newer tools that empower users seem to be aligned with the library mission.

After all, librarians blogging and allowing the catalogue to be 'mashed up' can be seen as an extension of current information services. But this abundance of new applications poses a challenge.

Given the speed with which new tools are invented, librarians may find it difficult to create strategies that include all the desired services that they make possible. For every new application that becomes available, library administrators must decide whether it can serve the library, how to use it, and how to find additional resources to manage it. This problem stems from focussing excessively on the technology. Librarians should, instead, focus on the phenomena made possible by the technology. Most important of these phenomena, the library invites participation.

As Chad and Miller state:

- Library 2.0 facilitates and encourages a culture of participation, drawing upon the perspectives and contributions of library staff, technology partners and the wider community.
- Library 2.0 means harnessing this type of participation so that libraries can benefit from increasingly rich collaborative cataloguing efforts, such as including contributions from partner libraries as well as adding rich enhancements, such as book jackets or movie files, to records from publishers and others.
- Library 2.0 is about encouraging and enabling a library's community of users to participate, contributing their own views on resources they have used and new ones to which they might wish access.

- With Library 2.0, a library will continue to develop and deploy the rich descriptive standards of the domain, whilst embracing more participative approaches that encourage interaction with and the formation of communities of interest.

The carte blanche statement that users participating in the library is 'good,' however, is insufficient. Library administers must ask, 'What is the ultimate goal?' In summary, current initiatives in the library world to bring the tools of Web 2.0 to the service of Library 2.0 are exciting and innovative, and more to the point, they are supportive of the library's purpose. They may, however, incur costs, such as monitoring blogs and Wikis and creating content and corresponding with users that stretch already inadequate resources even further. Ultimately, the value of Library 2.0 concepts requires us to answer some important questions: will they be used to further knowledge, or will they simply create more work for librarians? What does the 'next version' of Library 2.0 look like? Is its mission the same and just the tools different? What makes the library different from MySpace... simply a legacy? Should we incorporate new services into the current library offerings? How do we, as facilitators of conversations, point the way to the next generation of library? It is hoped that some of the concepts in participatory librarianship may answer these questions and help further the innovations of the Library 2.0 community.

PARTICIPATORY NETWORKS

The authors use the phrase participatory networking to encompass the concept of using Web 2.0 principles and technologies to implement a conversational model within a community.

Why not simply adopt social networking, Web 2.0, or Library 2.0 for that matter? Let us examine each term's limitations:

- Social networking: Social network sites such as MySpace and Facebook have certainly captured public attention. They have also proven very popular. In their short life spans these sites have garnered an immense audience and drawn much attention from the press. Some of that attention, however, has been very negative.
- MySpace, for example, has been typified as a refuge for pedophiles and online predators. Even the television show Saturday Night Live has parodied the site for the ease with which users can create false personas and engage in risky online behaviours. To say you are starting a social networking site in your library may draw either enthusiastic support, vehement opposition or simply confused looks.
- Add to the potential negative connotations the ambiguity of the term. Is a blog a social networking site? Is Flickr? To compound this confusion, the academic domain of Social Network Theory predates MySpace by about a decade.

- Web 2.0: Ambiguity also dogs the Web 2.0 world. For some, it is technology. For others, it is simply a buzzword for the current crop of Internet sites that survived the burst of the.com bubble. In any case, Web 2.0 certainly implies more than just the inclusion of users in systems.
- Library 2.0: As stated before, the term Library 2.0 is a vague term used by some as a goad to the library community. Further, this term limits the discussion of user-inclusive Web services to the library world. While this brief focuses on the library community, it also sees the library community as a potential leader in a much broader field.

So, ultimately, the authors propose 'participatory networking' as a positive term and concept that libraries can use and promote without the confusion and limitations of previous language. The phrase 'participatory network' also has a history of prior use that can be built upon. The phrase 'participatory networks' represents systems of exchange and integration and has long been used in discussions of policy, art, and government. The phrase has also been used to describe online communities that exchange and integrate information.

LIBRARIES AS PARTICIPATORY CONVERSATIONS

So where are we? We started with the abstract statement that knowledge is created through conversation. We then looked at the current landscape of technologies that can facilitate these conversations and showed examples of how libraries, other industries, and individuals are using these technologies. In this section we combine the larger framework with the technologies to see how libraries can incorporate participatory networks to further their knowledge mission.

PARTICIPATORY LIBRARIANSHIP IN ACTION

Let us look specifically at how participatory networks can be used in the library's role as facilitator of knowledge through conversation. An obvious example is libraries hosting blogs and Wikis for their communities creating virtual meeting spaces for individuals and groups, just as libraries do in the physical world. Indeed, these are increasingly useful functions for libraries. They meet a perceived need in the community, and can generate excitement both within the library and in the community.

The idea of creating online sites for individuals and organisations makes sense for a library, although it is not without difficulties. Libraries could also use freely available open source software to create library versions of Wikipedia. Another way for libraries to offer these services would be through a cooperative or other third-party vendor.

Such a service can easily be seen as a knowledge management activity capturing and providing local expertise while linking this expertise to that produced at other libraries. Another reason for libraries to engage in participatory networking is that one library can more easily collaborate with other libraries in richer dialogues. We currently have systems that connect our online catalogues and share resources through interlibrary loan. These conduits exist and can be used for the transferal of richer data, as has been proved through collaborative virtual reference systems.

In our current systems, as in traditional library practice, when users are referred to other libraries, they are sent out and not brought back. In a participatory library setting, libraries would facilitate a conversation between the user, the community of the local library, and then through the developed conduits, other libraries and their communities. The end result would be a seamless web of libraries where the user can ignore the intricacies of the library's organisation structure and boundaries, and in which the libraries are using the best local resources to meet local needs. Bringing libraries seamlessly together to participate in conversations with a single user has another significant advantage: the Library would make it easy for users to join the conversation regardless of where they are, through the presentation of a single façade.

There is, for example, only one Google, one Amazon, and one Wikipedia. Why should users have to search from among thousands of libraries to find the conversations they want? Participatory networking will be most effective when libraries work together, when the whole is greater than its parts. We currently see elements of The Participatory Library in the OCLC Open Worldcat project. For example, users searching Google may come across a listing provided by OCLC.

After selecting the entry for the book, the user can then jump to his or her own local library's information about the book. Users do not have to know which library to visit to find a book near them. Extending this concept to conversations, one goal of these participatory networks is to make it easier for the user to enter a conversation with The Library without having to work to discover their own specific entry points. However, ensuring this effective seamless access to the Library will require more than simply adding elements of participatory networking around the edges of the library. Adding services like blogs and Wikis may be seen merely as adjunct to current library offerings. As with any technological advance, scarce resources must be weighed against a desire to incorporate new services. Do we expand the collection, improve the Web site, or offer blogs to students? A better approach for making these kinds of decisions is to look at the needs of the community served in context with the commonly accepted, core tasks of a library, and see how they can be recast as conversational, or participatory tools.

In point of fact, every service, patron, and access point is a starting point for a conversation. Let's start with the catalogue. If the catalogue is a conversation, it is decidedly formal and, more importantly, one way. Think of today's catalogue as the educational equivalent of a college lecture. A formal system is used to serve up a series of presentations on a given topic. The presentations are rigid in their construction. They follow an abstract model and provide minimal opportunities to the receiver of the information to provide feedback or input.

They provide no constructive means for the user to improve or shape the conversation. Even recent advances in catalogue functions do little more than make the presentation of information more varied. They are still not truly interactive because they do not allow user participation; they do not allow for conversation. To highlight the one-way nature of the catalogue, ask a simple question: what happens when the user doesn't find something?

Do we assume that the information is there, but that the user is simply incapable of finding it? Do we assume that the information does not exist? Do we assume that the catalogue itself is limited? What if we assume that the catalogue is just the current place a user is involving in an ongoing conversation...what would that look like? How can such a traditionally rigid system be made more participatory? What if the user, finding no relevant information in the catalogue, adds either the information or a placeholder for someone else to fill in the missing information? Possibly the user adds information from his or her expertise.

However, assuming that most people go to a catalogue because they don't have the information, perhaps the user instead begins a process for adding the information. The user might ask a question using a virtual reference service; at the end of the transaction, the user then has the option to add the question, along with the answer and associated materials, to the catalogue. Or perhaps, the user simply leaves the query in the catalogue for other patrons to answer, requesting to be notified when an answer is posted. In that case, when a new user does a catalogue search and runs across the question, he or she can provide an answer.

That answer might be a textual entry, or simply a new query that directs the original questioner or new patrons to existing information in the catalogue. The catalogue can also associate conversations with any data point. For example, a user pulls up the record for a book s/he feels might be relevant to an information need s/he is having. This process starts a conversation between that user and the library, its users and authors of associated works. The user can see comments and ratings associated with this book from not only users of this library but users of other libraries. Also associated is a list of related works and the full audio of a lecture by the author. The user might also be directed to an in-person or online book group that is reading that book.

The point is that the catalogue facilitates a conversation as opposed to simply presenting what it 'knows' about a topic and then stepping out of the process. The catalogue, then, does not simply present information, but instead helps users construct knowledge by allowing the user to participate in a conversation. There are other means of improving systems in a conversational library. Take the implicit link between the catalogue and circulation. Of course these systems have always been linked in that items found in the catalogue can be checked out and checked out items have their status reflected in the catalogue. But this kind of 'state' information is a pretty meagre offering. Imagine using circulation data to improve the actual functionality of the catalogue. Take the example of a user who is searching the catalogue for fictional books on magic. Currently, a relevance score between an item's metadata and the query is computed and then all the items are ranked in a retrieval set. This relevance score can be computed in many ways, but is usually based on the number of times a keyword appears in the record and the placement of that keyword in the metadata record. What is missing is the actual, real-world circulation of an item. Wouldn't it make sense, given such an abstract query, to present the user with Harry Potter first? What if we added circulation data to our relevance rankings: how many times this item has been checked out? It turns out that using a simple statistic is amasingly powerful.

It is akin to Google's page rank algorithm that presents sites most linked to higher in the results. Also, for those worried that users would be flooded with only popular materials, studies show that while these algorithms do change the very top ranked material, the effect quickly fades so that the user can still easily find other materials. Another consideration for adjusting a search is to allow the user to tweak the algorithms used to retrieve works. In the example, a user could turn off the 'popularity' feature. The user could also toggle switches for currency, authority, and other facets of relevancy rankings.

The conversational model requires us to rethink the catalogue as a dynamic system, with data of varying levels of currency and, frankly, quality, coming into and out of the system. In a conversational catalogue there is no reason that some data can't exist in the catalogue for limited durations. Records of well-groomed physical collections may be a core and durable collection in the catalogue, but that is only one of many types of information that could exist in the catalogue space. Furthermore, even this core data can be annotated and linked to more transient media.

So, the user might see a review from a blog as part of a catalogue record on one day, but when s/he pulls the record up again in a few days, that review might be absent, the blog writer having withdrawn the comment. This is akin to weeding the collection; however, it would happen in a more dynamic fashion than occurs with the content on library shelves. The conversational model can also be used in other areas of the library. What do we digitise? What do we select? What programmes do we offer? What do we preserve? The empowered user can participate in answering all of these questions but does not replace the expert librarian; rather, the user contributes additional and diverse information and commentary. In fact, the catalogue scenario just proposed already assumes that the library catalogue does more than store metadata. In order for the scenario to work the 'catalogue' must store questions, answers, video, audio…in essence the catalogue must be expanded and integrated with other library systems so that a final Participatory Library System can present a coherent view of The Library to patrons.

FRAMEWORK FOR INTEGRATION OF PARTICIPATORY LIBRARIANSHIP

As has been noted, participatory networks and libraries as conversations are not brand new concepts sprung from the head of Zeus. Instead they are means to integrate past and current innovations, and create a viable plan forward. The figure below provides a sort of road map of how the library might make the transition from current systems to a truly participatory system. It includes current systems, systems under development, and new concepts. It seeks to capture current momentum and push the field forward to a larger view instead of getting bogged down in the intricacies of any one development activity.

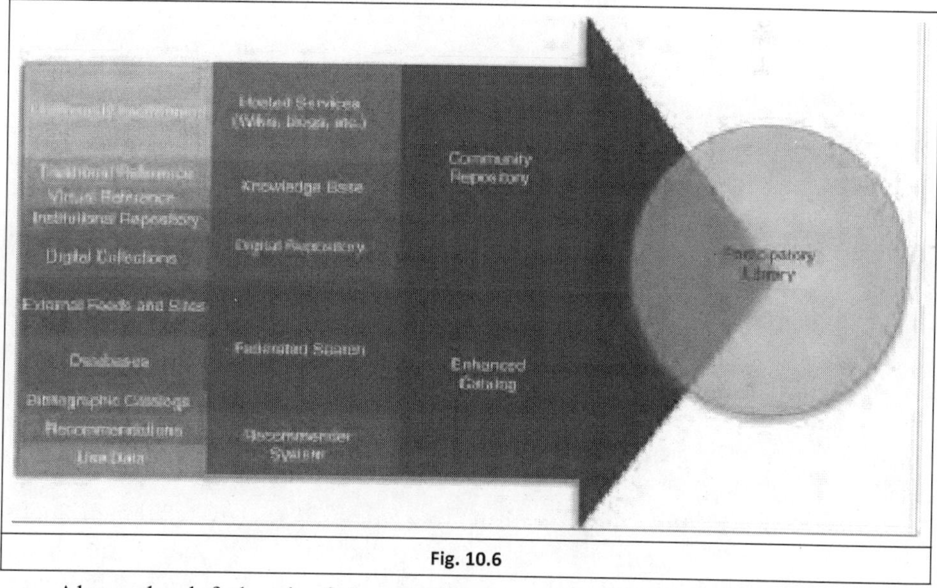

Fig. 10.6

Along the left hand of the graph are current library systems. While the terminology may differ from library to library, nearly every system can be found on today's library web sites. By showing the systems together, the problems of user confusion and library management burden become obvious. Users must often navigate these systems based on their needs, and often with little help. Should they search the catalogues first or the databases? Isn't the catalogue really just another database? Which database do they choose? In our attempts to better serve the users by creating a rich set of resources and services, we have instead complicated their information seeking lives.

As one librarian puts it, "don't give me one more system I, or my patrons, have to deal with." From the array of systems on the left hand, we can see that libraries have not been doing themselves any favours either. We are maintaining many systems, therefore making the calls for yet more systems not only impractical but unwise. The answer is to integrate systems, combining the best of each while discarding the complexity of the whole. The library world is in the midst of doing just that. This section seeks to highlight promising developments in integrating library systems well beyond the library catalogue and to highlight not only an ideal endpoint, but also how this ideal system is truly participatory.

Merging Reference and Community Involvement

The functional area furthest along in the integration of participatory librarianship is reference; since, reference is most readily recognisable as a conversation, this comes as no surprise. Over the last decade, reference services have gone online, and have led to shared reference services. More importantly, reference done online creates artifacts of reference conversations: electronic files than can be cleaned of personal information and placed in a knowledge base, and used as a resource for other users.

A new development in reference is the reference blog, in which multiple librarians and other users can be part of a question answering community with conversations that can live on beyond a single transaction. Another functional area of libraries that is already involved with participatory librarianship is community involvement. For decades, public libraries have supported local community groups through meeting spaces. Some libraries are now hosting Web spaces for local groups.

As libraries incorporate participatory technologies into their offerings, they can create virtual places such as discussion forums, Wikis, and blogs for these community groups to use. If there are standards for these discussion areas, then groups from different communities could also easily participate in shared boards; this makes sense for groups such as Weight Watchers or Alcoholics Anonymous that have local branches and national involvement.

In an academic setting, these groups can be student, faculty, or staff organisations or courses. In addition to reference and hosted community conversations, the library has been actively creating digital collections of materials. Parallel to the digital collection building of library materials is an active attempt to create institutional repositories of faculty papers, teacher lesson plans, organisational documentation, and the like.

These services are participatory systems in which collections come from users' contributions, and they may evolve into digital repositories that include both user-created and librarian-created artifacts. These different conversations can be archived into a single repository, and if properly planned, the reference conversations can live alongside, and eventually be intermingled with, the community conversations, and the digital repository into a community repository. Community repositories allow librarians to be more easily involved in the conversations of the community and capture important artifacts of these conversations for later use.

Merging Library Metadata into an Enhanced Catalogue

Participatory librarianship can be supported by another functional area of the library: collections. Traditionally, the collection comprises books, magazines, and other information resources paid for by the library. Electronic resources such as databases that are leased instead of purchased make up a large portion of library expenditures. More recently, Web-based resources have been selected and added to the virtual collection. Several kinds of finding aids are used to locate these information resources.

The catalogue and databases both contain descriptions of resources and searching interfaces. In order to improve access, libraries include records for databases within the catalogue. Conversely, federated searching tools combine the records from different databases and could allow the retrieval of both books and articles by combining records from both the traditional catalogue and databases into one tool. If community-created resources are part of the catalogue, then these resources would also be findable alongside other traditional library resources.

The tools for describing information resources can also be participatory. In traditional librarianship, the librarians provide metadata that patrons then use to make selections. By examining this use data, recommender systems can be created to help users locate new materials. In participatory networking, patrons will be encouraged to add comments about items. If standards are used for these comments, then they can be shared among libraries to create larger pools of recommendations. As these comments are analysed, they can be combined with usage databases to create stronger recommender systems to present patrons with additional choices based upon what is being explored.

The end result is an enhanced catalogue that allows users and libraries to find information regardless of which system the information resides in. However, the enhanced catalogue is still just that, a catalogue. It contains surrogates of digital information and is managed separately from the artifacts themselves. In the case of physical items, this may be all the library systems can manage, but in the case of digital content, there is one more step that needs to be taken. Namely, the artificial barrier between catalogue and content must come down.

Building the Participatory Library

At this point in the evolution of distributed systems into a truly integrated library system, the Participatory Library, we have two large collections: one of resources and one of information about the resources. The first collection of digital content, the community repository, is built by the library and its users collaboratively. The second collection, the enhanced catalogue, includes metadata, both formal and user-created. Both the community repository and the enriched catalogue are participatory. Yet to realise the dream of a seamless system of functionality, these two systems must be merged allowing users to find resources and, much more importantly, conversations. Furthermore the users must be able to add to both metadata and content. The result may be conceived of as a single integrated information resource, which, for the purposes of this conversation, is called the Participatory Library. Users may access the Participatory Library directly through the library, or they may access it as a series of services in Google, MySpace, or their own homepages. The point is that the access to the library takes place at the point of conversation, not at the point the user realises he or she needs information from the library.

CONVERSATIONS AND PRESERVATION

The conversation model highlights the need for preservation. Aside from simply providing systems that facilitate conversation, libraries serve as the vital community memory. Conversations construct knowledge, but someone must remember what has already been said, and know how to access that dialog. Scientific conversations, for example, are built on previous conversations. Capturing conversations and 'playing them back' at the right time is essential.

This might mean the preservation of artifacts but it also means the increasingly important tasks of capturing the digital dialogs. This highlights the need for institutional repositories. Specifically, Web sites, lectures, courseware, articles must be kept. Further, they must be kept in true conversational repositories that capture the artifacts the methods and the process. They must be kept in information structures that make them readily available as conversations: in other words, users must be able to search for materials, and be able to reconstruct a conversation in its entirety from one fragment.

BEING WHERE THE CONVERSATION IS

Imagine the conversations that are going on in your local library as you read this. Imagine the physicist chatting with the gardener, and the trustee talking with the volunteer who is reading the latest best seller. What knowledge can be gleaned from these novel interactions? Can you measure it? Can you enhance it? Can you capture it? Can you recall it when it would be precisely what a user needs to meet an information need? Note also that these conversations do not belong solely to the library. The library is only part of the conversation. Faced with the daunting variety of resources available on the Web, many organisations try to become the single point of entry into it. Remember that conversations are varied in their mode, places and players, and, more importantly, that they are intensely personal.

This means that participants need to have ownership in them, and often in their locations as well. This also means that the library, as facilitator, needs to be varied in its modes and access points. In many cases, it is better to either create a personal space in which users may converse, or, increasingly, to be part of someone else's space. What we can learn from Web 2.0's Mashups is that smaller sets of limited functionalities lead to greater incorporation of tools into people's lives.

In the ChicagoCrime Google Maps Mashup, combining maps from Google and Chicago crime statistics, it was important for the host of the site to brand the space and shape the interface for his conversation on crime. Can your library functions be as easily incorporated into these types of conversations?

Can a user search your catalogue and present the results on his or her Web site? The point is that libraries need to be proactive in a new way. Instead of the mantra, 'Be where the user is', we need to, 'Be where the conversation is. 'It is not enough to be at the users' desktops; you need to be in their e-mail programme, in their MySpace pages, in their IM lists, and in their RSS feed readers. All of these examples point to a significant mental shift that librarians will need to make in moving from delivering information from a centralised location to delivering information in a decentralised manner where the conversations of users are taking place.

The catalogue example presented earlier is an example of a centralised place for conversations. What if, Instead of only being in a catalogue, the same data were split into smaller components and embedded in the user's browser and e-mail programmes? Just as Google's mail system embeds advertising based upon the content of a message, The Library could also provide links to its resources based upon what a user is working on. By disaggregating the information within its system, The Library can deliver just what is needed to a user, provide connections into Mashups, and can live in the space of the user instead of forcing the user to come to the space of the library.

CHALLENGES AND OPPORTUNITIES

There is clearly a host of challenges in incorporating participatory networks and a participatory model into the library. This is to be expected when we are dealing with something as fundamental as knowledge and as personal as conversations. We consider four major challenges that must be met by libraries before they can truly get into the business of participatory librarianship.

Technical

There is a rich suite of participatory networking software that libraries can incorporate into their daily operations. Implementing a blog, a Wiki, or RSS feeds these days is not a hard task, and they can easily be used to deliver information about library services and conversations to the user's space. Furthermore, these systems are often tested in very large-scale environments and are, in some cases, the same tools used in large participatory networking sites such as Wikipedia and Blogger. Some of these packages are commercial, but others are open source software. Open source software is cheaper, easier to adapt, and, in some cases, more advanced.

The downside to open source is that it requires a considerable amount of technical knowledge by the library and does not come with a technical support hotline. The largest technological impediment, however, may be the currently installed base of software within libraries. Integrated library systems have a long history, and include a broad range of library functions. Legacy code and near monolithic systems have restricted the easy exchange of a diverse set of information. Were these systems written today they would use modular code and loosely coupled APIs and allow customers much more customizability of interface.

These changes may come to integrated library systems but it may take years. Several libraries are currently attempting to pick apart these integrated systems themselves. Often, libraries go to the underlying databases that hold the library metadata or create their own data structures, such as the University of Pennsylvania Data Farm project. Once components of this system are exposed, the catalogue simply becomes another database that can be federated into new and unified interfaces. However, such integration requires a great deal of technological expertise.

There is an opportunity for ILS vendors or large consortial groups such as OCLC to move quickly into this space. In the meantime, there is an opportunity for the larger library community. This technology brief was created in response to a perceived need. Whether evidenced in the Library 2.0 community or in conversations at LITA, libraries are now interested in incorporating new Web technologies into their offerings and operations.

The technologies under consideration here present platforms for experimentation. Rather than setting up thousands of separated experiments, however, the library community should create a participatory network of its own. The technology certainly exists to create a test bed for libraries to set up various combinations of communication technologies to test new Web services against pooled data and even to incorporate new services into the current library offerings. By combining resources in a single, large-scale test bed, libraries cannot only get greater impact for the their investments, but can also directly experience life as a connected conversation. These connections, if built at the ground level, will then make it easier for The Library to come into existence. Terminology can be clarified, claims tested, and best practices collaboratively developed, greatly accelerating innovation and dissemination.

Operational

In addition to being in the conversation business, libraries are in the infrastructure business. One of the most powerful aspects of a library is its ability not only to develop a collection of some type of information but to maintain it over time. Sometimes infrastructure can be problematic but more often than not, it provides a stable foundation from which to operate. There are many conversations going on that need infrastructure but have none. Think of the opportunities in your community for using the Web to facilitate a conversation. It might be a researcher wanting to disseminate the results of his or her latest study. It might be a community organisation seeking funding.

It might be a business trying to manage its basic operational knowledge. The point is that such individuals and community organisations are not in the infrastructure business and could use a partner who is. Imagine a local organisation coming to the library, and within a few minutes setting up a Web site with an RSS feed, a blog and bulletin boards. The library facilitates, but does not own, that individual's or organisation's conversation. It does form a strong partnership, however, that can be leveraged into resources and support.

The true power of participatory networking in libraries is not to give every librarian a blog; it is in giving every community member a blog. In addition, the library can play the role of connecting these conversations to other users when appropriate. Participatory libraries allow the concept of community centre to be extended to the Web. Many public libraries have no problem providing meeting space to local non-profits. Why not provide Web meeting space in the form of a Web site or Web conferencing? Many academic libraries attempt to capture the scholarly output of their faculties, why not help generate the output with research data stores? The answers to these questions inevitably come back to time and money.

However, there is nothing in this brief that says such services have to be free. In fact, the best partnerships are formed when all partners are invested in the process. The true problem is that libraries have no idea of how to charge for such services. Faculty would be glad to write library support into grants, but need a dollar figure to include and how long each task will take. Many libraries aren't used to positioning their services on a per item basis, and this makes it difficult to build partnerships. Sometimes it is not a lack of money, but a lack of structure to take in money that is the problem.

Policy

As always, it is policy that presents the greatest challenges. The idea of opening the library functions to a greater set of inputs is rife with potential pitfalls. How can libraries use the technologies and concepts of Facebook and MySpace without being plagued by their problems? How can users truly be made part of the collection without the library being liable for all of their actions? The answers may lie in a seemingly obscure concept: identity management. Conversations can range in their mode, topic, and duration. They can also vary in the conversants.

The library needs to know a conversant's status to determine policy; and requires a unique identifier like a library card, to uphold it. In traditional libraries, that is the extent of identity management. In a participatory model, distinctions among identities become complex and graduated, and require us to consider a new approach. This new model, of patrons adding information directly to library systems, is not as radical as it may first appear. We have become very used to the idea of roles and tiered levels of authority in many other settings. Most modern computer systems allow for some gradation in user abilities. Online communities have even introduced merit systems, by which continual high-quality contributions to a site equals greater power in the site.

Think about Amazon, Wikipedia, even eBay; as users contribute more to the community they gain status and recognition. From participants to editors, from readers to writers, these organisations have seen membership as a sliding scale of trust, and libraries need to adopt this approach in all of their basic systems. We currently do, to a degree, in the form of librarians, paraprofessionals, and other staff. Yet even these distinctions tend to be rigid and often class based, with high walls between the strata. Some of this is imposed by outside organisations but a great deal is there by inertia of the field. Skillful use of identity management will help libraries avoid the baggage of MySpace and Facebook.

As users grain greater access, greater responsibility, and greater autonomy, libraries need to be more certain of their identities. That is, for a user to do more requires the library to know more. Knowing about a user may involve traditional identity verification, or tracking an activity trail whereby intentions can be judged in relation to actions. These concepts may be expressed as, 'The more we know you, the more control you can have in valuable services such as blogging, or the catalogue."

The concepts are illustrated in Blogger and LiveJournal, both of which require some level of identity information. In another example: to join LiveJournal you must be invited, thus the community confers identity. The common theme is that verifying identity is community based. The difference between the library and MySpace is that the library works in an established community with traditional norms of identity, whereas MySpace is seeking to create a community. Both the library and the services, however, base their functions and services on identity.

Ethical

As knowledge is developed through conversation, and libraries facilitate this process, libraries have a powerful impact on the knowledge generated. Can librarians interfere with and shape conversations? Absolutely. Should we? We can't help it. Our collections, our reference work, our mere presence will influence conversations. The question is, in what ways? By dedicating a library mission to directly align with the needs of a finite community, we are accepting the biases, norms and priorities of the community. While a library may seek to expand or change the community, it does so from within. When Internet filtering became a requirement for federal Internet funding, public and school libraries could not simply quit, or ignore the fact, because they are agents of their communities. School libraries had to accept filtering with federal funding because their parent organisations, the schools, accepted filtering.

We see, from this example, that libraries may shift from facilitating conversations to becoming active conversant, but they are always doing both. Thus, the question is not whether the library shapes conversations, but which ones, and how actively? These questions are hardly new to the underlying principles of librarianship. And nothing in the participatory model seeks to change those underlying principles. The participatory model does, however, highlight the fact that those principles shape conversations and have an impact on the community.

WIRELESS NETWORKS IN MEDIUM-SIZED ACADEMIC LIBRARIES

Wireless networking offers a way to meet the needs of an increasingly mobile, tech-savvy student population. While many research libraries offer wireless access to their patrons, academic libraries serving smaller populations must heavily weigh both the potential benefits and disadvantages of this new technology. Will wireless networks become essential components of the modern academic library, or is this new technology just a passing fad? Prompted by plans to implement a wireless network at the Houston Cole Library (HCL), which serves a student enrollment close to ten thousand, this study was conducted to gather information about whether libraries similar in size and mission to HCL have adopted wireless technology. The study also sought to find out what, if any, problems other libraries have encountered with wireless networks and how successful they have perceived those networks to be. Other questions addressed include level of technical support offered, planning, type of equipment used to access the network, and patron-use levels.

REVIEW OF LITERATURE

A review of the literature on wireless networks revealed a number of articles on wireless networks and checkout programmes for laptop computers at large research institutions. Seventy percent of major research libraries surveyed by Kwon and Soules in 2003 offered some degree of wireless access to their networks. No articles, however, specifically addressed the use of wireless networks in medium-sized academic libraries.

Many articles can also be found on wireless-network use in medical libraries and other institutions. Library instruction using wireless classrooms and laptops has been another subject of enquiry as well. Breeding wrote that there are a number of successful uses for wireless technology in libraries, and a wireless Local Area Network (WLAN) can be a natural extension of existing networks.

He added that since, it is sometimes difficult to install wiring in library buildings, wireless is more cost effective. A yearly survey conducted by the Campus Computing Project found that the number of schools planning for and deploying wireless networks rose dramatically from 2002 to 2003. "For example, the portion of campuses reporting strategic plans for wireless networks rose to 45.5 per cent in fall 2003, up from 34.7 per cent in 2002 and 24.3 per cent in 2001."

The use of wireless access in academia is expected to keep growing. According to a summary of a study conducted by the EDUCAUSE Centre for Applied Research (ECAR), the higher-education community will keep investing in the technology infrastructure, and institutions will continue to refine and update networks. The move towards wireless access "represents a user-centred shift, providing students and faculty with greater access than ever before." In an article on ubiquitous computing, Drew provides a straightforward look at how WLANs work, security issues, planning, and the uses and ramifications of wireless technology in libraries.

He suggests, "Perhaps one of the most important reasons for implementing wireless networking across an entire campus or in a library is the highly mobile lifestyle of students and faculty." The use of wireless will only increase with the advent of new portable devices, he added. Wireless networking is the best and least expensive way for students, faculty, and staff to take their office with them wherever they go. The circulation of laptop computers is a frequent topic in the available literature.

The 2003 study by Kwon and Soules primarily focussed on laptop-lending services in academic-research libraries. Fifty per cent of the institutions that responded to their survey provided laptops for checkout. The majority indicated moderate-to-high use of laptop services. Positive user response and improved 'public reputation, image, and relations" were the greatest advantages reported with laptop circulation. The major disadvantages associated with these services were related to labour and cost. A study of laptop checkout service at the Mildred F. Sawyer Library at Suffolk University in Boston revealed that laptop usage was popular during the fall semester of 1999. Students checked out the computers to work on group projects. A laptop area was set aside on one library floor to provide wired Internet access for eight users. However, students wanted to use the laptops anywhere, not one designated place. The wired laptop areas were not popular, Dugan wrote, adding that "Few students used the wired area and the wires were repeatedly stolen or intentionally broken." An interim phase involved providing wireless network cards for checkout to encourage patrons to use their own laptops, and, when a wireless network was put into place in the fall of 2000, demand exceeded the number of available laptops for checkout.

METHOD

A survey was designed to find out how many libraries similar in size and mission to HCL have adopted wireless networks, the experiences they have encountered in offering wireless access, and, most importantly, whether they felt the investment in wireless technology has been worth the effort.

The National Centre for Education Statistic's Academic Library Peer Comparison Tool, a database composed of statistical information on libraries throughout the United States, was used to select institutions for this study.

A search on this database retrieved eighty-eight academic libraries that met two criteria: full-time enrollments of between five thousand and ten thousand, and classification by the Carnegie Classification of Higher Education as Master's Colleges and Universities I. The survey was administered to those thought most likely to be responsible for systems in the library; they were selected from staff listings on library Web sites. If such a person could not be identified, the survey was sent to the head of library systems or to the library director.

The survey was divided into the following sections:

- Implementation of wireless network
- Planning and installation stages
- User services
- Technical problems
- Benefits specific to use of network

Surveys were mailed out in March 2004. An Internet address was provided in the cover letter if participants wished to take the survey online rather than return it by mail.

An e-mail reminder with a link to the online survey was sent out three weeks after the initial survey was mailed. All letters and e-mails were personalised, and a self-addressed stamped envelope and a ballpoint pen with the JSU logo were included with the mail surveys. In the e-mail reminder, the authors offered to share the results of the project with anyone who was interested, and received several enthusiastic responses.

RESULTS

A total of fifty-three completed surveys were returned, resulting in a response rate of 60 per cent. The overwhelming majority responded that their library offered wireless-network access. Even if the thirty-five surveys that were not returned had reported that wireless networks were not available, more than 50 per cent would still have offered wireless networks. Survey results also pointed to the newness of the technology. Only four of the fifty-three institutions have had wireless networks for more than three years. The majority has implemented wireless networks just within the last two years.

When asked to identify the major reasons for offering wireless networks to their patrons, the three responses most chosen were:

- To provide greater access to users;
- The flexibility of a network unfettered by the limitations of tedious wiring; and
- To keep up with technological innovation.

Least significant factors in the decision to implement wireless networks were cost; use by library faculty and staff; to aid in bibliographic instruction; and use for carrying out technical services. Somewhat to the authors' surprise, wireless use in bibliographic instruction was not high on the list of reasons for installing a wireless network, identified by only 9 percent of respondents. The benefits of wireless for library instruction was stressed in the litreature by Mathias and Heser and Patton. In addition to obtaining an instrument for gauging how many libraries similar in scope and size to HCL have implemented wireless networks and why they chose to do so, questions on the survey were also designed to gather information on planning and implementation, user services, technical problems, and perceived benefits.

PLANNING AND IMPLEMENTATION

Although Tolson mentions that some schools have used committees composed of faculty, staff, and students to look into the adoption of wireless technology, responses from this survey indicated that the majority of the libraries did not form committees specifically for the planning of their wireless networks.

In addition, 49 per cent of the libraries took fewer than six months to plan for implementation of a network, 37 per cent required six months to one year, and 15 per cent reported more than one to two years. Actual time spent on installation and configuration of wireless networks was relatively short, 98 per cent indicating less than one year. One of the most important issues to consider when planning to implement a wireless network is extent of coverage—where wireless access will be available. Survey responses revealed varying degrees of wireless coverage among institutions. 20 per cent had campus-wide access, 55 per cent had some level of coverage throughout the entire library, 37 per cent provided a limited range of coverage outside the building, and 20 per cent offered access only in certain areas within the library.

Institutions vary in their approaches to networking depending on enrollment. Smaller colleges and universities with fewer than ten thousand students are “more likely to implement campuswide wireless networks from the start. Larger institutions are more likely to implement wireless technology in specific buildings, consistent with a desire to move forward at a modest pace, as resources and comfort with the technology grow.” Questions on the survey also queried respondents about the popularity of spaces in the library where users access the library’s wireless network. Answers revealed that the most popular areas for wireless access are study carrels, tables, and study rooms. 19 per cent indicated that accessing wireless networks in the stacks is popular. Of particular concern to HCL, a thirteen-story building, was how the environment of the library would accommodate a wireless network.

A thorough site survey is important to locate the best spots within the library to install access points and to determine whether there are architectural barriers in the building that might interfere with access. The majority of survey respondents indicated that the site survey conducted in their library for a wireless network was carried out by their academic institution’s IT staff. While library staff conducted 35 percent of site surveys, only 17 per cent were conducted by outside companies.

USER SERVICES

An issue to be addressed by libraries deciding to go wireless is whether laptop computers should also be provided for checkout in the library. After all, it might be hard to justify the usefulness of a wireless network if users do not have access to laptops or other hardware with wireless capabilities. While one individual reported working at a 'laptop university' in which campuswide wireless networking exists and all students are required to own laptops, not all college students will have that luxury.

In order to provide more equal access to students, checking out laptops has become an increasingly common service in academic libraries. Seventy percent of this survey's respondents whose institutions offered wireless access also made laptops available for checkout. Comments made throughout the survey seemed to imply that while checking out laptops to patrons is an invaluable complement to offering wireless access, librarians should be prepared for a myriad of hassles that accompany laptop checkout. Wear and tear of laptops, massive battery use, cost of laptops, and maintenance were some of the biggest problems reported. One participant, whose institution decided to stop offering laptops for checkout to patrons in the library, wrote, "It required too much staff time to maintain and we decided the money was better spent elsewhere.

The college now encourages students to purchase a laptop [instead of] a full-sized PC." One participant worried that the rising use of laptops in his library would lead to the obsolescence of its more than one hundred wired desktops, writing, "Our desktops are very popular and we think having them is one of the reasons our gate count has increased in recent years. What happens when everyone has a laptop?" The number of laptops checked out in the libraries varied. The majority of libraries had purchased between one and thirty laptops available for checkout.

Three institutions had more than fosrty-one laptops available for checkout. One library could boast that it had sixty laptops available for checkout with twelve pagers to notify students waiting in line to use laptops. When asked about the use of laptops in libraries, 46 percent observed moderate use, while 32 per cent reported heavy use of laptops. Only 3 percent indicated that they hardly ever noticed use of laptops in the library. For those students who chose to bring their own laptop to access the library's wireless network, half of the institutions surveyed required students to purchase their own network- interface cards for their laptops, while 19 per cent allowed students to check them out from the library.

In addition to laptops, personal digital assistants, (PDAs) were listed by 37 per cent of respondents as devices that may access wireless networks. One librarian indicated that cell phones could access the wireless network in his library. 56 per cent of respondents indicated that users are able to print to a central printer in the library from their wireless device. An important consideration for implementing a wireless network is how users will authenticate. Authentication protocol is defined by the Microsoft Encyclopaedia of Networking as "any protocol used for validating the identity of a user to determine whether to grant the user access to resources over a network." Authentication methods listed by the institutions surveyed varied greatly and the authors could not identify all of them.

Methods mentioned were Lightweight Directory Access Protocol (LDAP), virtual private network (VPN), and Media Access Control (MAC) addresses, Bluesocket, Remote Authentication Dial in User Service (RADIUS), pluggable Graphical Identification and Authentication (pGINA), Protected Extensive Authentication Protocol (PEAP), and e-mail logins. Out of the thirty-nine responses to this question, seven individuals indicated that they do not require any type of authentication at the present. Although some individuals noted that they are planning to enable some type of authentication in the future, one participant suggested that there were ethical issues involved in requiring users to authenticate. This person argued that "anonymous access to information is valued" and praised his institution's current policy of allowing "anyone who can find the network" to use it. A concern about offering wireless network access in the library is how library staff will be prepared to handle the flood of technical questions that are likely to ensue. The level of technical support offered to users varied among the institutions surveyed. More than half of the respondents indicated that users receive help specifically from IT staff or from the campus computer centre. 39 per cent of users received help from the reference desk, while 19 per cent received help from circulation staff. 33 per cent of the responding institutions offered technical help from a Web site, while 7 per cent indicated that they did not offer any type of technical support to users.

Technical Problems

The technical problems most often encountered with wireless networks centered on architectural barriers that cause black-outs or slow-spots where wireless access fails. This confirms the importance of carrying out thorough site surveys and testing prior to installation of access points. Site surveys may be carried out by companies specially equipped and trained to determine where access points should be installed, the most appropriate type of antennae and how many access points are needed to provide the greatest amount of coverage. Configuration of the network was the second most highly reported problem associated with installing wireless networks, seeming to suggest the need for librarians to coordinate their efforts and rely on the knowledge provided by the IT coordinator within their institution.

Lack of technical support available to users, slow speed, and authentication were also indicated as technical problems most encountered. Integrating the wireless network with the existing wired network was the least-mentioned problem associated with wireless networks. Although security problems, particularly concerning Wired Equivalency Protocol (WEP) vulnerabilities, have been pointed out as one of the major drawbacks of a wireless network, the majority of users had not as yet experienced security problems. Although one participant wrote, "Don't be too casual about the security risks," another individual wrote, "Talk to your networking department," as many of them are overly worried about security.

Perceived Benefits

Respondents reported that the number-one benefit of offering wireless access was user satisfaction. Giving patrons the ability to use their laptops anywhere in the library and do multiple tasks from one machine is simply becoming what more and more users expect.

The second largest benefit revolved around flexibility and ease of use due to the lack of wires. 35 per cent indicated that allowing students to roam the stacks while accessing the network was a significant benefit. Although a few studies have suggested the promise of wireless networks for aiding bibliographic instruction, only 9 per cent of respondents indicated this as a benefit of wireless technology. Use of wireless technology for instruction, it might be recalled, was not a significant factor noted by respondents in the decision to implement a wireless network.

Likewise, use of this type of network to carry out technical services was also low on the scale of benefits. 73 per cent of users claimed that wireless networks have thus far been worth the cost-benefit ratio. While 70 per cent indicated moderate to heavy use of the wireless network, 27 per cent reported low usage. When asked what advice they would give to others considering adopting wireless networks in their libraries, the overwhelming majority of responses were positive, recommending that HCL take the plunge.

As one individual wrote, "Offer it and they will come. It has really increased the usage of our library." Other individuals noted that it is simply necessary to offer wireless access to keep up with technological innovation, and that students expect it. The most significant warning, however, revolved around checkout and maintenance of laptops, which, from the results of this survey, seems be both a big advantage and a headache. Several individuals echoed the importance of doing site surveys to test bandwidth limitations and access. One particularly energised participant, using multiple exclamations for emphasis, shared a plethora of advice. "Throttle connection speeds! Allow only http access! Block ports and unnecessary protocols! Secure your network and disallow unauthenticated users! Use access control lists! Establish policies that describe [wireless fidelity] Wi-Fi risks and liabilities on your part!

Useful advice on wireless-access implementation gleaned from this surveyfell under the following categories:

- Be aware of slower speed.
- Create a policy and guide for users.
- Do it because more users are going wireless, it is necessary to keep up with technological innovation, and because students love it.
- Provide plenty of access points.
- Install access points in appropriate places.

- Ensure continuous connectivity by allowing overlap between access points.
- Purchase battery chargers and heavy-duty laptops with extended warranties.
- Get support from IT staff for planning and maintenance.
- Offering wireless will increase library usage.
- Perform or have an expert perform a careful site survey and do lots of testing to locate dead or slow spots in the library due to architectural barriers.
- Enable some type of authorisation.
- Be aware of security concerns.
- Although the majority of participants' networks support 802.11b, a few participants suggest using the 802.11g standard because it is 'the fastest' and 'backwards compatible to 802.11b'.

❐

11

Educating the Online Catalogue User

An issue which is central to planning for the impleme-ntation of online catalogue systems in libraries of all types, but which received little notice in the literature of the early 1980s on online catalogues, is that of the role of public services staff in the management planning process.'

Because much of the hard work in the early implemen-tation stages was on the technical and technical services side, it was perhaps natural that reference librarians and other public services personnel were not counted among those most responsible for bringing forward the technology in libraries. Now more than midway through a decade of tremendous change in libraries, however, it is clear that the public service aspects of online catalogue implementation are of considerable interest to the field and that reference librarians everywhere are seeking to forge new roles for themselves.

As public services librarians have sought to define their relation-ship to the online catalogue, it has been natural for them to view the relationship in terms of their role vis-à-vis the older card file technology that online technology supplants.

The historic relationship cast the public services librarian as "interpreter" of the catalogue, i.e., assisting users to locate items and teaching them how to use the card catalogue by themselves.

It has long been unclear how much such "interpretation" the card catalogue required, though it was long recognized that consistent and clear management of the catalogue on the technical services side relieved the burden considerably on the reference side in this regard. With the bibliographic instruction movement having gained consider-able force and influence on the field within the past fifteen years, the concept of catalogue "interpretation" has come to be understood as man-dating instruction, at least in academic libraries.

Do online catalogues require instruction in their use and, if so, how is that instruction best delivered? These questions do not have simple answers, yet from the early online catalogue implementations at the beginning of the decade library managers have taken positions that assumed a rather simple "yes" or "no" to the first question.

To approach answers to the two questions of whether the online catalogue requires instruction and what might be the best means of delivering it, Northwestern University Library undertook a research study, supported by the Council on Library Resources (CLR), to test the value of online catalogue user education.

In the pages that follow, the research undertaken at Northwestern will be summarized as to the research objectives, the rationale for the study, a description of the methodology and findings, and the study's major conclusions.

Though the research brings new findings to the specific question of how best to provide users with services that will enable them to make best use of an online catalogue, our work also addresses some larger questions:

- What is the role of the reference librarian vis-à-vis a catalogue that is now considered to be self-inter-preting?
- What do our experiences with online catalogue user education lead us to expect in the way of changes in our bibliographic instruction programmes overall?
- What is the future of reference services in an increasingly automated library?

It is hoped that these issues can continue to be seriously addressed as more and more libraries move from an initial "presentation" phase to an ongoing operational phase in online catalogue implementation.

The article begins with an overview of the primary objectives of the "Educating the Online Catalogue User" project. These objectives are described in the context of Northwestern's setting, with a brief description of LUIS (Library User Information Service), the online catalogue component of NOTIS (Northwestern Online Total Integrated System). Following this is a discussion of some of the underlying issues that prompted our interest in online catalogue user education.

The issues that surfaced in establishing broad learning objectives-the framework upon which the model programme was based-are described, and a description of the NOTIS transaction log facility-an important data gathering tool in the research-is provided.

Finally, the article closes by proposing that reference librarians and managers expand the scope of their online catalogue user education efforts to include more than the teaching of a single tool. They should take advantage of the brief historical opportunity presented by the online catalogue to use the novelty it provides as a vehicle for teaching users about other information retrieval systems that are becoming increasingly visible both within and beyond the library environment.

The overall purpose of the "Educating the Online Catalogue User" study was to provide a model for the development and evaluation of an online public access catalogue user education programme that could be employed by other academic libraries with any number of different online catalogues.

The model was developed by collaborative effort among the reference staff at Northwestern and librarians at the University of Wisconsin-Madison and Washington University in St. Louis. Though the project was centered at Northwestern, public services staff at these other institutions provided advice and feedback at several stages of the project in order to keep the research as broadly focused as possible. The experimental stage of the study was conducted exclusively at Northwestern University.

The study had four objectives:

- To develop a set of systematic and formalized instr-uctionalobjectives for teaching online catalogue use that could be adopted by other academic libraries seeking to develop an online catalogue instruction programme;
- To implement an instructional programme based on those learning objectives at Northwestern University;
- To evaluate the success of this programme through a variety of established evaluative techniques including the use of transaction log data; and
- To assess the viability of transaction log monitoring as a data sourcefor bibliographic instruction evaluation.

It was recognized at the outset that the study's objectives were constrained by the features of the online catalogue to which the researchers had the most complete access. Northwestern University Library uses the LUIS online catalogue, which has a number of features common to many other such systems but also lacks certain features that present significant instructional challenges.

LUIS offers title, author, and subject searching but at the time of the study did not provide keyword searching or the ability to use Boolean operators. A number of descriptions of LUISexist in the published literature on online catalogues, and LUIS is now available in over sixty libraries-academic, public, school, and special-in the United States and Canada.

ONLINE CATALOGUE USER EDUCATION ISSUES

The central question that directed this study, "What might be the components of a model programme to instruct users of an online catalogue?" challenges a commonly held view within the field of librarianship and information science. This view is that an effective "user friendly" inter-active computer system-such as an online catalogue-should not require instruction at all. While such a view is not universally held, it is common especially among system developers and others who are steeped in the use of computers in libraries and elsewhere.

A frequently articulated design specification for end user oriented systems is that all system use instruction should be provided as part of its interface-through such things as introductory help screens, user prompts, and labeling conventions-and should be all that even the most naive user needs to know to be able to effectively use that system.

A corollary of this view is that efforts to develop an instructional programme for the online catalogue suggest that the catalogue is not fulfilling its purpose and that its design is flawed. With this logic, any effort to provide instruction in onlin catalogue use by public services staffs might be viewed as wasted effort at the least, and provide implicit criticism of the designers as well.

Though the project from its inception questioned this view of the incompatibility of "user friendly" online systems and instruction pro-grams, it did not simply embrace the contrary view that formalized instruction must be given to all online catalogue users. Interactive systems for the general public are simply too new and untested for us to assume either of these positions without a period of considerable experimentation and practical examination of what works and what doesn't work for our users.

A certain amount of curiosity, fascination, or mystique naturally accompanies technological evolution. At this early stage of online catalogue implementation, learning from the practical experiences of others, as well as from more formal research findings, is essential if we are to move beyond these phases in our programme development. Baker and Nielsen review much of the early literature on the debate about the value of online catalogue user education, pointing out particularly the sampling bias in the widely cited CLR Online Public Access Catalogue (OPAC) studies, a bias which caused users who experienced difficulties in using online catalogues to be underrepresented in the findings.

We became interested in creating a model programme for educating online catalogue users for a variety of reasons:

- There was (and is) wide recognition that the perfect online catalogue simply does not (yet) exist.
- There was (and is) a perception by many librarians that the online user interface may not accommodate all user needs at present and may never do so.
- "User friendly" systems are not indeed friendly to all, judging from the experiences of many reference librarians who have worked with users trying to master such systems.
- The pace of change in interface improvements can seem painfully slow once any online catalogue system "works" in the sense that it meets managerial (not necessarily user) criteria for "satisfying."
- A general training programme that conveyed infor-mation retrieval concepts might aid users as they moved on to other automated systems both within and beyond the library setting.

- The numerous online catalogue instructional prog-rammes that had been initiated in various settings-particularly in academic libraries-suggested that making an effort for consistency in instructional 3planning was worthwhile and beneficial.

LEARNING OBJECTIVES

In order for a model online catalogue user education programme to be applicable to a variety of institutions and for the programme to be formally evaluated, it was critical to the Northwestern project that programme learning objectives be stated and generalized beyond those associated with a particular system.

The first step in the execution of this research project involved formalizing a set of such objectives which would serve as the basis for teaching the use of an online catalogue. Much of the conceptual work related to this aspect of the project is described by Baker.

In planning the framework of instructional objectives, there was extensive discussion with librarians at each of the participating libraries. These discussions centered on identifying a set of ideal objectives (or goals of instruction) without linking them to features of specific systems or tying them to specific methods of instruction. With the goal of developing a generic instruction programme with generalizable objectives, it was essential to look at online catalogue instruction as it could be applied across many systems. By focusing on such general expectations of online catalogue users, we felt that skills might be more easily transferred across systems.

WHAT TO TEACH: CONCEPTS OR PROCEDURES

In determining an appropriate direction for our online catalogue teaching, two concerns were raised. The first involved what technical aspects of the system's structure should be presented to users; the second questioned the manner in which such aspects should be included in the learning activity. With one of our project objectives being to work towards developing transferability of skills learned about one automated system to skills needed for another, an emphasis on teaching concepts and structure, rather than procedures, was endorsed. In addition to increasing the likelihood for transferability of skills, teaching system structure is useful for conceptualizing the workings of a system. When the way a system works is not transparent to the user, there is little opportunity for self-diagnosis of errors or decision-making for search strategy development.

This instructional approach has been supported by other research in the ways humans interact with computers. Works by Christine Borg-man, Ramsey and Grimes, and others discuss the importance of conceptual models in teaching interactive systems and the resulting mental model the user has available for error diagnosis and problem solving. Such conceptual models are often built around metaphors and often illustrate techniques designed to communicate an overall context for system behaviour to the learner.

Learning occurs whether it is structured in a systematic programme or whether it is coincidental. Coincidental learning of a system through the use of prompts and help screens may actually prove to be an effective means for learning procedures.

Focusing an instructional programme around conceptual models does not by any means diminish the necessity for a user to have a functional understanding geared towards learning system-specific searching techniques. These techniques may actually be more easily acquired from instruction embedded in the system once the conceptual model has been learned.

One of the most important functions of the user interface for online catalogues has been to provide this task-oriented training. With so many automated systems being used in libraries around the country, transferring skills learned about one system to another may prove quite difficult. Designing instruction around a conceptual v. procedural framework may provide ultimate transfer-ability of learning in the use of online catalogues.

EVALUATING THE MODEL

Because the objectives developed for online catalogue instruction involved acquisition of both cognitive and behavioural learning, it was important to develop an evaluation strategy that addressed objective achievement of a group of representative users at solving both cognitive and behavioural problems. Both pencil-and-paper responses and observation of "hands-on" online catalogue activity were deemed critical to assess the project.

Another issue important to the study was that of cumulative learning. Because the library patron often learns the use of research tools in stages (such as by trial use followed by assistance from a librarian), cumulative learning, or learning that builds on previous learning, frequently occurs.

In the case of learning to use a library catalogue, cumulative learning isespecially salient: many users are exposed to repeated instruction in the use of the catalogue in elementary school; many users rely on experience as the most available teacher of library use skills. Bibliographic instruction librarians are aware of the problems inherent in this situation, for they often must help students "unlearn" previously incorrect information concerning the card catalogue.This concern with the effects of cumulative learning led to the development of an experimental design which allowed us to examine and evaluate the effects of two types of bibliographic instruction methods-both individually and combined-taking into account the order of their presentation. The research design protocol called for the creation of two experimental groups (each of which took two tests and participated in two instructional sessions) as well as the use of a control group which only took two tests but received no instruction.

The instructional treatments included a classroom-like presentation on the online catalogue (what Northwestern has dubbed a "LUIS Workshop"), and the reading of a printed brochure designed to convey instructional content. As the tests themselves required participants to use the online catalogue to answer some of the questions, all three groups were exposed to the catalogue and its introductory (tutorial) and "help" screens. The two tests were composed of questions designed to test the same knowledge.

The control group took the first test followed by a "placebo" presentation (a short non-instructional film) and then the second test. The first experimental group, which as suggested, call Group "A," received the classroom instruc-tional session followed by the first test and then read the instructional brochure and took the second test. The second experimental group, which as suggested, call Group "B," read the brochure and took the first test and then received the instructional session and the second test.

SAMPLE SELECTION

A random sample subject population of ninety freshmen students was selected for participation in the study using a sampling technique that insured equal representation by sex and representation by academic major corresponding as much as possible to national norms derived from American Council on Education data.'

Only freshmen who had previously participated in LUIS workshops were excluded from participation. As an incentive for the subjects to commit to participation when they were contacted by telephone, each student was offered a free ticket to a commercial movie theater upon completion of the experiment.'

DATA COLLECTION

The principal means of data collection for the study were a battery of two written tests prepared for the study and transaction data collected by the NOTIS computer as subjects interacted directly with LUIS. The first test consisted of fourteen questions related to background characteristics of the students, forty-five questions tapping knowledge of LUIS-including some which required use of the terminal-and eight attitudinal questions asking how the students liked various features of the catalogue.

Eight catalogue search "practice questions" for which students had to use the terminals were also included. The second test included the same type of questions as the first except for the fourteen initial questions tapping demographic variables. Pretesting of the two tests with twenty randomly selected Northwestern students verified that the tests, though different, were measuring acquisition of the same learning.

Monitoring online catalogue transactions as a means of collecting data was accomplished through utilization of NOTIS software developed initially in connection with the CLR-sponsored OPAC studies of 1980-82 in which Northwestern was a Research Libraries Group participant. The room in which the experiment was conducted was equipped with sixteen online catalogue terminals, each having adjacent to it a copy of the Library of Congress Subject Headings.

Subjects were instructed to write on their test booklets the identification number of the terminal at which they were searching for the test but were not told that their transactions were being recorded. This protocol device provided a means of unobtrusive measurement of online catalogue use in which transaction data could be associated with user characteristics recorded on the test booklets.

This strategy is especially notable as a monitoring technique as it allows exemption from institutional and federal guide-lines for research on human subjects-due to the educational testing nature of the experiment-and yet is less obtrusive than other monitoring experimental designs in that subjects are led to assume that pencil-and-paper is the sole method of data collection.

ANALYSIS

Following the completion of the data gathering, the 178filled-out tests were first paired by student identification number and subsequently coded for machine processing. Eighty-seven usable pairs of tests were so coded and input for processing using the Statistical Package for the Social Sciences (SPSS). Tabulated responses were scored using a key of correct test items, and raw percentage correct scores were computed.

Analysis was also accomplished in regard to a number of study questions by grouping the raw percentage scores into "high", "middle", and "low" performance groups.

This grouping enabled as well the analysis of student performance considered in terms of degree of achievement of five important learning objectives established in conjunction with the model programme developed at Northwestern. A fuller description of the methods used to reduce the data, as well as detailed findings on the effect of demographic variables on perfor-mance, are provided in the authors' final report to the Council on Library Resources on the project."

An indicator of overall test performance for each of the three test groups is the average (mean) test score, again expressed as a percentage of questions answered correctly. Table provides a clear picture of group performance showing the score for each group on both test one and test two. On both tests the performance of the control group was the lowest. Group "A", which received the lecture instruction prior to test one, performed best on test one overall, and their score on test two surprisingly dropped.

Group "B", which read the brochure prior to test one, performed less well on the first test, but, following their receiving the live instruction, performed nearly as well on test two as group two had on test one. Analysis of variance tests with the test one and test two data for the mean score by group revealed that the within-group variation on both scores was less than the variation between groups indicating that the different means for each group are statistically significant.

Table. Average Test Score by Group

	Test 1	Test 2
Control Group	54.66	53.21
Group "A"	77.5	63.3
Group "B"	61.66	76.94
ANOVA Significance < .001		

These average scores represent overall test performance in only a general way and are presented in this manner as a way to look at the cumulative learning issue that was of interest in the study. Because of the length of the instruction period and the opportunity subjects were given to interact with the instructor, the superior performance of group "A" on test one was expected. Why the "A" group's performance dropped on the second test-following their exposure to the brochure-cannot be adequately explained by the analysis presented here, but we may hypothesize that test fatigue may have been an important factor.

Recalling that the "A" group's taking of the second test was nearly ninety minutes into the period set aside for the experiment, and that the intervening period between tests for this group was much shorter than for group "B," it seems highly likely that group "A" was simply tired of responding to questions on the second test. Group "B," while spending as long on the experiment overall as the "A" group, did have a consider-ably longer intervening period between the two tests.

In the matter of evaluating the achievement of specific learning objectives we were less successful. Although we established a means to analyse the result of the evaluative test in a way that treated the achievement of each objective separately, we must acknowledge that a conceptual dilemma exists. As certain objectives dealt more concretely with the learning of definitions and concepts that were easily tested for, while other objectives-concerned as they were with the execution of procedures-were inherently more difficult to test for, we cannot make clear conclusions regarding different levels of attainment on the test.

Different attainment levels may reflect more about the tests themselves than about actual superior performance in online catalogue searching. Because our knowledge of online catalogue users is still so incomplete, instructional evaluation is made difficult especially in respect to validation of the appro-priateness of certain cognitive learning tasks for successful performance in searching. There is some danger in evaluation studies of this sort to direct instruction to successful completion of the test rather than to the achievement of skills that the test has been designed to measure.

With these considerations in mind, an analysis of the data showed that the group that had the workshop first scored significantly higher on procedures such as using equipment than the group that had the brochure. One of the most interesting facts is that the control group scored higher than both of these test groups on procedural knowledge. But in interpreting and structuring searches the workshop group did significantly better. It was followed by the brochure group and then the control group. In terms of concepts, the control group fell far behind the other two test groups with the workshop group in the lead. Among our findings on the analysis of the transaction logging was that subjects who had a workshop presentation made fewer errors than those whose first instructional exposure was to the printed brochure.

What do these findings allow us to say about the cumulative effects of two learning experiences with online catalogue instruction? Because there is no clear pattern in improvement on all the objectives for any of the three groups it is difficult to say. The order of presentation of the two learning experiences-the brochure and the lecture-did not appear to affect group performance on all five learning objectives in the same way; for some objectives a score increase between test one and test two might have been the result of the lecture having been given first, for other objectives it might have been the brochure being presented first. Further work is in order to refine the analysis and sort out what factors may lead to improved test scores.

CONCLUSION

Through a close examination of the process of developing learning objectives, creating a programme to help meet them, and evaluating the outcome of the programme, there are a number of conclusions that we can make. This research has provided some answers to the question which initially motivated the study, "Why teach use of an online catalogue?" First of all, it is evident that teaching improves user performance on a written test. The development and use of learning objectives has further helped to define specific competencies which may lead to better online catalogue searching. We have further helped define for the field at large those specific competencies that lead to better performance.

Another aspect of our response to the "Why teach the online catalogue?" question must be that there are certain concerns that arise with teaching online catalogue use at this time. Of primary concern is the necessity to train users on some procedural matters on a case-by-case basis leading to possible difficulties in users' assimilating the information? For example, in any online system there will be details and peculiarities about the library's organization and physical layout which may appear in index displays online.

Providing instruction at this level of detail distracts from the overall flow of the presentation and adds only incidental information which the audience is not likely to remember. Perhaps a greater problem that we are confronted with is the fact that such an explanation reveals idiosyncrasy and inconsistency in the sys-tem possibly leading to loss of confidence among users that there is an understandable logic to the system that can be mastered. Such a situation tends to defeat the overall instructional goal.

Inconsistencies are numerous in online catalogues. Explana-tions for these features through printed guides, lectures, online help, or individual assistance may help ease the burden for many users. However, the explanation to a user of one odd feature in one catalogue does not prepare him or her for the next feature or the next catalogue. As important as making design improvements in online catalogues is at this time it must be recognized that each online catalogue will likely continue to present its own set of instructional problems with which public services librarians must somehow struggle.

There were limitations imposed by the study process itself that point to areas of difficulty in the way library public services staffs perceive the challenge of online catalogue user education and thus approach programme planning. Our experience and training as librarians has led us to view the online catalogue and its use in isolation from other information retrieval developments both within and beyond the scope of libraries."

Focusing only on online catalogue training may result in narrow programme planning. In this research project, we developed a model programme which demonstrated positive results in subjects' performance on tests of online catalogue knowledge. However, there are clear indications that instructional development which embodies objectives for generalized information retrieval may be a more appropriate teaching ideal.

As a new and very important tool, the online catalogue is the focus of a great deal of attention from public services staffs, but this concentration of attention should not necessarily lead to building programmes around the teaching of a single tool alone. Users are, on the whole, pleased with the online catalogue, but for them it is but one tool among many and, more to the point, a means to an end rather than an end in itself.

Our focus in the "Educating the Online Catalogue User" project was to develop a model programme for online catalogue instruction. In seeking a cognitive model or metaphor upon which to base instruction, we used the card catalogue because a number of valuable analogies and comparisons could be made. But as we librarians move further in our own thinking about the direction in which online systems are developing, the card catalogue analogies may become less and less appropriate or relevant.

The advances in computer communications make the acquisition of knowledge about information retrieval, broadly conceived, increasingly valuable for any library user. Many libraries provide public OCLC terminals in addition to an online catalogue of local holdings already in place or planned. Online searching of commercially vended bibliographic files is gradually working its way from behind the reference desk out into the room.

As an outcome of the Linked System Project, one may soon expect to provide the searching of remote files directly within the online catalogue interface now provided users. As these systems are introduced, we need to be aware of the more complex training needs such systems may require: building upon our online catalogue training experience may be a useful way to prepare ourselves, our staffs, and our users. But to do this, our conceptualization of what is most usefully conveyed about the online catalogue must be generalized beyond our traditional notions of catalogue teaching.

The online catalogue towards which the teaching would be directed would serve as an example of a particular implementation of general principles but not the only possible implementation. Bringing in another example-such as a general database management system now commonly available even on the microcomputer-would enrich the instruction. Such a training approach would be more challenging to students and have the great advantage of providing information that would be useful in other contexts.

This approach relegates to a secondary status many of the pieces of helpful information that may make a particular online catalogue easier to use, but we feel a broader view may gain both better acceptance by patrons in general and better trans-ferability to other systems. Overcoming the sense of insecurity that this situation may bring will perhaps be difficult at first, but as risks are taken, the rewards may reinforce the new approach suggested here.

❒

12

Computers, Online Environment and Cataloguing Principles

INTRODUCTION

It is often claimed that current cataloguing codes (cataloging codes) are based on concepts and principles from the pre-machine period and that they do not serve us well in giving guidance in the construction of electronic catalogues.

Thus, in organising bibliographic information for an electronicenvironment, it is essential to examine the validity and adequacy of the principles on which current cataloguing codes are based. By assessing the extent to which cataloguing principles accord with the capabilities of the online environment, this chapter will answer some of the questions that have been highlighted in the literature of the last two decades on the relevance of current cataloguing principles to the online environment. To many writers, for example, Martin the online catalogue has meant a re-examination of the principles and practice of cataloguing.
Carpenter and Svenonius raise the issue that:

- "At the time the Paris Principles were composed, there was some awareness that computers might change cataloguing. the direction of this change could not then be imagined. It remains to be seen whether this change will require the composition of a new set of principles, this time without ambiguity or compromise".

Another aim of this chapter is to establish whether cataloguing principles for the online environment should encompass a broader range of information sources, i.e., different bibliographic databases such as library catalogues, databases constructed by publishers, booksellers, library suppliers and A&I services.

Boll Asks

- "Whether there is now a need to include rules for A&I services, which constitute a major component of the online environment".

In general, the aim is to investigate whether the conceptual foundations developed over the last two centuries for the creation of bibliographic records and the construction of catalogues are still valid in the new environment. A similar question is posed by Svenonius who questions whether changes in technology call for changes in the conceptual foundations of cataloguing.

This chapter is in two parts. In Part one some of the basic cataloguing principles, which have been highlighted in the literature as those most likely to be influenced by the new technology, will be re-examined in the light of both the present and the potential characteristics and capabilities of the online environment. Part two will deal with a comparison of A&I conventions with library cataloguing principles and identify in what areas the same principles can be applied by both communities.

- What are 'Cataloguing Principles'

In terms of descriptive cataloguing, 'principles' are regarded as underlying concepts for the design and develop-ment of cataloguing rules and the construction of library catalogues. Principles can also be Cataloguing principles do not necessarily mean that we must have a single standard for descriptive cataloguing, or that all cataloguing codes must be the same. Cataloguing principles mean that we can have different, but compatible standards within the same framework. The Paris Conference was an international attempt to make national codes compatible. The Paris Principles are, in fact, an expansion of a few basic concepts developed over the last two centuries.

These concepts, which are repeated in various parts of the Statement of Principles are:

- The functions of the catalogue,
- The concept of multiple entries,
- The concept of uniformity in the choice and form of headings and entry words,
- The concept of functionality of entries and catalogues, and
- The concept of authorship, personal and corporate.

However, this chapter deals only with some of the principles that might be influenced by the new environment and that have been the subject of arguments among cataloguers for a long time, namely:

- The objectives and functions of the catalogue which influence all other principles,
- The structure of the catalogue and the kinds of entries and indexes, i.e., main entries, added entries and references,

- Uniform headings for works and uniform headings for authors, and
- The form of personal headings and corporate headings.

The concept of main entry will be dealt with in detail, because it has been considered important in the literature on the impact of computerised catalogues on cataloguing principles.

There are other pre-existing principles, unstated or overlooked, in the Paris Principles, such as the general assumption that catalogued items are almost always stand-alone publications rather than 'dependent works'. This issue, and other related questions, such as the 'basic unit of description' and the 'edition' issue, will be discussed in the next chapter in relation to their treatment in the online environment, particularly in shared cataloguing systems.

In the extrapolation of cataloguing principles, it is necessary to be aware of the context within which they were originally meant to operate. The Paris Principles have been indirectly influenced by both the characteristics and the limitations of the manual catalogue. They were principles for a catalogue which had limited capabilities in providing access to bibliographic information. Those who contributed to the formulation and compilation of earlier cataloguing principles implicitly assumed that the physical form of the catalogue would be the card or printed book catalogue, either as individual catalogues or national bibliographies. On the whole, the Paris Principles were formulated at a time when there was little perception of approaches other than the traditional ones of author, title and subject.

Major Developments and Changes in Descriptive Cataloguing Since the Paris Conference

Nearly 35 years have passed since the Paris Conference and cataloguers have witnessed profound changes in many aspects of bibliographic control in general, and in descriptive cataloguing in particular, during this period of time. There has also been a considerable increase in unconventional forms of publications as well as various types of information sources and a considerable growth in different presentations of documents which demand increasing detail to retain precision in identification. Martin reviews some of the major issues which influence bibliographic control and access in the new environment.

The cataloguing world has also faced major challenges such as the increasing costs of cataloguing and the need for simplified cataloguing or minimal level cataloguing (MLC), the question of duplicate records in cooperative cataloguing systems and the potential danger that cataloguing principles and concepts might be de-emphasised by those coming from the new technology environment. The cataloguing community is now working in an environment totally different from that of the early 1960s. Given the influence of all these changes and developments in the world of cataloguing, a fundamental re-examination of cataloguing principles seems very necessary.

A Re-examination of Cataloguing Principles in an Online Environment While current cataloguing principles deal with basic questions concerning the organisation of author/title catalogues, online catalogues have revolutionised access to bibliographic information beyond that approach. An important change in relation to providing access to bibliographic information in the online environment is that access is no longer controlled by cataloguing principles and rules to the same extent as previously but, to some extent, is now governed by various search/ retrieval capabilities that were not available in the manual catalogue.

For example, access through keyword searching, truncation, Boolean searching, hypertext searching and, most importantly, access to the full text of items, lie outside of cataloguing rules. This is one of the most fundamental differences between an online system and a manual system that should be taken into consideration when re-examining cataloguing principles.

Furthermore, while the boundary between description and access has faded in the online environment, cataloguing principles have traditionally placed little emphasis on description.

In the following parts some of the principles will be analysed with regard to the present and potential influences which the various capabilities of the new technologies might have upon them.

Objectives and Functions of the Catalogue in An Online Environment In our re-examination of cataloguing principles, major consideration should be given to the objectives and functions of the catalogue. Most cataloguing principles, such as the basis for description, the structure of the catalogue and the choice and form of access points are, to a great extent, influenced by the objectives and functions of the catalogue.

The present cataloguing objectives, which were proposed by Lubetzky to the Paris Conference, have their origin in the work of Panizzi and Cutter dating from the nineteenth century. The traditional approach in the Paris Principles towards the functions of the catalogue has not been able to solve the controversies between the 'finding function' and the 'collocating function' of the catalogue. It is often stated that the first and second objectives are inherently in conflict, and to consider one as primary means to sacrifice the other. While the first function puts emphasis on the finding of specific items within a library collection, the second function focuses on collocation of the works of a particular author and the editions and manifestations of a particular work.

These two different approaches influence the choice and form of main and added entries, references and the linking devices to connect related entities.

For example, in the finding function approach the focus of description and the basis for cataloguing data is the physical item in hand. Thus the main entry and added entries are provided according to the information on the title page because it is more familiar to readers. In this context, the relationship of the item to other works and its place in the bibliographic hierarchy is not identified and recorded.

Wilson presents a well account of the conflict between the two objectives and their implications for the functions of the catalogue.

It is further stated that these objectives are not fully achieved in the manual environment because of its limitations in finding the actual location of items and the huge cost of making analytics and assembling all the works of a given author, i.e., the collocating function.

A general question raised in the literature is whether the objectives and functions of the catalogue as set forth in the Paris Principles are still valid in the online environment. Another question which has to be addressed in this regard is: whether the catalogue in the online network environment should still maintain the same functions formulated for a pre-machine environment or should widen its scope to include new functions? While it is claimed by some writers that the current objectives and functions of the catalogue continue to be valid in the new environment and even that the new technology may help fulfil them more comprehensively and accurately others have challenged the validity and adequacy of the traditional objectives of the catalogue in the new environment.

Ayres states that the scope of the objectives must be expanded to include the impact that online catalogues have on the content of the catalogue. Buckland discusses the need to change our basic assumptions about the catalogue's purpose in order to design the catalogue of the future. He claims that we should pay more attention to bibliographic access and selection and should design the catalogue as a selecting aid. Heaney notes that library catalogues function not solely as descriptive lists of books but as elements of library management systems and as sophisticated information tools.

In addition to the finding and collocating functions, which are valid in any environment, the online catalogue helps to better identify and characterise entities in terms of their nature, scope and orientation through different data fields such as intellectual level, document type, genre, language code, geographic area code and additional notes. Similarly, a fuller description of the item helps the online catalogue to be used as a means for different users to choose one item over similar items. The locating of items is another function of the catalogue and, in this respect, online catalogues are far more capable of showing the location and status of the item(s) being sought.

In the following part, the functions of the catalogue will be analysed with regard to the impact of some of the major characteristics of the online environment. These are:

- The integration of library operations,
- Developments in networking and in global access to catalogues,
- Access to other types of bibliographic databases, and
- Online search/retrieval/display capabilities.

Integration of Different Library Operations

The integrated online library system has made it possible for different library modules to use the same bibliographic records within the same database management system. Acquisitions librarians, cataloguers, circulation librarians, serial librarians and reference librarians all have access to the same database and use it for different purposes. In an integrated system, the end user may have access to parts of acquisition status, circulations and holdings information. It is therefore necessary for the online catalogue to fulfil the various bibliographic needs of different operations, from housekeeping functions to reference services. In this context, not only should the catalogue function as a finding tool as well as a collocating tool but it should also help in the choice between one work and others.

The combination of approaches to an integrated catalogue not only makes it necessary to expand the current objectives but also to put more emphasis on principles for the choice and form of access points as well as for description, i.e., data elements beyond author/title information. For example, a reference librarian may need to find a specific item and at the same time identify different editions and manifestations related to that item to provide more help to the user.

Networking and Global Access to Catalogues

The fact that the resources and bibliographic information of hundreds of libraries participating in national and international networks are now accessible to any remote user calls for a reconsideration of the functions and objectives of the catalogue. The concept of 'catalogues on demand' extends the functions of the catalogue beyond providing access to a library's own collections.

With international access to individual catalogues, the question arises as to whether a catalogue should serve in the first place its local users, that is, to identify the holdings of a particular library, or to enable any user to access the collections of other libraries available through the network.

Buckland asks:

"What difference does it make that the catalogue now is concerned with the collectivity of collections rather than the local holdings of the individual library?" While catalogues should serve their local patrons well, they should also be useful to remote users. In such an environment, consideration should always be given to the fact that the item in hand for cataloguing may be a manifestation of another work known under a different title being held in another collection. With respect to the network environment, there is some support for the precedence of the collocating function of the catalogue over its finding function. In a conceptual approach to a catalogue's functions as presented by Lubetzky to the Paris Principles, Wilson proposes that, with regard to the availability of different catalogues in an online network and with respect to the significance of 'work' over 'publication', priority should be given to the collocating objective. He proposes a redefinition of 'work' to be taken as the basic unit of cataloguing.

Dempsey points out that a lack of sufficient attention to the collocating objective of the catalogue has resulted in two problems in large shared databases: difficulty in authority control and an increase in duplicate records. Ayres supports a similar concept. In general, in a network, online environment and with regard to the needs of different users, we cannot give precedence to any function. Rather, all functions of the catalogue should equally be taken into consideration.

On the other hand, while in a large shared database the potential number of editions and manifestations of a work increases, it is more likely that access to a very specific bibliographic manifestation of a work, for example, a particular version, would be a common need for some users. The result of a study of MELVYL at the University of California using transaction logs of remote users showed that known item searches constituted 40% of searches. It is evident that in a shared system or network of catalogues there will be a good chance for the user to select those that suit his/her needs best among different representations of a work. Copy cataloguing through bibliographic utilities, which is usually a known-item search, is another example of such a user approach.

With the availability of catalogues to different remote users, it is hard to give absolute priority to either of the two traditional functions of the catalogue. A catalogue accessible to all types of users through a network will be expected to satisfy, as far as possible, different needs.

Availability of Different Types of Bibliographic Database

With respect to the accessibility of different types of online and/or on-disk bibliographic databases to various users, a combination of approaches in terms of the functions of the catalogue should be considered.

With access to book trade databases, the catalogue goes beyond providing holdings information and becomes a gateway to explore what is newly published, what is to be published and what is in print. In such an environment, emphasis is also put on other functions such as the crucial choice of one item over another. From a different point of view, the functions of the bibliographic database in the library world and book trade world are similar in many respects, such as the finding function, the selecting function and housekeeping function. Even the bringing together of works by a particular author and also collocation of series, are functions wanted by the two communities. A major difference is in the collocation of different editions and manifestations of a work, which libraries appear to consider important enough to control by rules of entry.

Online Search/Retrieval/Display and Functions of the Catalogue

All a catalogue's functions can be achieved more comprehensively through the search/retrieval/display capabilities of the online catalogue. An interesting aspect of the online catalogue which is duplicated from A&I services is the ability of the searcher to choose and/or combine a number of different searching options.

For example, keyword searching on place of publication, name of the publisher, date of publication, series information and ISBN or ISSN not only facilitates the finding function but it can also help in the choice of one item over another. Boolean searching can facilitate both the finding function and the collocating function. Hypertext searching on any term or a combination of terms can extend a known-item search to other items which may be unknown to the searcher but may have some kind of relationship with the item first found.

There is an important difference between the manual environment and the online environment in terms of search/retrieval/display capabilities of the catalogue and their influence on the two objectives. Whilst collocation in the manual catalogue is achieved through the physical pre-arrangement of records of related editions and manifestations of a work, in the online environment it can be achieved through the pre-coding and display of search results.

With many more data elements in MARC records, additional indexes and extensive search and retrieval capabilities, the online catalogue can be used as a selecting aid to choose specific items. This function, i.e., the choosing function, which is of interest to different users such as acquisitions and reference librarians as well as the book trade, can be carried out more effectively. For example, combining key data elements, such as author or title with date of publication, country of publication, name of publisher and language of the item is a useful way to choose appropriate items.

Conclusion

The catalogue in the global online environment is supposed to satisfy all possible approaches. From the preceding paragraphs, it can be concluded that the functions of the online catalogue go beyond those laid down in the Paris Principles. The online catalogue with its extensive capabilities can widen the scope and content of the functions and fulfil new functions. It is therefore necessary that cataloguing principles for the online environment should cover all these different functions equally and should also take into consideration the influence of each function on other principles.

Structure of the catalogue and the concept of multiple entries

The structure of the catalogue has an important role in the fulfilment of its functions. Sections 3 (Structure of the Catalogue), 4 (Kinds of Entry), 5 (Use of Multiple Entries), 6 (Function of Different Kinds of Entry) and sub-sections 8.1, 9.1, 9.2, 9.5, 9.6 and also sections 10 and 11 of the Statement of Principles relate to the structure of the catalogue. The principles underlying the structure of the catalogue and choice of entries in the Paris Principles include statements concerning the determination and construction of necessary entries for a linear, alphabetical catalogue. Such a linear catalogue consists of main entries, added entries and references.

Online catalogues, on the other hand, go far beyond the linear author/title catalogue. they permit dynamic linking, merging and rearrangement of files. The structure of an online catalogue usually consists of bibliographic, authority and holdings records linked to one another, each of which is arranged in a given order. Multiple access points and related index files in an online system are not limited to traditional author/title headings. Since it is possible to specify more data elements in a record as access points, the structure of online catalogues may include other index files such as keywords, author/ any keyword from title, standard numbers, language of the item, country of publication, date of publication, type of material, genre and readership level.

Cataloguing principles should take into consideration the complex structure of the online catalogue and provide principles for the construction of different files and also for the indexing of different fields and sub-fields concerning access to required elements in the record. They should also suit the structure of the catalogue including different indexes for searching and browsing. A possible approach would be to provide principles for the construction of browsable indexes which can help the searcher to get a clear idea of what sort of indexes are available for searching and retrieval. It is also useful to provide name authority files for browsing, like those offered by SIRSI and PALS systems and a uniform-title authority file for making the catalogue more effective in its collocating function. A possible development in the structure of the catalogue is through the concept of 'super records'.

The Concept of Main Entry

As a typical example of the impact of the online environment on cataloguing principles, it has been claimed that the concept of main entry has lost its value. It was indicated that with the advent of computerised catalogues the value of the main entry concept, which developed in the context of book and card catalogues, has been questioned, but no satisfactory and practical solution has emerged as to how its functions can be otherwise fulfilled.

Svenonius asks:

- "If the main entry were to be abandoned, what would replace its role in the construction of uniform headings? what would take its place in the structuring displays in online catalogs? how would abandoning the main entry affect single-entry and minimal-level catalogs"?

A review of the related literature of the last two decades shows a developing discussion in favour of abandoning the main entry concept in the online environment. Although before the advent of automated catalogues there were some proposals for the no-main-entry concept such as 'Description Independent System (DIS)', 'alternative entry', and 'title main entry', developments in online catalogues of access to bibliographic information have given the issue a new dimension and the number of those who advocate the abandonment of the main entry concept has increased.

To many writers, the concept arose out of pre-machine systems and is said to be irrelevant in a developed online catalogue where the technology permits many more access points of equal value in the retrieving of bibliographic information. It is often also claimed that the process of determining main entries is one of the most complex, costly and time consuming processes in descriptive cataloguing.

In contrast to those supporting the simple abandonment of the main entry principle, others argue for its continued use in computerised catalogues. In a survey of the attitudes of cataloguers and cataloguing educators, Musavi found that more than half of the respondents disagreed with the abandonment of the main entry concept even in the online catalogue. The majority of respondents believed that online catalogues will not devalue the concept of main entry. Baughman and Svenonius assessed the implication of the possible abandonment of main entry in AACR2 and found that a number of problematic rules would result. Exploring the definitions and functions of main entry, Carpenter stated that some of the functions of main entry, particularly its collocating function, are still valid in the online environment.

The following part is an analysis of the main entry concept in terms of its functions in an online environment. The focus of this part is only on main entries for personal names.

Functions of Main Entry

Discussions of the main entry concept have been mostly concerned with the objectives and functions of the catalogue rather than merely its definitions.' Verona any consideration about the functions of the main entry has to be based on an evaluation of the general objectives and functions of the alphabetical catalogue. A similar idea comes from Carpenter who points out that: "If main entry is to have any function, it must be in the context of fulfilling an objective of a catalogue."

A major justification for the concept often lies in its collocating function, in bringing together both different editions of a work and the works of an author. Carpenter states that other functions, i.e.:

- Naming a work,
- Providing credit to the principal author,
- Providing the only full entry, and
- Being the entry to which all others refer, are of historical interest.

Looking from a database perspective, Brooks and Bierbaum consider the uniform main entry as an essential device to link all the occurrences of a bibliographic mutation. Tillett emphasises the role of main entry in specifying the nature of the relationship between a work and the person associated with it.

Heaney notes that the issue of the main entry is more complicated than its being only considered as a primary heading. it involves not the idea of "main" entry but also the adequate identification, within the record, of related works. As a collocating device, the concept of main entry has been retained not only in multiple-entry card catalogues but also with the same justification in automated catalogues.

In terms of collocation, main entry has two specific functions:

- Assembling and displaying works by an author, and
- Assembling and displaying different editions of a work.
- Assembling and Displaying Works by an Author

Assembling of the works of an author can be achieved through a uniform heading for the author, whether recorded as the main entry heading or as an added entry. This function is thus not exclusively achieved by the main entry heading. Furthermore, the main entry heading alone cannot assemble all the works by an author. In many cases where an author is a joint author, editor, compiler or author of one part, his/her name may be presented as an added entry heading.

Assembling and Displaying Different Editions of a Work

While the most important justification for the main entry is in its role of assembling and displaying, in a meaningful and logical order, the various editions of a work, it has been a complex and debatable concept in the history of descriptive cataloguing.

Although this function is attributed to main entry, it cannot be fully achieved through the main entry heading alone. In assembling the different editions of a work, the main entry heading is dependent upon a second collocating device: the uniform title. Without the inclusion of a uniform title following the main entry heading in the record, the assembling function of the main entry is only partially achieved: it would be limited only to those works whose editions and manifestations have identical titles proper. Thus, neither of the two functions perceived for main entry in the Paris Principles can be fully achieved through the main entry heading alone. As will be discussed further in this part, a combination of the author's uniform heading and the uniform title that is considered as a 'unifying mode of identifying' different editions of a work will fulfil the collocating function in a more comprehensive way.

Online Search/Retrieval/Display and the Concept of Main Entry

Keyword Searching

In an online database with keyword access, it is possible to retrieve a record through keywords, whether in main entries, added entries or any other significant word indexed from the text of the record. A major characteristic of keywords is that they are not controlled by cataloguing rules and they are not subject to authority control. Therefore, keyword searching on names will retrieve only those records that match the term(s) keyed in by the searcher. Keyword searching capability cannot replace the main entry in terms of its collocating function. It can, however, facilitate the collocating function: once access to one or more specific items has been provided through keywords, the searcher can extend the search by keying the exact form of the author heading or the uniform title found on the retrieved record(s) to search for related editions with the same terms only.

Boolean Searching

Boolean search is another capability for bringing together different editions of a work. This can be done by keying in two or more data elements such as the author heading and the title proper or the uniform title, by using the 'AND' operator. Since the title proper of different editions of a work may vary, titles proper in conjunction with author heading cannot be a useful element for the collocating function. The 'author/title' search key, which many systems provide, is an implicit Boolean search which has the same limitation. Instead, a Boolean search on the author uniform heading and the uniform title, including relevant qualifiers, can achieve the collocating function more effectively. This approach is another justification for the main entry concept.

Index Browsing

The browsing capability removes the burden of entering the exact search terms and enables the searcher to gain an overview of an index containing an alphabetical list of all headings. Browsing, for example, the author index will display together all the works by an author irrespective of his/her type of contribution. Nevertheless, for the uniform citation and display of entries in the browsable author index we need to identify the primary author. To link works, however, the primary author's name should be in a uniform heading. This is again another justification for the concept of main entry in an online environment.

It can be seen that, even with browsing capability, a useful collocation of different editions of a work is not possible with the present structure of entries. Browsable indexes could help solve the collocation problem if the author and the title indexes are pre-coordinated for meaningful arrangement and display of related entities.

Online Display and the Concept of Main Entry

Since the display format in online catalogues is independent of the storage format, when a number of records are displayed in response to a query, the retrieved titles need to be displayed in conjunction with a second primary identifier such as the author heading.

Otherwise, not only is the identification of the retrieved items not complete, but different works by an author are also not distinguished and assembled. This primary element is necessary in online displays of related works. Carpenter states that the primary key provides a unique identification of the record. He also points out that: "Discussions about main entry have changed focus from records to useful displays". Online displays, for instance, default listings in brief displays, require that, in addition to titles proper, another principal element must be displayed.

The following example may help to make this idea clearer:

- As the convention now exists in many OPACs, when there is an editor or a compiler for a work and the work goes under title main entry or a corporate heading and the editor or the compiler is given an added entry as opposed to main entry, his/her/its name would still need to be displayed in conjunction with the title proper in the brief display to uniquely identify the work and to differentiate between works with identical titles. From another perspective, that of the catalogue user who does not understand what main entry is, an editor or a compiler may seem to be the primary identifier or access point which should be displayed in conjunction with the title in brief displays and in single entry listings.

Conclusion

As a concept, the main entry relates rather to the nature of relationships between entities than to the physical medium through which those entities are to be described. Many works, particularly in the fields of literature, law and music, require such a uniform construct for identification and collocation.

Even if technology provides catalogues with sophisticated devices to link two or more related entities to one another, it would not help the user if catalogues do not show him/her the nature of these relationships. Without such a concept the catalogue, whether manual or computerised, would lose its integrity and usefulness.

From the preceding discussions concerning the possible influence of different online search/retrieval/display capabilities, it can be concluded that online catalogues still need a construct to carry out some specific functions which cannot be fulfilled thoroughly through other devices. Of great concern is the fact that the main entry concept is not meant to be a single function element but rather a concept that is essential to fulfil some basic functions. Thus it is in need of a re-definition that will focus on its multiple functions.

Main entry is a uniform construct for the naming and identifying of works and also for the useful collocation and arrangement/display of the different editions and manifestations of a work. In addition to the identification of the primary author, the concept of uniform citation is dependent on two key identifying elements: uniform titles for works and uniform headings for authors.

Uniform Headings for Titles

A work can potentially be produced in different editions, different versions, in various languages and/or in a variety of physical formats. This concept is intrinsic to the bibliographic universe and its control is an essential principle for catalogues. In this context, the name of the work, i.e., the 'uniform title', has been devised in descriptive cataloguing to control the conditions of a work.

For this reason, the use of uniform titles has greatly increased and their application has gone beyond anonymous classics, sacred scriptures and works of music. However, the Paris Principles are less concerned with the concept of uniform titles: principles 7.1, 11.3 and 11.4 only deal vaguely with the choice and form of uniform titles. In the following parts, the rationale and the functions of uniform titles will be examined in the context of the online senvironment.

Functions of the Uniform Title

- The functions of uniform titles are:
- To standardise the original title of a work,
- To standardise the form of the main entry heading for anonymous works,
- To group together all editions and manifestations of a work under one particular title, and
- To identify the relationships between an edition and a work.

The rationale for the principle of uniform titles, however, rests mainly with two functions:

- The uniform identification of a work; and
- The assembling of entities derived from or related to the same work.

Uniform titles support at least four types of bibliographic relationship: equivalence, derivative, whole-part, and sequential relationships.

Online Search/Retrieval/Display and the Concept of Uniform Titles

No research has yet attempted to study the influence of different search/retrieval/display capabilities of online catalogues on the principle of uniform title. Tillett states that some Western cataloguing practices that arise from the physical limitations of manual catalogues do not make sense in the online environment and should be rethought. Of such practices, the uniform title is one of the most important. Tillett states that we should simplify the entire issue of uniform titles to make it relevant to the online catalogue in a network environment. Vellucci emphasises the need to explore more fully the potential of uniform titles as linking devices and as foundation points for online catalogues.

She states:

- "As we move into the online environment, the uniform title will continue to evolve. The terminology might change again, and new functions might be identified. But the important role of the uniform title in identifying works and serving as a linking device for bibliographic relationships will no doubt be a primary focus for uniform titles of the future".

Boll points out that, in an online catalogue, both the primary heading and the uniform title "are needed to recall, as a group, manifestations of the same work that have different titles proper". As in the case of the main entry concept, the examination of individual search/retrieval/display capabilities in online catalogues reveals that not only do those capabilities not diminish the need for the concept of uniform titles but they also emphasise their role in the effective collocation and display of related works and items.

Without the uniform title associated with the main entry heading, one can see that different editions of the same work are scattered among the retrieved records for other works by the same author. For example, translations or selections of a work, while being scattered among different works by the same author, are treated as if they are new works by the same author. This problem is highlighted in online catalogues: they may need a number of screens to list all retrieved items and the searcher may have to spend considerable time to find his/her needed item. With regard to the catalogue's collocating function, uniform titles will play a more important role in the online catalogue. In an online environment, the linking of different editions and manifestations of a work is essential for increasing recall in response to user queries and could be a critical part of the file structure for new system designs. While uniform titles alone increase the search results, the addition of other data elements, such as version, language, date and part of the work, to the uniform title will narrow down the search results and will increase precision.

In their present state, formal or conventional titles, such as "Laws, etc." and "works", may not be useful in online retrieval unless in conjunction with, for example, a name or date. The search expression "Laws, etc. AND New South Wales" is useful in an online catalogue. In such systems some of the qualifiers can be specified by Boolean means or can be simplified into natural language terms.

While the occurrence of editions of the same work with different titles and different works with similar titles increases in large catalogues and union databases, the concept of uniform titles can help control this problem. In the context of searching a large bibliographic database, there should be a means for the user to realise that what has been retrieved in response to his/her query may be different editions of the same work.

Uniform Headings for Persons

Another principle that is essential to the fulfilment of the main entry's functions is a uniform heading for persons. A rigid ideal in modern cataloguing codes and one of the first principles in the Anglo-American cataloguing tradition has been to list all works by or about a given person under a uniform heading. In this context, uniform headings have been regarded as a necessary device for the integrity of the catalogue.

While the need for uniformity of headings in an online environment and for links among variant forms of a name has been reaffirmed by a number of writers, the necessity to enter an author's works under one uniform heading and the provision of references for other forms of a name for the same author has come into question in online catalogues.

In terms of the implication of adhering to the principle of uniform headings in an online environment Chan asks:

- ". . . does the principle of uniform heading have the same meaning or import in the automated catalogue as in the card catalogue?...What are the implications of the principle of uniform heading in the maintenance of the name authority file? To what extent does the designation of a focal point facilitate and economize such operations?"

However, as discussed in relation to the collocating function of the catalogue, the bringing together and display of an author's works require that all records be presented under a uniform heading for the author. Divergence in the form of headings is not consistent with the requirements of the online environment. Normalisation of names is a principle which is also essential to database management systems.

However, a major problem in the online environment is that there are different bibliographic databases and a wide variety of users. A difficulty in searching different databases is that, while there is a uniform approach in library cataloguing in relation to uniform headings, other communities such as the book trade and A&I services are less concerned with this principle. In many bibliographic databases it is often the case that the same person has been entered under a variety of unlinked names leading to irretrievability of all the works by a particular author.

Online Search/Retrieval/Display and the Principle of Uniform Headings

Keyword searching

Keyword searching facilitates the finding function of the catalogue through the form of an author's name that appears on the title page or in information sources, i.e., the form which is usually familiar to both the book world and the searcher. However, with keyword searching it is possible only to search names under the form in which they have been recorded in the bibliographic record. Keywords are not subject to authority control and therefore cannot always collocate all the works by or about an author in a catalogue, especially if the form of name differs. However, keyword searching facilitates the collocation of an author's works: once access is made to a record through any form of the name, it is possible to assemble works by or about a particular author through a further search on the uniform author heading.

Truncation

With right-hand truncation, the online catalogue is able to retrieve those names which begin with the characters defined by the searcher. In other words, names must be uniform, at least for the few beginning characters, to retrieve all the works by a given author. For example, truncation on a surname will retrieve works by those authors whose forenames or initials may differ from one another.

Truncation, particularly automatic right-hand truncation, influences uniform headings in two ways:

- It retrieves all the works by an author when only the surname is known to the searcher,
- It increases the number of retrieved records, some of which may not be relevant to the needs of the searcher.

In effect, not only does truncation not devalue the principle of uniform headings, but it also emphasises it, in that the more complete the uniform heading is, the more chance there will be for retrieval precision.

Index Browsing

In systems allowing the browsing of name indexes, it is necessary, in general, that works by an author be assembled under a single form of name. The browsing capability thus reinforces the need for the principle of uniform headings. The value of uniform headings can also be seen in single-entry printouts and lists both in library cataloguing and in publishers' activities. The 'author index' volume in the Books In Print is a good example of a name browsable index.

Authority Control Systems

In an online catalogue utilising name authority files, access to the works of a given author by any variant forms of the name would be as effective as access by the uniform heading. The distinction between the established form of a name and any cross reference to it is invisible to the user. It has been said that in future catalogues a complete listing of an author's works under any form of the author's name is quite feasible.

Even in authority control systems there is still a need to establish one form of a person's name as the uniform heading and others as references. In fact, uniform headings are still considered to be an important principle in authority work.

While name authority systems make it possible to achieve the finding function in a one-step search for any work by a given author, adherence to the principle of uniform heading is a means to maintain the one-to-many relationship in bibliographic databases and, thus, to achieve the collocation of all works available by a given author in the catalogue.

Online Displays and the Principle of Uniform Headings

With regard to differences in the physical forms of the manual catalogue and the online catalogue, the very rigid ideal in the card catalogue of assembling in one place all the works a library has by a given author has shifted, in the online catalogue, to the ideal of the system's ability to retrieve all the works of an author through any searched form of his/her name and to display them together under one uniform heading for the author. Under whatever form of name the works by a given author have been searched, the default listing of those works requires that the name of the author needs to be displayed in a uniform manner.

Networks and the Concept of Uniform Headings

Uniform headings are an essential principle in bibliographic control, especially in shared cataloguing environments and union catalogues, facilitating bibliographic cooperation between libraries.

The communication of bibliographic records for cataloguing purposes, reference services and inter-library loan depends to a large extent on the uniformity of headings. In searching the different catalogues accessible in a network, the patron, the technical services librarian and the reference librarian usually look for the works of a given author under the same heading.

The ability to look for particular bibliographic information in different catalogues irrespective of their size, type and location requires an ever- increasing need for standard bibliographic records.

Except for differences in user interfaces, a first requirement is to conform to the concept of uniform headings at the national level. National name authority files would be the most desirable answer to complications in the forms of authors' names and can provide consistent access to catalogues and other bibliographic lists. It is then possible to share bibliographic and authority records on the international level.

Criticising the way that cataloguers prepare headings as if they are cataloguing for a single library, Wajenberg states that:

- "The cataloguing code for the third millennium should rise the parochial emphasis on the local catalogue. It should provide instructions for preparing headings for a national online authority file, and eventually for an international equivalent".

Form of Headings in an Online Environment

In addition to the principle of uniform headings, which is essential to the integrity and the collocating function of the catalogue, the form of names in headings, as emphasised by IFLA/Unesco in 1961 should be agreed upon both nationally and internationally. This principle needs to be examined with respect to searchers' expectations and also to the searching/retrieval/display capabilities of the online catalogue. The form of personal and corporate names will be discussed with respect to the possible influence of the online environment.

Form of Personal Name Headings

The form of a name is an important factor in searching and retrieval, particularly in online systems in which the searcher has to key in the name as the search string. In online catalogues with many search/retrieval capabilities it is important to see whether this principle needs a rather different approach. In a manual environment, a problem with the form of heading is that searches for works of authors must be in the exact form and order of their name headings.

This requirement is no longer totally necessary since cross references in authority records and keyword searching allow for the searching of names in different ways.

If the searcher is not sure as to which part of the name forms the surname for efficient searching, for example, Jean De La Fountaine, Walter De La Mare, Dante

Alighieri, cross references or keyword access offers the possibility to search names in any order. Keyword searching capability also reduces the need for complete "surname+initials+(full forenames)+dates" headings as in AACR2R.

Truncation of headings, especially automatic right-hand truncation, can help retrieve works by authors whose complete heading is not known to the searcher. Variations in the fullness of forenames seem unimportant in systems with a truncation capability. Using 'Price, H H' and 'Grossman, Allen R.' as examples, Arlene Taylor proposes that an online catalogue with keyword searching of headings and automatic right-hand truncation needs rather different rules for the formulation of headings and references.

Wajenberg claims that, with keyword searching, the inversion of surnames and rules for the choice of entry-element in compound surnames and names with prefixes become unnecessary. Using the heading 'Mozart, Wolfgang Amadeus' as an example, he points out that the most useful form of name is the fullest form.

Kilgour on the other hand, proposes that for a single-screen miniature catalogue author entries can be reduced to surnames alone. His survey of two online catalogues in the North Carolina State University, containing approximately 3.4 million entries, showed that surname searches produced mini catalogues of one screen 12.6% of the time, two screens 22.5%, and three screens 30.1%. He claims that his finding, that nearly two-fifths of the cataloguing of books in a large university library produces entries that will be displayed in mini catalogues of one screen, demands revision and simplification of cataloguing practices in large research libraries For example, he proposes that with keyword search function no added author fields will be necessary for multiple surnames.

There are other factors, such as the need for default listings of the works of an author and the needs of the book world, citation traditions and international exchange of bibliographic data, which require the standard order of 'surname, forename' in full form for personal headings. There is at present no consensus on the form of headings among the different creators of bibliographic records. There are, however, to some extent similarities between library cataloguing and the book world: both tend to use the best known form of name with library cataloguing more inclined to use the complete form.

Form of Corporate Headings

The issue of corporate headings was one of the problems on which there was no international consensus at the Paris Conference. Even today different national codes have different approaches towards the form of headings.

Searching, retrieval and display of corporate names in online systems are often frustrating to the user. Many of the problems concerning the searching of corporate bodies' publications relate to the form of headings for these bodies. Little has been written on the form of corporate headings in an online environment. Some of the implications of searching corporate names in online systems have been briefly addressed by Arlene Taylor, Brunt and more fully by Greig. The result of a study by Henty, concerning unsuccessful keyword searching, indicates that the reasons for the users' search failures are, to some extent, due to the implications of variant forms of corporate names.

Some of the problems concerning the searching, retrieval and display of corporate headings in online systems are:

- It is particularly difficult to search under the exact form of corporate headings in online catalogues because the user has to key in the search string. How much of the heading should be keyed in by the searcher to initiate the search, since corporate names are usually long, often similar to one another and appear in different forms such as acronyms, initials and subordinations?
- In some cases, headings for subordinate bodies associated with the same parent body do not follow a uniform approach. While the 'World Health Organization' appears as the heading for this body, a number of subordinate bodies incorporating the acronym 'WHO' are treated as headings in the catalogue. for example, 'WHO Collaborating Centre on Environmental Pollution Control', 'WHO Commission on Health and Environment', 'WHO Expert Group on Pesticide Residues'. The same problem exists with the 'Food and Agriculture Organization of United Nations' and some of its subordinate bodies beginning with 'FAO'.
- Entering corporate bodies under the name of the higher body would often cause inconvenience for the searcher, especially in large catalogues and shared systems. The use of indirect corporate headings is not innate and could appear meaningless to catalogue users. They "can be considerably distorted because of re-arrangement of the elements of the name and, in many codes, by translating the name of the jurisdiction".
- The addition of a geographic name to the heading for corporate bodies often does not make sense in the online environment. Exact searching and truncation on headings beginning with the name of the jurisdiction often result in too many hits. Headings like 'Australia. Australian Parliamentary Observer Group', 'Canada.
- Canadian High Commission' and 'Canada. Canadian Armed Forces' which are problematic for searching could be more straightforward if 'Australia' and 'Canada', were omitted from the heading.
- Truncation on the name of the parent body will usually retrieve too many records that are not easy to distinguish from one another, especially in brief displays where, because of screen limitation, the name of the parent body alone may fill the allotted space.
- Clustering of all the publications of different departments and divisions of a corporate body is not usually sought by searchers.

- Also, it does not make sense in brief displays where, because of screen limitation, only the first few elements of the heading are displayed thus obscuring the name of the actual issuing body.
- Consider, for example, how frustrating the retrieval of publications of different subordinates bodies of the United Nations would be in an online catalogue.

ABSTRACTING AND INDEXING SERVICES AND LIBRARY CATA LOGUING: RECONCILIATION OF PRINCIPLES

Online and/or on-disk A & I databases are now a major component of the online environment. As indicated earlier, one of the aims of this research is to acknowledge the impact of the merging, integrating and accessibility of different types of bibliographic files, particularly library catalogues and A&I databases, on cataloguing principles and to see in what areas and how far similar principles might be applicable to the practices of the two communities.

Library cataloguing has over a century's history of establishing standards for the exchange of information whereas, due to the production of abstracts and indexes by publishers rather than by libraries, there is less standardisation within A&I services. Many indexing rules in the first half of the twentieth century were practically identical with those used in the preparation of library catalogues such as Cutter's Rules for a Dictionary catalogue and the ALA

Cataloguing rules for Author and Title Entries.

Because of the introduction of new technologies, library cataloguing and indexing services now have more impact on one another than before largely due to three major factors:

- The extensive and powerful searching and retrieval capabilities that computer technology has introduced to library catalogues, such as keyword searching, truncation, Boolean searching and hypertext searching, were first introduced in A&I services. Consequently, the indexing of more data fields, which requires the addition of more data elements such as language, type of material and readership level, is another indication of the impact of A&I services oncataloguing practices.
- The accessibility of different online library catalogues and A&I databases through a single terminal and the increasing ability of the searcher to go from one bibliographic database/file to another and to navigate the whole bibliographic apparatus.
- The evolution of CD-ROM versions of many A&I databases which are now available to end users.

These factors have now become a cause for concern over the possible use of the same or compatible standards for the creation of bibliographic records. Because of technological advances in providing integrated access to different bibliographic files and databases, it is time to think as to whether bibliographical control of these different practices should be done based on a single standard. A first step in a study of the possible use of a single standard in both communities is to acknowledge the similarities and differences between library cataloguing and A&I practices. Library cataloguing has come to a set of principles which are internationally agreed upon and has provided bibliographic standards for description of and access to bibliographic items and for the communication of bibliographic data, whereas A&I services have not. There are differences within A&I services about their approaches to description and there are different standards.

Some of the major areas of differences/similarities between the two communities that have to be considered are:

- Objectives and functions of the catalogue/database,
- Structure of the catalogue/database and of the bibliographic record, and Choice and form of access points.
- Objectives and Functions of the Catalogue/Database

Differences in the approaches of library cataloguing and A&I services towards creating bibliographic records are a result of different objectives which each of the two communities identifies for its bibliographic database. The major object of looking for an article's bibliographical citation in A&I databases is different from that of looking for bibliographic information in a library catalogue. While library cataloguing is traditionally concerned with the finding, identifying, collocating and organising of bibliographic entities, A&I services deal rather with the subject content of bibliographic entities and, to some extent only, the finding of works by a particular author.

In A&I databases, the assembling of all the works by a given author may be a common approach for some searchers, but there is usually no concept such as the assembling of all editions and manifestations of a work. Journal articles, patent documents, reports, dissertations and conference proceedings have fewer editions than books. Consequently, the concept of main entry, which is useful for bringing together different editions and manifestations of a work, has more justification in library catalogues than in A&I databases. A similar idea is present in the COSATI (the Committee on Scientific and Technical Information) standard with the policy of a main entry free environment: "The system works because only rarely are there technical reports that are about other technical reports and unrelated by contract number".

Structure of the Catalogue/Database and of the Bibliographic Record Because of the differences in their objectives and functions, library catalogues and A&I databases differ from one another in terms of the structure of the bibliographic record and the structure of the database. There is no concept such as multiple entries in A&I databases.

However, in terms of the structure of the record, there are similarities in some of the data fields which can potentially conform to the same standard: headings for persons and corporate bodies associated with an item, date of publication, title of analytic, title of monograph, title of collection or series, language of the item, ISBN/ISSN, conference identification information, abstract/summary, country of publication, target audience and subject headings. These data fields can be treated similarly by the two communities by using identical terms/phrases. The searcher can approach the catalogue or the database with the same search string.

Choice and form of Acces Points

This is one of the most important areas of possible reconciliation between cataloguing principles and indexing conventions. Because CD-ROM versions of A&I databases are becoming increasingly available to end users and have larger cumulations of citations in them, there is more need to reconcile variant names. Since there is usually no retrospective editing of headings when a CD-ROM is produced, such discrepancies are simply left alone.

Many A&I databases also include citations of monographs, such as conference proceedings, festschriften and books reviewed, that are duplicated in library catalogues. This also indicates the need for more consistency in name headings between library cataloguing and A&I practices.

In terms of the treatment of names for inclusion in the record for later retrieval, A&I conventions differ markedly both within themselves and from cataloguing conventions. In respect of the choice of names to be entered in the bibliographic record, A&I conventions usually provide author indexing in depth. They do not conform to principles such as main entry and the 'rule of three'. The names of persons associated with an item are entered as they appear on the item in hand. For example, the UNISIST Reference Manual prescribes that the names of all individual authors associated with a given item are to be entered in the record, unless there is a clear indication on the original that the chief responsibility for authorship lies with choosing only one or less than all of the persons cited, in which case only those indicated as chief contributors are to be entered.

There are other similarities or differences:

- Since A&I databases are not searched through the exact titles of items, title is not as common an access point as in library catalogues. Instead, a title keyword index is provided for title as well as subject searching.
- As a first principle in the indexing of names, both communities invert names of persons to secure alphabetic arrangement by family names.
- A&I conventions regard the names of editors of collections as an essential element for the identification of monographs whereas cataloguing conventions put less emphasis on the role of such contributors, in that they no longer consider editors and compilers as main entries.

- In terms of the names of persons associated with a monograph, A&I conventions regard the form derived from the item as essential and other forms as optional.
- Since A&I services do not normally use name authority files and do not maintain references, many of them prefer to include other forms of the name with initials immediately after the complete form:
- Wendt, Richard P. Wendt, R. P.
- Atkinson, H Craig Craig Atkinson, H
- Library cataloguing, on the other hand, treats names with initials differently.
- For example, AACR2R has the following approach:
- Wendt, R.P. (Richard P.)
- Eliot, T.S. (Thomas Stearns)

One reason why many A&I services do not conform to the principle of uniform heading may be that they are usually discipline-oriented and, therefore, the chance of similarity between the forms of names within a given discipline is not great.

There are usually not many identical names with identical forenames or initials within a given A&I database. for example, there were only two authors with the surname 'Buckland' in the LISA database and three in ERIC but none with identical forename or initial.

- A&I conventions emphasise the addition to names of two other elements: 1) the 'role', i.e., the type of intellectual responsibility, such as 'author', 'editor', 'compiler', 'translator', etc., and 2) the person's affiliation. Cataloguing rules, on the other hand, treat the role of persons in the statement of responsibility area and discard affiliations. With regard to corporate names, there are some similarities and differences between A&I conventions and cataloguing principles:
  - The full form of corporate names is entered by A&I services with the inclusion of an abbreviation or acronym of a corporate body as an optional element. AACR2R prescribes a similar approach without the optional inclusion of an abbreviation or acronym.
  - If the official or formal name of an organisation is usually quoted in the form of an acronym, this may be entered as the full form. AACR2R has the same approach.
  - The name of a corporate body should be entered in the language of the document, unless the name shown on the document is itself a translation, and the name in its original language is known, in which case the latter form should be entered if better known. AACR2R prescribes that the official language of the body should be used.
  - Where several levels of an organisation are cited, they should be given in descending order of scale from the larger unit to the smaller. In terms of entering at the intermediate levels, if their inclusion

does not add significant information to the entry, they may be omitted provided always that the most specific unit is cited and that the entry provides an unambiguous identification of the organisation. Similarly, AACR2R prescribes that a subordinate or related body should usually be entered as a subheading of the main body.

SUMMARY AND CONCLUSIONS

The following conclusions are derived from the examination of a number of cataloguing principles carried out in this chapter, in the light of the various capabilities of the online environment.

Functions of the catalogue:

- Conceptually, the objectives and functions of the catalogue are independent of its physical form and arrangement. Technology can, however, influence the way in which these functions are carried out: the more developments there are in the technology of catalogue construction and in the online environment, the more possibilities there are to achieve those objectives and functions.
- Due to the potential use of bibliographic records by a variety of users, the scope of catalogue functions should be expanded to encompass additional functions. The two basic functions remain valid in the online environment but the catalogue also can serve additional functions: to further identify entities, to choose one item over similar items, to locate items and copies of items and to maintain databases in terms of record updating.
- While the finding function is a general approach in almost all bibliographic databases, the collocating function is more important to library catalogues and, to some extent, to publishers' databases than to other communities such as A & I services. However, in the online environment, with a variety of users, all the functions of the catalogue need to be considered important. It is therefore necessary to elaborate on this issue and arrive at an international agreement, since the delineation of the objectives and functions of the catalogue influences other cataloguing principles.

The concept of main entry:

- Rather than being the locus of complete information for the bibliographic record or the primary access point, main entry is an important concept that maintains some basic functions of the catalogue, that of identifying and collocating, in a uniform way, different editions and manifestations of a work. In other words, if a major function of the catalogue is to identify and collocate works as well as their editions and manifestations, there is a need for a concept such as main entry. The lack of such a concept could result in failure to place a publication in the context of its bibliographic relationships.

- Unless we devise new mechanisms for the uniform identification and collocation of the different manifestations and editions of a work, it would be unwise to abandon the concept of main entry.
- Nevertheless, in order to delineate the concept more clearly and to avoid confusion as to its functions, main entry is in need of re-definition. The new functional definition should address the validity of the concept in terms of its various functions, irrespective of the catalogue's physical environment. Main entry is particularly needed in the online environment for the useful retrieval, display and arrangement of search results.

The concept of uniform titles:

- Similarly to the concept of main entry, uniform titles are needed to perform some basic functions such as providing links between different editions and manifestations of a work and to distinguish among works with identical titles proper. Because of present problems in the online retrieval of the various editions and manifestations of works, a concept such as a standardised form of the title of a work can serve to identify and collocate them. However, uniform titles need to be simplified in order to avoid online retrieval problems.

The principle of uniform headings:

- It is difficult to fulfil the collocating function of the catalogue/ database without maintaining the principle of uniform headings.Uniformity of headings for authors and titles is especially important in network environments, where different catalogues and other bibliographic databases are accessible to the user through the same terminal. The principle is also of particular significance in shared cataloguing systems and union databases. Library cataloguing, book trade bibliographic databases and A&I services should at least be consistent or compatible in certain areas such as uniform headings. In effect, standardisation or compatibility in the form of headings is an essential requirement for universal bibliographical control (UBC), particularly in the global online environment.

Form of name headings:

- In terms of the form of personal and corporate name headings for effective searching, retrieval and display, online catalogues need a simpler approach. The form of headings needs to be reconsidered in terms of its suitability for different searching patterns and for display. For example, given adequate software, full forms of name should satisfy searchers seeking either that form, or only the surname plus initials. But searching under single letters, such as initials, is still a problem for many library systems. For subordinate corporate bodies direct headings are usually more responsive to online search/retrieval/displays.

Number of contributors:

- As a consequence of the potential of the online system to incorporate more names as access points, the 'rule of three' is not sensible in the online environment. Removal of this outdated principle would add to the functionality of the catalogue, in that it would enhance access to and identification of works of all authors.

Wider application of the principles:

- Current cataloguing principles are not based on the overriding requirements of different users in a variety of environments. There are advantages if we can arrive at a body of principles which can serve to reconcile the bibliographical practices of publishers and booksellers with those of libraries, bibliographic utilities, national bibliographies and the archival community. It would also be advantageous if A&I services and library cataloguing practices could come closer in terms of providing consistent access to bibliographic information, particularly in terms of the form of name headings. Although the objectives and functions of book trade databases, A&I databases and library catalogues are different from one another, the entries created by each community need to be consistent or at least compatible for the purposes of record exchange and database searching. A possible solution is for each community to conform to national name authority files.

In terms of some fundamental questions such as the 'basic unit of description', 'the edition issue' and the display of bibliographic data, current cataloguing principles are not adequately responsive to the requirements of the new online environment. In considering basic concepts for further investigation, attention should be paid to a possible resolution of such questions.

CATALOGUING IN THE INTERNET AND DIGITAL ERA

This chapter explores those issues in greater detail. It begins by describing the motivations underlying the reuse of the term "library" to describe the new digital information research area. As will be described, those motivations reflected the expedient interests of each participant community and their respective definitions of a library. It next describes the influence of that term on the architectures and applications that were produced by the digital library research programme over the subsequent years. The chapter continues with an explanation of how the architecture of those digital library applications impacts the technical coexistence of digital libraries with the mainstream web.

Finally, the chapter describes how the evolution of the web from Web 1.0 to Web 2.0 has not only increased the technical incompatibilities between the two information environments, but has led to a fundamental conceptual difference in their infor-mation models.

"ORIGINS OF THE "DIGITAL LIBRARY

The decision in the early 1990's to extend the notion of the library forward into the emerging digital information context was the result of the collective and distinctive assumptions of three stakeholder communities: the funders, the technology-focused researchers, and the practitioner library community.

Each community responded to the opportunities offered by emerging networked computing technologies in a unique, opportunistic (and sometimes myopic) fashion. While they all agreed that "digital libraries" was an appropriate term for the new endeavour, they each had a different idea of the meaning of the term and different allegiances to the components of what they considered a library. The following parts demonstrate this "interpretive flexibility" by describing the different meanings attributed to digital libraries by the three major communities involved in the research effort.

PERSPECTIVE OF THE DIGITAL LIBRARY FUNDERS

The primary funders of digital library research in the U.S. were the NSF, within the Directorate for Computer and Information Science (CISE), DARPA, NASA, and NIH, with lesser contributions from NEH, IMLS (Institute of Museum and Library Services), and the Library of Congress. The notable characteristic of all the primary funders is their focus on technology-oriented science, in contrast to social science, humanities, or arts.

This focus is reflected in a research programme that funded mainly core computer science and its applications to networked information, with very little attention to network information as a sociotechnical phenomenon. In fact, the first phase of Digital Library Initiative (DLI) funding was exclusively technical.

This was moderated somewhat in the second phase. Influenced by the results of a 1996 NSF workshop that called for increased research on the social aspects of digital libraries, the NSF included social science research in the DLI-2 solicitation. An examination of documents published early in the digital library effort reveals the underlying assumptions and biases of the lead agencies that shaped the nature of the funding programmes and their vision of the digital libraries that would emerge from it.

Although it appeared in a visionary 1988 document from Kahn and Cerf, the term "digital libraries" was introduced into the national research agenda in February 1994 in a report from a task force on Information Infrastructure Technologies and Applications (IITA). This report was commissioned by the newly funded High Performance Computing and Communications programme, which was formed to leverage advances in computing and networking for the general social benefit. The report defines digital libraries as follows:

- "[Digital libraries are] both technologies and applications which will lead to significant advances in the generation, storage, and use of digital information of different kinds across high speed networks. A digital library is a knowledge center without walls, open 24 hours a day and accessible by way of a network. Research areas range from advanced mass storage, online capture of multimedia data, intelligent filtering, knowledge navigation, effective user interfaces, system integration, to prototyping and technology demonstration".

The list of research areas enumerated in this statement is notable for its omission of the implications of eliminating the "walls", or a being open "24 hours a day." Clearly, the impression of the task force, or at least the only concern, was that the transfer of information to an online form raised only technical issues and that the larger social issues raised by this transfer were either inconsequential, unforeseen, or not worthy of study.

Another report from the same era, authored by Gladney and Fox, demonstrates prevailing thinking of the time that perhaps underlies this decision by the funders to focus only on technical issues:

- "The concept "library" has been refined over several centuries. It would be injudicious to depart from what people expect merely because a digital service is replacing a material one. Except where explicit reasons suggest an improvement that is easily explained to ordinary users (e.g., in query services), library services should implement a familiar model".

Implicit in this text is the assumption that the nature of the institution and the information model it entails should remain as a stable overlay on a changed technical foundation. A digital library should, by nature, imply the same notions of integrity, trust, and quality, historically associated with libraries.

Books might turn into bits, the catalogue might become an online database, and shelves might turn into repositories, but the values, structures, and practices of the "institution" should be based on a "familiar model." Even as the web continue to grow in importance and scale, the notion that digital libraries were the focus for "serious" information-oriented activities persisted. The web was relegated to a more lowbrow status–an unfiltered mishmash of questionable and frequently objection-able content. For example, a 2001 (U.S.) President's Information Technology Advisory Committee report called the web a "rudimentary" information environment that "only hint[s] at the future of digital libraries".

Even if the funding agencies had decided that the broader implications of the transfer of information to the online environment deserved investigation, it is doubtful whether they were structurally configured to handle such investigations.

In a retrospective on the Digital Libraries Initiatives, Griffin takes note of the problem that agencies such as the NSF have with research that is by nature long-term: "The programme funding models did not work optimally, particularly for the mid-size, longer-term, interdisciplinary research and test bed projects."

PERSPECTIVE OF THE COMPUTER SCIENCE RESEARCH COMMUNITY

The computer science research community had every incentive to follow the funding agencies in this selective interpretation of digital library research. The DL initiatives were a new and relatively large stream of funding for extending their pre-existing database and information retrieval research into a new application area.

As stated by researchers: "The computer scientists] could see, or at least imagine, how current library functions would be moved forward by an injection of computing insight". The computer scientists who dominated DL research had little interest in examining the nature of "current library functions" or in understanding how the "injection of computing insight" might affect the foundations of these functions. The library was really only a convenient platform for technically focused work.

Indeed as researchers noted the computer science researchers had little patience for the less technically manageable aspects, and "nagging downsides" of digital library research. For example, issues related to copyright and intellectual property were perceived as an annoyance that interfered with work on more interesting technical problems.

Furthermore, the work often required collaboration with librarians who seemed overly focused on metadata "that the computer scientists felt would be replaceable by just another clever search algorithm improvement".

In hindsight, the attraction of the computer science research community to the field of digital libraries was really not based on special allegiance to the library notion, but was just a case of following the funding. When the funding disappeared and it became obvious that the web was a more attractive, and less restrictive environment for studying and exercising emerging computer science techniques such as machine learning, many of the former prominent members of the digital library community disappeared.

PERSPECTIVE OF THE LIBRARY COMMUNITY

The "real" librarians, those with over a century-long tradition collecting, curating, and preserving books and other materials, entered the realm of digital libraries with a consider-ably more institutionally-focused definition of the library and vision of what the digital library would look like.

From their perspective the library, as an institution, had successfully managed previous transitions to new media (the transition of the printed form from scrolls to the codex book to the printed book, the inclusion of recordings, etc.) and had a track record of incorporating new technology into established practices, such as the computer-based catalogue.

The "digital" library would be just another library and through all, the venerable institution would prevail:

- The functions of the librarian have always been to select the material that his constituents will require. to catalogue it so that those who would use it can know what is available and where it is. and to preserve it so that both contemporary readers and those who will follow will be able to use it… none of these tasks will disappear with the emergence of the electronic library. Somebody will have to perform them: if not the librarian, then his replacement. The anarchy of the Internet may be daunting for the neophyte, but it differs little from the bibliographic chaos that is the result of five and a half centuries of the printing press.

Because of this allegiance to the institutional basis of the library and the belief that it was a necessary component of a useful information environment, librarians vigourously resisted the encroachment of the web on the domain formally dominated by the library. For librarians the intrusion of the web into the work on digital libraries was much more difficult to integrate.

Initially, they were largely dismissive and disdainful of the web as a serious information space, declaring that the "web is not a library" and likening it to a bookstore in which "the entire stock is just piled up in the middle of the floor". As the amount of valuable content increased on the web, they responded with efforts to fold the web into standard operations, such as cataloguing.

While these efforts to catalogue the web were ultimately abandoned, they demonstrate how persistent traditional practices can be even in the face of a rapidly changing technical landscape. In summary, the application of the library concept to the uncharted and unruly context of networked information reveals the distinctly narrow and flawed assumptions of the three parties responsible for its origin and use.

The funding agencies mistakenly assumed tat they could fund (and shape) the development of a new information infrastructure as a mainly technical endeavour. The computer scientists followed suit by framing digital libraries by-and-large as applications of familiar distributed database problems in which "predictable, repeatable … access and retrieval is a prime value." In fact, the unpredictability of the web and its seemingly autonomous dynamism has not only affected our perceptions of information use and management, but it has had a far-reaching effect on computer science shifting it from its deterministic, algorithmic foundations to a more probabilistic and socially-oriented focus.

Finally, the librarians assumed that they could safely wrap radically new technology and traditional organizational values and structures in the same embrace. In combination, these flawed assumptions lead to a research area that by and large treads the middle ground.

At a fine granular level, it produced a number of interesting research results and applications of those results. But, at the higher level, it failed to explore the more far-reaching questions of how putting information online and giving people power over their information might change the nature of the information and the way people use it.

It is useful in closing this part to quote Agre who, "Information and institutional change", spoke of the dangers of naively mixing historical forms with innovations:

- A concept of "library" that is too fully rooted in past historical forms will make innovation impossible, but a superficial concept of "library" that draws out only a few aspects of those past historical forms (for example, a library as a big container of documents) will pass over phenomena whose absence in a newly designed system may be fatal. The middle ground between the maximal and simplistic conceptions of "library" is enormous and is not easily mapped.

INFLUENCE OF THE LIBRARY ON DIGITAL LIBRARY TECHNOLOGY

The previous part described the set of assumptions about libraries and networked information that led to the choice of the term "digital libraries." This part describes the manner in which that term and the presumptions underlying it have affected the nature of the technical artifacts produced by digital library research. This effect is reflected in both the overall architectural framework and on the individual architectural components of that framework.

Table. Comparison of Digital Library and Web Architectures

	Digital Libraries	Web Architecture
Core Architecture	Repository-centric	Resource-centric
User Model	Portal Searching	Browsing
Content Model	Digital Objects	Resources
Indexing Model	Surrogates	Full-text and links
Identification	Persistent IDs	URIs
Federation Model	Federated Search,	Centralized
	Metadata Harvesting	Indexing

CORE ARCHITECTURE: REPOSITORY-CENTRIC VERSUS RESOURCE-CENTRIC

Digital library systems are by and large based on the notion of the institutionallymanaged repository as the central architec-tural entity. The repository acts as the container for storage of and access to "digital objects", the content "within" the library. In this manner, the repository is a virtual boundary defining the locus of institutional management, curation, and preservation of the contained digital objects.

This virtual boundary is the functional equivalent of the physical boundary in the "bricks and mortar" library in which the physical structure defines the limits of library curation and stewardship of the information resources within it. In contrast, the resource is the central entity in the web architecture.

Uniquely identified resources are the nodes in a virtual directed graph, in which the edges are the hyperlinks that connect resources. Notably absent from this graph model is the notion of containment or location. There is no first-class entity that corresponds to the repository in digital architecture.

Although repositories are sometimes compared to websites, the comparison is incorrect due to the nature of the latter.

A website is an ambiguously defined, second-class technical artifact – it may be all the web pages served within the same DNS domain, or those accessible through a single server. Technically, it has no identity (URI) and therefore it cannot be the target of any protocol requests. Conceptually, it does not imply control or management in the same manner as a repository. The remainder of this part describes the major components of digital library systems that support this repository-centric architectural core.

PORTALS

The portal, or the "front door of the digital library", serves the same purpose as the physical entry to the traditional library. It provides the user with the clear notion of being "inside" the digital library. Services and content within the portal are thereby blessed with the imprimatur of the library, endowing them with a level of trust and integrity. This is commonly known as "branding".

Correspondingly, most digital library applications clearly indicate to the user when they are "leaving the library", for example by traversing a hyperlink to a page outside the boundary of the library. The focus of a portal is usually a search interface, that in most cases is field-based, providing more functionality than the single text box search paradigm employed by most web search engines.

This allows users to search on specific bibliographic fields such as title, author, or subject. This search paradigm reflects the influence of the library cataloguing tradition, which eschews simple keyword searching that is predominant in mainstream crawler-based search engines (e.g., Google) in favour of more targeted search capabilities.

Metadata, which is the basis of this field-based searching. In contrast to this "front-door" paradigm, the web user metaphorically "surfs" among linked information resources without regard for their location on the network. The informal notion of a "homepage" for a website does exist, but there is no presumption or enforcement of this as the uniform entry point to the collection of pages of that site.

The notion of uniform, location-independent sources has proven to be quite powerful. In its simplest form it makes it possible to aggregate information from multiple sources in a single webpage, in the manner that a page may include an image that is stored in some other location on the net. As I will describe later, location independence is leveraged in Web 2.0 in a much more powerful manner in the form of "mash-ups."

METADATA–CATALOGUING IN THE DIGITAL CONTEXT

The shaping effect of the library tradition on digital libraries is perhaps most evident in the focus on descriptive metadata. This focus has its roots in cataloguing, one of the core functions of the modern library. The traditional catalogue developed for a number of reasons. At the simplest level, in a library of physical resources it gave users an easy and compact tool for finding information resources without having to traverse the shelves.

However, describing the catalogue as merely a compact shelf list trivializes its complexity and intellectual content. Underlying cataloguing is the concept of information entities having uniform attributes, such as author, title, or subject classification, and the utility of those attributes for logical organization of those entities. This organization presents multiple access points based on those uniform attributes, and allows users to search and browse within those access points.

For example, a user may search for information by author name and then traverse the resources associated with that author, or alternatively they may search for information by subject classification and traverse the resources associated within that class. As a result, the organization of the catalogue and the manner in which it is made available to the user (e.g., cards in drawers or screens in an electronic catalogue) is independent of the manner in which the physical, or digital, resources are organized on shelves, or in repositories.

Furthermore, an individual information resource (e.g., a book) may have multiple catalogue instances, each accessible through specific access points (e.g., title, author, subject, etc.). Efforts to extend the practice of cataloguing into the context of online information reflects an ongoing belief that in a world where even the books that are part of library collections have been digitized and are available for full-text search, structured search over surrogates is more functional and ultimately preferred by users.

This is despite empirical evidence that users seem to prefer the "one text box" search paradigm of Google to the fielded-search paradigm employed in most digital library portals and online catalogs, and decades-old evidence of the frequent superiority in recall and precision of automated full-text search to human-assisted indexing and cataloguing.

Traditional library cataloguing is both complex and expensive, especially when applied to the rapidly expanding and diverse set of digital resources. The notion of metadata emerged as a simpler and less expensive alternative to traditional cataloguing records, perhaps making it possible for nonprofess-ionals to create structured bibliographic information.

The predominant digital library metadata effort is the Dublin Core Metadata Initiative. Ironically, the origins of Dublin Core lie in improving search and retrieval on the general web. However, this effort to develop easy-to-use bibliographic standards for networked information objects has been deemed irrelevant, ill-conceived, or even counterproductive by the mainstream web community and most notably the search engines that dominate it. As I describe later, the attempts to translate the benefits of cataloguing to the online domain via metadata have been compromised by problems with ensuring the quality of the metadata records that are produced by non-professionals and preventing so-called "metadata spamming" by unscrupulous agents trying to falsely lead information consumers to their sites.

DIGITAL OBJECTS — CONTAINERS FOR COMPLEX DATA AND METADATA

The content model of most digital library architectures is based on the notion of a digital object. an identified (first-class) information resource that is an aggregation of multiple information units consisting of multiple formats, multiple subsidiary units, versions, or document components (e.g., the text, data, images, etc. of a scholarly paper).

These are generally known as compound objects. These object models reflect an ongoing effort by the library community to account for the complexity of information in both its abstract form and the physical or digital manifestations of it. These efforts have focused on mechanisms to represent the various relationships among information resources. and to describe those resources at multiple levels of granularity, for various purposes, and in various descriptive formats. Access to compound objects and their components is frequently mediated by protocols unique to the particular repository architecture.

These protocols are usually embedded in the URLs that carry user requests from the digital library portal to the repository. These protocols allow operations such as access a digital object in a specific form, access a portion of a digital object such as its descriptive metadata, and the like.

The proliferation of these architecture-specific access protocols has spawned a virtual cottage industry of repository interoperability initiatives in the digital library community. In contrast, the web architecture includes a quite simple information model based on the atomic resource.

"Interoperability" is defined in the simple terms of the web architecture–resources, URIs, and HTTP. There is no architectural notion of a compound object, or aggregation of resources. Ad hoc and de facto aggregations exist, for example a logical document split into a set of interlinked web pages.

However, these aggregations are not first-class objects. they do not have a unique identity and are essentially ephemeral. There is, in fact, an increased awareness in the web community that more complex information models are appropriate in a number of instances. for example, scholarly publishing.

FEDERATION

The issue of federation arises because digital library systems are conceived as discrete institutionally-managed entities with distinct boundaries accessible to the user through branded portals. Sometimes, a user might want to search across multiple digital libraries when a selected resource is not available in their "local" library. In the physical library domain, this problem is solved by union catalogs such as WorldCat and by interlibrary loan.

Digital library applications employ two mechanisms to allow users to search for and access information outside the confines of a single digital library. The first is federated searching or meta-searching, in which a single search query is multicast to several digital library search engines.

The query is then individually processed at those search engines. the individual result sets are then returned and integrated at the site from which the original query was multicast. Federated searching was the subject of substantial work in the early years of digital library research describes our own work in this area. Although instances of federated search still exist, the technique has fallen into some disfavour because of problems with dependence on the reliability of multiple search sites and the problems with the ranking of search results from several sources. The second is metadata harvesting, in which bibliographic records from several distributed institutional sources are combined at a single indexing site, which provides a search interface across the resulting "union catalogue".

The most widely deployed mechanism for metadata harvesting is the Open Archives Protocol for Metadata Harvesting (OAI-PMH). That same chapter describes complica-tions with metadata harvesting. Neither of these techniques has achieved widespread deployment in the general web information space.

Boundaries and the repositories that implement them are not a part of the web architecture. Web search engines such as Google crawl the web via graph traversal, ignoring the notion of the location of a webpage, except as a tool for optimizing graph traversal strategies. In addition, ranking algorithms such as PageRank are designed to operate over a centralized index, and are difficult if not impossible in the context of distributed methods such as federated search,

PERSISTENT IDENTITY FOR NETWORK INFORMATION

A final example of the difference between digital library and web architecture is the notion of "persistent identity" for information stored in digital repositories. The attention to this issue in the digital library contexts reflects concerns about both preservation and control of intellectual property. The Handle System is the best known of this class of technologies.

Like many persistent naming systems, the Handle System depends on a hierarchy of identity resolvers, and therefore the notion of a central root name server. These efforts have gained little traction in the mainstream web community, which has historically resisted centralization and has comfortably adapted to the fragility of URLs, deeming identity persistence as a policy problem rather than a technical problem.

COEXISTENCE OF DIGITAL LIBRARIES AND THE WEB

The previous part described the distinction between the repository-centric digital library architecture and resource-centric web architecture. In addition, it described how these different core architectural principles affected the technical components of each architecture.

The digital library applications that have been assembled from these components are indeed quite powerful and include advanced searching capabilities, complex information models, and rich user interfaces.

Ironically, the same architectural features that enhance their functionality have often interfered with the interoperability of digital library applications with the mainstream web and thereby mitigated the impact of these applications in the broader web context.

The problem comes from the fact that the specialized, repository-specific access protocols that provide access to these digital library resources often do not follow the conventions of mainstream HTTP access methods. For example, in many cases the URLs used to access objects are conflated with query predicates, the syntax of which is unique to the digital library and is hardcoded into portal/repository interaction.

This is not a problem when access to the digital library resources occurs through the "front door" portal and through its respective search user interface that generates these query-based access URLs. However, mainstream crawler-based search engines, such as Google, do not access objects through the front door, but rely on generalized graph traversal.

The nature of the access URLs in digital libraries and their interdependence on the respective digital library search interface often makes these URLs unreachable via these graph traversal techniques. This is because the URLs of the digital objects in the repository are not explicitly linked to, but are generated by the digital library based on search engine queries.

These query-generated URLs are not visible in the web graph traversed by mainstream search engines and, as a result, the digital library resources are not crawled and are subordi-nated to an information black whole–the so-called "deep web". They fail to appear in result lists returned by main-stream search engines, which have emerged as the universal tool for discovery of information (much to the chagrin of the library community).

In an effort to increase search engine visibility, digital library providers frequently generate special link pages that expose the individual URLs of repository contents to crawlers as conven-tional hyperlinks. Digital library resources then appear as search results in Google and similar search engines.

As a result, a steadily expanding amount of access to digital library resources occurs through these commercial providers. But this reverse engineering to increase visibility of contained resources subverts the role of the digital library as a control zone, and the intention of the portal as a branded entry to that control zone

The "digital library collection" becomes just another set of web resources, with no joint identity or imprimatur. The digital library becomes "invisible infrastructure", barely evident through a web-dominated information paradigm.

DIGITAL LIBRARIES AND THE EVOLVING WEB

In addition to the technical incompatibilities between the digital library and web architectures that were described in the previous part, there is a widening gap between their underlying information models. The web that Tim Berners-Lee invented in 1989 has undergone an explosive growth in scale, measured in terms of number of URLs, servers, and traffic.

At the same time, it has experienced a radical change in form and impact, referred to as Web 2.0. In contrast to the relatively passive and transactional search/ access paradigm characteristic of the library and Web 1.0 in which the delineation between authors and consumers was relatively distinct, information interactions in Web 2.0 are highly inter-active and participatory.

Rather than just browsing and reading web pages, web users, acting as both authors and readers are writing reviews on Amazon, annotating and tagging pictures on Flickr, writing and updating articles on Wikipedia, publishing observations and research results in blogs, and mashing up online content into new content. This part examines the evolving web and the coexistence of digital libraries within that context.

The metaphor of versions – Web 1.0, Web 2.0, and the recently coined Web 3.0–is obviously artificial and overly simplistic. However, it is a useful rhetorical device. The predominant "features" of these versions are as follows. Web 1.0– called the document web, the "web of cognition", or the "read-only" web.

The time span of this version roughly extends from the invention of the web until 2000. It primarily consisted of hyperlinked, semi-static, atomic documents (HTML, PDF, GIF or JPEG images). Interaction and collaboration were minimal except for document authoring and querying. Content creation required specialized tools and, as a result, was restricted to a small subset of web users. Web 2.0-called the "web of communication" or the "read/write"web.

This "version" includes participation-oriented tools such as wikis, blogs, social applications like Flickr, and instant communication tools like Twitter. Another prominent feature is the notion of a "mash-up" whereby new information objects are created via the dynamic combination of existing information resources.

These features enable a phenomenon that Engestrom calls "object-centered sociality", in which information objects, people, and social exchanges are linked together in web space. This has effected a phase transition in the web's impact on economics, scholarship, learning, and most recently politics.

The effect of this impact on national politics is exemplified by the recent observation that "... Barack Obama's victories in the Democratic primary and in the presidential election would not have been possible without Internet-empowered fund-raising and social networking". Web 3.0–called the "web of meaning" or the "contextual web", this currently emerging web function-ality incorporates concepts of the semantic web, the under-pinnings of which Tim Berners-Lee and the W3C have been developing since the late 1990's. The key features of the semantic web include machine readability and interpretation of web data and the ability to reason over that data. The technological foundation of the semantic web is the Resource Description Framework (RDF) a data model for expressing statements about entities (web resources) and their properties (ontologically defined relationships).

Raffl et al. adopt the language of Evolutionary Systems Theory to illustrate how the features of these versions are cumulative: "[E]ach new layer is built upon a preceding one and …the new stage comprises not only the new layer, but parts of the old one". Figure illustrates the changing nature of the web through these versions.

As shown, Web 1.0 was primarily a one-way channel from producers to consumers. In Web 2.0, the bifurcation of web participants blurs into consumer/producers who collaboratively author, manage, and annotate content. This is enhanced in the Semantic Web (Web 3.0) in which machines (agents) process and interpret this collaboratively produced content and contribute new content back on the web.

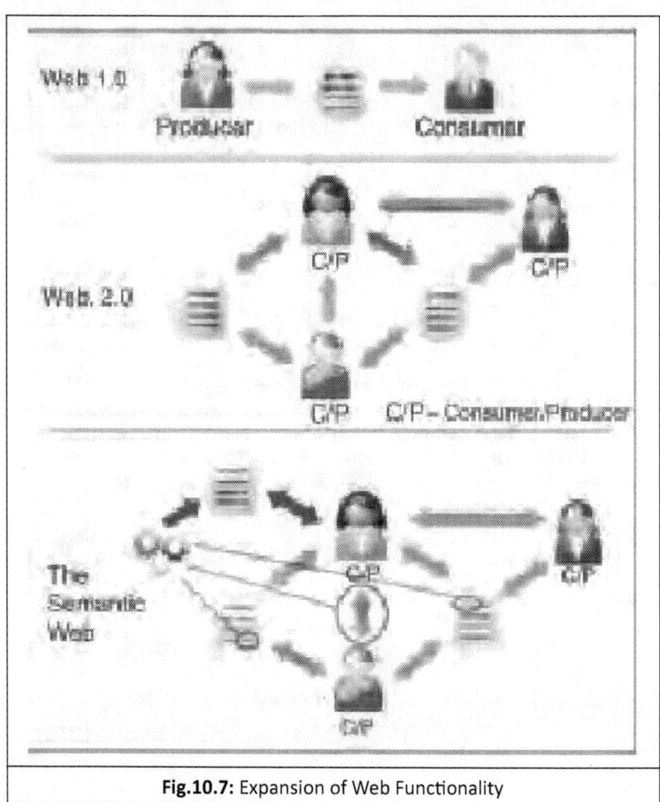

Fig.10.7: Expansion of Web Functionality

The participatory nature Web 2.0 should not be dismissed as just a popular phenomenon, manifested in increased use of mainly social sites like FaceBook.

Many experts in the field, we are witnessing a fundamental change in the prevailing information paradigm that is transforming all aspects of our culture.

Notably, this impact extends to the nature of scholarly research and communication, one of the backbones of the research library.

As pointed out by Paul Ginsparg, who create arXiv and is considered one of the icons of Internet-based scholarship:

- ...There are...objective reasons to believe that we are witnessing an essential change in the way information is accessed, the way it is communicated to and from the general public, and among research professionals-fundamental methodological changes that will lead to a terrain 10-20 years from now more different than it was 10-20 years ago than in any comparable time period.

Timo Hannay of Nature, one of the most prestigious scientific journals, makes the following observation of the impact of the current and future of the web on science scholarship:

- For all but a very small number of widely read titles, the day of the print journal seems to be almost over. Yet to see this development as the major impact of the web on science would be extremely narrow-minded–equivalent to viewing the web primarily as an efficient PDF distribution network... Though it will take longer to have its full effect, the web's major impact will be on the way that science itself is practiced.

In addition, there is mounting evidence that, for a number of important informationoriented activities such as education, the participatory information paradigm in Web 2.0 has advantages over the traditional consumption-based model. Fuchs and Raffl argue that Web 2.0 paradigms of collaboration, construction, and participation are more closely aligned with recognized models of human cognition and knowledge development than the more restrictive and controlled library model.

Downes and Ullrich describe the utility of the Web 2.0 model for education because of the manner in which it facilitates activities such as group collaboration, exploration, and manipulation that are key to learning according to cognitively-oriented constructivist theories.

Gee argues that the "affinity spaces" facilitated by the Web 2.0 environment are powerful tools for learning. Black identifies the notion of "beta-reading" in online fan communities where contributors grow as readers and writers based on mutual feedback. Finally, others see the general benefits of the "wisdom of crowds" that is enabled by the collaborative nature of Web 2.0.

ONLINE CATALOGUES AND CARD CATALOGUES: IDENTIFICATION OF AREAS OF SIMILARITIES AND DIFFERENCES

This chapter is prerequisite to the following chapters, in that it provides the background for the study of the possible influences of online catalogues on both the bibliographic record and on cataloguing principles.

A major aim is to explore the development of online catalogues, their basic features and capabilities and also to reveal the major differences that exist between them and manual catalogues.

This comparison will help identify the differences and similarities in the processes by which a bibliographic record and, on a larger scale, a catalogue, is created, manipulated and made accessible to the catalogue user for searching and retrieval.

In this context, the requirements of online systems which may influence cataloguing rules will also be discussed. A thorough understanding of the conceptual as well as the practical and technical differences and similarities between the online catalogue and the card catalogue will then help in an investi-gation of the relevance of current cataloguing principles and rules to the online catalogue. It is not the intention of the present chapter to discuss the influence of the features and capabilities of online catalogues on individual cataloguing principles or concepts..

In any comparison between the online catalogue and the manual catalogue, it seems appropriate to choose the card catalogue among the other forms of catalogues as an appropriate approach, because:

- The card catalogue has been and still is one of the most important manual systems in use for more than a century,
- It is the basis from which the present cataloguing standards have been developed, and
- It is the basis on which the structure and contents of online catalogues have been developed, i.e., online catalogues are the logical successors to card catalogues.

It is not the intention of this chapter to reject the merits of the card catalogue. A realistic approach in comparing the online catalogue with the card catalogue should reveal advantages and disadvantages in both catalogues.

Although there is overall support among librarians for online catalogues, most librarians consider having knowledge about the card catalogue to be very useful for an understanding of the origins of the present online system, particularly the structure of the MARC format and how individual records fit into the idea of a catalogue system.

This was clearly the case in the general discussions about the card catalogue on the AUTOCAT list, 20 November 1994 to 3 December 1994, commenting on the need to teach the card catalogue in library schools. In fact, an understanding of the origins and underlying concepts from which the present environment has evolved will help us develop catalogue systems based on substantive assumptions. In short, this understanding and comparison of the two environments will help us to reassess, refine and redesign our standards for the construction of catalogues. John Hickey states:

- "Even if nobody still uses catalogue cards, more of our professional assumptions that we recognize are based upon unit cards and card isplays. it helps to have some acquaintance with the previous technology."

It should be noted that online catalogues and card catalogues can be compared from different perspectives and according to different criteria. However, this study will compare them with regard to the processes by which bibliographic records and files are created, manipulated and organised on the one hand and searched, retrieved and displayed on the other. The differences between the online catalogue and the card catalogue will be explored in terms of the input, manipulation and output processes of bibliographic data.

ONLINE CATALOGUES: WHAT THEY ARE

Online catalogues are a norm today. they are not static. they have developed rapidly and will continue to evolve further. By utilising the various capabilities of computers and telecommuni-cations, online catalogues are adding new features that make them totally different from traditional catalogues. Online catalogues are now gateways to larger information systems or, as Hopkins says, they are the 'one-stop information store'.

The online environment is an environment encompassing a wide range of information tools, both bibliographic and non-bibliographic. Library catalogues are now a small but very important component of the evolving online environment and are accessible through different tools in the networked environment, the public access computer system (PACS).

The global network is the Internet including various PACS components such as Gopher, WAIS (Wide Area Information Servers), Netscape and Mosaic and other access modes such as Archie and FTP (File Transfer Protocol) tools. The Webpages created by libraries and other information providers are becoming very pervasive and are often used both by librarians and endusers as linking sources for library information.

The same workstation serves as a means of navigating the whole world of the Internet. In the online environment not only are the information tools different from the traditional tools but also the whole concept of access to bibliographic information has changed. Time and location are irrelevant in searching the online environment.

DEVELOPMENTS AND DIRECTIONS OF ONLINE CATALOGUES

As a result of a significant growth in scientific and technological information after the second world war and a resulting expansion in library collections, manual systems could no longer respond effectively to the ever-growing information needs of society.

In terms of fast and effective retrieval of bibliographic information, the card catalogue had many disadvantages. Its large size, complexity and high costs of maintenance made it more and more difficult for libraries to maintain as an up to date searching tool. It became obvious that a more flexible tool was needed to cope with the new conditions of libraries. It was thus necessary to think of alternative ways of constructing library catalogues that could be cost-effective, manageable and easy to use. Following on the application of computers in other fields, librarians became assured that the computer's theoretical capability to control library operations constituted adequate grounds for embracing a mechanised approach. As Weihs and Howarth point out, "It was necessary to investigate the computer as a relatively cost-effective tool to provide library catalogs."

Computer applications, however, first occurred in library activities other than the provision of public access to the catalogue. Computers were used in libraries mainly for house-keeping types of activities such as circulation control, acquisitions and serial control. This did not directly affect patrons' access to the library catalogue. Library automation began in the early 1960s with the rationale that "If a job could be done by computer, then the number of staff required to work at a defined level of expertise could be reduced".

Although some evidence of automation of library operations other than cataloguing is reported from the 1950s and 1960s, it is the MARC (Machine-Readable Cataloguing) project that has been considered as one of the most important factors in the development of automated catalogues.

With the beginning of the MARC Distribution Service in 1969, large libraries began to utilise MARC magnetic tapes mainly for automated cataloguing in the standard form provided by the Library of Congress. The usefulness of MARC services in cataloguing, along with the increasing availability of computer technology in the late 1960s, led to more developments in automated catalogues.

In response to the needs of small and medium-sized libraries without access to a mainframe computer, centralised cataloguing services gave way to the establishment of bibliographic utilities in the early 1970s.

The Online Computer Library Center, established in 1971, has been considered to be a significant factor in the development of automated catalogues. With the standard cataloguing services of such bibliographic utilities, libraries were able to utilise the power of computer technology in a cost-effective way.

The proliferation of MARC-based cataloguing led to the realisation of the importance of uniform, standardised bibliographic description as the nucleus of bibliographic services at national and international levels. The growth of bibliographic utilities in the early 1980s as well as developments in telecommunication technology accelerated the move towards centralised MARC-based cataloguing and the need for standardised descriptive cataloguing.

A significant factor further affecting the development of online catalogues was that some libraries began to use MARC bibliographic information for their circulation systems in an online mode. Using short bibliographic records rather than full MARC records for circulation operations, a number of libraries tried to help their patrons in checking whether an item was on loan, on order, or at binding.

This was a form of public enquiry module, which later developed into the online public access catalogue (OPAC). However, as Seal pointed out "The public enquiry module will often replicate the structure of a card or COM [Computer Output Microform] catalogue."

Another major factor leading to the rapid development of online public access catalogues was the contribution, by some library system vendors, of designing and developing public access modules as an important part of their turnkey systems. These vendors tried to incorporate a more sophisticated structure for the public enquiry module with more searching facilities. It should be noted that the early public enquiry systems were not integrated with other library modules, such as acquisitions and serials control.

Due to both the relative success and acceptability of online public enquiry modules, and pressures from patrons and librarians, libraries began to consider developing online public access catalogues (OPACs) with more bibliographic information, i.e., full MARC records and more searching capabilities, such as keyword access and Boolean searching.

The possibility of utilising MARC records as the foundation of bibliographic databases led to the development of the concept of the Integrated Online Library Systems (IOLS) in which "The information that was input at the acquisitions stage would form a basis for the catalogue record which, in turn, would support all library functions. Thus, a number of integrated systems, such as GEAC, ULISYS, ATLAS, DOBIS, NOTIS and VTLS, were established incorporating this modular design.

The overall factors relating to the growing interest in online catalogues have been numerous. It is generally agreed that the most important factors that led to the rapid proliferation and development of online catalogues in the early 1980s were those related to their search, retrieval and display capabilities. Moreover, the opportunity of feedback from librarians and library patrons has provided a continuing momentum for upgrading the structure, contents and capabilities of online catalogues.

Tracing the historical development of online public access catalogues, Hildreth and Matthews identify three generations of OPACs. This categorisation is based on the features and capabilities of online catalogues in the processes of input, storage and output of bibliographic information.

Matthews claims that most of the existing online catalogues are still in the first or second generations and only a few systems have moved beyond first-generation. Added to the three generations identified by Hildreth and Matthews, recent advances in OPACs using graphical user interfaces (GUIs) have introduced a fourth generation to online catalogues.

FIRST-GENERATION ONLINE CATALOGUES

Derived from circulation or cataloguing systems, first-generation online catalogues were in fact computerised card catalogues with almost the same traditional features. In contrast to the patrons' expectations from their use of computerised database systems, these new library catalogues provided limited author, title and controlled vocabulary subject heading access points. For this reason, first-generation online catalogues have been criticised as having no advantages over the card catalogue.

Searching in first-generation online catalogues was essentially based upon pre-coordinated information retrieval principles and was possible only through inputting the exact form of words or phrases. In contrast to searching in card catalogues, the patron had great difficulties as he/she had to input something into the system so that it could respond to his/her query.

As this was possible only through inputting the exact form of words or phrases, which was difficult to remember, searching was not as successful as the searcher expected. Keyword access was not available and refining a search by further limiting it to elements such as date of publication, language or country of publication was not possible. The interfaces, which were usually menu-driven, replicated traditional catalogues in their form of access by providing mainly phrase access to separate subject headings, title, and author indexes. Output and display of search results generally had a single format.

SECOND-GENERATION ONLINE CATALOGUES

With further developments in information technology, it was possible to provide a more sophisticated system for input, storage and output of bibliographic information. Second-generation online catalogues are a departure from traditional card catalogues and incorporate many new features for the provision of effective access.

In contrast to the limited input, storage and output capabilities of first-generation online catalogues, second-generation online catalogues are characterised as being powerful tools for the searching of bibliographic information. Keyword search, Boolean keyword search, cross index search and increasing or reducing of search results are among the features of second-generation online catalogues. Hildreth writes:

Today's second-generation online catalogs represent a marriage of the library catalogue and conventional online information retrieval (IR) systems familiar to librarians who search online abstracting and indexing databases via DIALOG, BRS, ORBIT, MEDLINE, etc.

Improved card catalogue-like searching and browsing capabilities have been joined with the conventional IR keyword and Boolean searching approaches. Many online catalogs support the ability to restrict searches to specified record fields, to perform character masking and/or right-hand truncation, and to limit the results by date, language, place of publication, etc. Also, bibliographic records may be viewed and printed in a number of different display formats.

However, it should be noted that there are a number of major differences between online catalogues and these IR systems that make second-generation online catalogues easier searching tools. With a combination of different search methods, the user is offered possibilities that were not available in first generation online catalogues.

Due to improvements in the design of database management softwares, the structure and content of bibliographic records in second-generation online catalogues may be enhanced by incorporating full records augmented by information such as tables of contents, summaries, content notes, abstracts and links to full electronic texts. Considerable increase in the length of fields was another improvement in second-generation systems.

Interfaces are usually in two modes, menu-driven and command-driven. this makes the interaction between the user and the catalogue more flexible. In terms of user assistance, these catalogues provide more options including, for example, help screens, error messages and suggestive prompts. Ease of use and user-friendliness are two major features of today's second-generation online catalogues.

THIRD-GENERATION ONLINE CATALOGUES

Only a few systems have moved beyond second-generation online catalogues into third-generation online catalogues with enhanced or more sophisticated features. Due to the growing sophistication and availability of technology, new capabilities are being added to online catalogues making them more adaptive to the needs of library patrons. Free text search, enriched database search and simultaneous journal citation searching are among the retrieval capabilities in third generation online catalogues. Furthermore, the mode of interaction has been developed to the point of conversational, adaptive dialogue and the bibliographic format can be tailored according to user preference. Operational assistance such as automatic, context-based correction is also available.

FOURTH-GENERATION ONLINE CATALOGUES

Beginning from the late 1980s, a most recent development in online public access catalogues has been achieved in providing easy access to bibliographic information by using graphical user interfaces (GUIs) such as Windows. These systems, which can be considered as fourth-generation catalogues, have moved away from the traditional menu-type interfaces and are more associated with client server and graphical user interface.

They use WIMP (windows, icons, mouse and pointers) interfaces to speed and simplify searching. With the Windows-style user interface available through PCs (personal computers, i.e., intelligent, and not dumb terminals), there is much more functionality. In these systems the user has the flexibility to click on various buttons, each of which carries a special function.

Nevertheless, these systems do not eliminate but augment the keystroke access. There is also the possibility of using function keys for different purposes when keyboards are involved. In general, access is via mouse or keyboard or a combination of both. Searching capabilities in the Windows version of OPACs are greater than those found in other generations of online catalogues. Pointer capabilities allow the searcher to select exactly the term he/she is looking for, while pull-down menus provide additional options to make searching even more useful. By using scroll bars and pull-down menus, browsing in different indexes is very simple.

With the capability of post-Boolean searching, the search software also attempts to interpret users' search requests in order to present matches of greater or lesser interest to the user. This is called relevance ranking of the search terms. Similar to second and third generation online catalogues, these systems search for terms through using an implicit Boolean 'AND'.

Other Boolean operators such as 'OR' and 'NOT' can also be used to narrow down search results or such search strings can be constructed using the mouse alone. In addition, access has been enhanced by text retrieval qualifiers such as 'language', 'date' and 'form' of the text.

With this feature, it is possible to include new data elements that help in the better identification of the sought item. Integral or add-on text retrieval modules to provide range searching, related term searching, wild card features, adjacency and proximity are supplied by some systems.

One of the recent additional advanced features of fourth-generation OPACs is the 'hypertext' function. Through this function, any word that the user selects or highlights can be used to search all the fields and subfields in all the records in the database for any occurrence of that word. This dynamic feature helps the searcher to navigate the database to find more relevant sources of information.

ONLINE CATALOGUES: HOW THEY DIFFER FROM MANUAL CATALOGUES

There have been some general attempts in the literature of the past decade to briefly compare different types of library catalogues. However, these comparisons have not been concerned with the concepts that underlie the nature and structure of the catalogue. In the following parts, the two types of catalogue will be compared in terms of the creation, manipulation and search/ retrieval/display of bibliographic records.

CREATION AND MANIPULATION OF BIBLIOGRAPHIC RECORDS

Structure and Content of Bibliographic Records

By 'structure of the record' is meant the bibliographic descri-ption consisting of data elements arranged and presented in a given order, such as card catalogue formats and MARC formats. It is generally understood that the medium, via which biblio-graphic records are created, manipulated and made accessible to the searcher, influences their structure and content.

The computer has made possible the enriching of the structure and contents of bibliographic records. While the space limitations of 3" x 5" cards generally restrict the level of data elements to be entered in a record, the content of a bibliographic record in an online catalogue makes it possible and desirable to include more data elements such as those fixed-length data elements indexed in field 008 in the USMARC bibliographic format and even data such as summaries, tables of content, and full texts. This issue has been of major interest to librarians and system designers during the past decade and there have been some proposals in this regard.

User studies of the early 1980s showed that most users of online catalogues would like to have access to tables of contents, back-of-the-book indexes and summaries. Other suggestions have included the titles of essays in collected works or festschriften, book introductions, book jacket material, and the assignment of more subject headings. With the advent and further development of online catalogues it has become possible to assign a larger number of access points to bibliographic records. In comparison to the conventional main and added entries in the card catalogue, any data element in a bibliographic record may be designated as an access point.

MARC Format and Categorisation of Data Elements

As a set of standards for the identifying, storing and communicating of cataloguing information, MARC has significantly contributed to the growth of library automation and to the development of online catalogues. Although the MARC record was conceived as an automated version of the catalogue card, the structure is flexible enough to store bibliographic information in more detailed fields and subfields due to the requirements of automated systems for separate identification of data elements.

While the medium for the card catalogue is the 3" x 5 " card with a fixed, less flexible format, most online catalogues use MARC as a communication format for the exchange of bibliographic information. In this regard, MARC communicates bibliographic information with more flexibility than the card catalogue.

With the machine-readable format, in which the biblio-graphic information on a record has been broken down into fields and subfields, it is possible to separately identify each data element. This approach also allows for inclusion or exclusion of data elements for output as desired. Based on the MARC format, bibliographic records can be created and tailored according to the specific needs of the library without either discarding standardisation or diminishing the quality of cataloguing.

In the card environment, cataloguing depends on a longer process of manual checking against other catalogues, the ordering of card sets and receiving and interfiling them in the catalogue. This process in online catalogues is done more comprehensively and easily by subscribing to bibliographic utilities or by purchasing MARC products and downloading the needed records into the library's automated system.

MARC records permit a fuller level of description. more data elements to be included in the description and many more data elements to be assigned as access points for retrieval. A MARC record also includes other data, including non-bibliographic data that are used for catalogue maintenance. There is now a trend towards preserving detailed bibliographic records in machine-readable form.

The amount and type of information that constitute a 'full bibliographic record' is certainly open to debate, but since the late 1960s the accepted standard has been the MARC format. The data that can be contained in a MARC record include the entire spectrum of information normally presented on catalogue cards plus a great deal of other potentially valuable categorizing information that can be encoded in fixed elements and elsewhere on record.

However, MARC format has been criticised for being an electronic version of the catalogue card and for its limited accommodation of hierarchically structured information. There are also some problems with the MARC tagging and indexing of data elements that influence retrieval in online databases. Systems may differ from one another in the indexing of fields and it is often difficult to find out what fields are indexed by a given system. This results in retrieval and display problems, leading to user confusion.

Bibliographic Standardization

In comparison to manual systems, the online environment gives much more emphasis to the concept of standardisation. Although the idea of standardised bibliographic description seems to have first appeared with derived cataloguing and the sale of Library of Congress cards in 1898 and later with the introduction of the National Union Catalogue (NUC), it was not until the 1970s that the application of computers to library operations and the advent of online catalogues gave to standardisation a much more significant role.

With regard to the description, choice and form of data elements to be included in a bibliographic record, conformity to standards, e.g., cataloguing codes, ISBDs and MARC formats, are vital to online catalogues.

Unlike libraries of two decades ago with their independent card catalogues, libraries of today often create their own catalogue records according to national and/or international standards for the purposes of easy communication of and access to bibliographic information. Now, it is common for libraries of any size to participate in networks. One result of this, as Wajenberg points out, is an ever-increasing pressure to conform to national and international standards.

Uniformity and consistency are basic requirements for effective bibliographical control. The rapid growth of shared cataloguing systems, developments in bibliographic utilities and the need for bibliographic exchange between databases in the last decade has led to a stronger reaffirmation of the value of standardisation in bibliographic records. Standardisation helps bibliographic records to be uniformly created, manipulated, exchanged and retrieved. As the cataloguing community moves closer to making the ideal of universal bibliographic control a reality through local, regional, provincial, national, continental and international networks, all libraries assume the responsibility of maintaining standards requisite to maintaining the network. Integration and standar-dization are the keywords in the increasing move-ments towards, and promotion of, interconnected telecommunicating automated systems.

Despite this emphasis on the significance of standardisation in the online catalogue, this concept has been considered only in the inputting of data elements in bibliographic description and not in the output and display, whereas in the card catalogue both input and output are standardised.

For example, both the card catalogue and the online catalogue conform to the ISBD standard for the input format, i.e., the order of areas, punctuation and levels of description. However, in online catalogues the output format is not fixed as in card catalogues and may be flexible.

As Gorman and associates state, the standardisation and formalisation of description and access points is crucial to the online environment and to the effective exchange of bibliographic records. As an important concept that has developed over the last hundred years to meet the changing forms of the catalogue and the needs of the profession, standardisation will continue in the future and as Wajenberg points out, at an accelerated pace.

Input Inconsistencies and Level of Tolerance

A major difference between a manual and an automated catalogue lies in the fact that the creation of bibliographic records for online catalogues demands more precision and logic in terms of typography, spelling, punctuation, spacing, coding of fields and subfields.

This is a critical requirement for computerised systems, since such errors can result in a serious separation or an improper sequencing of entries and therefore can lead to the irretrievability of records. In other words, any errors, even if very small, for instance a faulty keystroke, will be magnified in the online catalogue. However, in a manual system, when filing catalogue cards or when retrieving information, the human brain can often ignore such minor errors and treat them as if they are correct and file them in the right place.

Errors and inconsistencies can be corrected in the process of filing cards, whereas in the automated catalogue there is a lower level of tolerance towards such errors as variations in format, filing and indexing, and literal and logical inconsistencies within the catalogue. In general, the online catalogue is far less forgiving of cataloguing and typographical errors than is the card catalogue.

CONSTRUCTION AND MAINTENANCE OF THE CATALOGUE

Structure and Content of the Catalogue

By 'structure of the catalogue' is meant how the catalogue is built up, the kinds and content of files and indexes constituting it and the relationships of these files and indexes to one another.

For example, a card catalogue, whether in dictionary or divided form, may include different files such as:

- Authors
- References
- Titles
- Subject headings and
- Shelflists

The advent of the online catalogue has given new dimensions to the catalogue's structure. It is generally main-tained that the online catalogue can support a more complex yet more dynamic structure than that of the card catalogue. The online file may be independent and self-contained, it may be related to files of similar scope and structure or it may be integrated with other files such as holdings, circulations, acquisitions and authority files.

The online catalogue provides services that were not part of the traditional library catalogue. Access to circulation information, status information, holding information, indexing of special collections, serials and so on have become possible through the development of the contents and structure of the catalogue. While the structure of the card catalogue is based on the concept of several discrete entries for a single item, the online catalogue maintains a single-entry structure for a single item but with several indexes as access points to records in the master file.

Emphasising what constitutes the structure of an online catalogue, Svenonius states that:

- In its general sense structure refers to an aggregate of elements related, or arranged with respect, to each other . . . The structure of a catalogue or catalogue database consists of bibliographic, authority, and holdings records arranged in a given order and referencing one another through a variety of syndetic relationships. Thus, filing rules, together with ordering devices, such as the main entry and see and see also references, define a cataloguestructure....The structure of biblio-graphic descriptions consists of data elements arranged and presented in a given order. Thus, cardcatalogue formats and MARC format represent different but related bibliographic structures, the former intended for display and the latter for communication.

In terms of addition to the contents of the catalogue, the online catalogue has a growing ability to enlarge its own scope. Results of a nationwide survey on the use of online catalogues in the United States revealed that respondents were enthusiastic about accessing journal articles, newspaper articles, encyclo-paedias, dissertations, films and government documents through online catalogues.

Other studies showed that users wanted the catalogue to be expanded to include journal titles, government publications and dissertations and journal citations, indexes to collections, content services, abstracts and book reviews. Thus, it can be concluded that the contents of the online catalogue will be expanded in parallel with developments in the technology of catalogue construction.

Integration has been considered as an important feature of the recent online catalogue in the sense that different parts of the library automated system are integrated through the use and manipulation of the same record as the basis for different library operations. In such an integration, a single master bibliographic record is tagged and can be manipulated for different library operations, such as acquisitions, cataloguing and circulation. A consequence of integration of the online catalogue, as pointed out by Buckland is that bibliographic information in different parts of a library system, as well as other useful information, can be accessible to users and to other libraries. Such a concept indicates the impor-tance of uniformity and standardisation of bibliographic records in the online environment.

Another interpretation of integration in the online environment is related to various methods of access to bibliographic information. In such an integration, different files and databases can be accessible via the same terminal. This concept has opened up a new era in bibliographic services and is considered as a significant factor in the enhancement of the catalogue. There are increasing attempts to build information systems with integrated access to different types of information services. The trend towards the integration of book trade bibliographic databases and A and I services with the online public access catalogue is an approach which makes the library catalogue a window to the whole bibliographic apparatus, a concept not feasible in the manual catalogue. These different kinds of integration have implications for cataloguing principles.

Authority Control

Authority control ensures the consistent use of names, series and subjects. No bibliographic record can be entered into the system until all assigned headings under which it can be searched are verifiable against the approved authority file. In a manual system, it is a time-consuming and costly operation and requires the services of skilled staff.

There are many advantages to authority control in an online catalogue: in terms of maintaining cataloguing operations, it is particularly advantageous when major revisions to name and subject headings have to be done.

In terms of searching, the actual search that the user does is via an authority control file. What the user inputs to the system is automatically switched through the index to the correct form. In the online environment, the authority records are usually linked with bibliographic records.

There are a number of reasons for the resurgent interest in authority control in the online environment. The various difficulties that users have had with searching names and, as Potter points out, the inconsistencies and errors in the records used to build the databases for online catalogues have led to new attention being given to the concept of authority control. For example, the ability to search personal names in either direct order or through initials has led to the enhancement of the scope and structure of authority files.

Another major difference in the process of authority control between a manual system and an automated system is that correction or change of any heading in the card catalogue is a time consuming operation, whereas this task in some automated systems is to a great extent facilitated through a 'global change' which automatically generates a correction or change in all relevant records. Although authority control in the online environment is at an early stage of development and, at present, only a few systems have operational authority control modules, the online catalogue's features and capabilities have given a new dimension to the notion of authority control.

Much work needs to be done into the need for authority control in online catalogues. access by name will decrease and the concept of name references will change and the need for authority files in the traditional sense may become less important.

In making the concept of authority control in the online environment clearer, Gorman points out that:

- It is evident that traditional reference structure was designed for premachine catalogues. The ideas that underlie references have been taken over in machine systems and incorporated into the notion of authority files. An authority file consists, very simply, of the approved form of access point for a person, body, or title, together with the references to that approved form and links to other related authority records. We have already seen that, in the computer catalogue environment, the distinction between a main and added entry access point no longer has meaning. The authority record takes this progress a step further. It, in effect, abolishes the distinction between an access point and a reference.... In other words, two of the basic assumptions of traditional catalogue codes—the main entry and the distinction between a heading and a reference—have survived.

Filing Rules and Problems

In any library catalogue, access points are usually filed according to alphanumeric order, which is a conventional arrangement applicable to most information systems accessed by human beings. However, filing is different in the manual catalogue and the automated catalogue.

The arrangement of access points has always been of particular interest to librarians and there have been a number of specific filing rules published to date. The ALA Filing Rules, The Library of Congress Filing Rules developed by John Rather, and the rules developed by the British Library Filing Committee are among the most important. Although developments in filing rules have been strongly in the direction of commonsense and are oriented towards the intelligent user, users actually have major problems in identifying the exact location of a heading in the sequential order of a large card catalogue.

In a manual system, filing is flexible and can be executed according to the order which seems desirable to the catalogue user, whereas, in a computer catalogue, it must follow the logic of the computer.

Filing in a manual system follows the principle of file as if: that is, the form and order in which access points are arranged is according to the interpretation of the librarian with the supposition that the arrangement would be the most desirable to the user. For instance, the number 3 can be filed as if it were the word three.

The use of the computer has influenced filing practices and it is generally agreed that the principle of file as is, which is necessitated by the introduction of computer filing, has more validity in the computer environment. This principle states that characters or words should be filed as they are and not as if they were something else. for example, the number '3' as 3, and 'three' as three. This realisation of the logical as well as the practical differences between filing in a manual catalogue and a computer catalogue came with the earliest attempts in the application of computers to bibliographical work. Current filing rules, which were developed for manual systems, proved not to be effective in a computer environment.

Users of online catalogues can encounter many problems when searching for bibliographic information. Due to different software specifications, computer-based filing has not been entirely standardised and the burden of thinking, for example, about the exact form of access points and the way punctuation and non alphabetic symbols are treated is left to the user.

In manual filing it is possible, by a simple convention, to ignore stop words such as 'the', 'and', 'of', 'a', 'an', etc. at the beginning of titles whereas, in the computer catalogue, this issue demands special programming and in some cases they are difficult to handle. The treatment of punctuation poses another problem for the computer catalogue. while symbols, such as commas, apostro-phes, periods and hyphens, may cause problems in the manual catalogue, they are considered as characters and are located in their 'logical' places by the computer unless software is created to overcome these difficulties.

While the presence or absence of punctuation may be important in access points, they may or may not be important for online display. Diacritics and extended character sets to accommodate non-roman scripts are other important issues in computer filing of entries.

In sum, the logical arrangement of data elements in the computer has implications for the form of access points in the online catalogue. As an example, see the treatment of "Sir," which comes before forenames and thus interferes with filing. This can be seen in the change of some rules for the form of headings in the second edition of the Anglo-American Cataloguing Rules.

In fact, the incorporation/modification of some rules in AACR2 concerning the filing of data elements has arisen in response to the requirements of filing in the computer catalogue. For example, the inclusion of given names in parentheses in cases where the initials are not adequate for identification of authors with identical surnames is to respond to computer filing.

In terms of conference headings the form and order of the number, the date and the location of a conference in parentheses is an illustration of filing relevant to a computer. The place of numeric identifying elements in music uniform titles, e.g., "Pianos (2)" rather than "2 Pianos", is another example of this issue.

SEARCHING, RETRIEVAL, AND DISPLAY OF BIBLIOGRAPHIC RECORDS

User Interfaces

A significant difference between the online catalogue and the card catalogue comes at the stage in which the user interacts with the catalogue, i.e., bibliographic records can be searched, retrieved and displayed. Online catalogues are here considered to be a great departure from card catalogues and it seems that there will be more developments in this regard in the near future. While the card catalogue is a self-evident medium with a clear physical existence, the online catalogue is not revealed to the users and is not easy to grasp in their first interactions with it. In an online environment, the user cannot immediately understand the catalogue or its structure, coverage and searching mechanisms unless he/she interacts with the system and tries different options for searching and displaying of bibliographic information.

Despite these limitations of the online catalogue, users show a high degree of satisfaction with the variety of features and capabilities it has at the output stage. Graphical user interfaces (GUIs) have made interaction with and use of online systems easier and more desirable. It seems likely that, in the near future, new generations of online catalogues will incorporate intelligent interfaces and sophisticated search/retrieval/display facilities.

Interactivity

Online catalogues have often been defined in the literature as 'interactive' catalogues. In the Dictionary of Information Technology, 'interactivity' is defined as "system or piece of software that allows communication between the user and the computer in a conversational mode." Interactivity is considered as a major advantage of online catalogues over card catalogues. "It is this interaction between the user and the computer system that really sets apart the online catalogue from the other types of library catalogs"

Unlike in the card environment, if the user does not input a query in the system, the system will not respond to him/her. This process, namely the action of inputting a query by the user and responding by the computer, occurs quickly in real time and in a dynamic and progressive way.

In sum, the concept of interactivity in the online catalogue is well defined below:

- "Online catalogues can be reactive and able to respond to the user in an intelligent way. This can be used to indicate what searching options are available, to correct operational errors, to suggest alternative items which might particularly match the search criteria and to guide the user through a long search. The reader can then be given help and feedback from the system itself, without needing to consult library staff. This approach is impossible in a card or a COM catalogue".

With the introduction of the online interactive catalogue, it has also become possible to record how users interact with the system and search the catalogue. In this way, i.e., through 'transaction log' analysis, librarians are able to check how users approach the catalogue and how frequently search terms appear, as well as to examine other aspects of search/retrieval problems, e.g., users' errors and unsuccessful searches. Many catalogue use studies have been and are being done using transaction logs as a means of data collection.

User's Input Errors and the Catalogue's Level of to Lerance

As pointed out earlier, online catalogues are less forgiving than card catalogues in terms of any kind of error, either in the input stage by the cataloguer, or in the searching stage by the user. A general problem with computers is that they are usually unforgiving of errors. if the user makes the smallest of mistakes, they will not necessarily recognise it as a mistake, and even if they do they will often not offer help in correcting the mistake. However, there are systems being developed that recognise errors, display the type of error, and offer help to the searcher.

User Assistance

In comparison to card catalogues, online catalogues have the ability to provide user assistance in a variety of ways and at different levels. Mitev classifies such aids in four categories as 'retrieval aids', 'linguistic aids', 'navigational aids', and 'semantic aids'. This is a major advantage over the card catalogue in that the system can respond to the user's problems and help him/her as to what the next move to achieve the result would be. Online catalogues have developed, over the past decade, different devices for providing help to their users in the different stages of searching the system.

Most online catalogues have the ability to customise help messages, screen displays and system prompts according to the needs of the user. Online assistance enables the user to influence the dialogue at all times in a clear way. This is not possible in manual systems.

User Satisfaction

It is generally stated that there is a higher level of satisfaction with online catalogues than with card catalogues and that users prefer this new form of the catalogue to the traditional card catalogue. Matthews, Lawrence, and Ferguson, over 90% of users like the online catalogue and almost 75% of users rate the online catalogue as being better than the card, book or microform catalogue.

It is also interesting to note that this high level of satisfaction is consistent across all types of libraries. Lewis, in reporting the results of different user studies, states that: "Users have a strong preference for online catalogs over card catalogs, and they very much want the new technology to succeed".

Balaam and Burton and Hawkins report user satisfaction with OPACs despite their shortcomings.

A reason for preference of the online catalogue, even in its primitive form, to the card catalogue is related to its search and retrieval capabilities. It is also safe to assume that, as online catalogues continue to mature in terms of user interface, enhanced content and access, the level of satisfaction will be even greater.

Another point worth mentioning is that the result of different online use studies show that use of the catalogue and use of the collection have increased with the introduction of online interactive catalogues. This, in turn, leads to higher user satisfaction as he/she becomes able to fulfil his/her information needs in easier, faster and more effective ways.

A major group of OPAC users are librarians themselves who are among the strong supporters of such systems. In a series of discussions in the electronic mail discussion group PACS-L@UHUPVM1.UH.EDU, 7-20 April 1994 and in response to Nicholson Baker's "Annals of Scholarship: Discards" published in the New Yorker, 4 April 1994, concerning the closing or storing of card catalogues, most librarians supported online catalogues as being superior to card catalogues. Charles Hildreth considers Baker's article to be a nostalgic approach to the historical value of card catalogues. For Hildreth card catalogues represent a dead-end technology and their maintaining would be very expensive. Instead, online catalogues are open-ended, with a pure potentiality that will never reach its 'final' form.

Walt Crawford asserts that online catalogues are ever-evolving systems that, when reasonably well designed, offer substantially better access and, unlike card catalogues, can be maintained as well as improved.

Robin Alston supports online catalogues for their advantages over card catalogues in many ways and states that a major advantage is that most of the key elements on a record in an online catalogue are searchable, while massive amount of information on catalogue cards are not retrievable. Although there are deficiencies in OPACs, as Baker expresses very well from the point of view of a scholar, online catalogues will keep improving, while card catalogues have not any potential for improvement.

Searching and Retrieval Capabilities

With regard to searching capabilities, the online catalogue is a significant departure from traditional library catalogues. One of its most interesting features and a major advantage over the card catalogue, is the ability of the user to search for the needed item in a variety of ways that are not available in the manual catalogue.

Online catalogues are able to generate both a greater number of access points as well as new searching capabilities that enable the user to search the catalogue with little information to hand. In addition to controlled-vocabulary searches by author, title and subject headings, for which relevant indexes have been created and maintained in the online catalogue, it is possible to search bibliographic records through access points such as other title information, series, standard numbers and any other significant data through keyword searching.

In general, although there are still shortcomings in the searching capabilities of online catalogues, particularly in subject searching, the findings of various studies indicate that users show much enthusiasm in online catalogues' searching capabilities. The following types of searches in the online catalogue are not available in the manual catalogue and can help the user to execute a greater variety of searches:

Keyword Searching

Keyword access is a very powerful search tool and can create much greater flexibility for the user to search item(s) of which he/she has not exact information. This is extremely difficult in the card catalogue.

Keywords, i.e., every indexed word in the bibliographic description, mainly headings, titles, other title information, contents notes and subjects, are appropriate alternatives for the catalogue user who cannot match the exact bibliographic information in the catalogue.

When searching the catalogue, it is not necessary for the user to enter the exact form and order of words. while keyword searching is an alternative to controlled-vocabulary searching, it can also act as a complement to it. The potential value of keyword searching has often been highlighted in the literature.

For example, reporting the result of a transaction log analysis of the Colorado University Library OPAC, Wallace found that 53% of searches were keyword searches. In many online catalogues, there are options for limiting keyword searching to fields such as author, title, subject, or cross index. Among these options, title keyword searching provides a useful tool both as a substitute for subject access and for specific items when the exact or full title is not known.

Some online catalogues provide keyword searching of abstracts and a number of systems extend this capability to the entire text of a document, a trend that is becoming common in many online search services.

It is extremely difficult to search authors under their forenames in manual catalogues, whereas in online catalogues with keyword access it has become possible to execute such searches. The same capability is available in the online catalogue for searching compound words of which the exact, full form is not known. However, keyword searching has its disadvantages: in some cases too many records may be retrieved and some records may be irrelevant to the searcher's need.

Boolean Searching

Influenced by A&I (Abstracting and Indexing) services, many online catalogues have the ability to run Boolean searches. With the use of Boolean operators, such as AND, OR, NOT, it is possible to define subsets of the desired subject or concept when two or more sets are combined.

Specificity is what Boolean searching offers: the user can combine two or more terms in a search statement and narrow or broaden the parameters of the subject of his/her interest. Matthews points out that:

"In most OPACs, a Boolean 'and' is assumed when two or more terms are entered in a search statement, especially if the search is conducted on a single field or type of information, such as author, title, or subject".

Truncation

As in A&I services, some online catalogues permit the user to broaden the set of records to be retrieved by shortening the search word through entering a special truncation symbol immediately after the shortened search word, or before it, or within the word. Most online catalogues perform right-hand truncation implicitly rather than explicitly. This feature of online catalogues provides greater flexibility for the user to broaden access to the necessary information when character-by-character exact match does not help.

It should be noted, however, that users have difficulty in understanding and using this type of searching in online catalogues. In some cases, truncation also results in either too many hits or irrelevant records. This has implications for cataloguing principles and rules.

Browse Searching

When the search aim is not specific, the desired results are not precisely known in advance or the correct terms for representing the user's query are not known at the outset, "browse searching is the most useful and preferred approach". Browsing, which is a good feature of the card catalogue, is becoming available in the form of browsable indexes in more and more online catalogues.

The natural searchability that browsing offers satisfies users. In this type of searching, lists of index terms are usually presented in alphabetical order and the searcher can navigate the database by going forward or backward through the desired index until he/she finds the index term which may lead him/her to relevant records.

A novel interface for browsing, which can improve access and the effectiveness of end-user searching, has been developed very recently. Using a GUI, some advanced online systems offer improved searching functionality by providing a multi-windowed view of data stored on a relational database manage-ment system.

This novel interface can help the user to search bibliographic databases in a multi-windowed environment, each of which represents an index of the catalogue with scrollable windows. This approach has the advantage that the user can browse different indexes on the same screen to filter their content and find the most relevant items.

Among the indexes are: author, title, publication date, document type, language and subject headings. It would be possible, therefore, to match different indexes and find related documents which have the same values, i.e., identical data elements. This facility helps the user in appreciating the actual contents of the database through its different indexes and removes the problem of search specification using values that are not present.

Hypertext Searching

A most recent addition to searching capabilities in information retrieval systems, including advanced online catalogues, is hypertext searching or 'hypersearch'. Non linear, associative hypertext systems offer a search approach that attempts to more closely mimic human thought processes. It is stated that hypertext, when used with bibliographic records, could overcome the static nature of existing catalogues.

The hypersearch facility, such as that one offered by GoPAC from Data trek, can simply be applied by highlighting a term or clicking on a highlighted term in the record. The system will search for any occurrences of the highlighted term in all fields and subfields or all authority-controlled fields in all records in the database.

The number of postings associated with the term will be indicated or the system will show a brief display of those related records which contain the same term. The term is highlighted in the retrieved records so that the searcher can see in which field it is located and can decide on the relevance of the record to his/her information need.

During the display of related records, the possibility exists for the user to shift his/her focus and to continue a hypertext search on new and more relevant data elements. In this way, the hypertext facility helps users to navigate throughout the catalogue to find possible related works.

Author-title Search

In most online catalogues, there is an option for searching a known item through the author's surname combined with any keyword from the title. This is the clearest way to execute known-item searches. However, in those systems which restrict the search to author surname and the first word of the title, this type of search has the disadvantage of retrieving too many records when the author's surname is a common name, such as 'Smith', 'Johnson', and so on, or the title of the item begins with common words, such as 'Introduction', 'History', and so on.

Another disadvantage is that, in most cases, users do not remember the first word of titles and thus fail to use this type of search in online catalogues. Nevertheless, it is very useful, for example, for searching titles on reading lists and it emphasises the importance of surname field.

ID Numbers

Another type of search in some online catalogues is possible through ID numbers. Among possible ID numbers are: call number. International Standard Book Number (ISBN). International Standard Serial Number (ISSN). document number. computer system number, e.g., OCLC (Online Computer Library

Center), RLIN (Research Libraries Information Network) or WLN (Western Library Network). local system number, e.g., accession number. These types of search are usually performed by library staff.

Other Searching Sapabilities

Other types of searches in online catalogues include full-text searching, proximity searching, adjacency searching which are available only in a few online catalogues. These new searching capabilities in the online catalogue have revolutionised the way in which users search the library catalogue. The results of different use studies indicate that the searching patterns of users in online catalogues have changed. In other words, the online catalogue has affected the ways in which users search for bibliographic information in library catalogues.

Output and Display

Display of bibliographic information is another major aspect in which the online catalogue departs greatly from the card catalogue. Surveying OPACs in a number of Canadian academic libraries, Cherry report that screen display is the best developed area in online catalogues. The last step at the catalogue, viewing a search result through the display of the bibliographic record(s), is what the user actually gains from the system. The quality of such a display affects the overall usefulness of the catalogue. While the form and content of bibliographic records in the input/output format in the card catalogue are fixed, the online catalogue permits a flexible format, with the possibility of displaying bibliographic information in a variety of ways and at different levels.

The ways in which bibliographic information is presented in the online catalogue in response to searches vary from system to system. Each system has its own techniques for manipulation of a search result. This is impossible in the card technology where space limitations and the fixed form of bibliographic description do not permit any flexibility or manipulation of search results.

The level of bibliographic description is usually flexible and can be designed according to the user's needs. On the other hand and from a system perspective, as Boll points out, there is a range of display formats suitable for a computer screen or a page printout rather than a three by five inch card. Online display formats usually include:

- 'Brief-listing display' which shows, on one or more screens, the overall results of a search through 'author', 'title' and 'date' of publication, 'Medium-level display' containing the standard bibliographic description, access points and status and location information, and
- 'Full bibliographic display' which shows full description with all access points, including added entries, and may contain summary and/or table of contents of the item.

Another major difference between the online catalogue and the card catalogue is the way in which data elements in a record make up and represent a bibliographic record. Reynolds points out three functions in this regard: the labelling of data elements, the sequence in which data elements appear and the spacing between them.

The online catalogue can include identifying labels before data elements for distinguishing the bibliographic text in a record. Labels may be highlighted, or displayed in uppercase characters or in a different colour. In relation to the sequence of data elements appearing in a bibliographic record, there is a fairly high degree of uniformity among online catalogues.

As in the card catalogue, the arrangement usually follows the numerical sequence of MARC tags or the ISBD order. Some online catalogues do not incorporate ISBD punctuation on the basis that users do not comprehend such 'secret punctuation'. However, it should be noted that a number of problems may arise from the differences in the input and Encyclopaedia of Computers in Library Services output formats in the online catalogue. A problem which would be difficult for the user to understand is that the relationships of headings to bibliographic data may not be clear to him/her.

For example, the role of persons associated with the work or manifestations of a work may not be distinguished in the way these names are displayed on the screen in conjunction with the title of the work. Therefore, the user may miss what he/she is seeking. In short, output in online catalogues is not controlled by cataloguing standards.

Limiting Search Results

Limiting or restricting the search results is a good feature of online catalogues and seems to have been copied from A&I services. Crawford, this capability of online catalogues should be offered or performed only when the search yields a large result. Matthews points out that assisting the searcher in refining or expanding a search shows the powerful capability of the online information retrieval system over the card or COM catalogue.

In terms of refining the search results, the online catalogue has a great advantage over the card catalogue. When many records are retrieved in response to a search, the user may want to restrict them to certain aspects that might seem more relevant to his/her need.

This is not possible in the card catalogue whereas, in most online catalogues, due to the assigning of some subfields in the MARC format as active and searchable, the user has the opportunity of further restricting, reducing or narrowing the search results. For example, the searcher can limit all the search results to works in a particular language, in a particular type of material or all the works published prior to, during or after a given date, or even works of a certain level of difficulty. This is done by specifying certain control fields and other MARC elements that can be used for limiting search results.

With further developments in online catalogues it is expected that the limiting of search results will become more sophisticated and more flexible for the user. In addition to the usual access points available in the card catalogue, more data elements are being indexed and more indexes are likely to be created in the online catalogue.

Sorting Search Results

Another feature of online catalogues is the opportunity offered to the user to sort the search results in the way that will best fulfil his/her need. Most online catalogues can sort the retrieved records according to such data elements as the author, the title and the date. This sorting capability requires that, in addition to usual access points, more data elements be indexed in MARC records in the database.

Some systems, such as OKAPI (Online Keyword Access to Public Information) the experimental OPAC developed at the Polytechnic of Central London, SMART, the US National Library of Medicine catalogue CITE (Current Information Transfer in English), STATUS/IQ, CANSEARCH, PLEXUS provide ranked output and relevance feedback. They sort and display results of a search in order of highest occurrence of keywords. Given the searcher's judgments of retrieved items as either relevant or irrelevant, some of these systems can be asked to perform another search modified automatically by relevance feedback to provide a new ranked output list.

Status, Holdings and Location Information

A major feature of the online catalogue is its ability to link circulation information to bibliographic and holdings information and to show to the searcher the status and location of the sought item(s). The user of the online catalogue is able to see the status of any volume and/or copy of the item and whether the item he/she is looking for is available on the shelf or it is on loan, on order, at binding, missing or is not for loan.

The status information also displays the 'date due' of an item on loan. The online catalogue can also show the location of the item in the library, e.g., on which level and/or in which part it is located. All such information is useful also for stock taking and check-in purposes. These features help the patron, particularly the remote user, saving his/her time in knowing the status and location of the needed item(s).

Access and Availability

Unlike in a manual system, the user of the online catalogue has access to bibliographic, circulation, acquisition, holdings and location information at the same terminal, whether within the library or in other libraries through remote access. Again, this capability may be an indication of the need for uniformity and standardisation of data elements and also the importance of integrity in the structure of different files in the system.

In contrast to the possibilities for online consultation, card technology is a strictly localised medium with many physical restrictions to its use. Almost all libraries have a single set of catalogue cards for a document. To some extent a book catalogue or a COM catalogue might help in making the library catalogue available in different locations but these catalogues are costly to update at regular intervals, particularly when the collection is very large.

Unlike the card catalogue, the online catalogue is accessible through terminals located in different places in the library and outside the library via local area networks (LANs) and wide area networks (WANs). In the online environment it is possible for different users, whether inside the library building or outside it, to use the catalogue online and to even search the same record simultaneously. In terms of access to library catalogues, distance has now become irrelevant. Technology has enabled us to have decentralised access to bibliographic information.

Interconnectivity is one of the most important goals of libraries today and can take different forms. Many library catalogues are now accessible through the different tools in the Internet such as Netscape, Gopher, Mosaic and Telnet. This is a great advantage over the manual system and will continue to expand with further developments in telecommunication allied to a decrease in telecommunication costs.

There is also more flexibility with interconnectivity for the searcher to go from one catalogue to another. This is done through the same catalogue or other catalogues which have a WWW forms-based interface. These developments have brought with them new concepts such as globalisation of catalogues and the 'library without walls'.

With the availability of different types of OPAC systems to remote users over networks, for example, over the Internet, libraries need to conform to a new standard known as Z39.50. This standard is a protocol for information search and retrieval in a client-server environment, and is now moving from a standard to an operational reality. Z39.50 is used by libraries to access and search remote databases.

The WAIS system has implemented the standard to provide a consistent environment with consistent user interface, search and retrieval services. In environments supporting Z39.50 connectivity, the user sees remote catalogues as though they were additional databases available from the local system.

The standard is also being used in different library operations such as technical services, acquisitions and interlibrary loans. In this context, Z39.50 encompasses biblio-graphic databases, full-text documents, even numeric databases. For example, for bibliographic databases, a list of fields needed to exchange information and support those functions has been developed.

With advances in telecommunications and the rapid development of different facilities in the Internet it is now also possible to have access to electronic texts and files stored anywhere in the world. As we move to the end of the twentieth century, more full text services will become accessible through remote databases.

❒

13

Computers in Libraries: An Introduction

INTRODUCTION

Good things come in small packages. The old adage holds true for this new contribution to the field of library and information science by Wilson. At just under 200 pages, this book is densely packed with the information that library technicians and assistants need to understand the impact that computers and the Internet have had on library systems and procedures.

The State Library of New South Wales in Sydney, Australia, is the current location for Wilson's professional work and where she manages the digital and library systems. Clearly, her years of experience have informed her writing. A colleague encouraged her to put her extensive knowledge and experience in information technology and library systems into book form. In doing research for her book, she discovered older texts on library automation and realised the paradigm-shifting impact that the Internet has had on library operations.

As Wilson states in her preface, the "audience for this book is both practicing and new library technicians and library assistants." As with any discipline, library and information science has its own set of acronyms and field-specific jargon. By including acronym and abbreviation definitions with other terminology, Wilson attempts to remove the barriers to understanding.

Wilson begins her book with a discussion of the history of the Internet and its protocols and applications. The service areas in which the Internet is used in library settings are then reviewed, and public services, reference services, technical services, and collection development are covered. In fact, the overall strategy Wilson has employed to arrange the contents of her book follows this format. Chapter titles include “The Internet,” “Integrated Library Management Systems,” “Acqui-sitions,” “Cataloguing,” “Circulation,” “Serials,” and “The Online Public Access Catalogue.” Organizing the information in the book in this manner is helpful for readers, as new and changing technological innovations and systems are applied to each service area in which a library technician or assistant might work.

A chapter on resource sharing explains the world of consortial arrangements for the sharing of library materials and automated systems for interlibrary loan of print as well as electronic sources. Two very informative chapters are instructive on successful search processes and skills for both online databases and the Internet, including some brief explanations for creating Web-based content with codingin hypertext markup language (HTML).

Finally, “Future Directions,” looks at the trends in the use of computers in libraries. Wilson predicts the continued emphasis on the digitization of collections and the ensuing increased access to the collections by the public at large. Challenges in access and licensing will need to be addressed by developing new ways to preserve and manage those electronic resources.

Libraries may consider purchasing integrated library management systems that are more open sourced in nature. Bibliographic standards, including MARC, may be revised and expanded to increase their applicability. As the use of the online public access catalogue (OPAC) continues to decline, libraries will need to come up with new and innovative ways to deliver responses to users' information requests, such as through the creation of portals.

Wilson has an interesting take on the reference desk versus information desk quandary. She states that efforts in the 1990s to “rename reference and research departments and desks as Information Services have reversed”. She sees the focus of each as separate, with information residing in the physical structure and reference and research assistance moving beyond the physical building into the online environment. Lastly, library technicians and librarians alike must make efforts to keep up with the changing technologies required in their individual settings.

This reviewer conducted an informal survey with two instructors who teach in library technician programmes, one in a face-to-face environment and the other through a correspondence course format. The instructor of the “in-seat” course on computers in libraries is using Wilson's book for the first time. She also will draw from the Neal-Schuman Library Technology Companion: A Basic Guide for Library Staff by Burke. Her opinion is that the Burke book is more comprehensive but more expensive.

The correspondence course instructor was not familiar with Wilson's book. He used Introduction to Automation for Librarians by Saffady. However, he felt that it contained too much detail for his students' needs. He has also chosen Burke's book for his course. The Burke book provides questions for review at the end of each chapter, as does Wilson's, but Burke places his list of recommended readings with the chapters, instead of in a bibliography at the end. The content of Burke's book does not seem to be as practically organized.

Wilson's treatment, arranged by service area, is much more approac-hable and useful.

While this book is highly recommended for use as a textbook in library technician programmes, its scope is necessarily, and as claimed, an introduction to the topic. To truly understand and take to heart all that was presented in this volume, one must transfer the knowledge to practice.

Development of Digital Libraries in India: Socio-economic Problems and Prospects

Information and Communication Technology (ICT) has revolutionized the information management activities in the academic libraries during the past few years developing the Information Society. The Information society demands that all the relevant technologies; that are involved in Access to Information, Information collection, information processing, consolidation, repackaging and retrieval be merged so as to evolve an integrated system; capable of providing diversified services.

Advances in Computer Storage and telecommunication methods, online access to databases, electronic journals, electronic knowledge banks, direct ocument delivery, teletext, teleconferences, bulletin boards, Radio Frequency Identification Systems, Compact discs, Digital Versatile Disks, Networks including Internet, Smart Cards etc. are revolutionary developments in the last two to three decades that have brought a great change in the collection, communication, storage and management of information. As a result, the organization structure and functions of the libraries are changed. The libraries are termed as Conventional Libraries, Digital Libraries and Hybrid Libraries.

DIGITAL LIBRARIES

The digital libraries may be defined as the new way of carrying out the functions of libraries, encompassing new type of information resources new approaches to acquisition; new methods of storage and preservations; new approaches to classification and cataloguing; intensive use of electronic systems and networks; and dramatic shifts in intellectual, organizational and electronic practice.

Digital library is system providing a community of users with coherent access to a large, organized repository of information and knowledge. The digital library is not just one entity, but multiple sources seamlessly integrated. The digital libraries endow with a structural and planned entrance to information stuffing in a dispersed environment and assist users in searching evaluating and utilizing resources irrespective of their format.

Improved information retrieval and enhanced document delivery capabilities are widely acclaimed strength of digital library in a networked environment through internet and internet in library and information centre.

The US Association of Research Libraries Identified Five Elements Common to All Definitions of Digital Libraries:

- The digital library is not a single entity;
- The digital library requires technology to link the resources;
- Linkages between digital libraries and information services are transparent;
- Universal access to digital library must be a goal;
- Digital library collections are restricted to document surrogates but include digital artifacts that have no printed equivalent.

To use the digital format, the user population must be literate, preferably computer literates with Internet facilities. Further, there is adequate resources such as Electricity power generation in the country, higher standard of living, proper telecommunication facilities etc.

Today, in developing country like India the numbers of digital libraries are growing. Further, in various academic libraries, conversion and digitization of the collection from print to electronic format is also progressive.

But there are many social, economical and political problems, which have become obstacles to the development of the digital libraries in India.

SOCIO-ECONOMIC PROBLEMS

Of Course any of the nations in the world, is not completely free from its own problems like unemployment, Poverty, Illiteracy, Crime etc. In other words, every nation is having its own problems.

Similarly, India is also having certain Political, Economical and Social problems. These problems are the hindrance to the development of the digital libraries in India. They are discussed as under:

Growing Population and Illiteracy

India is the second largest country in growing population. Approximately 1/3rd of the population is illiterate and uneducated. The following table shows the population and literacy rate of different Countries in the world.

TABLE

S. No.	Country	Geographical Area (Sq. km)	Population (In Millions)	Literacy Rate (In %) Year
1.	China	95,96,960	1295	86 (2002)
2.	India	32,87,590	1049	65(2001)
3.	Gemany	3,56,910	82,4	99(2002)
4.	Japan	3,77,835	127.5	99(2002)

5.	Russia	1,70,75,200	144.1	100(2002)
6.	United Kingdom	2,44,820	59.1	99(2002)
7.	United States of America	96,29,091	291	98 (1991)

It is noted that the digital libraries are successful only if the complete population of the respective country is literate. In this case, it is observed from the table that literacy rate is higher in Russia, Japan, Germany, UK, USA AND China. But in India, the literacy rate is still 65.38% and it is a problem for the development of the digital libraries.

Standard of Living and Telecommunication Facilities

Growing population has caused unemployment and poverty in India. Consequently there is a lower standard of living and lower GDP per capita. Due to these factors, there is slow development in telecommunication facilities. The following table shown the GDP Per capita, number of fixed telephone links and Mobile Cellular available for people in different countries.

TABLE.: GDP Per Capita ($), Telephone Facilities and Cellular Phones in Different Countries

S.No.	Country	GDP Per Capita ($)	No. of Telephone Connections (in Thousands)	No. of Cellular Phones (in Thousands)
1.	China	4700	135000	65000
2.	India	2540	27700	2930
3.	Germany	24051	53720	60043
4.	Japan	31407	60381	56000
5.	Russia	8900	35500	17609

It is noted that India is having lowest GDP per capita and there are lower number of Telephone and Cellular Phone users. For the development of the digital libraries, there is need to develop the standard of living and improve telecommunication facilities for the people.

Demand and Supply of Power

It is noted that the electricity is the basic and main source of power for working of any electrical and electronic equipment. Adequate Production and supply of electricity helps the population to enable the use of telecommunication facilities and computers.

As per the Census of India 2001, of the total 191963935 households in India, only 107209054 (55.84%) households are having electricity and the remaining 84754881 (44.16%) households are powered with alternative energy sources such as Kerosene, solar power and others.

Further, the Energy and Power Supply in India in the years 2002-03, 2001- 02 and 2000-01 are as under table below.

From tshe data, it is clear that there is shortage in power supply and about half of the households in India are not using Electric power till now. Hence there is need to develop power sector in India, for the development of the digital libraries.

Table: The Demand and Supply of Power and Energy in India in Selected Years

Energy (MU)	2002-03	2001-02	2000-01
Requirement	45877	522537	507216
Availability	417090	483350	467400
Shortage (%)	9.1	7.5	7.8
Power (MW)			
Peak Demand	81492	78441	78037
Peak Demand met	71520	69189	67880
Shortage (%)	12.2	11.8	13.0

Computer and Internet Users

The awareness about the Information Technology, Computers and Internet is essential for the development of digital library. Hence for the development of digital libraries, the majority of the population must be able to use the computers and internet. The following Table shows the statistics about the Computer users in different countries in 2002 and 2005.

TABLE: Number of Computer Users in Different Countries in 2002 and 2005

S.No.	Country	2002 (%)	2005 (%)
1.	China	35	35
2.	India	6	21
3.	Germany	63	67
4.	Russia	19	35
5.	Canada	75	79
6.	United Kingdom	59	76

The Internet is popularly used media for communication in digital libraries. Hence, to access digital libraries, the internet usage is also a most important factor. Table shows the Statistics about the Internet users in different countries in 2002 and 2005.

TABLE: Number of Internet Users in Different Countries in 2002 and 2005

S. No.	Country	2002 (%)	2005 (%)
1.	China	35	35
1.	China	24	33
2.	India	47	60
3.	Germany	47	60
4.	Russia	7	15
5.	Canada	68	71
6.	United Kingdom	47	71
7.	United States of America	64	70

It is noted from the table above that only 21% of the population know about the Computers and only 14% of the population use Internet in India.

For operating and accessing digital libraries, the majority of the population must be able to use computers and able to search Internet. When compared to other countries, the majority of Indian population is unaware of these technologies. Hence it is a major obstacle for the development of digital libraries in India.

Status of Library and Professionals

It is noted that when compared to developed countries, the development of the Libraries is slow in India. Even after 60 years of Independence, many of the State Governments have not enacted Public Library Legislations so as to provide public library facilities to common public. In many colleges, the Library professionals are still considered non-teaching and supporting staff. A few academic libraries are managed by non-library professionals. Even though Dr. Ranganathan, emphasized Open Access system for the libraries, many academic libraries are working with closed access system for their collection.

PROSPECTS AND DEVELOPMENTS

The Government of India, Union Territories and State Governments already, formulated and executed various plans and policies to curb the growth rate of population, Literacy programmes, increase in standard of living, to achieve full employment, developing Agriculture and industrial sector, Improvement in Power Production and Supply, to increase the exports, etc., due to such efforts, India is developing in all respects. Even though many of social, political and economic problems proved to be obstacles and problems for the development of the digital libraries in India, the Government of India and different state governments initiated Information Technology projects to develop the application of Information Technology in administration and planned to educate the people.

Of course, it is not possible to discuss all the measures and policies undertaken by the Government of India for encouraging use of ICT and web in

India. Following are a few policies of the Government of India and developmental trends in promoting use and development of the Information and Communication Technology, electronic media and Information Sector.

The Prime Minister of India constituted a National Task Force on Information Technology and Software Development in May 1998 with the purpose of formulating a long term National IT Policy to convert India into an IT software superpower.

As it is not possible to mention all the developments, the developments stated in the following paragraphs are the only a few achievements made in different departments and parts of the Central Government:

- A Land Information System has already started using Geographic Information System (GIS) and remote sensing to help the farmers to plan their activities and facilitate decision making and planning at the local level. Government is also planned for a System known as "Agriculture Online" for the exchange of Ideas and Information between farmers, Agricultural Scientists, traders and exporters.
- The higher education institutions consisting of 310 Universities and academic institutions 16,000 affiliated colleges were networked with the help of INFLIBNET, an Inter-University Centre of UGC. In 28th December 2003, UGC-INFONET Electronic Journal Consortia was started by INFLIBNET and at present it is providing 4000+ Research Journals to 100+ Universities in India Online. The INFLIBNET is conducting regular training programmes in different applications of ICT to the information professionals. Now a days, every Indian University is using internet for its activities such as Admissions, Exams, Results etc.
- Postal Department got computerized and several new services based on Internet were introduced. E-Post is a new service available at 204 Post Offices at present in a few States — Andhra Pradesh, Gujarat, Goa, Kerala, and Maharastra to cater the postal service to the persons who do not have a PC or internet facilities. E-Bill post is a multipurpose web based facility for paying telephone bills, mobile phone bills, Electricity bills etc., online. Speed Net is another internet based tracking and tracing service for the customer at Speed Post Counters. The computerization and VSAT connectivity for the postal service is under progress.
- India has the fifth largest telecom network in the world comprising of 61.09 million telephone connections (basic and mobile) and over 1.48 million public call offices. There are over 16 million cellular subscribers in the country, growing at the rate of about 1 million per month. The number of digital electronic exchanges was around 300 increased to 36,772 in July 2003.
- The software and IT industry has grown significantly during 2003-04 by emerging as one of the fastest growing sectors with a growth rate of over

30.5% and an export value of US$12.5 billion. According to the National Association of Software and Services Companies (NASSCOM) estimate in 2002-03, the total revenue from the India IT market was ₹317 billion against ₹291 billion in 2001-02. The Indian IT and electronics industry recorded a production of ₹80,884 Crore during 2001-02 as compared to ₹68,450 Crore during 2000-01 showing a growth of 18 per cent. Software export alone has jumped by approxi-mately 10 per cent to ₹36,500 crores during 2001-02 from ₹3,700 Crore during 1996-97 with a compound annual growth of about 60 per cent.

- The Government of India computerized different departments under E-Governance programme. The departments are Customs and Excise department, Banks, Railways, Air Transport, Income Tax, and Telecommunications etc. so as to facilitate Online Transactions. Similarly the Electronic Voting Machines were introduced in Elections.
- Government also taken up development programmes in Mass Media, such as Television, Radio, Newspapers and Magazines. Electronic Media developed in such a way that the actual situations at various polling booths in Lok Sabha Elections 2004 were telecasted live through Video-Conferencing. Many of the News Channels in Television using Video Conferencing for Live Telecast of the News and Other events. The Collections of many of the Academic Libraries and Special Libraries were digitized already and can be accessible through the networks.
- Several Information Systems and Networks are developed connecting libraries. NISSAT developed several Metropolitan Area Networks such as ADINET, BONET, CALIBNET, DELNET, etc. The Other networks are INFLIBNET, ERNET, SIRNET, etc. Through networking of the Libraries, many libraries are sharing their resources online.
- On September 20, 2004 Geo-Synchronous Satellite Launch Vehicle (GSLV) is launched from Sriharikota and put EDUSAT, the educational Satellite. The EDUSAT is set to bring about revolutionary changes in distance education, converting homes into virtual classrooms. Through EDUSAT, a teacher from a television studio can simultaneously address hundreds of students in different schools and colleges in the various parts of the country if the educational institutions have a terminal to receive the programme.
- The EDUSAT has 12 transponders, which are capable of generating regional beams covering different parts of India. It is estimated that programmes from EDUSAT can reach 1,000 class rooms and 50,000 students.
- According to Essential Science Indicators (ESI) during 1997-2001, India produced 76,970 papers as against 1,14,894 by China. The Number of Scientific papers is just one measure of state of research in the country.

- India has joined a select club of six advanced countries with the Pune-based Centre for Development of Advanced Computing (C-DAC) developing the country's Super computer. CDAC developed 'Param Padam' a super computer which promises the creation of a seamless computing platform for supercomputing at an affordable price in the international market. India also ahead in production and export of the electronic products, as disclosed in table:

TABLE: Electronic Exports from India

S. No.	Items	1999-00	2000-01	2001-02	2002-03
1.	Electronic Hardware	1,400	4,788	5,800	5,600
2.	Computer Software	17,150	25,350	36,500	47,500
	Total	**18,550**	**33,138**	**42,300**	**53,100**

The Impact of Information Technology on Library Anxiety: The Role of Computer Attitudes

Computers and information technologies have experienced considerable growth over the past two decades. As such, familiarity with computers is rapidly becoming a basic skill and a prerequisite for many tasks. Although not every college student is equally prepared for the rising demand of computer skills in the information age, computer literacy is increasingly becoming a gatekeeper for students' academic success. Gaps in computer literacy and skills can leave many students behind not only in their academic achievement but also in their future job-market success.

The unprecedented pace of technological change in the development of digital information networks and electronic services in recent years has helped to expand the role of the academic library. Once only a storehouse of printed materials, it is now a technology-laden information network where students can conduct research in a mixed print and digital-resource environment, experience the use of advanced information technologies, and hone their computer skills. Yet, many students are struggling to cope with the changes brought on by the rapid advances of information technologies.

Academic libraries of various sizes have spent a large percentage of their material budget on electronic commercial content, and the trend will continue.

These days, college students are faced with the choices of ever-changing modes of electronic accessing tools, interfaces, and protocols along with the traditional print resources in the library. The fact that the same journal article may be available in multiple vendors' aggregator sites (such as EBSCOhost and Gale Group) makes the navigation through these bibliographic databases more complex and challenging.

Relevant sources must be identified and navigation protocols must be learned before appropriate information and contents can be found. Furthermore, students still have to search the library online catalogue to find out if the journal or book is available in the library and, if not, know how to make an interlibrary loan request either on paper or electronically. Anxiety levels can be high and patience levels can be low at varying times of conducting library research. That students experience various levels of apprehension when using academic libraries is not a new phenomenon. Indeed, the phenomenon is prevalent among college students in the United States and many other countries, and is widely known as library anxiety.

Mellon first coined the term in her study in which she noted that 75 per cent to 85 per cent of undergraduate students described their initial library experiences in terms of anxiety. Feelings of anxiety stem from either the relative size of the library; a lack of knowledge about the location of materials, equipment, and resources of the library; how to initiate library research; or how to proceed with a library search. Library anxiety is an unpleasant feeling or emotional state with physiological and behavioural concomitants that come to the fore in library settings. Typically, library-anxious students experience negative emotions, including ruminations, tension, fear, and mental disorganization, which prevent them from using the library effectively.

A student who experiences library anxiety usually undergoes either emotional or physical discomfort when faced with any library or library-related task. Library anxiety may arise from a lack of self-confidence in conducting research, lack of prior exposure to academic libraries, the inability to see the relevance of libraries to one's field of interest, and lack of familiarity with library equipment and technologies. Library anxiety is often accorded special attention because of its debilitating effects on students' academic achievement. Although many students continue to experience high levels of library anxiety, it is likely that the new technologies and electronic databases in libraries have led to students experiencing other forms of negative affective states. In particular, it is likely that library anxiety experienced by students is, in part, a function of their attitudes towards computers.

Consistent with this assertion, Mizrachi and Shoham and Mizrachi reported a statistically significant relationship between library anxiety and computer attitudes. They noted in their research that home and work usage of computers, computer games, word processors, computer spreadsheets, and the Internet are all related to the dimensions of library anxiety found among Israeli students to varying degrees. Similarly, Jerabek, Meyer, and Kordinak found levels of computer anxiety to be related to levels of library anxiety for both men and women. These studies focused exclusively on undergraduate students.

However, no study has examined this relationship among graduate students, a population that uses the academic library more than any other student population. Over the past fifteen years, a large body of research literature on computer attitudes has been generated. In particular, many researchers have studied the relationship between computer attitudes and computer use. The importance of beliefs and attitudes towards computers and technologies is widely acknowledged. Students' computer attitudes arguably impact their willingness to engage in computer-related activities in colleges and universities where effectively using library electronic resources represents an increasingly important part of college education.

Negative computer attitudes may inhibit students' interests in learning to use the library resources and thereby weaken their academic performance levels, while at the same time elevating levels of library anxiety. McInerney, McInerney, and Sinclair observed that negative perceptions about computers among student teachers may accompany feelings of anxiety, including worries about being embarrassed, looking foolish, and even damaging the computer equipment.

Further, there is often a negative relationship between prior experience with computers and computer anxiety experienced by individuals. Until recently, library anxiety has only been interpreted in the context of the library setting—that is, a phenomenon that occurs while students are undertaking library tasks. Researchers defined library anxiety as "an uncomfortable feeling or emotional disposition, experienced in a library setting, which has cognitive, affective, physiological, and behavioural ramifications." At the same time, unprecedented technological advancement has had a profound impact on the products and services offered by academic libraries. Students now are able to conduct sophisticated library searches from the comfort of their homes. It is clear that the construct of library anxiety needs to be expanded in the new library and information environment, incorporating into its definition other variables that are relevant for the changing library and information context.

Because many library users spend a significant portion of their time using computer-based technologies to conduct information searches, it is natural to ask, to what extent does library anxiety stem from students' prior attitudes and experiences with computers and library technologies? However, with the exception of the studies conducted by Mizrachi and Shoham and Mizrachi on Israeli undergraduate students, this link has not been examined. Thus, the present study investigated the relationship between computer attitudes and library anxiety in the rapidly changing library and information environment.

As such, the current enquiry replicated the works of library activists by examining the degree to which computer attitudes predict levels of library anxiety among graduate students in the United States. It was expected that findings from this study would help to increase the understanding of the construct of library anxiety. Indeed, research in this area has become critical in higher education where educators are responsible for graduating students with the skills necessary to thrive and to lead in a rapidly changing technological environment in the twenty-first century.

METHOD

Participants

Participants were ninety-four African American graduate students enrolled in the College of Education at a historically Black college and university in the eastern U.S. All participants were solicited in either a statistics or a measurement course at the time that the investigation took place. In order to participate in the study, students were required to sign an informed-consent document that was given during the first class session of the semester. The majority of the participants were female. Ages of the participants ranged from twenty-two to sixty-two years (Mean = 30.40, SD = 8.75).

Instruments and Procedure

All participants were administered two scales, namely, the Computer Attitude Scale (CAS) and the Library Anxiety Scale (LAS). The CAS, developed by Loyd and Gressard, contains forty Likert-type items that assess individuals' attitudes towards computers and the use of computers.

This instrument consists of the following four scales, which can be used separately:

- Anxiety or fear of computers;
- Confidence in the ability to use computers;
- Liking or enjoying working with computers; and
- Computer usefulness.

Loyd and Gressard reported coefficient alpha reliability coefficients of.86.91.91, and.95 for scores pertaining to computer anxiety, computer confidence, computer liking, and total scales, respectively.
For the present study, the score reliabilities were as follows:

- Computer anxiety.84 (95 per cent confidence interval CI =.79.88);
- Computer confidence.81 (95 per cent CI =.75.86);
- Computer liking.89 (95 per cent CI =.85.92); and
- Computer usefulness.76 (95 per cent CI =.68.83).

The LAS, developed by Bostick, contains forty-three 5-point Likert-format items that assess levels of library anxiety experienced by college students.
It also contains the following five subscales:

- Barriers with staff;
- Affective barriers;
- Comfort with the library;
- Knowledge of the library; and
- Mechanical barriers.

A high score on any subscale represents high levels of anxiety in that area. Jiao and Onwuegbuzie, in their examination of the score reliability reported on

LAS in the extant literature, found that it has typically been in the adequate to high range for the subscale and total-scale scores.

Based on their analysis, Onwuegbuzie, Jiao, and Bostick concluded that "not only does the produce scores that yield extremely reliable estimates, but also these estimates are remarkably consistent across samples with different cultures, nationalities, ages, years of study, gender composition, educational majors, and so forth."

For the current investigation, the subscales generated scores for the combined sample that had a classical theory alpha reliability coefficient of:

- 89 (95 per cent CI =.85.92) for barriers with staff,
- 84 (95 per cent CI =.79.88) for affective barriers,
- 53 (95 per cent CI =.37.66) for comfort with the library,
- 62 (95 per cent CI =.48.73) for knowledge of the library, and
- 70 (95 per cent CI =.58.79) for mechanical barriers.

Analysis

A canonical correlation analysis was conducted to identify a combination of library anxiety dimensions (barriers with staff, affective barriers, comfort with the library, knowledge of the library, and mechanical barriers) that might be simultaneously related to a combination of computer-attitude dimensions (computer anxiety, computer liking, computer confidence, and computer usefulness). Canonical correlation analysis is used to examine the relationship between two sets of variables whereby each set contains more than one variable.

In the present investigation, the five dimensions of library anxiety were treated as the dependent multivariate set of variables, and the four dimensions of computer attitudes formed the independent multivariate profile. The number of canonical functions (factors) that can be produced for a given dataset is equal to the number of variables in the smaller of the two variable sets.

Because the library-anxiety set contained five dimensions and the computer-attitude set contained four variables, four canonical functions were generated. For any significant canonical coefficient, the standardized canonical-function coefficients and structure coefficients were then interpreted.

Standardized canonicalfunction coefficients are computed weights that are applied to each variable in a given set in order to obtain the composite variate used in the canonical correlation analysis. As such, standardized canonical-function coefficients are equivalent to factor-pattern coefficients in factor analysis or to beta coefficients in a regression analysis. Conversely, structure coefficients represent the correlations between a given variable and the scores on the canonical composite (latent variable) in the set to which the variable belongs. Thus, structure coefficients indicate the degree to which each variable is related to the canonical composite for the variable set. Indeed, structure coefficients are essentially bivariate correlation coefficients that range in value between-1.0 and +1.0 inclusive. The square of the structure coefficient yields the proportion of variance that the original variable shares linearly with the canonical variate.

Results

Table presents the intercorrelations among the five dimensions of library anxiety and the four dimensions of computer attitude. Of particular interest were the twenty correlations between the library-anxiety subscale scores and the computer-attitude subscale scores. It can be seen from table below that, after applying the Bonferroni adjustment, four of these relationships were statistically significant.

TABLE: Inter-correlations among the Library-Anxiety Subscales and Computer-Attitude Subscales

S.No.	Subscale	2	3	4	5	6	7	8	9
1.	Barriers with Staff	64	63	49	46	-.02	.05	-.27	-.09
2.	Affective Barriers.	56	52	40	-.05	.02	-.37*	-.23	
3.	Comfort with the Library	.56	.44*	-.19	-.20	-.55	-.16		
4.	Knowledge of the Library	-39*	-.21	-.11	-.37	-32*			
5.	Mechanical Barriers	-.13	-.01	-.18	.04				
6.	Computer Anxiety		.77	.48	.46*				
7.	Computer Confidence							.67	36*
8.	Computer Liking							43*	
9.	Computer Usefulness								

Notes: *Indicates a statistically significant relationship after the Bonferroni adjustment

Specifically, computer liking was statistically significantly related to affective barriers, knowledge of the library, and comfort with the library. Using Cohen's criteria of.1.3, and.5 for small, medium, and large relationships, respectively, the first two relationships (involving affective barriers and knowledge of the library) were medium, and the third relationship (between computer liking and comfort with the library) was large. In addition to these three relationships, the association between computer usefulness and knowledge of the library also was statistically significant, with a medium effect size. The correlation matrix in table was used to examine the multivariate relationship between library anxiety and computer attitudes. This relationship was assessed via a canonical correlation analysis. The canonical analysis revealed that the four canonical correlations combined were statistically significant ($p<.0001$).

Also, when the first canonical root was removed, the remaining three canonical roots were not statistically significant. In fact, removal of subsequent canonical roots did not lead to statistical significance. Together, these results suggested that only the first canonical function was statistically significant, but the remaining three roots were not statistically significant.

This first canonical root also was practically significant (Rc1=.63), contributing 40.8 per cent (Rc12) to the shared variance, which represents a large effect size.

TABLE: Canonical Solution for Third Function—Relationship between Library-Anxiety Subscalesand Computer-Attitude Subscales

Theme	Standardization Coefficient	Structure Coefficient	Structure (%)
Library-Anxiety Subscale Barriers with Staff	.17	.82*	67.2
Affective Barriers	.40 •	.85*	72.3
Comfort with the Library	.39 •	.85*	72.3
Knowledge of the Library	.31 •	.78*	60.8
Mechanical Barriers Computer-Attitude Subscale	-.12	.39*	15.2
Computer Anxiety	-0.31*	-.00	4.8
Computer Confidence	0.98*	-.13	1.7
Computer Liking	-1.25*	-.80*	64.0
Computer Usefulness	-0.13	-.4.0*	16.8

Notes: *Loadings with the effect sizes larger than 0.3.

Data pertaining to the first canonical root are presented in Table, which provides both standardized function coefficients and structure coefficients. Using a cutoff correlation of 0.3, the standardized canonical-function coefficients revealed that affective barriers, comfort with the library, and knowledge of the library made important contributions to the library-anxiety set, with affective barriers and comfort with the library making similarly large contributions.

With regard to the computer-attitude set, computer anxiety, computer liking, and computer confidence made noteworthy contributions, with the latter two dimensions making the most noteworthy contributions.

The structure coefficients revealed that all five dimensions of library anxiety made important contributions to the first canonical variate. The square of the structure coefficient indicated that barriers with staff, affective barriers, comfort with the library, and knowledge of the library made similarly large contributions, explaining 67.2 per cent, 72.3 per cent, 72.3 per cent, and 60.8 per cent of the variance, respectively.

With regard to the computerattitude set, computer liking and computer usefulness made important contributions. These variables explained 64.0 per cent and 16.8 per cent of the variance, respectively.

Comparing the standardized and structure coefficients indicated that computer anxiety and computer confidence served as suppressor variables because the standardized coefficients associated with these variables were large, whereas the corresponding structure coefficients were relatively small. Suppressor variables are variables that assist in the prediction of dependent variables due to their correlation with other independent variables. Thus, the inclusion of computer anxiety and computer confidence in the canonical correlation model strengthened the multivariate relationship between library anxiety and computer attitudes.

EMERGENCE OF DIGITAL LIBRARY SERVICES IN INDIA

The digital library is an electronic or virtual library where information is selected, acquired, processed, organised, stored and retrieved in digital form.

The developed countries have already digitized their libraries. The developing countries are in the process of digitization of their libraries. The users of digital libraries are the universal users who should have facility to access to all created and acquired digital sources of information in the form of electronic text, image, map, sound, video and multimedia.

Thus the digital libraries are attributed to electronic databases and capable of handling large data and servicing users effectively in resource sharing environment.

DIGITAL LIBRARY INFRASTRUCTURE

A digital library has certain technological requirements such as:

- Locally developed database
- Local library system with adequate personal computers having LAN and CD-ROM Drives.
- Electronic mail service
- Network connection to have access to other data bases Various functions to coordinate, manage the entry and retrieve data.
- Multimedia Kit
- Well trained manpower
- Computer Hardware with Audio-Visuals, Video Conferencing Kit, Pentium Web Server, Laser Printer, Scanner, Barcode Scanner, Barcode Printer, Digital graphic printer and UPS.
- Software and its accessories.

The super structure of digital library rests on some important factors like:

- The human need for information especially that is timely and relevant and
- Accumulation of information, and all the supporting infrastructure that includes research community, professional associations, libraries and publishers, advances in methods and technology leading to developments in net working, information science, information storage and retireval, hyper-media, human-computer interaction, artificial intelligence and other areas of computer science that make digital libraries a possible proposition.

Always library services are followed by library works. But now the advancement in information technology has brought changes in the concept of traditional library work as well as service. The recent trend and change in the information related field especially in collection, storing, processing and dissemination of information have resulted in to the evolution of digital libraries. Now most of the reference books like encyclopaedias, dictionaries, directories, hand books, etc. are published in electronic form.

Similarly about 50% of the existing secondary resources like abstracting and indexing services are available in electronic form for example, Chemical Abstracts Service, Index Medicus, Engineering Index. At present most of the digital libraries have been highlighted mainly on providing access to diverse digital information resources. The provision of personalized reference and information services is considered as one of the important characteristics of the library and information profession.

However reference services include:

- Either finding the required information on behalf of users, or assisting users in finding information themselves;
- Instruction in the use of library resources and services, and User guidance in which users are guided in selecting the most appropriate information sources and services.

In this changing scenario, reference works of modern libraries are influenced by a set of related technical and economic factors, especially the increasing use of technology and techniques. To cite some examples, the recent developments in the INTERNET and in Web Technologies have brought significant changes in the concept of traditional reference services and a number of web-based "expert services", that are now offered by many non-library organisation.

Information services are provided to the users on demand as well as anticipating the user needs including various forms of current awareness and selective dissemination of informa-tion services. Such services are provided to the users to keep them abreast of the latest developments in their field of interest through on-line search services in digital information environment, even by the non-library organisations like Dialog.

PERSONALIZED SERVICES

Most of the researches on digital library development have focused on access to and retrieval of digital information but they have overlooked the personalized service aspects, as primary goal of library information services. However the technology and information resources, on their own, can not make up an effective digital library. On priority basis the personalized services in a digital library environment would help the users to find information resources available in a digitally chaotic world.

In a Delphy study it was revealed that:

- The primary roles library professionals play in digital libraries include organization of macro and micro-documents, selection and acquisition and acting as gateways to the provision of information services, and

- The best reasons of developing a digital library include: increasing access to information serving and users needs and bringing organization to the unstructured universe of electronically available information.

However there is a demand for end-user instruction on the use of digital libraries and the digital library professionals who are subject specialists should help users to formulate disciplinary search strategies and provide assistance in developing new digital information resources.

Web-Based Reference and Information Services

Several reference and information services are now available on the web and many of these services are provided by non-library organization. Also a web site that provides a categorized listing of libraries that offer real-time reference services using specific software, live interactive communication tools, call centre management software, bulletin board services and other INTERNET technologies.

Of course, most of these services are designed for registered users of some specific libraries in-digital information environment. HodgKin has made an aggregation approach to reference and information services.

According to which more than one reference sources is made accessible digitally and also it is more practicable in terms of visibility and profitability than a single reference source.

Further:

- It's reference service becomes much better known to professional users and thus easier to find, by providing access to several reference works,
- By tackling a number of reference works at a time, the publishers can achieve economics of scale in production and development
- The user's search session is likely to be much more powerful and fruitful.

Online reference and information services can be broadly categorized into three groups:

- Those from publishers, database search services and specialized institutions
- Those provided by libraries and/or experts through the INTERNET and
- Where the users need to conduct a search and find information through the web.

Also they have listed several online information services that belong to the first category comprising various current awareness, and SDI services, for example:

- Contents pages services from commercial publishers, such as Elsevier's Contents Direct Service and IDEAL Alert from Academic Press.
- Information on new books available for free from publishers and vendors, such as Wiley Book, Notification Service from Wiley, and Amazon.com.
- SDI services from online search services providers, such as Dialog (Dialog Alerts)
- Current contents and ISI Alerting Services from ISI and so on.

However some of these services, particularly the contents page services from publishers of journals, are free, while for others, such as Dialog Alerts, or Current Contents from ISI, users need to register and pay for the services. There are also some web-based reference services where users need to conduct a search in order to answer their reference query.
For example:

- The Internet Public Library,
- Britannica,
- The Electric Library and
- The Internet Library for librarians.

Most of these web-based reference services are available free of charge but some charge a small amount as fee. For example, the Electric Library charges an annual subscription fee.

SEARCH ENGINE SERVICES

like:

- Sherman made a comparision among three web-based reference services Ask Jeeves basically a search engine, is useful for complex questions and is a good choice for searchers who lack Boolean or other searching skills, because of its strong natural language parser and question-and-answer template structure. The users can ask a question on a given topic and it comes up with a list of questions on the same or similar topics; the users can select any of those predefined questions and then it provides further answers.
- It processes each query syntactically and semantically and then its answer processing engine provides the question template response.When the users click on a response, the answer-processing engine retrieves the answer template that contains links to the answer locations. Thus Ask Jeeves can help users to select a query from a pre- defined set of queries on a given topic. So it is considered as a useful model for reference and infor-mation services in digital libraries.
- The Electric Library is an excellent choice for a serious researcher in need of timely content from a wide array of otherwise unavailable sources. It provides access to various on line reference sources and allows users to either select a specific source or conduct a search on a range, or all, of the sources.
- Information please is a suitable tool for students and other researchers, as an authoritative source of facts and pointers for further investigation.

Moreover Chowdhury and Chowdhury have suggested some other useful search engine services like:

- Web help.com that claims to offer real time search assistance with a real live expertany time, day or night,
- About.com is a service that shows a number of pre-defined categories related to a search topic given by the user.

For example, a simple search on 'e-commerce' not only produces a list of sites, but also provides a set of topics related to e-commerce, such as e-commercedefinition, e-commerce security, the advantages and disadvantages of e-commerce, e-commerce statistics and so on.

DIGITAL REFERENCE SERVICES FOR GENERAL PUBLIC

Today web-based digital reference services are being provided by a network of public libraries. The users make their query on an enquiry page and it is automatically routed to one of the participating libraries which records it as an e-mail message to the user containing necessary and available information.

For example, the British Library, London provides special reference services for business, scientific, technical, medical, patent and environmental information which range from answering simple queries up to complex questions involving on line data base searches.

Of course some of these services are free if users put simple queries, but for complex queries users need to pay at the prescribed rate which covers the costs of staff time, on-line searching and value added tax (VAT). The British Library provides STM (Science, Technology and Medicine) Search Service for which users need to pay. Similarly New York Public Library (Digital Library), American Library of Congress, Alexandria Digital Library, Berkeley Digital Library, Bibliotheque Nationale de France, Victoria State Library, Vatican Library, etc. are some other libraries which provide digital reference services for users.

DIGITAL REFERENCE SERVICES OF ACADEMIC LIBRARIES

Web based reference services are also now being provided by academic libraries, Recently a study report on web-based reference services reflects the current practices of digital library services in seventy academic libraries of USA. The study shows that university libraries allow their patrons to put reference questions in a variety ways: 99% offer e-mail reference, 96% offer reference services by appointment while 29% of the libraries offer real-time virtual reference. These libraries use customer relationship management (CRM) software packages for providing web-based reference services in the virtual reference environment.

CO-OPERATIVE DIGITAL LIBRARY SERVICES

The rising cost of digital reference sources and its proper processing by the trained manpower and also the initial infrastructural investment for introducing new services in libraries have influenced different organisations to choose a co-operative model of digital reference services. As a result some co-operative projects have been launched for providing web-based reference services to the users who can ask for such services from a remote location at any time.

The Library of Congress, USA has launched the collaborative digital reference service with a mission to provide the users, anywhere anytime through an international digital network of libraries.

This network has three main components consisting of:

- Member Profiles
- Request Manager-Software for entering, routing and answering reference queries; and
- Knowledge Base-a searchable database of questions and answer sets.

In this network a participating library sends a question to the system on behalf of a user and the system looks in to the knowledge base for a match. Then a reply is sent to the relevant library through e-mail. Incase the question and its corresponding answer is not found in the knowledge base, then it is passed on to the Request Manager where using the profiles of participating libraries and their information resources collection, expertise etc, relevant query is passed on to an appropriate library.

This library receives the query, finds an answer and sends back reply to the results store and answer to the knowledge base. Thus the Knowledge Base and Request Manager become able to provide reference service in digital environment. However, the Library of Congress and OCLC have developed a co-operative "Question Point" the advanced generation of collaborative Digital Reference Service (CDTS) in June 2002 which integrates local as well as global electronic reference networks.

PRESENT SCENARIO IN INDIA

All the six IITs (Indian Institute of Technology) created as centres of excellence for higher training, research and development in science, engineering and technology, have automated their libraries and now they have access to more than one thousand electronic journals.

The Central Library IIT, Delhi has switched over to the Silver Platter's Electronics Reference Library (ERL) technology for providing access to bibliographic databases subscribed on CD-ROM.

The technology facilitates simultaneous and integrated access to ERL complaint reference databases to multiple users across the LAN/WAN Via TCP/IP. This library offers network-based CD-ROM search services from the CD-ROM databases subscribed in the central library. Most of its databases have now been transferred to ERL technology and its CD-NET system has been installed for searching of CD-ROM databases on the campus intranet. This Library has started subscribing to the web-based full-text electronic journals with availability of high speed INTERNET connection and about 1330 electronic journals are accessible full text.

In most of the higher learning and research institutes in India such as:

- The Regional Engineering Colleges (RECs),
- Tata Institute of Fundamental Research (TFIR),
- Indian Institute of Science (IIS),
- Indian Statistical Institute (ISI),
- Indian Agricultural Research Institute (IARI),
- Institute of Veterinary Research of India (IVRI),
- All India Institute of Medical Science (AIMS),
- Indian Institute of Management (IIMs),
- Institute of Physics, Institute of Life Science,
- Shaha Institute Nuclear Physics,
- The Medical College Libraries etc., have automated their library systems.

Some of them are in the process of digitization of rare and valuable documents. Digital library services in India are in developing stage. At present most of the university libraries have taken steps to provide web-based reference and information services in digital environment in addition to their traditional library services.

These services include:

- Access to library catalogues and union catalogues.
- Access to bibliographic databases
- Access to subject gate ways in specific disciplines
- Providing links to web sites
- Accessing and procuring e-reference sources
- Subscribing to e-journals
- Reference services provided by librarians and experts on the web
- Document delivery services
- On-line current awareness services
- Digitization of library resources, considering their intellectual value.
- The University Grants Commission (UGC) of India has launched the major initiative for setting up nation wide communication network for Indian universities called UGC-Infonet.

Each university was to establish a LAN in its campus linking all the teaching departments including library. ERNET of India and INFLIBNET Centre, Ahmedabad are conducting a series of training programmes for technical staff of each participating university library for managing and maintaining the network at their premises.

The INFLIBNET Centre will administer and monitor the E-Journal programme and will have independent electronic access to all the publications to help with the process. The INFLIBNET Centre has carried out training programmes in various places to spread awareness and to develop expertise in the University community in the use of E-Resoures under the networked environment. The INFLIBNET Centre has developed and also recently released library automation software package new version for university libraries (SOUL) for building up digital library services. Soul is Windows based user friendly software, based on client server architecture with multi-user and multi language facilities which supports internationally known standards such as CCF, AACR-II andMARC-21, etc.

Thus INFLIBNET centre is patronizing for digitization of college and university libraries and encouraging e-subscription and e-learning in Indian Universities and colleges. The DELNET (Delhi Library Network) created as a metropolitan network in 1988, has changed its name to Developing Library New Work (DELNET) in 2000.

The main objectives of DELNET are to promote resource sharing among its member libraries, develop a network of member libraries, collect store and disseminate information, offer computerized information services in digital environment

The DELNET presently avails the high speed satellite communication facilities of NIC spread across the country and its 620 member libraries can access about 35 lakh bibliographic records in machine readable form. Also it maintains an online union catalogue of books available in its member libraries in CCF format. Its union catalogue is continuously updated. DELNET has been networking the libraries of about 400 affiliated institutes of AICTE, New Delhi. DELNET presents two management software packages i.e. DELMARC and DELPLUS.

❐

14

The Role of Libraries in Modern Society

First, the general development of the information society is pushing to re-evaluation of all the institutions which work with information, data, and knowledge-indirectly also with culture.

In this connection the roles of education and media have been discussed already quite largely also in the European Union. But libraries-as well as other memory institutions like archives and museums-have not been considered.

Still, there is a clear need in the information society to maintain an institution which is concentrating in collecting and organizing information and offering general access to it. Until now, this work has been underestimated, but I argue the situation will change!

Libraries are especially important now when the whole idea of education is stressing more and more independent learning and acting. All citizens must be able to find and use information. It is the key raw material-but it is a zero resource, if there are no access points to it and if documents are in chaotic order.

Here we can see libraries enter the stage:

- The unique function of libraries is to acquire, organize, offer for use and preserve publicly available material irrespective of the form in which it is packaged in such a way that, when it is needed, it can be found and put to use. No other institution carries out this long-term, systematic work. Culture must be nominated especially: it has an important and unique role in mobilizing resources of human beings. It has been described: To some extent, culture makes its influence felt more indirectly than knowledge, but it is impossible to imagine how people's creative powers could be fully activated without the impact of culture, which extends into the depths of the mind.

The challenge to modern societies is that the basic resource, knowledge, is developing from information in very individual, capricious and unpredictable process. It cannot be commanded. Still, societies can support this desvelopment, e.g. by offering access to cultural and knowledge treasures.

This can even be translated into economic language: to get out the best from the human resources in Europe, this resource must be feeded up with rich and various cultural and information contents! I would like to stress especially the idea of organizing information by libraries.

It is often shadowed by the second important side of library work: offering access. But in the life-long learning and new technology context just all forms of organizing documents are getting more to the focus. This is clear to anybody who has tried to find something from not-so-often-used Internet websites.

NEW LINES IN THE EU-AND IN THE UNITED STATES

In accordance with these phenomenons, there are new political lines in the European Union: The Maastricht Treaty in 1992 launched the cultural aspects. This was only after a long discussion, which made it clear that we have to remember to separate the national view and the European view. The Amsterdam Treaty in 1997 declared citizenship as an important theme.

A significant part of this are a.o. granting information skills and access to information to every European. In addition to this, the European future strategies need to meet the democratic aspects of the information society development. One of the crucial points is again general access to information.

Libraries, especially public libraries, are a good tool in all of these new areas. But the European union does not support whichever cultural or citizen concentrated projects in Europe. In the interests of the European Union there is always to find the European element. So, what can be done in library policy on the European level, taking in account that libraries are primarily a part of national education and cultural policies? The own-initiative report "The role of libraries in modern societies," adopted by the European Parliament in October 1998, is the first effort to answer these questions.

The same topics have been discussed in the United States. They have reached the point where especially the problems of those lacking access to digital resources have been studied. The report Falling Through the Net: Defining the Digital Divide by the U.S. Department of Commerce was released earlier in July 1999. The report finds that minorities, low-income persons, the less educated, and children of single parent households, particularly when they reside in rural areas or central cities, are risk groups. The report calls for public policies and private initiatives to expand affordable access to critical information resources.

But it also shows,, for the first time as far as I know, that libraries and community centres really can diminish the information gap between haves and not-haves. The 1998 data from the U.S. demonstrates very clearly that community access centres, primarily public libraries, are particularly well used by those groups who lack access at home or at work: e.g. unemployed groups used Internet in libraries three times as often as an average citizen.

EARLIER ACTIONS IN EU

In the European Union, there have been some efforts to mobilize "the treasures of the European libraries" since the mid-80'ies. These discussions and resolutions led to two special library programmes under the 3rd and 4th Framework programmes of research and development. The later programme has been known as "Telematics for Libraries". They have been strongly concentrated in IT, because it has been seen as a good tool to produce better access to the existing, underused library resources.

These programmes have had a clear impact in the European library co-operation and development. Benefits of this work come to public libraries indirectly: common standards and working methods help in the end all kind of libraries. But a fact is, that nearly all the libraries active in these EU projects are national libraries or big research and university libraries. Two main exceptions are Publican, a network of European public libraries, and ECUP, which was a copyright awareness raising project, and reached public libraries as well.

A new beginning was the so called Morgan report in 1997. In this report libraries were for the first time put clearly onto the place where they belong in the information society. As one result of the Morgan report, the European Commission informed that it will produce a Green Paper about the role of libraries in the information society.

For one or another reason, this was made quite ready but was never published. In this situation the Committee on Culture, Youth, Education and the Media in the European Parliament decided to produce an own- initiative report about libraries.

The main reason was that they wanted to influence the big issues under work in the EU, first of all the copyright directive and the 5th framework programme, which will have a direct impact to libraries. I was nominated the rapporteur of the own-initiative report. The report was adopted almost unanimously and with a very encouraging discussion in the Plenary session of the Parliament in October 1998.

DECISIONS OF THE EP CONCERNING LIBRARY POLICY

In short, when adopting the own-initiative report, the EP was calling the Commission and/or the member states to following actions:

- Libraries must be taken in account in national and EU information society strategies and in the respective budgets.
- Libraries need more resources for acquiring expensive books.

- The Green Paper on libraries by the Commission must be completed.
- The users position must be taken in account in the copyright directive process, the balance must be maintained-this was politically the most important decision in short run.
- Support to libraries was demanded from the 5th Framework programme of research and development, e.g. for networking, drafting standards, preserving, and transferring information; there is no more named library programme under the 5th framework programme
- A clearing-house to solve problems of long-term conservation should be founded.
- Studies concerning permanent paper should be done on European level.
- The member states should take care of digitizing their cultural heritage for future.
- There should be studies and concrete support to libraries in licensing matters, which are–will be the next big issue in library work.
- The EU cultural and information budget should be opened to libraries as well, libraries and their co-operation should be taken in account in planning new programmes.
- Problems of legal deposit in international and multinational materials, especially in electronic materials should be solved.
- The member states should provide all types of libraries with modern equipment, particularly with Internet connections.
- Free of charge use of public libraries, in the spirit of the UNESCO Public Library Manifest, was demanded.
- Free and easy access via libraries to material produced with the aid of tax revenues was demanded.
- The members states should organize for their library professionals up-dating education and training.
- A European Union focal point for libraries should be set up The member states should found European information points at libraries in countries where they do not yet exist.
- Library statistics should be better and more comparable both on national and European level.
- The national Parliament libraries should be opened to the MEP's in countries where this is not yet the practice.

In addition to these, the report strongly stresses that the library financing must be re-thought in the information society. Without new resources libraries are unable to do everything they are expected to do! After the EP adoption of this report, the European Commission informed that it will next prepare a communication about actions to do. It was stated that the report had already served as a discussion paper, and so the need for the Green Paper had disappeared. The communication is in summer 1999 still under work in the Commission DGXIII/2.

TRADITIONS AND NEW FORMS OF WORK IN THE SAME HOUSE

The European Commission R&D framework programmes have concentrated in IT matters. The three cultural programmes, Caledoskope, Ariane and Raphael, have not been very useful for libraries, because their scope has been quite narrow. E.g. the books and reading programme Ariane has concentrated in translations. In the coming framework programme Culture 2000 libraries will have more possibilities to get support also for their cultural actions. What then will be the fate of the traditional tasks of libraries in general? Will the information society wipe out book loaning and poems?

THE PUBLIC LIBRARIES IN THE KNOWLEDGE SOCIETY

THE LIBRARIES IN A STATE OF FLUX

The municipal reform in 2007 had major consequences for the library service. The number of libraries decreased and the remaining libraries grew in size. The reform thus underlined and intensified various tendencies in library development over the past many years.

The public library is in a state of flux. Library service to children from 2008 that chose as its point of reference the changes in children's use of the library. Thus this report had a strong focus on one target group and on how the library can develop new services to that group.

The present report also focuses on the target group, but slightly more on the institution–the public library. Based on a number of societal needs and new opportunities the report also considers how the library can be developed as an institution. The library offer is changing rapidly, but it continues to be much sought after.

Two out of three Danes use the public library, and 29% of the adult population visit the library at least once a month. In 2008 the public libraries registered more than 34 mil. visits. This makes the library one of our most popular, public cultural offers, and this has been the case for many years. But the way we use the library is undergoing a change. On the one hand the loan of physical materials–books, CDs etc.–is falling.

In the period 2000-2008 the public libraries' loan of physical materials has thus fallen by 22%, from ca. 62 mil. to app. 48 mil. materials. On the other hand the use of digital offers is growing, an offer that spans from downloads of music and e-books to renewals of loans via the library's homepage. Bibliotekernes Netmusik, where as a library user you can via your municipality download music for free, experienced over 2,5 mil. downloads in 2008–an increase of 48% compared with 2007.

One explanation of the change in borrowing patterns could be that the technology and media development has resulted in new media habits on behalf of the library users. At the same time the libraries' consistently high visiting figures show that they have succeeded in reorganizing and revitalizing themselves and continue to be attractive.

This happens by developing new library services, particularly digital services, but also by turning the library into something more than just a collection of materials, so that the physical library maintains its desirability.

Today the library is also a place for being and meeting, where one for example gets instruction, uses the Internet or gets help in the local citizen service centre. However, borrowing books remains the main reason why Danes visit the library. The latest cultural habits survey from 2004 shows that 85% of adult library users visit the library to borrow books and journals. The same tendency becomes apparent in more recent studies.

In a Gallup poll conducted on behalf of the Danish Library Association, the Union of Danish Librarians and HK Kommunal (white collar workers' union (municipal) in 2009, "borrowing books" is the most frequent reason for visiting the library, followed by "borrowing electronic media", "taking the children to the library" and "watching events".

There is in fact also a growing interest in the library's non-users, as can be seen from the large number of new initiatives, which the libraries participate in at municipal level. In many cases these have a social aspect, and the library is here used as a partner in a targeted initiative towards certain target groups.

This effort is particularly relevant in the light of the challenges that globalization presents to less resourceful citizens. The focusing on non-users also has another angle, which is i.a. clearly expressed in former minister for culture, Carina Christensen's strategy Culture for everybody from 2009. Here the emphasis is on the value of participating in a cultural community and the individual citizen's benefit from cultural offers. The strategy suggests that all citizens should be able to take advantage of the cultural offers and consequently–that the cultural institutions focus more purposefully on non- users.

THE POLITICAL BASIS FOR THE COMMITTEE'S WORK

The appointment of the Committee on the Public Libraries in the Knowledge Society was decided by the minister for culture in connection with several consultations in Folketingets Kulturudvalg (parliamentary cultural committee), which took place in the wake of a large number of public library branches being closed down during the first year of the municipal reform. The discussion fuelled by this naturally included the media and technology development.

A suggestion for a more extensive, interdepartmental committee work was rejected by the minister, who referred to the work that had already been done by the Globalisation Council. The committee's work builds on the report Future library service to children from 2008. The report contains a number of recommendations as to how to make sure that a strong library offer continues to be available to all Danish children.

In 2008 the Danish Agency for Libraries and Media also published the report The public libraries after the municipal reform, which analysed the development within the public library area with particular focus on any consequences due to the municipal reform. The reposrt concluded that the closure of the branches in 2006-2007 was a natural adaptation of the library service, and that at the same time it demonstrated a prioritisation in order to deliver a more up-to-date and value-enhancing library offer.

With the report from the Committee on the Public Libraries in the Knowledge Society we now have a number of recommendations as to how this prioritisation can be made so that the public libraries also in future will be able to meet the public's need for enlightenment, education and cultural activity. The committee presents its recommendations within an expenditure- neutral framework with the perspective that it may be both necessary and correct with local changes of priorities within the library field in order to support and strengthen the public library in the knowledge society.

THE COMMISSION'S ASSIGNMENT: MANDATE FOR THE COMMITTEE ON THE PUBLIC LIBRARIES IN THE KNOWLEDGE SOCIETY

The committee must focus on continuous development of the public libraries in Denmark. This includes the public libraries' interaction with other libraries and relevant institutions. Focus must be on the libraries as an easily accessible offer to everybody. The committee must build on the report Future library service to children and pay particular attention to service to youngsters and adults.

The committee must assess the public libraries' role in relation to the challenges facing the knowledge society, the globalisation strategy's focus on education, lifelong learning and societal cohesive force. The committee must assess to which extent there is basis for establishing new concepts for a library service that meets the public's needs in terms of enlightenment, education and cultural activity, and close to the citizens.

Likewise the committee must asses the possibilities for continuous development of traditional core services such as literature dissemination. In particular, the committee must asses the need for further development of the libraries' digital infrastructure and the interaction between digital and traditional services.

The committee must furthermore describe models for the mediation of digital cultural heritage and licensed digital media and models for various forms of learning and inspiration activities (e.g. in relation to citizens with poor reading and IT skills). The committee must likewise give examples of new partnerships, including inter-institutional cooperations and binding networking commitments.

Finally the committee must assess the need for competence development of library staff. On the basis of its analyses the committee must put forward recommendations and suggestions as to how tshe strategy's objectives can be realised within the present legislation and existing division of labour between state and municipalities. The committee's suggestions must be expenditure-neutral.

The committee is composed upon appointment, so that the minister for culture appoints three members, while Local Government (KL), Danish Library Association, Association of Library Directors, Danish Research Library Association, the Regional Libraries, Union of Danish Librarians and Børne-og Kulturchefforeningen each appoints a member. The Danish Agency for Library and Media's director general is chairman of the committee, and the Agency is the committee's secretariat. The committee must have completed its work primo 2010.

DIGITAL LIBRARIES AND SOCIETY

Digital libraries are large, organized collections of information objects. Whereas standard library automation systems provide a computerized version of the catalogue—a gateway into the treasure-house of information stored in the library—digital libraries incorporate the treasure itself, namely the information objects that constitute the library's collection. Whereas standard libraries are, of necessity, ponderous and substantial institutions, with large buildings and significant funding requirements, even large digital libraries can be lightweight.

Whereas standard libraries, whose mandate includes preservation as well as access, are "conservative" by definition, with institutional infrastructure to match, digital libraries are nimble: they emphasize access and evolve rapidly.

The five stages in this part provide an excellent illustration of the hugevariety of interesting issues in digital library research that impacts the Asia Pacific region. Unlike the New World, where most of the research on technological aspects of digital libraries originates, Asia has an exceptionally rich cultural heritage. This manifests itself in a huge legacy of documents, in various forms—from paper to palm leaves—and in various different conditions.

The need to preserve this legacy is particularly pressing in today's world, where political instability is rife and climate change is beginning to have an effect. As recent events have shown, disasters, both manmade and natural, can have a devastating effect on fragile cultural artifacts.

S.M. Shafi from the University of Kashmir, India, surveys the many issues involved with digital archiving of medieval manuscripts in Asia. Libraries are pillars of education, and it is natural to expect that digital libraries will provide new opportunities for innovative educational practices.

These will be particularly relevant to the Asia Pacific region because of the huge disparities in access to education between the different communities there. Peer-to-peer learning has always been a crucial factor in personal development, although it is frequently ignored in educational studies.

Natalie Lee-San from Nanyang Technological University, Singapore, describes her studies of how digital libraries can provide an innovative, perhaps revolutionary, environment for peer-to-peer learning amongst youths. She touches on many practical issues: gender differences, different learning styles, different levels of media and computer literacy, and age-related differences.

Many economies in the Asia Pacific region are agriculturally-based. Modern agriculture is a knowledge-based activity that can benefit greatly from digital libraries. Mila Ramos from the International Rice Research Institute in the Philippines describes a large-scale digital library system designed to support the growth, nurturing, harvesting, and distribution of that most Asian of staples, rice.

This digital library supports an institute whose goal is to improve the well-being of present and future generations of rice farmers and consumers, particularly those with low incomes. The institute's library houses the world's most comprehensive collection of technical literature on rice, and provides a widely-used international reference service.

As in many specialized libraries, digital library technology is seen to have special advantages in a world of shrinking library budgets. Intellectual property issues are a central driving force behind the market in information of which libraries are a part. And the questions become more complex as the nature of today's information shifts from a primarily book-based culture to one that embraces all types of multimedia objects, and large, carefully-curated, collections of such objects.

The stage on "Multimedia digital library as intellectual property" by Hideyasu Sasaki and Yasujshi Kiyoki at Keio University in Japan clarify the copyright situation as it affects multimedia collections and compilations. They go on to discuss the patentability of particular retrieval mechanisms, an essential component of digital libraries. The fifth stage in this part on how digital library research impacts the Asia Pacific region is the present one, on digital libraries in society.

Most existing digital library projects, being research-oriented, are predicated on state-of-the-art equipment and interfaces, academic and research institutions, special collections. In contrast: digital library technology can and should be available to everyone, on all platforms, in all countries; and it can and should enable ordinary people to exercise their creative powers to conceive, assemble, build, and disseminate new information collections that are designed not just for western academics but for a wide diversity of different audiences throughout the world. Though less glamorous, this may, in the end, be a more important goal for society.

Digital libraries pose an inherent tension between the technologist's desire for advanced solutions that use the latest and greatest hardware and software, and the librarian's desire for wide, crossplatform availability and long-term preservation—as epitomized by the sustained success of paper as a delivery medium.

To achieve universal access for both information consumers and collection-builders is really a problem for HCI. We examine the social need for digital libraries, particularly in developing countries, by briefly sketching some trends in commercial publishing and contrasting them with a growing international perspective of information as a public good. We draw out the implications for the user interface, which is the principal bottleneck in allowing non-specialist people to make public information available in focused collections that are universally usable.

Then we introduce digital library technology and illustrate it with a particular example, the Greenstone digital library software, which is designed for a broad user base and is in widespread use in many corners of the world—from Uganda to the US, Kazakhstan to Canada, Nepal to New Zealand. Following that, we review a project that is applying digital library technology to the distribution of humanitarian information in the developing world, a context that is both innovative and socially motivated.

Next we discuss issues of universal access and illustrate them with reference to the Greenstone software. We include a brief demonstration of a prototype system that is intended to allow anyone to build and disseminate information collections, and illustrates some human interface challenges that arise when providing necessarily complex functionality to a non-computer-oriented user base.

We close with the hope that future digital libraries will find a new role to play in helping to reduce the social inequity that haunts today's world, both within our own countries and between nations.

BOOKS, LIBRARIES, AND THE SOCIALLY DISADVANTAGED

Today, the long-standing three-way tension between the commercial interests of publishers, the needs of society and information users, and the social mandate of public libraries, is being pulled and stretched as never before. First, the very notion of a "book" is evolving in many different directions: books become more interactive; publishers rent content; books are distributed under restrictive conditions that mechanically prohibit sharing.

While it would be premature to make specific predictions, it seems likely that these trends will further disadvantage the disadvantaged—particularly those in poorer countries who have yet to benefit from ready access to ordinary books. Second, a huge body of information is becoming freely available on the Internet.

Much is of questionable quality, but some is very good indeed. In many cases the information is provided for the "public good" rather than for commercial profit, and the redistribution of such information is likely to be encouraged, rather than prohibited, by those who make it available.

Initiatives like UNESCO's "Information for all" programme and the upcoming World Summit on the Information Society highlight the importance of public information; they are founded on the belief that information literacy will help alleviate many of the problems confronting human societies.

Third, the implications for libraries are mixed. Whereas new controls by publishers over how the content they own may be used presents libraries with significant problems, the ready availability of "public good" information meshes well with library philosophy.

A new role is emerging for information professionals who can select material, index it, add appropriate metadata, and redistribute it in added-value form for the good of society. Suitable technological infrastructure is being provided by the open source movement, which is making available high-quality software for repackaging and distribution of information (and not just on computer networks).

Books

What future has the book in the digital world? The question is a complex one that is being widely aired. Authors and publishers ask how many copies of a work will be sold if networked digital libraries enable worldwide access to an electronic copy of it.

Their nightmare is that the answer is one: how many books will be published online if the entire market can be extinguished by the sale of one electronic copy to a public library? To counter this threat, the entertainment industry is promoting new "digital rights management" (DRM) schemes that permit a degree of control over what users can do that goes far beyond the traditional legal bounds of copyright.

Indeed, the acronym is more aptly expanded as "digital restrictions management" because it is concerned solely with content owners rights and not at all with user's rights. It is, in effect, a "private governance system in which computer systems regulate which acts users are and are not authorized to perform".

Anticircumvention rules are sanctioned by the Digital Millennium Copyright Act (DMCA) in the US. The DMCA has been used, for example, to prosecute a Norwegian teenager for writing software to play a DVD that he had purchased on a computer for which no commercial playback systems exist.

Can DRM be applied to books? The motion picture industry can compel manufacturers to incorporate encryption into their products because it holds key patents on DVD players. Commercial book publishers are promoting e-book readers that, if adopted on a wide scale, would allow the same kind of control to be exerted over reading material.

Basic rights that we take for granted—such as the ability to lend a book to a friend, resell it on the second-hand market, keep it indefinitely, continue to use it when your e-book reader breaks down, donate it to charity, preserve it for your grandchildren, copy excerpts without resorting to a handwritten transcription—are in jeopardy. DRM allows such rights to be controlled, monitored, and withdrawn instantly, and DMCA legislation makes it illegal for users to seek redress by taking matters into their own hands. Fortunately, perhaps, lack of standardization and compatibility issues are delaying consumer adoption of e-books.

In the realm of scholarly publishing, digital rights management is more advanced. Academic libraries license access to content in electronic form, often in tandem with purchase of print versions too. They have been able to negotiate reasonable conditions with publishers—probably because they represent the lion's share of the scholarly market.

However, the extent of libraries' power in the consumer book market is moot. One can envisage a scenario where publishers establish a system of commercial, pay-per-view, libraries for e-books and refuse public libraries access to books in a form that can be circulated. These new directions present our society with puzzling challenges, and it would be rash to predict what society's response will be. But one thing is certain: they will surely increase the degree of disenfranchisement of those who do not have access to the technology.

Public Information

In parallel with publishers' moves to reposition books as technological artifacts with refined and flexible control over how they can be used, an opposing trend has emerged: the ready availability of free information on the Internet. Of course, the world-wide web is an unreliable source of enlightenment, and undiscriminating use is dangerous—and widespread.

As early as 1996 complaints arose that the Web's contents are largely unattributed, undated, unannotated, unreliable; information about author and publisher is unavailable or incomplete; far too many resource catalogues are chasing far too few original or non-trivial documents—complaints that are very familiar today. But one thing has changed: search engines and other portals have enormously increased our ability to locate information that is at least ostensibly relevant to any given question.

Teachers complain bitterly that students view the Web as a replacement for the library, harvesting information indiscriminately to provide answers to assignments that are at best shallow and at worst incoherent and incorrect. One consolation is that the very same search facilities can be used to detect plagiarism.

Nevertheless, the Web abounds with accessible, high-quality information. Many social groups, non-profit societies and charities make it their business to create sites and collect and organize information there. To take a single example at random, a Google search for diabetes returns three national diabetes associations in the top ten hits, and of course many more exist.

Each of these sites offers a cornucopia of valuable information on the disease, which is not commercial and provided for the public good. Widespread use is strongly encouraged, and it seems likely that arrangements could be made for re-distribution of the material presented there, particularly it was intended as a not-for-profit service and appropriate acknowledgement was made.

One of the key problems with information distribution via the Web is that it disenfranchises developing countries. Although the Web does not extend into the homes of the socially disadvantaged in developed countries either, various national programmes are working to provide access.

But network access varies enormously across the world. Whereas in 1998 more than a quarter of the US population were surfing the Internet, the figures for Latin America and the Caribbean was 0.8%, for Sub-Saharan Africa 0.1%, and for South Asia 0.04%. Schools and hospitals in developing countries are poorly connected.

Even in South Africa, the bestconnected African country, many hospitals and 75% of schools have no telephone line. Universities are better equipped, but even there up to 1,000 people can depend on just one terminal. The Internet "is failing the developing world".

Prompted by this inequity, the importance of information, and particularly public information, is today being highlighted by prominent international bodies. For example, UNESCO's "Information for all" programme was established in 2001 to foster debate on the political, ethical and societal challenges of the emerging global knowledge society and to carry out projects promoting equitable access to information.

It reflects a growing awareness that information is playing an increasing role in generating wealth and human capital, and that participation in the "global knowledge society" is essential for social and individual development. Information literacy is described as "a new frontier" by the Director of UNESCO's Information Society Division. The International Telecommunications Union has established a World Summit on the Information Society, held in Geneva in December 2003 and Tunis in 2005, to promote a global discussion of the fundamental changes that are being brought about in our lives by the transformation from an industrial to an information society, and to confront the extreme disparities of access to information between the industrialized countries and the developing world.

Libraries and their Role

What is the librarian to make of all this? The mandate of today's public libraries, in sharp contrast to that of publishers, is to facilitate the open distribution of knowledge. Librarians strive to enable the free flow of information. Their traditions are liberal, founded on the belief that libraries should sesrve democracy.

To help fulfil their mission as resource centres for citizens, public libraries maintain collections of records, policy statements, government documents, and so on.

A recent psromotional video from the American Librarian's Association exults that "the library is democracy's place of worship".

Clearly, the impending redefinition of the book as a digital artifact that is licensed rather than sold, tied to a particular replay device, with restrictions that are clearly laid out and mechanically enforced, is an innovation that goes right to the heart of libraries.

The changing nature of the book may make it hard, or even impossible, for libraries to fulfil their mandate by providing quality information to readers. And on the other hand, the emergence of a vast storehouse of information on the Internet poses a different kind of conundrum. Librarians, the traditional gatekeepers of knowledge, are in danger of being bypassed, their skills ignored, their advice unsought.

Search engines send users straight to the information they require—or so users think—without any need for an inter-mediary to classify, catalogue, cross-reference, advise on sources. The ready availability of information on the Internet, and its widespread use, really presents librarians with an opportunity, not a threat.

Savvy users realise they need help, which librarians can provide. A good example is Infomine, a cooperative project of the University of California and California State University. Infomine contains descriptions and links to a wealth of scholarly and educational Internet resources, each of which has been selected and described by a professional academic librarian who is a specialist in the subject and in resource description generally.

Participating librarians see this as an important expenditure of effort for their users, a natural evolution of their traditional task of collecting and organizing information in print. What kind of technical infrastructure is needed to support and promote this kind of work?

Open source software is a powerful ally for librarians who wish to extend liberal traditions of information access. These systems make the source code freely available for others to view, modify, and adapt; and the very nature of the licensing agreement prevents the software from being appropriated by proprietary vendors. But the open-source movement is more than just a vehicle for librarians to use: its link with library traditions goes much deeper.

Public libraries and open source software both enshrine the same philosophy: to promote learning and understanding through the dissemination of knowledge. Both are pervaded by a sense of community, on the one hand the kind of inter-institutional cooperation exemplified by interlibrary loan and on the other teams of designers and programmers that frequently cross national boundaries.

New trends in information access present librarians in developed countries with difficult and conflicting challenges. Meanwhile, however, the situation in the developing world is dire. Here, traditional publishing and distribution mechanisms have failed tragically.

For example, whereas a US medical library subscribes to about 5,000 journals, the Nairobi University Medical School Library, long regarded as a flagship centre in East Africa, last year received just 20 journals. In Brazzaville, Congo, the university has only 40 medical books and a dozen journals, all from before 1993, and the library in a large district hospital consisted of a single bookshelf filled mostly with novels.

Digital Libraries and the Challenge for HCI

Traditional libraries are substantial institutions that occupy physical space, present a physical appearance, and exhibit tangible physical organization. When standing on the threshold of a large bricks-and-mortar library you gain a sense of presence and permanence that reflects the care taken in building and maintaining the collection inside. Digital libraries, in contrast, are lightweight. But they provide potentially far greater accessibility, which means that they will have even greater social effects.

Once created, they can, without significant institutional support, continue to serve users. They can be distributed throughout most of the developed world over the Internet. In developing countries and remote corners of the developed world they can be circulated on removable media—CD-ROM, DVD, or 100 Gb disk units the size of videocassettes—and updated over radio. Issues of copyright pose difficult problems, but they are manageable.

For example, there is plenty of non-copyright material, or material whose owners are prepared to donate copyright for socially useful purposes, and trends towards more open access to academic and humanitarian information are visible. Not everyone sees digital rights management and the DMCA as the way forward, and in the longer term publishers, to remain viable, will have to investigate alternative revenue models for the information they own.

No wonder international organizations such as the United Nations, along with many smaller non-government organizations (NGOs), are keenly interested in digital library technology. Advances in digital library technology are radically lowering the bar for the design and production of richly-organized, coherent, focused collections of information.

Now, anyone with access to sufficient source material can use public-domain software to build large, fullysearchable, collections the size of traditional personal or institutional libraries—in minutes. Let the minutes stretch to hours and the collection can be polished, organized, branded, distributed. It can include fully-illustrated text, images, video, music.

It can present attractively-designed pages with consistent use of icons. Keywords, key phrases, even acronyms and their definitions, can be extracted—automatically—and used to underpin novel means of access. Let the hours stretch to days and metadata can be manually added that permits further levels of organization. Given access to programming skills, creative new facilities that stretch the imagination can be rapidly integrated into the system. All this, one might say, can be done with ordinary Web sites: there is no need for digital library technology.

However, bitter experience has shown that all but the most rudimentary sites do require significant institutional support—for organization and maintenance. The Web is littered with incomplete, unfinished, unmaintained, out-dated, inconsistently-organized, useless information collections.

Just as traditional library cataloging procedures integrate new works into existing collections with minimal overhead so that they immediately become first-class members of the collection, so digital libraries allow new documents to be added completely automatically.

In the case of traditional libraries this is done through the small but nonnegligible overhead of generating a new catalogue entry. With ordinary Web sites it requires inserting links manually into index pages and the like, and may involve adding links not only into the new document but also into existing ones that ought to reference it—it's like rewriting the book, and maybe revising all other books in the library too!

In contrast, digital libraries bring access structures instantly and effortlessly up to date whenever new documents are added. The challenge for HCI is to design and build digital library systems that fulfil the potential of digital libraries as a "killer app" for computers in developing countries, which will bring concomitant benefits in almost every other sphere of application.

For the information consumer we need access to information that is guaranteed across space, time, and culture. We need flexible distribution mechanisms for documents, and for information objects of all types, that can be accessed on all computer platforms—including the lowliest. We need a choice of distribution over the Web or on removable media such as CD-ROM or DVD.

Digital libraries can incorporate flexible presentation that caters to individual differences, such as large-font displays or spoken output for the visually impaired. Libraries are places where information is preserved, not rendered obsolete, and digital libraries must instill confidence that information prepared today can be accessed next week, next decade, next century—regardless of technological changes.

An important aspect of digital libraries is their ability to work in local languages, promoting pluralism and reducing the risks of homogeneity. Because language is the vehicle of thought, communication, and cultural identity, this will encourage diversity and strengthen individual cultures. But there is a long way to go: even Unicode is woefully incomplete in certain areas, such as African languages. Naturally, today's digital library systems focus principally on the reader: the consumer of the material stored in the library's treasure-house. But digital libraries make a more radical, and perhaps ultimately more important, contribution by empowering ordinary users to conceive, assemble, build, and disseminate new information collections themselves.

In principle, modest computing resources are quite sufficient to enable users to build new collections by gathering together material in local files or on the Web; augmenting it with appropriate metadata that supports convenient search and browsing operations; incorporating advanced features like key-phrase extraction, document summarization, and metadata extraction; designing an attractive and functional interface; and publishing the collection on a variety of different media that are suitable for the intended readership.

The HCI challenge is to realise this potential for users—such as most librarians—who have a strong understanding of information and its organization, but no more interest in computers than they have in papermaking technology, last millennium's vehicle for information dissemination.

WHAT ARE DIGITAL LIBRARIES

A digital library is an organized collection of information:

- A focused collection of digital objects, including text, video, and audio, along with methods for access and retrieval, and for selection, organization, and maintenance of the collection.

This definition deliberately accords equal weight to user and librarian. The latter functions are often overlooked by digital library proponents, who often work from a technology perspective rather than from the viewpoint of library or information science, but it is precisely these aspects that allow digital libraries to be used to democratize information dissemination.

As a concrete example, consider the Humanity Development Library, a collection of some 1,200 authoritative books and periodicals, produced by many disparate organizations—UN agencies and other international organizations—on various areas of human development, from agricultural practice to economic policies, from water and sanitation to society andss culture, from education to manufacturing, from disaster mitigation to micro-enterprises.

It contains 160,000 pages and 30,000 images, which if printed would weigh 340 kg, cost $20,000, and occupy a small library book stack. Instead, it takes the form of a digital library and is distributed on a CD-ROM throughout the developing world at essentially no cost. The Humanity Development Library is produced using the Greenstone software, a freelydistributed open-source project whose aim is to create novel digital library technologies and make them available for others to use.

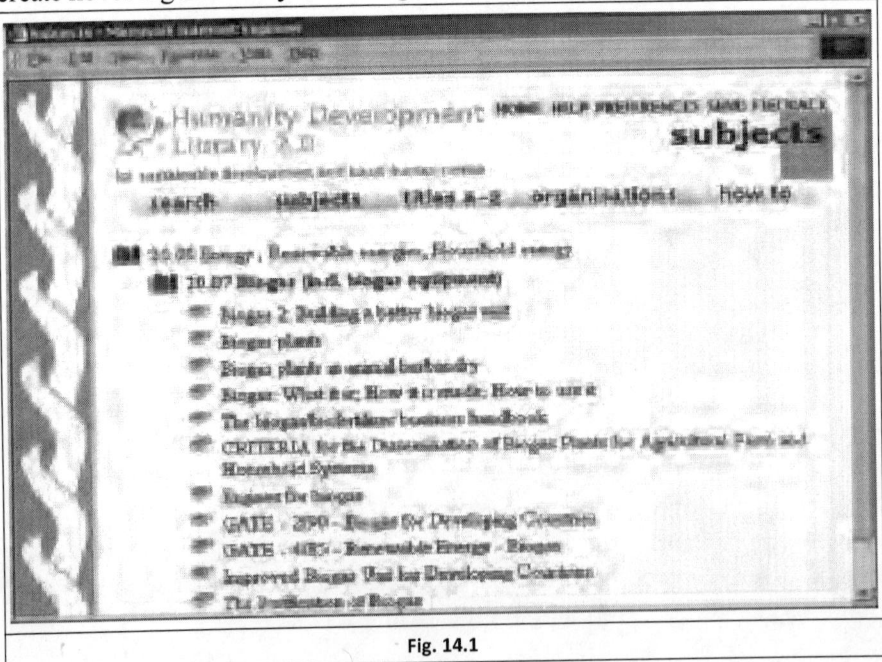

Fig. 14.1

Greenstone digital libraries are arranged in collections. A collection comprises several documents, and a library may include several collections, each organized differently. Collections built with Greenstone offer simple but effective searching and browsing facilities based on metadata and the full text of electronic documents. Each collection is individually designed to take advantage of whatever metadata is available.

All collections support full-text searching and most provide several different browsing options, although they differ depending on the collection design and the metadata available. Typically you can search for particular words that appear in the text, or within a section of a document, or within a title or section heading.

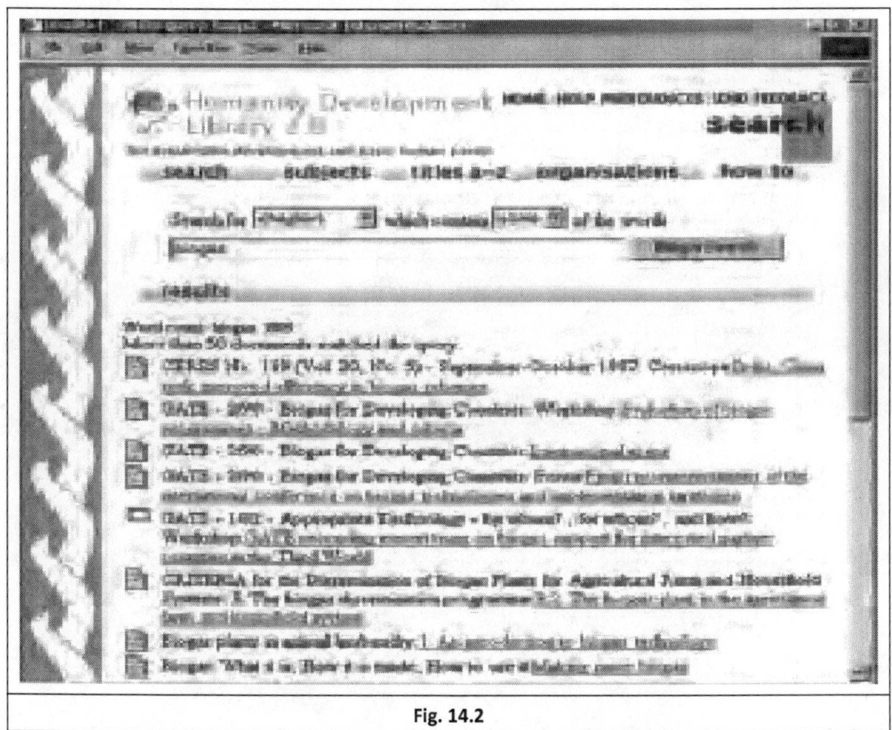

Fig. 14.2

A variety of interfaces exist for browsing collections by title, subject, date, or any other metadata chosen by the collection designer.

Figure shows snapshots of the Humanity Development Library. In figure documents are being searched for stages containing the word biogas. In figure the collection is being browsed by subject: Energy, Renewable energies, Household energy. Pursuing an interest in energy from biogas, the user selects a book by clicking on its book icon. All the icons in the screenshots of figure are clickable.

The navigation bar beneath gives access to the searching and browsing facilities, which differ from one collection to another. This particular collection can be searched by book, chapter, or section, and browsed by subject, title, organization, and "how to" metadata as indicated by the navigation bar.

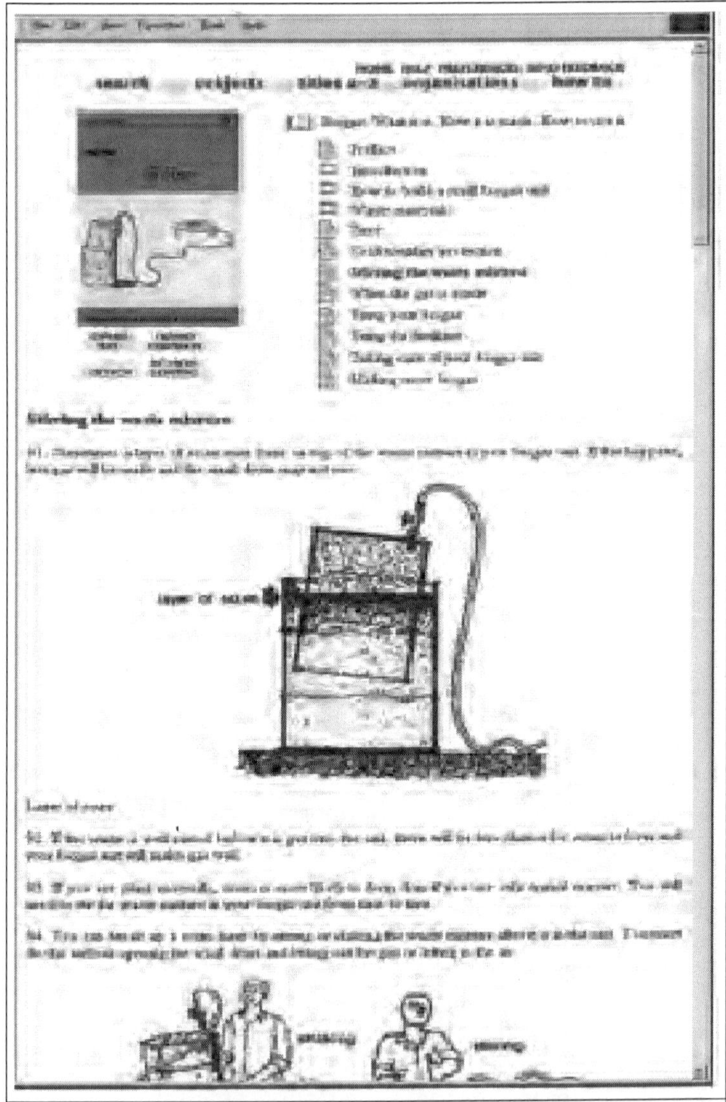

Fig. 14.3: The Humanity Development Library: (a) Searching for Biogas; (b) Browsing by Subject; (c) Reading a Document

Documents are presented as Web pages generated by Greenstone from the source material.

In figure, the book's cover is displayed as a graphic on the left, and an automaticalsly constructed table of contents appears at the start of the document. The current focus, Stirring the waste mixture, is written in bold in the table of contents; its text starts further down the page.

Incidentally, the material in this collection on building household biogas plans is fascinating, though it is not directly relevant to this chapter. Greenstone collections present documents as automatically-generated Web pages.

This allows documents in different source formats to be presented in a consistent manner, and lets users view the entire collection with a standard Web browser—no special viewing applications are required. However, the collection maintainer may choose to present the original source document instead of, or as well as, the HTML version, and rely on the user's web browser to select a suitable application to display the document. In general, Greenstone deals well with documents and metadata in a wide variety of different formats.ss

USING DIGITAL LIBRARIES TO DISSEMINATE sHUMANITARIAN INFORMATION

Digital libraries provide perhaps the first really compelling raison d'être for computing technology in the developing world. Priorities in these countries include health, agriculture, nutrition, hygiene, sanitation, and safe drinking water. Though computers per se are not a priority, simple, reliable access to practical information relevant to these basic needs certainly is.

In an article entitled "The promise of digital libraries in developing countries"

Witten mention ten information collections, available on the Web and CD-ROM, from organizations ranging from UN agencies to small NGOs, in which Greenstone is being used to deliver humanitarian and related information in developing countries.

For example, the Humanity Development Library described is a compendium of practical information aimed at helping reduce poverty, increasing human potential, and giving a practical and useful education. We describe four new ones that have been created recently, and distributed in the same way.

Fig.14.4: A Selection of Recent Humanitarian Digital Library Collections on CD-ROM

The Researching Education Development library is a project of the Department for International Development (DFID), a British government department responsible for promoting development. Its central focus is a commitment to an internationally agreed target of halving the proportion of people living in extreme poverty by 2015.

Associated targets include ensuring universal primary education, gender equality in schooling, and skills development. It works in partnership with other governments and multilateral institutions, with business and the private sector, with civil society and the research community. It has created a CD-ROM library containing many education research papers and other documents.

Each one represents a study or piece of commissioned research on some aspect of education and training in developing countries. The Energy for Sustainable Development library was initiated as part of the outreach phase of the World Energy Assessment, which was initiated jointly by the United Nations Development Programme (UNDP), the United Nations Department of Economic and Social Affairs (UNDESA), and the World Energy Council (WEC), along with funding from the United Nations Foundation. This library contains a broad and valuable collection of 350 documents from UNDP, UNDESA, WEC and many other organizations.

It includes titles that all these organizations have published on the subjects of energy for sustainable development—technical guidelines, journals and newsletters, case studies, manuals, reports, and other training material. The documents are in English, Spanish and French, and one document has Arabic, Russian and Chinese translations as well.

The UNAIDS Library contains publications in the "Best Practice" collection which form a unique resource for those working in planning and practice. It is produced by the Joint United Nations Programme on HIV/AIDS, whose globa ission is to lead, strengthen and support a response to the AIDS epidemic that will prevent the spread of HIV, provide care and support for those infected by the disease, reduce the vulnerability of individuals and communities to HIV/ AIDS, and alleviate the socioeconomic and human impact of the epidemic.

The Health Library for Disasters is the result of a collaboration between the emergency and disaster programmes of the World Health Organization (WHO) and the Pan American Health Organization (PAHO), with the participation of many other organizations: the United Nations High Commissioner for Refugees (UNHCR), the United Nations Children's Fund (UNICEF), the International Strategy for Disaster Reduction (EIRD); the Red Cross Movement (ICRC and IFRC); the SPHERE Project; non-governmental organizations such as OXFAM; and national organizations such as the National Emergency Commission of Costa Rica.

It contains more that 300 technical and scientific documents on disaster reduction and public health issues related to emergencies and humanitarian assistance. A follow-up to the Spanish-language Biblioteca Virtual de Desastres discussed by Witten et al., it includes technical guidelines, field guidelines, case studies, emergency kits, manuals, disaster reports, and other training materials.

UNIVERSAL ACCESS

Universal access to digital libraries presents huge challenges to software engineers and HCI practitioners. The Greenstone digital library software allows us to glimpse some of the issues, although it certainly does not yet effectively address them all.

Platforms and Distribution

Most digital libraries are accessed over the web, using any web browser. However, in many environments, particularly in developing countries, web access is insufficient and the system must run locally. And if people are to build and control their own libraries, a centralized solution is inadequate: the software must run on their own computers.

Thus digital library systems intended for broad access should run on a wide variety of computer systems, particularly low-end ones. Developed under Linux, the Greenstone server runs on any Windows, Unix, or MacOS/X system. All versions of Windows are supported, from 3.1 up.

Supporting primitive platforms poses substantial challenges of a rather mundane nature: for example, Microsoft compilers no longer support Windows 3.1 and it is necessary to acquire obsolete versions. Under Windows, pre-built collections can be viewed on any system with at least 8 Mb RAM, but collections cannot be built under Windows 3.1/3.11—for this at least a Pentium processor is generally required, except for very small collections.

The fact that Greenstone does not run on early Macintosh systems is a serious drawback in certain environments. In an international cooperative effort established in August 2000 with UNESCO and the Belgium-based Human Info NGO, Greenstone is being distributed widely in developing countries with the aim of empowering users, particularly in universities, libraries, and other public service institutions, to build their own digital libraries.

UNESCO recognizes that digital libraries are radically reforming how information is acquired and disseminated in its partner communities and institutions in the fields of education, science and culture around the world, and particularly in developing countries. Their hope is that this software will encourage the effective deployment of digital libraries to share information and place it in the public domain.

The UNESCO distribution of Greenstone is a CD-ROM that contains the full source code and executable binaries for Windows and Linux, along with all necessary associated software. Full documentation and five demonstration collections are included.

The current CD-ROM is trilingual, with complete interfaces, instructions, and documentation in English, French and Spanish. For those with Web access, the same package is also available for download from the Greenstone Web site, often in a form that is slightly ahead of the CD-ROM version—for example, many other language interfaces are included and full documentation is available in Russian and Kazakh too.

Providing accessibility in different languages is more difficult than one might at first realise. As well as the manuals, installation instructions and installation prompts, the licensing agreement, and the readme files have to be translated too.

Access for Readers

Greenstone collections like the Humanity Development Library can be published as standalone collections on removable media such as CD-ROM, or presented on the Web. CD-ROM is a very practical format in developing countries.

Any Greenstone collection can be converted into a self-contained Windows CD-ROM that includes the Greenstone server software itself and an integrated installation package. The installation procedure has been thoroughly honed to ensure that only the most basic of computer skills are needed to install and run a collection under Windows.

Even standalone Greenstone users interact through a Web browser: Netscape is supplied on each CD-ROM for those who do not already have a browser. In standalone mode the software runs locally but incorporates a Web server so that if the system happens to be connected to a network—say a hospital or school intranet—information is available to other machines that may not possess CD drives.

This happens automatically: no special configuration is necessary. Another difficult engineering challenge is checking for the existence of a network. While installed network software is easily detected, it is hard to determine non- intrusively whether it is operational. Incorrectly installed or configured software is endemic in developing countries, because computers there are often cast-offs whose software is inappropriate to their present environment, yet system support to rectify the problems is unavailable.

It is essential for universal access that such problems are addressed properly and solved satisfactorily without involving the user, even though they are mundane and timeconsuming. Greenstone provides some support for the visually impaired by incorporating a "textual" mode of access that replaces all images by textual prompts. This output is suitable for users with speech synthesizers or other specialized access devices. However, the facility is not well advanced: in particular, we have not yet refined it through usability testing and interface improvement.

Building New Collections

Effective human development blossoms from empowerment rather than gifting. As the Chinese proverb says, "Give a man a fish and he will eat for a day; teach him to fish and he will eat for the rest of his days." Disseminating information originating in the developed world, like the Humanity Development Library, is a useful activity for developing countries.

But a more effective strategy for sustained long-term human development is to disseminate the capability of creating information collections, rather than the collections themselves. This will allow developing countries to participate actively in our information society, rather than observing it from outside.It will stimulate the creation of new industry. And it will help ensure that intellectual property remains where it belongs, in the hands of those who produce it. Users whose skills resemble those of librarians rather than computer specialists should be able to build and distribute their own digital library collections. As an initial step in this direction, Greenstone includes an interface called the "Collector" that is intended to help people build their own library collections.

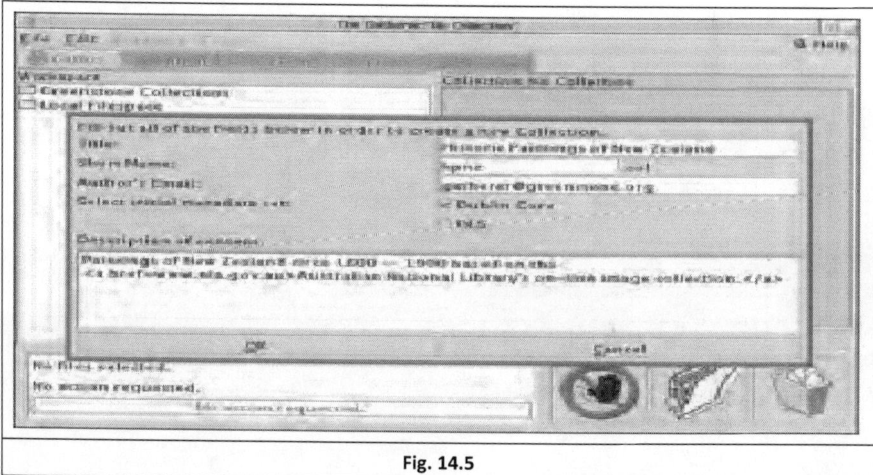

Fig. 14.5

Collections may be built and served locally from the user's own web server, or remotely on a shared digital library host. End users can build new collections styled after existing ones from material on the Web or from their local files—or both, and collections can be updated and new ones brought on-line at any time.

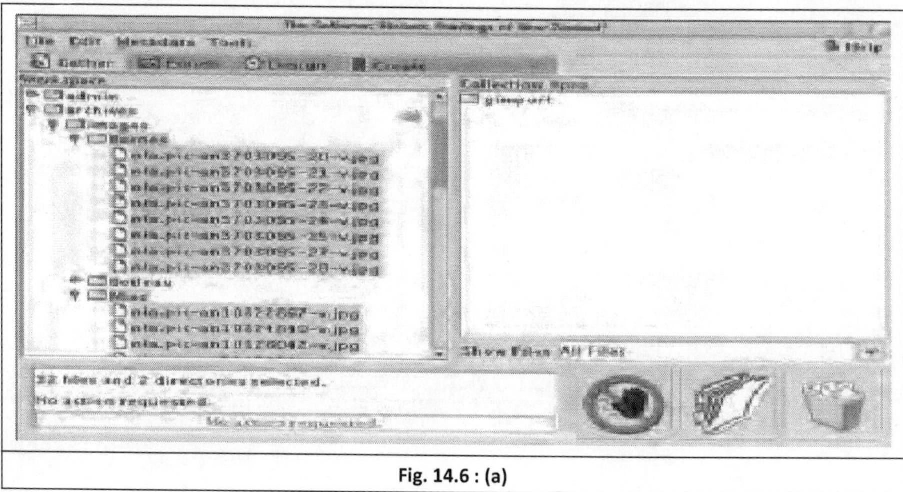

Fig. 14.6 : (a)

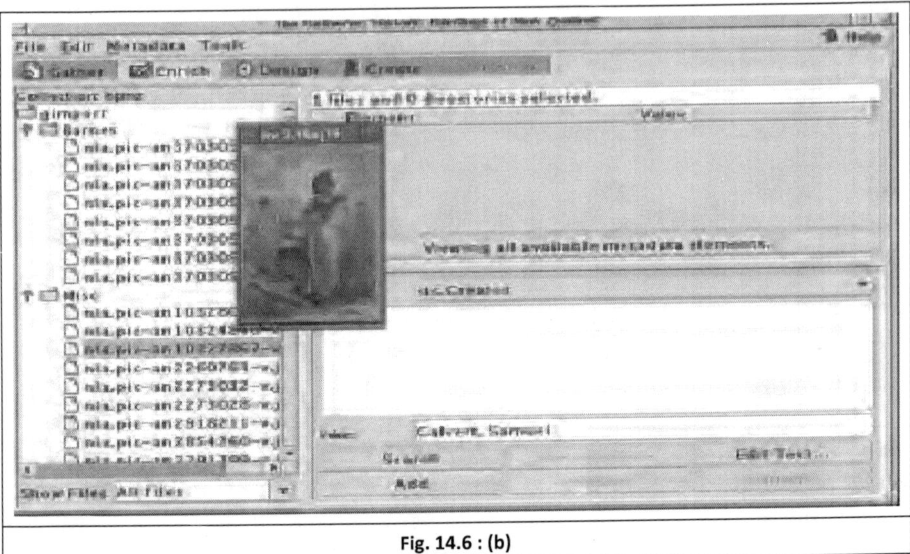

Fig. 14.6 : (b)

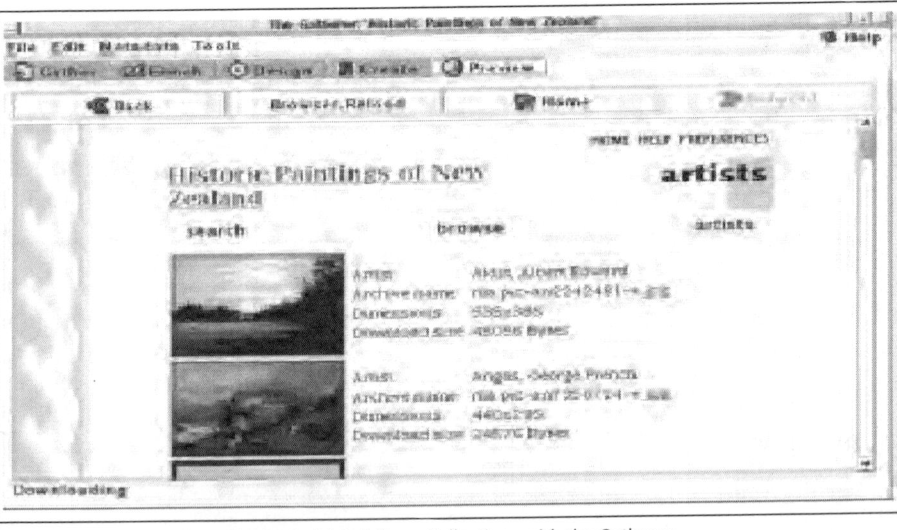

Fig. 14.6 : (c) Building a Collection wsith the Gatherer

The interface, which is intended for non-professional end users, is modeled after widely used commercial software installation packages, frequently called software "wizards"—a term we deprecate because of its appeal to mysticism and connotations of utter inexplicability. We chose this interaction style because it simplifies the choices and presents them very clearly.

Figure shows a new Greenstone librarian interface, currently undergoing beta testing by UNESCO at sites in Argentina, India, Kazakhstan, Mexico, and South Africa, which builds on lessons learned from the Collector. It incorporates a great deal of additional functionality, particularly the ability for users to associate metadata with any item or group of items, and to reuse metadata elements without retyping them.

In figure, it is being used to collate a selection of images for a digital library collection, augment these source documents with textual metadata and then build and view the collection. From here, it is a matter of a few further clicks to produce a self-installing CD-ROM version of the collection.

In this illustration the user is developing a digital library collection of historic paintings of New Zealand. The user creates a new collection using the file menu, and a resulting popup window prompts for some general information about the collection. Once the user has filled out this form the main window becomes active. A series of panels guide the user through the processes required to build the collection.

The left-hand pane of the Gather panel shows the file system and the right-hand one represents the contents of the collection, initially empty, which the user populates by dragging and dropping files. In figure, the user has moved to the Enrich panel and is adding textual metadata to the selected documents. The next two panels, Design, Create, help the user structure the collection, control its appearance, and build it.

On completion the result is viewed in the Preview panel. Figure shows a page from the newly built collection, in which source documents are alphabetically listed by artist. Shown alongside each thumbnail are the artist's name, its catalogue number, image dimensions, and its download size.

The full-size image is shown by clicking on the thumbnail. The user may skip backwards and forwards through the panels using them to augment and enhance the collection, perhaps adding further source documents, editing metadata values, and altering the collection's appearance.

Customization

An important component of access is allowing people to control the appearance of the collections they create. Many who build digital libraries want to brand them to ensure that they with an appropriate personal, institutional, or corporate image, and some can only contemplate software solutions that allow them to do so.

Although Greenstone comes with the standard appearance shown in figure—a distinctive bar down the side of all pages except those that show documents in the library, a green access bar with yellow buttons, etc.—the interface is highly configurable. Greenstone creates all pages that appear on the screen on the fly: none are stored in advance. They are generated using macros, written in a simple language specially designed for the job, that perform textual replacement.

One reason is that Greenstone accommodates a large number of different interface languages and macros help cope with this. All text fragments are couched as macro definitions. To add a new language, just the macro contents need to be translated—no web pages need be reworked.

Every page displayed by the system is passed through a macro interpreter that expands all the macros on the page. The interpreter checks a language variable and uses the macro definitions pertaining to it, which loads the page in the appropriate language.

Macros can have parameters. In this case, the parameter is the language variable: it causes the appropriate text fragment to be used for the macro's expansion. If there is no Arabic version for a particular macro, the interpreter will automatically substitute the default version.

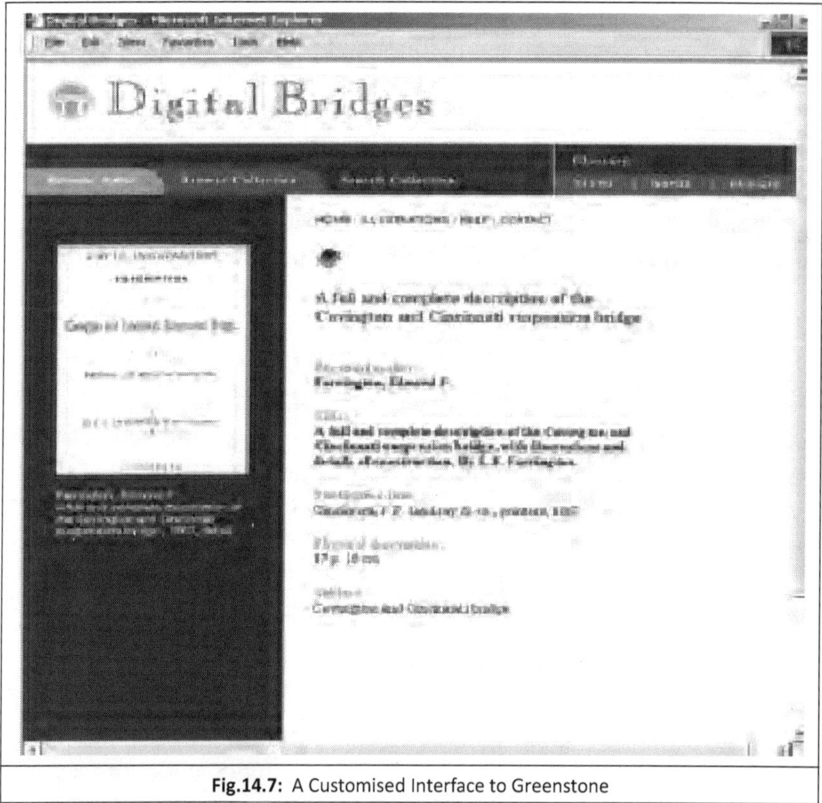

Fig.14.7: A Customised Interface to Greenstone

This lets system developers experiment with the interface without having to worry about translating every little bit of new text immediately. Defaulting to English is not ideal—it reflects an Anglo-centric mindset—but it seems better than displaying nothing. Macros are also used to deal with display variables.

Whenever a web page contains information that is not known in advance—like the number of documents returned by a search, or the value of a particular metadata item, or the content of a document page—a macro name is used in the page description.

Unlike language macros, these macros are dynamic: their content is not stored in advance but generated by the system in accordance with the value of the variable in question. Users can completely alter the form of the user interface by rewriting the macro files—or even by writing their own web pages which embed the dynamic macros that generate bits of Greenstone output.

Figure shows a Greenstone interface that has been heavily customised by Lehigh University Library, Pennsylvania. The standard Greenstone appearance has been completely obliterated in favour of an in-house style, yet all the Greenstone functionality is available. Figure shows a thumbnail of a book cover on the left, and full bibliographic information on the right. Entering a book displays facsimile images of its pages.

Internationalization

The international Unicode character set is used throughout Greenstone, and documents in any Unicode-supported language and character encoding can be imported. Collections of documents in Arabic, Chinese, Cyrillic, English, French, Spanish, German, Hindi, and Maori are publicly available.

The New Zealand Digital Library Web site hosts many of these, and the Greenstone Web site links to sites that contain further examples. It makes little sense to have a collection whose content is in Chinese or Russian, but whose supporting text—instructions, navigation buttons, labels, images, help text, and so on—are in English.

Consequently, the entire Greenstone interface has been translated into a range of languages, and the interface language can be changed by the user as they browse from the Preferences page. All the language fragments in the interface are stored in macro files. These have been translated by Greenstone users in other parts of the world and contributed back to the project.

Figure shows an example: a Russian collection. Currently, interfaces are available in Arabic, Czech, Chinese, Dutch, French, Galician, German, Hebrew, Indonesian, Italian, Kazakh, Maori, Portuguese, Russian, Spanish, Turkish, and English. Managing the organizational and software complexity of any comprehensive and evolving open source software system presents a significant challenge.

However, the challenge is greatly magnified when the interface is available in different languages, for enhancements to the software and changes to the interface must be faithfully reflected in each language version. No single person knows all interface languages; no single person knows about all modifications to the software—indeed there is likely no overlap at all between those who translate the interface and those who build the software.

Currently, Greenstone has about twenty interface languages and there are around 600 linguistic fragments in each interface, ranging from single words like search, through short phrases like search for, which contain, of the words, to sentences like More than... documents matched the query, to complete paragraphs like those in the on-line help text.

Fig. 14.8: A Russian Digital Library Collection

Maintaining the interface in many different languages is a logistic nightmare. The solution adopted by Greenstone is to incorporate a language translation facility, which allows autho-rized people to update the interface in specified languages. A standard version control system is used to manage software change, and from this the system automatically determines which language fragments need updating and presents them to the human translator.

❐

15

Computers and Children's Section in Public Library

INTRODUCTION

In The Historical Society of Cotuit, Sheila Bourbeau writes: "A library is books and somewhere to put them and some people to want them there". Yet increasingly, this simple definition doesn't apply to the modern public library. More often, today's public libraries are bustling community centers, offering not only books, but also computers with online catalogues, databases, various software, and internet access. Indeed, computer use in the public library is becoming more prominent and pervasive.

Moreover, technological services are available to a wider audience of adults and children than ever before. In particular, computers with educational or recreational software and internet access are especially popular in the children's section of the public library.

Given this recent shift towards computer use in the children's section, it is essential that library and information science professionals examine the way in which these services are implemented, utilized, and promoted. Children's librarians are in a unique position to provide observations and suggestions regarding the role of computers in the children's section of the public library. In addition, they are more likely to be able to identify trends in computer use. Collecting their impressions signifies an important step towards offering better computer services to children in the public library.

Through personal interviews, this research project considers children's librarians' perceptions of the following: quality of computers and computer software; staff knowledge of and involvement with computers; procedures for computer use; patron use of computers; and children's librarians' attitudes and responses to computer use in the children's section of the public library. Ultimately, this study's findings have the potential to benefit both children's librarians and their young patrons by highlighting ways computer services are successful and ways in which they require improvement. This research project employed a flexible, rather than a fixed design. More specifically, it comprised a set of individual case studies. In Real World Research, Colin Robson defines the case study approach as a "strategy for doing research which involves an empirical investigation of a particular contemporary phenomenon within its real life context using multiple sources of evidence". Further, this study focused on a "small number of individuals with some features in common". These common features included: location; workplace; and job description. Because multiple libraries and librarians were represented in this study, the results are more reliable and more generally applicable. Moreover, this approach provided multi-layered, qualitative, and empirical evidence.

Personal interviews constituted this study's research method. Robson explains that personal interviews offer a "flexible and adaptable way of finding things out," providing potentially rich and illuminating material. Further, he suggests that personal interviews promise several advantages, including "modifying one's line of enquiry" and "following up interesting responses and investigating underlying motives in a way that postal and other self-administered questionnaires cannot". This study is based on personal interviews, each lasting approximately a half an hour in length, with four children's librarians from North Carolina public libraries. In addition, physical observations provided a visual dimension to this study.

The process for initiating this research project involved several steps: first, after submitting a proposal, UNC's Institutional Review Board granted permission to conduct a study involving human participants; second, four children's librarians at North Carolina public libraries were invited to participate in the study; and finally, research participants were asked to sign informed consent forms at the time of their scheduled interviews. Three out of four sessions were taped with a handheld recorder to ensure precision and complete-ness. Interviews consisted of both closed and open-ended questions related to five broad headings: computers, staff, procedures, patrons, and attitudes and responses.

This study produced a combination of quantitative and qualitative data. A small portion of this data, such as the number of computers available in the children's section, was quantitative in nature. The majority of data collected, owever, was qualitative. Since the purpose of this research project was to gather a sample of children's librarians' perceptions of computers in the children's section of the public library, the qualitative results of this study were emphasized.

An interpretive and flexible editing approach, rather than a quasi-statistical, template, or immersion approach, was utilized for analysis. Informal coding was applied to the results of the personal interviews, highlighting "similar phrases, patterns, themes, relationships, sequences, differences between sub-groups, etc." Finally, the emergence of these relationships was used to describe trends in children's librarians' perceptions of computers in the children's section of the public library, as well as to identify strengths and weaknesses in practice.

RESULTS AND DISCUSSION

LIBRARY A

Library A offers two non-OPAC computers specifically designated for children. While posted signs stipulate that these computers are intended for users between the ages of two and fourteen, other patrons are allowed to use them as well. At one time, these computers were located at the entrance to the children's section, making them immediately visible to incoming patrons. Now, the computers are still within view of the children's information desk, but they occupy a less central part of the children's section. As Children's Librarian A explains: "… the problem we were having with our old location was that it was so prominent, that as soon as kids entered the children's section, they'd be drawn, like a television, to the computers, and they often would have to be pulled away."

Indeed, because the computers are so popular, the library is planning to add at least two more to the children's section in the near future. Moreover, although the current computers are perhaps only two or three years old, both will be replaced in the next year in accordance with the town's computer replacement policy.

Further, as gifts of the Gates Foundation, Library A's computers came with a variety of software, including Microsoft's Office package, Encarta Encyclopedia, three Arthur games, three Barney games, three Magic Schoolbus games, Living Tales, Success Builder Algebra and Geometry, Experiment Science, and Big Science Ideas. Most of the games range in age appropriateness from two to ten years old, while the more educational software is appropriate for young adults. Currently, Library A's children's section does not have a budget for computers since both computers were gifts.

Library A's children's section is staffed by three full-time and two part-time librarians. While acknowledging that "you could use one person just to do the computer cue," Children's Librarian A stresses that she would like more staff for activities unrelated to computer use, such as community outreach. She describes monitoring computer use as a "pretty constant" staff responsibility, but "not excessive."

She mentions one instance in which this task becomes problematic: "The only time it's troublesome is when you get a lot of people coming in, and you have a whole lot of people on the wait list, and people are up and down, and you're trying to find the person who's next."

Library A uses a manual sign-in procedure and limits patrons to thirty minutes on the computer at a time. Children's Librarian A explains: "We have a list, a purple sheet at the desk … where patrons are supposed to, if it's their first time, read the guidelines for use, and then sign in with the adult name, if the child is nine or younger, the child's name, age, and the time they're starting to use the computer, and which computer they're on."

If other patrons are already using the computers, this sign-in sheet acts as a wait list. When a computer becomes available, staff in the children's section call on patrons who are waiting. For this reason, most of the interactions Library A's children's staff have with the computers consist of "keeping an eye on the clock and showing people where to sign in." Children's Librarian A describes the procedure for using computers as relatively problem-free, although there are "complications sometimes."

Usually, these complications arise when a patron does not sign in, but expects to be able to use a computer when it becomes available. For this reason, Children's Librarian A would like an automated sign-in procedure installed eventually, mentioning a company called Library Guardian that offers software with a timing component.

While noting that this type of procedure requires patrons to have their library cards with them to access the computers, she suggests that this system would be advantageous overall. In the mean time, she comments: "For the most part, our procedure works pretty well, and we haven't been able to think of how we might improve on it."

Library A does not have a strict age requirement for computer use, although they suggest that children be at least two years old. Children's Librarian A feels that this recommen-dation is appropriate, if only because children under two do not have the manual dexterity to use a mouse successfully. Still, she points out that "some two year olds really will just sit and listen to the whole Stellaluna story [a read-along story programme]…And other [children] just want to bang on the keyboards!" Children who are nine years old and younger are required to be with an adult in the library building, so they are also required to be supervised by an adult on the computer.

Children's Librarian A agrees with this policy, too, noting that the children's section has had a problem with parents leaving their children at the computers unattended. In terms of written policy regarding computer use, Library A has a safe child policy, guidelines for using the computers, rules of conduct, and an internet use policy.

Children's Librarian A designed the safe child policy to apply to the computers in the children's section specifically, "covering all your basic safeguards," which was approved by her library director. This policy is posted beside the sign-in sheet at the children's information desk, as well as beside the computers.

Computer use in the children's section at Library A is constant. Children's Librarian A estimates that many children would stay on the computers longer than their allotted thirty minutes if possible. When asked if she would prefer to see her young patrons spending their time in other ways, like reading books and attending programmes, Children's Librarian A says she feels "pretty good" about the level of computer use. She explains that her library supports a strong base of readers: "I think a lot of people who are coming, that are using the computers, are also big readers…we're real lucky to have readers."

In addition, she suggests that many patrons who would not ordinarily visit the library are drawn in by the computers. She describes a scenario in which a nanny told her: "I used to try to bring the kids, and they never really wanted to come here, but now that you have the computers, it gets them excited to come and visit the computers, and then once I have them here, we can also grab some books." She hypothesizes that computers may be related to the children's section's dramatic rise in circulation statistics. She thinks that the Barney and Arthur games are the most popular applications because even the youngest children are able to play them. She feels that almost all the games and read along stories are both age appropriate and appealing to children.

On the other hand, she criticizes the Magic Schoolbus programmes, which attract younger children, but are intended for six to eleven year olds. She estimates that three to five year olds spend the most time on the computers.

Although she does not have a preference for which age group uses the computers most or least, she wishes that the educational software, such as the Encarta Africana, were available more often: "I'd like to see the more educational products, which are really great, being used more, and they would be helpful to upper elementary, middle school students, but I think that most of the time [when] the elementary and middle school students walk by, they see Arthur and Barney there, [and] they assume that's all there is."

Children's Librarian A lists several reasons for having computers in the children's section. First, she suggests that the public library has an obligation to provide access to computers to patrons who don't have them at home. Second, she argues that the computers act as a gateway, drawing in patrons that might not visit the library otherwise, in effect, increasing "use of the library by having different resources."Third, she asserts that computers are a "really great service [the library] can provide."

For example, she mentions being able to offer free word processing for children to complete homework assignments, rather than having to refer them to a for-profit business, like Kinko's. When asked what she considers to be the mission and goals of children's services, she explains: "I think it's to get kids excited about reading… and [to] get kids excited about learning." She feels that the inclusion of computers in the children's section is in keeping with these mission and goals.

While pointing out that there are some patrons who disapprove of "technology in general or things changing in general," she feels that it is useful to have computers in the children's section at Library A. Indeed, her impressions of computers are positive: "On the whole, I think that most people are happy that we have [computers], and making your public happy and satisfied with the services you offer is obviously what's going to keep you in business."

LIBRARY B

Library B offers six non-OPAC computers specifically for children in the children's section. Like Library A, these compu-ters are intended primarily for children's use, but they are also available to adults. Located immediately adjacent to the children's information desk, four of the six computers are internet access only, while the other two are for word processing. A printer is also available for patron use.

When asked if the children's section would benefit from a greater number of computers, Children's Librarian B asserts that they are able to meet their patrons' needs successfully with their six current computers: "We have the ability to see how many reservations we might have for people waiting [for a computer], and we don't have a waiting line." While it does not offer any educational software, Library B does subscribe to several online sources, such as Gale Source's Biography Resource Center and World Geography Online, that arrive via the internet.

Children's Librarian B notes that while children would probably enjoy "wilder video games," the amount of software the library offers meets the standards specified in the library's mission statement. Finally, Library B's children's section does not have a budget of its own for computer technology, but rather is encompassed by the library's Computer Operations budget.

Two full-time librarians, one part-time librarian, one full-time library assistant, two part-time library assistants, and several floaters staff Library B's children's section. Children's Librarian B explains: "To meet the daily needs of [the patrons that] come through the door, we do our best to balance, so we do OK," but implies that she would like more staff. She estimates that the children's staff spends about ten per cent or less of its work day "giving directions" about the computers.

She notes, however, that before the implementation of their current automated sign-in procedure, they were devoting a much higher percentage of their time to this activity: "... we were spending probably a third of our time everyday monito-ring computer use, because we signed everybody up at the desk, and we also were trying to place limitations on how long they could use the computers, so we were spending a lot more time paying attention to it, and now we don't."

At Library B, the procedure for using computers in the children's section is the same as the procedure used in the adults' section. Children's Librarian B explains: "We require our users to bring a library card, and to use that library card to sign themselves up at an available computer ... If all the stations are busy, then they come to a library staff member who can make a reservation for them, and they will get the next available opening." Although young patrons sometimes forget their library cards, Children's Librarian B claims that this system "works very well." She reflects that at one time, the staff in the children's section acted as a "reservation station," signing children up manually for time on the computer.

Now, they find that having children sign themselves up requires certain skills that act as "kind of a test" of appropriateness. In effect, the automated sign-in procedure helps screen out children who are physically or develop-mentally unready to use the computer without an adult. Further, she notes that the automated sign-in procedure frees up staff in the children's section to spend valuable one-on-one time with patrons who need assistance: "It allows us to be able to spend time with the people who can really take advantage of the expertise we have."

There is no age requirement for using the computers in the children's section at Library B. Children's Librarian B explains that at one time there were certain guidelines they required patrons to read before using the computers, specifying that "if you were a non-reader, that you have a reader with you." Children's Librarian B feels that their new policy works well. She argues that just as children are not required to be supervised in the stacks, they should not be required to be supervised at the computer unless their behaviour demonstrates that they need such supervision: ". . . if they show that they don't have the skills to use [the computer], then we ask that they [do it with] an adult or someone that can help." While Library B does not have a standard acceptable use policy, there is a statement on the automated sign-in page that patrons must click on or agree to before accessing the internet. This statement was developed by the county library system, and appears on all branch computers. Children's Librarian B estimates that the average child spends thirty to sixty minutes on the computer in the children's section of Library B, while pointing out that patrons can spend up to three hours on the computers. She explains that she would like to see "more of a mix" between computer use and other library-related activities, especially reading. When asked what computer applications are most popular among her patrons, Children's Librarian B mentions several game sites.

She does not feel comfortable evaluating "how good they are at what they are," but says that children seem to enjoy them. She thinks that six to twelve year olds spend the most time on the computer, noting that young children "think they want to [use the computer], but then they get on there, and it's not quite what they thought it was." Finally, when asked which age groups she would like to see spending the most and the least amount of time on the computer, Children's Librarian B claims to have no preference.

Children's Librarian B suggests that having computers in the children's section supports the library's mission and goals: "Our mission statement is to promote the love of reading and foster the pursuit of knowledge, and [computers are] an avenue of knowledge." Further, she sees the inclusion of computers in the children's section as a positive extension of library services, not only because it is an expectation that public libraries provide computers, but also because children get excited about them.

In addition to the formal interview, Children's Librarian B shared some unique insights about computers afforded by her long-time career in the public library system. She mentions some of her past frustrations related to computer use in the children's section. First, she describes observing staff struggling with the way children use computers.

She explains that children's librarians are trained to help children "find information to support homework or to support a hobby or a special interest," but that children rarely use the computers for these purposes. Second, in the past, she recalls being irritated at the computers freezing up, particularly on game sites: "… [it got] to the point where you were spending much more than a third of your time shutting them down, starting them up, and you [felt like asking], 'Why are we doing this?' We didn't have Scrabble, we didn't have pinball, and now we're spending a lot of time doing this." Third, she touches on the issue of appropriateness, mentioning that older children sometimes use chat rooms in an unacceptable manner. She points out that although Library B uses filtering software, this mechanism "limits sites," but not "what people can type."

Interestingly, she says that she and her staff have been very satisfied with filtering: "It's relieved a lot of responsibility from our staff, of having to watch and watch and watch, which has been nice. And we all did not want it. We did not want filtering at all, we felt like that would be the wrong way to go, but once it came, nobody wanted to go back."

LIBRARY C

Unlike the other libraries represented in this study, Library C does not have any non-OPAC computers in the children's section. Instead, it offers six computers for both children and adults. Four are available beside the adults' information desk, while two others are located inside a small private room. Children's Librarian C explains that this branch was, at one time, slated for renovations that would have expanded the physical space, thus allowing room for both a children's desk and computers in the children's section. In the mean time, however, one of the computers in the back room does include several "animated games," as well as the online Encarta Encyclopedia for children.

Library C employs only one full-time children's librarian. Children's Librarian C explains that one part-time position is informally assigned to children's services, but that "it's a little problematic because [the part-time employees] don't always come as a person that has any experience and training in children's [services], and they don't really emphasize that when they advertise, so. . . I have to sort of go with the flow." She says that she would like more staff, especially for programming. When asked how much time staff spends directing children to computers and offering instruction, she explains that because they don't have "software that self-times," staff is constantly assisting patrons with the computers. She claims, however, that staff spends a "really, really small" amount of time offering more extensive help, such as helping a child with a paper.

Library C utilizes a manual sign-in procedure and limits computer use to thirty minutes. Children's Librarian C reflects that in terms of procedure, the time limit poses the biggest challenge: ". . . we only have four [computers], and you know, it's becoming more and more popular.

People come here first thing in the morning to use the computers." She considers the potential benefits of an automated sign-in procedure, noting that it might be less work for Library C's small staff, but suggests that "it's kind of hard [to judge] until you get there."

At Library C, children under eighteen are not allowed to use the computers without adult supervision or signed parental consent. Children's Librarian C explains that at one time the age requirement was sixteen, but they raised it because all of Library C's computers have unfiltered internet access. She mentions that the county's central branch has software that blocks certain internet sites according to age, but explains that Library C chose not to adopt this option because so many adults need full access to the internet. Library C does have an acceptable use policy, developed by the county library system, which is posted by the sign-in sheet at the adults' information desk.

To answer the series of questions about patrons, Children's Librarian C relies partly on her weekend experience at the county's central branch, where she has observed greater computer use. She argues that because the children at the county's central branch come from a lower socioeconomic level that "it's a little bit more fascinating to them, and it's a little bit harder to tell them to get off because, you know, it's kind of new and exciting." At Library C, she suggests that many patrons have computers at home. She worries that her young patrons don't find books to be as exciting as computers: "I guess my fear is that they're just so hooked into it, and it's sort of an interactive thing that they don't really get involved in the whole book thing."

In spite of these concerns, however, she feels that Library C needs more computer opportunities for children. She says that children at Library C use the computers most often for homework and to play games. She estimates that older children, from nine years old to the early teens, use the computers most often. In contrast, she thinks that eight to twelve year olds spend the most time on the computers at the county's central branch. When asked what age groups she would like to see spending the most amount of time on the computers, she says five to six year olds, because they stand to gain the most from these interactions: ". . . people talk about kids improving their reading skills when they're just learning to read, and you know, I've heard some good results from that, so I think that's something that could be an opportunity for them."

Conversely, she feels that older children "often gravitate towards the computer when the book is right there." Also, at the county's central branch, she mentions older children printing off "music to rap songs" and "all kinds of stuff that's kind of a waste of time." She wishes that older children "could just be more inclusive in using books" and not be so quick to "discount" them.

Children's Librarian C feels that inclusion of computers in the children's section would complement the mission and goals of children's services. She tempers this response, however, by suggesting that children's use of computers should be "controlled." She argues that the children's section would require space for a children's information desk in order to provide support and supervision for computers designated solely to children.

She stresses that children, like adults, should have access to computers. Further, she asserts that computers have the potential to "help with reading or help with homework," by providing "timely," as well as "obscure" information. Ultimately, she agrees that her impressions of computer use are generally positive, emphasizing that she thinks children should "definitely have access [to computers] and more so than [they do at Library C]."

LIBRARY D

Library D offers one non-OPAC computer specifically designated for children in the children's section. Unfortunately, this computer is at least three years old, and therefore breaks often due to hard and frequent use by young children. Children's Librarian D notes that it would be nice to have more computers, especially since children enjoy using the computer, but feels that space and shelving are more pressing issues.

In addition to the designated children's computer, a Gates and a bilingual computer, both purchased with Smart Start money, are popular among children. In fact, Children's Librarian D explains that most new computers come to Library D through grants, such as Gates or LSTA, because although the county has a computer replacement policy, there is currently no budget. Reading games and read along programmes are most popular with children, although Children's Librarian D stresses that the children's section would benefit from having new and different story CD-ROMs.

At Library D, the staff hours for the children's section are split into two jobs, so that there is one full-time librarian and one part-time librarian. Children's Librarian D feels that she does not have enough staff to meet the demands of the children's section. When asked how much time staff spends monitoring computer use, Children's Librarian D says that "it's like twenty four-seven, all day, everyday," because patrons often run into problems when using the computers. Further, she characterizes the demands of monitoring computer use as "labour-intensive" and "bothersome," because she believes that patrons spend too much time on activities like e-mail, which aren't sresearch-oriented.

Unlike the other libraries in this study, Library D's procedure for computer use in the children's section is first come, first serve, with no time limit, although there's an informal thirty minute rule when other patrons are waiting. For the other computers with internet access, there is a manual sign-in procedure, which Children's Librarian D describes as "staff-intensive." Interestingly, while acknowledging that patrons are "pretty good" about following these procedures, she hints that they could be improved, but admits that staff is reluctant to confront patrons.

There is no age requirement for using the computer in the children's section at Library D because it only offers educational CD-ROMs. Twelve year olds and younger can use the computers with internet access with a parent, while thirteen year olds and older may use them independently with signed parental consent on file. Children's Librarian D feels that these requirements are appropriate, not only for safety reasons, but also because she thinks that children do not need to spend "all their time" on the computer.

Further, she stresses that librarians are not babysitters, noting that internet use opens up a number of safety and legality issues. Library D does have an acceptable use policy. While the county and state set certain guidelines that must be followed for determining this policy, the library itself is responsible for particular details, such as age requirements. This policy is posted with support documentation at the adults' information desk.

Children's Librarian D describes the amount of time children spend on computers as constant. She feels that although a little time on the computers is appropriate, she would prefer to see them reading books. Interestingly, however, she says that the most popular computer applications are reading activities, such as Curious George Does the Alphabet and Mom and Me. When asked what age group spends the most time on the computer, Children's Librarian D says that younger children tend to use the computer most often because it is the first thing they encounter when entering the library and the children's section.

Moreover, she claims to have mixed feelings about this age group using the computer so often. She thinks that younger children need to be aware of computers and how to use them, since many of them do not have computers at home.

Further, she acknowledges that they enjoy using the computer. On the other hand, she feels that the computer might be more appropriate for school age children, especially if it had a greater number of applications. She is particularly interested in the idea of creating a permanent room for computers, suitable for homework help and online research.

When asked to describe the purpose of computers in the children's section, Children's Librarian D answers in ideal terms, emphasizing that the computer should act as an educational and informational resource, rather than as a recreational opportunity only. She suggests that computers should enhance research and reading skills, as well as help children explore areas of interest.

She feels that the computer in the children's section complements the mission and goals of children's services at Library D, which include "providing a wide range of programmes and services to supplement the schools, curriculum, [and promoting] literacy, appreciation of cultural and artistic diversity, environmental awareness, creative expression, and life-long learning." Children's Librarian D admits to having mixed impressions about the use of computers in the children's section. She reiterates the need for increased staff, more space for leisure reading, and child-friendly shelving, over OPACs and computers with internet access for the children's section.

COMPUTERS

The number of non-OPAC computers designated specifically for children in the children's sections of Libraries A, B, C, and D varies from zero to six. Most of these computers, however, are similar in age, ranging from two to three years old. Three out of four children's librarians felt that the children's section would benefit from having more computers, while only one expressed a need for newer computers. Children's Librarian B, with six computers in the children's section, insisted that at this time, her staff needed computers more than her patrons.

All four libraries distinguish between computers intended for children versus computers intended for adults, although they do not necessarily prohibit adults from using computers in the children's section. Library C stands out for not making computers available in the children's section. This distinction, however, is the result of limited physical space, rather than a philosophical choice. Moreover, all four children's librarians mentioned space issues when discussing inclusion of computers in the children's section.

In addition, they reported placing computers near the children's or adults' information desk. Likewise, they suggested that placement of computers contributed to use significantly. At Libraries A and D, where the computers are or were located at the entrance into the children's section, both children's librarians described active computer use. Indeed, they alluded to the almost magnetic effect of computers on young children in particular.

Libraries A, B, C, and D differ in the amount and variety of software available on computers in the children's section. Library A offers word processing and educational prog-rammes/games; Library B offers internet access only; Library C offers internet access primarily, as well as word processing and some educational programmes/games; and Library D offers educational CD-ROMs only. Children's Librarians A and B suggested that children might enjoy having a greater selection of games to choose from, but neither felt that more software was necessary.

Children's Librarian D wanted more CD-ROMs related to reading, but was particularly interested in developing a homework center for more research- oriented computer use. For the most part, Children's Librarians A, B, C, and D agreed that most of the software available in the children's section is age-appropriate and appealing to their audience, although each librarian gave at least one anecdotal example of inappropriate use of computers.

For instance, Children's Librarian A highlighted a game about dinosaurs intended for older children, which appeals to younger children who are unable to use it successfully. Similarly, both Children's Librarians B and C noted observing older children engaged in questionable internet activities, such as using chat rooms in an inappropriate manner or printing out explicit song lyrics. sIn terms of money allocation for technology, all four librarians demonstrated little knowledge concerning budge-ting for computers in the children's section.

Children's Librarian A suggested that she and Library A's director would decide on the amount of money she could spend on computers; Children's Librarian B explained that the children's section's budget for computers was determined by the Computer Operations department; and Children's Librarian D said that her county library system established the amount of money designated for computers. Clearly, allocation of money for computer services varies, especially in a year of budget cuts and crises.

Interestingly, children's Librarian A called attention to a unique concern for children's librarians regarding staff training and new technology. While acknowledging that Library A "could come up with some money" for staff training on computers, she suggested that most "workshops offered by the state library usually have to do with online reference questions and NC Live."

Seesmingly, little training exists for the computer interactions children's librarians are most likely to observe, monitor, and guide in the children's section.

STAFF

The children's sections of Libraries A, B, C, and D employ a range of full-time, part-time, professionally trained, and non-professionally trained staff. Library B's children's section supports the largest staff, with two full-time librarians, two part-time librarians, one full-time library assistant, two part-time library assistants, and floaters, while Library A's children's section supports the second largest staff, with three full-time librarians and two part-time librarians.

Both Libraries C and D employ only one full-time librarian and one part-time library assistant in their children's sections. While staff numbers certainly reflect the size of each library's children's section, they also affect the quality of computer services these libraries are able to offer. It is not surprising that Libraries A and B not only provide more computers, but also report high levels of computer use among their patrons. Despite variation in staff numbers, however, all four children's librarians consistently expressed a desire for more staff, especially for assistance with programming.

Children's Librarian C, in particular, explained that until Library C has a children's information desk, the inclusion of computers in the children's section will not be possible. It is noteworthy that all four children's librarians to participate in this study feel that they are understaffed to meet the demands of the children's section.

While three out of four children's librarians described monitoring computers to be a constant staff responsibility, few viewed it as an overwhelmingly demanding task. Despite feeling understaffed, when asked if they spent a dispropor-tionate amount of time monitoring computer use two out of four children's librarians disagreed. In fact, most of the time staff spends monitoring computer use appears to be related to procedure.

For example, Library B, which uses an automated sign-in procedure, demands a markedly smaller portion of children's staff's time. Indeed, Children's Librarian B reported spending only ten per cent of her day addressing computer-related issues. This finding indicates that a combination of offering more computers, more staff, and automated sign-in reduces staff involvement in monitoring computer use dramatically.

PROCEDURES

Libraries A, B, C, and D utilize a variety of procedures for using computers in the children's section. Both Libraries A and C use a manual sign-in procedure, in which patrons sign their names and other pertinent information to a list in order to use the computers. Library B uses an automated sign-in procedure, in which patrons enter their library card numbers to gain access to computers. Library D operates on a first come, first serve basis, allowing patrons to use the children's computer any time it is available.

Library D's internet access computers, however, involve a manual sign-in procedure. All four children's librarians report that these procedures work fairly well, with patrons following the rules properly, although Library B's procedure stands out as the most problem-free. While Children's Librarians A, C, and D must devote a significant part of their time to monitoring procedure, Library B's children's staff's involvement with computer procedure is notably hands-off.

Accordingly, Children's Librarians A, C, and D suggest that their procedures could be improved, although they also express some hesitancy about changing current practices. These findings demonstrate a need for improved procedure for computer use in the children's section, but a reluctance to depart from the status quo.

Most libraries require patrons to be a certain age to use computers independently. Library A insists that children nine years old and younger be supervised by an adult while using the computer. Because Library B's computers are filtered, children of any age may use the computers independently. Library C requires patrons to be eighteen years old or older, or have signed parental consent, to use their internet access computers without supervision.

Library D allows children of all ages to use the computer located in the children's section, since this computer is not connected to the internet, but uses educational CD-ROMs only. They require children to be twelve years old or older, or have signed parental consent, to use their internet access computers independently. Children's Librarians A, B, C, and D unanimo-usly support these age requirements for a variety of reasons.

For example, Children's Librarian D speaks to both safety and legality issues related to the internet, noting that there is a lot of information on the internet that children "don't need to get into." Similarly, Children's Librarian A points out that younger children often do not have the manual dexterity or the maturity to operate computers without adult help. All four children's librarians demonstrate both a keen sensitivity and a vigilant awareness about children's safe and acceptable use of computers.

In turn, Libraries A, B, C, and D all have written policies dictating appropriate computer use. Library A's "Rules of Conduct for Children's Personal Computers" stipulates fifteen guidelines for using computers in the children's section. Library B's "Internet Use Statement" offers county and state statutes regarding internet use, and appears on both its website and its automated sign-in page.

Library C posts a county "Policies and Procedures: Computer Use Policy" sheet, which includes specific information about computer use by children. Library D requires parents with children twelve years old and under to read and sign its "Internet Use Guidelines." All of these policies are determined by library, county, and state authorities, and posted with computers and at sign-in stations. Indeed, it is evident that all four libraries take child protection and responsible computer use seriously.

PATRONS

Children's librarians A, B, C, and D estimate that children spend different amounts of time on the computer, ranging from thirty minutes to several hours.

At Libraries A and C, however, computer use is limited to a certain length of time. For instance, at Library A, children may only stay on the computer for thirty minutes, unless no one else is waiting for a turn. According to all four children's librarians, educational and recreational games are by far the most popular applications. Even on Library B's internet access computers, Children's Librarian B reports that children most frequently visit online game sites.

At both Libraries A and D, reading games/programmes are especially well-liked by children. Three out of four children's librarians say that they would prefer to see their patrons spending their time engaged in activities other than using computers, such as reading books, doing research, and attending programmes. In particular, Children's Librarians B, C, and D mention that they would like their patrons to show more interest in books and reading, or at least demonstrate an equal balance between time spent with computers and time spent with books. Interestingly, Children's Librarian. A describes her young patrons as "big readers," so perhaps it is not surprising that she is unconcerned by the amount of time they spend on the computers. Children's Librarians A, B, C, and D observe different age groups using the computers most often. Children's Librarians A and D report that three to five year olds are their most enthusiastic computer users; Children's Librarian B reports that six to twelve year olds are her most enthusiastic computer users; and Children's Librarian C reports that children nine years old to the early teens are her most enthusiastic computer users. Children's Librarian A speculates that preschoolers may appear to use the computer most often simply because they patronize the library most frequently.

Similarly, Children's Librarian B has the impression that six to twelve year olds show more persistence on the computers than three to five year olds. It is interesting to note that computers are most popular among young children in the libraries with educational games/programmes and CD-ROMs, whereas they are most popular among older children in the libraries with internet access. Although this distinction may be related to age requirements regarding internet use, it is possible that games are more appealing to younger children, while the internet is more appealing to older children.

In addition, Children's Librarians A and B both claim not to have any preference for which age groups use the computers. Children's Librarian C feels that younger children should spend more time with educational, reading-related games/programmes, while older children should spend less time on the computers in general. Children's Librarian D, on the other hand, believes that young children should have access to and experience with computers, but wishes that their interactions did not revolve around play alone. Overall, Children's Librarians A, B, C, and D feel mixed about which age groups should be spending the most and least amount of time on computers in the children's section.

ATTITUDES AND RESPONSES

When asked what they consider to be the purpose of having computers in the children's section, Children's Librarians A, B, C, and D offer a variety of thoughtful and compelling responses. These purposes include providing access to children who do not have computers at home; attracting patrons to the library; offering resources in a variety of formats; promoting a love of reading and fostering the pursuit of knowledge; supplying timely and sometimes obscure information; enhancing research and reading skills; and helping children explore their areas of interest.

Interestingly, none of the children's librarians repeated the same potential reason for offering computer services in the children's section. This array of responses not only indicates the different ways children's librarians perceive computers, but also demonstrates the plethora of opportunities that computers can afford in the children's section of the public library.

Further, while three out of four children's librarians express some ambivalence about the fulfillment of these potential purposes, most appear to feel that computers are a positive addition to the children's section. Similarly, all four children's librarians believe that computers complement the mission and goals of children's services, which most often included inspiring children's excitement about reading and learning. Finally, when Children's Librarians A, B, C, and D were asked to characterize their overall impressions of computer use in the children's section as positive or negative, three out of four claimed to feel positively. Children's Librarian D's impressions were mixed based on her opinion that computers should be used primarily for educational, rather than recreational purposes. She acknowledged, however, the potential benefits of inclusion of computers in the children's section. Children's librarians' positive impressions act as a promising predictor of the future of computer services in the children's section of the public library. Indeed, these results reflect children's librarians' commitment to providing exemplary computer services to their patrons.

CONCLUSION

This study addresses many of the issues discussed in current literature about children and computers. First, it offers further anecdotal evidence of children's librarians' perceptions of computers. In particular, it shows that children's librarians are demonstrating increased comfort and enthusiasm for computers. Although Children's Librarians A, B, C, and D observed some problems related to computer use, they are working to remedy these challenges. Further, they showed attention to the developmental needs and abilities of young children by implementing age and adult supervision requirements, as well as by creating thoughtful policies dictating computer use.

Moreover, quality computers and software appeal to their patrons' educational and recreational needs. In addition, all four children's librarians underscored the importance of providing computer access to children who do not have computers at home. Such actions affirm the suggestions of children's services experts. They speak to the concerns of authors who worry about the potentially negative effects of computer use on young children. Children's Librarians A, B, C, and D exhibited careful consideration, sensitivity, and responsibility to children regarding computer services in the children's sections of their libraries.

Specifically, the results of this study yield patterns and similarities that reveal the strengths and weaknesses of current practices in the children's section of the public library. Strengths include: availability of quality computers and software in the children's section; children's staff's level of interaction with computers; improved sign-in procedures for using computers; clear and prominent policies guiding computer use; appropriate age requirements for computer use; and children's librarians' positive attitudes towards the inclusion of computers in the children's section. Weaknesses include: children's librarians' involvement in budgeting for computers; lack of staff; outmoded sign-in procedures for computer use; inappropriate use of computers by children; and children's diminished interest in books and reading.s

Thus, this research offers several implications for future practice in the children's section of the public library. First, it is apparent that many libraries must address larger concerns, such as providing adequate space, child-appro-priate shelving, and a children's information desk, before incorporating computers into their children's sections. For those libraries that already include computer services in their children's sections, most require both more and newer computers to meet the demands of their patrons. Second, children's staff need better training on how to provide excellent computer services.

Computer training should focus on applications that children's librarians will encounter on the computers in the children's section, thus engendering confidence and enthusiasm. Third, children's librarians should have the opportunity to participate in developing a budget for computer services. Further, they should be involved in shaping all aspects of library policy that affect the children's section. Fourth, children's services in most public libraries require more staff. Increased staff would benefit all parts of the children's section, including reference, reader's advisory, programming, and outreach, in addition to computer services.

Fifth, procedures for computer use should be improved. Automated sign- in procedures appear to be most effective and efficient. Sixth, children and young adults require guidance when using the computers in the children's section of the public library. While most libraries insist that young children be supervised by an adult, it would be helpful for older children to be reminded of what constitutes appropriate computer use. Lastly, the children's section of the public library must attempt to strike a compromise between computer services and other more traditional services, such as the promotion of recreational reading.

The results of this study also reveal a number of tensions regarding computers in the children's section of the public library. For instance, three out of four children's librarians claimed to need more computers. Yet based on current evidence, having more computers would result in the need for greater staff involvement monitoring their use, when children's librarians already report being understaffed.

Moreover, several children's librarians expressed ambivalence about children's current interactions with computers. Perhaps it is necessary for children's librarians to address these concerns before introducing not only more computers, but also a greater variety of software or internet access. At this crucial stage of growth and development, it is particularly important that children's librarians define children's services' role in offering computers. Implementing good procedures for computer use represents another step towards ensuring children's staff's increased satisfaction with computers. Also, while all four children's librarians felt that having computers in the children's section complements the mission and goals of children's services, most were anxious to see a better balance between computer use and reading.

In addition, they noted that games are by far the most popular computer activity in the children's section. It is unlikely that when children's librarians speak of promoting access and providing service, that they are referring to computer game use. For this reason, children's services must attempt to reconcile their conflicting attitudes towards informational, educational, and recreational computer use. In many ways, the tensions children's librarians face in introducing computers to the children's section reflect larger issues for children's services as a whole. Some of these issues include appropriate adult supervision of children, the children's section's role as a place of education or recreation, and children's librarians' commit-ment to promoting reading.

This study's findings also demonstrate the symbiotic relationship between computers, children's staff, procedures for computer use, patrons, and, in turn, children' staff's attitudes and responses to computers. To be sure, placing computers in the children's section of the public library necessarily demands the time and consideration of children's librarians. Next, procedure functions as the vehicle for negotiating the level of interaction between computers and children's librarians in making this service accessible to children. Further, children's use of the computers demands the attention of children's staff. Thus, children's librarians involvement with patrons, proce-dures, and computers shape their overall attitudes and responses to computers in the children's section. Indeed, children's librarians represent the frontline of children's services at the public library.

For this reason, their perceptions of computers are of considerable significance. Children's librarians have enormous influence over the way in which computers are implemented, utilized, and promoted. Because they act as a filter between the needs of children and the services the library provides, they are in an excellent position to gauge the degree to which computer use among their young patrons is successful, as well as to suggest ways in which it could be improved.

Although computer use in the children's section of the public library is on the rise, insufficient literature exists to document this phenomenon. By consulting children's librarians in North Carolina public libraries, this study not only reflects children's librarians' perceptions of computers, but also offers a portrait of computer services in the children's section of the public library today. In turn, these findings have the potential to shape future practices and to illuminate note-worthy tensions in the field of children's librarianship.

FUTURE RESEARCH

As with any research based on case studies, the results of this study reflect only a small sample of the target population of children's librarians in the public libraries of North Carolina. For this reason, interviewing a greater number of children's librarians would ensure more reliable and conclusive data. Further, a national, rather than a regional, study might reveal significant trends in children's librarians' perceptions of computers.

Current literature indicates a growing disparity in computer access between more affluent public libraries and their less fortunate counterparts, which could in turn affect children's librarians' attitudes and responses towards new technology. Also, employing a different research method, such as conducting telephone or mail surveys, would make it possible to reach a greater number of research participants, although results would surely provide less detail.

Another study might involve children more directly, through observation, interviews, or surveys. In some ways, by removing the children's librarian or intermediary from the equation, this kind of research would address issues, such as appropriateness, more explicitly. Another study might compare computer use in the children's section of the public library with the school media center. Lastly, an additional approach to this area of research would address computer services geared towards adults. Such a study might utilize the insights of reference and reader's advisory librarians in the adult section of the public library.

In addition, each category of research in this study could be its own focus in a future study. For instance, procedures for computer use in the children's section of the public library alone, offer many potential avenues of exploration. Research projects related to this topic could include a study of the effectiveness of manual versus automated sign-in or the examination of various acceptable use policies. Similarly, research geared even more exclusively towards gathering children's librarians' perceptions of computers could prove useful to the field of children's librarianship. Attention to specific aspects of children's computer use, such as OPAC use, internet use, or educational game use might demonstrate whether the children's section is meeting the needs of its young patrons ssuccessfully.

Finally, conducting follow-up interviews with this study's research participants could be valuable. It would be interesting to chart levels of computer use over time, changing staff responsibilities with regard to computers in the children's section, revised procedures and policies related to computers, patterns of patron use, and ultimately, children's librarian's changing perceptions of computers. Also, it would be useful to gather more information about the children's librarians included in this study.

Experience, level of training, and professional background could be related to their perceptions of computers. For example, it is telling that the most recently graduated children's librarian involved in this study is also the most excited about computers in the children's section of the public library. Perhaps this distinction indicates that comfort with and enthusiasm for computers is, in part, related to age and experience with them. It is clear that the implementation, utilization, and promotion of computer services in the children's section of the public library is in a state of flux. As these services become a more integrated part of the public library, it is especially important that library and information science professionals document and respond to this phenomenon. Children's librarians should play a primary role in this process.

❒

16

Network Models

Digital Library systems are the computerized information storage and retrieval systems connected to computer networks and have maximum flexibility, durability, immunity, stability, scalability, accessibility and compatibility with other media at minimum cost, space and maintenance.

Library network provides transmission of information dissemination of catalogues; abstract and full text formats as well as various basic functions of libraries like acquiring, digitizing and archiving of contents.

The networking of library resources means that users or patrons can access the information from their desktops irrespective of their physical location. The library networks provides library without walls.

TRADITIONAL LIBRARY NETWORK MODEL

Traditional library network setup was established with Ethernet technology and fewer clients and server machines. Ethernet has become the most commonly used LAN (Local Area Network) technology worldwide.. More than 85% of all installed network connections are using Ethernet technology, according to International Data Corporation. As a transport protocol, Ethernet operates at 10Mbps data transmission speed and Layers 1 and 2 of the 7-layer OSI networking model, delivering its data packets to any device connected to the network cable. This type of network have very limited infrastructure.

The hardware and software is used make library network it includes one server machine and 5 to 10 client machines connected to gather. The server is responsible for all library related activities and like storage and retrievals. The same server runs library management software like SOUL and provides resources to the clients.The other hardware requires is hub/switch, network interface card

(NIC) etc. while software need is generally network client software and network card drives. The figure shows the typical library network. This setup has only one server, which provides library management information, database storing and retrieving, running library software for library with limited support for services.

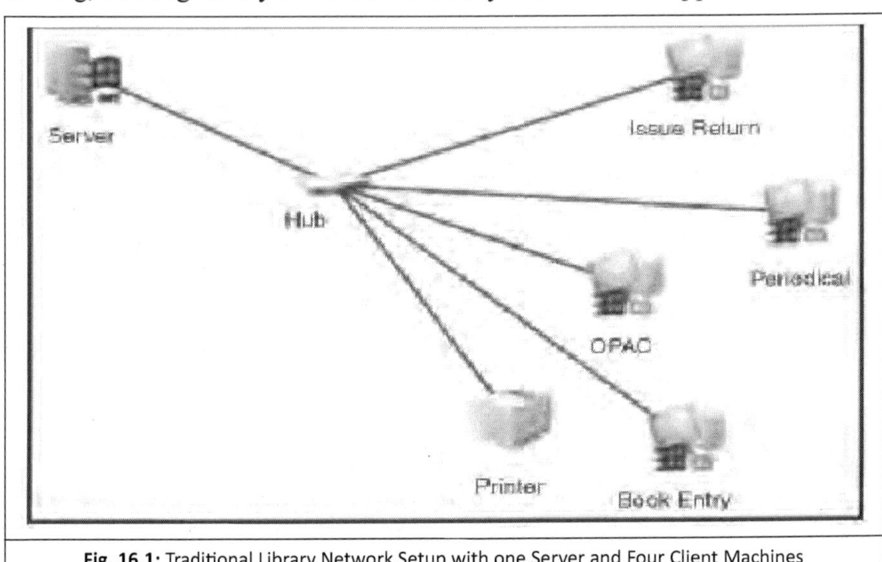

Fig. 16.1: Traditional Library Network Setup with one Server and Four Client Machines

GENERAL NETWORK MODEL

Traditional library networks model operate at 10Mbps speed. At these speed libraries that use extremely large files such as transferring audiovisual contents to desktop, can experience long delays when sending such data across the network. This model uses the extended version of Ethernet called fast Ethernet, which is simply, an extension of existing Ethernet technology, running 10 times faster at 100 Mbps. The general network setup for libraries is shown in figure. This setup model has two servers one for library applications and the other is for Internet access through remote location. These two servers provide information to switch, which is of 100Mbps.

Both the server NIC are of 100Mbps, which is little, bit higher then the traditional network setup. The figure shows four machines like issue return, periodical, OPAC and Admin machine are directly connected to switch with 100Mbps NIC installed on each machines, giving total bandwidth of 100Mbps. The Windows NT server provides user authen-tication and library management services to the various clients connected to it. While Internet server provides Internet services with remote online libraries, and Internet services .

HIGH SPEED NETWORK MODEL

Traditional and general setup model operates at 10/100Mbps speed, while high speed network operates at gigabit 1000Mbps speed. Easy and straightforward migration to higher performance level without disruption, low cost of ownership including purchase and support cost and flexibility in network design are prime criteria for the high speed network model. This model is 100 times faster than regular 10 Mbps Ethernet and 10 times faster than 100Mbps fast Ethernet. The high-speed model as shown in figure shows the server farm to switch connection is of 1000Mbps gigabit Ethernet.

This also employs the same protocol, same frame format and same frame size as its predecessors like 100Mbps fast Ethernet. This model setup has three main server connected to central switch with 1000Mbps gigabit data transmission speed. All three-server has gigabit Ethernet card Installed. The high speed network switch has 1000Mbps network link and distributes network traffic to four hub/switch segments like Internet services, digital content reading room, audiovisual learning and finally library management. Out of four hub/switch segments three are working at 100Mbps speed with 100Mbps fast Ethernet cards installed on each desktop machines.

The hub connection has also 100Mbps link support. The fourth segment named audiovisual self-learning as shown in figure needs more than 100Mbps because the data transmission is of high-end audio and video graphics files. Transferring this high bandwidth intensive file on the shared Ethernet makes network busy or low so that this segment must of 1000Mbps. This high-speed network segment provides simultaneous access to all the clients with streaming audio and video without any hustle form network speed. The high-speed performance is possible because the traffic is segmented. The figure shows library management, user authentication etc. services from windows-NT sever while NAS (Network Attached Storage) server provides database, digital books, thesis, journals audio and video learning material storage.

The NAS server has very large capacity storage with 1000Mpbs gigabit card installed on it. This server provides automatic storing and transfer of data on network with supporting domain server. IIS server provides Internet access and web services of any other digital library from Internet.

NETWORK SECURITY

The process of securing your library network begins with realizing what the library stands to lose if security is not pursued. Network security is not just "another thing to do." Its importance lies in protecting the library's network resources. Network resource means the equipment, software, and data that make up a networking system, including the user data that is shared over the network.

In terms of network communication, this includes the servers, workstations, hubs, switches, routers, firewalls, and telecommunications links that make up a network. In terms of usage, this includes shared printers, database systems, shared software, user accounts, the shared or user-specific files stored on a central server, and the keystrokes and form information that travel across the network.

IMPLEMENTING NETWORK SECURITY

We divide the realm of network security in libraries into seven main categories: physical security, password security, hardware security, server security, workstation security, perimeter security, and financial security These areas are expanded in the Checklist by separating out specific configuration issues related to web servers and general administrative issues related to budgeting, planning, and policy development.

There are many sections in the security checklist:

- General security.
- Physical security of computers and network equipment.
- Password security.
- Hardware security.
- Workstation security.
- Network server security.
- Network equipment security.
- Switch/Router/Hub security.
- Web server security.

LOCAL AREA NETWORK SECURITY

Securing any computer in a library must be achieved without any compromise to these three basic concepts: public service, user privacy and legal access. In an office or business environment, security is a matter of making sure those documents and transactions haven't been tampered with, corporate information is protected, personal employee information is kept private, and data is available when the business wants it to be. Network and computer security in a library setting faces these same challenges and a few additional ones. The major local area network security points are: Password Security, Hardware Security, Workstation Security, LAN/Domain Server Security, and Network Equipment Security. As a librarian we have to protect these levels of security in the network.

PASSWORD SECURITY

The least expensive and most important aspect of network security is the use of appropriate passwords.

Password protection is inherent in various aspects of the network:

- Administrative access to server functions
- Workstation access to various files and services (such as the Internet)
- Administrative access to network hubs, switches, routers, and firewalls
- Access to administrative files, such as confidential personnel files or reports

Here are the checklist items related to password security:

- Develop written password policy and provide to all staff and patrons using specific user logons

- Develop written instructions in creating strong passwords and provide to all staff and patrons using specific user logons
- Document passwords for all network equipment, servers, and workstations
- Store password documentation in secure location known only by library director and one other person

HARDWARE SECURITY

Hardware security is a convenient category used to classify miscellaneous items related to your computer and network hardware. The first set of items relate to the BIOS (the Basic Input/Output System) of your servers and workstations. The BIOS is a well-known feature on all Intel/AMD PCcompatible servers and workstations. It performs basic tests of internal components to be sure they are working satisfac-torily. It also stores and manages the configuration of many of the parts inside the CPU case.

WORKSTATION SECURITY

Properly securing workstations is a very important part of the overall network security in a library. There are a large number of configuration issues to address when securing workstations. Using the Windows NT Workstation/2000 Professional operating system provides a better security foundation than does Windows 98.

Those libraries using Windows 98 on public workstations are highly encouraged to install special software to secure many of the workstation functions:

- Configure NT Workstation/2000 Professional partitions with NTFS file systems.
- Windows NT/2000, unlike Windows 98, includes a feature known as file system security.

LAN/DOMAIN SERVER SECURITY

This chapter assumes the use of Windows NT/2000 as the library's server operating system. In most small library local area networks, there will be one or two servers: a main server, usually a domain controller under Windows NT/ 2000, which verifies the logins of all users, and a file server used with the library automation system. In some libraries, these two services are combined on one server.

It is possible to operate in a very small environment with just Windows NT Workstation/2000 Professional-based computers and no server at all, but it is more difficult to maintain security in this environment. So this base level of security assumes the presence of at least one server.

The following items are needed to secure the local area network servers in the library:

- Configure all NT Server partitions with NTFS file systems.
- Configure separate operating system and data partitions (both NTFS).
- Mirror server drives (or implement RAID), if funding allows, for redundancy.
- Configure servers with private IP addresses (LAN-wide recommendation).
- Remove unnecessary services.
- Remove unnecessary files/programmes.
- Configure file system with proper file/folder access permissions.
- Restrict access to the Network Monitor Agent.
- Disable anonymous user logons.
- Disable caching of user logons.
- Configure account policy to restrict unauthorized logon attempts.
- Create logon-warning message (a warning against unauthorized logon or access and use of restricted resources).
- Create alternative Administrators group and restrict membership.
- Restrict privileges of default Administrators group
- Create alternative Administrator account (with new name) with full privileges.
- Disable default Administrator account.
- Configure auditing of Administrator account logon attempts (to track hacking attempts).
- Set a strong password for current administrator account.
- Use different passwords for domain/server accounts than for local workstation accounts, or use different account names.
- Restrict access permissions for the everyone group.
- Disable Guest account if enabled.
- Create appropriate user and group accounts (minimum of three groups: Patrons, Staff, and Administrators).
- Set appropriate group access permissions.
- Implement procedures for file backups according to backup plan.
- Restrict access to backup programme.
- Create and maintain current Emergency Repair Disks, and store in a controlled location.
- File all server component documentation (papers/manuals/disks) for use by service technicians.

NETWORK EQUIPMENT SECURITY

Network equipment refers to all the devices required to get data signals from one computer to another. Generally, these include hubs, switches, routers, and firewalls. Libraries should be purchasing network equipment that provides management capabilities.

This provides the possibility of remote management of the network even if the library does not contract for that service initially:

- Set appropriate network management protocol (SNMP) passwords/ community strings
- Record and secure any password settings created by staff or contractors

These two items minimize the risk of network equipment configurations being altered by unauthorized personnel. When the library hires a vendor to install and configure network equipment, be sure to document all passwords used to secure the equipment. It is the library's responsibility to secure these passwords by documenting them and storing the documen-tation in a secure (preferably locked) location.

- Configure audit logs properly, if available
- Implement procedure for monitoring audit logs
- Schedule periodic installation of firmware updates
- Document equipment settings for future use in reconfiguring equipment
- File all network equipment documentation (papers/manuals/disks) for use by service technicians.

CONCLUSION

A Library network service is an assemblage of digital computing, storage and communication machinery together with the software needed to reproduce, emulate and extend the services provided by the conventional libraries.

The analysis of depicted models indicates that scalability in the increasing processing capabilities of digital computing of workstations and servers providing services to the clients, larger and larger storage needs and effective management of storage and increasing requirements of network bandwidth and high speed data transfer are the prime issues of infor-mation technologies. The library network once established is not secured from the administrators' point of view but must provide network security policy for servers, clients and other connectivity devices to provide satisfactory level of network security.

❒

17

Information Science and Library

THE ROLE AND PURPOSE OF THE PUBLIC LIBRARY

DEFINING THE PUBLIC LIBRARY

Public libraries are a world-wide phenomenon. They occur in a variety of societies, in differing cultures and at different stages of development. Although the varied contexts in which they operate inevitably result in differences in the services they provide, and the way those services are delivered, they normally have characteristics in common, which can be defined as follows. A public library is an organisation established, supported and funded by the community, either through local, regional or national government or through some other form of community organisation. It provides access to knowledge, information and works of the imagination through a range of resources and services and is equally available to all members of the community regardless of race, nationality, age, gender, religion, language, disability, economic and employment status and educational attainment.

THE PURPOSES OF THE PUBLIC LIBRARY

The primary purposes of the public library are to provide resources and services in a variety of media to meet the needs of individuals and groups for education, information and personal development including recreation and leisure. They have an important role in the development and maintenance of a democratic society by giving the individual access to a wide and varied range of knowledge, ideas and opinions.

Education

The need for an agency available to all, which provides access to knowledge in printed and other formats to support formal and informal education, has been the reason for the foundation and maintenance of most public libraries and remains a core purpose for the public library. Throughout their lives people require education either at formal institutions, for example, schools, colleges and universities, or in a less formal context related to their employment and daily life.

Learning does not end with the completion of formal education but is, for most people, a lifelong activity. In an increasingly complex society people will need to acquire new skills at various stages of their life. The public library has an important role in assisting this process. The public library should provide material in the appropriate media to support formal and informal learning processes.

It should also help the user to make use of these learning resources effectively as well as providing facilities that enable people to study. The ability to access information and make effective use of it is vital to successful education and, where possible, public libraries should co-operate with other educational organisations in teaching the use of information resources. Where adequate library facilities exist to support formal education the public library should complement them rather than duplicating library provision available elsewhere.

The public library should also actively support literacy campaigns, as literacy is the key to education and knowledge and to the use of libraries and information services. Newly literate people need easy access to appropriate reading materials to maintain and develop their skills. In some countries the need for educational development is seen to be paramount and the focus of public libraries is to support formal education. There are, however, a variety of ways in which public libraries can support both formal and informal education. How this is achieved will depend on the local context and the level of available resources.

Information

It is a basic human right to be able to have access to and an understanding of information, and there is now more information available than ever before in the world's history. As a public service open to all, the public library has a key role in collecting, organising and exploiting information, as well as providing access to a wide range of information sources. The public library has a particular responsibility to collect local information and make it readily available. It also acts as a memory of the past by collecting, conserving and providing access to material relating to the history of the community and of individuals. In providing a wide range of information the public library assists the community in informed debate and decision-making on key issues. In collecting and providing information the public library should, wherever possible, co-operate with other agencies to make the best use of available resources. The rapid growth in the volume of available information and the continuing technological changes, which have radically affected the way information is accessed, have already made a significant effect on public libraries and their services. Information is very important to the development of the individual and of society, and information technology gives considerable power to those able to access and use it.

Despite its rapid growth it is not available to the majority of the world's population, and the gap between the information rich and the information poor continues to widen. A vital role for the public library is to bridge that gap by providing public access to the Internet as well as providing information in traditional formats. Public libraries should recognise and exploit the opportunities provided by the exciting developments in information and communications technology. They have the opportunity to become the electronic gateway to the information world.

Personal Development

The opportunity to develop personal creativity and pursue new interests is important to human development. To achieve this, people need access to knowledge and works of the imagination. The public library can provide access, in a variety of different media, to a rich and varied store of knowledge and creative achievement, which individuals cannot acquire on their own behalf. Providing access to major collections of the world's literature and knowledge, including the community's own literature, has been a unique contribution of the public library and is still a vitally important function.

Access to works of the imagination and knowledge is an importantcontribution to personal education and meaningful recreational activity. The public library can also make a fundamental contribution to daily survival and social and economic development by being directly involved in providing information to people in developing communities; for example, basic life skills, adult basic education and AIDS awareness programmes. In communities with a high illiteracy rate the public library should provide services for non-literates and interpret and translate information where necessary. It should also provide basic user education.

CHILDREN AND YOUNG PEOPLE

The public library should attempt to meet the needs of all groups in the community regardless of age and physical, economic or social circumstances. However, it has a special responsibility to meet the needs of children and young people. If children can be inspired by the excitement of knowledge and by works of the imagination at an early age, they are likely to benefit from these vital elements of personal development throughout their lives, both enriching them and enhancing their contribution to society. Children can also encourage parents and other adults to make use of the library. It is also important that young people who experience difficulty in learning to read should have access to a library to provide them with appropriate material. Public Libraries and Cultural Development

An important role of the public library is providing a focus for cultural and artistic development in the community and helping to shape and support the cultural identity of the community. This can be achieved by working in partnership with appropriate local and regional organisations, by providing space for cultural activity, organising cultural programmes and by ensuring that cultural interests are represented in the library's materials. The library's contribution should reflect the variety of cultures represented in the community. It should provide materials in the languages spoken and read in the local community, and support cultural traditions.

The Social Role of the Public Library

The public library has an important role as a public space and meeting place. This is particularly important in communities where there are few places for people to meet. It is sometimes called 'the drawing room of the community'. Use of the library for research and for finding information relating to the user's education and leisure interests, brings people into informal contact with other members of the community. Using the public library can be a positive social experience.

AN AGENCY FOR CHANGE

In carrying out its role in these key areas the public library is acting as an agency for social and personal development and can be a positive agency for change in the community. By providing a wide range of materials to support education and by making information accessible to all, the public library can bring economic and social benefits to individuals and to the community. It contributes to the creation and maintenance of a well–informed and democratic society and helps to empower people in the enrichment and development of their lives and that of the community in which they live. The public library should be aware of the issues that are being discussed within the community and provide information that will inform that debate.

FREEDOM OF INFORMATION

The public library should be able to represent all ranges of human experience and opinion, free from the risk of censorship. In some countries a Freedom of Information Act will help to ensure these rights are maintained. Librarians and governing bodies should uphold these basic human rights and resist pressure from individuals and groups to limit the material available inthe public library.

ACCESS FOR ALL

A fundamental principle of the public library is that its services must be available to all and not directed to one group in the community to the exclusion of others. Provision should be made to ensure services are equally available to minority groups who for some reason are not able to use the mainstream services, for example, linguistic minorities, people with physical and sensory disabilities or those living in remote communities who are unable to reach library buildings.

The level of funding, development of services, the design of libraries and their opening hours should all be planned with the concept of universal access as a basic principle. The development of collections should also be based on the principle of access for all and include access to formats appropriate to specific client groups, for example, Braille and talking books for blind people. Information and communications technology should be used to allow access to the library's collections and those of other information sources, both from within the library or from remote sites.

LOCAL NEEDS

Public libraries are locally based services for the benefit of the local community and should provide community information services. The services and collections they provide should be based on local needs, which should be assessed regularly. Without this discipline the public library will get out of touch with those it is there to serve and will, as a result, not be used to its full potential. Librarians should, therefore, be aware of the changes in society arising from such factors as social and economic development, demographic change, variations in the age structure, levels of education, patterns of employment and the emergence of other educational and cultural providers.

LOCAL CULTURE

The public library should be a key agency in the local community for the collection, preservation and promotion of local culture in all its diversity. This can be achieved in a variety of ways, for example, the maintenance of local history collections, exhibitions, storytelling, publishing of items of local interest and developing interactive programmes on local themes. Where the oral tradition is an important method of communication the public library should encourage its continuation and development.

THE CULTURAL ROOTS OF THE PUBLIC LIBRARY

It is important to the long-term success of the library that it should be based on the culture, or cultures, of the country or area in which it operates. It is less likely to succeed if the form and structure of the public library are introduced from a country or area with a very different cultural background.

LIBRARIES WITHOUT WALLS

In developing policies to fulfil the role and purpose of the public library the emphasis should be on the services it provides. In meeting the needs of its community the public library will provide a range of services, some of which can be most effectively delivered from a library building. However, there will be many circumstances where it is more effective to provide the service beyond the walls of the library.

Examples will vary in different societies but the principle of planning library development from a service rather than a building perspective is important in all public library policy development. The provision of services using information and communications technology also presents exciting opportunities to take library and information services direct to the home and the workplace. A variety of forms of transport are used to deliver services to sparsely populated areas. The provision of library and information services to people unable to visit a library due to physical or sensory disability or lack of transport, for example, ensures that access to these services is available to all at their home or workplace regardless of their circumstances.

LIBRARY BUILDINGS

Library buildings play an important part in public library provision. They should be designed to reflect the functions of the library service, be accessible to all in the community and be sufficiently flexible to accommodate new and changing services. They should be located close to other community activities, for example, shops and cultural centres.

Wherever possible the library should also be available for community use, for example, for meetings and exhibitions and in larger buildings for theatrical, musical, audiovisual and media performances. A well used public library will make a significant contribution to the vitality of an urban area and be an important learning and social centre and meeting place, particularly in scattered rural areas. Librarians should, therefore, ensure that library buildings are used and managed effectively to make the best use of the facilities for the benefit of the whole community.

RESOURCES

To fulfil its roles satisfactorily the public library must have adequate resources, not just when it is established but also on a continuing basis, to enable it to sustain and develop services that meet the needs of the local community.

This means it should provide materials in all formats, up-dated regularly to meet the changing needs of groups and individuals, including newly-published and replacement materials. It should also provide adequate levels of staff with appropriate training and sufficient funds to support whatever methods of service delivery are needed for it to meet its vital role in the community.

THE LEGAL AND FINANCIAL FRAMEWORK

Public libraries are a community agency providing access at local level to a range of knowledge and information for the benefit of the individual and society as a whole. In order to maintain the level of service required to fulfil their functions public libraries should be supported by legislation and sustained funding.

THE PUBLIC LIBRARY AND GOVERNMENT

There are many different models of the relationship between public libraries and government. Equally, the laws that govern their activities and funding arrangements are varied and complex. In different countries, provinces, regions, states or municipalities are, either in whole or in part, responsible for library services. As public libraries are a locally based service local government is often the most appropriate place in the government structure for them. However, in some countries public libraries are provided at regional or state level and the national library sometimes has responsibility for providing the public library service. There are instances of two or more levels of government co-operating in the provision of the service.

Alternative Structures

In some countries, although the local authority has nominal responsibility for the public library, it does not have the required funds and non-governmental organisations or private foundations undertake the practical operation of the public library services.

However, to ensure sustained development and its role in the information network, the public library should be closely related to and funded by the appropriate level of government. The eventual aim should be to bring public libraries into the formal government structure operating under national legislation and with appropriate levels of funding.

National Information Policies

In order to make the most effective use of available library and information resources, and take full advantage of the opportunities offered by the development of electronic information sources, many countries are developing national information policies.

Public libraries should be a key element in such policies and public librarians should ensure they are fully involved in their development.

PUBLIC LIBRARY LEGISLATION

Public libraries should be based on legislation, which assures their continuance and their place in the government structure. Public library legislation takes various forms. In some countries or regions the legislation is specific to public libraries whereas in others it is part of wider legislation which includes different types of libraries. Public library legislation is also varied in its provisions. It can be simple, allowing the establishment of public libraries but leaving standards of service to the level of government directly responsible for the library, or more complex, with specific detail on what services should be provided and to what standard. Examples of public library legislation are available on the IFLA web site. Because governmental structures vary so much in different countries the form and detail of public library legislation is also likely to vary significantly. However, legislation governing public libraries should state which level of government is responsible for their provision and how they should be funded. It should also place them in the framework of libraries in the country or region as a whole.

Related Legislation

Public libraries are subject to a range of legislation apart from the specific legislation relating to them. This can include legislation on financial management, data protection, health and safety and staff conditions and there will be many other examples. Library managers should be aware of all legislation affecting the operation of the public library. They should also be aware of global trade negotiations, which can result in policies and agreements, which could have a serious impact on public libraries. In such cases librarians should take every opportunity to bring the effect of such policies on public libraries to the notice of the public and politicians.

Copyright

Copyright legislation, especially that relating to electronic publications, is of particular importance to public libraries. It is constantly subject to amendment and review and librarians should keep up-to-date with the legislation in relation to all media. Librarians should promote and support copyright legislation, which achieves an equitable balance between the rights of creators and the needs of users.

Public Lending Right

In some countries, public lending right legislation has been introduced which provides a payment to authors and others involved in the creation of a book, related to its provision in, and loan from, public libraries. It is important that funds for payment of public lending right should not be taken from libraries' funds for the purchase of materials. However, public lending right, if separately funded, does provide support for authors without affecting public libraries' budgets. In some schemes it can also provide useful statistics on the loans of books by specific authors. Librarians should participate in the development of public lending right schemes to ensure they are not financedfrom library budgets.

FUNDING

Adequate levels of funding are crucial to the success of a public library in fulfilling its roles. Without suitable levels of funding over the long-term it is impossible to develop policies for service provision and make the most effective use of available resources. This can be seen in number of examples: a new library building without adequate funds to maintain it, collections of new books with no money for their replacement and computer systems without funds to maintain and update them. Funding is required not only when a public library is established, but should also be sustained on an assured and regular basis.

Priorities

A public library and the services it provides is a long-term investment on behalf of the community and should be funded appropriately. It is recognised that even in the wealthiest of societies it may not be possible to provide appropriate levels of funding for every service requirement. It is vitally important, therefore, that service development should be conducted on a planned basis with clear priorities. This process is necessary whatever level of funding is available to the library service. To determine strategic planning and the maintenance of agreed priorities, written policy statements should be developed for services. They should be reviewed at regular intervals and revised where necessary.

Partnership

No public library, however large and well funded, can meet all the needs of its users on its own. Participation in partnerships and networks with other libraries and related organisations, and the provision of access to other sources of information, enables the public library to satisfy the information needs of its users by increasing the range of available resources.

Sources of Funding

A number of sources of funding are used to finance public libraries but the proportions of funding from each source will vary depending on local factors in each country.

The primary sources are:

- Taxation at local, regional or central level
- Block grants from central, regional or local level.
- Secondary sources of income may include:
- Donations from funding bodies or private individuals
- Revenue from commercial activities, e.g., publishing, book sales, sale of works of art and handicrafts
- Revenue from user fees, e.g., fines
- Revenue from charges to users for individual services, e.g., photocopying and printing facilities
- Sponsorship from external organisations
- Lottery funds for specific initiatives.

Charging the User

The IFLA/UNESCO Public Library Manifesto states: 'The public library shall in principle be free of charge'. Charging users for services and membership should not be used as a source of revenue for public libraries, as it makes the ability to pay a criterion in determining who can use a public library. This reduces access and therefore breaches the fundamental principle that the public library should be available to all. It is recognised that in some countries subscriptions to join the library or charges for specific services are levied. Such charges inevitably deny access to those unable to afford them.

They should be seen as an interim situation and not as a permanent feature of public library funding. It is common in some countries to ask users to pay a fee or fine when keeping an item after it is due for return to the library. This is sometimes necessary to ensure that items are kept in circulation and not retained for a long time by one user. The fine should not be set at a level that would deter anyone from using the library. Charges are also sometimes levied for personalised services, for example photocopying or use of a printer. These charges should also not be set at a level which will deter the user.

Funding for Technology

Public libraries must, whenever possible, make use of the new technologies to improve their services and provide new ones. This means a considerable investment in various kinds of electronic equipment, and a reliance on this equipment for the delivery of services. To continue to perform effectively equipment should be upgraded and replaced. This has significant funding consequences and a plan for the replacement and upgrading of technological sequipment should be developed.

External Funding

Librarians should be imaginative in seeking external sources of funding for the public library. However, they should not accept funding from any source if, by so doing, the fundamental status of a public library as an agency available to all is compromised. Commercial organisations, for example, may offer funding with conditions which might prejudice the universal nature of the services provided by the public library.

THE GOVERNANCE OF THE PUBLIC LIBRARY

Public libraries should be governed by a properly established body made up largely of representatives of the local community including those elected either to the local council or to the library board. Library committees and boards should have rules of procedure and their proceedings should be open to the general public. They should meet on a regular basis and publish agenda, minutes, annual reports and financial statements. Normally the governing body will be responsible for matters of policy rather than the day-to-day operation of the library. In all cases the chief librarian should have direct access to the meetings of the governing body of the library and work closely with it. Policy documents should be made available to the public and, where possible, steps should be taken to involve local citisens in the development of the public library.

Public librarians must be fully accountable both to their governing bodies and local citizens for their actions by providing reports, holding public meetings and through consultation. They must also maintain the highest professional standards in carrying out their duties and in advising the governing body.

Although the final decisions on policy will be taken by the governing body and the librarian, ways should be sought to involve the local citizens who are the actual or potential library users. The concept of a 'library charter', which identifies and publicises the level of service the public library provides has been developed in some countries. This establishes a 'contract' between the public library and the users. Library charters have more credibility if they are developed in consultation with users.

THE ADMINISTRATION OF THE PUBLIC LIBRARY

Public libraries should be well managed and administered. The administration of a public library should be directed towardss improving the quality of service to the users and not as an end in itself. It should be efficient and accountable.

To get best results the administrative and manageent staff of a large public library service should be multidisciplinary, involving staff with specialist skills, for example, librarians, accountants, public relations officers and system managers. It may also be necessary to draw on the expertise of staff of the parent authority or other related organisation in certain areas, for example, lawyers, payroll and pensions staff.

PUBLICITY AND PROMOTION

Public libraries operate in an increasingly complex society, which makes many calls on people's time and attention. It is important, therefore, that libraries publicise their presence and the range of services they provide. Publicity ranges from simple techniques, like signs on library buildings stating what they are, and leaflets advertising opening hours and services, to more sophisticated methods like marketing programmes and the use of web sites to promote the library's services and activities.

MEETING THE NEEDS OF THE USERS

To be successful in fulfilling its goals the public library service must be fully accessible to all its potential users. Any limitation of access, whether deliberate or accidental, will reduce the ability of the public library to fully achieve its primary role of meeting the library and information needs of the community it serves.

The following are important elements in delivering an effective public library service:

- Identifying potential users
- Analysing users' needs
- Developing services to groups and individuals
- Introducing customer care policies
- Promoting user education
- Co-operating and sharing resources
- Developing electronic networks
- Ensuring access to services
- Providing library buildings.

IDENTIFYING POTENTIAL USERS

The public library has to aim to serve all citizens and groups. An individual is never too young or too old to use a library.

- The public library has the following potential target groups.
- People at all ages and at all stages of life:
- Children
- Young adults
- Adults.

Individuals and groups of people with special needs:

- People from different cultures and ethnic groups including indigenous people
- People with disabilities, e.g., blind and partially sighted, hearing impaired Housebound people
- Institutionally confined people, e.g., in hospitals, prisons.

Institutions within the wider community network:

- Educational, cultural and voluntary organisations and groups in the community
- The business community
- The governing body of the parent organisation, e.g., local authority.

As resources are limited in even the wealthiest society it is not always possible to serve all users to the same level. The library must establish priorities based on an analysis of user needs and related to their access to alternative sservices.

ANALYSING NEEDS WITHIN THE COMMUNITY

It is important to establish who uses and who does not use the library service. It is also necessary to collect and analyse data that identifies those needs of individuals and groups within the community that can be met by the public library.

SERVICES TO USERS

The public library must provide services based on an analysis of the library and information needs of the local community. In planning services, clear priorities must be established and a strategy be developed for service provision in the medium to long term. Services should be developed for identified target groups and only provided if such groups exist in the local community.

The services of the library should not be subject to any form of ideological, political, religious or commercial pressure. Services must be able to adjust and develop to reflect changes in society, for example, variations in family structures, employment patterns, demographic changes, cultural diversity and methods of communication.

They should take account of traditional cultures as well as new technologies, for example, support for oral methods of communication as well as making use of information and communication technology. In some countries the services that the public library must provide are defined in library legislation.

Service Provision

Public libraries provide a range of services, both within the library and in the community, to satisfy their users' needs. The library should facilitate access to its services for all, including those who have difficulty reading print.

The following services, which should be easily accessible to the user in a variety of formats and media, should be provided:

- Loan of books and other media
- Provision of books and other materials for use in the library
- Information services using print and electronic media
- Readers' advisory services including reservation services
- Community information services
- User education including support for literacy programmes
- Programming and events.

This is not an exhaustive list but an indication of some of the key services of the public library. The range and depth of provision will depend on the size of the library and the community it serves.

Every library should aim to be an active participant in one or more networks, which will give the user access to a wide range of material, however small the access point. Service provision should not be confined to the library building but also taken direct to the user where access to the library is not possible. In providing services, both within the library and beyond, use should be made of information and communications technology as well as the printed word.

Services to Children

By providing a wide range of materials and activities, public libraries provide an opportunity for children to experience the enjoyment of reading and the excitement of discovering knowledge and works of the imagination. Children and their parents should be taught how to make the best use of a library and how to develop skills in the use of printed and electronic media. Public libraries have a special responsibility to support the process of learning to read, and to promote books and other media for children. The library must provide special events for children, such as story telling and activities related to the library's services and resources.

Children should be encouraged to use the library from an early age as this will make them more likely to remain users in future years. In multilingual countries books and audiovisual materials for children should be available in their mother tongue.

Services for Young Adults

Young people between childhood and adulthood develop as individual members of society with their own culture.

Public libraries must understand their needs and provide services to meet them. Materials, including access to electronic information resources, that reflect their interests and culture should be provided.

In some cases this will mean acquiring materials that represent youth culture, in a variety of media that are not traditionally part of a library's resources, for example, popular novels, book and television series, music, video tapes, teenage magazines, posters, computer games, graphic novels.

It is important to enlist the help of young people in selecting this material to ensure that it reflects their interests. In larger libraries this material, with appropriate furniture, can form a special section of the library.

This will help them to feel that the library is for them and help to overcome a feeling of alienation from the library, which is not unusual among this age group. Relevant programmes and talks to young adults should also be provided.

SERVICES FOR ADULTS

Adults will have different requirements of an information and library service related to the variety of situations they will encounter in their studies, employment and personal life. These requirements should be analysed and services be developed on the outcome of that analysis.

They should include support for:

- Lifelong learning
- Leisure time interests
- Information needs
- Community activities
- Cultural activity
- Recreational reading.

Services meeting these needs should also be available to children and young adults.

Lifelong Learning

The public library supports lifelong learning, working with schools and other educational institutions to help students of all ages with their formal education. The challenge of providing educational support provides an opportunity for public libraries to interact and network with teachers and others involved in education.

The public library should also provide a range of materials on a variety of topics which will allow people to follow their interests and support their formal and informal education. It should also provide materials to support literacy and the development of basic life skills. In addition the library must provide study facilities for students who have inadequate or no access to these facilities in their homes. The development in distance learning is having an impact on the public library. Distant learners, studying at home, are likely to make use of their local library as their primary source for material. Many will require access to the Internet which the public library should provide. Public libraries play an increasingly important role within the educational network and should provide space and access to materials to meet this demand.

Leisure Time Interests

People need information to support their leisure time interests and meeting this need by a range of resources in a variety of formats is another key role of the public library. Public libraries must be aware of the cultural, social and economic changes in the community and develop services that are sufficiently flexible to adjust to these changes. The public library should also help to preserve the culture, history and traditions of the local community and make them readily available. The public library, by organising activities and exploiting its resources, should encourage artistic and cultural development in people of all ages. The library is also an important social centre for individuals and groups to meet both formally and informally. This is of special importance in communities where other meeting places are not available.

Information Services

The rapid development of information technology has brought a vast amount of information within reach of all those with access to electronic media. Information provision has always been a key role of the public library and the ways in which information can be collected, accessed and presented have changed radically in recent years.

The public library has a number of roles in providing information:

- Providing information about the local community and making it readily accessible, often in co-operation with other organisations.
- Training people of all ages in the use of information and the associated technology.
- Guiding users to the appropriate information sources Providing opportunities for disabled people to have independent access to information.
- Acting as a gateway to the information world by making it accessible to all, thus helping to bridge the gap between 'the information rich' and 'the information poor'.

The dramatic development of the Internet has been largely unstructured and uncontrolled. The vast amount of information that can be accessed via the Internet is of variable quality and accuracy and a key role of the librarian is to guide users to accurate information sources, which will meet their requirements.

Services to Community Groups

The public library should be at the centre of the community if it is to play a full part in its activities. It should, therefore, work with other groups and organisations in the community. This will include departments of government and local government, the business community and voluntary organisations.

An analysis of the information needs of these bodies should be conducted, and services be provided to meet these needs. This will not only help the organisations involved but will also demonstrate, in a practical way, the value of the public library to people in the community who are likely to have some influence on the future of the library service.

Many public libraries, for example, provide an information service to local government politicians and staff, giving a practical demonstration of the value of the public library.

Services to Special User Groups

Potential users who, for whatever reason, are unable to use the regular services of the library have a right to equal access to library services. The library should, therefore, establish ways of making library material and services accessible to these users.
These will include:

- Special transport, e.g., mobile libraries, book-boats and other forms of transport to serve those living in isolated areas.
- Services taken to the home of those people who are housebound.
- Services taken to factories and industrial premises for employees.
- Services for those confined in institutions, e.g., prisons and hospitals.
- Special equipment and reading materials for those with physical and sensory disabilities, e.g., hearing impaired and visually impaired people.
- Special materials for people with learning difficulties, e.g., easy-to- read materials and cassettes.
- Services for immigrants and new citizens to help them to find their way within a different society and to provide access to media of their native culture.
- Electronic communication, e.g., Internet catalogues.

Services for people with special needs can be enhanced by the use of new technology, for example, speech synthesisers for the visually impaired, online access catalogues for those in isolated areas or unable to leave their home, connections to remote sites for distance learning. Mainstream service provision, for example, public access catalogues (OPACs) can often be adapted to meet the needs of those with physical and sensory disabilities. Those who can benefit the most from technological developments are often the least able to afford the investment needed.

Innovative schemes should, therefore, be developed by the public library to exploit the new technology in order to make services available to as many people as possible. Services for ethnic groups in the community and for indigenous peoples should be developed in consultation with the group concerned.
They are likely to include:

- The employment of staff from the group in the library.
- Collections including the native literature of the group and reflecting the oral tradition and non-written knowledge of the people.
- The application of special conditions, developed in conjunction with local people, to culturally sensitive material.

Reading Promotion and Literacy

Reading, writing and the ability to use numbers are basic prerequisites to being an integrated and active member of society. Reading and writing are also the basic techniques needed for making use of new communication systems.

The public library should support activities that will enable people to make the best use of modern technology. It should support other institutions that are combating illiteracy and promoting media competence.
It can achieve this by:

- Promoting reading.
- Providing appropriate materials for those with poor literacy skills.
- Working with other agencies in the community involved in combating illiteracy.
- Participating in campaigns to combat illiteracy and improve numeracy
- Organising events to promote an interest in reading, literature and media culture.
- Promoting and providing training in the use of computer technology
- Promoting awareness of new developments in the media market.
- Helping people to find the information they need in the appropriate format.
- Co-operating with teachers, parents and other contact persons to help new citizens acquire the necessary educational skills that will help them to manage their lives in the new context.

The public library provides a range of creative literature and can use promotional techniques to bring its variety and range to the attention of its users. It can also organise interactive programmes that enable users to exchange views about books that they have read.

CUSTOMER CARE

The policies and procedures of the library should be based on the needs and convenience of the users and not for the convenience of the organisation and its staff.

Quality services can only be delivered if the library is sensitive to the needs of its users and shapes its services to meet those needs. Satisfied users are the best advocates of the library service. The public library should have a positive policy of customer care. This means ensuring that in all policy planning, design of libraries and of systems, preparation of operational procedures and drafting of information and publicity material, a positive effect on the user should be a prime objective. The following actions should be elements in a customer care policy:

- The image projected by all libraries must be neutral and objective.
- Staff should be courteous, friendly, respectful and helpful at all times.
- There should be a regular programme of staff training in customer care.
- All staff should receive basic awareness training on how to deal with people with disabilities or from ethnic minorities.
- Jargon should be avoided in all forms of communication, verbal and written.
- Staff should have a friendly and informative telephone manner.
- Methods of communication with the users must be provided, e.g., billboards, bulletins, web site.
- Library services should be properly planned, adequately prepared and reliable.
- The design of the library should be as convenient and inviting as possible.
- Opening hours should be convenient for the users.
- Open public access catalogues should be available on the Internet so that the user can access services from home and outside opening hours.
- There should be efficient renewal and reservation services.
- Services should be delivered beyond the library building when users' needs require it.
- Users should receive a response in the shortest possible time; letters and other forms of communication should be answered promptly and courteously.
- Equipment should be provided to make library use convenient, e.g., drop-in boxes for returning materials out of hours, self-service issue and return equipment in the library, answering machines for communicating with the library out of hours.
- All printed information about services should be available in appropriate alternative formats, e.g., large print, tape; they should also be available in minority languages.
- When resources allow, good quality electronic equipment should be provided in the library including special equipment for the partially sighted and hearing impaired.

User Participation

Customers should be involved in service development:

- By asking them through surveys what services they use and require.
- By analysing and responding to users' complaints.
- By monitoring users' reactions to services and new initiatives.
- By ensuring the input received from users is considered in the development of policy and procedures.
- By providing feedback to users about the effects of their input on service development.
- By providing suggestion boxes and a complaints and commendations procedure.

USER EDUCATION

The public library should help its users develop skills that will enable them to make the most effective use of the library's resources and services.

Library staff must act as information navigators to help users of all ages to make the most effective use of information and communications technology, and programmes of user education should be developed. As the new technologies become more commonly available, the role of the public library both in providing access to these technologies and in helping people learn how to make best use of them is of vital importance.

Guided tours of the library should take place regularly to introduce people to the library building and services and how to use its tools, for example, catalogues and technical equipment. These guided tours have to be carefully planned according to the needs of those taking part. Tours for groups should be organised in co-operation with the institution from which they come.

CO-OPERATION AND RESOURCE SHARING

Overall service to the community is enhanced when libraries develop links for exchanging information, ideas, services and expertise. Such co-operation results in less duplication of service, a combining of resources for maximum effect, and an overall improvement in community services. In addition, individual community members may in some cases be of great assistance in helping the library to carry out special tasks or projects.

Formal Links

The library should establish formal links with other organisations in the local community, for example, schools, cultural institutions such as museums, galleries and archives, literacy programmes, chambers of commerce or boards of trade.

The links should be used to co-ordinate the resources and efforts of each partner and thereby jointly improve services to the community.

Relations with Schools

One of the most important institutional relationships for a public library is that with the local schools and the education system in the service area.
Types of linkages and/or forms of co-operation include:

- Sharing resources
- Sharing staff training
- Co-operative collection development
- Co-operative programming
- Co-ordination of electronic services and networks
- Co-operation in the development of learning tools
- Class visits to the public library
- Joint reading and literacy promotion
- Programme of web-awareness for children
- Sharing of telecommunications and network infrastructures
- Jointly arranged authors' visits.

Resource Sharing

Each library collection is in some degree unique. No collection can contain all the materials that the members of its public require. Libraries, therefore, can greatly enhance services to their users by providing them with access to the collections of other libraries. Libraries can participate in resource-sharing schemes at any level, local, regional, national and international, involving libraries of a wide range of organisations with information resources. The library should also make its collection available for loan to other libraries through participation in a network, for example, in a union catalogue or in a local network of information providers, such as schools, colleges and universities.

Bibliographic Records

The library should classify and catalogue its resources according to accepted international or national bibliographic standards. This facilitates their inclusion in wider networks.

Borrowing from Other Libraries

In order to meet the information needs of users the library should borrow materials from other libraries both within the same organisation and beyond.
The library should establish interlending policies, which address such issues as:

- Lending materials to other public libraries
- The type of materials it is prepared to lend or not to lend
- The length of time for which materials will be lent
- When it will request materials from other libraries
- Methods of shipment
- How the costs of the service will be met

- Action to be taken if materials are lost or damaged.

ELECTRONIC NETWORKS

Public libraries are instruments of equal opportunity and must provide a safety- net against alienation and social exclusion from technological advance by becoming the electronic doorway to information in the digital age. They should enable all citizens to have access to the information that will enable them to manage their lives at the local level, to acquire essential information about the democratic process and to participate positively in an increasingly global society.

The library should provide access to the resources of the library and to those of other libraries and information services through the creation and maintenance of and participation in effective electronic networks at all levels from local to international.

This can include participation in community networks, programmes to develop technologically advanced communities and electronic networks linking two or more agencies. They should also be part of national information policies.

User Access

The library should provide free public access to the Internet/world wide web to enable all citizens, regardless of economic means, to have access to information available in electronic form. It should have at least one public-access workstation with Internet access and a printer that is not shared with staff.

Remote Access

The library should exploit information and communications technology to enable the public to gain access to as many of its electronic resources and services as possible from their home, school or workplace. If possible they should be made accessible 24 hours a day, seven days a week. Making the library catalogue available on the Internet increases its accessibility to the public, and to other libraries, and improves the quality of the service.

Staff Access

Library staff should have access to the Internet/world wide web to enable them to provide better reference and readers' advisory service to users. Staff should have regular training in using the Internet.

Information Navigator

The public library's role is becoming one of mediator, of being the public's electronic doorway to digital information and of helping citizens cross the 'digital divide' to a better future. The librarian's role is increasingly one of 'information navigator' ensuring that the user gets accurate and reliable information.

ACCESS TO SERVICES

Physical accessibility is one of the major keys to the successful delivery of public library services. Services of high quality are of no value to those who are unable to access them. Access to services should be structured in a way that maximizes convenience to users and potential users.

Location of Service Outlets

Public library service outlets should be located for the maximum convenience of residents of the community. If possible they should be near the centre of transport networks and close to areas of community activity, for example, shops, commercial centres, cultural centres. Where appropriate the public library may share buildings with other services such as arts centres, museums, art galleries, community centres and sports facilities. This can help to attract users and achieve capital and operational economies. The outlet should be highly visible and easily reached by foot, public transport, where available, or by private vehicle. In well-developed urban and suburban areas a public library should be available within a journey by private vehicle of about 15 minutes.

Opening Hours

In order to provide the best possible access to the library service, the library must be open at times of maximum convenience to those who live, work and study in the community.

LIBRARY BUILDINGS

In general when planning a library, the librarian and governing body should consider the following elements:

- The function of the library.
- The size of the library.
- Designated spaces.
- Design features.
- Accessible shelving.
- Sign-posting.
- The ambience of the library.
- Electronic and audiovisual equipment.
- Safety.
- Parking.

The Function of the Library

The library should have adequate space to implement the full range of library services that are consistent with the library's strategic plan and that meet local, area or national standards/guidelines.

The Size of the Library

The amount of floor-space required by a public library depends on such factors as the unique needs of the individual community, the functions of the library, the level of resources available, the size of the collection, the space available and the proximity of other libraries.

Because these elements will vary significantly from country to country and between different building projects it is not possible to propose a universal standard on the space required for a public library.

Designated Spaces

The library should include space for services to adults, children and young adults and for family use. It should aim to provide a range of materials to meet the needs of all groups and individuals in the community.

The range of functions provided and the space available for each will depend on the size of the library.

In planning a new library the following should be considered for inclusion:

- The library collection including, books, periodicals, special collections, sound recordings and video cassettes and other non-print and digital resources.
- Reader seating space for adults, children and young adults to use for leisure reading, serious study, group work and one–one tutoring; quiet rooms should be provided.
- Outreach services: space should be provided to house special collections and preparation areas for outreach services.
- Staff facilities, including work space rest space for eating and relaxing during breaks and meeting rooms where staff can meet with colleagues and supervisors in private.
- Meeting room space for large and small community groups, which should have separate access to the washrooms and to the exterior to enable meetings to be held while the library is closed
- Technology, including public access workstations, printers, CD-ROM stations, copiers, microfilm/fiche readers, public typewriters and facilities for listening to recorded sound.
- special equipment, including atlas cases, newspaper racks, self-service book circulation, dictionaries, wall-mounted display racks, display stands, filing cabinets, map cases, etc.
- Sufficient space for ease of circulation by both public and staff; this can be 15 per cent–20 per cent of public areas and 20 per cent–25 per cent in staff areas.
- In larger libraries a café area for the public is a desirable facility.
- Space must be allowed for the mechanical services of the library, e.g., elevators, heating, ventilation, maintenance, storage of cleaning materials, etc.

Design Features

The library should guarantee easy access for all users and in particular spersons with physical and sensory disabilities.

The following features should be included in the planning of a new library:

- The exterior of the library should be well lit and identified with signs clearly visible from the street.
- The entrance of the library should be clearly visible and located on that part of the building that most users approach.
- The library should focus on eliminating barriers to use.
- There should be no design features that limit the ability of an individual or groups to use any part of the library.
- Care should be taken to avoid steps as much as possible in both interior and exterior design.
- Lighting levels should comply with those stated in international or national standards.
- Libraries that occupy two or more floors should provide elevators that are close to the library entrance and that easily accommodate wheelchairs and child strollers.
- The library should provide facilities for the return of library materials when the library is closed; after-hours deposit boxes should be both theft and waterproof.
- A library should undertake an 'accessibility' audit on a regular basis to confirm that there are no barriers to easy use.
- Local, national or international standards on making public buildings accessible to the disabled should be followed, wherever possible.

Accessible Shelving

Materials should be displayed on open shelves and arranged at a height within easy reach for users. All shelving should be adjustable and preferably on lockable wheels so that it can easily be moved. The furniture in the children's section should be appropriately sized. Shelves should be of accessible height and width for persons using a wheelchair.

Sign-posting

The library's exterior signs not only identify the particular function of the building but are also the library's most basic form of publicity. Signs should therefore be carefully planned to communicate an appropriate image of the library. Internal areas of the library and parts of the collection should be clearly identified by signs of a professional standard so that users can easily find them, for example, the library catalogue, magazines, reference services, the children's area, washrooms, Internet stations, copy machines, etc. Signs should also be posted in Braille where necessary. Where appropriate, signs should be provided in languages used by ethnic groups in the community. A sign displaying the opening hours of the library should be clearly visible from outside the library. Talking kiosks could also be considered to help all users find their way in the library. Directional signs should be erected in nearby streets and town centres to guide the public to the library.

The Ambience of the Library

The library should provide a physical setting for the library service that is inviting to the public and that provides:

- Adequate space to store and display the library collection.
- Adequate, comfortable and attractive space for the public to make proper and convenient use of the library's services.
- Sufficient space for the library staff to carry out their duties in an efficient and comfortable setting.
- Adequate space and flexibility for the future.

The climate of the library should be maintained at a comfortable temperature, using efficient heating and air conditioning. Humidity control helps to protect the stock as well as increasing the comfort of the library. Larger libraries may include a café open either throughout the opening hours of the library or for special occasions. Such facilities are sometimes contracted out to a commercial provider.

As a major function of the public library is to bridge the gap between the information rich and the information poor, it has also to provide access to the necessary electronic, computer and audiovisual equipment. This will include personal computers with Internet access, public access catalogues, microform readers, tape recorders, slide projectors and equipment for the visually and physically handicapped. Wiring should be up-to-date and easily accessible for alterations at a later date. It should also be inspected regularly.

Safety

Every effort should be made to ensure that the library is safe for the public and the staff. Smoke and fire alarms should be provided and security protection for staff and resources. The location of fire extinguishers and emergency exits should be clearly marked. Staff should be trained in first aid and first aid supplies be made readily available. Evacuation drills should be carried out regularly.

The library manager in co-operation with the emergency services should prepare a disaster plan to be put into action in the event of a serious incident, for example fire.

Parking

Where users travel to the library in private vehicles there should be sufficient safe and well lit parking either at or close to the library with appropriately identified spaces for persons with disabilities. If bicycles are a common mode of transport, secure cycle racks should be provided outside the library.

COLLECTION DEVELOPMENT

The public library should provide equality of access to a range of resources that meets the needs of its users for education, information, leisure and personal development. The library should provide access to the heritage of its society and develop diverse cultural resources and experiences. Constant interaction and consultation with the local community will help to ensure this objective is achieved.

COLLECTION MANAGEMENT POLICY

Each public library system requires a written collection management policy, endorsed by the governing body of the library service. The aim of the policy should be to ensure a consistent approach to the maintenance and development of the library collections and access to resources. It is imperative that collections continue to be developed on an ongoing basis to ensure that people have a constant choice of new materials and to meet the demands of new services and of changing levels of use.

In the light of today's technological advances, the policy must reflect not only a library's own collections but also strategies for accessing information available throughout the world.

The policy should be based upon library standards developed by professional staff related to the needs and interests of local people, and reflecting the diversity of society. The policy should define the purpose, scope and content of the collection, as well as access to external resources.

Content of the Policy

The policy may proceed from statements of universal applicability that are relevant to all library services, through more general statements that are relevant to particular countries, or regions, to statements that are specific to particular library services and could include the following elements.

Universal

- Article XIX of the Declaration of Human Rights.
- IFLA statement on freedom of access to information.
- Statements on intellectual freedom, free access to library collections.
- Freedom of information.
- Consideration of the International Copyright Convention.
- IFLA/UNESCO Public Library Manifesto.
- Purpose of the collection management policy and its relation to the corporate plan of the library service.
- Long and short term objectives.
- Access strategies.
- History of the collection and/or library service.
- Identification of relevant legislation.

General

- Purpose of the collection management policy and its relation to the corporate plan of the library service.
- Long and short term objectives.
- Access strategies.
- History of the collection and/or library service.
- Identification of relevant legislation.

Specific

- Analysis of community needs.
- Priorities of the library service.
- Parameters of the collection, including special collections and collections for special needs, such as multicultural material, literacy and resources for people with disabilities.
- Selection and discard principles and methods.
- Budget allocation.
- Responsibility within the organisation for collection development, selection and discard.
- Access to electronic resources including online access to periodicals, databases and other information sources.
- The role of the library as an electronic gateway to information.
- Co-operative relationships with other libraries and organisations.
- Preservation and conservation policies.
- Auditing requirements: accessioning, recording, control, discard, sale or disposal.
- Financial accountability.
- Donations policy.
- Complaints procedure.
- A resource management plan assessing the current and future needs of the collections.
- Review and assessment of the policy.

This is not an exhaustive list but an indication of some of the issues that may be included.

RANGE OF RESOURCES

The public library should provide a wide range of materials in a variety of formats and in sufficient quantity to meet the needs and interests of the community. The culture of the local community and society must be reflected in the resource collection. Public libraries must keep abreast of new formats and new methods of accessing information. All information should be as readily available as possible, irrespective of format. The development of local information sources and resources is vital.

Collections

The following categories of library materials may be represented in a typical public library, although this list is not exhaustive:

- Fiction and non-fiction for adults, young adults and children.
- Reference works.
- Access to databases.
- Periodicals.
- Local, regional and national newspapers.
- Community information.
- Government information, including information by and about local administrations.
- Business information.
- Local history resources.
- Genealogical resources.
- Resources in the primary language of the community.
- Resources in minority languages in the community.
- Resources in other languages.
- Music scores.
- Computer games.
- Toys.
- Games and puzzles.
- Study materials.

Formats

The following formats may be included in a public library collection although this list is not exhaustive and new formats are continually appearing:

- Books, both hard and soft covers.
- Pamphlets and ephemera.
- Newspapers and periodicals including cuttings files.
- Digital information through the Internet.
- Online databases.
- CD-ROM databases.
- Software programmes.
- Microforms.
- Tapes and compact discs (CDs).
- Digital versatile discs (DVDs).
- Videocassettes.
- Laser discs.
- Large print materials.
- Braille materials.
- Audio books.

- Electronic books.
- Posters.

COLLECTION DEVELOPMENT

Collections complement services and should not be seen as an end in themselves, unless their specified primary purpose is the preservation and conservation of resources for future generations. Large collections are not synonymous with good collections, particularly in the new digital world. The relevance of the collection to the needs of the local community is more important than the size of the collection.

Collection size is determined by many factors, including space, financial resources, catchment population of the library, proximity to other libraries, regional role of the collections, access to electronic resources, assessment of local needs, acquisition and discard rates, and policy of stock exchanges with other libraries.

Criteria for Collections

The main criteria for collections should be:

- A range of resources that cater for all members of the community.
- Resources in formats that enable all members of the community to make use of the library service.
- Inflow of new titles.
- Inflow of new books.
- A wide range of fiction categories and of non-fiction subject coverage.
- Provision of non-print resources.
- Access to external resources such as libraries of other institutions, electronic databases, local societies, government departments or the community's knowledge of oral cultures.
- Discard of old, worn and outdated books, non-print resources and information sources.

COLLECTION MAINTENANCE PRINCIPLES

Public libraries of any size will contain materials in a variety of formats. Collection maintenance applies equally to all materials whatever their format.

Materials on open access should be in good physical condition and contain current information.

A smaller, high quality stock will result in more usage than a large stock with a high proportion of old, worn and outdated books, in which newer titles can be lost among mediocre stock. Using outdated reference material can result in the user being given inaccurate information. Materials in electronic formats complement book collections and will replace them in certain areas. Reference works and periodicals on the Internet and on CDs are viable alternatives to printed formats.

Acquisition and Discards

The library collection is a dynamic resource. It requires a constant inflow of new material and outflow of old material to ensure that it remains relevant to the community and at an acceptable level of accuracy. Acquisition rates are more significant than collection size. The acquisition rate is often determined largely by the size of the resource budget.

However, it can also be affected by other factors, for example:

- The number of books published in local languages.
- The population served.
- The level of use.
- The multicultural and linguistic diversity.
- Age distribution of the population.
- Special needs such as people with disabilities or older persons.
- Access to online information.

The size and quality of the stock should reflect the needs of the community.

Reserve Stocks

It may be necessary to maintain a collection of older and lesser-used books on shelves not directly accessible to the public. This should only contain books that have a current or future use and that cannot be replaced or found in any other format. This may include special subject collections that are used on a regular, if limited, basis and out-of-print fiction. Books that contain outdated information or are in poor condition and can be replaced, should be discarded and not held in a reserve stock. It is efficient to maintain a cooperative reserve with other libraries. The maintenance of a reserve stock should be a regular and on-going activity. The availability of a wide range of information on the Internet and electronic databases reduces the need for public libraries to keep extensive reserve stocks.

Interlending

No library or library service can be self-sufficient in stock, and an efficient and effective interlibrary loan system should be an essential part of every public library service. Within a library service with several outlets a regular programme of exchange of stock between libraries makes maximum use of the stock and provides users with a greater variety of titles from which to choose.

STANDARDS FOR BOOK COLLECTIONS

The following proposed standards relate to book collections. Local and financial circumstances could lead to variations in these proposed standards. Where resources are severely limited these may be regarded as target figures and medium and long-term strategies should be developed to work towards achieving these standards in the future. In the smallest collections materials for children, adult fiction and adult nonfiction may be provided in equal proportions. In larger collections the percentage of non-fiction titles will tend to increase. These ratios can vary according to the needs of the local community and the role of the public library.

Relevant collections to serve the needs of young adults should be developed. Where the library has a strong educational role this is likely to be reflected in the composition of the stock.

Where reliable population figures are not available alternative methods of developing standards are needed. The estimated size of the community served, the size of the library, and the number of current and anticipated users can be used as a basis for developing standards for the size of the collection. Comparisons with a number of existing libraries serving communities of a similar size and make-up can be used to determine a target figure for the size of the collection and the resources needed to maintain it.

STANDARDS FOR ELECTRONIC INFORMATION FACILITIES

The development of standards for the provision of electronic information facilities is at an early stage.

Current standards include the following:

- An assessment is required of the demographics of the community in the catchment areas of proposed new library developments to determine the initial mix of collections. The development of local and regional standards should be undertaken to take account of variations in the catchment population to be served by the new library. The following recosmmended standards relate to book provision. Additional standards will be required for other media.

Establishment Phase

A basic collection should be established in new libraries to serve the needs of the general population within the catchment area. A sufficient range and depth of resources to meet general needs should be the aim at this stage rather than comprehensive coverage.

The interlibrary loan system should be at its peak utilisation during this phase to supplement the developing collections. In some countries materials from a national or provincial centre are used to supplement the local stock.

Where this is not achievable a modest growth plan should be implemented to establish this minimum base stock over a period of three years. Access to electronic information sources should also be included in this phase of development.

Consolidation Phase

The objective under this phase is to achieve growth in the stock size, range and depth. Special conditions of the population are taken into account and collections developed to meet the more in-depth needs of the population served. The book discard factor comes into play and the collection growth rate decreases as discards begin to offset acquisitions.

Steady-state Phase

The collections meet the needs of the community in depth, range and quantity. The quality of collections is maintained by acquisition rates matching discard rates. New formats are accommodated within the collections as they become available and access is provided to the widest possible range of resources through the use of technology.

Content Creation

The service should become a content creator and a preserver of local community resources. Content creation includes publication of information booklets and the development of web content by providing access to information about the library or held by the library in printed formats. This positions the library as an electronic gateway by the creation of links to useful web pages.

ACQUISITION AND DISCARD RATES

For general book stock in an established library service the following acquisition rates may be applied:

TABLE

Population	Books Per Capita Per Annum	Books Per 1000Population Per Annum
Below 25000	0.25	250
25000-50000	0.225	225
50000+	0.20	200

The following examples suggest the size of book stock for communities of different sizes.

Scenario 1:

- Established libsrary service serving 100 000 population.
- Median book stock of 200 000 volumes.
- Annual acquisition rate of 20 000 volsumes.

Scenario 2:

- Established library service serving 50 000 population.
- Median book stock of 100 000 volumes.
- Annual acquisition rate of 11 250 volumes.

Scenario 3:

- Established library service serving 20 000 population.

- Median book stock of 40 000 volumes.
- Annual acquisition rate of 5000 volumes.

Small Libraries and Mobile Libraries

The general acquisition rates would be inadequate to meet the needs of small libraries and mobile libraries where stock numbers are limited. All libraries require a certain minimum stock in order to provide a sufficient range of books from which users may make their selection. The acquisition rate of 250 books per 1000 population may not be relevant in the smallest service points, where physical limitations may reduce stock levels below the minimum recommended level of 2500 volumes. In these cases the acquisition rates, renewal rates or exchange rates should be based upon the collection size rather than the population served, and be in the order of 100 per cent or more per annum. An efficient interlibrary loan system is essential in these situations.

Special Collections

General acquisition and discard rates may not be relevant to some parts of the collection or to particular special collections or where special circumstances prevail. In these cases the collection policy must reflect the special needs.
Particular examples of these exceptions are:

- Indigenous Resources – the public library has a role in maintaining and promoting collections of resources related to the culture of indigenous people and ensuring access to them.
- local History Resources – material relating to the history of the locality should be actively collected, preserved and made available.
- Libraries in Communities with a high proportion of particular groups, e.g., children, retired people, young adults, indigenous peoples, ethnic minorities or unemployed people should reflect the needs of these groups in their collections and services.
- Reference Collections – older reference material may need to be retained to provide historical data for research.

HUMAN RESOURCES

Staff are a vitally important resource in the operation of a library. Staff expenses normally represent a high proportion of a library's budget. In order to provide the best possible service to the community it is necessary to maintain well trained and highly motivated staff to make effective use of the resources of the library and to meet the demands of the community. Staff should be available in sufficient numbers to carry out these responsibilities. The management of library staff is itself an important task. All staff should have a clear understanding of the policy of the library service, well-defined duties and responsibilities, properly regulated conditions of employment and salaries that are competitive with other similar jobs.

THE SKILLS OF LIBRARY STAFF

The public library is a service aimed at all members of the community who will have varied and changing needs. Public library staff will require a range of skills and qualities, including interpersonal skills, social awareness, teamwork and leadership and competence in the practices and procedures of the organisation.

The fundamental qualities and skills required of public library staff can be defined as:

- The ability to communicate positively with people.
- The ability to understand the needs of users.
- The ability to co-operate with individuals and groups in the community.
- Knowledge and understanding of cultural diversity.
- Knowledge of the material that forms the library's collection and how to access it.
- An understanding of and sympathy with the principles of public service.
- The ability to work with others in providing an effective library service
- Organisational skills, with the flexibility to identify and implement changes.
- Imagination, vision and openness to new ideas and practice.
- Readiness to change methods of working to meet new situations.
- Knowledge of information and communications technology.

STAFF CATEGORIES

The following categories of staff are found in public libraries:

- Qualified librarians.
- Library assistants.
- Specialist staff.
- Support staff.

In some countries there is an additional category of library technician, or para-professional, with an intermediate level of qualifications. Staff in all categories may be appointed on either a full-time or part-time basis. In some countries two or more people share a single post, a practice known as job-sharing. This provides the opportunity to appoint and retain experienced staff who may not be able to work full-time.

Qualified Librarians

Qualified librarians are professional staff who have undertaken a course of study in librarianship and information studies to degree or post-graduate level. A librarian designs, plans, organises, implements, manages and evaluates library and information services and systems to meet the needs of the users of library and information services in the community.

This will include collection development, the organisation and exploitation of esources, the provision of advice and assistance to users in finding and using information and the development of systems that will facilitate access to the library's resources.

Qualified librarians will have regular contact with members of the community that they serve. In order to fulfil its functions staff with expertise in specific areas, for example, children's librarians, information officers and reference librarians should form part of the professional team. The following is a list of some of the duties of the qualified librarian.

This list is not exhaustive nor is it likely that the qualified librarian will undertake all these activities simultaneously:

- Analysing the resource and information needs of the community.
- Formulating and implementing policies for service development.
- Planning services to the public and participating in their delivery.
- Retrieving and presenting information.
- Answering reference and information enquiries using appropriate material.
- Assisting users in the use of library resources and information.
- Developing services to meet the needs of special groups, e.g., children Creating and maintaining databases to meet the needs of the library and its users.
- Designing library and information services and systems to meet the needs of the public.
- Developing acquisition policies and systems for library resources.
- Managing and administering library and information systems.
- Cataloguing and classification of library materials.
- Promoting library services.
- Evaluating library services and systems and measuring their performance.
- Selecting, evaluating, managing and training staff.
- Budgeting.
- Strategic planning.
- Participation in planning the design and layout of new and refurbished libraries and of mobile libraries.
- Keeping up-to-date with current developments in librarianship and information services including the relevant technologies.

Library Assistants

The duties of the library assistant include routine circulation functions and operational library tasks such as shelving, shelf-checking, processing library materials, data entry, filing, secretarial support and basic level reader enquiry work. Library assistants are the staff the public will come into contact with most frequently. It is essential, therefore, that they should have a high level of interpersonal and communication skills and receive appropriate straining.

Specialist Staff

Large public library services may employ specialist staff to carry out specific functions, for example, computer system managers, administrative, financial, training and marketing staff. Specialist staff may have a qualification in their specialism rasther than in librarianship.

Support Staff

Support staff include caretakers, cleaners, drivers and security staff. They carry out important functions, which contribute to the smooth operation of the library service. They should be regarded as an integral part of the library's staff.

The Composition of the Staff

The composition of the staff should, as far as possible, reflect the make-up of the population it serves. Where, for example, there is a significant number of people from a particular ethnic group within the community, the library staff should include members of that group. This demonstrates that the library is a service for all members of the local community and will help to attract users from all sections of the public.

ETHICAL STANDARDS

Public library staff have a responsibility to maintain high ethical standards in their dealings with the public, other members of staff and externalorganisations. All members of the public should be dealt with on an equal basis and every effort must be made to ensure that information provided is as full and accurate as possible. Librarians must not allow their personal attitudes and opinions to determine which members of the public are served and what materials are selected and displayed.

The public must have confidence in the impartiality of the library staff if the library is to meet the needs of all members of the community. Library associations in some countries have developed codes of ethics, which can be used as models to introduce similar codes elsewhere.

THE DUTIES OF LIBRARY STAFF

The operation of a library should be a team effort with a close working relationship between all members of staff. It is important, however, that staff are used primarily for tasks related to their skills and qualifications. It is a wasteful use of scarce resources, for example, for qualified librarians to regularly carry out routine circulation functions. For the same reason it is not necessary to have a qualified librarian in every library regardless of size or circulation rate.

Small libraries open for limited hours do not require the continuous presence of a qualified librarian. They should however be under the supervision of a member of the qualified staff. All users should have the opportunity of access to a qualified librarian. Staff should have a written contract at the time of their appointment, which clearly states their duties and responsibilities. These should not be changed without consulting the member of staff involved.

STAFFING LEVELS

The number of staff required in each library service will be affected by a range of factors, for example, the number of library buildings, their size and layout, the number of departments within each building, the level of use, services provided beyond the library and requirements for specialist staff. Where some services are provided or supplemented by a regional or national central agency this will have an impact on the number of staff required at local level. The level of available resources is also a critical factor. Allowing for these and other local differences the following basic staffing level is recommended:

- These are basic recommended levels, which will be affected by local circumstances. Where reliable population figures are not available staffing levels can be related tos the size of the library, the range of its functions and the number of users. Another method of developing an appropriate staffing level for a library service is to carry out bench-marking with libraries of comparative size and similar characteristics.

EDUCATION OF LIBRARIANS

Qualified librarians will have undertaken a degree or post-graduate course in librarianship and information studies at a school of librarianship. To ensure that they remain in touch with the latest developments, librarians should maintain a process of continuing professional development on a formal and informal basis. It is important that public librarians maintain close links with the schools of librarianship in their country and are fully aware of course content. Whenever possible they should participate in the work of the schools, for example, by contributing lectures, assisting in interviewing of prospective students and other appropriate forms of co-operation.

TRAINING

Training is a vital element of the activities of a public library. There must be a planned and continuous programme of training for staff at all levels, which should include both full-time and part-time staff. The rapid developments in information technology make the need for regular training even more essential, and the importance of networking and access to other information sources should be included in training programmes. Specialist and support staff should receive induction training in the functions and purpose of the public library and the context in which it operates. In budgeting for the implementation of new systems, an element should be included for training.

In large library services a post of training officer should be created to plan and implement the training programme. To ensure funds are available for training a set percentage of the budget should be earmarked for this function. This level of funding for training should be maintained at times of budget reductions as the need for a well-trained staff is very important in such circumstances.

Mentoring

An effective and economical method of training is to introduce a system of mentoring. New staff work with a more experienced colleague who provides guidance and training. The mentor should be able to advise the new member of staff about issues relating to their work and employment. A checklist of the training provided by the mentor should be maintained to ensure that it is carried out effectively.

Contacts

In addition to in-service training staff should be given opportunities to attend short courses and conferences relevant to their ability to carry out their work. They should be encouraged to be active members of the relevant library association, as this creates links with other library staff and provides opportunities for an exchange of ideas and experience. It may also be possible to arrange staff exchanges with staff in other libraries, either in the same country or in a similar library in another country, which can be a valuable experience for all those involved.

Career Development

In order to motivate and retain skilled staff opportunities for career development should be available at all levels. A scheme of performance appraisal should be in place that provides staff with an evaluation of current performance and guidance in improving and developing their skills. It also presents an opportunity to review career progression.

WORKING CONDITIONS

All library staff should have satisfactory working conditions and the conditions of employment should be clearly stated in the contract given to the new member of staff when they are employed. Salaries should be at a level appropriate to the level of work being undertaken and competitive with other similar jobs in the community.

Health and Safety

The health and safety of staff must be a high priority and policies and procedures put in place to reduce risks.
Consideration should be given to:

- Good working conditions for staff.
- Ergonomically designed furniture and equipment.
- Availability of technical aids for employees with special needs and disabilities.
- The drawing up of evacuation plans and their testing on a regular basis.
- Identified health and safety risks being rectified at the earliest opportunity.
- Ensuring that all equipment and cabling conforms with recognised safety standards.

- The establishment of a staff health and safety committee.
- Appointment and training of staff as first-aid officers and fire wardens.
- Provision of safety devices for staff, particularly when staff work at nights or away from the library.
- Providing advanced driver training for staff who drive library vehicles
- Protective clothing when required.
- Limiting the weight of cartons and loads on book trolleys.

Public libraries are often open for long hours including evenings and weekends. In creating work schedules for staff every effort should be made to ensure that their working hours provide them with adequate time off at appropriate times for social activity. It is vital that good labour relations are maintained and fostered with staff.

Anti-social Behaviour

In any building freely accessible to the public, staff will occasionally encounter users who behave in an unpleasant and anti-social manner. Staff should be trained in how to deal with such situations and have alarm systems that can alert other staff.

Senior staff should be immediately available to assist staff and full records of such occurrences should be kept. A support system involving other staff and people from other agencies, for example, social workers, should be developed to help library staff deal with these situations.

VOLUNTEERS

Where a library uses volunteer help from individuals in the community to assist library staff, a written policy should be in place defining the tasks of these volunteers and their relationship to the library operation and staff. Volunteers should not be used as a substitute for paid staff.

THE MANAGEMENT AND MARKETING OF PUBLIC LIBRARIES

A successful public library is a dynamic organisation working with other institutions and with individuals to provide a range of library and information services to meet the varied and changing needs of the community. To be effective it requires experienced, flexible and well trained managers and staff able to use a range of management techniques. This chapter deals with the key elements of public library management.

MANAGEMENT SKILLS

Management of a public library involves a number of different skills:

- Leadership and motivation.
- Maintaining effective relationships with governing and funding bodies.
- Planning and policy development.
- Building and maintaining networks with other organisations.

- Budget negotiations and management.
- Management of library resources.
- Staff management.
- Planning and development of library systems.
- The management of change.
- Marketing and promotion.
- Community liaison and lobbying.

Leadership and Motivation

The library manager has a vital role in advocating the value of public libraries as an integral part of an international, national and local infrastructure. He/she must promote public libraries to politicians and key stakeholders at all levels in order to ensure they are aware of the importance of public libraries and to attract adequate funding for their maintenance and development. The library manager must ensure that governing authorities are informed of new developments that may impact on public library services and are made aware that the library service is a key player in providing access to the delivery of new services.

The library manager is responsible for the motivation of staff and bringing energy, vitality and strength into the library service and its staff. The manager also plays a key role in managing the development of physical facilities and ensuring that the most effective use is made of resources, including information technology, to enable the library service to meet the library and information needs of the community.

Relationships with Governing and Funding Bodies

To achieve its goals the public library needs adequate and sustained funding. It is very important that the library manager establishes and maintains a close and positive relationship with the bodies that govern the library service and provide its funding. The library manager as head of the public library service should have direct access to and involvement with the board or committee that is directly responsible for the library service. As well as formal meetings there should be regular informal contacts between the library manager and members of the governing body, and they should be kept well informed about the library service and current and future developments.

Planning and Policy Development

Planning ensures that:

- The library responds to the needs of the community.
- The governing body, management and staff understand what the library is trying to achieve.
- Community funds are spent in an effective and responsible manner.
- Continuity of service is maintained regardless of changes of personnel.

- The library expands the expectations of the community as new services are developed.
- The library is able to respond effectively to change.

The determination of public library goals, short and long term objectives, strategies and performance measurement is necessary to ensure equitable, effective and efficient library service provision with access for all sectors of the community. Strategic and operational plans require formulation, documentation and adoption. Planning should not take place in isolation but in conjunction with the governing and funding bodies, the library staff and the actual and potential clients served.

A strategic plan must be user-focused and should include the following elements:

- Review of achievements.
- Examination of needs.
- Identification of priorities and short term goals.
- Development of strategies for achieving goals.
- Identification of critical success factors.
- Budget allocation.
- Deployment of resources to achieve optimum performance.
- Measurement and evaluation of input and output performance.
- Reassessment of needs and policies.

Operational Planning

An operational plan is necessary to ensure that the activities of the library service are focused on achieving the priorities and goals identified in the strategic plan. The plan should reflect the following elements:

- A focus on service to users.
- The implementation of the priorities and goals of the strategic plan.
- The formation of operational elements of the agreed strategies.
- The development of clearly identified goals with manageable and achievable time frames.
- The definition of achievable outputs for the level of inputs.
- The participation of library staff who carry out the activities.
- The allocation of responsibility to identified staff members for achieving outputs.
- A programme for monitoring, evaluating and amending the plan at regular intervals.

By-laws or local legislation, specific policies and procedures may be needed and should be properly formulated, documented and communicated to all those involved. Business and marketing plans, market research, community needs analyses and surveys of users and non-users should form part of the management process. Planning for the future should advocate positive change and flexibility and aim to minimize the impact of transition on services, staff and users. To achieve effective change, all stakeholders must be involved in the change process.

BUILDING AND MAINTAINING NETWORKS

The library manager must ensure that networks are developed and maintained at national, regional and local level, using information and communications technology wherever appropriate.

This enables a very wide range of resources to be brought to the user at a local level. The library manager should also develop good working relationships with other agencies in the community, for example, schools, other local government departments and voluntary organisations for the benefit of the users, and to confirm the public library's role at the centre of community activity.

The library manager should, wherever possible, ensure that the library takes an active and positive role within the corporate structure of the parent organisation.

FINANCIAL MANAGEMENT

Financial management and financial planning are vitally important to ensure that the library operates efficiently, economically, and effectively. In order to achieve these aims the library manager should:

- Look for wasys of improving levels of funding from national, state or local government or from other sources.
- Prepare 3–5 year business plans based on the library's long term plans, including bids for the required funds.
- Allocate funds to support activities identified in the library's policy statement and based on the priorities previously determined.
- Establish partnerships, where appropriate, for co-operative purchasing to maximize the use of available funds.
- Undertake activity-based costing to determine the cost of activities and programmes and to facilitate future planning.
- Maintain a policy for the sustainable renewal of plant and equipment.
- Evaluate and implement automated techniques, wherever appropriate, to improve efficiency and effectiveness.
- Introduce systems that will ensure that all staff with responsibility for any part of the budget will be fully accountable for the expenditure of funds for which they are responsible.
- Improve staff productivity and efficiency.

MANAGEMENT OF LIBRARY RESOURCES

A major element of a library's budget is expenditure on library materials. The library manager should ensure that these funds are spent properly and in accordance with the agreed priorities of the library and that the materials are maintained and made available so that they can be of maximum benefit to the library user.

STAFF MANAGEMENT

Library staff are a vital element of the library's resources and staff salaries are normally the largest part of the library budget. It is very important that the management of staff should be sensitive, consistent and based on sound principles if staff are to work most effectively and with high levels of motivation and job satisfaction.

The following are important elements of staff management:

- An equitable procedure for staff appointments. Job and person specifications should be drawn up prior to a post being advertised.
- Interviews should be conducted in a way that is fair to all applicants.
- Appointments should be based solely on professional judgement and suitability for the post and not be prejudiced by any other factors.
- Good communication between staff at all levels. Managers should review internal communication systems regularly to make sure staff are well informed about the policies and procedures of the library service.
- The opportunity for staff to participate in the development of policy and operational procedures. Initiative should be encouraged to make the best use of the skills and experience of staff. By bringing staff into the decision-making process they will feel they 'own' the policies and procedures of the service.
- The principles of affirmative action, including the creation of nominated positions for special needs areas, may be adopted.

PLANNING AND DEVELOPMENT OF LIBRARY SYSTEMS

To make the most effective use of resources the public library will require a variety of systems, for example circulation control, financial management, internal communications. The library manager should ensure that appropriate systems are introduced, making use of specialist staff for their development where necessary. Staff must be given adequate training in the use of such systems, the effectiveness of which must be reviewed regularly.

THE MANAGEMENT OF CHANGE

In common with many other organisations public libraries are going through a period of unprecedented and ongoing change as a result of the rapid development of information technology and social and demographic change. This presents tremendous opportunities for the public library, as information provision is one of its primary roles.

It also presents challenges to managers and staff to ensure that change can be introduced with the maximum effectiveness and the least stress on staff and the organisation. Library managers must be aware of the issues arising from continuous and fundamental change and establish methods of dealing with them.

Planning for the Future

Library managers should be aware of developments both within and outside librarianship that are likely to have an impact on service development. They should make time to read and study so that they can anticipate the effect of changes, particularly technological, on the future shape of the service. They should also ensure that policy-makers and other staff are kept informed of future developments.

DELEGATION

The library manager in charge of the public library service has ultimate responsibility for the service, in conjunction with the governing body. However, all library staff with responsibility for any resources of the library, whether materials, staff or library premises, have a managerial role, and this should be recognised by the library manager and the member of staff concerned.

They should be given appropriate managerial training and participate in the policy development of the library whenever possible. Managerial responsibility should be delegated to staff at an appropriate lower level. It should be made clear what responsibilities are being delegated and what the reporting mechanism to senior managers is.

Staff must be given training to enable them to carry out the delegated responsibilities effectively. A planned system of delegation makes best use of the skills and experience of a wide range of staff and provides opportunities for professional development. It also increases the number of people fully involved in the development and operation of the library service, improves job satisfaction and prepares staff for promotion when opportunities arise.

MANAGEMENT TOOLS

A wide range of management tools can be used in a public library. Their relevance will depend on a number of factors, for example, the cultural context, the size and character of the service, the management style of other departments in the same organisation and available experience and funding.

The following are however important tools for public libraries in almost any situation:

- Community needs analysis.
- Monitoring and evaluation.
- Performance measurement.
- Community Needs Analysis

In order to provide services that meet the needs of the whole community, the public library has to establish the extent of those needs. As needs and expectations will change, this process will need to be repeated at regular intervals, perhaps every five years. A community needs assessment is a process in which the library collects detailed information about the local community and its library and information needs. Planning and policy development are based on the results of this assessment and in this way a match between services and needs can be achieved. In some countries the preparation of a community needs assessment is a legislative requirement of the local authority.

The information to be collected will include:

- Socio-demographic information about the local community e.g., the age and gender profile, ethnic diversity, educational level.
- Data about organisations in the community, e.g., educational institutions, health centres, hospitals, penal establishments, voluntary organisations.
- Information about business and commerce in the locality.
- The catchment area of the library, i.e., where library users live in relation to the library.
- Transport patterns in the community.
- Information services provided by other agencies in the community.

This is not an exhaustive list and further research would be required to establish what information is needed to form a community needs assessment in each situation. However, the principle of preparing a community profile, which will enable the librarian and the governing body to plan service development and promotion on the needs of the community, is an important one whatever the local context. The assessment should be complemented by regular customer surveys to establish what library and information services the public wants, at what level, and how they judge the services they receive. Survey work is a specialist skill and, where resources are available, a more objective result will be gained if the survey is carried out by an external organisation.

Monitoring and Evaluation

As the library service moves towards its goals, management must be accountable in terms of financial control and the monitoring and evaluation of library activities. Management must continually monitor the performance of the library service to ensure that strategies and operational results are achieving the set objectives. Statistics should be collected over time to allow trends to be identified. Community needs and satisfaction surveys, and performance indicators are valuable tools in monitoring the achievements of the library. Techniques should be developed to measure the quality of the services provided and their impact on the community.

All programmes and services should be evaluated on a regular basis to ascertain whether they are:

- Achieving the objectives and declared goals of the library.
- Actually and regularly provided.
- Meeting the needs of the community.
- Able to meet changing needs.
- In need of improvement, new direction or redefinition.

- Adequately resourced.
- Cost effective.

Procedures and processes operating within the library also require constant evaluation and revision to increase efficiency and effectiveness.

Performance Indicators

The availability of reliable performance information is a necessary tool for evaluation and the improvement of efficiency, effectiveness and quality of service. The collection of statistics related to resources, staff, services, circulation, activities, etc., will provide data for planning, show accountability and assist informed management decision-making. The following key performance indicators may be used to evaluate and monitor the achievement of the library's objectives.

Usage indicators:

- Loans per capita.
- Total library visits per capita.
- Membership as a percentage of the population.
- Loans per item, i.e., turnover resources.
- Reference enquiries per capita.
- Loans per opening hour.
- Number of accesses to electronic services and other non-print materials.

Resource indicators:

- Total stock per capita.
- Provision of terminals/personal computers per capita.
- Provision of online public access computers (OPACs) per capita.

Human Resource Indicators:

- Ratio of full time equivalent (FTE) staff to population
- Ratio of professional staff to population.
- Ratio of full time equivalent (FTE) staff to library use.

Qualitative indicators:

- User satisfaction surveys.
- Enquiries satisfied.

Cost indicators:

- Unit costs for functions, services and activities.
- Staff costs per functions, e.g., books processed, programmes.
- Total costs per capita, per member, per visitor, per service point, etc.

Comparative indicators:

- bench-mark statistical data against other relevant and comparable library services, internationally, nationally and locally.

In addition to the collection and analysis of input and output service statistics, the unstated needs of non-users should be established by carrying out market research including the use of focus groups and community surveys. Where reliable population statistics are not available it becomes more difficult to develop reliable performance indicators.

Use can be made of estimated population totals, the comparison of costs with user and visitor statistics and bench-marking with other libraries with similar characteristics.

Performance Measurement

Performance measurement has been used in public libraries for some years. Measurements or performance indicators are established to measure the input to libraries, that is the resources devoted to the whole or particular services, and the output: what is achieved as a result of the activity being carried out.

For example, the establishment of an enquiry service for users requires the input of staff, materials, equipment and floor space.

The output is the number of enquiries received, the number satisfied, the level of use made of the resources and the use of other services, for example, the reservation service, arising from the original activity.

These measures can then be compared each year to see if the effectiveness of the library service is improving. Computer technology makes performance measurement a simpler task and enables sophisticated models of library use to be established and used in service development. Performance measurement should be a planned process carried out with consistency over a period of time.

Further information about library performance indicators can be found in ISO 11620:1998 Information and documentation. Library performance indicators. Another way of gaining a useful indication of the success of a library service is to compare key input and output measurements with other public libraries of similar size and characteristics. This is usually known as benchmarking and is a useful adjunct to performance measurements carried out internally.

MARKETING AND PROMOTION

Library managers can use marketing techniques to enable them to understand the needs of their users and to plan effectively to meet those needs. The library should also promote its services to the public to ensure that they are kept informed of the services provided to meet their library and information requirements.

Marketing and Promotion Policy

The library should have a written communications, marketing and promotions policy to enable it to undertake a planned promotion of its services to the public. The policy should include a marketing and communication strategy and methods of evaluating promotional programmes.

Marketing and Promotion Plan

To enable the library to achieve its marketing strategy, a coherent marketing and promotion plan should be developed based on the agreed policy.

- It could include the following elements:
- Making positive use of print, electronic and communications media.
- Displays and exhibits.
- Effective interior and exterior sign-posting.
- Regular publications and the preparation of resource lists and pamphlets.
- Reading and literacy campaigns.
- Designing campaigns to meet the needs of people with physical and sensory disabilities.
- Book fairs.
- Library web sites.
- Links to and from related web sites and portals.
- Friends of the library groups.
- Annual library week celebrations and other collective promotional activities.
- Special years of celebration and anniversaries.
- Library listings in the telephone book and other community directories.
- Fund-raising activities and campaigns.
- Public-speaking activities and liaison with community groups.
- Special library publications, e.g., history of the library, history of the community.

This list is not exhaustive and other elements can be added depending on local circumstances.

Working with the Media

Library staff should be trained to use communication media to promote the library service and respond to media enquiries. They should be able to write articles for local newspapers and prepare press releases. They should be familiar with the techniques of speaking and being interviewed on radio and television.

They should also be able to promote the library and its services via computer and telecommunication networks including the creation of library web sites.

Community Support

The library managers must ensure that the community is aware of the importance of the library service. Municipal, regional and national funding bodies should be made fully aware of the important place that the library occupies in the community, and support its development.

Gaining Community Support

The library should have an agreed policy and a sustained programme for developing community support.

This can include:

- Maintaining a 'friends of the library' organisation for fund-raising and general support.
- Working with community advocates in support of major initiatives such as new buildings and services.
- Forming liaisons with community groups to enhance parts of the collection or strengthen specific services.
- Working with groups that wish to speak out on behalf of the library service and its development.
- Participation by library staff in activities aimed at increasing awareness of the variety and value of the library service.

The support of the community also depends on the library delivering the services it has promised to deliver.

Advocacy

The library should have established and adopted written policies that define its role in generating public support for the library service. A well informed public can provide valuable support for the public library service and actively promote it within the community.

Getting people to talk positively about the library and its services is one of the most effective marketing tools. Lobbying involves interaction with decision-makers to secure specific objectives at an appropriate point in the legislative, policy-making or budget process.

Working with Governing Bodies

Library managers should meet at least annually with the library's principal governing and funding body to review the library's services, development plans, achievements and obstacles. Librarians should look for as many opportunities as possible to involve its governing body in its major activities. Events such as the opening of a new library, the launching of a service, the installation of public Internet access, the opening of a new collection and the inauguration of a fund-raising drive can be used for this purpose.

Participation in Community Life

One of the most effective promotional strategies is the participation of wellinformed library staff and committee or board members in community activities.

Examples include:

- Presenting book and activity reviews on radio and television.
- Working with adults and children's literature and cultural groups.
- Writing a newspaper column.
- Supporting literacy organisations and campaigns.
- Participating in the activities of local organisations.
- Assisting with school-based initiatives.
- Participating in local history and genealogy societies.
- Being a member of a service organisation, e.g., Rotary.
- Visiting local organisations to promote the library service.

Evaluation

The library should carry out a regular evaluation of its marketing and promotion programme and ensure the results of the evaluation are taken into account when planning future programmes.

❐

18

Establishment of Library Services: Statement of the Problem

The Emuhaya Constituency Strategic Development Plan 2008-2018, the general trend in education in the constituency has been declining. Among the reasons cited for this negative trend are inadequate learning and teaching resources.

Among these inadequate resources are libraries and even the books themselves, where libraries do not exist. Schools and entire community of Emuhaya constituency have a serious shortage of reading materials. Most of the schools in the constituency are day schools with small or no libraries.

Yet the students in these schools are expected to compete with their counterparts in national and provincial schools well endowed with library facilities. Consequently, the performance of students in final exams like KCSE and KCPE has consistently been compromised by the continued lack of adequate information resources in form of books, past examination papers and other pertinent information materials.

In addition, even the rest of the community members in the larger parts of the constituency do not have resource centres where they can access information and benefit from the poor of information. This has in turn contributed to the deterioration of the reading culture.

PROJECT SIGNIFICANCE

Establishment of community libraries in the constituency will ma tremendous contributions to boosting education and literacy levels in the constituency. First the project will complement school efforts in providing learning materials to school-going generation.

This will address the strain the pupils have to go through to access any useful materials for referral for their studies. By providing an alternative channel for accessing literature for educational and academic work, the libraries will reduce the stress imposed on schools and provide the school going youths and children opportunities to access libraries even if they are day scholars.

Secondly, provision of resource materials like newspapers, storybooks and novels and economic-based materials like farming literature and literature on socio-econo-political issues like HIV & AIDS, drug abuse and sexual harassment will be useful to the community. This will boost the knowledge base of the community and reduce levels of ignorance by exposing community to information. Thirdly, the rate of unemployment in Emuhaya constituency is as high as in most parts of the country.

Consequently, idleness resulting from this unemployment drives most youth into crime and immoral behaviour. The libraries will provide an avenue where youths can engage in constructive readership initiatives that will reduce idleness hence improve security. Fourth, community libraries can serve as centres for dissemination of important information from government, NGOs and development partners. By making the library a central repository, dissemination of information from development agencies and government becomes easy to administer and control. Fifth, with the government's effort to establish Information Centres and Digital villages country-wide, the community libraries can offer an ample place to set up an information centre or establish a digital village. Sixth, under the Africana section of the library, the libraries can be excellent points to collect all artifacts and other literatures that preserve the culture of Banyore people.

PROJECT OBJECTIVES

- To provide educational textbooks that can be accessed by secondary and primary school pupils to support their education activities.
- To ensure students who do not have libraries in their home areas have alternative source of information to facilitate studies during holidays or weekends for those in day schools and primary schools.
- Provide materials relevant to the general community – non-school going members- on economic, social and political issues to improve knowledge base and awareness of the people.
- Provide fictional materials for general readership to promote reading culture and control idleness amongst the unemployed youth.

- Keep and provide relevant audio-visual materials on important aspects of socio-economic and political development that can be used for education of the community.
- Provide both in-house and outdoor reader services to students and community in general.
- Ensure availability of relevant information materials-textbooks, general monographs and journals to the users.

IMPLEMENTATION STRATEGIES

LOCATION

The target of the initiative is to have a community library in every sub-location. However for a start, the libraries will be establish in each of the eight locations. This translates to 8 libraries for a start before cascading the project to sub-location level subject to availability of funds. The project will first roll out a pilot project of one library in West Bunyore Location, which is among worst hit locations in terms of inadequacy in education resources. This pilot will then provide insights on how to roll-out and manage subsequent libraries in the constituency.

IMPLEMENTATION APPROACH

It is recommended that for cost effectiveness and ease of security, the libraries be set up at selected secondary or primary schools where library facilities can be constructed. The library once set up in the school will then be open to the community in the location where the school is based, subject to agreed terms with the hosting school. Use of the library facility will be free for individual members.

However for institutional registration, an agreeable administrative fee may be levied for sustainability. During implementation, the CDF office and the CLPB shall source for reputable persons or firms to support both technical and professional aspects of the project. Individual consultants or consultant firms in library management could be sought to inject professionalism in the implementation of the project especially on collection development, management and marketing strategies.

RECOMMENDED LIBRARY COLLECTION

- Textbooks-approved by K.I.E.
- Higher education and tertiary texts.
- General readership texts and story books.
- Children books-texts and story books.
- Journals and other periodicals.
- Past papers from other schools and KNEC.
- Audio visual materials.
- Artifacts – especially representing the Banyore culture and various Kenyan communities.

SOURCING FOR INFORMATION MATERIALS

- Direct purchase of relevant texts, especially school texts approved by K.I.E.
- Donations from Kenya National Library Service.
- Donations from Ministry of Education.
- Donations from NGOs like Children International and Centre for Literacy Development.
- Donation from Private corporate companies and civil society groups.
- Donations from International agencies like CODE and Book Aid International.
- Donations from teaching institutions-universities and polytechnics.
- Donations from individuals within the community.
- Collaborative initiatives from benefiting schools – joint requisitions.

PROJECT MANAGEMENT

ADMINISTRATION

The project shall be managed by a Community Libraries Project Board (CLPB) appointed by the area MP in conjunction with CDF Committee and reporting to the Constituency Development Office. Every library shall have a designate staff employed and remunerated by the Constituency Development office out of the budgetary allocation for the library.

Where a school is hosting the library, the host school will have discretionary powers in regard to overall security and safety of the library and the school may use some of its human capital to support aspects like cleanliness to complete those of designate library manager.

The project team shall from time to time seek opinion from professional experts in Library management at Kenya National Library Services and private consultants with regard to management of the community libraries.

FINANCIAL MANAGEMENT

All financial management for the community libraries shall be controlled by the Constituency Development Fund (CDF) office and overseen by the CLPB. This is because the CDF office has necessary personnel, systems and experience in managing community projects. All payments to contractors, consultants and staff shall be made by the CDF office as per the existing systems of payment.

All necessary structures, systems and documents for financial expenditure shall be put in place and monitored by the CDF office. The Librarian shall be trained appropriately on financial management aspects, especially where petty cash may have to be utilised.

FUNDING NEEDS

The project will require some funding to:

- Set up the library rooms.
- Set up the library layout, arrange and describe materials, i.e., source
- for consultant.
- Compensation of Library staff.

BUDGETARY ESTIMATES

The budget indicated here-i-under is the initial costs required to set up one library.

Important Notes to the budget estimates:

- The budget is drawn on assumption that there shall be found an available space at any of the local secondary schools which can be converted into a library.
- Incentives for use of such space for the school shall be waiver of any administrative fees applied to institutional membership for sustainability.
- The costs for wages, security and recurrent costs have been calculated for a period of 2 years.
- The books budget for are initial stock required to start up the library service and that subsequent collections shall be solicited from donations and gifts. Further funding shall be sort for restocking form the CDF kitty.

TABLE

Description	Quantity	Unit Cost	Total
Books	–	–	1,000,000,00
Renovation of Building	1		1,500,000,00
Furnishing (chairs, tables, shelves, burglar proffing)			800,000,00
Wages for Librarians Security	2	10,000,00 pm	480,000,00
Recurrent Costs-lighting Miscellaneous	2	5,000,00 pm	240,000,00
			50,000,00
			100,000.00
Total			**4,170,000.00**

Summary

Total costs for 1 library - Kishs, 4,170,000.00

Available funds = nil

Total funding required for eight libraries in the eight locations will be Kishs. 33,36,000.00

PROJECT MONITORING AND EVALUATION

The Constituency Development Office in collaboration with the CLPB shall provide objective monitoring and evaluation of the project to ensure that the project serves the objectives for which it has been setup. This should also be done in line with the Strategic development Plan for the Constituency.

PROJECT SUSTAINABILITY

In order to ensure that the projects are sustained for longer periods, it is anticipated that:

- There shall be continuous efforts by the Constituency Development Office to lobby and solicit more financial and material support.
- All benefiting schools will make subsidised contributions towards sustenance of the libraries.
- The Constituency Development Fund shall make some allocations of the CDF annual budget towards sustaining the libraries as part of its budget on education in the constituency.
- The CLPB shall continue to lobby the surrounding community, in conjunction with the provincial administration, to attract support from the community.

FUTURE PLANS

The libraries would be automated and also be used as digital villages to facilitate diffusion of ICT knowledge in the community and exposure to Internet. The GOK is facilitating availability of sufficient bandwidth which should be harnessed. GOK can easily fund this process through Ministry of Information. The constituency can also source for donors on this plan.

CONCLUSION

It is envisaged that with implementation of this essential service in the constituency, education levels with be scaled-up. The community will also be exposed to information for socio-economic empowerment.

❒

19

e-Resources Management and Modern Library

WIRELESS LOCAL AREA NETWORKS

The WLAN market is exploding, with reported yearly growth figures of 300 per cent. WLAN systems are a technology that can provide very high data rate applications and individual links (e.g., in company campus areas, conference centers, airports and in libraries) and represents an attractive way of setting up computers networks in environments where cable installation is expensive or not feasible.

LANs and mobile computing, have recalling the attention of equipment manufactures. This shows their high potential and justifies the big attention paid to WLAN by equipment manufacturers. Whereas in the early beginning of WLANs several proprietary products existed, nowadays they are mostly conforming to the Institute of Electrical and Electronics Engineering (IEEE) 802.11b (also known as Wi-Fi) standard. It operates in the unlicensed 2.4-GHz band at 11 Mbps and it is currently extended to reach 54 Mbps. A description of the MAC can be found in.

WLAN STANDARDS

802.11A

A physical layer standard in the 5 GHz radio band. It specifies eight available radio channels (in some countries, 12 channels are permitted). The maximum link rate is 54 Mbps per channel; maximum actual user data throughput is approximately half of that, and the throughput is shared by all users of the same radio channel.

The data rate decreases as the distance between the user and the radio access point increases.

802.11B

This is a physical layer standard in the 2.4 GHz radio band. It specifies three available radio channels. Maximum link rate is 11 Mbps per channel, but maximum user throughput will be approximately half of this because the throughput is shared by all users of the same radio channel. The data rate decreases as the distance between the user and the radio access point increases.

802.11D

This standard is supplementary to the Media Access Control (MAC) layer in 802.11 to promote worldwide use of 802.11 WLANs. It will allow access points to communicate information on the permissible radio channels with acceptable power levels for user devices.

The 802.11 standards cannot legally operate in some countries; the purpose of 11d is to add features and restrictions to allow WLANs to operate within the rules of these countries.

802.11E

This standard is supplementary to the MAC layer to provide QOS support for LAN applications. It will apply to 802.11 physical standards a, b, and g. The purpose is to provide classes of service with managed levels of QOS for data, voice, and video applications.

802.11F

This is a "recommended practice" document that aims to achieve radio access point interoperability within a multivendor WLAN network. The standard defines the registration of access points within a network and the interchange of information between access points when a user is handed over from one access point to another.

802.11G

This is a physical layer standard for WLANs in the 2.4 GHz and 5 GHz radio band. It specifies three available radio channels. The maximum link rate is 54 Mbps per channel whereas 11b has 11 Mbps. The 802.11g standard uses orthogonal frequency-division multiplexing (OFDM) modulation but, for backward compatibility with 11b, it also supports complementary code-keying (CCK) modulation and, as an option for faster link rates, allows packet binary convolution coding (PBCC) modulation

802.11H

This standard is supplementary to the MAC layer to comply with European regulations for 5 GHz WLANs. European radio regulations for the 5 GHz band require products to have transmission power control (TPC) and dynamic frequency selection (DFS). TPC limits the transmitted power to the minimum needed to reach the farthest user. DFS selects the radio channel at the access point to minimize interference with other systems, particularly radar.

802.11I

It will apply to 802.11 physical standards a, b, and g. It provides an alternative to Wired Equivalent Privacy (WEP) with new encryption methods and authentication procedures. IEEE 802.1X forms a key part of 802.11i

WIRELESS NETWORK CONFIGURATIONS

There are two kinds of wireless networks:

1. An ad-hoc or peer-to-peer wireless network consists of a number of computers each equipped with a wireless networking interface card. Each computer can communicate directly with all of the other wireless enabled computers. They can share files and printers this way, but may not be able to access wired LAN resources, unless one of the computers acts as a bridge to the wired LAN using special software. This is called "bridging". Each computer with a wireless interface can communicate directly with all of the others.
2. A wireless network can also use an access point, or base station. In this type of network the access point acts like a hub, providing connectivity for the wireless computers. It can connect (or "bridge") the wireless LAN to a wired LAN, allowing wireless computer access to LAN resources, such as file servers or existing Internet Connectivity.

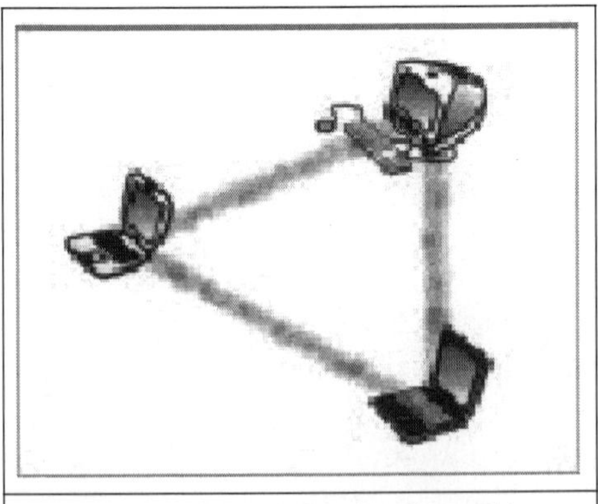

Fig. 19.1: Ad-Hoc or Peer-to Peer Networking.

There are two types of access points:

1. Dedicated hardware access points (HAP) such as Lucent's Wave LAN, Apple's Airport Base Station or Web Gear's Aviator PRO. The figure shows Hardware access points offer comprehensive support of most wireless features.

2. Software Access Points which run on a computer equipped with a wireless network interface card as used in an ad-hoc or peer-to-peer wireless network which is shown in figure. The Vicomsoft Internet Gateway suites are software routers that can be used as a basic Software Access Point, and include features not commonly found in hardware solutions, such as Direct PPPoE support and extensive configuration flexibility, but may not offer the full range of wireless features defined in the 802.11 standard.

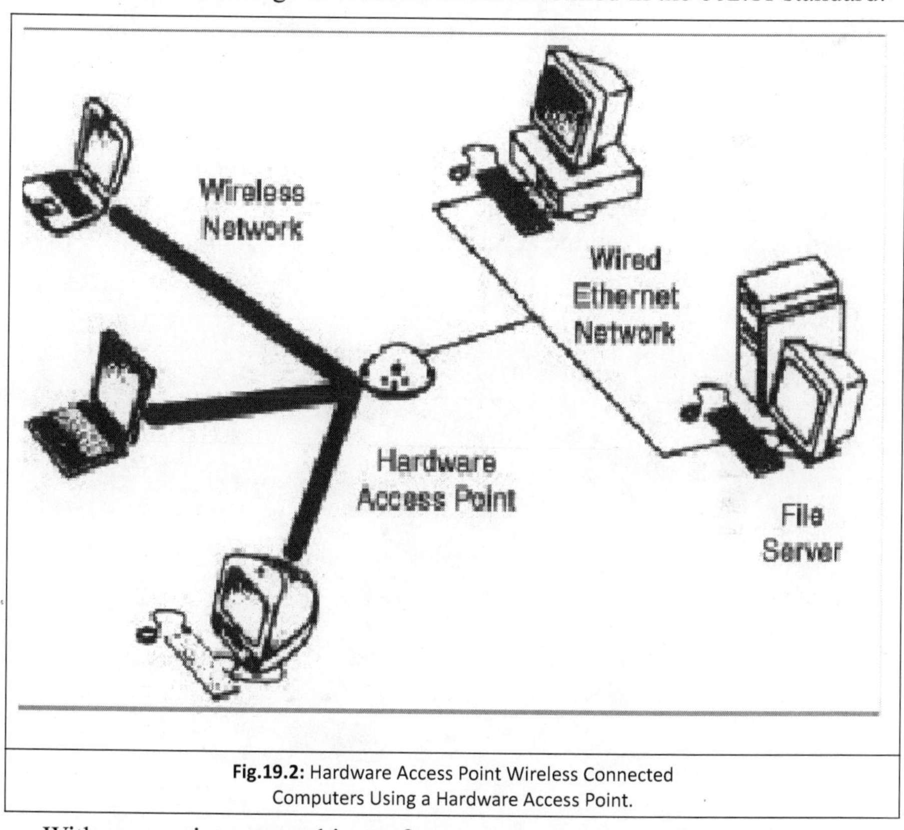

Fig.19.2: Hardware Access Point Wireless Connected Computers Using a Hardware Access Point.

With appropriate networking software support, users on the wireless LAN can share files and printers located on the wired LAN and vice versa.

APPLICATIONS OF WIRELESS LANS

When computers were first built, only large universities and corporations could afford them. Today we may find 3 or 4 personal computers in our neighbour's house. Wireless LANs have taken a similar path, first used by large enterprises, and now available to us all at affordable prices. As a technology, wirelesses LANs have enjoyed a very fast adoption rate due to the many advantages they offer to a variety of situations. As suggested, discuss some of the most common and appropriate uses of wireless LANs.

ACCESS ROLE

Wireless LANs are deployed in an access layer role, meaning that they are used as an entry point into a wired network. In the past, access has been defined as dial-up, ADSL, cable, cellular, Ethernet, Token Ring, Frame Relay, ATM, etc. Wireless is simply another method for users to access the network. Wireless LANs are Data-Link layer networks like all of the access methods just listed. Due to a lack of speed and resiliency, wireless networks are not typically implemented in Distribution or Core roles in networks. Of course, in small networks, there may be no differentiation between the Core, Distribution, or Access layers of the network. The Core layer of a network should be very fast and very stable, able to handle a tremendous amount of traffic with little difficulty and experience no down time. The Distribution layer of a network should be fast, flexible, and reliable. Wireless LANs do not typically meet these requirements for an enterprise solution. Figure illustrates mobile clients gaining access to a wired network through a connection device (access point).

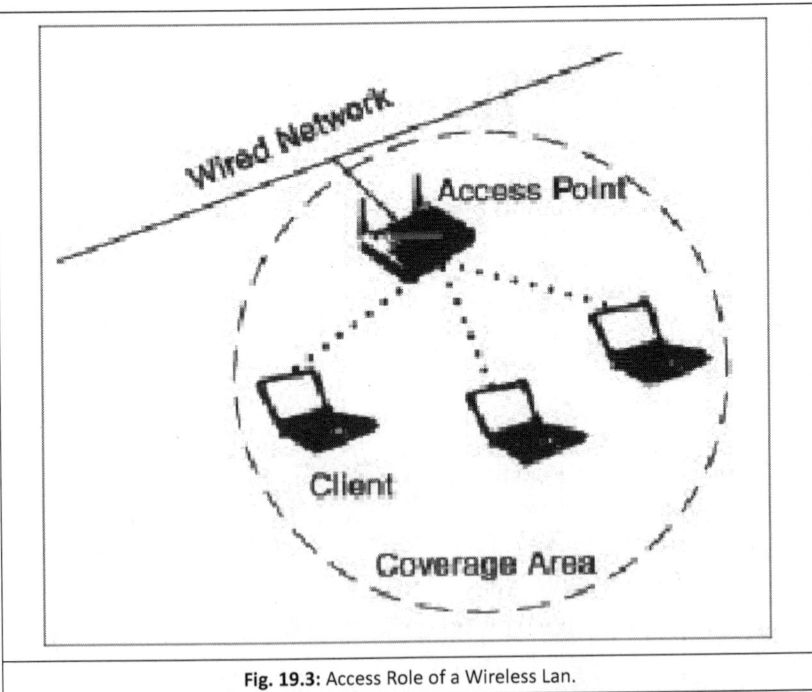

Fig. 19.3: Access Role of a Wireless Lan.

Wireless LANs offer a specific solution to a difficult problem: mobility. Without a doubt, wireless LANs solve a host of problems for corporations and home users alike, but all of these problems point to the need for freedom from data cabling. Cellular solutions have been available for quite some time, offering users the ability to roam while staying connected, at slow speeds and very high prices. Wireless LANs offer the same flexibility without the disadvantages. Wireless

LANs are fast, inexpensive, and they can be located almost anywhere.

When considering wireless LANs for use in network, keep in mind that using them for their intended purpose will provide the best results. Administrators implementing wireless LANs in a Core or Distribution role should understand exactly what performance to expect before implementing them in this fashion to avoid having to remove them later. The only distribution role in a network that is definitely appropriate for wireless LANs is that of building-to-building bridging. In this scenario, wireless could be considered as playing a distribution role; however, it will always depend on how the wireless bridging segments are used in the network.

NETWORK EXTENSION

Wireless networks can serve as an extension to a wired network. There may be cases where extending the network would require installing additional cabling that is cost prohibitive. You may discover that hiring cable installers and electricians to build out a new section of office space for the network is going to cost tens of thousands of Rupees. Or in the case of a large warehouse, the distances may be too great to use Category 5 (Cat5) cable for the Ethernet network. Fibre might have to be installed, requiring an even greater investment of time and resources. Installing fibre might involve upgrades to existing edge switches. Wireless LANs can be easily implemented to provide seamless connectivity to remote areas within a building, as illustrated by the floor plan image in figure. Because little wiring is necessary to install a wireless LAN, the costs of hiring installers and purchasing Ethernet cable might be completely eliminated.

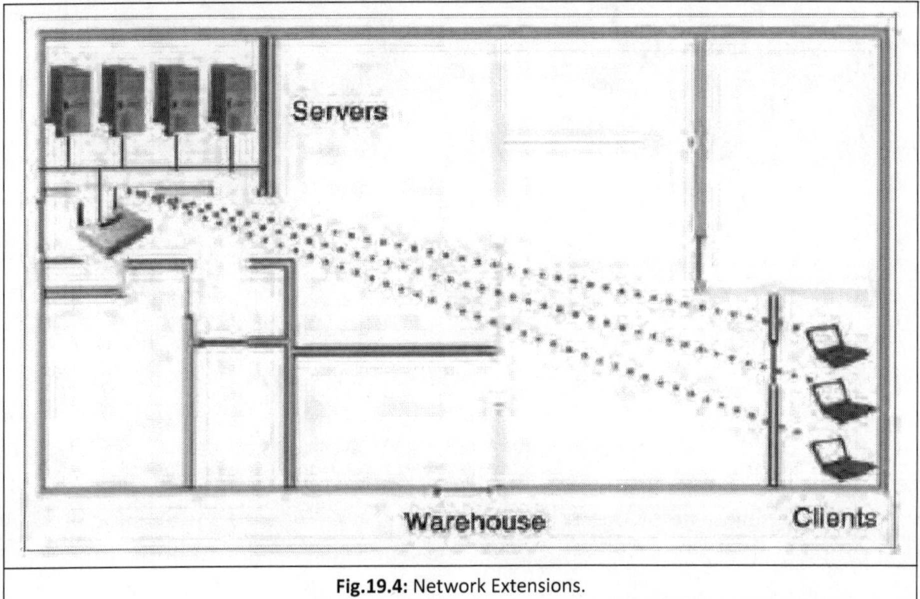

Fig.19.4: Network Extensions.

BUILDING-TO-BUILDING CONNECTIVITY

In a campus environment or an environment with as few as two adjacent buildings, there may be a need to have the network users in each of the different buildings have direct access to the same computer network. In the past, this type of access and connectivity would be accomplished by running cables underground from one building to another or by renting expensive leased-lines from a local telephone company.

Using wireless LAN technology, equipment can be installed easily and quickly to allow two or more buildings to be part of the same network without the expense of leased lines or the need to dig up the ground between buildings.

With the proper wireless antennas, any number of buildings can be linked together on the same network. Certainly there are limitations to using wireless LAN technology, as there are in any data-connectivity solution, but the flexibility, speed, and cost-savings that wireless LANs introduce to the network administrator make them indispensable. There are two different types of building-to-building connectivity.

The first is called point-to-point (PTP), and the second is called point-to-multipoint (PTMP). Point-to-point links are wireless connections between only two buildings. PTP connections almost always use semi-directional or highly-directional antennas at each end of the link.

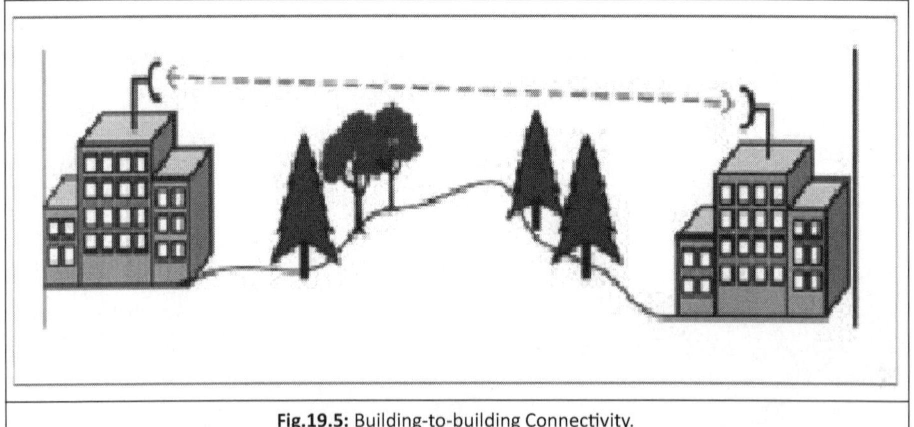

Fig.19.5: Building-to-building Connectivity.

Point-to-multipoint links are wireless connections between three or more buildings, typically implemented in a hub-n-spoke fashion, where one building is the central focus point of the network.

This central building would have the core network, Internet connectivity, and the server farm. Point-to-multipoint links between buildings typically use omni-directional antennas in the central "hub" building and semi-directional antennas on each of the outlying "spoke" buildings. There are many ways to implement these two basic types of connectivity.

LAST MILE DATA DELIVERY

Wireless Internet Service Providers (WISPs) are now taking advantage of recent advancements in wireless technology to offer last mile data delivery service to their customers. "Last mile" refers to the communication infrastructure wired or wireless that exists between the central office of the telecommunications company or Cable Company and the end user. Currently the BSNL and cable companies own their last mile infrastructure, but with the broadening interest in wireless technology, WISPs are now creating their own wireless last mile delivery service, as illustrated in figure.

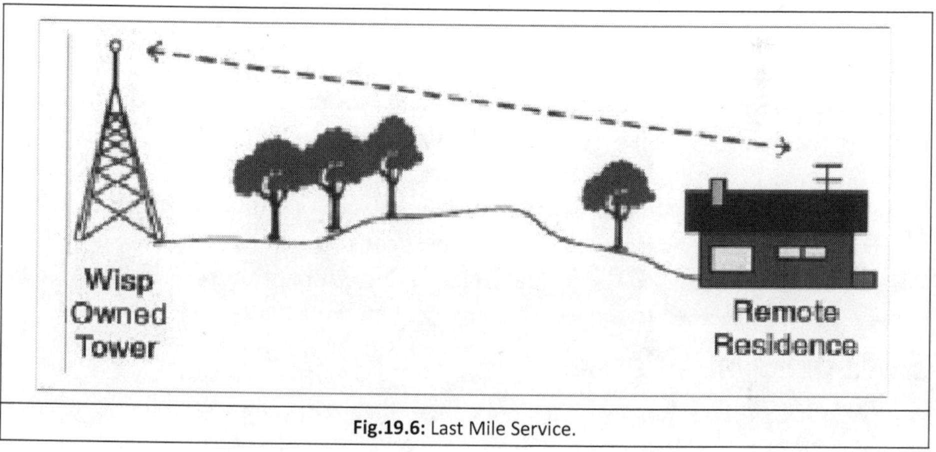

Fig.19.6: Last Mile Service.

MOBILITY

As an access layer solution, wireless LANs cannot replace wired LANs in terms of data rates (100BT at 100Mbps versus IEEE 802.11a at 54Mbps). What wireless LANs do offer is an increase in mobility as the trade off for speed and quality of service.

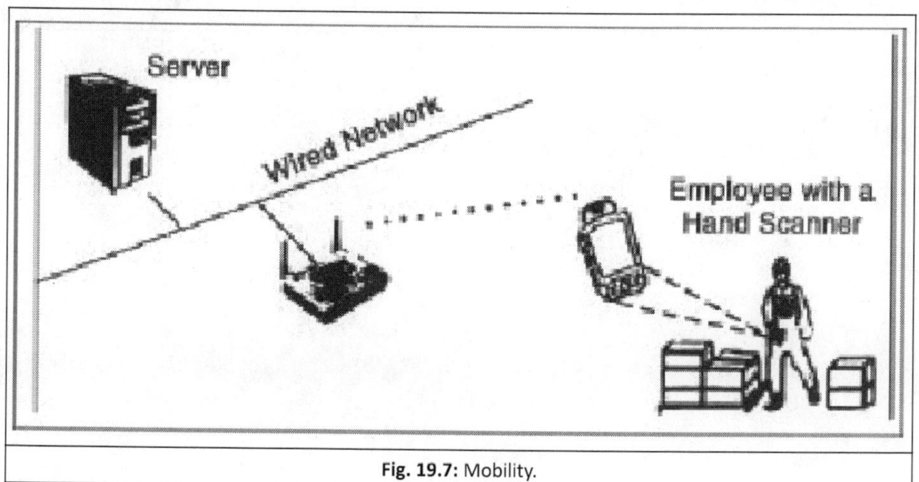

Fig. 19.7: Mobility.

For example, a parcel delivery company uses wireless technology to update parcel tracking data immediately upon the arrival of the delivery vehicle. As the driver parks at the dock, the driver's computer has already logged onto the network and transferred the day's delivery data to the central network. In warehousing facilities, wireless networks are used to track the storage locations and disposition of products. This data is then synchronised in the central computer for the purchasing and shipping departments. Handheld wireless scanners are becoming commonplace in organisations with employees that move around within their facility processing orders and inventory.

In each of these cases, wireless networks have created the ability to transfer data without requiring the time and manpower to input the data manually at a wired terminal. Wireless connectivity has also eliminated the need for such user devices to be connected using wires that would otherwise get in the way of the users. Some of the newest wireless technology allows users to roam, or move physically from one area of wireless coverage to another without losing connectivity, just as a mobile telephone customer is able to roam between cellular coverage areas. In larger organisations, where wireless coverage spans large areas, roaming capability has significantly increased the productivity of these organisations, simply because users remain connected to the network away from their main workstations.

SMALL OFFICE-HOME OFFICE

As an IT professional, one may have more than one computer at the home. And if you do, these computers are most likely networked together so you can share files, a printer, or a broadband connection. This type of configuration is also utilised by many businesses that have only a few employees. These businesses have the need for the sharing of information between users and a single Internet connection for efficiency and greater productivity. For these applications – small office-home office, or SOHO – a wireless LAN is a very simple and effective solution.

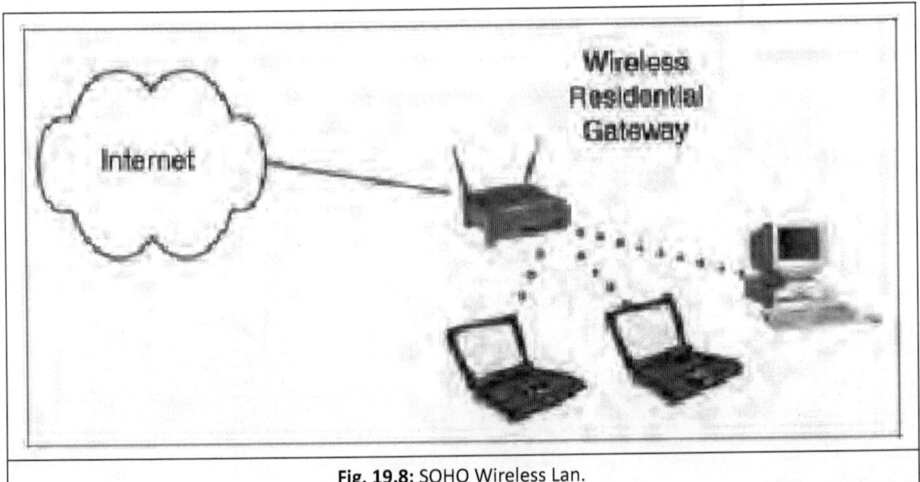

Fig. 19.8: SOHO Wireless Lan.

Figure illustrates a typical SOHO wireless LAN solution. Wireless SOHO devices are especially beneficial when office workers want to share a single Internet connection. The alternative of course is running wires throughout the office to interconnect all of the workstations. Many small offices are not outfitted with pre-installed Ethernet ports, and only a very small number of houses are wired for Ethernet networks. Trying to retrofit these places with Cat5 cabling usually results in creating unsightly holes in the walls and ceilings. With a wireless LAN, users can be interconnected easily and neatly.

MOBILE OFFICES

Mobile offices or classrooms allow users to pack up their computer equipment quickly and move to another location. Due to overcrowded classrooms, many schools now use mobile classrooms. These classrooms usually consist of large, movable trailers that are used while more permanent structures are built. In order to extend the computer network to these temporary buildings, aerial or underground cabling would have to be installed at great expense. Wireless LAN connections from the main school building to the mobile classrooms allow for flexible configurations at a fraction of the cost of alternative cabling. A simplistic example of connecting mobile classrooms using wireless LAN connectivity is illustrated in figure.

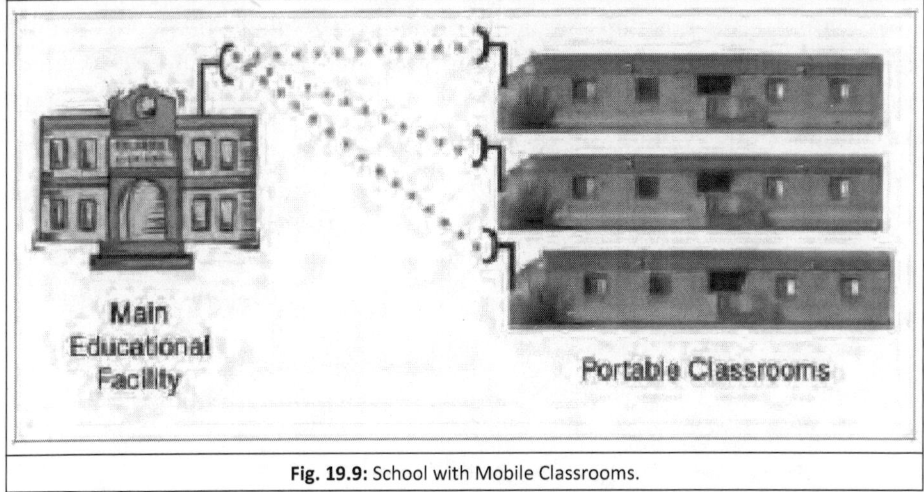

Fig. 19.9: School with Mobile Classrooms.

Temporary office spaces also benefit from being networked with wireless LANs. As companies grow, they often find themselves with a shortage of office space, and need to move some workers to a nearby location, such as an adjacent office or an office on another floor of the same building.

Installing Cat5 or fibre cabling for these short periods of time is not cost-effective, and usually the owners of the building do not allow for the installed cables to be removed. With a wireless network, the network components can be packed up and moved to the next location quickly and easily.

Wireless LANs are well suited to these types of environments. Hospitals and other health care facilities benefit greatly from wireless LANs. Some valuable uses of wireless LANs within these facilities include doctors using wireless PDAs to connect to the networks and mobile diagnostic carts that nurses can move from room to room to connect to the patient and the network. Wireless networks allow doctors and nurses to perform their jobs more efficiently using these new devices and associated software. Industrial facilities, such as warehouses and manufacturing facilities, utilise wireless networks in various ways.

A good example of an industrial wireless LAN application is shipping companies whose trucks pull into the dock and automatically connect to the wireless network. This type of networking allows the shipping company to become automated and more efficient in handling the uploading of data onto the central servers.

CONCLUSION

The purpose of this thesis has been to describe and discuss the wireless technology in accessing information in the hope that libraries and librarians will benefit from using this technology. This thesis will help us in understanding the capabilities of WLAN. The evolution of wireless technology has perceived as a powerful tool for getting fast information which will become universal in the near future. The goals of libraries are to provide information to their users. But the way users receive that information is changing. By integrating more effective delivery tools with current university infrastructure, libraries can help to attract more students and faculty to access information from inside or outside the library, 24 × 7 days a week. WLAN and its applications provide this extension possible to make "Library without Walls".

❐

20

Computer Technical Processing Services in Library

CATALOGUING

AACR2 defines a catalogue as:

- A list of library materials contained in a collection, a library, or group of libraries, organized according to some definite plan.

Obviously, cataloguing, or bibliographic control, is the process of preparing such a list.

The catalogue consists of a description of each item, which is retrievable by several of its important characteristics used as headings, or access points: the author, title or subject matter. In a manual system, there are several copies of each description which are filed under the appropriate access points for the respective item.

But in an automated system there is only one copy of the description which can be displayed using any access point for searching. The description is now called bibliographic record or just record. Preparing and maintaining a catalogue require:

- Intellectual activity for the cataloguing process based on selected standards and rules, or for locating and using bibliographic records created externally.
- Choice of an overall organization of records within the catalogue and their specific filing sequence.

- Choice of the physical form(s) for the catalogue and the production of records in that form.
- Developing procedures for adding new records and modifying existing ones.

CATALOGUING PROCESS

Descriptive Cataloguing

This embraces the description of the bibliographic or physical significance of the item except its subject content. The cataloguer also decides here which bibliographic elements should be used as access points for the item in the catalogue and determines the appropriate form of access points used. The description normally has many different elements arranged in standard formats.

The rules that should be followed for descriptive cataloguing in a medical library are the Anglo-American Cataloguing Rules, second edition (AACR2) and its revisions. As these rules are more or less the most used rules internationally in both manual and automated systems, using them will enable the user to see the same descriptive record format in any library he may use, and enable the library to use records produced in other libraries.

Defining the Subject Content

This is normally done using two types of tools which produce a subject description in a coded form or in the language(s) used in the catalogue, which is the only difference between using them, otherwise the processes are identical. The two processes are:

- **Classification:** Classification, through the notation of the classification scheme used, decides the general area in the collection where the item will be shelved. Most classification schemes lead to an arrangement of items based on their subject content. This allows the user to browse the shelves. Normally, a more specific shelving number or symbol must be added after the class number to give the item a unique place among other items in the same class. The resulting number is called " call number ".
- Standardization in classification, contrary to descriptive cataloguing, has not yet been achieved internationally. The library may choose a generalized scheme or a specialized one.

The general schemes most widely used in medical libraries are:

- Dewey Decimal Classification (DDC), which is now in its 21st edition and the second on CD-ROM.
- Library of Congress Classification (LCC), which is continuously subjected to revision.
- Universal Decimal Classification (UDC), which is widely used in Europe.

- Among the specialized schemes the most widely used one in medical libraries is NLM Classification. Subject Cataloguing or Indexing. The problem of this process is that it is language dependent and thus no standardization can possibly be achieved.

The process depends on two types of tools:

- Lists of subject headings: These may be general or specialized. Among the general ones, the most widely used list is Library of Congress List of Subject Headings (LCSH), while Medical Subject Headings (MeSH) is the most widely used list by medical libraries. It is now available in many languages.
- Thesauri: These are more recent than lists of subject headings and are more associated with automation in libraries. Most thesauri are specialized in their nature.

The choice between lists and subject headings and thesauri is mostly dictated by the indexing method, whether it is pre-coordinated or post-coordinated, as the former favours the lists while the latter adopts thesauri.

Automation has introduced yet another way of indexing using free text search or selecting keywords as access points. Cataloguing may involve original cataloguing, that is the creation of cataloguing records in the library from scratch, or using existing records elsewhere which is known as copy cataloguing.

This may be carried out manually or automated. The sources for copy cataloguing may be:

- **Cataloguing-In-Publication (CIP):** The data in CIP is created on the basis of prepublication galley proofs or preproduction information for the item. This data is usually given on the verso of the title page. CIP data has to be handled with care and should be compared carefully with the item itself when it is used as the basis for a cataloguing record, as it may have erroneous elements or is not in conformance with standards and rules adopted by the library.
- **Published Bibliographies:** Whether these bibliographies are catalogues of library holdings or published bibliographies, such as national bibliographies, they may be used for creating cataloguing records.
- **Machine-Readable Records on Tape:** Some major libraries, such as NLM, may distribute their records on tapes in MARC format. The subscribing library may get such tapes, then use local computer system to select the records needed for the local catalogue. This approach requires significant local hardware and software. Recent development for this is the use of CD-ROM instead of tapes which is cost-effective.
- **Online Services:** Some files simply offer copies of cataloguing records, other online services allow user libraries to modify or create cataloguing records in a variety of formats for incorporation into their local catalogues.

Among these are OCLC, RLIN, WLN, UTLAS, and BCMP. NLM has three online files with cataloguing data: CATLINE (Catalogue-on-line) for printed materials, AVLINE (Audiovisualson-line) for audiovisuals since 1975, and NAF (Name Authority File) for name and series authority records.

- **Service Bureaus:** Several agencies and companies in some countries produce catalogue cards or other catalogue formats on demand.
- The cataloguing copy is provided in a form that is immediately usable in a local catalogue.
- **Book Suppliers:** Some book suppliers provide catalogue records (cards or otherwise) with the books they ship to their library customers.

Regardless of the source of the cataloguing copy, individual libraries may modify or augment cataloguing records they find in order to make them more useful in local catalogues.

Among such amendments the following are necessary:

- If the copy has subject headings and/or classification which the library does not use.
- If the edition of cataloguing rules used for the copy is different from the one applied by the library.
- If the library may wish to add further access points and explanatory notes to records to emphasize some local interest.

But if the cataloguer comes across an error in an access point or in another part of a cataloguing record, he should write to the appropriate institution and ask for clarification.

Other kinds of modifications are probably unnecessary, such as:

- Eliminating data to simplify records.
- Deleting data that the library feels does not assist users very much, such as ISBN or ISSN.

ORGANIZATION OF THE CATALOGUE

In a manual system, most library catalogues are divided into at least two parts:

Shelflist

The shelflist contains one record for each item in the collection. It is usually arranged by call number in exactly the same order of items on the shelf. It is useful for assigning individual shelving numbers, in making an inventory of the collection, provided it is annotated when the library has multiple copies in the same order. This shelflist may not be available for serials when they are not classified. A list of serials may replace it.

Main Catalogue

The main catalogue contains several copies of the record for each item in the collection. A copy of each record is entered: under the author's name, the names of any of the other persons or corporate bodies associated with the work described, its title, its series title, and various subject headings. It also includes cross-references, guiding users from unused forms of names and subject headings to those that have been used.

Many catalogues may also include guide or special heading to enable a user to determine quickly where in the overall sequence of records a particular catalogue file drawer, page of book catalogue, or part of a microform catalogue is located.

DICTIONARY VERSUS DIVIDED CATALOGUE

There are three major arrangements for manual main catalogues:

- Dictionary catalogue, in which author, title and subject access points are interfiled.
- Divided catalogue, in which subject access points are arranged in a separate sequence from author and title sequence. Some libraries divide even author and title access points as well.
- Classified catalogue, in which the call numbers serve as subject access points and are in a separate sequence from author and title access points. This arrangement usually requires a language subject index to class numbers used in the catalogue, although some libraries may be satisfied with the published index of the classification scheme used.

In an online catalogue there will be no need for such arrangements although the automated systems produce any arrangement as a by-product.

AUTHORITY FILES

The authority file is the file that contains the forms of names (of persons, corporate bodies or places), title, series, or subject headings and descriptors used in the bibliographic record, as well the required cross-references to and from these forms, and their relationship with other used forms.

Authority records may be interfiled in the main catalogue, or may be kept in separate authority files, in a manual system. They must be accessible to cataloguing staff. In automated system, they are usually separate from the bibliographic records database but transparently interlinked with the number or symbol of the authority record.

The following is a brief description of the types of authority files:

- Name Authorities: A name authority record consists of:
  - The authoritative name form chosen for use in the catalogue.
  - Alternate forms of the name, and an indication as to whether cross-references from these forms are maintained in the catalogue.

- Any related names such as previous names of an institution.
- Source of the authoritative name.
- Any historical or biographical information about the name necessary to distinguish it from another name.
- An indication as to which set of cataloguing rules was used to establish the authoritative form.

Name authorities may be imported from cooperative ventures or from major libraries that have such files, such as NLM. They may be initiated also on cooperative basis particularly among libraries with a common language such as Arabic, because the forms of names may differ among the speakers of that language, and the library in the respective country is the best to verify them. With automated systems, it may be easier to use as a search tool as well if the file is constructed in a thesaurus form. These systems and the thesaurus structure will enable making the file multilingual.

- **Title Authorities:** These files will be particularly useful if the library uses uniform titles in its catalogue, or when variant titles exist among various editions of the same work.
- **Series Authorities:** A series authority record is required only for a monographic series, where individual works bear individual title and authorship information, in addition to an overall series title.
- This file should record the decision on how to handle series.
- **Subject Authorities:** The library may consider the list of subject headings or the thesaurus it applies as a subject authority, or restrict the file to the subject headings or descriptors it actually uses. This latter type has been eliminated when an automated system is used as it is going to do both purposes.

Catalogues of Special Collections

Some libraries maintain separate catalogue for special types of materials, such as audiovisuals, in addition to their inclusion in the main catalogue. In automated systems, such catalogues may be produced as by-product from the bibliographic database.

Filing Rules

Records in main catalogue in a manual system must be filed alphabetically according to standard filing rules, while those in the shelflist according to the filing order of the classification scheme in use. In an automated system, the system itself contains filing values for the elements of description that are considered in filing. These values are in fact interpretation of the filing rules adopted. As filing is always language dependent, the rules must cope with all languages represented in the catalogue, whether the characters are in roman or non-roman alphabets.

The major existing filing rules are:

- ALA filing rules/Filing committee, Resources and Technical Services Division, American Library Association. Chicago: ALA, 1980.
- Blaise filing rules/British Library Filing Rules Committee. London: British Library, 1980.
- BS 1749: 1985-British standard recommendations for alphabetical arrangement and filing order of numbers and symbols. London: BSI, 1985.
- ISO 7154-ISO bibliographic filing rules. Geneva: ISO, 1985. and ISO/ TR 8393-1985, Exemplification of bibliographic filing principles in a model set of rules. Geneva: ISO, 1985.
- Library of Congress filing rules/prepared by John C. Rather and Susan C. Biebel. Washington, DC: Library of Congress, 1980.

The set of filing rules for Arab libraries discusses the agreement and disagreement of these filing rules and those used in some major libraries in the Arab region as well as standard rules for the region:

- ARIS-Net filing rules for catalogues, bibliographies and directories.
- Tunis: ALDOC, 1989.

The basic principles behind all these rules are:

- Filing is word by word rather than letter by letter.
- Filing must be strictly as is rather than as if which means that the word is filed as written not as it sounds or means, whether written in full or abbreviated form.
- A numeral files before the alphabet.
- Order of characters must be strictly adhered to.
  - Space, dash, hyphen and diagonal slash are given equal filing character and come first
  - Ampersand
  - Arabic numerals
  - Alphabet letters
- Different forms of the same letter have equal value and must be interfiled.
- All records in the same catalogue must be filed according to the same principles-the same rules.

PHYSICAL FORMS OF CATALOGUES

Card Catalogues

This form is still prevalent in medical libraries. It can include all records regardless of their source. Records are on cards which file into drawers housed in cabinets. Standards are 12.5 x 7.5 cm. Rods may be inserted through holes in the bottom of the cards to help retain them in drawers.

Sheaf Catalogues

A loose-leaf binder format providing some of the convenience of the book. Usually each record is on a separate slip of paper. There may be a number of records on each slip.

Visible Index

This form consists of strips mounted in a frame, or cards held flat, hinged, and with the edge of each card protruding to make the heading visible. This form is used for displaying the list of serials holdings of a library.

Microform Catalogues

This is a form in which records are greatly reduced and "printed" upon a film. So a suitable reader which magnifies the film and project it on to a screen is required. It may be a microfilm or a microfiche.

Machine-readable Catalogues

This is a form which permits input and storage for manipulation in a computer. Access may be online or offline. Data are displayed on a screen or visual display, and may also be output to magnetic tape, disk or printed in hard copy. An offshot of the machine-readable form is the CD-ROM. Another is the computer output microform (COM). But the form which facilitates continuous updating, with amended records being available to the user as soon as they are input, is the online public access catalogue (OPAC). It can be accessed from outside the library through remote terminals.

Finally, the form the library decides to choose should possess as many as possible of the following:

- It must be easy to use.
- It must be easy to keep uptodate.
- It must be easy to scan.
- It must be easy to produce multiple copies.
- It must take up as little space as possible.
- It must be easy to guide.

DESCRIPTIVE CATALOGUING

International Efforts

The major contribution in cataloguing at the international level is that of IFLA. This is in the form of international standard bibliographic descriptions (ISBDs) which have influenced almost all existing cataloguing rules.

IFLA has so far issued the following ISBDs and is continuously subjecting them to revision:

- ISBD (G)-General

- ISBD (M)-Monographs
- ISBD (NBM)-Non-book Materials
- ISBD (CM)-Cartographic Materials
- ISBD (A)-Antiquarian Books
- ISBD (PM)-Printed Music
- ISBD (S)-Serials
- ISBD (CF)-Computer file, Machine-Readable files (MRF)
- ISBD (CP)-Component parts
- ISBD (ER)-Electronic Resources (replaced ISBD(CF)

Other international efforts include those of Unesco particularly the creation of the International Serials Data System (ISDS). ISDS seeks to develop a registry of world serials publications. containing sufficient bibliographic information for their identification and bibliographic control.

The cornerstones of ISDS are the ISSN and a corresponding "key title", to which geographic qualifiers may be included in parentheses at the end of the title when necessary to make the key title unique. Another international organization is the International Standardization Organization (ISO) which is responsible for many relevant international standards, in addition to those previously cited on filing rules:

- ISO 690, Bibliographic references: contents, form and structure.
- ISO 9115, Bibliographic identification (biblid) of contributions in serials and books.
- ISO 2108, International standard book numbering (ISBN).
- ISO 3297, International standard serial numbering (ISSN).
- ISO 3901, International standard recording code (ISRC).
- ISO 2709, Format for bibliographic information interchange on magnetic tape.
- ISO 10444, International standard technical report number (ISRN).

AACR2

AACR2 incorporates the ISBD system aiming at eliminating inconsistency in the descriptive treatment of various types of materials. It allows local cataloguers to choose among three levels or degrees of detail in constructing descriptive cataloguing data and also includes some optional rules. This flexibility improves the utility of the rules by a wide range of sizes and types of libraries.

Levels of Description

Rule 1.OD of AACR2 specifies these levels as follows:

- **First level:** Title proper/first statement of responsibility if different from main entry in form or number or if there is no main heading.—Edition statement.—Material (or type of publication) specificdetails.—First publisher, etc., date of publication, etc.—Extent of item.—Note(s)—Standard number.

- **Second Level:** Title proper [general material designation] = Parallel title: other title information/first statement of responsibility.—Edition statement/ first statement of re-sponsibility relating to the edition.—Material (or type of publication) specific details.—First place of publication, etc: first publisher, etc, date of publication, etc.—Extent of item: other physical details. dimensions.—(Title pro-per of series/statement of responsibility relating to series, ISSN of series. numbering within the series. Title of subseries. ISSN of subseries. numbering within subseries).—Note(s).—Standard number.
- **Third Level:** All the elements set out in the rules that are applicable to the item being described.

The information stated here is considered the minimum to be given by the cataloguer, as he may add additional elements in the first two levels. Moreover, the cataloguer may use different levels for different materials. if he does he must be consistent. It is noted that a punctuation pattern is used, which is very important element in bibliographic standardization. This pattern is defined for every element of description.

Areas of Description

The description is divided in both AACR2 and ISBDs into eight areas or fields.

They are as follows:

- **Area 1:** Title and Statement of Responsibility Area
  - 1.1 Title proper
  - 1.2 General material designation
  - 1.3 Parallel title(s)
  - 1.4 Other title information
  - 1.5 Statement(s) of responsibility
- **Area 2**: Edition Area
  - 2.1 Edition statement
  - 2.2 Parallel edition statement(s)
  - 2.3 Statement(s) of responsibility relating to the edition
  - 2.4 Statement relating to a named revision of an edition
  - 2.5 Statement(s) of responsibility relating to a named revision of an edition
- **Area 3:** Material (or Type of publication) Specific Details area (Used only for cartographic materials, printed music, computer files, and serials).
- **Area 4:** Publication, production, Distribution, etc, Area.
  - 4.1 Place(s) of publication, distribution, etc.
  - 4.2 Name(s) of publisher, distributor, etc.

  - 4.3 Date of publication, distribution, etc.
  - 4.4 Place of manufacture
  - 4.5 Name of manufacturer
  - 4.6 Date of manufacture
- Area 5: Physical Description Area
  - 5.1 Specific material designation and extent of item
  - 5.2 Other physical details
  - 5.3 Dimensions
  - 5.4 Identification of accompanying material
- Area 6: Series Area
  - 6.1 Title proper of the series
  - 6.2 Parallel title(s) of the series
  - 6.3 Other title information of the series
  - 6.4 Statement(s) of responsibility relating to the series
  - 6.5 International Standard Serial Number (ISSN) of the series
  - 6.6 Numbering within the series
  - 6.7 Enumeration and/or title of subseries
  - 6.8-The same as for 6.2 through 6.6 for subseries
  - 6.12
- Area 7: Note(s) Area (repeatable, each note being a separate area)
- Area 8: Standard Number, etc Area (a repeatable area)
  - 8.1 Standard number: ISBN, ISSN, ISRC etc.
  - 8.2 Key-title (associated only with an ISSN)
  - 8.3 Terms of availability and/or price
  - 8.4 Qualification(s) following 8.1 and/or 8.3

Access Points (Headings) and References

AACR2 is of two parts: The first covers descriptions as stated before and consists of (13) chapters where the first covers all types of materials, and chapters 2-12 cover a certain type each, while chapter 13 concerns analytical cataloguing. The second part starts with chapter 20 which is an explanation of the rules of this part, while no chapters 14-19 exist.

Chapter 21 covers the choice of access points, chapter 22 deals with headings for persons, chapter 23 deals with headings for geographic names, chapter 24 deals with headings for corporate bodies, chapter 25 deals with uniform titles, while chapter 26 collects together the various rules for references.

The rules are completed by four appendices:

1. A: Capitalization
2. B: Abbreviations
3. C: Numerals
4. D: Glossary

Numerous handbooks and illustrations have been published in different languages, as well as in the local formats adopted such as CEHANET procedures manual.

SUBJECT ANALYSIS

CLASSIFICATION

Classification is basically grouping similar objects or ideas together. This grouping is done through the notations assigned as class numbers from the classification scheme adopted. There are three major general classification schemes that may be encountered in some medical libraries.

Library of Congress Classification (LCC)

This is a general enumerative scheme consisting of 21 classes in individual schemes, although they are now available on CD-ROM as well. The main classes and subclasses are designated by capital letters. Further subdivision is by integral numbers ranging from 1 to 9999, which may be extended decimally.
The classes of this classification that concern medical libraries are:

- GN: Anthropology
- HN: Social History and Reform
- QR: Bacteriology
- TC: Hydrology
- TD: Sanitary and Municipal Engineering
- TH: Building construction
- TX: Domestic Sciences

Note here that medicine is assigned class R which is not recommended for medical libraries.
This class is subdivided as follows:

- R: Medicine in General
- RA: Government Medicine and Public Health
- RB: Pathology
- RC: Practice of Medicine
- RD: Surgery
- RE: Ophthalmology
- RF: Otorhinolaryngology
- RG: Gynecology and Obstetrics
- RJ: Paediatrics
- RK: Dentistry
- RL: Dermatology
- RM: Therapeutics
- RS: Pharmacy
- RT: Nursing

- RV: Herbalism
- RX: Homeotherapy
- RZ: Various Schools and Arts

The LCC uses auxiliary tables for individual classes, but not for the scheme as a whole. There are five types of these tables: form, geographic, historical, topical and mixed.

Dewey Decimal Classification (DCC)

Knowledge in this scheme is divided into ten major classes using arabic numerals 0-9 provided that the number is of three digits. After this base number numbers may be expanded decimally.

Medical sciences are placed in the main class 600-Technology as follows:

- 610: Medical Sciences Medicine
- 611: Human Anatomy, Cytology, Histology
- 612: Human Physiology
- 613: Hygiene
- 614: Forensic Medicine, Disease Incidence, General Preventive Medicine
- 615: Pharmacology
- 616: Diseases
- 617: Various Medicine Branches. Surgery
- 618: Other Medicine Branches. Gynecology and Obstetrics
- 619: Experimental Medicine

In addition, there is a large number of class numbers relevant to health sciences, among which are:

- 334: Social Law, Social welfare, Labour, Health, Safety, Education and Culture Law
- 363: Social Issues and Services
- 574: Biology
- 628: Sanitary and Municipal Engineering, Environ-mental Protection Engineering
- 632: Plant Injuries, Diseases, Pests
- 636: Veterinary Medicine

The scheme has seven auxiliary tables for using with the various class numbers as instructed in the schedules. The scheme is now in its twenty-first edition in four volumes, of which the fourth volume is an alphabetical relative index and a manual. It is also on CD-ROM.

Universal Decimal Classification

This scheme is originally based on DDC but deviated from it in many aspects particularly the obligation of using the three digits base numbers. But the major classes are nearly the same except for cancelling class 4 to be combined with class 8.

Medical sciences have 61 and its subdivisions are as follows:

- 61: Medical Sciences (Medicine)
- 611: Anatomy. Human and Comparative Anatomy
- 612: Physiology. Human and Comparative Physiology
- 613: Hygiene in General. Personal Health and Hygiene
- 614: Public Health and Hygiene. Accident Prevention
- 615: Pharmacology. Therapeutics. Toxicology
- 616: Pathology. Clinical Medicine
- 617: Surgery. Orthopaedics. Ophthalmology
- 618: Gynecology. Obstetrics
- 619: Domesticated Animal Diseases. VeterinaryMedicine
- Class numbers related to health sciences are also scattered in nearly the same way as DDC. The scheme also uses ten auxiliary tables. The latest medium English edition was published in 1993, and its amendments in 1996. It is also on CD-ROM.

NLM Classification

This scheme covers medicine and other related sciences using the classes QS-QZ and W-WZ permanently excluded in LCC. So, LCC may be considered supplementary to this scheme for classifying other disciplines, except QM (human anatomy), QR (microbiology) and R (medicine) in LCC which cannot be used in this scheme.

The classes are subdivided as follows:

- QS-QZ Preclinical Sciences
  - QS Human Anatomy
  - QT Physiology
  - QU Biochemistry
  - QV Pharmacology
  - QW Microbiology and Immunology
  - QX Parasitology
  - QY Clinical Pathology
  - QZ Pathology
- W-WZ Medicine and Related Subjects
  - W Health Professions
  - WA Public Health
  - WB Practice of Medicine
  - WC Communicable Diseases
  - WD100 Nutrition Disorders
  - WD200 Metabolic Diseases
  - WD300 Immunologic and Collagen Diseases. Hypersensitivity
  - WD400 Animal Poisons
  - WD500 Plant Poisons

- WD600 Diseases and Injuries caused by Physical Agents
- WD700 Aviation and Space Medicine
- WE Musculoskeletal System
- WF Rispiratory System
- WG Cardiovascular System
- WH Hemic and Lymphatic System
- WI Digestive System
- WJ Urogenital System
- WK Endocrine System
- WL Nervous System
- WM Psychiatry
- WN Radiology. Diagnostic Imaging
- WO Surgery
- WP Gynecology
- WQ Obstetrics
- WR Dermatology
- WS Paediatrics
- WT Geriatrics. Chronic Disease
- WU Dentistry. Oral Surgery
- WV Otorhinolaryngology
- WW Ophthalmology
- WX Hospitals and Other Health Facilities
- WY Nursing
- WZ History of Medicine

In addition the scheme has two types of auxiliary tables, the first covers form subdivisions which are listed under main class numbers, and the other is list (G) which is common to all schedules and covers the geographic subdivision. This list divides the world into nine geographic regions, and one notation for international organizations that publish materials related to medicine. It has an alphabetical relative index, which uses terms derived from Medical Subject Headings (MeSH), and includes subjects outside the scope of the scheme and have LCC numbers. The scheme is now in its fifth edition.

CONTROLLED VOCABULARY

There are two types of tools for controlling vocabulary to be used in subject cataloguing and indexing:

- Lists of Subject Headings; and
- Library of Congress Subject Headings (LCSH)

This is the largest list of subject headings in English. It is a general list originally constructed for the use of the Library of Congress. Now it is published annually, as well as quarterly on CD-ROM under the title: CDMARC subjects.

Recent development include:

- The use of accepted abbreviations such as BT and NT, generally used in thesauri.
- Eliminating inverted forms of subject headings gradually.
- Gradual elimination of subject headings that have the conjunction " and " or qualifiers.

The list has four types of subdivision:

- Topical subdivision
- Form subdivision
- Geographic subdivision
- Chronological subdivision

The list is not recommended for medical libraries as it is too general and lacks the subject headings required in health sciences.

Medical Subject Headings (MeSH)

This is the largest list of medical subject headings in English and in other languages to which it has been translated. It is published annually by the NLM, and is used in Medline and in most large medical libraries in the world. It is unique in having the following features that are absent in traditional lists of subject headings:

- Subject headings have classification numbers based on the tree structure of the list. Some headings bear more than ten different numbers each.

The major categories of the tree structure are:

- A Anatomy
- B Organisms
- C Diseases
- D Chemicals and Drugs
- E Analytical, Diagnostic and Therapeutic Techniques and Equipment
- F Psychiatry and Psychology
- G Biological Sciences
- H Physical Sciences
- I Anthropology, Education, Sociology and Social Phenomena
- J Technology, Industry, Agriculture
- K Humanities
- L Information Science
- M Named Groups
- N Health Care
- Z Geographic Locations

Each main category is further subdivided once or more as required using arabic numerals and decimal points:

- The list has an index to the tree structure which is published as a separate volume.
- The list has a KWOC index for the terms used. This feature is used in thersauri.
- The topical, geographical, chronological and form subdivisions are not repeated in the list under the related headings but the notes give instruction on their use.

The print edition has the following lists as appendices:

  - Types of publications. The types are also listed in the main list.
  - Topical subdivisions which are only used with main headings. They are also given in the main list.
  - Form subdivisions for cataloguers with annotations. They are also given in the main list.
  - Geographical locations for cataloguers. They are not given in the main list.
  - Language subdivisions. These are not given in the main list.

Entries of MeSH are of three types:

- Entry of the main heading which typically includes the following information as required:
  - The Heading
  - Consider also cross-reference to other terms
  - Tree number(s)
  - Indexing annotation
  - Cataloguing annotation
  - History note
  - Online note
  - See related
  - X See cross-reference, for entry vocabulary
  - XR See related from other headings
- Subheading: This is printed in lower case and preceded by a slash. The entry includes the following information:
  - Subheading
  - Indexing annotation
  - History note
  - Online note

Vocabulary Terms: These include synonyms, near-synonyms, abbreviations, alternative spelling and alternate forms that may be more familiar or easier to type. The entry includes the following information:

  - The vocabulary term
  - The word "see"

- The main heading preferred
- The tree number(s) of the main heading

Thesauri

A thesaurus is the vocabulary of a controlled indexing language, formally organized so that the relationships between concepts are made explicit. Fortunately the establishment and development of thesauri have been handled by ISO:

- ISO 2708, Documentation-Guidelines for the establish-ment and development of monolingual thesauri.
- ISO 5964, Documentation-Guidelines for the establishment and development of multilingual thesauri.
- ISO 5963, Documentation-Methods for examining documents, determining their subject and selecting indexing terms.

These standards, the relationship or function of term or note which follows is expressed by the following abbreviations and symbols:

- SN: (Scope note). A note attached to a term to indicate its meaning within an indexing language.
- USE: The term that follows the symbol is the preferred term, when a choice between synonyms or quasi-synonyms exists.
- UF: (Use for). The term that follows the symbol is a non-preferred synonym or quasi-synonym.
- TT: (Top term). The term that follows the symbol is the name of the broadest class to which the specific concept belongs. It is sometimes used in the alphabetical part of a thesaurus.
- BT: (Broader term). The term that follows the symbol represents a concept having a wider meaning.
- NT: (Narrower term). The term that follows the symbol refers to a concept with a more specific meaning.
- RT: (Related term). the term that follows the symbol is associated, but is not a synonym, a quasi-synonym, a broader term or a narrower term.

Although these abbreviations have acquired status as generally recognized conventions, some agencies have developed different symbols such as using ® instead of USE, = instead of UF, < for BT, > for NT and—for RT.

The concepts that are represented by indexing terms may be:

- Concrete entities:
  - Things and their physical parts
    - a. Limbs
    - b. Microforms
  - Materials
    - a. Adhesives
    - b. Drugs

- Abstract entities:
  - Actions and events
    - a. Treatment
    - b. Marketing
  - Abstract entities, and properties of thing, materials or actions
    - a. Elasticity
    - b. Speed
  - Disciplines or sciences
    - a. Chemistry
    - b. Microbiology
  - Units of measurement
    - a. Hertz
    - b. Kilometers
- Individual entities', or classes-of-one, expressed as proper nouns
  - World Health Organization
- The indexing term should preferably consist of a noun or a noun phrase.

The latter occurs in two forms:

- Adjective phrase: Handicapped children
- Prepositional phrase: Hospitals for children

UNCONTROLLED VOCABULARY

Uncontrolled, or natural language, words and terms can be of considerable value as subject access points when they come from such sources as the title of a document, cataloguer's note on its bibliographic record, abstract or full text.

Such words are often called keywords. Use of these keywords was made for creating KWIC (Keyword-incontext) and KWOC (keyword-out-of-context) indexes particularly by using the computer. In addition they are used for searching databases particularly those without controlled vocabulary. This requires compiling stop-list to identify those words of natural-language text which the computer programme is not to make accessible in an index, thus marking accessible only those words which are highly significant for retrieval purposes.

But natural language indexing compared to that of controlled vocabulary has some stronger and weaker characteristics:

- **Synonym Control:** Suppose that we consider "renal stone" as the keywords to be searched. We must look into several places if our search is to be fairly comprehensive. We have look under renal calculi, kidney calculi, and kidney stones, as well as their singulars.
- If the system develops some sort of synonym control then searching will be efficient.

- **Singular and Plural:** The same problem occurs here as in synonym control. This has to be solved through truncation and other devices that enable the retrieval of singulars and plurals.
- **Different Spelling:** An important example is the different spelling in British and American English.
- **Hierarchical Relationships:** Prevalent in controlled vocabulary.
- **Specificity:** This is represented better in natural language indexing than in controlled vocabulary.
- **Uptodate Vocabulary:** Natural language indexing is always uptodate.
- **Ease:** Natural language is easier to use than controlled vocabulary, if the need is for few articles, but is very hard if the need is for comprehensiveness.
- **Lower Cost:** Natural language is quicker and cheaper for the index producer to develop. There is no need for well-trained indexers.
- **Compound Terms:** The controlled vocabulary takes care of this problem fairly easy. Natural language should have the required capability in the system.
- **Inconsistency of the Indexer:** This is not existing in natural language indexing.

❒

Index

❑❑❑